THE STUDY
OF TEACHING

THE STUDY
OF TEACHING

MICHAEL J. DUNKIN
Macquarie University
Sydney, Australia

BRUCE J. BIDDLE
University of Missouri
Columbia, Missouri

HOLT, RINEHART AND WINSTON, INC.
New York Chicago San Francisco Atlanta
Dallas Montreal Toronto London Sydney

Library of Congress Cataloging in Publication Data

Dunkin, M. J., 1936–
  The study of teaching.

  1. Teaching. 2. Educational research. 3. Teachers,
Training of. I. Biddle, Bruce Jesse, 1928–   joint
author. II. Title
LB1025.2.D86   371.1′02′072   74-1251

ISBN 0-03-088099-8

Acknowledgments

The authors are indebted to the following for permission to reproduce materials in this text:

Addison-Wesley Publishing Company, Reading, Mass. Figure 3–8, page 85, from *Analyzing Teacher Behavior* by N. A. Flanders. Copyright 1970.

American Educational Research Association, Washington, D.C. Excerpts from pages 50–51, 52–53, 54, "Contemporary models of teaching" by G. Nuthall and I. Snook, in *Second Handbook of Research on Teaching*, R. M. W. Travers (ed.). New York, Rand McNally. Copyright 1973 by the American Educational Research Association.

American Educational Research Journal. Page 665 from "A computer investigation of verbal characteristics of effective classroom lecturing" by J. H. Hiller, G. A. Fisher, and W. Kaess, 6, 661–675, 1969. Copyright 1969 by the American Educational Research Association. Page 34 from "An experimental investigation of the effects of pupil responding and teacher reacting on pupil achievement" by D. C. Hughes, 10, 21–37, 1973. Copyright 1973 by the American Educational Research Association. Page 2 from "Classroom behavior and underachievement" by H. V. Perkins, 2, 1–12, 1965. Copyright 1965 by the American Educational Research Association. Excerpts from "Relationships between teacher behaviors and pupil achievement in three experimental elementary science lessons" by C. J. Wright and G. Nuthall, 7, 447–491, 1970. Copyright 1970 by the American Educational Research Association.

American Psychological Association, Washington, D.C. Excerpts from "The development of a technique for the measurement of social-emotional climate in classrooms" by J. Withall, *Journal of Experimental Education,* 17, 347–361, 1949. Copyright 1949 by the American Psychological Association. Reprinted by permission.

Association for Productive Teaching, Minneapolis, Minn. Page 14 from *The Role of the Teacher in the Classroom* by E. J. Amidon and N. A. Flanders. Copyright 1963.

Beacon House, Inc., Beacon, N.Y. Page 158 from *Who Shall Survive?* by J. L. Moreno. Copyright 1953.

B. B. Brown. Excerpts from *The Florida Taxonomy of Cognitive Behaviors,* Institute for Development of Human Resources, University of Florida, Gainesville.

David McKay Company, Inc., New York. Excerpts from pages 201–207, *Taxonomy of Educational Objectives: The Classification of Educational Goals, Handbook I: Cognitive Domain* by B. S. Bloom, M. D. Engelhart, E. J. Furst, W. H. Hill, and D. R. Krathwohl. Copyright 1956 by David McKay Company, Inc.

J. J. Gallagher. Excerpts from *Productive Thinking in Gifted Children,* ERIC Clearinghouse, Bethesda, Md.

P. V. Gump. Excerpts from *The Classroom Behavior Setting: Its Nature and Relation to Student Behavior.* Final Report, Contract No. OE-4-10-107, U.S. Bureau of Research, Department of Health, Education and Welfare.

W. H. Hawkins. Figure from "Teacher reactive behavior related to class size and to the teaching of mathematics, social studies, and English," paper presented at the annual meeting for the Australian Association for Research in Education, Canberra, 1972.

Holt, Rinehart and Winston, Inc., New York. Excerpts from pages 9–10, 16 of "The integration of teacher effectiveness research" by B. J. Biddle, *Contemporary Research on Teacher Effectiveness,* B. J. Biddle and W. J. Ellena (eds.). Copyright 1964. Excerpts from pages 9–10, 65, 67–78, 82, 85, and Appendix figures 4.1 and 4.2 from *Discipline and Group Management in Classrooms* by Jacob S. Kounin. Copyright © 1970.

Journal of Educational Research. Page 148 from "Classroom feedback behavior of teachers" by J. A. Zahorik, *62,* 147–150, 1968. Copyright 1968.

M. D. Loflin. Excerpts from *Sex, Race, Social Class and Language in the Classroom* by M. D. Loflin, B. J. Biddle, N. Barron, and M. Marlin, Technical Report No. 88, Center for Research in Social Behavior, University of Missouri, Columbia. Excerpts from personal communication, 1973.

G. A. Nuthall. Excerpts from personal communication, November 1972

New Zealand Council for Educational Research. Excerpts from pages 6, 9, 10, 20, 21, 23, 58, 59, *Thinking in the Classroom: The Development of a Method of Analysis* by G. A. Nuthall and P. J. Lawrence. Copyright 1965.

Pacific Books, Palo Alto, Calif. Excerpts from pages 144–145, *Teacher Effectiveness and Teacher Education: The Search for a Scientific Basis* by N. L. Gage. Copyright 1972.

Peabody Journal of Education, Nashville, Tenn. Excerpts from "Cognitive objectives revealed by classroom questions asked by social studies student teachers" by O. L. Davis and D. C. Tinsley, *45,* 21–26, 1967. Copyright 1967.

S. Levine and F. F. Elzey. Excerpts from *Thinking in Elementary School Children* by H. Taba, S. Levine, and F. F. Elzey. U.S.O.E. Cooperative Research Project No. 1574, San Francisco State College.

Edward Scott. Transcript provided by personal communication, 1971.

B. O. Smith. Excerpts from *A Study of the Strategies of Teaching* by B. O. Smith, M. O. Meux, J. Coombs, G. A. Nuthall, and R. Precians, Bureau of Educational Research, University of Illinois, Urbana.

Stanford University Press. Figure from "Studies of teachers' classroom personalities, I: dominative and socially integrative behavior of kindergarten teachers" by H. H. Anderson and H. M. Brewer, *Applied Psychology Monographs,* 1945, No. 6. Copyright 1945.

Teachers College Press, New York. Reprinted by permission of the publisher from *The Language of the Classroom,* excerpts from pages 4, 22ff, 24, 25, 112, 194, 195, 204–205. Copyright 1966 by Teachers College, Columbia University. Reprinted by permission of the publisher from *A System for Analyzing Lessons* by J. Herbert, page 39. Copyright 1967 by Teachers College, Columbia University.

University of Chicago Press, Chicago. Excerpts and figure from pages 308–316, "Learning by discovery: psychological and educational rationale" by H. Taba, *Elementary School Journal, 63*. Copyright 1966 by the University of Chicago Press.

University of Kansas Committee on Scholarly Publications. Excerpts from page 73, *Specimen Records of American and English Children* by R. G. Barker, H. F. Wright, L. S. Barker, and P. Schoggen. Copyright 1961, reprinted by permission of the Committee.

University of Illinois Press, Urbana. Excerpts from A *Study of the Logic of Teaching* by B. O. Smith and M. O. Meux. Copyright 1962.

John Wiley & Sons, Inc., New York. Page 384 from "The nature of verbal discourse in classrooms and association between verbal discourse and pupils' understanding in sciences" by R. P. Tisher, in *Scholars in Context: The Effects of Environments on Learning*, W. J. Campbell (ed.). Copyright 1970 by John Wiley & Sons, Inc.

PREFACE

This book concerns *the study of teaching*. Such a phrase connotes at least three different meanings, and each applies to this book. In it the reader will find a summary of knowledge concerning teaching that has been developed through research; a discussion of methods and issues associated with the study of teaching; and a plea for the expansion of research in this vital field. This book is intended primarily as an advanced text for students of education. As such, it should find uses in courses concerned with the methods of teaching, with educational psychology and sociology, and with educational research. As far as we know, this is the *first* text yet written that concerns the study of teaching. And as such, it should also have meaning for educators and citizens concerned with education, for what could be more central to the improvement of education than the study of teaching? It also provides researchers concerned with teaching a review of recent research in this lively field.

To paraphrase a famous American, we have a dream—and in addition, a belief and a presumption. Our dream is of an educational system whose procedures are governed by research and by theories that are empirically based. Our belief is that the study of teaching is the heartland of the research effort that should govern education. Our presumption is that sufficient research has already been completed concerning teaching that a text should now be written on that topic. Each of these is an arguable proposition, of course. As most educators would attest, our dream of an education based on research is no nearer realization than is the dream of racial fraternity in America. Surely the study of teaching is crucial to education—but so is the study of learning, and of educational administration.

Research on teaching is as yet a young science. Its methods, which depend on the observation of classroom events, are but a generation old. Serious studies of teaching so far number less than half a thousand, surely a drop in the bucket by standards of most sciences. Moreover, some of this research is flawed and confused, so that investigators and reviewers alike have found it difficult to interpret findings from this field. Why then write a text?

First, because there is such an obvious need for information concerning teaching. Such a need is expressed in several quarters. Our students, many of whom are or intend to be teachers, want to know how knowledge is derived for their profession, what claims can now be made about teaching, and how they can apply this information to their own performances. Our colleagues have shown an interest in recent research on teaching and have asked where they might turn for a discussion of this field. Parents and citizens in our communities, too, have continued to ask us what is known concerning teaching, its determinants, its effects. Indeed, so patent is this need that isolated studies of teaching have become classics in their time, and innovations in educational practice are now being urged on their meager evidence. Books of readings are now available for this field, as well as reviews of selected aspects of the research (written for scholars). But as yet, no text has appeared that puts it all together.

A second reason concerns the state of the art in research on teaching. Perhaps because no text was available, standards for conducting and reporting studies of teaching have varied from investigation to investigation. Scores of instruments have been used for observing classroom events, along with literally hundreds of different concepts, and investigators have sometimes appeared unaware of problems of methodology or of conceptual overlap. Worse, many authors have seemed ignorant of, or unconcerned about, the relevant findings of others in the field. Indeed, a few have seemed ignorant of their own research findings! Given such a state of affairs, it seems time that someone prepared a text that would serve as a guide to methods, concepts, and findings of research on teaching.

Our third reason is more personal. Quite frankly, we began the review that became this text out of curiosity. We too have labored in the vineyard of research on teaching, and oft we have wanted to know what others had found in their research, what their findings meant, or how we might best expand on their efforts in our own studies. This book, then, represents our initial effort to satisfy that curiosity. It will surely not be the last such effort. Research on teaching to date raises more questions than it provides answers. In many ways it tells us more about what *not* to do in teaching than what to do, and more about how *not* to conduct research than how to conduct it properly. For these reasons, much of the research so far conducted (including our own) looks precursive rather than definitive. If readers share our values, they will not be satisfied until *theories* are available that enable the assembly and explanation of empirical findings concerning teaching. So far we are more certain of a few findings than we are of theories that might explain them. And in this sense our curiosity is far from satisfied.

This book represents a long-standing, trans-Pacific cooperation. It began in friendship during 1965 when we were both temporarily at the University of Queensland. During the next several years it became clear that both of us felt the need for a serious review of resarch on teaching. Accordingly, in December 1970 we began a six-month intensive search through the literature at the Center for Research in Social Behavior of the University of Missouri.

Whatever innocent ideas we had concerning the simplicity of the task were shortly dispelled! Several times as many additional studies were unearthed as we had previously known of. Countless problems of methodological confusion, conceptual unclarity and overlap, and ambiguity of findings were met. As a result, what we had hoped to accomplish in six months was merely well started by June 1971. Each of us has crossed the Pacific twice since then for planning and revision meetings. But most of the work has been done under the handicap of a 10,000 mile separation. As a result, our next book will surely concern the joys and miseries of international collaboration, the efficiency of our mailing systems, and the differences between Australian and American English!

It would be impossible to thank the literally dozens of persons who helped us in this task at one time or another. We owe much to our respective universities for making it possible for us to come together, to our many colleagues who have reacted to our ideas and enriched them or who did our teaching while we were away, and to our students whose reactions gave us guidance in using materials and ideas in the teaching situation. Special thanks are due to Ellen H. Biddle who aided our conceptualization and gathered and abstracted research reports for us. Thomas Good, Philip Jackson, Jacob Kounin, Graham Nuthall, and Louis Smith all struggled through draft versions of the manuscript and made dozens of helpful suggestions. Raymond Adams, Marvin Loflin, N. L. Gage, Barak Rosenshine, Edward Scott, Robert Precians, Stanley Doenau, and Neil Baumgart also helped by responding to specific issues taken up in the book. Invaluable encouragement was given by the Holt editorial staff, and in particular Richard Owen and David Boynton. Frances Head and Susan Gunn provided yeoperson service in typing (and retyping, and retyping) the manuscript. Finally, thanks are also due our wives and families, without whose tolerance the concentrated and chauvinistic tasks of authorship would have been quite impossible.

Sydney, Australia   M. J. D.
Columbia, Missouri   B. J. B.

CONTENTS

THE STUDY
OF TEACHING

I
OUTLOOK AND ORIENTATION

This is a book about teaching. It is directed at senior undergraduate students, graduate students, and serious researchers in education. Its subject matter is the classroom behavior of teachers, the response of pupils, and the determinants and effects of these events. In this it is similar to many other education texts—for teaching is the core process through which education happens, and most books concerned with education discuss it sooner or later.

But in contrast with most other texts, the present book is concerned with teaching as researchers have conceptualized it. It is, in fact, a summary of the methods, concepts, and findings of observational research on teaching. It is addressed to students of education who seek scientifically derived knowledge about instruction. In it the reader will find:

> a discussion of the problems and potentialities of observational research on teaching;
> a number of different concepts that have been found useful for describing the teaching process;
> a collection of notions that have been advanced for the "improvement" of education, and evidence bearing on those claims;
> a number of findings concerning strategies for teaching that have been found to work in some contexts;
> other findings that concern the influence of teacher, pupil, and context on classroom events;
> and still other findings concerned with the effects of differing teaching strategies on pupil growth.

What a radical notion—to base a text on teaching upon research evidence! For years student teachers have been exposed to quite different traditions. Nearly all of us were taught the history and philosophy of education. Most of us also studied the psychologies of white rats and preschool children, as well as "individual differences" and "tests and measurement." We also learned the dynamics of nonclassroom groups, the sociology of educational communities, the organization of schools, and the laws pertaining to education in our states.

Were this all, each of us might well have been subjected to a conspiracy to instruct future teachers in all matters educational—except the subject of teaching. But we were surely taught about teaching too. We were told that "good" teaching is democratic and that we should provide for individual differences in the classroom. Moreover, our "success" in teaching, we were taught, would depend on our ability to provide positive reinforcements, maintain appropriate discipline, inspire interest in the subject matter, and present an exciting and challenging lesson. Were these not enough, we were also counseled to use appropriate logic, diction, and a pleasant tone of voice, exhibit warmth and humor, and provide a bright and cheerful classroom!

Quite apart from whether *any* teacher could possibly achieve these many and sometimes contradictory objectives, how do we know that they work? Where is the evidence that democratic classrooms are happier or better learning environments than autocratic ones? How do we know that teachers whom we might characterize as logical, warm, or humorous are more likely to have pupils who learn and love their subjects than teachers who possess these attributes to a lesser extent? Unfortunately, most texts on teaching provide no evidence to back their recommendations. Instead, their claims are advanced through argument, example, and enthusiasm.

However, we should not dismiss out of hand the ideas presented in these texts simply because they are not accompanied by supporting research evidence. Until quite recently very little evidence was available concerning the processes of teaching. As will shortly be discovered, the research on which this text is based was primarily conducted during the past two decades. Lacking evidence, and faced with the enormous task of motivating and instructing the teachers of the next generation, it is small wonder that teacher-educators have built their texts upon irrelevant information, examples, and exhortation.

But things they are a-changin'. Evidence is now beginning to accumulate concerning the effectiveness of different teaching strategies. Perhaps for the first time, ever, we are able to consult studies that have examined such matters as classroom democracy, the use of reinforcement, or teacher manipulation of classroom logic to see how these affect pupil behavior and learning. Thus, it is now possible to construct a text on teaching that is based on research evidence pertaining to classroom behavior. This is the first such text that we know of. It is surely not the last of its breed.

Of course, a book of this kind is bound to pose a challenge for students used to other traditions in education. For one thing, it presupposes the usefulness of applying scientific methods to teaching. (Those who question this assumption will want to look at Chapter II fairly quickly.) For another, it requires students to learn some of the complexities and problems associated with conducting research on teaching. Again, it is restricted to educational theories and notions that have actually been investigated in observational research and, as we shall see, this is still a limited universe. Moreover, the answers provided by this research so far are often incomplete and fragmentary and frequently appear to tell us which teaching strategies make little or no difference rather than which ones are clearly effective. Finally, sophisticates will be dissatisfied—as we are—that no overarching theory of teaching can be provided in this text to complement the concepts and findings presented. In part this lack reflects the immature state of knowledge yet developed concerning teaching; in part it mirrors our own deficiencies as prophets.

Educational research takes many different forms, most of which do *not* concern *research on teaching* as we shall use the term in this book. Among the kinds of studies with which we are *not* concerned are:

> investigations conducted with white rats, monkeys, planaria, or preschool children;
>
> observations of teacher or pupil behavior in nonclassroom contexts;
>
> studies of the backgrounds and characteristics of teachers, pupils, or others concerned with education except as they have been related to classroom behavior;
>
> field surveys of school characteristics such as size of classrooms or per-pupil expenditures unless they have included observations of classroom behavior;
>
> experiments in which an innovation is introduced into the classroom (such as a new curriculum or teaching device) and evaluated against the criterion of pupil achievement without study of the actual teaching process with which it was mediated;
>
> investigations in which teachers, pupils, school principals, or others are asked to report or rate classroom events which they saw—but the investigators did not.

While this may seem to leave a rather small field, it is the central and most crucial field of research if one wants to learn something definitive about teaching. Thus, all of the studies reviewed here have involved *systematic observation of teaching in classrooms*.

To say that these studies involved "observation" means that the investigator actually looked at the processes of classroom interaction—although his observations may have taken place through mechanical means such as audio or videotape recordings. To say that these observations were "systematic" means that instruments were developed for noting or measuring events that took place in those classrooms observed—and usually that a number of different classrooms or lessons were studied.

We give little of our story away by noting that only a "handful" of studies have been conducted to date that meet these criteria. In preparing this text we reviewed somewhat less than 500 studies. Not all of these proved to concern research on teaching, according to our definition, and not all of those that did were sufficiently well conducted to be worth citing. Although not exhaustive, our search unearthed the majority of applicable publications. Thus this research effort is as yet a far cry from the more than 10,000 studies that have been published to date on "teacher effectiveness," or the literally hundreds of thousands of studies conducted in well-researched areas of chemistry or medicine.

Given the youth and size of this research effort, why do a text *now*?

Isn't the production of such a book premature? In some ways, it is. We too are concerned with the inability of the research so far conducted to answer a number of crucial questions concerning teaching. When these questions arise we shall note them and make suggestions for research that might answer them. Indeed, one of our motives for writing this book is to affect the course of research in this vital field, and one of our two summary chapters is devoted to suggestions for those who expect to enter this area of research in the near future. However, even the limited investigative effort made so far has borne fruit. In part this fruit is a series of negative findings concerning panaceas that have been argued for improving teaching—and for which the evidence is inconclusive or negative. In part it consists of a number of new and useful concepts that teachers can apply to the understanding of their own classroom efforts. And in part it involves a number of findings concerning the processes, determinants, and effects of teaching.

These findings are no accident. Although this text is built around studies that involved the systematic observation of teaching, it turns out that the majority of these studies also involved the measurement of non-teaching variables. Many investigators were concerned with the effects of teacher background or experience on the teaching process—for example, how teachers trained with one curriculum compared with others having different experiences, or how men and women differed with respect to their own or their pupils' classroom behavior. Other studies took up the effects of context—how teaching varies as a function of grade level, subject matter, or ethnic composition of the classroom. Still others concentrated on the effects of different teaching practices on pupil outcomes—on pupil learning of the subject or pupil attitudes. However, most of the studies gave their greatest attention to classroom *inter*action—to the give and take of teaching and the effects of teacher behavior on pupil behavior (and vice versa). Indeed, we shall see that some of the strongest evidence for "successful" teaching concerns the criterion of pupil classroom response rather than pupil learning or other product variables.

This book is organized into three quite different parts. The first introduces tools the student will find useful for understanding the substantive material to follow. It is composed of three chapters. *Chapter II* concerns itself with the basic, ideological posture of this text, with the ineffectiveness of earlier educational research to answer most questions concerning teaching, and with some of the notions that have grown up in education concerning teaching and its improvement. In this chapter we take up some of the beliefs we feel are likely to hamper students in their orientation to this text, and we attempt to counter them.

Chapter III concerns a model for classroom teaching. As will be discovered, the way in which we have organized our substantive chapters, and, in particular, the conventions we have adopted in presenting empirical findings reflect a model for research on teaching that should be made explicit. The chapter opens with a section on common characteristics of classroom teaching. We next present the model and define its various components. Finally, we take up the complex issue of *Commitments* that are held by many educators for the improvement of teaching by specific means, and we discuss how these have affected research on teaching.

Chapter IV presents methodological matters we believe students need to understand if they are to deal with research on teaching. Some readers will already have a good background in statistics and research methods. For them, this chapter will be a "snap." (We recommend they read it, nevertheless, since our verbal conventions may not be quite those they have learned from other sources.) Readers who have a weaker background in research will find the chapter packed with ideas. Despite these, the chapter contains no statistical jargon or symbols. From the beginning we decided to write this text with students in mind who despair of mathematics. As a result, throughout the book concepts, methods, and findings are presented in ordinary English rather than in statistical language. After an introductory section in which the general problems of research on teaching are exemplified, Chapter IV devolves into four substantive sections. These concern, respectively, problems of measurement, sampling, design of investigations, and interpretation of results. Conventions for the presentation of findings are then set forth.

The second part of this text constitutes six chapters in which concepts are advanced, studies are reviewed, and findings are presented. These six chapters are the heart of the book, and each deals with a somewhat different "theory" or "orientation" toward teaching. *Chapter V* concerns research generated by those who consider teaching to be a matter of leadership and classroom climate. Of the orientations reviewed here, this one, which arose out of the progressive education movement, has generated the largest number of research studies. (Whether the orientation is equally strong in generating consistent findings we leave to Chapter V.)

Chapter VI deals with the management and control of pupil behavior in the classroom—surely an issue of great concern to the beginning teacher. Three different orientations are reviewed, each of which has its strengths. The first, which also sprang from the traditions of progressive education, views successful teaching as a matter of reducing teacher domination and encouraging classroom democracy. The second focuses on the ways in which teachers are successful in controlling deviant behavior and managing classroom groups. The third reflects the field of behavior modification and sees teaching as a matter of teacher manipulation of classroom reinforcements.

Chapter VII represents a quite different orientation, one that looks first to the description of classroom events rather than to the immediate improvement of teaching. Various types of concepts are advanced for this description, including concepts for lesson format, teacher roles, pupil roles, classroom group structure, group functions, ecological features of the classroom, and rules and activities for The Classroom Game. As we shall see, studies using these concepts have generated a wealth of findings concerning the interlocking processes of teaching, although we are somewhat less certain of their relation to product variables to date.

Chapter VIII is the first of two chapters concerned with the intellectual aspects of teaching. Three different research traditions are reviewed, each of which has sprung from psychological orientations. First, we review studies that have reflected Bloom's *Taxonomy of Educational Objectives*. Next, we take up those that were stimulated, in part, by Guilford's model for the structure of intelligence. Finally, we look at a set of studies that was influenced by Piaget, among others. Although independently developed, these three research traditions have a number of common concepts, and some of their findings dovetail neatly.

Chapter IX is also concerned with intellect, but here the concepts were taken from logicians and linguists. Two different research traditions are reviewed that concerned themselves with the use of logic by teachers and pupils. Next, we examine a number of different studies that have used concepts from structural linguistics for the description of classroom events. Concepts and findings reported for both traditions are complex, and in many ways this chapter constitutes a "progress report" for research fields that are currently active.

The notion of a progress report is even more applicable to *Chapter X*, which reports research that has dealt with the *sequence* of events in classroom teaching. As may be appreciated, much of the success in teaching depends not so much on whether a teacher does or does not smile or compliment the pupil as it does on whether he smiles or compliments on appropriate occasions. Several different approaches to the study of classroom sequences are explored, each of which is represented by but one or two studies, and a number of exciting findings are reviewed. We attribute considerable importance to this last approach and speculate on next steps for the study of classroom sequence.

The six substantive chapters of this text, it will become apparent, provide scores of concepts and literally hundreds of findings. But what does it all add up to? Which of these concepts are most useful? Which of the findings are worthy of implementation if not of further research? And where should we be going next in our research on teaching? Part Three attempts to answer these legitimate questions. *Chapter XI* provides a summary of concepts, findings, and conclusions for teachers based on the evidence that was developed through review. Tabular summaries of major notions are provided, together with an evaluation of the several *Commitments* to the improvement of teaching that have so far appeared in research on teaching. *Chapter XII* provides a review of the culture of research on teaching and sets forth recommendations for future research, both general and specific. Finally, a methodological Appendix is also provided concerning procedures used by the authors in reviewing studies of teaching.

It would be presumptuous in the extreme to advertise this text as "everything you've always wanted to know about teaching." For one thing, we suspect that many of the things you've always wanted to know are as yet untouched by classroom research. For another, much of what we present concerns not what we know but what we genuinely *don't* know about teaching—despite claims to the contrary by advocates. Perhaps through study of this text the serious student will learn not only what we now know and don't know but, more important, how that knowledge was acquired, its limitations, its likely state in the near future, and what he might do about it personally. Perhaps the beginning of wisdom is to discover how very little we know as yet and what to do to rectify that lack.

ONE
NECESSARY
TOOLS

III
RESEARCH FAILURE
AND IDEOLOGICAL RESPONSE

What do we *really* know about teaching? Young people who are about to become teachers are anxious to acquire the substantive knowledge of their chosen field; those who are already teachers would like to improve their skills; and teacher-educators would like to supply both with knowledge that has been verified through rigorous research. Unfortunately, most of these persons will be disappointed in their search for knowledge. Most of the questions they will ask have yet to be studied at all, and much of the research on teaching conducted so far does not provide adequate answers.

The list of things we as yet know little about in teaching seems endless. Why do boys do less well than girls in reading tasks? How can the classroom teacher best help a disturbed pupil? What kinds of persons make good teachers of high school mathematics? Of grade school mathematics? How can teachers motivate pupils from broken homes or overcome the effects of an impoverished background? What is the relationship between the teaching practices pupils encounter and their later, adult behavior?

Such vexing questions lie at the heart of a person's motivation to become a teacher. Many young people are disappointed when they discover that we do not yet know the answers to them. And often, too, this disappointment turns to resentment when teacher trainees discover that their curriculum is based on "little but" philosophy, uplift, and the specifics of their supervised practice teaching. It is not that the curriculum of teacher training is "wrong." Young teachers can benefit from knowledge of the history and philosophy of education, from correlative information from psychology or sociology, and from supervision in their first fumbling attempts to handle a classroom of pupils. But young teachers and their mentors, indeed the society that supports and benefits from education, deserve factual information about teaching. Where is the knowledge that should constitute the core of teacher training? Where is the empirically based information that represents the *science of teaching*?

Once upon a time, perhaps twenty years ago, there would not have been means to counter these complaints. Although the social sciences are now more than a century old, and although information concerning such related fields as learning or child growth and development extends back to the turn of the century, until quite recently almost no empirical knowledge about teaching was available. Much research on teacher effectiveness had been conducted, but little knowledge had been developed from the effort. Indeed, so little has been known that some educators have concluded that teaching is unknowable—one of the mystic skills, akin to preaching or artistic creativity. Other educators have considered the activities of teaching to be so obvious as to need no research at all. Thus, master teachers write books in which they recommend the strategies they have found workable in the classroom, novelists such as Jonathan Kozol or Bel Kaufman entertain us with archetypical descriptions of teaching practices from a single school, and curriculum innovators outline new teaching programs in the expectation that they will be conducted in the manner specified and that they have the effects desired. Still other educators have, in a sense, given up on teaching and have concluded that pupils will learn regardless of—or in spite of—the teacher's effort, or that good teaching consists merely in the provision of a "supportive learning environment."

Let us lay our cards upon the table. The authors of this book assume that the activities of teaching are reasonable, natural, rational events. They have discoverable causes and effects. Though conducted by human beings who have unique perspectives and aspirations for them, the activities of teaching have an observable, existential reality that is not divergent from any other set of observable events. Further, it is not only possible to conduct research on the activities of teaching, but considerable research effort has taken place in the past two decades. And while this research is complex, as is teaching, it has already developed both concepts and findings. Although not yet sufficient to construct an empirically based *science of teaching*, these findings are already sufficient to provide useful information for educators. In particular, young teachers can find in this research concepts for thinking about their own teaching and that of others that *work*, together with a selection of findings concerning the causes, contexts, and effects of teaching.

Since this is the first text that we know of which attempts a comprehensive review of the research on the activities of teaching, we feel somewhat diffident about the task. In particular, we will shortly ask readers to learn something about the conditions and limitations of research-based knowledge so as to appreciate what we can or cannot actually claim to know about teaching. Before imposing this discipline, however, it is wise to clear the undergrowth. Readers come from many backgrounds and have been subjected to various viewpoints concerning teaching and the value of research-based knowledge. Some of these views are based on presumptions that educational research has yet to develop useful knowledge concerning teaching. Others question the value of even doing such research. It is wise that we face these issues directly.

EARLY RESEARCH ON TEACHER
EFFECTIVENESS

Although research on *teaching* is quite new, research on *teacher effectiveness* has been conducted for many years in this country and elsewhere. Indeed, so popular has been this research field that more than 10,000 published studies have appeared for it. As Gage (1960) has noted, not only is the literature on this subject overwhelming, but even bibliographies on the subject have become unmanageable (see, for example, Barr, 1948; Domas and Tiedeman, 1950; Morsh and Wilder, 1954). In general, this research has provoked poor reviews. As the Committee on Criteria of Teacher Effectiveness of the American Educational Research Association (1953) commented:

> The simple fact of the matter is that, after 40 years of research on teacher effectiveness during which a vast number of studies have been carried out, one can point to few outcomes that a superintendent of schools can safely employ in hiring a teacher or granting him tenure, that an agency can employ in certifying teachers, or that a teacher-education faculty can employ in planning or improving teacher-education programs. (p. 657)

Something surely must have been amiss in this early research. What can have been so wrong with it? And why is research on *teaching* more likely to produce useful knowledge than research on *teacher effectiveness*? Several reasons have been offered by critics for the failure of this early research effort. These include:

1. failure to observe teaching activities;
2. theoretical impoverishment;
3. use of inadequate criteria of effectiveness; and
4. lack of concern for contextual effects.

Failure To Observe Teaching Activities

Perhaps the most significant shortcoming of these early studies is that they assiduously avoided looking at the actual processes of teaching in the classroom. In the typical study some "causative" factor, for example, classroom size, a curriculum innovation, or a new teaching "method," was studied against some criterion of teacher effectiveness, for example, a rating given to teacher subjects by school principals, without any attempt to assess what was actually going on in the classroom. As was suggested by Gage (1963a), such approaches treated the classroom as a "black box" into which were fed teachers, pupils, hardware, and software and out of which came various results—and more or less pupil learning. The crucial events within the classroom, the point at which teachers, pupils, tasks, and equipment come together and at which results must be determined, was ignored, if not denied. If teachers do vary in their effectiveness, then it must be because they vary in the behaviors they exhibit in the classroom. To shed light on this point one must study classrooms—where the action actually is.

Theoretical Impoverishment

Many early studies were also of the "shotgun" variety, in which teachers' scores on a battery of tests which happened to be available were correlated with a criterion of effectiveness. In most cases little or no rationale was provided for the inclusion of an item in the test battery, and in many cases there seemed to be no justification for even suspecting a relation between a particular item and teacher effectiveness. Thus, studies have appeared in which nearly all conceivable teacher characteristics have been examined for their relationships to effectiveness. Among these have been, for example, teachers' eye color, voice quality, clothing style, musical ability, and even strength of the teacher's grip!

These studies, examples *par excellence* of "dust-bowl empiricism," often yielded no better than chance relations between test scores and effectiveness criteria. In the main they were stimulated by the desire to provide objective bases for selection, training, employment, and promotion of teachers. By the same token they offered minimal scope for *understanding* teaching effectiveness. Even had they succeeded in identifying reliable predictors, they could not have provided teacher-education programs with guidance regarding the types of experiences desirable for student teachers. In general, they told teacher-educators no more than that performance on college examinations and practice teaching are apparently unrelated to subsequent teaching effectiveness.

Inadequate Criteria of Effectiveness

Schools exist and teachers are employed in them for the purpose of promoting desired learnings in pupils. There seems to be no more obvious truth than that a teacher is effective to the extent that he causes pupils to learn what they are supposed to learn. Yet the early studies of teacher effectiveness seldom employed pupil learning as a criterion. More often they used ratings of teacher effectiveness that were given by principals, pupils, supervisors, and others who are notoriously prone to disagree.

Let us not argue that rating methods are inherently invalid or unreliable. Rather, the early approaches to research on teacher effectiveness misused these methods. Raters were either asked to rank teachers in order of their teaching "effectiveness" with no definitions offered for the concept, or they were expected to differentiate among the teachers on the basis of the learnings of their pupils, or they were asked to scale teachers on qualities such as "enthusiasm" and "confidence" which were presumed to relate to pupil learnings. In the first case the raters themselves were given the very difficult problem of establishing what constitutes teaching "effectiveness." In the second the raters were asked to display knowledge which they did not possess. In the third little evidence was offered suggesting that the qualities concerned were aspects of effective teaching.

Lack of Concern for Contextual Effects

Most of the early studies also sought universal qualities of effective teachers. Thus, it was assumed that teachers who are warm, intelligent, well organized, responsive, or good disciplinarians would be more "effective" as teachers than persons who possess these characteristics to a lesser extent. Such statements sound reasonable on first reading, yet will they hold for all types of subject matter, for both first- and twelfth-grade pupils, or for both inner-city and suburban schools? It may be that teacher "warmth" is a more important quality for first-graders than for twelfth-graders, while "discipline" might be a greater determinant of effectiveness for inner-city than for suburban schools. Thus, what makes for effective teaching probably varies from context to context. But most early studies ignored context and lumped together all teachers of a given school or school system for purposes of analysis.

It is possible, of course, that some qualities may make for effectiveness of teaching regardless of context. But others, perhaps the majority, will be context related. And if we are to evaluate the effectiveness of teachers, train teachers for their specific jobs, or assign teachers to schools and curricula where they will be most effective, it would be wise to take contextual information into account.

The Current Scene

Much of the research on teacher effectiveness took place prior to 1950. Did efforts of the succeeding twenty years come closer to providing useful information concerning teaching and the effectiveness of teachers?

Clearly, the answer is *yes*. Partly in response to the barren picture painted by reviewers such as Barr, research on teaching has undergone considerable reorientation in the past two decades. Above all, present research focuses more often on the processes of teaching. Many researchers have turned from the study of teacher qualities or training to the observation of actual instances of instruction in the classroom. Teachers and pupils are now being studied, in interaction, in many classrooms in the United States and other countries. Hundreds of research reports have now been published of investigations involving systematic observation of classroom behavior. So widespread has been this development that reviews of the literature concerning observational studies in the classroom have become almost annual events (see Withall, 1960; Medley and Mitzel, 1963; Meux, 1967; Biddle, 1967; Nuthall, 1968a, 1970; Flanders and Simon, 1970; and Rosenshine, 1971). A recent publication (Simon and Boyer, 1970) reports 79 different systems for observing the classroom, almost all of them developed in the last twenty years. Clearly, classrooms are no longer black boxes of mystery as far as research is concerned. Rather, these days they seem to be more like goldfish bowls.

Recent research is also more likely to reflect theory and to take into account contextual effects, as we shall see throughout this book. But does this research provide useful information concerning teacher effectiveness? In terms of relationships between teacher behavior and pupil learnings, our answer must be tentative. In spite of the sharp increase in studies of classroom events, most recent research has focused on the *activities* rather than the *effects* of teaching. Thus, researchers have appeared to retreat from the study of teacher effectiveness. Presumably this does not indicate loss of interest or lack of courage. Rather, researchers may simply be more aware of the difficulties involved in providing valid information concerning the teacher effectiveness problem. These difficulties are so substantial, in fact, that we devote much of the next two chapters to their discussion. Those who are seeking simple answers to the problem of teacher effectiveness are only slightly better off today than they were twenty years ago (however, see Rosenshine, 1971).

Awareness of difficulties is probably not the only reason for a slowing down in teacher effectiveness research. Developments of a conceptual nature involving logical relationships between teaching and learning probably played an important role in influencing the interests of researchers. Smith's (1960) argument that teaching and learning are conceptually independent established teaching as a phenomenon worth studying in its own right, so that researchers could concentrate on describing and understanding it without becoming involved in the more complicated issues of teaching-learning relationships. Many studies conducted over the last fifteen years reflect this orientation and have contributed newly conceived variables of teaching processes about which new questions involving teaching and learning can be asked and investigated.

Other problems in contemporary research can also be cited. As we shall see, some current research is also handicapped by the desire to "prove" that one prescribed method of teaching is superior to other methods. Other studies have made use of weak or confused observational tools, and most have collected data from only small samples of classrooms and teachers. But above all, contemporary research is underfinanced. As has often been noted (see Rosenshine and Furst, 1971, for example), we spend but a minute fraction of the funds available for education on research, and most of the funds committed to research are spent on investigating areas other than teaching. In comparison with expenditures for teacher training, curricular innovations, performance contracting, development and promotion of new educational devices, or laboratory studies of human learning, support of teaching research is not merely anemic, it is leukemic!

While not denying these problems, current classroom research has already provided substantial knowledge concerning the *processes* of teaching. This knowledge involves concepts that apply to instruction as well as information concerning instructional processes. Thus, we know substantially more about *teaching* than we did two decades ago as a result of classroom research. In addition, we are accumulating a small but growing store of knowledge concerning the causes and effects of classroom events. It is the presence of this knowledge concerning teaching that justifies this textbook— although we will return to the problem of teacher effectiveness again and again, whenever evidence pertaining to it is available from the literature.

One more implication of the current research scene is also worthy of mention. Given the lack of hard knowledge concerning the effects of teaching, it comes as a surprise to discover that some researchers have lent their names to grandiose claims concerning the state of this knowledge. It is sometimes claimed, for example, that certain programs of curriculum innovation have been found to produce sharp increases in either the quality of teaching or pupil performance. Another claim made is that teachers can improve their teaching by learning some of the concepts or by using some of the research instruments we shall discuss and review in this book. Instructional kits are actually provided by some researchers for these purposes, with the claim made or implied that the user can improve his teaching by using them. As will be seen, most of these claims are poorly supported by data. Although we surely hope that young teachers' efforts will be improved by review of the empirical knowledge available concerning teaching (indeed, it is one of our motivations in writing this book), we know of no evidence to indicate that this will happen. Let us assume, with charity, that researchers who have made these claims are guilty of nothing more than excessive zeal in seeking the ultimate goal of improving teaching.

BELIEFS CONCERNING TEACHING AND TEACHING RESEARCH

Given the poor state of our knowledge concerning teaching, one wonders what substitutes for this information in the employment, promotion, and training practices in education today? What substantiates the textbooks and recommendations of teacher-educators, the decisions of those who evaluate or innovate in the realm of teaching? Apart from common sense, such decisions are presently based on plausible beliefs or ideological commitments concerning teaching that are held by groups of educators.

It is small wonder that teachers and teacher-educators have developed ideological commitments concerning teaching. After all, classrooms must be met on a daily basis, schools must be staffed and organized, communities must be persuaded to fund needed improvements in education, a new generation of teachers must be motivated and trained for their profession. All of this takes commitment, and commitment is generated by the sharing of ideologies. Most of the shared beliefs of educators are either irrelevant to the content of this book or complement its purposes. However, some of these beliefs bear directly on the topics of classroom teaching and teaching research. Some concern the likelihood that improvements in pupil learning will follow from increased knowledge and control of classroom behavior. Some question the feasibility of research. Some, indeed, question the very assumption that generalized knowledge about teaching is attainable at all. Let us examine some of these beliefs that have developed during the decades when we have lacked scientific knowledge concerning teaching.

Teaching as an Art

There can be no doubt but that teaching is an extraordinarily complex task, as any teacher knows. But is it possible to subject such a complexity to the vagaries and generalizations of scientific inquiry? Some critics have suggested that this effort is either futile or dangerous.

> It seems to me very dangerous to apply the aims and methods of science to human beings as individuals. . . . Teaching involves emotions, which cannot be systematically appraised and employed, and human values, which are quite outside the grasp of science. . . . "Scientific" teaching, even of scientific subjects, will be inadequate as long as both teachers and pupils are human beings. Teaching is not like inducing a chemical reaction: it is much more like painting a picture or making a piece of music, or on a lower level like planting a garden or writing a friendly letter. (Highet, 1954, pp. vii–viii)

While it would be interesting to hear the reactions of teachers to the suggestion that teaching is like painting, composing, gardening, and letter-writing, more pertinent is Gage's (1964) reply to Highet.

> Painting and composing, and even friendly letter-writing and casual conversation, have inherent order and lawfulness that can be subjected to theoretical analysis. . . . The artist whose lawfulnesses are revealed does not become an automaton; ample scope remains for his subtlety and individuality. . . .
> So it is with teaching. Although teaching requires artistry, it can be subjected to scientific scrutiny. The power to explain, predict, and control that may result from such scrutiny will not dehumanize teaching. . . . And for the work of those who train, hire, and supervise teachers, theory and empirical knowledge of teaching will provide scientific grounding. (pp. 270–271)

The extent to which teaching ought to be an art has also been questioned, especially by Gallagher (1970).

> Is teaching an art? Indeed it is. Perhaps too much of one. Surgery was once too much an art and many people died as a result. Cooking is an art, and while few people die of it these days, drugstores do a thriving business in remedies for misbegotten creative culinary efforts. For when a set of skills is in a developmental stage where people say, "It is an art," they mean several things. First, that there are only a very few persons who have the skills that can identify them as highly effective practitioners, as "artists." Second, even these artists cannot give a systematic account of how they practice their art, and they are reduced to modeling their performance for those who would learn from them. But it is hard to imitate the true artist, and his genius too often dies with him. . . .
> Those interested in the improvement of education and teaching would like to remove some of the mystery of the art of effective teaching through systematic study. (p. 30)

The controversy between art and science can be resolved only when it is known to what extent scientific objectives are achievable with respect to teaching. One aim of science is the discovery of order or patterns which permit generalizations about the phenomena under study; without such order study of causes or effects is impossible and scientific investigation is futile. Such a state would exist if teaching behaviors, and therefore teaching effectiveness, were truly idiosyncratic—the private preserve of the individual teacher. Abundant evidence is cited in this book to challenge such a conclusion. Although teachers may be unique in the combination of qualities they exhibit in their classroom behavior, those qualities are measurable in terms of concepts that apply to many teachers. To consider teaching "merely" an art is to turn one's back on these concepts and the evidence supporting them. Such a posture seems futile.

Teaching as Obvious

Another contention sometimes leveled at teaching is that its activities and effects are too obvious to require research. Consider the following propositions concerning education that are "obviously true."

1. More intelligent children tend to receive less social acceptance from their peers in the classroom; that is, there is a negative correlation between IQ, or scholastic achievement, and sociometric status. (This is easy to understand, because as is well known, children resent the greater success, higher grades, and teacher acceptance of the more able pupils.)

2. If a group of pupils is given a considerable amount of practice and instruction in developing a skill, the pupils will become more alike in that skill. (Certainly, if a group of persons is subjected to a uniform experience, their homogeneity on dimensions relevant to this experience will become greater.)

3. If a teacher wants to measure how much her pupils have learned from a given kind of instruction, she should subtract the pupils' score on a pretest from their score on an equivalent posttest on the given kind of achievement. (Nothing could be simpler than following the same procedure that a parent uses in measuring how much his children have gained in height over a period of time.)

4. When growth in achievement is measured by the "posttest minus pretest" method just described, it will usually be found that the brighter pupils have gained more than the pupils who had less of this kind of achievement to begin with. (Of course this is true, just as taller children at a given age become taller by growing faster, and until they approach the end of the growing period, they will continue to grow faster.)

5. If you want to strengthen a kind of behavior, you should reward it, and if you want to eliminate an erroneous kind of behavior, you should punish it. And if the pupil repeats his error, he should be punished more severely than for the first error. (And, of course, many parents successfully control their children's behavior in exactly this way.)

6. The only way to secure transfer of learning from one situation to another is to increase the similarity, or the number of so-called identical elements, between the learning situation and the application situation. (Ever since William James and E. L. Thorndike, we have known that there is no general transfer and that schooling should therefore be made as much like real life as possible.) (Gage, 1972, p. 144)

The only difficulty with these "obvious truths" concerning education is that they have *all*, without exception, been contradicted by repeated research. "More intelligent pupils are [in fact] *better* accepted by their classmates. Individual differences *increase* with training. [Etc.]" (Gage, 1972, p. 145). Similarly, common sense is likely to be a poor guide to good teaching. We need research on teaching no less than we need it in medicine, industrial relations, social rehabilitation, or any other human activity.

Teaching as Ineffective

Another, more sophisticated, reaction to our lack of knowledge concerning teaching is to conclude that teaching is inherently ineffective. This reaction appears in several quarters. Some educators (such as Stephens, 1967) believe that pupils learn primarily because of their own maturing abilities and forces that appear in their backgrounds, home, and community. Thus, the task of the teacher is merely to provide an appropriate "learning environment," and if this minimal environment appears, then pupils will learn spontaneously. The reason we have found so little from the decades of research on teacher effectiveness, it is argued, is that differences in teaching style simply make little difference in the spontaneous processes of pupil learning.

A related argument has been advanced by the authors of the now-classic study of pupil achievement in black, white, and racially integrated schools, *Equality of Educational Opportunity* (Coleman *et al.*, 1966). This study, based on a national sample of schools, concluded that pupils' social class background was the single most important determinant of pupil achievement and that school characteristics were relatively unimportant. This finding has been interpreted by Coleman (1972) and others to indicate that attempts to improve teaching will be ineffective in producing significant changes in the level of pupil achievement, particularly for those pupils from impoverished backgrounds.

Regarding Coleman's data, it turns out that the findings cited are statistically artifactual and are based on differences among schools rather than among individual teachers or classrooms. In the United States there is a high positive correlation between social class in the community and per-pupil expenditure in the schools. If one examines first the effects of social class on pupil achievement and only then the residual effects of school characteristics (as did Coleman *et al.*, 1966), one is bound to conclude that social class was the more important variable. But apart from this problem, it is safe to assume that most schools will feature a range of both capable and less capable teachers. To assess pupil achievement on a per-school basis washes out the effects of individual teachers.

Another difficulty with both Stephens' and Coleman's arguments is that they contradict logic. One does not have to look far within school curricula to identify knowledge and skills that pupils would not learn unless presented to them by a teacher. This is not to say that teaching guarantees learning or that no learning occurs without teaching. What it does say, however, is that the learning of organized curriculum material will not occur unless someone presents that material to the learner. Teaching, therefore, must make a difference.

Teaching as a Reflection of Learning

As we have seen, during the first half of the twentieth century research-ers interested in *teaching* assiduously avoided the classroom—and generated little knowledge concerning teaching. During the same period, however, other researchers conducted a great deal of research in certain types of *learning*—with considerably more success. Thus, until quite recently we have known much more about learning than about teaching. This imbalance was noted dramatically by Gage (1963a), who pointed out that the entry under "learning" in the *Comprehensive Dictionary of Psychological and Psychoanalytical Terms* (English and English, 1958) occupied three pages, while that under "teaching" was confined to only five lines. Further, a quick perusal of recent textbooks in educational psychology suggests their greater concern with learning and characteristics of pupils than with teaching and characteristics of teachers.

In defense of earlier researchers, it was surely easier to study learning, which could be measured by objective tests or animal behavior, than teach-ing, which required observation of classrooms. Nevertheless, curricula for teacher education have had to depend far more on information concerning learning than on information concerning teaching. And "theories of teaching" have often turned out to reflect little more than the concepts and knowl-edge developed in research on animal or human learning.

At least two difficulties have been generated by this reliance on knowl-edge about learning. The first, suggested by Gage (1963b), is that theories of learning do not make explicit the processes by which teachers might provide optimal conditions for learning in the classroom:

> teachers need to know how children learn, and how they depend on motiva-tion, readiness, and reinforcement. But . . . teachers similarly need to know how to teach—how to motivate pupils, assess their readiness, act on the assessment, present the subject, maintain discipline, and shape a cognitive structure. Too much of educational psychology makes the teacher *infer* what he needs to do from what he is told about learners and learning. Theories of

teaching would make *explicit* how teachers behave, why they behave as they do, and with what effects. (p. 133)

A second difficulty concerns the types of learning about which most has been known. Researchers of learning have often been castigated for their apparent disregard for human subjects and the types of learning emphasized in the objectives of classroom education. Techniques for inducing salivation in dogs, proficiency at ping-pong in pigeons, and lever-pressing in rhesus monkeys appear to have little application to such human tasks as writing books or exploring space. And while knowledge about the learning of nonsense syllables is relevant to rote memorization, "nonsensyllaby" is to be found as a formal curriculum entry only in the classrooms of a recent piece of educational satire (Doenau, 1970).

Learning theorists have also gleaned much of their knowledge of learning in settings that are strikingly unlike classrooms.

> Although he might wince at the appelation, the learning theorist is a private tutor par excellence. Rarely if ever does he deal with a group—a flock of pigeons, or a tribe of monkeys. Imagine his horror if faced with a pack of rats to instruct in bar-pressing! (Jackson, 1966, p. 19)

If this were not enough, meaningful verbal learning, which is a major concern of schools, has only recently attracted concerted attention by learning theorists (Ausubel, 1963). Since most of this latter research has been conducted in laboratory rather than classroom settings, its applicability to the classroom is unknown. Periods of instruction, sizes of learning groups, and the extent to which the experiences are structured in these laboratory studies all depart significantly from normal conditions in classrooms (see Rosenshine and Furst, 1971).

A somewhat different insight into the problem of applying the results of learning research to the classroom situation is provided by Nuthall. He suggests that learning researchers have tended to focus their efforts on special kinds of learning, while various kinds of learning are required in the classroom. Nuthall (1972, personal communication) elaborates as follows:

> Research on learning is characteristically undertaken in order to find out how a particular kind of learning takes place. . . . The result of this orientation is that while someone like Skinner can show how best to achieve operant conditioning because of his extensive research into the nature of operant conditioning, he is not in a position to show whether in any particular set of circumstances, operant conditioning is the appropriate kind of learning. The problem that faces the teacher is, given a particular curriculum objective (such as the learning of multiplication tables in arithmetic), which is the best form of learning in order to ensure that the curriculum objective is best achieved . . . ? So long as research on learning is devoted to the understanding of particular instances of learning, and does not address itself to the ques-

tion of what is the general nature of learning or attempt to provide a map of all the different types of learning that may operate in any set of circumstances, then learning research cannot hope to provide teachers with the kind of information they need.

A major criticism of learning research, then, is that it does not meet the challenge provided by the sheer complexity of the classroom setting and of the learning tasks pursued there. But, say some learning theorists, these criticisms assume that teaching and learning must continue to be provided in the complex classroom environment as we know it today. Why not alter the setting so as to make the implementation of knowledge about learning easier? Conventional classrooms, they argue, are unnecessarily complex, and it is for that very reason that research on teaching effectiveness has failed to produce meaningful results. Furthermore, even if it were possible through research in conventional classrooms to identify teaching skills by comparing effective teachers with less effective ones, we would be limited to a knowledge of the best teaching only as it exists today.

> The most significant conclusion that can be drawn from efforts to use teachers as a basis for information about teaching is that effective instruction can be produced by a variety of combinations of characteristics and conditions rather than by one unique combination. If this were not the case, efforts to enumerate the characteristics of good teachers would have resulted in the identification of at least one or two critical characteristics. However, neither the observation of master teachers nor that of a large number of effective teachers . . . has led to findings that are either substantial or sufficient for the understanding of teaching as a process. Thus, an alternative approach is needed. (Stolurow, 1965, p. 226)

The "alternative approach" suggested by Stolurow and many learning theorists is the use of programmed instruction together with computer-assisted instruction. Through such means, it is argued, instruction can be tailored to the needs of individual pupils, thus allowing us to eliminate the mass classroom experience altogether. If such advocates are indeed prophets, it may not be particularly useful to study classroom teaching, for this particular social form will shortly disappear!

We are not very excited by this argument, however, because it appears that all it amounts to, in Stolurow's case, is an attempt to convert classrooms into instances of a particular kind of learning, that is, behavioral learning. We doubt that this is the most appropriate type of learning for more than a narrow range of curriculum objectives. We doubt, too, that either citizens or educators are ready to abandon some curriculum objectives simply because they do not lend themselves to behaviorist techniques. With Gage (1966) we suspect that some forms of computer-based instruction will gradually appear in the classroom, supplementing and helping the teacher, but that live teachers and classroom experiences will persist for some decades to come.

As long as live teachers in conventional classrooms remain, the problem of training them more effectively will depend upon identifying those aspects of teaching that contribute to effectiveness in the complex classroom setting. This does not necessarily mean that it will be impossible to go beyond what is best today, for there appears scope for synthesizing a better model from the best of present-day teaching practices and knowledge developed concerning programmed learning and other classroom innovations.

Discovery Learning

Learning theorists have not been alone in advocating the improvement of teaching by applying insights from a related field of inquiry. Another such approach may be found in those who advocate *discovery learning*.

The discovery-learning approach seems an attempt to supply a psychological rationale for the "inspired performance of the master teacher" (Nuthall and Snook, 1973, p. 59). Its proponents have ranged from psychologists such as Bruner (1966) to curriculum writers and theorists (Taba, 1963) to experienced teachers (Hendrix, 1961). Given this diverse background, it is not surprising that the message of discovery learning is not always clear. Common to these writers, however, is the notion that teachers should encourage pupils to discover rules, principles, and generalizations for themselves. Thus, the teacher should avoid providing these directly and foreswear the use of those external reinforcements so dear to advocates of programmed instruction. Rather, the teacher must structure the learning situation so that pupils discover motivation, principles, and errors themselves.

Discovery learning appears to have made its major impact on new curricula in mathematics, the physical and biological sciences, and the social studies. One of the main claims of this approach is that learning becomes exciting and thus pupils participate with high motivation. By the same token the maintenance of this motivation and excitement probably depends on the subjective feelings of success experienced by pupils. Thus, the teacher faces the problem of ensuring success without "taking over" in the manner of expository teaching.

One major difficulty with the approach is that it is easier for the teacher to see what he is *not* supposed to do than what he is supposed to do (see Wittrock, 1966). Clearly, the teacher must not state principles and become a personal source of sanctions. But should he use the inductive method, encourage verbalization of principles, seek and reward examples of "insights," or what? Another problem concerns the apparent difficulty of conducting a classroom by means of discovery learning. Surely it is easier to be a traditional teacher and to follow a set curriculum than it is to be consistently "inspiring." At their best discovery-learning materials are exciting, innovative, and challenging for pupils. However, one wonders whether the method will succeed with teachers of limited motivation or with pupils from inner-city neighborhoods.

The discovery-learning approach is similar to many other prescriptive approaches which have been espoused on grounds other than their demonstrated effectiveness in classrooms (however, see Anastasiow et al., 1970; and Worthen, 1968). Such approaches have been advocated in teacher training either because they are consistent with a fashionable set of educational values or because of favorable subjective impressions by someone who has tried to implement them. Clearly, observations of the behaviors of teachers claiming to be following "the method" are desirable—first, to establish that such teachers are alike in doing things that can be regarded as "the method" and second, to test the effectiveness of "the method" in contrast with other styles of teaching. Those who have sought to improve teaching, whether they have favored discovery learning, phonics, team teaching, language laboratories, or open schools, have traditionally based their enthusiasms on plausible argument rather than evidence. Unfortunately, most contemporary innovations in education seem to be established by such means (see Chall, 1967).

Curricular Innovations

The same general comments may be applied to most recent programs of curriculum innovation. A number of educators have attempted to improve the quality of pupil learning by developing programs for changing curricula so that they would be more consistent with existing objectives of education or so that different objectives might be pursued. Such large-scale curriculum projects as the School Mathematics Study Group (SMSG), Harvard Project Physics (HPP), Physical Sciences Study Committee (PSSC), and Biological Sciences Curriculum Study (BSCS) are excellent examples of programs that select and organize subject matter for such purposes. However, for us the crucial issue must be the way in which these programs are translated into classroom experiences.

Curriculum developers need to ask themselves three questions regarding the implementation of their work: (1) Do different teachers implement the curriculum in the same way? (2) Are the experiences provided consistent with the aims of the curriculum? and (3) Do these experiences induce the effects desired in pupils? All of these questions are related to classroom research, of course. Unfortunately, none is adequately researched in most programs of curricular innovation.

With respect to the first question, Gallagher (1970) studied a group of teachers who were supposedly implementing part of the "Blue Version" of the BSCS curriculum. He found striking differences among the performances of trained teachers and found it doubtful that such a curriculum could be even said to "exist." Reminiscent of Gallagher's findings were those of Balzer

(1969), who compared biology teachers who had been trained using BSCS materials with those using other curricula. Numerous differences were found in teaching that could not be attributed to the curricula used. Earlier, Bellack and his co-workers (1966) had a similar experience in a study we shall review in detail in Chapter IX. Fifteen tenth- and twelfth-grade teachers were given the same four lessons to teach on international trade. Yet Bellack *et al.* found great variability in the subject matter actually covered in these supposedly identical lessons! Evidently, common curricular training is no guarantee of common teaching performance.

Regarding the second question, Gallagher (1970), Balzer (1969), and Moore (not dated) all found that teachers who were supposedly trained in a new curriculum stressing high levels of thinking (BSCS or PSSC) gave considerable emphasis to low levels of thinking in their classrooms. Some curricular instructions may be easy to follow; others are so difficult that months of training would be required for their implementation. But sorting these out would appear problematic without classroom research.

Concerning the third question, most curriculum projects are either not validated with research on pupil effects or are tested with research designs similar to those used in early research on teacher effectiveness. In the typical study an experimental group of teachers trained with the new materials is compared with another group that has not received training for effects on pupil gain scores, with no attention given to what the two groups do in the classroom. Such designs leave us in doubt concerning the features of the curriculum actually implemented and are often influenced by the "Hawthorn effect." (This effect concerns the influence of experimenter enthusiasm on the experimental group. Nearly *any* innovation in teaching can be found to produce higher pupil gain scores during its first year of implementation if its teachers are energetic advocates!) Once again, knowledge concerning the impact of curricular innovation on pupils would appear to require classroom research.

It seems clear that curriculum developers need to consider the behaviors of teachers who will implement their programs. We would suggest that curricular programs follow a three-phase model in their activities: conceptualization of objectives for teaching; development of procedures that will induce teachers to exhibit these in their classroom practices; and validation of the latter with research on pupil effects. An approximation to this model has, in fact, been followed in the program led by Taba and McNaughton at San Francisco State College (Taba *et al.*, 1964; Taba, 1966). Unfortunately, classroom research in support of newly proposed curricula is only too rare.

Generality of Teaching Skills

Yet another ideology concerning teaching questions the generality of teaching skills. Some teacher-educators believe that teaching is uniquely different for each grade level or subject area. Thus, whereas at one time most schools of education offered a single course in Methods of Teaching, they now tend to offer different methods courses for various grade levels within the primary curriculum and for some twenty or more subject-matter specializations in the secondary curriculum. Surely there are differences between the teaching of mathematics to twelfth-graders and the conducting of "show and tell" in the first grade. But are there not also similarities?

Let us consider some of the latter. Wherever it is found classroom discourse is always conducted using the language of the community; rules for classroom discipline and procedure are remarkably similar everywhere; teachers at all levels may be found asking questions while pupils struggle to answer them in the company of their peers; and classroom noise, smiles, chalkboards, tests, and routines have standardized uses that are familiar to all. Thus, while teaching obviously varies depending on grade level, there are patterns within this variation and similarities that cut across all grade levels.

The same conclusion probably also applies to subject-matter differences in teaching. Recent research evidence has appeared suggesting that the nature of effective teaching varies according to the level of abstraction of the learning tasks set for pupils (see Taba, Levine, and Elzey, 1964; and Soar, 1966). However, if tasks have a similar level of abstraction even though they involve different substantive topics, the pattern of effective teaching behavior remains relatively constant (see Dell and Hiller, 1968; and Hiller, Fisher, and Kaess, 1969). Thus, effective explaining of a cause-and-effect relationship in physics may be similar to effective explaining of similar relationships in social studies or biology, but each may be different from effective explaining of a routine procedure in both physics and social studies.

However, speculations about the specificity or generality of effective teaching have but little support from research to date. As we shall see, most research on classroom events has involved a limited range of grade levels or academic subjects, yet most researchers have assumed their findings to apply to a wide range of classroom types. Sometimes this assumption has proved a good one; sometimes additional evidence has contradicted it. Since this is a book about the *generalities* of teaching (and since science presumes generalization of results to similar events not yet studied), we shall assume that findings that have been documented for several grade levels or subjects will apply to others too. However, exceptions to such generalizations will be noted and commented upon when they appear.

Performance Criteria for Teaching

One last substitute for scientific knowledge on the effectiveness of teaching has been the appearance of *performance criteria* in education. If we cannot provide clear evidence that teaching behavior of a given sort leads to pupil learning, then we can at least state standards for the classroom behaviors of teachers and pupils that presumably reflect "good education." Thus, the newer curricula tend to state tangible behavioral objectives for teaching such as "asking evaluative questions" or "providing reinforcement for student answers" rather than such vague goals as "providing meaningful experiences" or "educating the whole child." Performance criteria are also sometimes encouraged for pupil classroom behavior, such as "making certain that each pupil reaches criterion at the end of the lesson."

As is pointed out by Rosenshine and Furst (1971), performance criteria appear to dominate the recent model teacher education programs funded by the U.S. Office of Education (see Schalock, 1968; Houston, 1968; Allen and Cooper, 1968; Hough, 1968; and Joyce, 1968). There are several apparent reasons for this emphasis, two of which are suggested by Rosenshine and Furst (1971).

> The first is the emphasis in the current literature on behavioral objectives in instruction. The second source is undoubtedly the series of experimental studies which have been conducted in teacher education. These studies were designed to determine whether training procedures could modify the behavior of the teacher as measured by systematic observation. The results of these investigations indicated that training procedures which focused on denotable, specific behaviors were more effective than traditional methods courses in changing teaching behavior. (p. 38)

Another reason may be the (belated) recognition by some educators that objective tests may not be the sole or best means of establishing pupil growth, if not pupil worth. Teachers often speak of pupils who "did not do as well as they should have" on a given test at the end of the semester. Such judgments are based on the teacher's knowledge of the pupil and his capabilities, which are gained, in turn, from observing his performance in class. This leads to the suggestion that performance criteria for the pupil might actually have their own validity as a measure of educational success. Still another reason may stem from the growing importance of education as a pleasurable experience in itself. As people are spending more and more time in classrooms, as leisure increases, as greater focus is placed on continuing and adult education, characteristics of classrooms are being examined for their own qualities rather than in terms of whether they lead to specific pupil learning. Thus, it may matter little in an adult education classroom whether testable learning results so long as those present are obviously "interested" and "participating."

Whatever the source of performance criteria—whether they be educational philosophy, findings from laboratory studies, subject-matter research, experimental classroom studies, process-product research, demands from the public, or shared values concerning "the good life" or "educational quality"—those who state performance criteria must ultimately seek to establish whether behaviors matching the specifications can be observed, and, if so, under what conditions they appear. The stating of performance criteria for teaching absolves us of the necessity of studying pupil outcomes, but does not free us from looking at classroom behavior. Indeed, if classroom behavior is our measure of success, looking at the evidence becomes all the more important.

Ideologies in the Future

As we have seen, a number of competing ideologies have appeared concerning the nature of teaching and teaching research. We have interpreted these to be altogether human and understandable responses to our lack of scientific knowledge about the teaching field. Teachers must confront their classrooms and teacher-educators must prepare them for this task. Superintendents and school board members must make hard decisions concerning whom to hire and fire and whether to adopt a newly proposed curriculum or educational device. To carry these decisions forward each educator will draw on beliefs concerning teachers that are plausible to him—whether or not they are now validated by research.

At the same time we have stressed that ideologies concerning teaching cannot replace evidence from research. At best such ideologies are unsupported by evidence; at worst they are monstrously in error. The only way we can tell for sure is to subject them to research in which the actual processes of teaching are observed. Enough research evidence has already accumulated to cause us to question some of the ideological tenets we have reviewed. But most of the beliefs cited have simply not been subjected to research as yet.

Needless to say, we should like to advocate tentativeness with respect to all systems of belief concerning teaching until they are based on evidence. It seems to us that such a posture would help to minimize error and promote additional research. We rather doubt that this advice will have much effect, however. The temptation to believe in simple explanations is almost universal in human experience, and a thousand years of medical research has not yet eradicated quackery in that profession! Most educators hold strong beliefs concerning teaching, and we think it unlikely that they will abandon these tomorrow just because we tell them to do so. Perhaps a more realistic aspiration is to encourage readers to adopt a generally open mind concerning the several and competing theories of teaching for which we present the evidence in this book. If some of the evidence cited causes readers to question their own ideological commitments, so much the better.

Above all, we hope by now that readers are convinced of the need for research on teaching. The classroom activities of teachers and pupils are observable events. They have discoverable causes and consequences. Not only is it possible to investigate them by observational means, but considerable research has already been conducted in this area. Among the tangible results of this research are the development of new concepts that apply to teaching, the discovery of information concerning instructional processes, and a few tentative findings concerning the causes and effects of teaching. Educators need this information; and the entire educational community needs continuation and expansion of the research effort.

Although it will not cure racial injustice or pollution, the study of teaching is a necessity for education. Moreover, research in this field has now produced concepts and findings needed by educators. The knowledge is, however, far from complete and there are many questions yet to be asked, let alone answered. These are the challenges to researchers, and we emphasize them in the chapters that follow.

A MODEL FOR CLASSROOM TEACHING

Of models for teaching there appears a never-ending supply. Most readers will already have been exposed to one or more models in the form of a diagram or listing of the factors presumably involved in the teaching process. (If not, see Mitzel, 1957; B. O. Smith, 1960, 1963; Ryans, 1960, 1963; Taba, Levine, and Elzey, 1964; Biddle, 1964; Strasser, 1967; Campbell, 1968; or most recent textbooks in educational psychology.)

The fact that such models appear should surprise nobody. For one thing, teaching is a complex activity that reflects many factors. Most of these relationships have not been adequately studied, nor indeed do we always have an agreed-upon set of terms with which to express them. Those who wish to teach about or study education find it convenient, therefore, to set forth a model for their efforts. In addition, many of us are interested in improving education, and often that interest is reflected in a commitment we make to some innovation—a new curriculum, a new educational device, a theory, a particular means for reaching and inspiring pupils. These commitments, too, may often be expressed and encouraged by models for teaching. Again, to set up a model for something complex is often the first step in the development of a genuine theory concerning it. Thus construction of models for teaching is heuristic.

Our task is a somewhat different one. In this text we consider not what teaching is about theoretically, nor what it should be like, but rather what has been found out about it in empirical research. Our aims are neither those of synthesis, though we shall review various theories of teaching as we go along, nor exhortation, though we shall consider the evidence for several innovative programs in teaching and teacher education. Rather, we shall take a long, hard, cold look at teaching from the viewpoint of those who have studied the actual behaviors of teachers and pupils and then seek knowledge from and about this research that will be of use to teachers, teacher-educators and researchers.

But this research is no less complex than the complex subject it investigates. Thus, we should find in it not only a wide variety of different conceptual schemes for expressing the behaviors of teachers and pupils but also many different types of variables that are presumed to bear relationships to the teaching process. If we are to consider this research in an economical and thoughtful manner, we must find a way of assembling concepts and information. And so we too shall use a model.

Before turning to the model itself it is useful to consider the boundaries of our problem. Although each teaching situation, each classroom, indeed each pupil, is a unique event, in many ways the process of teaching is surprisingly invariant across the United States and throughout the Western world. Clearly, classroom teaching is different from the kinds of events that normally take place in the operating room, in the military staff conference, at the family dinner table, in the boxing ring. Each of these settings has its own pattern of typical activities, its own equipment, its own cast of characters who usually appear. So does the classroom, and it will help the building of our model if we consider these in the beginning.

WHAT CAN WE ASSUME ABOUT CLASSROOMS?

Let us begin with the cast. Most classrooms feature but a single teacher and a group of 30 or more pupils of approximately equal age. The teacher is an adult and is given legal responsibility not only for the physical welfare of the pupils but also for providing curricular experiences for them. The teacher is usually a part of an administrative hierarchy that includes higher-ranking teachers, the school principal, curricular specialists, a superintendent of schools, and a school board which bears ultimate responsibility for the operation of education in the community. At all levels the teacher is more likely to be a woman. Up until World War II most teachers were also spinsters; at present this is no longer true. Most teachers in the United States are certificated to their professions by virtue of completing a four-year course of teacher education in an accredited college—and hence are considered "experts" by both their colleagues and their pupils, though not always by parents and others within the community who support the school. Most primary teachers are subject-matter generalists, although they may have been trained to teach a particular age level. Most secondary teachers are subject-matter specialists.

Pupils vary in age, ability, sex, and color, and classrooms have a tendency toward homogeneity in most pupil variables. However, while homogeneous grouping accorded to some pupil variables is accepted by educators and the public alike, homogeneity with respect to other pupil variables is viewed as either questionable, immoral, or illegal. Segregation by race is now illegal in the United States, although the separation of city and suburban school systems more or less guarantees its continuation in many cities, and segregation by social class and ethnic background appears in many communities. Most public schools in America practice co-education, while those private schools and colleges that were originally set up for the education of either young women or young men are declining in number. Segregation by ability is practiced in many localities—under such labels as "streaming" or "ability grouping"—and is generally supported by parents who are wealthy or have high aspirations for their children and decried by those who are disadvantaged.

Unlike hospitals, prisons, or the army, schools are not "total institutions." On the other hand, schools occupy more of the pupil's life than does any other institution.

> Aside from sleeping, and perhaps playing, there is no other activity that occupies as much of the child's time as that involved in attending school . . . there is no single enclosure in which he spends a longer time than he does in the classroom. From the age of six onward he is a more familiar sight to his teacher than to his father, and possibly even to his mother. (Jackson, 1968, p. 5)

Nevertheless, pupils and teachers begin and end their days in private pursuits and only enter the school for a period of from four to seven hours. At the primary level a single teacher and a group of pupils tend to remain together in a given classroom for this entire period, although the school day is broken up by periodic events such as recess and the lunch hour, which take pupils into other realms and other hands. However, the school day is usually organized into a prescribed set of "lessons" whose titles and content are set forth in curricular guides that apply throughout the school or school system. Sometimes the primary teacher has flexibility in scheduling these lessons. In other schools rigid times are prescribed for the teaching of each subject.

At the secondary level "lessons" are conducted by specialist teachers who occupy a classroom that is designed for their specialty and that often contains teaching aids such as vocabulary cards, maps, pickled animal organs, or bunsen burners. Pupils move from teacher to teacher and from setting to setting at the ringing of a bell, and each pupil and teacher must contend with a half-dozen classroom groups a day. For this reason the extent to which a secondary pupil is exposed to a given teacher during the school year is far less than for the primary pupil. This may be one reason for expecting that primary teachers have a greater effect on pupils than secondary teachers. (Another reason concerns the fact that secondary pupils probably spend more of their time in school in nonclassroom contexts—such as in study halls, gymnasia, play rehearsals, and club meetings— and are more likely to be influenced by the culture of their peers. Still another concerns the primacy of early learning and the fact that primary pupils are less mature.)

Despite innovations in school architecture, classrooms are also surprisingly similar. Most are rectangular, contain a desk for the teacher and smaller desks for each pupil, are surrounded by windows, chalkboards, and bulletin boards, and have tile or wooden floors. They all tend to have a flag, patriotic pictures, a waste basket, a pencil sharpener, supply cupboards, and exhibits of work by pupils or of materials pertinent to the subjects taught.

Classrooms are also similar in their cultures—in the activities that take place in them. Citing Herbert (1967), Nuthall and Snook (1973) have suggested that the activities of lessons usually fall into three basic forms.

> The first form [*lecturing*] is one in which the teacher is in control of the treatment of subject matter. The teacher is lecturing, performing, demonstrating or exhibiting materials. In the second form [*teacher-pupil interaction*] both teacher and pupil have some control over the treatment of subject matter. Usually this involves verbal interaction with variations in the degree to which teacher or students control the course of the interaction. In the third form [*seat work*] the students are displaced from the direct control of the teacher and are engaged in assigned or unassigned exercises, practical work, or study. In this last form of lesson the teacher's control is indirect. (pp. 50–51)

Further, proportions of time spent in these three types of activities tend to be quite stable. In most classrooms roughly one fifth of the time is taken up by lecturing, perhaps a third by seat work, and the rest by teacher-pupil interaction, either by itself or in combination with the other two forms (see Chapter VII).

Of these three lesson-activity forms the second, teacher-pupil interaction, is the one especially characteristic of classroom teaching. (Lecturing is found in the university, the church, and the political rally; seat work may be performed in private as well as public.) It is not surprising that most theories and research on the teaching process have concentrated on this form. According to Bellack *et al.* (1966), the process of teacher-pupil interaction may be considered a "game" with rules for both the teacher and pupil players. Again we quote from Nuthall and Snook (1973).

> They [Bellack *et al.*] characterize the game as one in which the object is to engage in verbal discourse about subject matter. The teacher obeys a set of rules which stipulate that *he* must do most of the talking and must structure the specific form and content of the verbal game at any one time. If he plays in the way expected of a teacher he will spend most of his time asking questions and commenting on pupil responses. From time to time he will spend time structuring the content and providing summaries of previous discourse.
>
> The rules for the pupils are much more restrictive. The pupil's primary task is to answer questions, to reply when called on. The pupil must respond as though the teacher always asks questions which a pupil *should* be able to answer. He may not respond evaluatively, but may, under certain conditions, ask the occasional question.
>
> The pupil is expected to pay attention to the progress of a lesson even though he will not be expected to respond more than six or seven times in an hour. When he is asked to respond his response will be repeated, praised, or

commented on by the teacher. Most of his time will be taken up listening to other pupils' responses and the teacher's comments to those responses.

The evidence gathered by Hoetker and Ahlbrand (1969) strongly suggests that this classroom language game has had a long and persistent history. Records of observational studies from the turn of the nineteenth century indicate that the game has not changed substantially in approximately 60 years. What may have changed is the nature of the questions asked by teachers. It is probable that the frequency of questions calling for recall of information and repetition of practiced responses has declined, and the frequency of questions requiring pupils to give opinions, make and draw conclusions, has increased proportionately. . . .

What is the purpose of this apparently laborious and complex pattern of verbal interaction? Underlying it there is a kind of pedagogical folklore, a set of rationalizations for practices that have survived the passing pressures imposed by parents, administrators, curriculum innovators and teacher-training programs. Some of the elements of this folklore are:

(a) pupils must be kept active and busily engaged in intellectually relevant activities;

(b) teachers should avoid telling pupils when pupils can tell themselves;

(c) questions stimulate pupil thinking and pupils should be made to think about the subject matter;

(d) it is the teacher's duty to monitor pupil understanding of subject matter by asking further appropriate questions. (pp. 52–53)

Other elements of the classroom culture are so familiar that anyone who has been exposed to more than a year of classroom education is familiar with the rules they represent. Pupils must learn to take turns, since only one person can be heard at a time, and to enter the conversation one must raise one's hand and be called on by the teacher. Departure from the classroom is strictly regulated, even for purposes of biological necessity. Ceremonies are performed in ritualistic fashion, such as singing the national anthem. Tardiness and absence must be excused with a note, and so forth. So important are these rules that much of the teacher's effort in the kindergarten year is spent in training children to be "good classroom members." Individual teachers, too, have their foibles and tend to create elements of culture that are perpetuated from class to class. Thus, teacher A demands formality, teacher B can be diverted from the topic by questions about her vacation last summer, teacher C has mannerisms which indicate that she has (at last) lost her temper, teacher D gives good grades to those who can pun in class. Even pupils can sometimes create elements of classroom culture, for we have all experienced one or more pupils who were classroom clowns or dunces and who set the tone of interaction for an entire year (see L. M. Smith and Geoffrey, 1968).

As was suggested by Nuthall and Snook above, the classroom has been a remarkably stable social form, resisting demands for change made by educators and parents alike. Thus, intruders into the classroom receive short shrift (even teacher trainees, for whom a role, of sorts, is prescribed). Curricular innovations which call for teachers to abandon the stance of authority, programs for team teaching, calls for pupil-centered and self-motivated instruction, revolutionary educational media such as television sets and teaching machines—all tend to be absorbed into and washed out by traditional modes of teaching.

Why should this be so? Why should the practice of teaching have changed so little during a century that has seen such sharp changes in other social forms? Many answers can be suggested to this question. For one, it has been claimed that student teachers tend to recall and build upon their own experiences as pupils, and later to model their practice teaching after the classroom performance of a supervising teacher. For another, at a minimal level classroom teaching appears to "work." Thus, given the limited financial resources of the school, it seems reasonable to closet groups of similarly aged pupils with a single teacher and to give her the responsibility of intriguing, cajoling, or threatening these individuals into knowledge. Further, most pupils seem to learn to read, to cipher, and even to pass on to higher education through such means. For another, many of the classroom innovations proposed by educators or citizens simply do not work or turn out to be too expensive.

The fact that teaching has not changed does not make it a dull or boring business any more than the fact that we have not yet done much research on teaching means that teaching is unresearchable. Teaching is an exciting, challenging job, rewarding when performed well. discouraging when performed poorly. The number of master teachers in this world is too few, the number of pupils who cannot play the Classroom Game probably too many, the tragedies engendered by failure to conduct research on teaching too serious. We have no doubt but that the practice of teaching will evolve in the next several decades, perhaps partially in response to research on its determinants and outcomes such as are reviewed (and called for) in books like this one. But for the present it behooves teachers to understand what is known about teaching as it is practiced today.

THE MODEL

With these facts in mind let us now construct a model that will enable us to organize the findings of research on teaching. Clearly, the model must concern itself with properties of teachers and pupils. Characteristics of the classroom must also be considered, together with those of its enfolding school and community. We must also consider the outcomes of education, those changes in pupils for which we are presumably conducting the enterprise. But most important, we must concern ourselves with the processes of teaching itself, with the actual behaviors of teachers and pupils as they play out the complex drama of classroom teaching.

A model reflecting these concerns is given in Figure 3.1. As may be seen, there are several "regions" in the model. The central region is the classroom itself, symbolized, appropriately, by a rectangle. To the left of the classroom are three sets of variables that will surely have at least some influence on classroom events: variables associated with the teacher, variables associated with pupils, and variables representing the contexts of community, school, and classroom. To the right are some of the hoped-for products of education.

Throughout the model appear arrows. Each presumes a causative relationship. Thus, we presume that teacher formative experiences occurred prior to, and tend to have a causative effect on, classroom events—and not vice versa. Most of the arrows are laid in time (as would be true for teacher formative experiences, for example, which surely occurred prior to the appearance of classroom events). However, some of the arrows indicate causative sequences we presume, even though the events thus linked are nearly contemporaneous. Thus, we presume that school and community contexts affect the classroom, and not vice versa. Sometimes these latter presumptions will turn out to be in error, although they are usually made by those who think about or conduct research on teaching. For example, it is possible for a given teacher to become so excellent or so notorious that she generates a response in the community. Again, classroom activities also have an impact on the noise level of the school, on the reputation and career of the principal, on the economy of the school and community, on the status of the teaching profession. Thus, teaching has other functions than fostering pupil growth, and some of these may form feedback chains that will, in turn, affect the teaching process in the classroom. Most of these are ignored in classroom research, however, partly because they are too complex to study easily and partly because they are presumed to be remote from the basic purposes of education.

Each arrow is but a source of hypotheses, however, and not a symbol of invariant truth. Let us assume, for example, that a relationship has been established between a teacher formative experience and teacher classroom behavior. For example, let us assume that teachers who come from middle-class backgrounds are known to approach pupils somewhat differently than those with lower-class backgrounds. Does this mean that social class "causes" differential classroom behavior? Indeed, this interpretation might be correct. But it might also be true that teachers who come from middle- and lower-class backgrounds are more likely to attend different colleges and thus to have had different experiences in teacher training; this latter factor, then, would be the actual cause of their different behavior in the classroom. To establish a relationship of covariance between two classes of variables within the model is a first step, albeit a large one. To discover that the relationship is causative is quite another matter and generally calls for experimental research. We return to this problem in the next chapter.

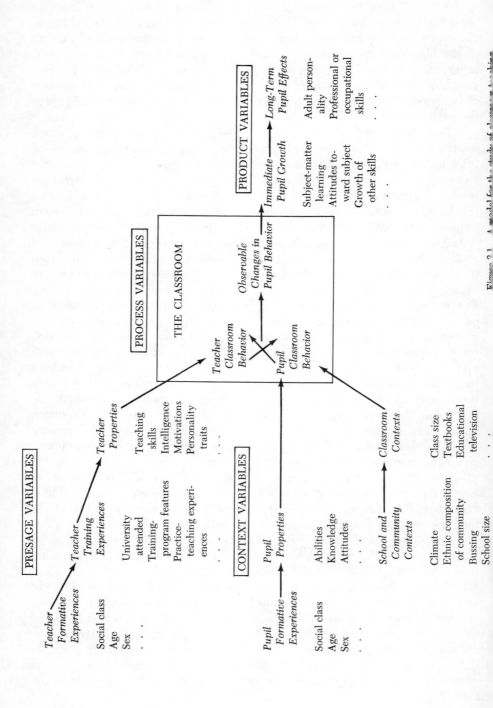

PRESAGE VARIABLES

Teacher → *Teacher* → *Teacher*
Formative   *Training*   *Properties*
Experiences   *Experiences*

Social class   University   Teaching
Age   attended   skills
Sex   Training-   Intelligence
. . .   program features   Motivations
  Practice-   Personality
  teaching experi-   traits
  ences   . . .
  . . .

CONTEXT VARIABLES

Pupil → *Pupil*
Formative   *Properties*
Experiences

Social class   Abilities
Age   Knowledge
Sex   Attitudes
. . .   . . .

School and → *Classroom*
Community   *Contexts*
Contexts

Climate   Class size
Ethnic composition   Textbooks
of community   Educational
Bussing   television
School size   . . .

PROCESS VARIABLES

THE CLASSROOM

Teacher
Classroom
Behavior

Pupil
Classroom
Behavior

Observable
Changes in
Pupil Behavior

PRODUCT VARIABLES

Immediate → *Long-Term*
Pupil Growth   *Pupil Effects*

Subject-matter   Adult person-
learning   ality
Attitudes to-   Professional or
ward subject   occupational
Growth of   skills
other skills   . . .
. . .

Figure 2.1. A model for the study of classroom teaching

Altogether there are some thirteen classes of variables suggested in the model of Figure 3.1. This list is neither exhaustive nor definitive. Other models with which the reader may be familiar will tend to cover the same ground, although they may present more or less detail than our model at certain portions of the paradigm. Given the present state of research on teaching, thirteen variable classes is too many for convenient review. Let us reduce these to *four* larger classes (see Mitzel, 1957). Following the terminology suggested by Mitzel (1960), we will distinguish *presage, context, process, and product* variables for research on teaching.

Presage Variables

As we shall use the term here, *presage variables* concern the characteristics of teachers that may be examined for their effects on the teaching process—thus, teacher formative experiences, teacher-training experiences, and teacher properties. As a general rule, such variables have a potential for control by administrators or teacher educators. For example, teacher trainees may be selected or rejected for their profession in terms of known background experiences, the teacher-training program can be altered, or teachers may be selected or assigned to different jobs in the school depending on their properties.

Teacher formative experiences include every experience encountered prior to teacher training, and for older teachers subsequent experiences as well. Teachers, like other persons, will have been treated differently if they were born a man or a woman, if they are white or black, if they lived in a lower-class or upper-class home, if they came from a large city or a small town, if they lived in an ethnic ghetto, if they were an only child or the last child in a big family. Some of these experiences presumably terminated with the ending of childhood, although their impact may persist in the teacher's adult personality. For example, the fact that a teacher grew up in a lower-class home is not a contemporaneous experience faced by the teacher, since nearly all teachers are now paid lower-middle-class wages. Again, the fact that the teacher may have grown up an only child provided her unique experiences as long as she lived in her parental home, but these experiences will have passed for most teachers. However, other formative experiences lead to the classification of teachers into ascribed positions within the society which provide continuing pleasures or problems. Thus, teachers who speak with an accent, who are male or black, or who have an obvious infirmity or a peculiar face or body are likely to be treated differently both within and without the school. Thus, some formative experiences are both historical *and* contemporaneous.

Teacher-training experiences include the college or university attended by the teacher, courses taken, the attitudes of instructors, experiences during practice teaching, and in-service and postgraduate education, if any. We should not be too surprised to learn that these variables are more often studied for their effects on classroom teaching than any others. After all, those who do research on teaching are likely to be teacher-educators themselves. For such persons not only are the conditions of teacher education convenient for study but often they can be manipulated, thus making experimental studies of the effects of new programs possible. Thus, presage research has appeared concerning the effects of "new and improved" methods of teacher education, such as fifth-year programs, in-service training, model teaching programs, microteaching, the use of videotape for teacher training, or new curricula. Whether such variables can, in fact, be more influential in determining the teacher's classroom behavior than, let us say, the teacher's age or sex or intelligence is moot. As we shall see in later chapters, most of the evidence "favoring" specific teacher education programs is weak, and it might be that as much improvement can be generated by recruiting and assigning the right teachers to the right jobs as by changing teacher training. The evidence is simply not available to answer the question yet, but on the assumption that formative experiences do influence teaching behavior, teacher-education programs might be more successful if they were tailored to take account of these factors.

Training and formative experiences cannot affect the teacher's classroom performance unless she retains traces of these experiences in her attitudes or behavior. Thus, we conceive of a third variable class, *teacher properties,* which consist of the measurable personality characteristics the teacher takes with her into the teaching situation. A legion of psychological traits, motives, abilities, and attitudes have been investigated for their potential effect on teaching.

> Such properties have two features in common: they are hypothetical constructs in psychology, thus they are presumed to characterize the individual teacher in a consistent fashion, over time, and serve to explain her behavior in response to a variety of situations. It is also presumed that such properties are laid "within" the teacher and are not amenable to direct observation in the same way that behavior can be observed. Contemporary American ideology [also] stresses the alterability of teacher properties. We know that warmth, authoritarianism, hostility—and even intelligence and physical aptitudes—are influenced by early learning and can be altered through appropriate educational experiences (including psychotherapy) in later life. (Biddle, 1964, pp. 9–10)

It is not clear why teacher properties such as authoritarianism, anxiety, attitudes toward pupils, personality inventory scores, and the like, should be studied more often than observable teacher characteristics such as age, sex, or race. One explanation might be the common view that teaching is largely a matter of personal relationships and personality, that such effects as teachers have are functions of their personalities (Nuthall, 1972, personal communication). Perhaps, too, there is joy in administering standardized instruments that purport to provide "secret" information about

respondents; perhaps the instruments for assessing personality characteristics have a mystique of their own. Although demographic variables have
long been known to be major influencers of job performance in other
contexts (see, for example, Helmreich, 1971), they have not often been
studied by those interested in teaching.

Context Variables

As we shall use the term here, *context variables* concern the conditions
to which the teacher must adjust—characteristics of the environment
about which teachers, school administrators, and teacher-educators can do
very little. Normally the teacher, indeed the school administration, has
little choice in its pupil population, inherits a well-used school building,
must live within a budget, and must contend with the aspirations, angers,
and beliefs of the community that supports the school. These, then, are the
contexts of classroom education. Whether seen as a welcome challenge or
an irrelevant annoyance, teachers must cope with contexts; and thus variables within the contextual sphere are likely to affect the processes of
teaching.

Pupils have also experienced *formative experiences*. Like teachers,
pupils will differ depending on whether they come from lower- or middle-
class homes, have experienced socialization as a boy or girl, have suffered
the loss of a parent, or come from a stimulus-rich or stimulus-deprived
environment. Some of these events took place in the pupils' past lives.
However, most of these conditions will continue to be present throughout
the teaching year, thus modifying and in some cases defeating the efforts
of the teacher. There can be few contextual experiences more disturbing
to the teacher than a hostile, retarded, or withdrawn child, and much of
the curriculum of educational psychology concerns strategies for meeting
such problems. Teaching is also strikingly different in the urban ghetto
and the affluent suburb, a fact that is now generating special curricula
for those who are to teach in the ghetto. Pupils who speak nonstandard
English or another language entirely, pupils who have physical or learning
disabilities, pupils who are hyperkinetic or stout—all pose special problems.
In part such problems are presented by the behaviors of these pupils,
but in part they appear to be caused by the prejudices and expectations
held by teachers and other pupils. Hostility among pupils representing
different ethnic groups is only too common, of course, but teachers may
also sort pupils into learning groups on the basis of social class backgrounds.
We shall have more to say on the subject of teacher expectations for pupils
in later chapters.

Educators are even more prone to measure *pupil properties* than they
are teacher properties. In fact, the periodic measurement of pupil abilities
and pupil achievements by means of standardized tests is now a well-
entrenched feature of most school systems. Such scores are used for various

purposes, notably as an aid in deciding whether to promote or retain a pup at his grade level, and for placing pupils within educational "streams" c "learning groups." Thus, a "fortunate" teacher might end up with a clas room of bright, well-scrubbed, highly motivated pupils, while anothe might have to contend with a classroom composed of the surly, stupid, an disruptive. Standardized measures of pupil achievement and pupil intell gence are both often used in research on teaching, usually for "adjusting or "regressing" a subsequent achievement score so as to provide a measur of effect for a given classroom experience. But these measures were usuall *not* designed for research, are known to co-vary with social class and ethni background, and are generally employed improperly in the statistics used b researchers (see Cronbach and Furby, 1970). (We return to their use i the next chapter.) Once again, surprisingly little use has been made c demographic variables concerning pupils in research on teaching. Thos few researchers who have studied pupils on the basis of race or sex hav nearly always uncovered substantial differences in treatment by teacher One hopes that more research will be forthcoming on such variables i the near future.

Pupils are not the only context for teaching, of course. Addition contextual variables may be found within the *school* and *communit* Schools differ from one another in many ways, and some of these are no coming to be studied for their effects on teaching. In small, isolate schools, for example, teachers may have to contend with a multigrade classroom. Larger schools are more specialized, and their activities mo expert, although pupils in them may experience less pressure to participat in those activities (see Barker and Gump, 1964). Schools differ dependin on their physical facilities, the homogeneity of their teacher and pupil popu lations, the personalities and practices of their principals, the impact c their athletic programs (see Coleman, 1961), and so on. Schools are als constrained both by law and custom. One school system features a rigi curriculum imposed by an authoritative hierarchy, another a militar teachers' union, another a tyrannical and bigoted school board, still anothe a tradition of experimenting with both school architecture and classroo education. Each of these contexts is likely to affect the conduct and exper ences of classroom participants.

> The school also bears functional relationships with the larger communit
> School systems are expected to serve citizen needs ranging from entertai
> ment, to the desire to learn, to the need for status advancement, to bab
> sitting. . . . Further, the school interacts with other institutions in the con
> munity. It provides employment for a number of people, consumes certai
> kinds of goods, keeps "wild youth" off the streets, provides an avenue f
> social service, and so on. The school building is sometimes stockpiled again
> the threat of tornadoes or nuclear fall-out. Often, particularly in small con
> munities, the school may be the only institution attracting the attention of
> majority of the citizenry; and observers have noted the demise of some sma

communities when their schools were consolidated with others. In low population areas a citizen may carry his community status into school settings, such as the PTA. Similarly, school personnel often may find their occupational positions carrying into the small community, such as when teachers are expected to lead in Sunday school or to be paragons of public virtue. Urban schools appear to be more isolated, and professional affiliation there may be easier to shed at the end of the day. (Biddle, 1964, p. 16)

Possibly because most classroom research is conducted by psychologists, or because it is expensive, few studies have investigated the relationships between either school or community variables and classroom teaching. A recent review of research on the properties of schools that might be relevant for their impact on teaching is provided by Biddle (1970), but we are unaware of more than a handful of studies concerned with the impact of community variables on teaching.

Fortunately, such is not the case with our final contextual category, *classroom contexts*. Classrooms also differ in size, and this variable has been investigated endlessly for its effects on the outcomes of teaching, with but indifferent success. Classrooms also differ in terms of lighting, equipment, and layout. Unfortunately, most of these variables have not yet been studied for their effects on teaching (although studies have been made of the impact of new educational media such as teaching machines and television). This is certainly too bad. One needs only to enter a crowded, poorly lighted, poorly equipped ghetto classroom to begin to understand why teaching is less successful in such an environment. Consider also the simple variable of classroom noise level. Most classrooms are quite noisy environments; with more than 70 feet, most of them restless, movable desks, excited voices, and with but minimal sound-absorbing surfaces, it is not surprising that teachers must often use a loud voice to command attention. Moreover, some less-talented school principals seem to evaluate the effectiveness of their teachers' efforts in terms of the low noise level of their classrooms. Some time ago one of the authors made videotapes of teaching in two carpeted classrooms and was struck by the quiet, order, attention, and relaxation they seemed to exhibit. Yet we know of no formal research that has been conducted on the effects of carpeting (and quiet) on classroom teaching. Other classroom contexts include the curriculum, the customs pertaining to conduct accepted by class members, the tasks promulgated for the group, and so forth. As these examples illustrate, some aspects of the classroom context are partially subject to the teacher's control. For instance, teachers may bring displays of wildlife or ship models to the classroom or set up conventions for conduct, entertainment, or competition that are not found in other classrooms. However, once these displays or customs are set, classroom participants, including the teacher herself, are likely to be affected by them. Once again, most of these effects have yet to be studied.

Process Variables

As we shall use the term, *process variables* concern the actual activities of classroom teaching—what teachers and pupils *do* in the classroom. By "actual activities" we mean to focus attention on *all* of the observable behaviors of teachers and pupils rather than upon only those that are productive of pupil growth or upon intangible or unobservable relationships between teachers and pupils. Some teachers appear incapable of keeping order in the classroom, some pupils engage in horseplay or whisper to others; as long as these events are observable they may be judged as components of teaching-process variables.[1] However, such factors as the teacher's like or dislike for a given pupil, or the classroom "we feeling," or whether a pupil is actually paying attention to the lecture cannot be judged as process variables unless they can be measured by overt behavioral signs.

Much of this book is taken up with various ways of conceptualizing process variables, so we will spend but little time on the subject here. It is convenient, however, to distinguish *teacher classroom behavior* as a category. As we shall see, most systems for studying teaching have concentrated on teacher behavior, assuming, reasonably, that much of the success of teaching is in the teacher's hands. Moreover, it is also assumed that the behaviors of the teacher must be primarily a function of presage variables— thus teacher formative experiences, teacher-training experiences, or teacher properties.

Are these presumptions adequate? Surely teachers not only induce but also react to pupil behavior. (If they are incapable of responding to pupils, the act of teaching is debased. The wife of one of the authors once observed an elderly teacher who was nearly deaf. Her strategy in conducting discussions was to ask a question, then to call for a class vote on the answer, and then to announce the right answer herself. Thus, apart from the collective exercise of voting, these pupils were subjected to little more than the teaching display characteristic of educational television.) In some ways, therefore, teacher behavior is also a function of pupil behavior, and the success of the teaching enterprise rests with pupils as well as with teachers.

For these reasons many systems for studying teaching have also investigated *pupil classroom behavior*. However, the study of pupil behavior involves several problems not encountered for the teacher. For one, the classroom has 30 or more pupils, all of whom are "behaving" at any

---

[1] In making this distinction we part company with those who would restrict teaching to activities the teacher introduces "with the intention that pupils will learn something" (Hudgins, 1971, p. 4; also see Gage, 1972, p. 18). We find it difficult to distinguish classroom events in terms of the teacher's "intent" and are quite as interested in classroom events that are *un*intended or that occur when the teacher has nonlearning goals in mind.

given moment, although usually only one of them is actually speaking. Investigators have solved this problem in several ways. Some have confined their attention to the target pupil who is addressed by the teacher, ignoring the other, audience pupils. Others have studied the reactions of pupils as a mass audience, making judgments about the collective or average state of pupil behavior for a given unit of time. Still others have studied the reactions of randomly selected pupils. As we shall see, these solutions have reflected the particular interests and concepts of investigators and have led to somewhat different conclusions concerning the effects of teaching.

Another problem concerns the fact that pupils are constrained by the Rules of the Classroom Game to sit in silence much of the time, hence their behavior tends to be dull and uninteresting in comparison with that of the teacher, and much of what we hope is going on within the pupil is not exhibited externally. Most classrooms would be disturbed if pupils were to shout "Eureka!" when suddenly seeing the point, although teachers strive valiantly to induce just such experiences in pupils.

Still another problem is posed by the rapid pace of teacher-pupil interaction. As anyone who has ever prepared a transcription of classroom interaction can testify, classrooms are wordy, and the words come thick and fast. Since the detailed analysis of transcriptions is costly, investigators have adopted several strategies that represent shortcuts. One of these is to develop concepts that are applied to units of time rather than to units of behavior. In other analytic systems coders must ignore the distinction between teacher and pupil behavior in favor of coding the "content" or "emotional quality" of the exchange, regardless of who was responsible for it. In still other methods, the distinction between teacher and pupil behavior is maintained, but only a few categories are provided for judging each. Another type of solution to the problem involves the study of neither teacher nor pupil actions but rather their *inter*actions. Thus, the typical classroom sequence, teacher question—pupil response—teacher assessment, is noted whenever it appears, and judgments are made concerning properties of the exchange as a whole. None of these procedures is without its difficulties. Time intervals simply do not correspond to boundaries of teacher and pupil actions. To make judgments about interaction units requires us to ignore aspects of causative influence of teachers upon pupils.

Still another problem concerns the relationship between (prior) teaching activities and (subsequent) classroom events. As was suggested in Figure 3.1, it is possible to assume that observable changes in pupil behavior are a function of teaching and hence evidence of the success or failure of the teacher's efforts. Such an assumption is involved in designs for various studies (for example, that of Kounin, 1970), and surely it is subscribed to by most teachers. After all, what can be more self-evident than the experience of working on dull Johnny for some minutes until he finally sees the point of the lesson? Such an assumption also appears in recent model teacher-education programs that emphasize performance criteria for judging the success of teaching. Yet are changes in pupil behavior truly a function of teacher activities alone? Once again, it seems to us that this is a risky conclusion. It may be that pupils learn as much from other pupils as from the teacher, or that dull Johnny will get the point by himself if only given enough time. For this reason we must assume that conclusions concerning cause-and-effect relationships in the classroom are unvalidated unless checked with manipulative experiments.

Given these problems, it is not surprising that classroom processes have been conceptualized in many ways. Each of the substantive chapters of this book takes up one or more ways of viewing classroom processes, thus generating a set of process variables. In Chapter IV we consider some of the assumptions and difficulties underlying these systems. In Chapters XI and XII we review the system competitively and summarize the strengths, weaknesses, and findings for each.

Product Variables

As we shall use the term, *product variables* concern the outcomes of teaching—those changes that come about in pupils as a result of their involvement in classroom activities with teachers and other pupils. Although we normally think of these changes in positive terms, and label them "growth" or "learning," it is possible that pupils might actually be hampered or harmed by classroom experiences. For example, a teacher might be so punitive that she causes pupils to become disturbed, or so confused in her presentation that pupils come to doubt knowledge they have brought with them to the classroom. These too would be products of the teaching experience, however we might decry them.

The product variables most often investigated are subject-matter learning and attitudes toward the subject, both of which involve *immediate pupil growth*. Both variables seem obvious ones to choose for evaluating the success of teaching. Standardized tests are available for assessing pupil growth in most subjects, and measurement of pupil attitudes can be accomplished by means of one or two multiple-choice questions. Moreover, if education is successful, surely it results in increased subject-matter competence and positive attitudes. But there are difficulties. Most standardized tests measure knowledge of facts rather than ability to synthesize and use that knowledge. And most attitudinal questions require only superficial judgments. Above all, some of the grandiose claims made for the effects of really good teaching have not been researched at all. We, therefore, are very limited in our ability to measure pupils' creativity, their learning of adult roles, their ability to practice democracy, their values. Given these lacks, our research on the effectiveness of various kinds of teaching experiences has a strange, one-dimensional quality. For example, strong evidence has now accumulated demonstrating that pupils can learn from both teaching machines and educational television. But what is *not* known is how they react to the boredom and dehumanization of these experiences in comparison with classroom activities involving a live teacher. In her classic study Ann Roe (1953) discovered that students' decisions to become scientists resulted in part from close contact and identification with a scientist-teacher during their late-adolescent and young-adult years; and yet educational television, which precludes any direct contact between students and faculty, has had its greatest adoption in undergraduate courses in the large universities!

For these reasons and others some educators (and some classroom researchers) have abandoned the task of validating teaching in terms of product variables. As we suggested earlier, some educators seek changes in observable behavior of pupils as the products of education. Jackson, for example, has questioned whether teachers themselves are primarily concerned with inducing measurable gains in pupil learning. Rather, teachers appear to be

> making some kind of an educated guess about what would be a beneficial activity for a student or a group of students and then doing whatever is necessary to see that the participants remain involved in that activity. The teacher's goal, in other words, is student involvement rather than student learning. It is true, of course, that the teacher hopes the involvement will result in certain beneficial changes in the students, but learning is in this sense a by-product or a secondary goal rather than the thing about which the teacher is most directly concerned. (Jackson, 1966, p. 24)

Other educators appear to give teaching a high rating if it exhibits certain characteristics, regardless of whether these are ever found to lead to pupil change. Thus, teaching should be stimulating, democratic, or warm because of the obvious inherent superiority of these qualities. This latter position is generated by at least three arguments. For some people these desirable teaching objectives are too obvious to be worth further discussion. For others commitment is generated by psychological, social, or philosophic positions—for example, the nondirective philosophy of Carl Rogers, or popularizations of psychoanalysis. Still others, particularly adult educators, are beginning to see the classroom as a consummatory rather than an instrumental activity, as a desirable way of spending time, as a useful alternative to idleness or drug addiction. For these people, classrooms should be pleasant places to be in, regardless of whether one learns anything there or not.

Regarding all of these advocates we shall here take the position that the traditional and continuing task of teaching is to promote learning. Thus, for our purposes, classroom activities will be deemed *successful* if they induce desired changes in pupils. Such a position requires us—eventually— to validate the practices of teaching with product variables.

The ultimate goal of education is not high test scores, although parents and educators sometimes appear to forget this fact. Rather, education is conducted for its *long-term effects on pupils*. Thus, we subject our sons and daughters to the tender mercies of classroom experiences in the hope that thereby they will become fit citizens, acquire the information and motivation needed to enter a profession, learn to meet the complex demands of a rapidly changing society, and contribute to the betterment of others. Unfortunately, the establishment of relationships between teaching and such laudable aims lies mainly in the future. Although anecdotal evidence may be found wherein an individual describes the signal influence a given teacher had on him, and although one can find the occasional master teacher who is known to have "produced" several stellar pupils, to our knowledge no researcher has yet attempted to establish relationships between teaching variables and long-term product variables. Consider the difficulties one would face in such research. For one thing, the research would have to be longitudinal—unless one just happened upon a set of recordings or transcriptions for a large group of classrooms and teachers that was assembled, let us say, at least ten years ago. For another, the influence of a given teacher or classroom is inevitably mitigated by the teaching efforts of other teachers and other contexts. Even a master teacher can be defeated by the stultifying effect of a generally poor school, while pupils who truly succeed in later life are probably the products of many fine teaching efforts. It is wise to keep in mind the long-term goals of education, but we should not be too surprised if contemporary research in teaching does not tell us much about them.

CLASSES OF KNOWLEDGE ABOUT TEACHING

As we have suggested, the model presented in Figure 3.1 was designed not only to aid understanding of the teaching process but also to enable a summary of research knowledge. How can this be done? Given the model, what kinds of knowledge can we discover concerning the teaching process, its antecedents, and its consequences?

In general, we will consider knowledge about teaching to fall into six classes. The first class of knowledge concerns the *conceptualization* and *study* of teaching processes. At a minimal level we must have concepts to use when thinking about events, and those concepts must enable us to sort out examples of the events in which we are interested. Many educators, and most teacher-educators, are convinced that they *already* have workable concepts for describing teaching. And yet when we examine them carefully we find that some terms that are supposed to describe teaching are merely slogans or propaganda. Thus, "teaching the whole child" does not denote any particular set of activities one can point to in the classroom any more than does "providing meaningful experiences" or "accommodating individual pupil differences." On the other hand, as we shall see, such concepts as "level of cognitive processes," "teacher evaluation of pupil response," and "maintaining group focus" not only denote observable teaching activities but variations in these activities tend to be associated with other classroom processes and pupil products. Our first task, then, is to discover and understand the concepts that have been found useful in research for studying the teaching process.

The second class of knowledge concerns the rate at which teaching *processes occur* in the typical classroom. Earlier in the chapter we provided a description of the typical classroom. For the most part our description was based not on data but on assertion, and if the reader found it a reasonable one, this may reflect the fact that he just happened to have experienced roughly the same types of classrooms as have the authors. But are our experiences typical of the average classroom today? This question is an important one. Nearly all critics of education begin by assuming that drastic things are "wrong" with the classroom. Teaching is too "cold" or "harsh" or "undemocratic" or "phonic" or "low level" or "discriminatory" or "dull"—and teachers must be trained (and school administrators encouraged or forced) to rectify these conditions. But are these criticisms valid? To find out we must study and report the processes that occur in a variety of classrooms for many contexts. Our second task, then, is to discover what kinds of teaching processes are typical of classrooms today.

The third class of knowledge concerns the relationship between *contexts* and *processes* in teaching. To what extent is teaching differentiated for boys and girls, for black and white pupils, among classrooms differing in subject matter, between upper- and lower-class communities, in small and large schools? These questions are also important to the public. A common complaint one hears from parents is that education is conducted "unfairly." Thus, minority-group children are being "discriminated against," bright children are being "held back," boys are more likely to be "picked on" than girls, teaching is "clearly better" in one community than in another, and so on. Such complaints are subject to research. Moreover, most teaching theories and curricular plans suggest that teaching should be differentiated in terms of pupil age and ability. Our third task, then, is to discover how teaching varies depending on context.

The fourth class of knowledge concerns the relationship between *presage* conditions and teaching *processes*. The entire business of teacher education is founded on the assumption that we can "improve" teaching practices by providing appropriate educational experiences for young teachers. School administrators would like to select the best available candidates for teaching positions and then assign them to jobs wherein they will be effective. Teachers, too, want to acquire information that will help them improve their teaching. Such needs presume that the teacher's prior experiences can influence the practice of teaching. Although this is a reasonable presumption, we usually have no direct evidence to back it up. Thus, innovations in teacher-education programs, decisions of school administrators, and programs of in-service training for teachers are usually engendered without evidence; and however "reasonable" may be the rationales for them, they may or may not produce better teaching. Our fourth task, then, is to discover relationships between the experiences and properties of teachers and the type of teaching they practice in the classrooms.

The fifth class of knowledge concerns relationships *among processes* occurring in the classroom. Many of the things we learn in teacher-education programs concern such processes. We learn to manage a room full of young pupils, to lead class discussions, to ask questions and respond appropriately to the responses of pupils. Moreover, to the extent we find teaching a rewarding and successful business, it will probably be found here too. But can we stimulate interest in pupils? Are our classrooms lively and interesting or dull and apathetic? Can we reach the withdrawn child or bring out the best in the talented? Such questions suggest relationships between our activities as teachers and the responses of pupils. And as we saw earlier, model teaching programs of the present decade tend to advocate goals for teaching that are stated in terms of resultant pupil behaviors. All of these require that we gain knowledge concerning the relationships among events in the classroom. Our fifth task, then, is to discover how teacher and pupil behaviors co-vary and influence one another in the classroom.

The sixth and last class of knowledge concerns relationships between the *processes* and *products* of teaching. Surely this class requires the least justification of any we have discussed. If we are to be successful teachers, we must not only maintain a bright and cheerful atmosphere, a schedule, a disciplined and orderly environment, but we must also *teach*. Thus, we should also seek to discover teaching strategies that will maximize pupil growth. Our sixth task, then, is to discover how the processes of teaching affect the growth and development of pupils.

The above discussion, and our model, suggest that these six classes of knowledge are independent of one another. This is not the case, of course. It is possible, for example, that the same teaching strategy will not be equally effective with first- and eleventh-graders, with both boys and girls, with the talented and the handicapped. Thus, contextual variables should affect not only the *occurrence* of various teaching practices but also the *relationship* between practices and products. Presage variables may also serve as conditions that affect the success of teaching, for a strategy that works for the teacher who is a young man may not work for the one who is an older woman. Although such contingencies are possible, they have only rarely been studied in research to date. Thus, it is convenient for us to summarize knowledge concerning teaching using the six classes we have indicated above. At the end of Chapter IV we set forth formal procedures for making summaries of each type.

THE COMMITMENT

Most educators are dedicated to the improvement of their profession. This impulse they share with other professionals, such as doctors and social workers—or, for that matter, scientists and businessmen. For years, however, the knowledge of educators has largely rested on personal experience, philosophy, and plausible argument rather than on research and evidence. For this reason some educators have become used to advocating innovative ideas for improving education that are attractively argued but unsupported by data.

Most educational researchers were originally trained as teachers themselves. They too matured in an atmosphere of advocacy, and they too are often dedicated to the improvement of teaching. Thus, we should not be surprised to discover that much of their research is designed to "demonstrate" the validity of a given program for improving education. We shall refer to such motivations on the part of researchers as *Commitments*.

Commitments are not necessarily bad things, of course. Among other advantages, they provide much of the motivation that drives researchers to invest their time and energy (and someone else's money) in complex research designs that require months or years for their accomplishment. But we should be aware of some of the problems involved in *Commitments*. First, not all researchers share the same *Commitment*. For some the improvement of education is to be accomplished through raising the cognitive level of classroom discourse, for others teachers should be warmer or more democratic, for still others teaching should exhibit clearer logic, and so forth. At best these different prescriptions are independent of one another; at worst they are antithetical.

Second, because they hold a *Commitment*, some researchers have chosen to conduct research that has turned out to be ineffective, or they have been unable to contemplate results that violate their *Commitment*. For example, we will see that some researchers have chosen to focus on presage-process research, assuming that a given classroom process has good effects on pupils even though no evidence has accumulated to support this assumption. Others have clung to weak research instruments or orientations, despite confusing and contradictory evidence and in defiance of severe criticism, apparently because they could not abandon their *Commitments*. Still others have simply ignored evidence accumulated by others that contradicts their *Commitments* or, worse, have become advocates for a particular program of teacher training or curricular innovation in violation of their own published results. (We shall note some of the more heinous examples of these problems where appropriate in our substantive chapters.)

We are no less interested in improving education than are other researchers or our readers. However, we shall adopt a somewhat more stringent position concerning *Commitments* than is indicated above. In general, we demand evidence for three types of relationships before we become advocates of a given *Commitment* concerning teaching:

1. evidence that a given teaching practice is presently occurring in typical classrooms;
2. evidence that an alternative teaching practice can be encouraged by changes in teacher-education programs (or through some other presage or contextual condition);
3. evidence that the alternative teaching practice produces more desirable classroom processes or (preferably) products in pupil growth than the present practice.

Given such evidence, we too will become advocates. Without such evidence we remain skeptical.

As was suggested in Chapter II, although the authors hope that readers will improve their teaching through reading this text, we know of no evidence to support this hope. (In the worst of all possible worlds teachers might actually be better off not knowing about teaching!) Thus, we reserve our *Commitment* until the evidence is in—and gently encourage readers to do likewise.

IV
METHODOLOGICAL PROBLEMS
IN CLASSROOM RESEARCH

This chapter examines some of the many problems faced by investigators in their search for generalizations about teaching. Since our focus in this book is on research involving process variables of teaching, this chapter concentrates upon them to the exclusion of other types of variables that are discussed extensively in other books. We will also dip into areas that some readers have been avoiding since their first unhappy experiences with mathematics and formal logic—such dread topics as measurement, sampling, and the design of scientific investigations. In so doing our aim is not to torment the helpless but rather to acquaint readers with information they need in order to understand what is and what is not known concerning teaching and what is involved in conducting research on that topic.

We sincerely wish that this approach were not necessary. Wouldn't it be convenient if one could say definitively that teaching strategy A leads to better results than teaching strategies B or C. But life is not so simple, at least where human beings are concerned. We shall find, for example, that sometimes teaching strategy A appears to work for some pupils but not for others; that it has desired consequences within the classroom but does not appear to affect longer-term pupil learning; that it has been explored with only a handful of teachers; or that it appears associated with other phenomena we would not want to encourage. In some cases we might not even be able to identify teaching strategy A at all! Thus, knowledge concerning teaching is complex, as is any knowledge derived from research, and we must study the conditions of the research with which it is developed in order to understand it.

Two extreme positions may be taken with regard to scientific knowledge concerning teaching. Some educators worship research and are inclined to espouse new educational devices and programs on the barest research evidence imaginable. Others have decided that the findings of educational research have no use at all and that teachers should be considered inscrutable artists. We prefer the stance of knowledgeable skepticism which resides between these two extremes. To develop empirical knowledge concerning teaching is surely possible, but that task has barely begun. Knowledge concerning teaching is complex and limited in scope, and if we are to use it to plan our own approaches to teaching, we must understand its complexities and limitations.

At the same time, we shall not deal with methodological problems in any depth here. Our aim is to provide readers with understanding rather than with the ability to conduct research themselves or even to read research reports that are written in technical jargon. The summaries of research findings presented in this book use the words and phrases of ordinary English and not such terms as "regression coefficients," "factor loadings," "levels of confidence," or "path analyses." Indeed, except for a brief discussion of statistical problems in the last section of this chapter, our presentation requires no prior knowledge of methodological issues in the social sciences. In the event that the reader's appetite is whetted for more knowledge concerning methodological problems, we refer him to sources cited in the chapter, to any of several good texts on the subject (such as Kerlinger, 1964), or to courses in the methodology of educational research.

THE CRUX OF THE PROBLEM

One of the best-known series of generalizations stated about teaching is the so-called "law of two thirds" posited by Flanders (1963). According to this "law," two thirds of the time spent in classrooms is devoted to talk, two thirds of this talking time is occupied by the teacher, and two thirds of teacher talk consists of direct influence.

How *true* is this "law"? What criteria might be invoked in evaluating its truth?

The first generalization involves just one concept of teaching behavior, *talk*; one measuring scale, *time*; one set of phenomena, *classrooms*; and one statistic, the fraction *two thirds*. The acceptability of the generalization, therefore, depends on the answers to questions that might be asked about these four elements.

First, the concept of *talk*. Is its meaning clear? Can instances of talk be reliably identified? Is talk relevant to the classroom?

Everyone knows what talk is. Talk is what a person is doing when he uses his vocal apparatus for the production of verbal symbols. There can be no clearer concept for behavior than talk. But if we want to measure talk in a context like a classroom, we have to make decisions about making this concept operational. For example, should we include *sotto voce* talk? Should we include recorded talk as it is produced by the sound track of a film, a videotape, or a phonograph record or the noise made by the principal when he interrupts the normal stream of activity to make an announcement on the intercom? Unless talk is explicitly defined to include or exclude such occurrences, attempts to quantify it may be unreliable. If explicit operational definitions are provided, are they clear enough that the same competent observer would make the same observations if he listened to the same events on another occasion?

Second, the measuring scale, *time*. Is it objective? Is it precise? Does it permit meaningful quantification?

Can talk be measured objectively and precisely in terms of time? Most assuredly yes, provided the timepieces employed are in proper working order. Moreover, the units by which time is measured, whether they are split seconds or years, are meaningful. Of course, human beings operate stopwatches, and error can creep in despite the quality of the stopwatch. No doubt we could eliminate the possibility of human error in such measurements, but this might involve expensive and impractical equipment.

Third, *classrooms*. What are they? How many of them are there? How varied are they? How many and what types need to be observed in order to generalize about them?

What is a classroom? Is a gymnasium a classroom? a woodworking shop? a chemistry laboratory? What about the normal third-grade classroom when involved with a test or the Annual Christmas Party? If we want to generalize about a class of phenomena called classrooms, presumably we cannot observe them all, yet we should observe more than one. How should we go about selecting the number and types of classrooms in order to be able to claim that an observation is generally true of classrooms? No one has ever counted the number of classrooms in the world, let alone classified them in any systematic way. Even assuming that this had been done and that a truly representative sample of classrooms could be selected, could all of them be studied? Given human problems, it seems unlikely that all the teachers, administrators, and others concerned would agree to participate in the investigation. At best one would finish with a sample of volunteer classrooms without any knowledge of the possible differences in classroom behavior between cooperating and non-cooperating teachers. Thus, any generalizations about classrooms could be assumed to apply only to something less than the whole population of classrooms.

Then again, how do we go about studying classrooms without inducing changes in the behaviors of their teachers and pupils by the presence of our observers or recording equipment? It is at best "difficult" to gauge observer effects upon classrooms because this knowledge presupposes observation of nonobserved classrooms. The problem is analogous to that faced by the inquisitive child who wants to know whether the light in the refrigerator is really out when the door is closed and who will be satisfied only by the direct evidence of his senses. Of course, the child might persuade his father to drill a hole in the side of the refrigerator and thus be satisfied. But normally the researcher of classrooms may not, on ethical grounds, observe without the teacher's knowledge and permission, even if he were permitted to drill a hole in the wall. Normally, the best we can hope for is to minimize the effects of observation by avoiding disruption of the classroom and providing assurances of significance and confidentiality in our research. While it might be true that most subjects appear to forget about the fact that they are under observation in a short time (see Barker and Wright, 1955), one researcher found that teachers who knew they were being observed were more responsive to pupils than teachers who could not be certain whether or not they were being observed (Samph, 1968).

Fourth, the fraction *two thirds*. What statistical technique was used in obtaining it? Is it an acceptable statistic?

Even given that talk is a valid concept of behavior with respect to classrooms, that it can be made operational and measured reliably, that a truly representative sample of classrooms is observed, and that there are no observer effects, there are still problems concerning the meaning of two thirds. Does the generalization that two thirds of classroom time is spent in talk mean that in *every* classroom two thirds of the time is so spent? Or does it mean that, *on the average*, talk takes up two thirds of classroom time? Often this type of generalization is formed on the basis of an arithmetic mean, and in some circumstances the arithmetic mean can lead to generalizations that are not valid.

The second part of Flanders' "law" says that two thirds of the talking is done by teachers. The same problems discussed above also apply to this generalization. In addition, another problem arises from the introduction of the concept "teacher." One would be surprised if two observers disagreed in identifying the teacher in the classroom, or if the same observer were inconsistent in identifying the same teacher observed at different times. There are times, however, when the teacher vacates the center of the stage and a pupil engages in behavior which is identical to teaching behavior— such as explaining the solution to a mathematical problem with the aid of the chalkboard to the rest of the class with the intention that others should learn. One could ask whether the pupil in question has temporarily "become" the teacher.

The third generalization, that two thirds of teacher talk is direct influence, introduces the most difficult problem yet encountered concerning the "law of two thirds." What is "direct influence"? This concept is discussed at length in Chapter V and is used here only as an example of a type of problem frequently encountered with concepts employed in classroom research. Meaty, educationally significant concepts such as "influence," "control," and "discipline" are more abstract than concepts such as "talk," "hand-raising," and "sitting." To claim that a teacher is exerting "influence" requires more inference, more interpretation, of the relationships between the activity of the teacher and other classroom events. The observer must perceive and integrate a complex pattern of acts in order to judge "acts of influence" from other teacher acts. To judge that "influence" is "direct" requires an additional abstract judgment on the part of the observer, for he must now sort examples of "influence" into at least two classes—those that are "direct" and those that are not.

The difficulty with such high-inference concepts is that it is difficult to provide operational definitions of them. This means that studies which call for observers to use such concepts may not be objective, since the judgments called for may be unreliable. Two different observers may both state that they are studying "direct influence" and yet be reporting incidents of quite different types of teaching. On the other hand, low-inference concepts, such as "talk" or "sitting," are of less interest to us than high-inference concepts. This leaves the researcher in a quandary. If he uses high-inference concepts, he must present clear operational definitions for them and data demonstrating that observers can make the judgments called for with reliability. If he uses low-inference concepts, he must engage in complex manipulation of his findings in order to give them meaning for educators.

None of these observations means that the "law of two thirds" is invalid. In fact, we suspect that the general notion it conveys is supported by more evidence than is usually presented to support generalizations about classrooms (see Chapter V). Rather, we have chosen this generalization to introduce readers to the host of problems encountered in arriving at knowledge about teaching. Let us now turn to the details of these problems. For convenience our discussion is divided into four sections: problems of measurement, sampling, design, and interpretation. We will dwell a little longer on the problems of measuring behavior in classrooms because they have special relevance to the research discussed in this book and because they are not often given adequate treatment in books on research methodology.

PROBLEMS OF MEASUREMENT

Measuring things is something we have done ever since we were very young; there is no mystery to the basic notion of measurement. To measure something we hold up to it a ruler, a caliper, or some kind of instrument and make a judgment concerning some aspect of it. We judge how long, how broad, how hot, how rough, how sweet, or how new it might be. Thus, to make a measurement three elements are required: something we want to measure, an instrument for making the measurement, and an act of judgment on our part. Sometimes we are inclined to forget about the instrument, for it is possible to make rough, intuitive guesses concerning length, breadth, or temperature using only our eyes and hands. In this case we have substituted our own judgment for the use of an instrument. But as everyone knows, we can get more accurate and reliable measurements from instruments than from our unaided eyes.

Measuring some aspect of teaching is done in exactly the same way. First, we must provide ourselves access to examples of teaching so that we may examine them. Second, it is necessary to develop an instrument for making judgments concerning some aspect of teaching. Third, we must judge (or code) examples of teaching in terms of the instrument we have developed. However, few of us have ever tried to measure teaching, and each of these steps has unfamiliar problems associated with it.

Collecting Data About Teaching

For several reasons, it is difficult to collect good examples of teaching for study. Perhaps the most obvious one is that since teaching usually involves a group of more than 30 persons in rapid interaction, the units of teaching—that is, the activities of the teacher and pupils—are many and complex. Moreover, they flash past at an astonishing rate. This has been noted by both Jackson (1968) and Adams and Biddle (1970), who suggest that the number of discriminable acts, utterances, or sentences spoken by classroom participants may be in the thousands for a given lesson. Because of this complexity it is difficult for the investigator to apply an instrument, such as a rating scale, directly to the on-going lesson. Instead, many investigators are now taking advantage of such technological tools as audio and videotape recorders to make stabilized records of the teaching process that can be studied at leisure. This suggests that the collection of data concerning teaching may actually involve two steps: *recording* and *encoding* (see Weick, 1968). However, not all investigators use recording; indeed, as we shall see, not all investigators use formal instruments for encoding either.

Another problem concerns the fact that teaching is not normally performed in public. Pupils are surprised at, and teachers may resent, our attempts to study their activities. Since teaching is normally found in closed classrooms, to observe it we must intrude ourselves into an environment in which other adults or recording equipment are not normally found. Still another problem concerns the fact that in studying teaching we must observe human beings rather than physical objects or baboons. While in theory it is fairly easy to measure aspects of mountains, daffodils, or butterflies without disturbing them (even this is not really easy!), it is more difficult to do so when observing people. Human beings are also observers and may adjust their activities when aware that we are observing them. Neither of these problems is insurmountable, but each has generated concern for those who want to study teaching. For example, some studies have made use of classrooms with one-way mirrors or hidden microphones, while most investigators have taken great pains to explain the purposes of the study to teachers and pupils and to restrict examination of data to research personnel.

Informal observation   The simplest method for collecting data about teaching is informal observation. Whenever the principal, a parent, or another teacher enters the classroom, the potential for informal observation is present. Each of these persons may come away from the experience bearing some impression of what he or she has seen there. Usually these impressions will reflect something that is striking or odd about the classroom. An observer might note that one lesson appears intense, that another seems noisy and disorganized, that the teacher is using harsh discipline, or that the room is messy. In informal observation the observer performs the tasks of recording and encoding (and, for that matter, data analysis, synthesis, and interpretation of results) in his own mind. Thus, the conclusions he reaches may be biased. This does not mean that we should eschew informal observation of teaching. Should we do so as educators we are fools, for many insights can be gained by studying others' teaching on an informal basis. Moreover, in the hands of anthropologists the art of informal observation has been systematized as "participant observation" and serves as a major technique for generating hypotheses about previously unresearched settings. A particularly good example of this appears in the work of L. M. Smith and W. Geoffrey (1968), who used intensive informal observation to study and develop insights concerning a junior high classroom in a slum school. Nevertheless, when we want to test hypotheses or to establish the validity of relationships among variables for a range of classrooms, informal observation is not a particularly good technique for the task.

Rating scales   For decades school principals and inspectors have been asked to make ratings of teachers. Sometimes these ratings are made on the basis of observing the teacher in action for one or more lessons. Sometimes they are made at the end of the school year. Instruments designed for this purpose usually provide a series of scales against which the teacher is to be rated. For example, teachers might be assigned a number or letter indicating how "industrious" or "sensitive" they are or how well they "manage their classrooms." These instruments were originally designed to provide means for evaluating and encouraging teachers. Moreover, they have enjoyed an unrivaled status for such practical purposes as hiring, granting tenure, placing and promoting teachers, and evaluating the performance of student teachers (Davis, 1964). The fact that no investigators have ever been able to provide much evidence that rating scales can be used validly for these purposes is irrelevant. School boards and school administrators have had to make decisions such as these, and it has seemed reasonable to them to use techniques similar to those used to evaluate and motivate pupils—namely, the assigning of grades. (Nor need it be added that use of rating scales has generally been an anathema to teachers.)

Rating scales have also been used extensively (see Gage, 1960) in research on the "effectiveness" of teaching. As was suggested in Chapter II, most of this research concentrated on designs in which relationships between a presage variable and a rating given to teachers was sought, ignoring altogether the process variables of teaching. Not too surprisingly, much of this research was fruitless. At least four difficulties may be cited in connection with the use of rating scales in research on teaching. First, the rating instrument often calls for observers to make high-inference judgments Moreover, in many cases the instrument provides only minimal information as to what one must observe if a teacher is to be rated highly for, say, "industriousness" or "sensitivity" (see Rosenshine, 1970). Second, sometimes only a single rating is made for each teacher, and thus the observer is asked to integrate his observations over one or more lessons, or even an entire school year, in order to make the rated judgment. (What does the observer do when a given teacher varies sharply in "industriousness" during the period observed?) Third, most of the studies have not made use of trained observers but rather have used ratings generated by administrators, pupils, or even teachers themselves. Apart from their lack of training, such observers are also likely to be involved with the teachers rated and therefore to be biased. Fourth, the qualities chosen for inclusion in rating instruments usually have not been validated against product variables, but have represented some "expert's" notion of what constitutes excellence in teaching (see Medley and Mitzel, 1963).

Despite these difficulties, some evidence has appeared which suggests that rating scales can indeed be used to predict pupil growth. According to Rosenshine and Furst (1971), ratings of the following teacher qualities have been validated against criteria of pupil growth in various studies: *clarity, variability, enthusiasm, task orientation,* and *student opportunity to learn criterion material* (also see Rosenshine, 1971). In perhaps the most extensive rating study yet published, Ryans (1960) was able to identify three apparently independent characteristics of teachers from rating scales and to validate them against a variety of presage, context, and process variables: teacher *warmth or understanding,* teacher *responsible or businesslike classroom behavior,* and teacher *stimulation or imaginativeness.* The usefulness for teacher education of knowledge gained through rating methods is, however, a matter of doubt. Knowing, for example, that warmth is a desirable quality in teachers is one thing. Developing procedures for engendering warmth in student teachers is quite another, and knowledge developed from rating studies provides us with little guidance in this matter. Teacher educators and teacher trainees can probably put such knowledge to much greater use if the specific behavioral referents of qualities such as warmth are known and agreed upon. Student teachers need to know what acts they must perform in order to demonstrate warmth. Unfortunately, rating methods have not contributed much of this latter type of knowledge. For this reason, as well as for others cited earlier, *we will ignore research based on rating methods for the remainder of this book.*

Live observation   In live observation the investigator or his assistant sits within the classroom lesson and makes coding judgments about the events he observes there *as they are occurring.* Live observation is similar to the use of rating scales in that neither method employs recordings. In both cases the observer is asked to encode information and to make judgments about teaching activities that he has witnessed personally. The two approaches differ, however, in the level of inference required of the observer and in their potential for studying the sequential processes of teaching. Whereas rating scales usually call for high-inference judgments and require the observer to integrate whatever he has witnessed over the lesson or year, in live observation observers must make judgments while the activities of the classroom are in progress. Most instruments for live observation call for quite rapid decision-making by the observer. Thus, judgments may be required after each teacher statement or question, or following each pupil response, or every few seconds of time. Since the observer must make many judgments, instruments used for live observation usually are quite simple, involve relatively few categories among which the observer must judge, and often attempt to represent only one dimension of classroom happenings. By the same token, when properly handled, data from live observation may be viewed as a sequential record of classroom events. Thus, live observation allows us to look at the ebb and flow, the highs and lows of the classroom lesson, the give and take between teacher and pupil in a way that is impossible with rating techniques.

Apart from rating scales, live observation is the most popular method for collecting data concerning teaching. More than 100 studies are summarized in this text that were based on live observation, and many others are being reported each year. It is easy to see why live observation should be popular. Since it usually involves only simple instruments and a single observer, studies using live observation are relatively easy to conduct. Observers can be used who are but minimally trained, and data generated are simple and easy to analyze. For these reasons live observation has appealed not only to those seeking to conduct research leading to their doctorates in education but also to teachers, teacher trainees, and teacher educators who would like to participate in honest, reputable research on teaching but who have little money or time.

At the same time, live observation has serious drawbacks as a method for collecting data. Most of these stem from the complexity and rapid pace of classroom events. Because exchanges between teachers and pupils are rapid, the observer may be overwhelmed when asked to judge as few as two independent aspects of the teaching process. As an example of this, the reader might try to keep track of the exact sequence of speakers (using a checklist of the names of all persons in a given classroom) during a classroom lesson. Even when he is trained and uses a number or letter code for each pupil, the reader will probably have difficulty with the task. Now try to code each utterance for its warmth, wit, or wisdom!

The other side of this problem concerns the simplicity of live observation data. Most of the truly interesting questions we would like to ask about teaching require complex data for their answers. Does use of warmth or humor by teachers induce more responsiveness in pupils? To answer this question we need to measure (1) teacher warmth or humor and (2) pupil responsiveness. But if it should turn out that pupils respond differently, we may also want to measure (3) pupil identity and (4) contexts or activities in which the teacher is behaving. The first two of these tasks would burden most live classroom observers, let alone either or both of the latter. Thus, studies involving live observation have usually involved simple, one-dimensional instruments—and their results have been limited accordingly.

There is still one more reason for the popularity of live observation. It has also been thought that teachers or teacher trainees might benefit from training in the use of instruments for live observation. Thus, practice in live observation has begun to appear in the curricula of schools of teacher education, and trainees may be required to use this technique as part of their requirements for practice teaching or educational psychology. In Chapter V evidence for these latter claims is examined.

Use of recordings Given the rapid pace and complexity of classroom events, investigators are turning to the use of recordings for "freezing" those events for subsequent study. If done properly, recordings offer the advantage of providing the researcher with a stable, static source of data that can be studied again and again. Thus, rapid exchanges between teachers and pupils may be studied more reliably, and investigators may study *many* aspects of the exchange rather than just one or two.

Various forms of behavioral recordings have been used in classroom research. One of these, the *specimen-record* technique, obviates the need for portable electronic recording equipment. As developed by Barker and Wright (1955), specimen records are running narratives of everything that happens to an individual and his responses to those events. Originally used for studying children's behavior, specimen records have now been applied to teachers (Hughes, 1959b), to pupil behavior in the classroom (Barker *et al.*, 1961), and to wholistic descriptions of classrooms (Gump, 1967). Specimen records are normally generated by an observer who sits in the classroom for the duration of a lesson, or for a shorter, arbitrary time period. Copious notes are taken, and at the conclusion of the lesson the observer retires and dictates a detailed, running account of everything that was said and done during the period of his observation. These observations are then typed in a standard format. Thus, when completed, specimen records become detailed, interpreted transcripts of classroom events. An example of such a record appears in Figure 4.1.

A second technique for recording behavior, *sound recordings,* has also been used by a number of classroom investigators, including Bellack *et al.* (1966), Nuthall and Lawrence (1965), and Taba, Levine, and Elzey (1964). Although various means are available for making recordings, all of these studies used electronic tape recordings. Use of sound recordings is subject to two difficulties. First, despite teachers' best efforts, most classrooms remain noisy environments, and audio records are often unintelligible. This is particularly true, for example, for *sotto voce* or whispered comments, which may or may not be comprehended by others in the classroom either. Second, teaching involves not only verbal events but also gestures, chalk drawings, and visual displays. These do not appear in the sound record, thus the transcriptions of sound recordings may or may not make sense without supplementary information. For example, the teacher may say in an annoyed voice: "Stop that!" (What was "that"?) Or again, the mathematics instructor may "complete his sentence" by drawing on the chalkboard. Perhaps the best way of meeting these two problems is to hang a transmitting microphone (that is, one without a cord) around the teacher's neck and then to place an observer in the back of the room who will dictate a running account of classroom events into a second microphone that comments on and explains what is happening. Such a procedure requires a two-track tape recorder, and a sample transcript prepared in this manner appears in Figure 4.2.

FIGURE 4.1 Excerpt from specimen-record transcript. Subject: Betty Pearson; grade V; Kansas, U.S.A. (From Barker et al., 1961, p. 73)

Reading in Reader

11:18 Betty occupied the last seat in the west row in the room.

She was holding a reader in her hands, rather lackadaisically.

She gazed about the room idly.

Commenting to Shirley

Shirley Vey, who sat directly across the aisle to her left, leaned over and whispered in a friendly way to Betty.

Betty tossed her head rather complacently.

She announced in a stage whisper, "I've finished."

Evidently she was referring to what she had been expected to finish in her reader.

She closed her reader quietly, with finality.

She was gazing absently around the room.

She casually poked the book into the desk.

Writing

11:19 She rather abruptly leaned over and peered

Finding Tablet

into her desk, as if to check on its contents.

Then she sat up very straight.

She searched persistently in the desk, without looking.

Evidently she could tell what she was after by feeling.

She coughed slightly as she searched.

In a moment she brought out a thin, writing book.

11:20 She placed it on her desk.

Her desk also held two pencils, one an iridescent red and the other a brilliant chartreuse green.

The green pencil was just a stub.

Betty sat up quite straight with her left foot in the aisle.

R — She absently reached around with her left hand and scratched her back a second with her left thumb.

She looked down at the writing pad curiously.

Then she glanced querulously at Shirley Vey.

11:21 She looked at the writing book as if trying to decide which page she wanted.

R — Unconsciously, apparently, she tapped her foot in rhythm to the march music that could be heard from the music room across the hall.

She gave no other sign that she was hearing the music.

Noting Mary

11:22 Mary Ennis, who sat across the aisle in the seat ahead of her, got out of her seat and walked to an empty seat just back of Betty.

> This was an empty desk packed full of supplies, inside and on top.

Mary knelt down to peer into and poke around in it.

Betty turned around halfway in her seat.

She watched curiously.

Mary softly whispered something to her, but I could not hear.

Betty looked disapproving; she frowned and pursed her lips.

Then Mary shrugged and pulled out a box of Kleenex from the desk and returned to her seat.

11:23 Betty immediately bent over her writing tablet attentively.

She leafed through until she found the page she wanted.

The sentence on the page read, "which is best?"

At the top of the page was a line in a very large green writing, then there were several blank spaces and then a line or two in smaller writing, followed by more blank lines.

Blowing Nose

Betty abruptly stopped looking at her writing tablet.

She reached over and picked up an empty Kleenex box and got a fresh Kleenex from the box underneath it.

She blew her nose quite vigorously and noisily.

Then she put the soiled Kleenex in the empty box.

She did this in a very businesslike way, as if she had no idea that anyone was paying any attention to her.

Noting Mary

11:24 She glanced around the room as if finding it difficult to settle down.

Mary Ennis went up to the teacher's desk.

She asked the teacher something in a quiet tone and came back.

Betty watched her idly until she returned to her seat and sat down.

Writing

Then she conscientiously bent over her paper again.

She picked up her chartreuse pencil.

With a very firm grip she began to trace over the large writing at the top of the page.

11:25 She abruptly changed from the green to the red pencil in the middle of the line.

She continued with the red pencil, which was some longer than the green one.

Shirley Vey went to the desk behind Betty.

Shirley immediately raised the cover on an Easter egg candy box which was on top the desk.

Betty glanced around to see what she was doing, but showed no particular interest.

She immediately turned her attention back to her writing.

Shirley took out a paper doll which she looked at for a second and then she put it back in the box.

She abruptly shut the box and returned to her desk.

Betty did not glance up.

11:26   The teacher asked hopefully, "How many of you have finished with your reading?"

Betty immediately and casually lifted her left hand.

She continued to write with the pencil in her right hand.

The teacher suggested that each child read the bold type on page 164 of the arithmetic text.

She added, "Douglas, you read it aloud for us and we'll all follow it."

11:27   Betty let her hand down.

She continued to write in the writing book.

Douglas Crawford started to read.

Evidently Betty had been somewhat aware of what was going on while she wrote.

Still holding the pencil in her right hand, Betty belatedly and hurriedly thrust her left hand in her desk.

She pulled out her arithmetic book.

She turned pages and found the place in the book very quickly.

With her feet stretched far under the desk, she conscientiously followed with her eyes the bold type which Douglas was reading.

She held the pencil in her right hand and kept intent her gaze on the book.

R— Her feet were crossed below the desk and were swaying rhythmically as if she still were feeling the beat of the music which was coming from across the hall.

11:28   The teacher queried, indicating a particular problem in the book, "Now, how do we change this to simple form?"

They were studying a certain section in fractions.

Then she asked in a louder tone, "What do we do, Betty, to get the numbers to their simplest form?"

Betty immediately began to answer "4/3 = 1 1/3."

65

FIGURE 4.2   Excerpt from two-track audiotape transcript. Grade I; Queensland, Australia. (From E. Scott, 1971, personal communication)

Now, we're going to talk about all of those things that are not good for your teeth. Oh, I'll bet little people of today know all about these things that are not good for their teeth. You tell me, Craig.

Craig: Biscuits.

Biscuits, they're no good for your teeth. Debrough?

Debrough: Lollies.

Right, no lollies, biscuits, or . . .

Mark: Sugar.

Hmm.

Neil: Cordial.

Yes, all those things that are too sweet are not good for your teeth. But mummy often gives them to you for a treat, doesn't she. If you've been very good, she'll give them to you for a treat.

If you do eat biscuits or cakes or lollies and things like that, you chew a piece of apple after it and that'll get rid of all the old pieces. Then they won't hurt your teeth, will they?

David: Mrs. _____, Mrs. _____, Dirt.

Pardon? Dirt? Oh, David, I don't think you're listening.

David: Lemonade.

We said all of those things. Sweet drinks and sweet lollies and sweet cakes are no good for your teeth. Well, you think tonight when you go home, and you're having your tea and your lovely vegetables, what do they do. They help to make your teeth strong.

Voices: They help to make your teeth strong.

For chewing, that's right. Now, it's time for our day. Oh, I wonder who's awake this morning. No. Hands down first. I'm going to look and find a nice person who's sitting very tall this morning. Stephen, I like the way you're sitting. You stand up and tell us what day it is today.

Stephen: Today is Monday.

We all know that because it's the first day we come back after our two little holidays, isn't it. We'll all say that together. Come on.

Children chant with the teacher.

That appears to be the end of the health session. The teacher moves to her table.

Voices: Today is Monday.

I'm going to write the story on the blackboard for you. You're going to tell me, what does that say?

Voices: Today.

What comes after that?

Voices: Is.

Yes, the magic word, "is." I wonder what sound "Monday" makes. You think. Oh, don't tell, just think. I hear someone.

I'll say it again, you listen. Monday. What kind of a sound does that make, Jillian?

Jillian: Mmmm.

Everyone say it?

Voices: Mmmmmmmm.

Do we know anything else that starts with "mmmm"? Rikkie?

Rikkie: Mother.

Good boy. Now we'll read the whole story. Ready now, all looking this way? Right.

Voices: Today.

Oh, but I don't think that was everybody. Come on.

Voices: Today is Monday.

Oh . . . What is the name of the month? Now remember, none of those funny hicking noises this morning. I don't know who makes them all the time but they're not nice. Christine? Do you know the name of the month?

Christine: March.

Oh, I think you've been asleep. Sharon might know.

Sharon: April.

Good girl. We'll all say it. Here it is up here. Come on. The month is . . .

Voices: The month is April.

April. We'll say it again.

Voices: The month is April.

Right. Now, we've got to find out what kind of a day it is, today. Put your hand up if you had a look when you were coming to school. The little people who walk to school would have had plenty of time for looking, wouldn't they? Glen, what could you tell me about today? Big loud voice, Glen.

Teacher writes on the board, "Today." As the children chant the word "is," the teacher writes "is" on the board.

Teacher now writes the word "Monday" on the board.

Christine stands and says "March."

The teacher points to the board where the word "April" is already written.

About half the hands are up. Maybe three-quarters now.

Figure 4.2 (continued)

Glen: There is a blue sky.   *Teacher gives him a*
Good, well you come out and make your blue   *piece of blue chalk.*
sky. Here you are. Everybody else think of   *Glen goes across to the*
something else they saw today coming to   *board. Draws an arc*
school. Good boy, Glen.   *blue to represent the*
Susan, you tell us something else.   *sky. Returns to his*
Susan: A cloudy day.   *place.*
Oh, did you tell me a big story?
Susan: Today is a cloudy day.
Lots of clouds or just a few clouds.
Voice: Lots of clouds.
I'm speaking to Susan. Now, you're rude to in-
terrupt.

A still more complex form of recording is the *audiovisual record* that can be either a sound motion picture (see Kounin, 1970) or a videotape recording (see Kounin *et al.*, 1966; or Scheuler, Gold, and Mitzel, 1962). Audiovisual recordings have an immediate appeal for research purposes because they provide a wealth of details of the two media in which most classroom interaction takes place. Such recordings can be viewed with instant understanding of most classroom events. At the same time, they are not the clear, unambiguous experience we are used to seeing on the television or motion picture screen. Most audiovisual recordings are technically inferior, and many are composed using two cameras and a split-screen image (so that the faces of all participants appear in the recording). Because of the "completeness" of the information in audiovisual recordings, it is possible to make coding judgments by viewing them repeatedly (see, for example, Adams and Biddle, 1970), but most investigators have also made transcripts from them for coding purposes. It is possible, also, to use the visual portion of the recording to provide information that clarifies the verbal record. Thus, notations concerning the references of verbal symbols may be added to the transcript. An example of a transcript prepared from videotape appears as Figure 4.3.

Which of these methods is best? It depends, of course, on one's research objectives and finances. Specimen records are relatively inexpensive to prepare. They do not involve the purchase or maintenance of electronic gear, and the record that is typed comes out in readable format, since the observer dictates and thinks in units that constitute grammatical sentences. On the other hand, the record dictated is filtered through the selective and integrative mechanisms of the observer. This introduces bias, because all human beings tend to simplify, categorize, unify, and distort their impressions of events. Depending on what aspects of teaching one wishes to study, this may or may not be important. Audio recordings are slightly more expensive than specimen records. They require equipment (albeit inexpensive and reliable machines), and if transcripts are desired they must be typed,

FIGURE 4.3 Excerpt from edited videotape transcript; grade XI; Missouri, U.S.A. (From Loflin et al., 1973, personal communication)

(*T*) To open the discussion today though on uh our questions: _____, if the democratic process requires the existence of political parties, what is the role of the unaffiliated voter? Who wants to start? Anyone? All right, Deborah.

(*Deborah*) Uh, if he's unaffiliated he should vote for the man who he feels would best fit the job instead of being loyal to his particular political party.

(*T*) What does the unaffiliated man do? What's his role?

(*Deborah*) His role is to vote for the best man possible.

(*T*) How can he make sure we have the best man?

(*Deborah*) _____.

(*T*) Okay. /calls on pupils/

(*Girl*) Uh, also he /DIS/ between, . . . uh, you know, I mean people like George Wallace, . . . /Boy INT./

(*Boy*) _____.

(*Girl*) The unaffiliated voter, you know, . . .

(*Levi*) He can uh /Girl INT./

(*Girl*) Try to, . . .

(*Levi*) Try to start his own political party.

(*T*) But we're assuming that he's unaffiliated, Levi.

(*Boy*) As long as he could do, . . . What he should do is, to uh vote for the man of the best interest to his needs or his wants, but he should always vote.

(*Boy*) I'd like to ask a question. On this question is uh, is the question in reference to an individual or to whole, . . . the whole party?

(*T*) Well, no. If, you're, . . . if, . . . /self INT./ We uh, we assume that we have political parties. Right?

(*Boy*) Yes.

(*T*) But there are a large, there's a large segment of the American population that does not claim to be a Democrat, does not claim to be a Republican. Now what's his role? We say that in the democratic processes we require political parties. But what do, . . . does this guy who doesn't claim to be of any political party fit it?

(*Boy*) The role of the individual voter, not the party as a whole?

(*T*) What did you think?

(*Boy*) Well, . . . uh well, I think that, . . . well, he's just, . . . well, he really doesn't favor any party, so therefore he uh votes for the man of his choice. He doesn't favor any party, you know.

(*T*) Clarence. I'm not going to call on you by hands, just speak out.

(*Boy*) Well, uh I feel that uh, you know, there are enough of them that uh when they, you know, vote for the one of their choice, vote for the one of their choice, they aren't affiliated, well there'll be some that'll vote, you know, for the ones, the things that they'd be able to make in one party, and another one might hear something he needs, and that's another party. So really it's, . . . I'd, I would say it's almost never split almost down the middle.

(*T*) Go ahead, Donnie.

interpreted, and sometimes retyped before they can be used for research. Furthermore, the audio record may sometimes be inaudible or ambiguous. Audiovisual recordings offer far more information and are clearly irreplaceable for the study of such visual information as facial expressions. However, they are far more expensive than either specimen or audio records. They also require the acquisition and maintenance of costly, touchy equipment. Specimen records require placing a human observer in the classroom (as does live observation). Audio recordings require microphones and perhaps an observer too. Videotape recordings require microphones, television cameras (preferably that can be remotely controlled), cables, and sometimes supplementary lighting. The choice is really dictated by one's research needs and resources. Most of the studies reported in this text used live observation. In terms of measurement criteria, the half-dozen most sophisticated studies all used—and needed—audiovisual recordings.

Instruments for Studying Teaching

Let us assume that we have now solved the problem of obtaining examples of teaching for study. Either we have access to live classrooms, or we have obtained a set of recordings or transcriptions of classroom lessons. Now we must decide what aspects of teaching we are to study. It is all very well to assert that we wish to study teaching, but what aspects of teaching are we to study? More than 30 people appear in the standard classroom, and it would be at least theoretically possible to attempt to observe the behaviors of each. Teachers (and pupils) speak words, ask questions, give answers, exhibit facial expressions, stand, move, gesture, touch themselves and others, write on the chalkboard, yawn. Are we to study *all* of these events, and if not, which? Moreover, classroom behavior is somewhat different when viewed from the standpoint of the teacher, the pupil, the psychologist, the sociologist, the educator. What conceptual posture should we adopt for our study?

Problems of this sort require decisions by the investigator, and once these decisions have been made they are "frozen" into the form of a research instrument that may be used not only by the investigator but also by others interested in the study of teaching. Nobody can study *all* aspects of teaching. Each instrument represents a decision to focus on certain aspects and to avoid others. Given this fact, all research-based knowledge concerning teaching is limited by the advantages and shortcomings of the instruments with which it was developed. And in order to understand this knowledge, we must appreciate both the advantages and shortcomings of the instruments. In effect, we must constantly ask ourselves, "So this is true. What else is true?"

Our task would be simpler if only a few instruments had been developed for measuring classroom events. Such is not the case. During the past decades a staggering number of instruments has appeared for studying teaching. In their presumably comprehensive anthology Simon and Boyer (1970) report 79 separate instruments. Rosenshine (1970) claims knowledge of 40 instruments that were somehow missed by Simon and Boyer and suggests that "no estimate can be made of the additional category systems which could be located" (p. 283).

It is possible to classify instruments for purposes of analysis in terms of various features. For convenience, we will deal here with their content, format, persons studied, unit of analysis, and conceptual posture.

Content of instruments The most basic way of sorting instruments is in terms of their content, or the aspects of teaching they choose to study. As we shall see in subsequent chapters, some instruments are designed to study the emotional content of teacher-pupil exchange, some the problems of classroom management, some classroom ecology, some the logic and ideas exchanged in lessons, and on and on. There is no magic to the classification of content we have used in the chapters of this text. A great many theories of teaching exist, any of which is capable of generating instruments for classroom research. But not all of these theories have as yet generated research, and some instruments represent more than a single orientation. For this reason any content classification for instruments will be arbitrary— a compromise between theory, insight, research published to date, and convenience. Readers might be interested to contrast the classification found in Chapters V through X with that proposed by Simon and Boyer (1970), who sorted research instruments into six classes: the affective domain, cognitive materials, psychomotor events, classroom activities, subject content, sociological structure, and the physical environment of the classroom.

Format of Instruments Following a suggestion made by Medley and Mitzel (1963), we shall distinguish here between two types of formats appearing in instruments: sign observation and categorical observation. In sign observation the observer is given a list of events to watch for in the classroom and is asked to check off those events that occur during a given time period. An example of such an instrument is OScAR (Medley and Mitzel, 1958). In contrast, in categorical observation the observer makes judgments among a set of categories into which the events he observes are to be classified. Examples of categorical instruments may be found in such studies as those of Flanders (1960), Kowatrakul (1959), and Perkins (1964). Categorical observation provides more data and appears to be more flexible than sign observation. It also lends itself more readily to the study of sequential events in the classroom, such as the appropriateness of responses to questions. Nevertheless, coders are usually "busier" when using categorical systems for observation and generally cover fewer "dimensions" than is true for sign systems.

To illustrate the difference in application of sign and category systems, take the case of an observer who is interested in "praise" as it occurs in the classroom. Under a sign system the observer might decide to register his observations every 30 seconds. The decision he makes with respect to praise every 30 seconds is: did praise occur during that interval? Now praise might have occurred only once or it might have occurred ten times, but the observer under a sign system is merely interested in whether it did or did not occur. Thus, praise can be checked only once in any one 30-second interval. Should the lesson last 45 minutes, the maximum "praise score" would be 90. Under a category system, however, the observer will try to tally every instance of praise occurring during that lesson. Theoretically, there is no maximum score for praise under a category system. Thus, whereas under the sign system the score for praise might be 60, under a category system it could be 120 or more for the same example of teaching.

It would appear, then, that category systems are more sensitive, precise instruments than sign systems. By the same token, sign systems might be more reliable, since they eliminate the extreme scores sometimes obtained with category systems.

By far the majority of instruments developed for classroom research are categorical systems designed for use with live observation. Typically, they are developed for use by one observer and may be used at any grade level or for any lesson content. Usually only verbal behavior is to be coded, and one judgment is to be coded for each such unit of observation. Before embarking upon formal observation the observer is expected to receive training, at the end of which his observations are to agree closely with those of an expert who has applied the system to specimen tape recordings of classroom discussions. The training involves memorizing the categories, their codes (for example, numbers), a set of ground rules for their application, and the mechanics of entering code symbols on a data sheet.

A common difficulty with the sets of categories contained in these instruments is that explanations of why the categories of a particular set should be mutually exclusive of one another, or just what it is that is being coded, are lacking. For example, consider a commonly used instrument, the Flanders Interaction Analysis Category system (FIAC). This instrument asks us to consider as mutually exclusive such categories for coding teacher behavior as "accepts or uses ideas of students," "praises or encourages," and "asks questions" (see Figure 5.3). However, to the uninitiated it appears that a teacher might simultaneously both accept ideas *and* encourage, or encourage *and* ask a question, although these appear as independent categories in the instrument. Because some sets of categories do not appear to be mutually exclusive, researchers who have used these instruments have had to develop policies or ground rules to resolve problems of precedence. For example, we discover from Flanders (1970) the following comments on FIAC:

> Teacher questions can be coded in any one of the seven teacher categories: in Category 1 if they are objective, nonthreatening inquiries involving attitudes or emotions and designate the feeling or emotion; in Category 2 if they are intended to praise; in 3 if they are based on ideas previously expressed by pupils; in 5 if they are categorical and no answer is expected;

in 6 if they are directions; and in 7 if they are critical, or designed to catch pupils who are day dreaming. Usually the questions which are coded 4 are genuine invitations to participate. (p. 45)

ince the meaning of a category depends on (1) the terms describing it nd (2) the terms describing other categories with which it is apposed, uch ground rules appear to be crutches supporting a questionable enter- rise.

Let us pose a concept and a rule for handling problems such as these. 'ollowing the terminology suggested by Guttman (1954) and Foa (1965), /e will describe a set of categories as a *facet* if they form a clear, mutually xclusive set, and all examples of the events in which we are interested can e coded in one of them. For example, if we are categorizing examples of erbal behavior, we might use the categories *talking* and *not talking*. They /ould surely form a facet. Another facet is indicated by the categories we light use for judging teachers' approaches to pupils: *warm, neutral*, and ool. As these two examples have indicated, many facets represent a series f rank-ordered alternatives along some underlying dimension in which we re interested. However, this is not true for all facets. Consider the interesting ategorical set posed by Bellack *et al.* (1966): *structuring, soliciting, esponding, reacting*. These four categories are designed for the classification f teacher or pupil utterances and are defined so that their boundaries do ot overlap, and all utterances can be classified within them. They too form facet.

Clearly, we are better off with categorical systems that form facets. At east three kinds of problems are likely to appear when our categorical list oes not form a facet. For one, our coding operations are likely to be some- /hat unreliable. For another, since those aspects of teaching we are inter- sted in measuring with our instrument are not measured crisply, we would xpect to find weak and sometimes contradictory findings when attempting o relate results for teaching with other variables. We will see evidence of hese in subsequent chapters.

But, most important, for nonfaceted instruments it is difficult to know vhat kinds of events are actually coded into the categories of the instru- nents and what to make of "findings" reported for them. To interpret a inding for the FIAC category "Asks Questions," for example, is difficult inless one knows whether questions asked by the teacher were actually oded there or whether what was coded was merely a residuum after "six ther kinds of questions" detected by coders had actually been coded else- vhere. All of this seems self-evident once one thinks about it, but a surpris- ng number of the instruments developed for live observation do not form acets, and investigators have often appeared unaware of the problems aused by this fact.

To summarize, then, observational instruments for research on teach- ng may be classified as *sign* or *categorical* systems, depending on whether the coder is given the task of looking for the occurrence of independent events (from a list) or whether he must judge all events of a given class for the category into which they fall (from a list provided). If the latter the category set should form a *facet*; that is, the categories provided should be mutually exclusive and provide an unambiguous classification for each event that is to be coded. It is also possible, of course, that the categorical instrument may provide two or more facets for which the events of teach ing may be coded. (For example, pupil answers could be coded for their accuracy, their originality, their warmth, and the identity of the pupil who spoke. To do so would require an instrument having four facets for making judgments about pupil answers.)

Most instruments that have been developed for research on teaching so far are single-faceted categorical instruments. This presumably reflect the fact that most research has collected data by means of live observation Most of the studies making use of recordings have taken advantage of their more complete data and have used multifaceted categorical instruments.

Persons studied   More than 30 people appear in the typical classroom each of whom is continuously "behaving" throughout the span of the lesson Theoretically, it would be possible to study the behaviors of each of these persons independently, although such a task appears expensive and of questionable usefulness for answering most of the questions we should like answered concerning teaching. Consequently, we must make decisions con cerning whom to study in the classroom and upon which occasions to switch our attention to others.

To researchers concerned with teaching the key figure in the classroom is the *teacher*, and most instruments call for the coding of teacher behavior at least part of the time. In some cases teacher behavior is studied through out the lesson; in others the teacher is studied only while she is actively speaking or otherwise emitting symbols in a public manner. Let us consider the case when a pupil is responding to the teacher's question. If what we are interested in is teacher behavior, we will continue to watch the teacher —perhaps, for example, coding her facial expression for response to the pupil's answer. In contrast, if we are concerned with characteristics of the public stream of communication, we will turn our attention to the pupil and abandon the teacher until she speaks again. This suggests that instruments may be classified into those concerned with *teacher behavior* and those con cerned with *teacher-as-emitter behavior*.

A similar distinction may be made for pupils, of course. Some instru ments call for the continuous observation of a selected pupil, while others require us to study only the pupil nominated by the teacher to speak or who is actually speaking. However, there are many pupils in the classroom, and sometimes we are concerned not with the response of individual pupils but with the behavior of the classroom group. For example, the pupil group may be coded for its excited interest, its apathy, its noisiness. This suggests that instruments may also be classified into those concerned with *individual pupil behavior, pupils-as-targets* or *emitters*, and *pupil-group behavior*.

Depending on the interests, concepts, and theories of investigators, these various treatments of persons may be combined in different ways within a given instrument. In FIAC, for example, attention is given to teacher-as-emitter or to pupil-as-emitter, depending on who is speaking. The same focus on teacher-pupil interaction appears in the work of Smith and Meux (1962); Nuthall and Lawrence (1965); and Taba, Levine, and Elzey (1964). In contrast, those concerned with cognitive aspects of teaching (such as Davis and Tinsley, 1968; or Gallagher, 1965) have often looked at either teacher questions or pupil responses in isolation. Other investigators, such as Kounin (1970), have concerned themselves with the responses of individual pupils to classroom events, such as strategies of management or incidents of deviancy control by the teacher. Still others have concerned themselves with the classroom group, either for its own qualities (see Adams and Biddle, 1970, for example) or as a context or function of teacher-pupil interaction.

Unit of analysis Instruments also differ in their units of analysis—in the events of teaching they choose for study. Thus some instruments concern themselves with acts, some with questions and answers, some with gestures or facial expressions, some with sentences spoken, some with "teaching cycles" or "episodes," some with arbitrary units of time. Let us consider some of these possibilities.

Sentences, questions, and gestures are all examples of *phenomenal units*. Such units are "natural" in that classroom members and investigators are both trained to perceive them and share a vocabulary for describing them. Once we know the grammatical rules of English, for example, we have little difficulty recognizing a "sentence." Again, "questions" can normally be easily discriminated from other forms of enunciation, certain gestures, such as the raising of one's hand, have unambiguous meaning in the classroom, a smile can be sorted out from a frown, and so forth. Phenomenal units are used in two ways in instruments for studying teaching. Some instruments require coders only to discriminate certain selected events for coding and to ignore others that do not fall into their ken. For example, Kounin (1970) singled out incidents of deviancy control in the classroom for study. Again, Davis and Tinsley (1968) investigated the characteristics of teacher and pupil questions. Other instruments break the teaching lesson into a series of phenomenal units that are theoretically exhaustive of the events with which we might be concerned. Thus, in linguistically oriented studies (such as that of Loflin *et al.*, 1972) the lesson transcript is considered to be a string of sentences that are coded for various properties.

Phenomenal units have several advantages for research purposes. Identification of phenomenal units may be done reliably, and when findings are reported for phenomenal units they are easy to understand. For example, we would find little difficulty in interpreting the following (fictitious) result:

On the average, boys were asked approximately twice as many questions as girls during the lesson.

As a result, phenomenal units are popular with investigators, coders, and the uninitiated customers of research alike. They also have their drawbacks. Of these perhaps the most serious is that our language simply does not provide commonly learned terms for some educational events with which we are concerned. Let us recall the Rules of the Classroom Game that we examined in Chapter III. As played in most classrooms, these involve the asking of questions by teachers, the provision of answers by pupils, and (sometimes) an evaluative statement by the teacher. This cycle of events—question, response, evaluation—appears over and over during the lesson. But what is it to be called? Unfortunately, our language does not provide us a common term for this cycle of events, although once our attention is drawn to it we recognize it as an experience we have all encountered.

For this reason some of the more sophisticated research instruments make use of analytic rather than phenomenal units. *Analytic units* use a vocabulary that is not immediately familiar to us. Sometimes this vocabulary is suggested by theories drawn from psychology, sociology, or the other social sciences. Sometimes investigators have had to invent new terms for the analytic units they wish to study because no prior vocabulary is available. For example, the cycle of events we discussed above—question, response, evaluation—seems to have been mainly ignored prior to the advent of observational studies of teaching. Since it is an obvious feature of classroom teaching, it has been "discovered" and named by various investigators. Smith and Meux (1962) termed it an "episode," Bellack *et al.* (1966) a "teaching cycle," Waimon and Hermanowitz (1965) a "teaching episode," and so forth. Although use of analytic units may be utterly essential for some research purposes, coders must be carefully trained to recognize them, reliability for the identification of units may be low, and uninitiated readers may have more difficulty understanding the results of research. Most educators would have at least some problems with the following (again fictitious) result:

> On the average, teaching cycles involving boys involved more abstract content and less positive affect than did teaching cycles with girls.

Nevertheless, we suspect that analytic units will continue to be used in research and thinking about teaching, if only because our common language is insufficient. Every other field of science has had to develop its own vocabulary, and research on teaching is unlikely to prove an exception.

Still another solution to the problem of choosing a unit for analysis is illustrated by FIAC and various other instruments that were designed for live observation. Instead of concentrating on actual classroom events, these instruments have used *arbitrary units of time* for analysis. In FIAC the coder is given the task of judging the category or categories of verbal behavior occurring during a three-second interval and ignoring successive reoccurrences of the same category in the same three-second interval. Other instruments have used shorter or longer units of time, depending on the complexity of the tasks given to the coder and the interests of the investigator. When carried to its lengthy extreme the arbitrary unit might be the classroom lesson itself, in which case we have changed the investigation from an observational to a rating study.

This illustrates the major problem encountered with time units. Since classroom events have a rhythm of their own, their boundaries may or may not correspond with the arbitrary time boundaries we are attempting to force on them. Since classroom events tend to occur rapidly, normally several events, such as teacher and pupil utterances, will occur in even the shortest arbitrary time intervals. When events come thick and fast judgments must be made as to which event one chooses for coding for a given interval. This introduces subjectivity and error into the coding process. It is sometimes suggested that use of arbitrary time intervals provides rhythm for the coder in live observation and that it provides a record of "how long" a given classroom emphasis lasted or "what proportion of time" was given to events of a given sort during the lesson. This information, however, can be provided by other means, such as the use of coding sheets that are marked off in units of time.

Conceptual posture Still another problem faced by those who design instruments for studying teaching is that of conceptual posture.

> What should be observed—the *intent* of behavior, its *objective characteristics,* or its *effects?* The problem may be illustrated by observing an incident in which a younger child attempts to strike an older child. The motive of the younger child is *hostility,* his action is *aggression,* but its effect is to create *amusement* in the older child. Each of these qualities—hostility, aggression, amusement—may be coded with reliability. But are all equally useful? (Biddle, 1967, pp. 344–345)

Various answers have been given to this problem. If we are concerned with establishing the determinants of classroom behavior, for example, we might find judgments about the intent of behavior more appropriate, and for Schoggen (1963) an act is identified by inferring the intent of the actor. In contrast, if we aim to establish relationships between process and product variables, judgments about behavioral effects would appear more appropriate. Thus, Medley, Schluck, and Ames (1968) argue:

> Since the pupil whom the behavior is supposed to affect must react to it in terms of how it looks to him, we may say that the observer's task is to put himself in the pupil's shoes and attend to only those aspects of teaching behavior a pupil would see. (p. 3)

However, the answer that impresses us most is the one that stresses our need for coding the objective characteristics of classroom events. At least two reasons may be advanced for this practice. For one, the coding of objective characteristics is likely to involve fewer inferences on the par of the coder, and hence it is less likely to be biased and more likely to be reliable. For another, objective codes may be related equally well to context presage, and product variables, thus simplifying the task of developing knowledge concerning teaching. Although we surely *can* code intent, objec tive characteristics, or effects, our judgments will be different depending or the posture we adopt. Hostility, aggression, and amusement are simply not the same qualities. We had better decide which of these is of interest to us and stick to that judgment.

Making Judgments About Teaching

Given a set of teaching events and an instrument for measuring them our problems of measurement reduce themselves to the application of the latter to the former. Usually this is a simple matter, so much so that it is often ignored in reports of research on teaching. However, research instru ments cannot be used by coders until they have received at least some training, and normally we should like to know something about the reli ability and validity of the judgments made with the instrument.

Training programs It seems truistic, but the more complex the instru ment, the more training is required before coders are able to use it reliably Thus, instruments requiring more than one judgment for a given teaching event, that use analytic units, that require coders to look at more than one person, that demand judgment be made of rapidly occurring events require substantial training of coders. At one end of the training continuum we find studies wherein little or no explicit training is required, whereas at the other we encounter instruments for which months or years of disciplinary education is a necessity. As an example of the latter, in the studies reported by Loflin *et al.* (1972) the transcript of classroom events must be "recon structed" into a string of "simplex sentences" for subsequent analysis. Coders who do this processing must have several months of training in structural linguistics. When instruments are used by several teams of investigators sooner or later a training manual is published for their use (for example, see Amidon and Flanders, 1967b).

Reliability and validity The terms reliability and validity have tech nical meanings when used to describe instruments for the measurement of teaching. To say that an instrument is *reliable* means that it provides the same score or measurement for repeated applications to the same teach ing events. To say that an instrument is *valid* means that it measures what we think it is measuring. Interestingly, an instrument may be reliable without being valid, but not vice versa. We might have an instrument that was supposed to be measuring the teacher's *warmth* and that was found to give stable scores for a given set of observers. However, when the observers' ratings were looked at more closely, it was discovered that they were actually coding teachers for their *directiveness* and not their warmth. In this case the instrument was reliable but not valid.

Reliability of teaching instruments is normally assessed by asking two coders who have had similar training to code the same samples of classroom events. When one has recordings of classrooms this is a simple matter. It is more difficult in situations of live observation, since we must then place *two* (or more) observers in a single classroom. For this reason reliability for live observation instruments is sometimes assessed against recordings or transcripts of classrooms, a method that appears invalid. It is much easier to generate reliability for recordings or transcripts, since the events of teaching may be examined again, and even complex judgments may be made with assurance by coders—if the units and concepts specified in the instruments have even minimal validity.

Many different statistics are used for reporting reliability. The usual statistic is some sort of proportionate measure showing what percentage of the judgments called for were agreed to by pairs of coders. However, correlation coefficients are sometimes used for the same purpose, along with other measures of association. In addition, reliability figures are reported for various aspects of the coding process: for individual categories of instruments, for an entire facet of judgments, for the identification of units for coding, for derivative measures that are assembled from instruments, and so forth. Unfortunately, some investigators report no reliabilities for their instruments at all! Clearly, we should like to know whether or not a given instrument measures some aspect of teaching reliably, and our confidence in the findings of a study are enhanced when high reliability is reported.

To assess validity for an instrument one normally compares scores generated by it against some criterion measure that is known to reflect the phenomenon in which we are interested. To validate a new test of intelligence, for example, we compare scores it generates with those of an accepted measure of intelligence, such as the Stanford-Binet. This is all very well, but suppose we are studying a new phenomenon that has not previously been measured. How do we establish validity for our instrument when no criterion is available? Two answers are given to this question. The more sophisticated one requires that we have a theory suggesting a relationship between the phenomenon and something else. If our investigation produces the predicted relationship, it is then assumed that the measurement we have made was also valid. The less sophisticated answer is that of "face validity." Given the problem of measuring the phenomenon in which we are interested, our scale is surely the most "obvious" and "straightforward" way of measuring it.

Formal discussion of validity appears rarely in reports of research on teaching. Studies during the past two decades have generally been termed "exploratory," and their instruments presumed a first attempt to measure the teaching aspect in question. Few formal theories have been stated that would allow validation of instruments by confirmation of hypotheses. Most investigators have seemed to feel that their instruments have "face validity" and bear obvious relationships with the concepts or *Commitment* that generated the research, although even "face validity" is not often discussed.

For our purposes we will consider evidence of validity for instruments to fall into two classes. Some instruments are difficult to interpret because their categories are poorly defined or because the latter do not form a facet. Other instruments generate findings that are weak or conflicting when assessed against presage, context, or product variables, despite reasonable theories suggesting otherwise. Either is likely to cause us to question the validity of the instrument.

PROBLEMS OF SAMPLING

To sample something, say a keg of wine, one draws a small bit of the universe for study. To be most useful the sample should be representative. In other words, we should mix the wine well before drawing our sample so as to avoid either the froth at the top or the dregs at the bottom of the keg. When studying teaching we should also like to draw representative samples of the teaching process so that our findings might apply to the universe of teachers, pupils, and classroom contexts. Unfortunately, to our knowledge *no* studies of teaching have yet made use of representative samples. Let us see why this has not yet occurred.

The basic difficulty with research on teaching is that it is expensive. Even live observation entails the salary of the coder who is to sit in the back of the classroom, while preparation of transcripts from audiotapes can cost well over $25 a lesson, and videotapes six to ten times that amount. This would still not be an insurmountable problem were we content to seek relationships among the several thousand events that may occur during the individual lesson. However, we are seldom willing to settle for such information. Rather, we should like to know how typical the lesson we have examined is of other lessons conducted by that teacher with those pupils, how the teacher compares with other teachers, how contextual variables affect the teaching process, or how pupils have reacted to various lessons. For these latter questions the lesson is, in fact, but a single unit, an N of one, and if we are to provide meaningful answers we must study many lessons. Unfortunately, only a few investigators have managed to secure resources sufficient to process data from more than a handful of lessons.

A second problem concerns the fact that teaching is conducted by and for human beings—and usually in the privacy of the closed classroom. Some teachers view the prospect of their efforts being observed with alarm, while administrators and parents may consider the prospect of conducting research on their pupils with asperity. For these reasons most research on teaching has concerned itself only with teachers who volunteered to participate, and who thus may have been better-than-average teachers, on the average.

Still another problem concerns the enormous number and variability of classroom lessons available for study. More than two million primary and secondary teachers operate in the United States today, with at least as many more of their confederates in other Western European societies. Perhaps a hundred different subjects are regularly offered in contemporary schools. Classrooms differ depending on whether they are urban, suburban, or rural; northern or southern; Canadian, French, or Australian; first, sixth, or twelfth grade; conducted in a traditional manner or using one of the newer curricula or media. With such numbers and variability it is difficult to define a universe from which one might sample, let alone draw a sample that might be representative of that universe.

Given these problems, it is no wonder that only small samples of classrooms have been systematically observed to date, and generally these have represented but limited universes and variables. Various criteria have been used to define a sub-class of classroom lessons for study. Commonly these have included grade level and subject matter. Thus, a given investigator would tell us that he had studied "only fifth-grade English language lessons" or "American history at the secondary level." Other criteria used have included social class of pupils, selected experimental curricula, pupil achievement and adjustment, or specific training programs for teachers. All sorts of classrooms have simply not been looked at to any great extent. These include classrooms with nonstandard curricula, rural classrooms, urban ghetto classrooms, classrooms for exceptional children, and classrooms representing various ethnic minorities.

The same limitations have characterized the choice of presage and context variables that have been studied in classroom samples. Most studies have concentrated on differences by grade level and subject matter or have differentiated the effects of an innovative curriculum or teacher-training technique with traditional practices. Few studies of either teacher or pupil sex are reported, or teacher age, or pupil social class. Consequently, in comparison with relationships among classroom processes, or between presage variables and classroom processes, we have as yet little information on the effects of contextual variables on teaching.

But does this mean that our supposed "findings" concerning teaching are invalid due to small samples? On the contrary, we suspect that much of the knowledge already developed concerning teaching is valid and will hold up when research with better samples is completed. Many findings to date are negative or descriptive in tone—they concern themselves with the rejection of plausible theories that turn out to have no empirical validity or with the conceptualization and interaction among classroom processes. Many also concern gross effects rather than fine processes that should respond to context. Other findings have been validated in two or more studies using different varieties of classrooms. In fact, readers may want to check our substantive chapters to see how often a given finding originally obtained for, let us say, mathematics at the primary level is replicated for social studies at the secondary level in another study. Exceptions may be found, of course, and when they pop up we will note and comment upon them. But on the whole we suspect that much of the knowledge we will review in this text will generalize. Thus, small samples have reduced our knowledge of contextual effects, but this has not necessarily meant that findings were invalid.

PROBLEMS OF DESIGN

Studies of teaching come in many designs. Some involve nothing more than the systematic observation of a single classroom over many lessons. Others contrast the lessons offered by a single teacher to several groups of students, or one subject matter with another. Still others involve the contrasting of a hundred or more classroom lessons chosen to represent a wide universe of types. Still others feature the manipulation of presage variables, such as innovative curricula or innovations in teaching training, in complex, factorial designs. A few even feature the direct manipulation of classroom events.

For simplicity we shall concentrate our discussion here on a single design feature—the distinction between field surveys and experiments in teaching research. Most studies of teaching feature *field surveys* of naturally occurring classroom events. In such studies the rule is that we measure the processes of education with as little disruption as possible. Minimally, in studies of teaching, this will involve observation of classrooms. But we may also measure presage, context, or product variables that may be associated with the processes of teaching. For example, it is possible to study the teaching efforts of trainees who have been exposed to a new method of training as opposed to the efforts of those exposed to more traditional methods. Or the learning of pupils at the end of the semester may be compared for teachers who are observed to be "warm" versus those who are "cold."

The strength of field surveys is that they provide us a slice of reality against which we can sharpen our concepts, theories, and instruments. Thus, they are most useful for initial exploration or for the *in*validation of a conceptual or theoretical scheme that has not yet had the cold, cruel light of empiricism cast upon it. The major difficulty with field surveys is that it is difficult to establish cause-and-effect relationships with them. Consider the problem of establishing the effects of teacher "warmth" on pupils. Suppose we find that warm teachers have pupils who score higher on achievement examinations at the end of the year than do cold teachers. Does this mean that teacher warmth causes pupil achievement? Not necessarily. It is possible that teachers may respond more warmly to pupils who are obviously going to achieve more highly, or even that both warmth and achievement may reflect some third event, such as the philosophy of the school principal or the choice of the textbook.

Two methods appear in social science research for establishing cause-

and-effect relationships. The first, and weaker, method is to conduct complex statistical manipulations with large samples in order to "control" or "partial out" the effects of other variables that might have affected the relationship between the independent and dependent variables in which we are interested. Since large samples have not featured in classroom research to date, this method has seldom been used. The second method involves *experiments* in which selected events are manipulated and investigated to see whether they affect other events. Those events manipulated are called *independent variables*, while those whose effects are measured are termed *dependent variables*. In the typical experimental design, for example, an investigator might compare the influence of two different methods of teacher training on the level of sophistication exhibited by teachers in the classroom. In such an experiment the independent variable is training procedure, while the dependent variable is level of sophistication of teaching. A design of this sort illustrates the *presage-process experiment* in which the dependent variable is laid within the classroom. Because of the concern most investigators have with teacher training (and because of the ease with which they can conduct such experiments), most experiments concerning teaching are of the presage-process variety.

A second type of experiment concerns *process-process* relationships. Examples of experiments of this sort may be found in Chapter VII, where investigators manipulated the classroom behavior of the teacher and observed pupil behavior as a dependent variable. Experiments of this type are difficult to control because teacher behavior is complex and, in part, responsive to pupil behavior. Nevertheless, they are essential if we desire definitive information concerning the processes of classroom information.

A handful of *process-product experiments* has also appeared, in which events are manipulated and the effects of differential classroom experiences are examined in pupil learning or attitudes. Since most of us would seek the ultimate validation of our efforts as teachers in pupil growth and development, this means that we have as yet little truly unambiguous evidence concerning the impact of teaching. And, as we shall see, when evidence of field surveys is compared with evidence from process-product experiments, the results are not always the same.

It would also be possible to conduct research on teaching by means of *context-process experiments*. For example, it would be possible to investigate the classroom impact of bussing pupils to a consolidated or racially integrated school by means of experiment. Unfortunately, no such experiment has been performed to our knowledge.

To summarize, then, research on teaching may be classified into four major design types: field surveys, presage-process experiments, process-process experiments, and process-product experiments. By far the majority of investigations fall into the first class, so that most of our knowledge concerning teaching to date is concerned with frequencies of occurrence and co-variation. To justify a cause-and-effect interpretation of these latter requires experimental evidence, which is only occasionally available.

PROBLEMS OF INTERPRETATION

Problems of measurement, sampling, and design are alike in that they are concerned with the conditions under which data are collected. Problems of interpretation concern the conversion of data into meaningful results. When instruments are applied to the measurement of events, data are generated in the form of numbers. But numbers are not meaningful in and of themselves. None of us (the authors, the readers, or even the investigators) thinks in numerical terms. In order to understand what was found in our investigation we must convert those numbers into meaningful information. In general, this process of conversion involves two steps: representation of the data in some form such as a figure, a table, or (usually) a derivative statistic; and verbal interpretation of that representation. Problems appear in both of these steps.

Liars, Damn Liars, and Statisticians

In general, a statistic is a number that represents a specific measurement or, more often, a score that is derived from measurements. Some simple statistics have been familiar to us for years. For example, we learned the idea of a sum or total of scores in Grade I, and the notion of an average not more than two or three grades later. Few of us would have any difficulty in interpreting research results were they reported only in sums and averages. But such is not the case. Rather, researchers have tended to ask more complex questions of their data—questions that require the computation of complex statistics that are not familiar to us unless we have had them explained in a course on the subject. Thus, most of us tend to gloss over the statistical portions of research reports and to assume that the investigators knew what they were doing when they chose statistics and then interpreted those statistics for us in words. The only difficulty with this is that some investigators, unfortunately, do not know what they are doing. Let us look at some of the more common statistical errors made in research on teaching.

Statistics fall into two classes, those concerned with description and those concerned with induction. *Descriptive* statistics provide us with measurements of something: a number representing a total, an average, a correlation, a range of scores. But each of these statistics requires us to make assumptions about the data, and the more complex the statistic, the more demanding the assumptions that must be made of its data. Probably the most common errors made by investigators are in using statistics that are inappropriate for their data. To form an average of measures the measures must lie along a common scale that provides firm and equal intervals, yet many investigators will construct averages for data that are merely rank-ordered. Most correlation coefficients assume that variables are related together in a linear fashion, and yet we shall discover evidence in later chapters that some relationships between teaching and other variables are not linear at all.

Two difficulties appear with the use of inappropriate statistics. Sometimes findings are obscured or voided by selection of the wrong statistic, while at other times the statistic itself will generate results that are spurious. The latter is particularly true for statistical processes that involve a great deal of inference, such as *factor analysis* or the *analysis of co-variance*. Unless used with great care such techniques can be used to generate apparent results when none actually was present in the data. Another example appears in the use of "gain scores" for assessing pupil achievement. Many investigators assume that it is more accurate to relate teaching variables to measures of pupil growth during the year than to unadjusted pupil achievement scores, and thus results are often given in terms of "gain scores" or "adjusted gain scores." But Cronbach and Furby (1970) have pointed out that most studies simply do not meet the assumptions necessary to utilize such complex statistics, or misuse the statistics when they are employed. Instead, they recommend the use of simple pupil achievement scores which just happen to be easier to comprehend (together with any of several analysis of variance forms depending on study design).

Inductive statistics are concerned with such questions as whether a given result is "big enough to count." Tests of statistical significance such as those based on χ^2, the t test, or the F distribution, illustrate such statistics. In general, inductive statistics are designed to tell us whether the results obtained by comparing or relating a group of descriptive statistics are sufficiently unlikely that we would not have expected to find them by chance alone in a random sample. Thus, when using inductive statistics we are asking ourselves whether our results are large enough that we can count on a relationship being there in the population.

Inductive statistics involve even more assumptions than do descriptive statistics, assumptions that are simply not met in the typical study of teaching. Of these the most fundamental is the assumption of randomness of the sample. As we have seen, samples of classrooms are usually small and invariably chosen in a nonrandom manner. Thus, if we were truly compulsive, no inductive statistics should be used at all in classroom research! Another problem concerns the appropriate choice of an N for computing significance. Consider the typical study that involves 60 lessons, 6 each from 10 teachers, each of which involves 30 pupils and an average of 1,000 discriminable utterances. What is the appropriate N for establishing statistical significance—6, 10, 30, 60, 1,000, or some other figure? No simple answer can be given to this question until we know something about the distribution of utterances among pupils, teachers, and lessons.

Still another problem concerns the use of inductive statistics for descriptive purposes. Should one want to express the degree to which two variables are found related to one another, for example, a descriptive statistic such as a correlation coefficient is appropriate (for example, $r = +.39$). Unfortunately, many researchers do not bother to tell us how strongly the two variables are found to be related, but only that the degree of their association exceeds a given level of statistical significance, which is inductive information. When carried to its extreme we occasionally find investigators who report to us that "74 percent of the results were significant at $p<.05$." Such reports are almost meaningless, since they depend on the size of the investigator's sample and his choice of N for analysis as much as on the strength of the relationships established.

Despite these problems, the establishment of statistical significance has become a status-validating fetish in the social sciences. This is so well entrenched that journal editors will sometimes refuse to publish articles that do not provide indication of the statistical significance of results, while at the same time insisting that investigators delete data tables and descriptive statistics from their articles "to save space." This means that the reader is often left in the dark as to whether the relationship obtained was a weak, moderate, or strong one, particularly for those studies that used a large N for establishing significance. (To illustrate this problem, the authors began the review effort which became this text by attempting to note for all findings the degree of association between variables found in the study. We had to give up tabulating this information, however, because it simply was not provided by many investigators—see the Appendix). At this stage of research on teaching descriptive statistics are probably more valuable than inductive statistics.

Deceivers and Self-Deceivers

It would be unreasonable to require investigators to be dispassionate concerning their research. Time, money, and ego have been invested in it, and in part the influence of each study will depend on the skill with which its results are interpreted. However, as we know, some investigators hold a *Commitment* that colors not only the research they design but also the claims they make for results. Others have a financial interest in a test, curriculum, text, or training program that may achieve greater sales if claims are made for its salubrious effect on teaching. Still others appear to make unreasonable claims concerning their data out of ignorance or misplaced enthusiasm. Let us consider some of the common errors of interpretation made in teaching research.

Errors of omission are surely more forgivable than errors of commission. As has been suggested, some studies fail to report reliability figures for their instruments, some use a poor research instrument when a better one is available, some fail to see obvious results in the data reported in their tables, some—perhaps most—fail to interpret results in terms of theoretical or practical significance. Nearly all samples used in classroom research are small and fail to meet criteria of randomness. Nevertheless, most investigators appear ready to make claims that their findings will generalize to all classrooms or all teachers. Perhaps the strangest omission of them all is failure to publish findings, and yet we shall discuss several studies wherein great effort was spent in instrumentation and data collection, but few (and in some cases no) findings seem to have been reported from the effort to date.

More serious are claims made by investigators that violate evidence from the design or findings of the study. As we shall see, some investigators are prone to interpret findings from field surveys in terms of cause and effect. Others seem incapable of discriminating the processes from the products of teaching and claim to have "improved" teaching when their only evidence concerns differences in the behavior of teachers. Still others claim results for grade levels or subject matters they have not yet examined, or in some cases, particularly in advertising brochures, claim results that violate their own data or that have never been published. Fortunately, the number of studies in which errors of commission appear is small.

Again, we would not want to leave readers with the impression that those who investigate teaching are charlatans or fools. Most are men and women of high purpose, dedicated to education, whose results speak in loud and honest voice. Hundreds of studies were reviewed in preparing this text, and in most cases the authors were able to accept the verbal interpretations investigators made of their data—indeed, these formed the basis of our own verbal summaries. Where obvious exceptions appear to these generalizations, we will say so.

RESEARCH BOXES

When preparing this book the authors thought a long time about how best to summarize research knowledge for readers. Several options were open to us, including the use of tables, graphs, or extended discussions of major and minor studies. Eventually we decided to use *Research Boxes* in which summaries of the design features and findings of studies are provided in verbal form. Why verbal form? Two reasons. As was suggested earlier, nearly everyone (including readers and ourselves) thinks in verbal terms and finds a verbal summary easier to digest and comprehend, and we wanted to keep the use of statistical jargon to a minimum.

The *Research Boxes* follow a standard format. Not only are the same headings to be found in each box, but entries within the boxes follow a standard pattern of wording. In order, the headings are:

Studies Reviewed
Instrument, Method of Gathering Data, Coding System, Unit Studied,
    Reliability
Design of Study, Subjects, Contexts
Findings
    Process Occurrence

Context-Process Relationships
Presage-Process Relationships
Process-Process Relationships
Process-Product Relationships

The first section of the box, *Studies Reviewed,* simply lists the studies reviewed in the box. Each study is also assigned an acronym, indicated in parentheses, which is used throughout the box to indicate design features or applicable findings.

The second section deals with five kinds of design features that are normally associated with the instrument used in one or more studies. First the instrument is named. Next we consider the usual way in which data are gathered for it, with the possibilities including live observation, audio-tapes, videotapes, and transcripts. Then we note the coding system used, whether it is a sign or category system, and if the latter, whether it involves one or more facets. Unit studied is next indicated—if units of behavior are coded, which; if given in arbitrary units of time, how long the unit. Finally, if the author gave some indication of reliability, this is paraphrased; if not, the fact that no information about reliability was given is noted.

The third section considers design features of the various investigations. Field surveys, presage-process experiments, and process-product experiments are all listed under separate subheadings. The identity of subjects is indicated—whether, for example, student teachers or teachers were observed—together with how many of them were involved in the design. Finally, the grade level, subject matter, and other contextual limitations of the sample are indicated.

The five *Findings* sections are similar in format. Each provides a list of propositions in verbal form that have been investigated in one or more studies, and all propositions listed are numbered sequentially within the box. However, propositional format differs slightly as we go from section to section. *Process-occurrence* propositions deal with the overall frequency of events observed in the lessons studied and are existential in format (thus, "More units are characterized by X in the classroom than by Y or Z"). Each of the other four sections presents propositions that involve two or more variables. In general, context and presage variables are listed as independent variables (thus, "Teacher-training program A raises the use of X in the classroom"). Product variables appear as dependent variables (thus, "Use of X in the classroom raises pupil academic achievement"). In addition, we use a verbal convention to differentiate between findings that were generated by field surveys and those generated by experiments. If the former, we use a passive verb such as "is associated with" (thus, "Higher use of X in the classroom is associated with greater pupil academic achievement"); if the latter, an active verb is used such as "raises" or "lowers." Studies supporting a given finding are indicated by the appearance of their acronyms after the proposition. Should a given finding be obviated or reversed in another study, a *new* proposition is listed immediately below the one it contradicts, giving the alternative information.

Several things should be borne in mind when reading the research boxes. First, findings listed are subject to the limitations of instrumentation and design appearing elsewhere in the box. Thus, should a given proposition read, "Use of X in the classroom raises pupil academic achievement," but this proposition is supported by only one study, we must turn to the details of that study to find out whether the finding holds for both primary and secondary pupils, for several subjects, or for a more limited population.

Second, without exception, findings were originally expressed in some other format in the studies we have summarized. Usually the format was another wording, but in some cases we have converted findings that were expressed originally in tables or statistical jargon to standard English phrases. Inevitably there was some "slippage" in this process of conversion. In particular, where several studies are listed as supporting a given proposition we may possibly have done some violence to the substance of findings in an effort to simplify.

Third, most of the propositions listed involve only two variables. Occasionally one encounters findings that involve three or more variables in research on teaching. For example, one might find a finding such as, "Use of X in the classroom raises the academic achievement of boys, but lowers the academic achievement of girls." If easy to express, we have included propositions of this sort in the research boxes. However, a number of the more complex findings from studies involving such tools as factor analysis or multivariate analysis were ignored because they are too difficult to express verbally.

Fourth, there is a fair amount of arbitrariness in our organization of studies for inclusion in each chapter and each research box. As was suggested earlier, the organization of concepts for expressing classroom events is still an unresolved matter. Our organization reflects a compromise between the ideal conceptual scheme we would like to impose on the field and the research completed by others to date. Findings expressed in some studies are difficult to interpret, because insufficient detail was provided by investigators, because of disjuncture between their results and interpretation, or because the investigators' writing is obscure. We have made arbitrary judgments to ignore weak studies. Another reviewer might make somewhat different decisions.

Again, readers should not be overly concerned with these problems. Where they bear significantly on the interpretation of findings, we shall call them to the readers' attention in our discussion.

TWO
SUBSTANTIVE
REPORTS

V
CLASSROOM CLIMATE

Teacher: O.K. That's enough for the moment. Close your books and look here . . . (*pause*) . . .Terry, I'm waiting for you to pay attention . . . (*pause*) . . . Thank you. No, Mary, let's save the questions for later. Put your hands down . . . (*pause*) . . . Now everybody sit up straight . . . (*pause*) . . . Michael, did you find out what year it was when Captain Cook died?

Michael: 1770.

Teacher: No. That was the year he discovered Australia. You didn't read carefully enough . . . (*pause*) . . . Graham, can you tell us?

Bill: Sir! Sir! I know.

Teacher: Take it easy, Bill. I asked Graham. Graham?

Graham: I'm not sure when it was, but I know where it was.

Teacher: Well, we'll get to that later. Let's find out when it was first. Does anyone know? . . . (*pause*) . . . Yes, Kevin?

Kevin: 1779.

Teacher: Now, then, how was he killed?

In the preceding segment of classroom interaction we see a situation in which the teacher is very much the master of ceremonies. There are commands, reprimands, and admonitions. An activity is terminated by declaration, pupil inquiries are postponed, volunteers are discouraged. In all, we might say that the social climate of that classroom seems authoritarian, or dictatorial, or teacher-centered and not at all democratic or learner-supportive. We might go further and decry this type of climate on a number of grounds.

It could be argued that this type of social situation is at odds with the values upon which a democratic society is built and has no place in such a society. We might go further and consider the effects of such a climate upon pupils. How can they learn participation in society if their very schooling discourages it? When antidemocratic behavior is held up to them by a teacher, how can they be expected to value democratic behavior? Under such repressive conditions what happens to their motivation to learn? And finally, what is the effect of this type of classroom climate upon achievement in reading, mathematics, and so on?

This chapter is concerned with research that has addressed itself to these types of issues. Much of the research reviewed here presents the view that teaching is leadership exerted to influence the behavior of the classroom group and that teaching can best be described using such terms as "autocracy," "permissiveness," "domination," "democracy," "classroom climate," "learner-centeredness," or "direct-indirect influence." Moreover, there is a tendency for this outlook to accompany a *Commitment* that the "good" teacher is one who is democratic, integrative, or learner-centered, while a "bad" teacher is one who is autocratic, dominative, or teacher-centered.

Such terms should certainly be familiar to readers, for they have formed the backbone of the progressive educational ideology that has dominated our philosophical training since early in the century. They have also featured prominently in textbooks and courses offered in educational psychology. Moreover, they have also appeared in other disciplines outside of education, such as group dynamics, social work, and the mental health movement. Thus, productivity, morale, and personal adjustment are all presumed to be functions of democratic leadership—not only in classrooms but also in problem-solving groups, therapy sessions, factories, and encounter groups.

As we shall see shortly, there are difficult problems associated with the use of such global concepts for describing teacher behavior. In particular, it would appear questionable that teachers fall along a *single* continuum from "good" (democratic, integrative, learner-centered) to "bad" (autocratic, dominative, teacher-centered). Rather, at least two major dimensions appear to be involved in teachers' efforts to influence classroom events. One refers to the teacher's affective response to pupils, which we shall term *warmth*. The other concerns the teacher's control over pupil activities, and we shall refer to this latter as *directiveness*. (Neither term is original with us, of course, nor is the distinction made here unique; see Ryans, 1960.)

This chapter constitutes our major review of the research tradition that has reflected these tenets of progressive education. We first consider the research evidence bearing on the idea that teaching might be arrayed along a single, global dimension, here termed "indirectness." Next, we turn to evidence taken from these same studies that pertains to the more specific concept of *warmth*. We delay evidence pertaining to *directiveness* until the next chapter, because it makes more sense (to us) to present it together with other evidence bearing on the problems of classroom management.

BACKGROUND

Where does one search for the roots of progressive education in the United States? Do they lie in historical experiences of affluence, violence, and the frontier? Are they a reflection of the values of independence and democracy? Were they influenced by such educators as Horace Mann or William James? These and other forces were surely involved in the progressive education movement which was responsible for freeing U.S. classrooms from the harsh, punitive, teacher-dominated practices they had inherited from The Dame School and British and Germanic models of repression.

But the message of progressive education was not always a clear one. As it turns out, at least two things were "wrong" with nineteenth-century American classrooms, and some educators to this day have difficulty in sorting out the independence of these two ideas. On the one hand, many early classrooms were reputed to be harsh, punitive, cold environments in which there was no place for laughter and the rod was not spared. On the other, many classrooms were also teacher-centered autocracies in which pupils could only respond to teacher directions—and often only in unison. Thus two things were simultaneously wrong—classrooms had a *cold climate* and were *automatically controlled*—and the task of the progressive educator was to rectify both of these conditions in present and future classrooms.

It is small wonder that early classroom research was influenced by the *Commitment* of progressive education. But surely this was not the only experience motivating classroom researchers. The international political situation of the 1930s seems to have had an influence on the ways in which concepts of teacher behavior were defined. In addition, correlative developments in the social sciences also had an impact. Withall and Lewis (1963) have argued that three of the latter had an early impact on classroom research. The field of *educational psychology* produced concerns for the influence of teacher characteristics, pupil characteristics, curricular issues, and methods of presentation—such as lecture versus discussion and optimum sequencing and pacing of learning experiences. The *mental health* movement saw the school as an important influence upon personality adjustment and emotional development and, thus, produced concern over emotional blocks to learning and unconscious motivation in the classroom. In addition, *social psychology* focused attention upon characteristics of the classroom group such as its social climate, decision-making processes, and patterns of participation and leadership. Each of these fields not only traded ideas and commitments during its formative stages, but such trade off appears to be continuing today: thus a Carl Rogers appears to have had as much influence on educational thought as on mental health, while a Jerome Bruner has influenced thinking in both social psychology and education.

In particular, one classical study of leadership appears to have generated enthusiasm in both group dynamics and educational research. This is the famous autocracy-democracy study of Kurt Lewin and his associates conducted at the University of Iowa in the 1930s (see Lewin, Lippitt, and White, 1939). These researchers were interested in the impact of *autocratic* (or authoritarian), *democratic*, and *laissez-faire* (or permissive) styles of leader behavior upon groups of boys engaging in clublike activities such as making masks. The three styles of leadership were presented, as experimental treatments, to different groups of boys. In general, it was found that *autocracy* was accompanied by either rebellion or submission. Moreover, when the autocratic leader was present productivity was high, but in his absence productivity gave way to aggression and destructiveness. Under *democratic* leadership groups were more task-oriented, cooperative and friendly, showed more independence and initiative, especially in the leader's absence, and endured frustration more effectively. *Laissez-faire* leadership, however, was least conducive to productivity, which tended to be higher in the absence of the leader, and was also accompanied by intragroup hostility and scapegoating. In almost every case the democratic style of leadership was preferred by the groups.

The Lewin-Lippitt-White research stimulated both interest and questions among social psychologists and educators. One obvious question was to what extent the findings might apply in *classrooms*, where groups are bigger, more enduring, and oriented to somewhat different types of tasks. Another question was an interpretive one. The concepts of *autocracy*, *democracy*, and *laissez-faire* are global ones that encompass a number of categories of behavior whose unidimensionality is a matter of controversy. Scholars have wondered which were the really crucial differences among the three leadership styles.

McCandless (1961), who was one of the group leaders in the experiments, has suggested that the crucial variable may have been the degree of emotional support, or *warmth*, which was transmitted:

> The four leaders were graduate students or postdoctoral fellows in child and clinical psychology. All were convinced and liberal equalitarians, living at a time when Hitler, the arch-authoritarian, was consolidating his power and preparing for world conquest. Each preferred and put his heart into his *democratic* leadership role, becoming perhaps the *warmest* and most dedicated democratic leader in recent history. But, when his turn came to play the authoritarian, he tended to become *cold* and *hard*—a veritable Captain Bligh. In the *laissez-faire* role, detachment of a profound sort became the order of the day. In other words, the crucial variable involved *may* have been warmth. (p. 438)

Other commentators have agreed with McCandless in attributing significance to warmth, although this term is not used universally. Among them are Smith and Hudgins (1964), who suggest, in addition, that a second dimension may also have influenced the boys' reactions.

> A second idea . . . is the *directiveness* or *nondirectiveness* of the teacher or leader in interaction with the children. Logically this dimension seems independent of sentiment. . . . Lippitt and White's autocratic group leader was highly directive, the democratic teacher [sic] was less directive but determined the course of events in part, and the *laissez-faire* teacher did little or

no directing. . . . Leaders with the best groups did some directing in their interaction, although not to the one extreme of complete domination or the other of complete submission to or abandonment of the group. (pp. 217–218)

In short, then, the confusion between *warmth* and *directiveness* seems to have appeared in these early studies in group dynamics as well as in the ideology of progressive education. Moreover, the Iowa research, no less than progressive education, also suggested a necessary, negative correlation between warmth and directiveness. No treatment group was given "benevolent autocracy," in which high degrees of warmth and directiveness occur together. Therefore, the possibility that this style of leadership has different, even desirable, effects was not researched.

CONCEPTS OF TEACHING BEHAVIOR

At about the same time as the autocracy-democracy studies another group of researchers under the leadership of H. H. Anderson began applying similar concepts to the study of teaching behavior in classrooms. Anderson's research was designed to study the effects of "dominative" versus "integrative" teacher behavior on pupil classroom performance. Figure 5.1 provides an adapted version of the original categories used by Anderson for coding the extent of teacher domination versus integration.

In an unusually emotive description of these two extremes of behavior, H. H. Anderson (1939) reveals his *Commitment.*

The use of force, commands, threats, shame, blame, attacks against the personal status of an individual are called dominative techniques of responding to others. Domination is characterized by a rigidity or inflexibility of purpose. . . . Domination is behavior that is based on a failure to admit the psychological inevitability of individual differences. Domination stifles differences. . . . Domination obstructs the natural growth processes. . . . Domination is consistent with a concept of self-protection. . . . Domination involves force or threats of force or of some other form of the expenditure of energy against another. Domination is behavior of one who is so insecure that he is not free to utilize new data, new information, new experience. Domination is an attempt at atomistic living. . . . Domination is the antithesis of the scientific attitude; it is an expression of resistance against change; it is consistent with bigotry and with autocracy. It is the technique of a dictatorship. (p. 73)

In contrast:

Integrative behavior is thus consistent with concepts of growth and learning. . . . It is behavior that makes the most of individual differences. . . . Socially integrative behavior respects differences, advances the psychological processes of differentiation. Integrative behavior is flexible, adaptive, objective, scientific. It is an expression of the operation of democratic processes. (p. 74)

FIGURE 5.1   Anderson categories for coding domination and integration. (Adapted from Anderson and Brewer, 1945)

1. Domination
   1. Determines a detail or acts for the child in carrying out a detail.
   2. Direct refusal.
   3. Relocating, repeating, or placing children in different relations to each other or to property.
   4. Postponing, slowing up the child.
   5. Disapproval, blame, or obstruction.
   6. Warning, threats, or conditional promises.
   7. Calls to attention or group activity.
   8. Rations material.
   9. Lecture method (defining a problem or anticipating a question).
   10. Questions: lecture method (one-answer questions) recitation.
   11. Perfunctory questions as statements (indifference).
2. Integration
   1. Approval.
   2. Accepts differences.
   3. Extends invitations to activity.
   4. Question or statement regarding child's expressed interest or activity.
   5. Builds up (helps child to better definition or solution without giving final answer).
   6. Participates in joint activity with children.
   7. Gives sympathy.
   8. Gives permission.

While it might appear from the above that Anderson's research was no more than a comparison between the "goodies" and the "baddies," the categories shown in Figure 5.1 suggest that domination and integration were operationally defined in more moderate terms and that a teacher classified as predominantly dominative need not be an ogre. At the same time, Anderson also appears to have collapsed the warmth and directiveness concepts into a single dimension, assuming that a teacher who is warm will also be nondirective, and one who is cold, autocratic.

Although the studies involving Anderson's concepts (Anderson, 1939; Anderson and Brewer, 1945; Anderson and Brewer, 1946; Anderson, Brewer, and Reed, 1946) were conducted with small numbers of teachers, they seemed to demonstrate that dominative teacher behavior, in contrast with integrative behavior, produced less pupil independence, less spontaneity and initiative, less participation, and less involvement in problem-solving. Furthermore, these studies found evidence suggesting that teachers were consistent in their domination-integration patterns of behavior from one class of pupils to another and that the effects of these behaviors were similar from one class to the next.

In 1949 Withall (1949) published the results of another attempt to measure the "social-emotional climate" of classrooms. He defined this concept as follows:

Climate is considered in this study to represent the emotional tone which is a concomitant of interpersonal interaction. It is a general emotional factor which appears to be present in interactions occurring between individuals in face-to-face groups. It seems to have some relationship to the degree of acceptance expressed by members of a group regarding each other's needs or goals. Operationally defined it is considered to influence: (1) the inner private world of each individual; (2) the *esprit de corps* of a group; (3) the sense of meaningfulness of group and individual goals and activities; (4) the objectivity with which a problem is attacked; and (5) the kind and extent of interpersonal interaction in a group. (pp. 348-349)

As illustrated in Figure 5.2, Withall developed seven categories of teacher verbal behavior as indicators of classroom climate. These ranged from "learner-supportive" statements through "neutral" statements to "teacher self-supporting" statements. Withall also put forward a "climate index" which was the ratio of "learner-centered" to "teacher-centered" statements. Once again, the concepts of warmth and directiveness appear to have been elided in this research.

FIGURE 5.2   Withall's classroom climate categories. (From Withall, 1949, p. 349)

1. Learner-supportive statements that have the intent of reassuring or commending the pupil.
2. Acceptant and clarifying statements having an intent to convey to the pupil the feeling that he was understood and help him elucidate his ideas and feelings.
3. Problem-structuring statements or questions which proffer information or raise questions about the problem in an objective manner with intent to facilitate learner's problem-solving.
4. Neutral statements which comprise polite formalities, administrative comments, verbatim repetition of something that has already been said. No intent inferable.
5. Directive or hortative statements with intent to have pupil follow a recommended course of action.
6. Reproving or deprecating remarks intended to deter pupil from continued indulgence in present "unacceptable" behavior.
7. Teacher self-supporting remarks intended to sustain or justify the teacher's position or course of action.

By now we have accumulated quite a vocabulary of terms that appear to have been used for the same hypothetical dimension of teaching. Although different words were used, the underlying notion involved in classifying teacher behavior as either *autocratic* or *democratic* (Lewin-Lippitt-White), *dominative* or *integrative* (Anderson), and *teacher-centered* or *learner-centered* (Withall) seems to be the same. Moreover, in each case the dimension thus designated seems to elide the concepts of warmth and directiveness, assuming that teachers who are cold are also dominative, and vice versa.

Conceptual confusion is not the only difficulty with this tradition of classroom research. In a devastating review of studies built upon these concepts and carried out in a variety of school and nonschool settings, R. C. Anderson (1959) called for the abandonment of this research effort on several grounds. He suggested, among other things, that findings from the research were weak and contradictory, that research efforts lacked rigor and tended to ignore the findings of others, that operations for defining observational categories were imprecise, that experimental studies provided extremes of treatments unlikely to be found in the real world, and that there was no theory whatsoever behind any of the effort—merely the *Commitment*. Thus,

> behind the facade of objectivity expressed in less-loaded words there lurks an essentially moralistic interpretation of leadership by many researchers and theorists and the bulk of the popularizers. . . . Much of the research . . . seemed bent on discovering whether "The meek shall inherit the earth," or whether, on the other hand, "Nice guys lose." (R. C. Anderson, 1959, pp. 210–211)

But bad press does not always have the same effect on research as it does on the theater, and this research tradition has survived and prospered. Where one might have expected Anderson's criticisms to inhibit further research in this tradition, the evidence of this chapter is that it has flourished. Why?

First, sincere *Commitments* are durable and, since they are matters of basic social values, empirical evidence might seem to be only marginally relevant to them. Second, modification, rather than abandonment, is one way of meeting the criticisms. One could, for example, moderate the *Commitment* by inserting between the black of autocracy and the white of democracy a shade of grey and by dropping emotive terms. Moreover, one could acknowledge that in some circumstances autocracy might be appropriate. Third, one could sharpen the concepts, refine the methodology, improve the research designs, and try very hard to obtain significant findings. Fourth, while doing all the above, one could continue what had really just begun—the investigation of classroom events by means of observational research.

Indeed, all of these developments have taken place during the past two decades of research in this tradition. Much of this effort has reflected the influence of N. A. Flanders. Flanders' contribution to research in classrooms has been important and pervasive. Not only did he develop the single most-often-used instrument for observing classroom behavior, but he has also made important attempts to utilize research findings to improve teaching through teacher education. In addition, Flanders and his students have conducted and stimulated a wide variety of studies concerned with the classroom. More studies have appeared in this research tradition, in fact, than in any other to date.

What changes did Flanders introduce to this orientation to classroom research? First, Flanders (1967) has reconceptualized the continuum along which teacher behavior is hypothesized to vary. He has actually used several vocabularies for this purpose, but most often the terms *direct* and *indirect* influence. Thus

> *Direct influence* consists of stating the teacher's own opinion or ideas, directing the pupil's action, criticizing his behavior, or justifying the teacher's authority or use of that authority.
>
> *Indirect influence* consists of soliciting the opinions or ideas of the pupils, applying or enlarging on those opinions or ideas, praising or encouraging the participation of pupils, or clarifying and accepting their feelings. (p. 109)

On the one hand, one notices that emotive, value-laden terms like "autocracy" and "democracy" have been replaced. On the other, however, these definitions do not seem much different from those employed in the earlier research, and it would appear that the confusion between warmth and directiveness continues. The continuum seems the same but the names have been changed. Flanders has continued to elaborate upon these global concepts in recent writings (see Flanders, 1970).

Second, Flanders (1967) has moderated the *Commitment* in that it is no longer assumed that classroom democracy is inevitably to be advocated and domination to be avoided: "Anyone with teaching experience recognizes that there are situations in which an integrative teacher behavior pattern is less appropriate than a dominative pattern" (pp. 106-107). Flanders has also argued that flexibility of teacher influence is important, and he developed hypotheses about the conditions under which direct influence might be preferable to indirect influence.

Third, Flanders developed a new observational instrument which was in some ways an improvement over earlier ones. This instrument, the Flanders Interaction Analysis Categories system (FIAC), is given in Figure 5.3 and was mentioned in Chapter IV. It contains seven categories for coding teacher verbal behavior. When compared with those of Withall (see Figure 5.2), they seem almost identical. However, Flanders added two categories for judging pupil verbal behavior, "response" and "initiation," and another for "silence and confusion."

On the whole, then, FIAC itself was not very different from earlier instruments, especially Withall's. However, FIAC by no means represents the penultimate instrument to have appeared within this research tradition. Rather, FIAC has been modified and extended by various groups of researchers for their own purposes. For example, Amidon and Hunter (1967) have developed the Verbal Interaction Category System (VICS) by sub-

FIGURE 5.3   Categories provided in FIAC. (From Amidon and Flanders, 1963, p. 14: reprinted in Amidon and Hough, 1967, p. 125)

		1. *Accepts feeling:* accepts and clarifies the feeling tone of the students in a nonthreatening manner. Feelings may be positive or negative. Predicting and recalling feelings are included.
		2. *Praises or encourages:* praises or encourages student action or behavior. Jokes that release tension, not at the expense of another individual, nodding head or saying "uh huh?" or "go on" are included.
	Indirect influence	3. *Accepts or uses ideas of student:* clarifying, building, or developing ideas or suggestions by a student. As teacher brings more of his own ideas into play, shift to category five.
Teacher talk		4. *Asks questions:* asking a question about content or procedure with the intent that a student answer.
		5. *Lectures:* giving facts or opinions about content or procedure; expressing his own idea; asking rhetorical questions.
	Direct influence	6. *Gives directions:* directions, commands, or orders with which a student is expected to comply.
		7. *Criticizes or justifies authority:* statements, intended to change student behavior from nonacceptable to acceptable pattern; bawling someone out; stating why the teacher is doing what he is doing, extreme self-reference.
Student talk		8. *Student talk-response:* talk by students in response to teacher. Teacher initiates the contact or solicits student statement.
		9. *Student talk-initiation:* talk by students, which they initiate. If "calling on" student is only to indicate who may talk next, observer must decide whether student wanted to talk. If he did, use this category.
		10. *Silence or confusion:* pauses, short periods of silence, and periods of confusion in which communication cannot be understood by the observer.

scripting Flanders' original categories so as to make distinctions between *narrow* and *broad* teacher questions on the basis of whether the response sought is predictable (narrow) or open-ended (broad). An example of the former is, "How much is three and three?" An example of the latter is, "Can you tell me some things about number three?" Accordingly, pupil responses are coded either as *predictable* or *unpredictable*. Divisions were also made within the accepting and criticizing categories to allow for information concerning the type of pupil behavior accepted or rejected.

Another modification has been attempted by Hough (1967), who distinguished between lecturing and answering pupils' questions, between criticism and corrective feedback, and between pupil initiations. Still other modifications appear in the anthology by Simon and Boyer (1970). One interesting aspect of many of these modifications is that they have been achieved by subscripting within the original FIAC categories, so that their validity is dependent upon the validity of FIAC. Furthermore, the modified versions of FIAC have not been used in research nearly as much as FIAC itself, and even where they have been used results are often still reported in terms of that basic continuum, *direct-indirect influence.*

What about procedures for applying FIAC? Has the definition of categories been sharpened to avoid the vagueness criticized by R. C. Anderson? Indeed, Flanders and his associates have given considerable attention to this problem. At least five separate statements of ground rules to be followed in applying the instrument have been published since 1960 (Flanders, 1960; Amidon and Flanders, 1963; Amidon and Flanders, 1968–1969; Flanders, 1970; Werner *et al.*, 1971). These provide guidelines for many intricate decisions the investigator must make when using FIAC.

The fact that changes in the ground rules have occurred over a decade of use indicates a continuing concern with improving FIAC. Unfortunately, they also raise doubts about the viability of the instrument, doubts concerned with the meaning and mutual exclusiveness of its categories. For example, changes regarding the coding of teachers' repetitions of pupils' answers have occurred. In 1960, they were to be included in Category 3—*acceptance of pupils' ideas,* or Category 5—*lecturing,* depending upon whether they contained evidence of true acceptance and development of pupils' ideas. In 1963, they were not mentioned in connection with Category 3. In 1968–1969, the following statement was made: "When a teacher repeats a student's idea, indicating that the student's idea is one that should be considered rather than that it is the correct answer, record a 3" (Amidon and Flanders, 1967, p. 9). Furthermore, repetition of a pupil's answer would be included in Category 2—*praise,* "when this repetition communicates to the child that his answer is correct" (Amidon and Flanders, 1967, p. 8). In 1970, "acknowledging the pupil's idea by repeating the nouns and logical connectives just expressed" is included in Category 3 (Flanders, 1970, p. 42). In 1971, it is again included in Category 3, but is regarded as "minimum," as distinct from "king size" 3's (Werner *et al.*, 1971). Since some teachers often repeat pupils' answers, their score for Category 3 will vary greatly depending upon which set of ground rules is followed. Unfortunately, researchers have not always indicated which ground rules they have followed in using FIAC.

Where earlier instruments were designed for live observation, so too was FIAC. However, the application of FIAC involves judgments made every three seconds rather than a single judgment for each utterance. Therefore, comparisons of the occurrence of the categories of FIAC can be made on the common basis of the number of three-second interval tallied.

In addition, the fact that FIAC contains categories for judging pupi behavior (as well as those provided for teacher behavior in earlier instru ments) makes possible the study of teacher-pupil interaction. By lookin at the sequence of classroom events coded in FIAC categories, we ar able to discover what kinds of teacher behavior precede or follow "respon sive" talk on the part of pupils, or the occasions upon which pupils ar coded as "initiating" content. In fact, Flanders has enlarged considerabl on the idea of studying sequences of classroom events using FIAC. Le us see how he does this. Suppose we had a sequence of events from a give lesson that was coded, in part:

8, 6, 5, 6, 8, 4, 8, 4 · · ·

For this sequence the first sequential pair constitutes the numbers (8, 6) the second pair (6, 5); the third pair (5, 6); and so forth. Each of thes pairs of numbers can then be treated as entries in a 10 × 10 square matrix as illustrated in Figure 5.4. And by making such entries, the frequency o all one-step sequences for a given lesson may be charted.

The matrix so formed has a number of interpretable features. For ex ample, the major diagonal of the matrix consists of cells in which classroon events were stable for more than three seconds of time. Similarly, compari sons between rows 8 and 9 can be made to test whether teacher behavio following teacher-initiated pupil talk is different from teacher behavio following pupil initiations. The region of the matrix indicated by column 4 and 5 has been designated by Flanders the "content cross" and provide an indication of the proportion of time spent in teacher talk about the content of the lesson. The area bounded by columns 6 and 7 and rows 6 and 7 yields a measure of "extended direct influence," that is, direct teache behaviors lasting more than three seconds. The interested reader will find a full discussion of the possibilities in interpreting such matrix data i Flanders' recent book (1970).

On the whole, then, it can be said that significant changes have oc curred in this research tradition since the early studies so trenchantly criti cized by R. C. Anderson (1959). However, there are still several problems associated with research using instruments such as FIAC. Perhaps the most significant of these is conceptual confusion. For one thing, it is not clear that the categories of these instruments ar mutually exclusive and fall along a single continuum. For another, nearly all of the instruments appear to elide the dimensions of warmth and directiveness. In Chapter IV we stressed that concepts for describing teaching should be clear and unambiguous, should be capable of being studied, and should be found to relate to contextual, presage, process, or product measures. It would seem that the research instruments representing this tradition fail to meet

Second Number

Category	1	2	3	4	5	6	7	8	9	10	Total
1											0
2											0
3			1		1						2
4				2	1			12		1	16
5				5	22	3					30
6					1	5		3		4	13
7											0
8			1	7	4	4		14		1	31
9											0
10				2	1	1		2		3	9
Total	0	0	2	16	30	13	0	31	0	9	101

Teacher (columns 1–7); Pupil (columns 8–9); X (column 10)
First Number — Teacher (rows 1–7); Pupil (rows 8–9); X (row 10)

Figure 5.4   Matrix for tabulating sequential pair frequencies from FIAC. (From Flanders, 1970, p. 85)

the first of these criteria—conceptual clarity. Given this problem, we would expect results generated by their use to be weak or contradictory. Let us see how this prediction fares in the evidence.

CLASSROOM RESEARCH

Approximately 100 studies are to be reviewed in this chapter. Each of these studies has concerned either the global dimension of "indirectness" or the more specific concepts associated with *warmth*. Most, but not all, were generated by application of FIAC and related instruments. This is a substantial amount of research publication, and our review is by no means exhaustive. In preparing it we have been dependent upon the earlier reviews of Rosenshine (1970) and Flanders (1970), supplemented with other and more recent studies. Given the large number of studies reviewed we have departed slightly from the box format to be used in later chapters. Box 5.1 provides a complete listing of studies and deals with instrumentation, methods of gathering data, coding systems, units studied, reliabilities, designs, subjects, and contexts of research. Box 5.2 presents findings for the global dimension of "indirectness," while Boxes 5.3, 5.4, and 5.5 deal with categorical findings related to *warmth*.

BOX 5.1   Studies of Warmth and Directiveness

STUDIES REVIEWED

Alexander (1970)	(Alx70)
Allen (1970)	(All70)
Altman (1970)	(Alt70)
Amidon and Flanders (1961)	(A&F61)
Amidon and Giammatteo (1967)	(A&G67)
Bondi (1969)	(Bon69)
Brophy and Good (1970)	(B&G70)
Brophy et al. (1973)	(B&a73)
Campbell (1970)	(Cam70)
Carline (1970)	(Car70)
Claiborn (1969)	(Cla69)
Conners and Eisenberg (1966)	(C&E66)
Cook (1967)	(Coo67)
Cornbleth et al., (1972)	(C&a72)
Dalton (1969)	(Dal69)
Dahllöf and Lundgren (1970)	(D&L70)
Davis and Slobodian (1967)	(D&S67)
Emmer (1967)	(Emm67)
Evertson et al. (1972)	(E&a72)
Evertson et al. (1973)	(E&a73)
Felsenthal (1970)	(Fel70)
Finske (1967)	(Fin67)
Flanders, Project 1 (1970)	(Flan1)
Flanders, Project 2 (1970)	(Flan2)
Flanders, Project 3 (1970)	(Flan3)
Flanders, Project 4 (1970)	(Flan4)
Flanders, Project 5 (1970)	(Flan5)
Flanders, Project 6 (1970)	(Flan6)
Flanders, Project 7 (1970)	(Flan7)
Fortune et al. (1966)	(F&a66)
Fowler and Soar (undated)	(F&Sun)
Furst (1967a)	(Fu67a)
Furst (1967b)	(Fu67b)
Furst and Amidon (1967)	(F&A67)
Goldenberg (1971)	(Gol71)
Good and Brophy (1972)	(G&B72)

Good *et al.* (1973)	(G&a73)
Gunnison (1968)	(Gun68)
Harris and Serwer (1966)	(H&S66)
Harris *et al.* (1968)	(H&a68)
Herman (1967)	(Her67)
Herman *et al.* (1969)	(H&a69)
Hill and Furst (1969)	(H&F69)
Hill (1967)	(Hil67)
Hoehn (1954)	(Hoe54)
Hough and Ober (1967)	(H&O67)
Hughes, D. (1973)	(HuD73)
Hughes, M. (1959a, 1959b)	(HuM59)
Hunter, C. P. (1968)	(HuC68)
Hunter, E. (1969)	(HuE69)
Jackson and Lahaderne (1966)	(J&L66)
Johns (1966)	(Joh66)
José (1970)	(Jos70)
Kirk (1967)	(Kir67)
Kranz *et al.* (1970)	(K&a70)
LaShier (1965)	(LaS65)
Lohman *et al.* (1967)	(L&a67)
McGee (1955)	(McG55)
Measel (1967)	(Mea67)
Medinnus and Unruh (1971)	(M&U71)
Medley and Hill (1968)	(M&H68)
Medley and Hill (1970)	(M&H70)
Medley and Mitzel (1959)	(M&M59)
Meichenbaum *et al.* (1969)	(Me&a69)
Mendoza *et al.* (1971)	(M&a71)
Meyer and Thompson (1956)	(M&T56)
Mood (1972)	(Moo72)
Moskowitz (1967)	(Mos67)
Pankratz (1967)	(Pan67)
Penney (1969)	(Pen69)
Perkins (1964)	(Per64)
Perkins (1965)	(Per65)
Powell (1968a)	(Po68a)
Powell (1968b)	(Po68b)
Rexford *et al.* (1972)	(Re&a72)
Rian (1969)	(Ria69)
Rothbart *et al.* (1971)	(Ro&a71)
Rowe (1973)	(Row73)
Rubovits and Maehr (1971)	(R&M71)
Rubovits and Maehr (1973)	(R&M73)
Schantz (1963)	(Sch63)
Schluck (1971)	(Shl71)
Sharp (1966)	(Sha66)
Silberman (1969)	(Sil69)
Simon (1967)	(Sim67)
Smith, M. B. (1965)	(SmM65)
Snider (1966)	(Sni66)
Soar (1966)	(Soa66)
Soar (1968)	(Soa68)
Soar and Soar (1969)	(S&S69)

(Box 5.1, continued)

Soar *et al.* (1971)	(S&a71)
Sorber (1967)	(Sor67)
Spaulding (1963)	(Spa63)
Sprague (1971)	(Spr71)
Thompson and Bowers (1968)	(T&B68)
Tisher (1970)	(Tis70)
Torrance (1966)	(Tor66)
Traill (1971)	(Tra71)
Tuckman *et al.* (1969)	(T&a69)
Wallen (1966)	(Wal66)
Wallen and Wodtke (1963)	(W&W63)
Weber (1968a)	(We68a)
Weber (1968b)	(We68b)
Wright and Nuthall (1970)	(W&N70)

INSTRUMENT, METHOD OF GATHERING DATA, CODING SYSTEM, UNIT STUDIED, RELIABILITY

FIAC (or modified *FIAC*), live observation, single-facet category system, T and P utterances in three-second intervals, moderate to high reliability (A&F61), (A&G67), (Bon69), (Car70), (Coo67), (Dal69), (D&L70), (Emm67), (Fin67), (Flan1), (Flan2), (Flan3), (Flan4), (Flan5), (Flan6), (Flan7), (F&Sun), (Fu67a), (Fu67b), (F&A67), (Gol71), (Gun68), (H&F69), (H&S66), (H&a68), (Her67), (Hil67), (H&O67), (HuE69), (Joh66), (Kir67), (L&a67), (Las65), (Mea67), (M&H68), (Moo72), (Mos67), (Pan67), (Po68a), (Po68b), (Re&a72), (Ria69), (Sch63), (Shl71), (Sil69), (Sim67), (SmM65), (Sni66), (Soa66), (Soa68), (S&S69), (Sor67), (Tor66), (Tra71), (T&a69), (We68a), (We68b).

Withall Schedule, live observation or audio recordings, single-facet category system, T statements, moderate reliability (Alx70), (Cam70), (HuC68), (Tis70).

OScAR, live observation, multifacet category and sign system, T and P verbal and nonverbal behaviors in five-minute intervals, high reliability (for emotional climate scale) (All70), (F&Sun), (H&a69), (M&H68), (M&H70), (M&M59), (Shl71).

SCOR, live observation, multifacet sign system, T and P verbal and nonverbal behaviors, reliability not reported (Soa66), (Soa68), (S&S69).

FLACCS, live observation, two-facet sign system, T and P verbal and nonverbal behaviors, reliability not reported (S&a71).

Perkins System, live observation, two two-facet category systems, T and P utterances in two-minute intervals, high reliability (Per64), (Per65).

Brophy-Good System, live observation, multifacet category system, questions, responses and reactions, verbal and nonverbal, high reliability (B&G70), (B&a73), (C&a72), (E&a72), (E&a73), (G&a73), (G&B72), (M&a71), (Row73).

COR, live observation, single-facet category system, T and P response dyads, high reliability (Fel70).

Provo Code, transcripts, multifacet category system, T verbal behavior, moderate reliability (HuM59).

TSC, live observation and audio recordings, multifacet category system, T and P verbal and nonverbal behaviors in 10–15 second intervals, moderate reliability (Spa63).

Other Systems, mostly live observation (Alt70), (Cla69), (C&E66), (D&S67), (F&a66), (F&Sun), (H&S66), (H&a68), (Hoe54), (HuD73), (Jos70), (J&L66), (K&a70), (McG55), (Me&a69), (M&T56), (M&V71), (Pen69),

(Sha66), (R&M71), (R&M73), (Ro&a71), (Sil69), (Spr71), (T&B68), (Wal66), (W&N70), (W&W63).

DESIGN OF STUDY, SUBJECTS, CONTEXTS

Field Surveys

(All70)	18 teachers and pupils, grade I
(Alt70)	13 inner-city and 15 suburban teachers and pupils, grades III and IV, science
(A&G67)	153 teachers and pupils, elementary grades, language arts
(B&G70)	4 female teachers and pupils, grade I
(B&a73)	5 teachers and pupils, grade V
(Cam70)	12 teachers, grades V–VII
(C&E66)	32 public school teachers and 6 private school teachers, nursery school classes in Head Start program
(Coo67)	8 teachers and pupils, grade X, biology
(C&a72)	7 student teachers and pupils, secondary grades, social studies
(Dal69)	1 teacher and pupils, grade IV
(D&L70)	9 teachers and pupils, grade XI, mathematics
(D&S67)	10 female teachers and pupils, grade I, reading
(E&a72)	9 teachers and pupils, grade I
(E&a73)	6 teachers and pupils, grade II
(Fel70)	20 female teachers and pupils, grade I, reading
(Flan1)	9 teachers and pupils, grade VII, English and social studies
(Flan2)	10 teachers and pupils, 10–12-year-old pupils
(Flan3)	16 teachers and pupils, grade VIII, mathematics
(Flan4)	15 teachers and pupils, grade VII, social studies
(Flan5)	30 teachers and pupils, grade VI
(Flan6)	16 teachers and pupils, grade IV, social studies
(Flan7)	16 teachers and pupils, grade II
(F&a66)	40 teachers and pupils, grades VIII–XI, social studies
(F&Sun)	53 teachers and pupils, elementary grades
(Fu67a)	15 teachers and pupils, grades X and XII, economics
(F&A67)	approximately 150 teachers and pupils, grades I–VI, arithmetic, social studies, and reading
(Gol71)	20 teachers and pupils, elementary grades
(G&a73)	8 female and 8 male teachers and pupils, grades VII and VIII, mathematics and social studies
(G&B72)	9 teachers and pupils, grade I
(H&S66)	46 teachers, grade I, reading achievement
(H&a68)	38 teachers, grade II, reading achievement
(Her67)	6 teachers and above-average I.Q. classes, 6 teachers and average I.Q. classes, 2 teachers and below-average I.Q. classes, grade V, social studies
(H&F69)	12 teachers and pupils, secondary grades, biology and developmental reading
(Hoe54)	19 teachers, grade III
(HuM59)	25 "judged good" and 10 "representative" teachers, grades K–VI
(HuC68)	11 teachers and pupils, 8–14 years old, emotionally handicapped pupils
(J&L66)	2 male and 2 female teachers and pupils, grade VI
(Joh66)	6 teachers and pupils, grades X–XII, English
(K&a70)	11 teachers and pupils, elementary grades
(LaS65)	10 student teachers and pupils, grade VIII, biology

(Box 5.1, continued)

(McG55)	150 teachers, elementary and secondary grades
(Mea67)	15 teachers and pupils, grade II
(M&H68)	70 teachers and pupils, secondary grades, science, mathematics, English and social studies
(M&H70)	53 teachers, secondary grades, science, mathematics, English and social studies
(M&M59)	49 teachers and pupils, grades III–VI, reading
(M&a71)	4 teachers and pupils, grade VII, mathematics, reading and social studies
(M&T56)	3 female teachers and pupils, grade VI
(Moo72)	15 female teachers and pupils, grade II
(Pan67)	6 teachers and pupils, secondary grades, physics
(Pen69)	32 teachers, grades VIII and IX, social studies and English
(Per64)	14 teachers and pupils, grade V, language arts, arithmetic, social studies and science
(Per65)	27 teachers and pupils, grade IV, underachieving pupils
(Po68a)	9 teachers and pupils, grade III, reading and arithmetic
(Po68b)	17 teachers and pupils, grade IV, reading and arithmetic
(Re&a72)	24 teachers and pupils, secondary grades
(Row73)	700+ teachers and 2,000+ pupils, grades I–VI, 5 top-achieving and 5 low-achieving pupils, science
(Shl71)	70 graduate student teachers, secondary grades
(Sha66)	31 teachers, secondary grades, biology
(Sil69)	10 female teachers, grade III
(SmM65)	7 female teachers and pupils, grade VI
(Sni66)	17 teachers and pupils, grade XII, physics
(Soa66)	55 teachers and pupils, grades III–VI
(Soa68)	54 teachers and pupils, grades III–VI
(S&S69)	189 pupils and teachers, grades V and VI
(S&a71)	70 teachers and pupils, grades K and I, experimental programs for disadvantaged children
(Sor67)	16 traditionally prepared first-year teachers and pupils and 14 graduate interns and pupils, elementary grades, several subjects
(Spa63)	13 male and 8 female teachers and pupils, grades IV and VI
(Spr71)	16 teachers and pupils, secondary grades, social studies
(T&B68)	15 teachers, grade IV, vocabulary and social studies
(Tis70)	9 teachers, grade VIII, science
(Tor66)	10 teachers and pupils, grades VII–XII, mathematics
(Wal66)	36 teachers and pupils, grade I; and 40 teachers and pupils, grade III
(W&W63)	65 teachers and pupils, grades I–V
(We68a)	9 teachers and pupils, grade III
(We68b)	17 teachers and pupils, grade IV
(W&N70)	17 student and in-service teachers and pupils, grade III, nature study

Presage-Process Experiments

(Bon69)	20 experimental and 20 control teachers and pupils, elementary grades
(Car70)	23 experimental and 20 control teachers and pupils, grades I–V, mathematics
(Cla69)	6 experimental and 6 control teachers and pupils, grade I
(Emm67)	16 teachers and pupils, grade II

(Fin67)	9 experimental and 9 control student teachers and pupils, elementary grades
(Fu67b)	10 experimental, another 10 experimental, and 10 control student teachers and pupils, secondary grades, English and social studies
(Hil67)	35 teachers and pupils, elementary and secondary grades
(HuE69)	11 experimental and 11 control teachers and pupils, grade I, science
(Jos70)	18 teachers with experimental and control groups of pupils, grades I and II
(Kir67)	15 experimental and 15 control student teachers and pupils, grades IV–VI, social studies
(L&a67)	30 experimental and 30 control student teachers and pupils, secondary grades
(Me&a69)	4 teachers and 14 institutionalized adolescent female offenders
(Mos67)	44 student teachers, their cooperating teachers and pupils, secondary grades, English, social studies, science and mathematics
(M&V71)	20 Head Start teachers, each with two boys from their own classes
(R&M71)	26 undergraduates teaching one lesson each to 4 pupils, grades VI and VII, social studies
(R&M73)	66 undergraduates teaching one lesson each to 2 white and 2 black pupils, grades VII and VIII, social studies
(Ro&a71)	13 student teachers each with four pupils, grades VIII and IX
(Sim67)	28 experimental and 28 control student teachers and pupils, secondary grades
(Tra71)	27 experimental and 27 control student teachers and pupils, elementary grades
(T&a69)	24 teachers and pupils, secondary grades, science, mathematics, social studies, and language arts

Process-Product Experiments

(Alx70)	one role-playing teacher, 58 pupils, grades VII-IX, mechanical drawing
(A&F61)	one role-playing teacher, 28 groups of 20 pupils each, grade VIII, geometry
(Car70)	23 trained and 20 control teachers and pupils, grades I-V, mathematics
(Gun68)	5 trained student teachers and 5 untrained student teachers, grade IX, social studies
(H&a69)	18 role-playing teachers, social studies
(HuD73)	1 role-playing teacher, 65 pupils, grade VII, nature study
(Ria69)	3 role-playing student teachers, 6 groups containing 181 pupils, grade VII, history
(Sch63)	one role-playing teacher, 61 pupils (one high- and one low-ability group), grade IV, science

Numerous instruments are represented in the research reviewed (see Box 5.1)—so many, in fact, that we can provide only a partial listing of them here (a fuller listing is provided in Simon and Boyer, 1970). Clearly, the research instrument most often used is the Flanders Interaction Analysis Category (FIAC) system and its modifications. As we know, FIAC is designed for live observation and requires coders to make judgment about behaviors occurring in each three-second interval. It has also been reported to generate moderate to high reliability.

Many of the rest of the instruments reviewed are similar to FIAC in format and application. That is, they consist of a set of categories that are presumed to form a single facet, they are designed for live observation, and for them adequate reliability is also reported.

Several instruments constitute exceptions to the above. OScAR (see Medley and Mitzel, 1959) is a multifaceted sign system, only a portion of which pertains to classroom climate. So is SCOR (Soar, 1966) as well as FLACCS (Soar et al., 1971). Perkins (1964, 1965) designed four, uni-faceted category systems that were to be used simultaneously by two live observers—two each for observing the behaviors of teachers and pupils. The Provo Code (see Hughes, 1959a, 1959b) is a multifaceted category system designed for observation of teacher verbal behaviors, and again only part of the content concerns the variables reviewed here. The Brophy-Good (1970) system is also multifaceted and represents a distinct research tra-dition that is reviewed later in the chapter. Again, we find a few cases in which these instruments have been applied to audio recordings (Tisher, 1970; Spaulding, 1963; Hughes, 1959a, 1959b). However, the majority of findings to be reported were generated by simple, categorical instruments presumed to represent but a single facet and were applied by observers in situ to acts occurring during short intervals of time. Thus, on the basis of distinctions made in Chapter IV, these instruments may be judged as methodologically primitive.

In sharp contrast, and in contrast also with the research reported in other chapters, the studies reviewed represent a wide range of designs, subjects, and classroom contexts. Grades studied have ranged from K through XII although elementary grades feature more than do secondary grades, and nearly all curriculum subjects found in standard classrooms are repre-sented. A few of the studies have actually dealt with non-American class-rooms (such as ones studied by Flanders, 1970; and those of Allen, 1970; Campbell, 1970; Dahllöf and Lundgren, 1970; Wright and Nuthall, 1970; Rian, 1969; and Tisher, 1970). Emotionally handicapped and delinquent pupils have also been studied, as well as the disadvantaged and Head Start classrooms. However, most of the studies reported have come from white, middle-class schools. Classroom interaction in either black ghettos or lower-class schools is underinvestigated. As is true in other chapters, most of the research reviewed consists of field surveys. However, various presage-process experiments also appear, most of which were designed to test the efficacy of a particular training program, and even eight process-product experiments. Thus, these research instruments have been validated, and findings generated, in a variety of designs and contexts.

Teacher "Indirectness"

We shall first summarize findings applying to the global dimension of instruments using Flanders' terms, "indirect" and "direct" teacher influence, although it should be understood that other investigators have used different terms. Even given this convention, we are still involved in a dilemma. Since instruments differ in the categories they feature, there is no standard way of judging how "indirect" or "direct" a lesson may be from categorical frequencies. Then again, several methods have been used for making this judgment for even FIAC, ranging from methods in which scores for "indirect" and "direct" teacher behaviors are calculated separately from ones in which a ratio (or balance) score is calculated. Each of these measures is derivative, and controversies have arisen among researchers as to the implications of the various methods of deriving scores. Rather than enter into these controversies, we have attempted to summarize findings verbally in Box 5.2, assuming that "indirectness" is the antonym of "directness" except where separate findings were reported for each. However, occasional anomalies will be found to have crept into our summaries (as, for example, where a given study is reported to have both found and not found a given relationship) when two or more methods were used for calculating scores for "indirectness," or when alternative techniques of statistical analysis produced contradictory findings (for example, Flanders, Project 5, 1970).

BOX 5.2 Findings for Teacher "Indirectness"

Process Occurrence

5.2-1 *More teacher behavior is "direct"* (that is, stresses lecturing, criticism, and direction giving) than "indirect" (use of praise, questioning, acceptance of pupil's feelings, acceptance of pupil's idea) (D&L70), (Flan1), (Flan2), (Flan3), (Flan4), (Fu67b), (F&A67), (L&a67), (Per64), (Sor67), (Tis70).

5.2-2 *Pupils talk* about 25 percent of the total time (Flan2), (Fu67b), (L&a67).

Context-Process Relationships

5.2-3 *Higher social class of pupils* is associated with *greater teacher "indirectness"* (Hoe54).

5.2-4 *Higher intelligence of pupils* is associated with *greater teacher "indirectness"* (Her67).

5.2-5 *Classrooms having computer-assisted instruction* are similar to traditional classrooms in *amount of teacher "indirectness"* (H&F69).

5.2-6 *Reading lessons* exhibit *more teacher "indirectness"* than do other lessons (Sor67).

Presage-Process Relationships

(a) *Teacher Academic and Professional Background*

5.2-7 *Teachers judged "superior"* by their administrators and supervisors are not different in amount of *"indirectness"* from other teachers. (HuM59). *In contradiction*, it is also found that

    5.2-7a *Teachers judged "superior"* by their administrators and supervisors exhibit more *"indirectness" than do other teachers* (A&G67).

5.2-8 *Higher teachers' scores on NTE History and Philosophy examination* are associated with *greater teacher "indirectness"* (M&H70).

5.2-9 *Teachers "traditionally trained"* exhibit *more "indirectness"* than graduate interns (Sor67).

(b) *Sex of Teacher*

5.2-10 *Sex of teacher* is unrelated to *amount of "indirectness"* (Spa63). *In con-*

(Box 5.2, continued)

---

tradiction, it is also found that

    5.2-10a *Female teachers* use *greater "directness"* than do male teachers (McG55).

(c) *Teacher Personality Variables*

5.2-11 *Teachers' scores on MTAI* are unrelated to *teacher "indirectness"* (Cam70), (C&E66). *In contradiction*, it is also found that

    5.2-11a *Higher teachers' scores on MTAI* are associated with *greater teacher "indirectness"* (F&Sun).

5.2-12 *Higher teachers' ego strength* (using MMPI) are associated with *greater teacher "indirectness"* (F&Sun).

5.2-13 *Higher teachers' authoritarianism* (using F scale) are associated with *greater teacher "directness"* (McG55).

5.2-14 *Teachers' scores on EPPS* are unrelated to *teacher "indirectness"* (Sor67).

5.2-15 *Teachers' humanistic and custodial* attitudes toward pupils are unrelated to *teacher "indirectness"* (Gol71). *In contradiction*, it is also found that

    5.2-15a *Higher teachers' humanistic attitudes* toward pupils are associated with *greater teacher "indirectness,"* and *higher teachers' custodial attitudes* toward pupils are associated with *lesser teacher "indirectness"* (Re&a72).

(d) *Teachers' Expectations (or Perceptions)*

5.2-16 *Teachers' expectations for pupil achievement* are unrelated to *teacher "indirectness"* (Cla69)E, (Dal69), (Jos70)E, (Me&a69)E.* *In contradiction*, it is also found that

    5.2-16a *Higher teachers' expectations for pupil achievement* are associated with *less directness" by teachers* (Dal9).

(e) *Teacher Training*

NOTE: The following treatment conditions appeared:

1. Training in use of research instrument (FIAC or modified FIAC)
2. Feedback from self
3. Feedback from others
4. Directions given for changing teacher's behavior
5. No treatment.

These treatments were combined as follows in experiments:

EXPERIMENTAL GROUP	COMPARISON GROUP	
1	3	(T&a69)
1	5	(Fin67), (Fu67b), (H&O67)
		(L&a67), (Mos67)
1+2	1	(Tra71)
1+2	2	(Sim67)
1+2	5	(Kir67), (Hil67)
1+3	1	(Bon69)
1+3	5	(Hil67)
4	5	(Emm67)
1+2+3+4	5	(Car70)

5.2-17 *Experimental treatment* does not produce change in *teacher "indirectness"* (T&a69)E. *In contradiction*, it is also found that

    5.2-17a *Experimental treatment* increases *teacher "indirectness"* (Bon69)E, (Car70)E, (Fin67)E, (Emm67)E, (Kir67)E, (L&a67)E, (Mos67)E, (Sim67)E, (Tra71)E; and also

---

* Findings generated experimentally are indicated with an E.

5.2-17b *Experimental treatment* increases *teacher "indirectness"* in the short term but *decreases* it in the longer term (Hil67)E.

5.2-18 *Experimental treatment* does not produce change in *teacher "directness"* (Car70)E, (T&a69)E. *In contradiction*, it is also found that

5.2-18a *Experimental treatment* decreases the use of *teacher "directnesss"* (Fu67b)E, (L&a67)E, (Sim67)E, (Tra71)E.

5.2-19 *Duration of training in FIAC* is unrelated to changes in *teacher "indirectness"* (Hil67)E.

5.2-20 *Mode of feedback* is unrelated to changes in *teacher "indirectness"* (Hil67)E.

Process-Process Relationships

5.2-21 *Greater teacher "indirectness"* is associated with *greater total amounts of pupil talk* (A&F61)E, (Fu67b)E, (Spr71).

5.2-22 *Teacher "indirectness"* is unrelated to *amount of pupil responses to teacher initiations* (L&a67)E. *In contradiction*, it is also found that

5.2-22a *Greater teacher "indirectness"* is associated with *greater amounts of pupil responses to teacher initiations* (Ria69)E; and also

5.2-22b *Greater teacher "indirectness"* is associated with *lesser amounts of pupil responses to teacher initiations* (Bon69)E, (Tra71)E.

5.2-23 *Greater teacher "indirectness"* is associated with *greater amounts of pupil initiations* (Bon69)E, (Joh66)E, (L&a67)E, (Ria69)E, (Tra71)E.

5.2-24 *Teacher "indirectness"* is unrelated to *teacher "directness"* (M&H68), (Soa66), (S&a71). *In contradiction*, it is also found that

5.2-24a *Greater teacher "indirectness"* is associated with *lesser teacher "directness"* (Cam70).

5.2-25 *Teacher "indirectness"* is unrelated to *cognitive level of classroom discourse* (Mea67). *In contradiction*, it is also found that

5.2-25a *Greater teacher "indirectness"* is associated with *higher cognitive levels of classroom discourse* (Joh66), (Moo72).

Process-Product Relationships (Field Survey Findings)

5.2-26 *Teacher "indirectness"* is unrelated to *pupil achievement* (All70), (Coo67), (Flan3), (Flan4), (Flan5), (Flan6), (Flan7), (Fu67a), (M&M59), (Po68b), (Sni66), (Soa66), (S&a71), (T&B68), (Tor66). *In contradiction*, it is also found that

5.2-26a *Higher teacher "indirectness"* is associated with *greater pupil achievement* (Flan3), (Flan4), (Flan5), (Fu67a), (HuC68), (LaS65), (Pen69), (Po68a), (Soa66), (We68a). *In addition*, it is also found that

5.2-26b *Higher teacher "indirectness"* is associated with *greater achievement of pupils* with low-achievement orientation (Tis70); and that

5.2-26c *Teacher "indirectness"* has a curvilinear relationship to *pupil achievement*, but the optimum degree of teacher "indirectness" is lower for concrete learning tasks than for more abstract learning tasks (Soa68); and that

5.2-26d *Higher teacher "indirectness"* is associated with *greater pupil growth* during the summer vacation in vocabulary, but not in reading and arithmetic (S&S69).

5.2-27 *Teacher "indirectness"* is unrelated to *pupil attitudes* (All70), (Flan4), (Flan7). *In contradiction*, it is also found that

5.2-27a *Higher teacher "indirectness"* is associated with *more positive pupil attitudes* (Flan1), (Flan2), (Flan3), (Flan5), (Flan6), (LaS65), (Sni66), (Soa66).

(Box 5.2, continued)

5.2-28 *Higher teacher "indirectness"* is associated with *greater pupil achievement motivation* (Cam70).

5.2-29 *Higher teacher "indirectness"* is associated with *greater pupil creativity* (Soa66).

5.2-30 *High teacher "directness"* following three years of high teacher "directness" is associated with *greater pupils' figural creativity* (than high "indirectness"—high "directness," high "directness"—high "indirectness," or high "indirectness"—high "indirectness" combinations) (We68b).

5.2-31 *Higher teacher "indirectness"* is associated with *lower pupil anxiety* (Soa66).

Process-Product Relationships (Experimental Findings)

5.2-32 *Teacher "indirectness"* is unrelated to *achievement of average pupils* (A&F61)E, (Car70)E, (Gun68)E, (H&a69)E, (Ria69)E. *In contradiction,* it is also found that

  5.2-32a *Higher teacher "indirectness"* raises the *manipulative performance of average pupils* (Alx70)E; and that

  5.2-32b *Higher teacher "indirectness"* slightly raises the *achievement of dependent-prone pupils* (A&F61)E; and that

  5.2-32c *Higher teacher "indirectness"* slightly raises the *achievement of high-ability pupils* (Sch63)E.

5.2-33 *Teacher "indirectness"* is unrelated to *pupil satisfaction* (Ria69)E.

5.2-34 *Higher teacher "indirectness"* raises *pupils' attitudes toward the teacher* (Gun68)E.

5.2-35 *Teacher "indirectness"* is unrelated to *pupils' attitudes toward industrial arts* (Alx70).

Not surprisingly, Box 5.2 lists a great many findings. Regarding process occurrence, it is discovered that teacher behavior is predominantly "direct." Thus, if we accept the *Commitment*, the natural state of teaching is poor, and matters can surely be improved by encouraging teachers to become more "indirect." We also discover, as a correlative finding, that pupils are speaking publicly not more than 25 percent of the time.

Only four findings appear within the context-process category, of which one is really not a finding at all. One study reports a positive relationship between social class of pupils and the degree to which teachers are "indirect," although there was evidence that pupil achievement, rather than social class, could have been the stimulus to which teachers were responding (Hoehn, 1954). A second finding is that the presence of computer-assisted instruction does *not* change the balance between "indirect" and "direct" teaching, in spite of the freedom from routine tasks it is supposed to give the teacher. Another finding suggests that teachers differ in "indirectness" according to the subject taught. Perhaps most interesting, however, is that teachers tend to be more "indirect" toward classes of higher intelligence than toward those of lower intelligence. If higher-intelligence classes are also higher-achieving classes, it should follow that teachers will be more "indirect" toward higher-achieving classes than toward lower-achieving classes. This possibility has interesting implications for the interpretation of process-product findings, to be discussed below. It seems, however, that investigators in this particular tradition have not generally concerned themselves with contextual influences on teaching behavior.

In contrast, greater attention has been paid to presage-process relationships, and these were generated by both field surveys and experiments. Among the former, we discover that "indirect" teachers are (and are not) more likely to be judged superior by others, score higher on the National Teachers' Examination history and philosophy examination, are more likely to be traditionally trained, are (and are not) more likely to be men, are (and are not) more likely to earn higher scores on the Minnesota Teacher Attitude Inventory Scale, have greater ego strength, are less authoritarian, are (and are not) more likely to have humanistic attitudes toward pupils, and have (or do not have) higher expectations for the achievements of pupils.

Most presage-process experiments have been conducted to test the efficacy of using FIAC as a training device to induce teachers to become "more indirect" in their teaching—hence "better" teachers. As indicated in Box 5.2, training in use of the FIAC has been combined with at least three other educative strategies in a number of experimental designs. Most studies report that teachers *do* become more "indirect" or less "indirect" in response to the experimental treatment, although two studies report no significant differences in "directness," and one even found that after initial gains there was actually a net loss in "indirectness." All of this suggests that adjustments in the "indirectness-directness" balance may indeed be induced for teachers. However, there is evidence to suggest that some of these inductions are lost.

However, the educational significance of "indirectness" depends on establishing a relationship between teacher behavior and its effects in process or product variables. Does such a relationship exist? Let us first consider process variables. In all, five groups of findings are summarized in Box 5.2: (1) Teacher "indirectness" appears to affect the amount of pupil talk. (2) Teacher "indirectness" is reported to be *unrelated* to amount of pupil responses to teacher initiations, to *raise* the amount of pupil responses, and to *lower* the amount of pupil responses(!). (3) Teacher "indirectness" is reported to raise the amount of pupil initiations (by five different studies). (4) Teacher "indirectness" is reported *unrelated* to their "directness" in three studies, and the commonly assumed negative relationship is reported in only one study. (5) Finally, teacher "indirectness" was found *related* to the cognitive level of classroom discourse in two out of three studies (see Chapter VIII). Most of these findings were interpreted by investigators in terms of cause-and-effect relationships, with the causative factor being the teacher's behavior. Moreover, as Box 5.2 indicates, some of the findings stem from experimental studies, thus tending to support the interpretation.

It is difficult to explain the contradictory findings reported for amount of pupil responses to teacher initiations. Either this variable is weakly related to teacher use of "indirectness," or the relationship is nonlinear, or it is susceptible to contextual influences that have as yet to be explained (note that the reversal of the relationship occurred in primary classrooms), or teacher "indirectness" is not measured in a constant fashion.

Perhaps the most significant process-process finding was obtained in three independent studies out of four. It is that "indirectness" and "directness" are independent of each other. As we suggested on conceptual grounds earlier in this chapter, the "dimension" presumed to underlie these concepts and instruments seems not a single dimension at all. On this point Soar (1968) was led to conclude that

> the term "permissiveness" has seemed to involve aspects of both emotional climate (warmth) and teacher control (directness). These results (and others, Soar, 1966) indicate that the two aspects of permissiveness are independent, and differ in their effect on pupils. (pp. 279–280)

In the long run, however, we would want to validate the concept of "indirectness" with product variables, thus demonstrating that "indirect" teaching had consistent effects on pupil learning or attitudes. Once again, process-product findings are available in Box 5.2 from both field surveys and experiments. Among field survey findings we discover that teacher "indirectness": is (and is not) associated with greater pupil achievement; is (and is not) associated with more positive pupil attitudes; is associated with greater pupil achievement motivation; is associated with greater pupil creativity; and is associated with lower pupil anxiety. Apart from the continuing (and vexing) problem of findings confirmed and denied, most of these results would appear to suggest that "indirectness" is indeed a cause of desired pupil learning. Two findings, in particular, are worth noting—both stemming from careful, thoughtful studies. In one (Tisher, 1970) teacher "indirectness" was found to be associated with greater achievement of pupils with low achievement orientation (only). In the other (Soar, 1968) "indirectness" was found to have a curvilinear relationship with pupil achievement, but the optimum degree of "indirectness" was found to be lower for concrete learning tasks than for more abstract learning tasks (see Chapter VIII). These latter findings suggest that the relationship between "indirectness" and pupil learning may not be a simple one.

At the risk of repeating a message given earlier, these findings were *not* based on experimental evidence. Given the lack of control inherent in field surveys, findings of a relationship between teacher "indirectness" and pupil learning might have reflected the causative influence of some third variable. What about the experimental findings for process-product relationships? Do they also show a relationship between teacher "indirectness" and pupil learning? In general, the experimental evidence does *not* show a relationship between teacher "indirectness" and the achievement of average pupils. This finding is true of five out of six experimental studies. Three relationships, only, are found between "indirectness" and pupil achievement: one study reported a slight increase in achievement for dependent-prone pupils, another a slight increase for the high-ability pupils, and the third an improvement in manipulative performance for pupils studying manual arts. Thus it would seem that where "indirectness" does have an influence upon pupil achievement, it is quite small. The score is no more encouraging for the *Commitment* when it comes to affective outcomes in pupils, for only one of the three experimental studies concerned found in favor of teacher "indirectness."

How then can we account for the process-product findings appearing in field surveys but not in experiments? If teacher "indirectness" does not induce greater pupil achievement, why should the two co-occur? Perhaps the simplest explanation is to be found in the context-process finding reported above that teacher "indirectness" varies with the intelligence level of the class. It is possible that the direction of causation is from pupil achievement to teacher behavior, and that experiments need to be devised with pupil achievement as the independent variable and teacher behavior as the dependent variable, instead of *vice versa*. The general question of the influence of pupil behavior on teacher behavior has been sadly neglected in educational research. The study by Good *et al.* (1973) was concerned with this question and found evidence consistent with the view that lower pupil achievement produces greater teacher "directness" than higher pupil achievement.

Another possible explanation is that of differential quality in different schools. As is well known, per-pupil expenditure in America varies depending on the affluence of the neighborhood, with the richest schools turning up in the richest suburbs. Rich schools can hire younger, more intelligent, more qualified teachers, who also probably happen to be more "progressive" in outlook. But the sons and daughters of rich persons are also more likely to earn higher grades on achievement examinations—for many reasons. Hence, teachers scored as more "indirect" should be found paired with pupils who achieve. This is but speculation, of course, since controls for social class have not featured in these studies, but the fact remains that evidence of a causative relationship between "indirectness" and pupil achievement is weak.

Perhaps, too, the answer lies in the suggestion that the relationship is not a linear one and that there can be too much "indirectness" as well as too little. Experiments have tended to contrast a very low degree of "indirectness" with a degree of "indirectness" which is so great that it should be hard to find in existing classrooms. Perhaps, therefore, these experiments have contrasted a less than optimal treatment with a more than optimal treatment and consequently have found no difference in effects on pupil achievement. If this explanation is correct, there would appear to be need for experiments that compare three treatments: low, medium, and high "indirectness."

Another interesting point about most of these experiments is that they assumed a negative relationship between "indirectness" and "directness." Thus, the "indirect" treatment took the form of high amounts of praise, acceptance, and questioning—and low amounts of lecturing, directing and criticizing—while the reverse was true of the "direct" treatment (see Amidon and Flanders, 1967b). Only two studies (Rian, 1969; Carline, 1969) avoided this assumption by having the amount of criticism similar in both treatments. The fact that they found no significant difference in effects upon pupil achievement raises the interesting possibility that where significant differences have been found, the crucial variable might have been the amount of criticism, although our review below of process-product relationships involving criticism does not single it out as an especially valid predictor to pupil achievement.

Let us now attempt a summary of what is known concerning teacher "indirectness." First, this concept reflects the *Commitment* of progressive education. Second, it is conceptually confused, in particular it elides the phenomena of warmth and directiveness, which are not necessarily related. Third, it is presumed to be measured by a number of single-faceted categorical instruments that are designed for live-observational use, although measuring "indirectness" or "directness" from these instruments requires a derivative statistic. Fourth, these instruments are reported to be reliable. Fifth, findings generated for "indirectness" have the annoying habit of being denied (or reversed) in other studies, although whether this is due to curvilinearity, to weakness of concepts or methods, or to contextual effects is not known. Sixth, teachers in standard classrooms are primarily "direct" in their operations. Seventh, teachers who are "indirect" are associated with pupils who initiate more. Eighth, teachers who are "indirect" score differently from others on a number of personality and teacher-assessment schedules. Ninth, teachers may be induced to be more "indirect" by various means, particularly training with the FIAC. Tenth, teachers who are "indirect" are found paired with pupils who achieve more and have more positive attitudes, atlhough this finding does not seem to be a simple cause-and-effect one.

Teacher Warmth

It turns out that many of the studies listed in Box 5.1 report findings for individual categories of their instruments rather than (or in addition to) findings for a "dimension" presumed to underlie it. Of these, three FIAC categories have generated substantial findings that appear to relate to the global concept of warmth. These are teacher *praise*, teacher *acceptance of pupils' ideas*, and teacher *criticism*. In terms of the *Commitment*, praise and acceptance should be positive components of warmth, while criticism should be its antonym. Thus, findings for the first two concepts should be similar and opposite in sign to those for the third. Categories expressing these same concepts also occur in other instruments, although in some cases the instrument may represent no assumption concerning the involvement of these concepts in a single, global dimension.

Praise We turn first to teacher *praise*. Box 5.3 reports a number of findings for this aspect of teacher behavior. It appears that teachers use praise sparingly in standard classrooms. It is also found that teachers give more praise to higher-achieving pupils; pupils to whom they feel more attached, or less indifferent; pupils whom they say they favor; white pupils for whom they have expectations of high achievement, but black pupils for whom they have expectations for low achievement; pupils for whom they have expectations of high future occupational status. It is also found (and not found) that boys receive more praise than girls; teacher

---

BOX 5.3   Findings for Teacher Praise

Process Occurrence

5.3-1 *Teachers use praise* no more than six percent of the total time on the average (Alt70), (D&L70), (Flan1), (Flan2), (Flan3), (Flan4), (F&A67), (L&a67), (Per64), (Tis70).

Context-Process Relationships

5.3-2 *Sex of pupils* is unrelated to *teachers' use of praise* (B&G70), (B&a73), (D&S67), (M&T56). *In contradiction,* it is also found that
5.3-2a *Boys* receive *more teacher praise* than do girls (E&a72), (E&a73), (Fel70), (G&a73), (Spa63).

5.3-3 *Location of school* (inner city versus suburban) is unrelated to *teachers' use of praise* (Alt70). *In contradiction,* it is also found that
5.3-3a Teachers in *lower social class schools* use *more praise* than teachers in middle social class schools (B&a73).

5.3-4 *Black pupils* receive *less teacher praise* than white pupils (R&M73).
5.3-5 *Higher (prior) pupil achievement* is associated with *greater teachers' use of praise* (G&a73).

Presage-Process Relationships

(a) *Teachers' Personality and Expectations*
5.3-6 *Teachers' dogmatism* (Rokeach scale) is unrelated to *teachers' use of praise* (R&M71)E,* (R&M73)E.
5.3-7 *Higher teachers' attachment to pupils* is associated with *greater teachers' use of praise* (Sil69), (G&B72).
5.3-8 *Higher teachers' indifference to pupils* is associated with *less teachers' use of praise* (G&B72).
5.3-9 *Higher teachers' favoring of class* is associated with *greater teachers' use of praise* (Sim67).
5.3-10 *Teachers' expectations for pupil achievement* are unrelated to *teachers'*

---

* Findings generated experimentally are indicated with an E. See the text and Box 5.2 for a description of experimental treatment.

(Box 5.3, continued)

---

use of praise (C&a72), (E&a72), (E&a73), (M&a71), (Ro&a71)E. *In contradiction*, it is also found that

5.3-10a *Higher teachers' expectations for pupil achievement* are associated with *greater teachers' use of praise* (B&G70), K&a70), (M&V71)E, (R&M71)E, and

5.3-10b *Higher teachers' expectations for pupil achievement* are associated with *less teachers' use of praise* (B&a73), (Row73), and

5.3-10c *Higher teachers' expectations for white pupils' achievement* are associated with *greater teachers' use of praise* (R&M73)E, and

5.3-10d *Higher teachers' expectations for black pupils' achievement* are associated with *less teachers' use of praise* (R&M73)E.

5.3-11 *Teachers' expectations for pupil behavior* are unrelated to *teachers' use of praise* (Fel70).

5.3-12 *Higher teachers' expectations for pupils' future occupational status* are associated with *greater teachers' use of praise* (SmM65).

(b)   *Teacher Training*

5.3-13 *Experimental treatment* does not produce change in *teachers' use of praise* (L&a67)E. *In contradiction*, it also found that

5.3-13a *Experimental treatment* raises *teachers' use of praise* (Bon69)E, and

5.3-13b *Experimental treatment* does not produce change in *teachers' use of praise* in the short term but lowers it in the longer term (Hil67)E.

5.3-14 *Duration of training* in FIAC is unrelated to changes in *teachers' use of praise* (Hil67)E.

5.3-15 *Mode of feedback* is unrelated to changes in *teachers' use of praise* (Hil67)E.

5.3-16 *Teacher training in experimental elementary science programs* does not produce change in *teachers' use of praise* (HuE69)E.

Process-Process Relationships

None reported.

Process-Product Relationships

5.3-17 *Teacher praise* is unrelated to *pupil achievement* (Fel70), (Flan3), (Flan4), (Flan6), (Flan7), (H&S66), (H&a68), (HuC68), (Per65), (S&a71), (Wal66). *In contradiction*, it is also found that

5.3-17a *Higher teacher praise* is associated with *greater pupil achievement* (Flan4), (S&a71), (W&N70), and

5.3-17b *High teacher praise and low teacher acceptance following correct pupil responses* increases *pupil achievement* more than low teacher praise and high teacher acceptance following correct pupil responses (HuD73)E.

5.3-18 *Teacher praise* is unrelated to *pupil attitudes* (Flan3), (Flan4), (Flan6), (Flan7). *In contradiction*, it is also found that

5.3-18a *Higher teacher praise* is associated with *more positive pupil attitudes* (Flan5).

5.3-19 *Higher teacher praise* is associated with *more positive pupil self-concepts* (Spa63).

5.3-20 *Higher teacher praise* is associated with *lower pupil nonverbal creativity* (W&W63).

---

praise varies with the social class status of the school's location; teachers give more praise to pupils for whom they have expectations of high achievement; and teachers give more praise to pupils for whom they have expectations of low achievement. Furthermore, teachers' praise appears unrelated to teachers' dogmatism and teachers' expectations for pupils' behavior and training in innovatory elementary science curricula. It is also reported, as an experimental finding, that use of praise by teachers can be increased by experimental treatments, including training in FIAC, though one study raises doubt about the durability of the change. Field studies of process-product relationships report that teacher praise is (and is not) associated with greater pupil achievement; is (and is not) associated with more positive pupil attitudes; is associated with more positive pupil self-concepts; and is associated with *lower* pupil nonverbal creativity. To our knowledge only one of these last results has been tested in experimental research. That study (Hughes, 1973) found that high teacher praise, with low teacher acceptance, following correct pupil responses, was more effective in relation to pupil achievement than low praise and high acceptance following correct pupil responses.

Acceptance of Pupils' Ideas   Box 5.4 reports findings for teachers' *acceptance of pupils' ideas*. Once again, it would appear that this aspect

---

BOX 5.4   Findings for Teachers' Acceptance of Pupils' Ideas

Process Occurrence

5.4-1   Teachers are scored for *acceptance of pupils' ideas* less than eight percent of the total time on the average (D&L70), (Flan1), (Flan2), (Flan3), (Flan4), (Fu67b), (F&A67), (Per64), (Tis70).

Context-Process Relationships

None reported.

Presage-Process Relationships

(a)   *Teacher Attitudes*

5.4-2   *Higher teachers' scores on MTAI* are associated with *greater teacher acceptance of pupils' ideas* (F&Sun).

5.4-3   *Higher teachers' concern for pupils* is associated with *greater teachers' acceptance of pupils' ideas* (Sil69).

5.4-4   *Higher teachers' humanistic* (rather than custodial) *attitudes toward pupils* are associated with *greater teachers' acceptance of pupils' ideas* (Gol71).

(b)   *Teacher Training*

5.4-5   *Experimental treatment raises teachers' acceptance of pupils' ideas* (Bon69)E,* (Car70)E, (Emm67)E, (Fin67)E, (Fu67b)E, (L&a67)E, (Mos67)E. *In contradiction*, it is also found that

5.4-5a   *Experimental treatment* failed to produce change in *teachers' acceptance of pupils' ideas* (Hil67)E.

---

* Findings generated experimentally are indicated with an E. See the text and Box 5.2 for a description of experimental treatments.

(Box 5.4, continued)

5.4-6   *Teacher training in experimental elementary science program* is unrelated to *teachers' acceptance of pupils' ideas* (HuE69)E.

Process-Process Relationships

5.4-7   *Greater teacher acceptance of pupils' ideas* raises the *amount of pupils' initiations* (Emm67)E.

Process-Product Relationships

5.4-8   *Teachers' acceptance of pupils' ideas* is unrelated to *pupil achievement* (Flan3), (Flan4), (Flan5), (Flan6), (Flan7), (Soa66). *In contradiction*, it is also found that

    5.4-8a   *Greater teacher acceptance of pupils' ideas* is associated with *higher pupil achievement* (Per65), and

    5.4-8b   *Low teacher acceptance and high teacher praise following correct pupil responses* increases *pupil achievement* more than high teacher acceptance and low teacher praise following correct pupil responses (HuD73)E.

5.4-9   *Teachers' acceptance of pupils' ideas* is unrelated to *pupil attitudes* (Flan3), (Flan4), (Flan7). *In contradiction*, it is also found that

    5.4-9a   *Greater teachers' acceptance of pupils' ideas* is associated with *more positive pupil attitudes* (Flan5), (Flan6), (Soa66).

5.4-10   *Greater teachers' acceptance of pupils' ideas* is associated with *lower pupil anxiety* (Soa66).

5.4-11   *Greater teachers' acceptance of pupils' ideas* is associated with *higher pupil creativity* (Soa66).

---

of teacher behavior appears sparingly in standard classrooms. Greater acceptance by teachers appears to be associated with higher teacher scores on the MTAI; higher teacher scores on the attitude of concern for pupils and higher scores on humanistic (rather than custodial) attitudes toward pupils. We also learn that experimental training with FIAC raises teachers' acceptance of pupils' ideas—and, moreover, the relationship is reported in seven studies with only one contradicting finding. Greater acceptance appears to raise the amount of pupil initiations. In contrast, seven studies (there is one exception) report that acceptance of pupils' ideas is unrelated to pupil achievement, despite the fact that it is (and is not) associated with more positive pupil attitudes. It also occurs with lower pupil anxiety, and greater pupil creativity. Once again, these process-product relationships are reported from field surveys only and are unvalidated with experimental research. The only experimental process-product study indicates that acceptance of correct pupil responses is less effective than praise following correct pupil responses (Hughes, 1973).

Criticism   Presumably teacher *praise* and teacher *acceptance of pupils' ideas* are GOOD things to do, while teacher *criticism* is a BAD thing. Findings from Box 5.5 suggest, however, that teachers *also* use criticism sparingly in the standard classroom. (Elsewhere we will discover that teachers often let pupil errors slip by without comment—see Chapter IX.) Boys

BOX 5.5   Findings for Teacher Criticism

Process Occurrence

5.5-1   Teachers use *criticism* less than six percent of the total time on the average (Alt70), (D&L70), (Flan1), (Flan2), (Flan3), (Flan4), (F&A67), (L&a67), (Per64), (Tis70).

Context-Process Relationships

5.5-2   *Sex of pupils* is unrelated to *teachers' use of criticism* (D&S67). *In contradiction, it is also found that*

    5.5-2a   *Boys* receive *more criticism* from teachers than girls (B&a73), (B&G70), (E&a72), (E&a73), (Fel70), (G&a73), (J&L66), (M&T56), (Spa63).

5.5-3   *Black pupils* receive *more criticism* from teachers than white pupils (R&M73).

5.5-4   *Lower primary grades* exhibit greater *teacher criticism* than do higher primary grades (HuM59).

5.5-5   *Social studies* exhibits *less teacher criticism* than do other subjects (G&a73), (HuM59).

5.5-6   *Location of school* (inner city versus suburban) is unrelated to *teachers' use of criticism* (Alt70). *In contradiction, it also found that*

    5.5-6a   *Lower social class schools* exhibit greater *teachers' use of criticism* than do middle social class schools (B&a73).

5.5-7   *Lower (prior) pupil achievement* is associated with greater *teachers' use of criticism* (G&a73).

Presage-Process Relationships

(a)   *Teacher Personality and Expectations*

5.5-8   *Higher teacher scores on NTE English A and Literature examinations* are associated with greater *teachers' use of criticism* (M&H70).

5.5-9   *Teachers' scores on MTAI* are unrelated to *teachers' use of criticism* (Cam70), (F&Sun).

5.5-10   *Higher teacher anxiety* and *hypochondria* (using MMPI) are associated with greater *teachers' use of criticism* (F&Sun).

5.5-11   *Teachers' dogmatism* (Rokeach scale) is unrelated to *teachers' use of criticism* (R&M71). *In contradiction, it is also found that*

    5.5-11a   *Higher teachers' dogmatism* (Rokeach scale) is associated with greater *teachers' use of criticism* (R&M73).

5-5.12   *Higher teachers' rejection of pupils* is associated with greater *teachers' use of criticism* (G&B72), (Sil69).

5.5-13   *Higher teachers' indifference to pupils* is associated with *less teachers' use of criticism* (G&B72).

5.5-14   *Teachers' expectations for pupil achievement* are unrelated to *teachers' use of criticism* (B&a73), (C&a72), (E&a72), (E&a73), (K&a70), (R&M71)E,* (Ro&a71)E. *In contradiction, it is also found that*

    5.5-14a   *Higher teachers' expectations for pupil achievement* are associated with *lower teachers' use of criticism* (B&G70), (Dal69), (M&V71)E, (Row73), and

---

* Findings generated experimentally are indicated with an E. See the text and Box 5.2 for a description of experimental treatments.

(Box 5.5, continued)

5.5-14b *Teachers' expectations for white pupils' achievement* are unrelated to *teachers' use of criticism of white pupils* (R&M73)E, and

5.5-14c *Higher teachers' expectations for black pupils' achievement* are associated with *greater teachers' use of criticism of black pupils* (R&M73)E.

5.5-15 *Higher teachers' expectations for female pupils' obedience and cooperativeness* are associated with *lower teachers' use of criticism* (Fel70).

5.5-16 *Higher teachers' expectations for female pupils' destructiveness* are associated with *greater teachers' use of criticism* (Fel70).

5.5-17 *Higher teachers' expectations for pupils' future occupational status* are associated with *less teachers' use of criticism* (SmM65).

(b)   *Teacher Training*

5.5-18 *Experimental treatment* failed to produce a change in *teachers' use of criticism* (Car70)E, (L&a67)E. *In contradiction*, it is also found that

5.5-18a *Experimental treatment* lowers *teachers' use of criticism* (Bon69)E, (Fu67b)E, and

5.5-18b *Experimental treatment* failed to produce change in *teachers' use of criticism* in the short term, but decreased it in the longer term (Hil67)E.

5.5-19 *Teacher training in experimental elementary science program* is unrelated to *teachers' use of criticism* (HuE69)E.

Process-Process Relationships

5.5-20 *Teachers' use of criticism* is unrelated to *teacher use of praise* and *teacher acceptance of pupils' ideas* (M&H68), (Soa66).

Process-Product Relationships

5.5-21 *Teacher criticism* is unrelated to *pupil achievement* (Coo67), (Fel70), (Flan3), (Flan5), (Flan6), (Flan7), (S&a71). *In contradiction*, it is also found that

5.5-21a *Greater teacher criticism* is associated with *lower pupil achievement* (Flan4), (H&S66), (H&a68), (HuC68), (Soa66), (Spa63), and that

5.5-21b *Teacher criticism* has a curvilinear relationship with *pupil achievement*, but the optimum degree of teacher criticism is higher for more concrete learning tasks than for more abstract learning tasks (Soa68).

5.5-22 *Teacher criticism* is unrelated to *pupil attitudes* (Flan4), (Flan6), (Flan7). *In contradiction*, it is also found that

5.5-22a *Greater teacher criticism* is associated with *less positive pupil attitudes* (Flan3), (Flan5).

5.5-23 *Greater teacher criticism* is associated with *lower pupil achievement motivation* (Cam70).

5.5-24 *Greater teacher criticism* is associated with *higher pupil fear of failure* (Cam70).

5.5-25 *Greater teacher criticism* is associated with *lower pupil self-concept* (Spa63).

5.5-26 *Greater teacher criticism* is associated with *higher pupil dependency* (Soa66).

5.5-27 *Greater teacher criticism* is associated with *lower pupil anxiety* (Soa66).

are also reported to receive more criticism than girls in nine studies (there was only one study reporting no difference). Thus boys are both *praised* and *criticized* more than girls! Teachers of lower grades also appear to use more criticism, while rather less of it appears in social studies than in other subjects. One study found that teacher criticism occurs more in lower-class schools than in middle-class schools, but another found no such difference between inner-city and suburban schools. Lower achievers were found to receive more criticism than others. Teachers who use more criticism tend to have higher scores on the NTE English A and Literature examinations; to be more prone to anxiety and hypochondria; to have (and not to have) higher scores on dogmatism; to have higher scores on the attitude of rejection of, but lower scores on the attitude of indifference to pupils; to have (and not to have) lower expectations for pupils' achievements; to have higher expectations for the achievement of black pupils; to have lower expectations for pupils' future occupational status; and to have lower expectations for obedience and cooperativeness, and higher expectations for the destructiveness of *girl* pupils. In contrast, teachers' use of criticism appears unrelated to scores earned on the MTAI or special training in innovatory elementary science curricula. Experimental training in FIAC has been found to lower the use of criticism by teachers, although these results are fewer than those for teacher acceptance of pupils' ideas. Two studies report no decrease, while another suggests a delayed effect of training. Turning to process-product relationships, we find that teacher criticism is (or is not) associated with lower pupil achievement, is (or is not) associated with less positive pupil attitudes, and is associated with lower pupil achievement motivation, greater pupil fear of failure, lower pupil self-concept, greater pupil dependency, and *lower* pupil anxiety! These findings were not tested in experimental research.

What can we make of these various findings? First, let us consider the question of whether or not they reveal a single dimension of warmth. Recall that we originally supposed *praise* (or approval) and teacher *acceptance of pupils' ideas* to be positive components of warmth, while *criticism* (or disapproval) should be its negative component. If this is the case, findings for the first two categories should be similar to one another and opposite in sign to those for the third category. Data to check this supposition can be apposed from Boxes 5.3, 5.4, and 5.5.

Unfortunately for the *Commitment*, findings for these three concepts do not fall into such a simple pattern. Praise and acceptance occur but infrequently, but so does criticism. Teacher use of praise and criticism are strongly associated with teacher attitudes toward, and expectations for, pupils, while evidence concerning these matters is missing for teacher acceptance. Experimental training appears to have the effect of inducing greater teacher acceptance, while few effects are reported for either praise or criticism. More relations are reported for the effects of criticism on product variables than for either praise or acceptance. On balance, then, it would appear that these three concepts represent independent phenomena.

Now let us consider three general issues that have generated quite a bit of the research for these concepts. These concern the treatment of pupils by sex, the effects of teachers' expectations for pupil achievement, and the effects of praise, acceptance, and criticism on pupil outcomes.

Concerning sex of pupils, six out of nine studies found that boys received more praise than girls, while nine out of ten studies found that boys received more criticism than girls. This suggests either that boys are generating these teacher reactions by behaving differently from girls or that teachers have differential reactions to boys regardless of their behavior. Contemporary educational ideology would suggest the first explanation. "Boys are treated differentially because they are 'less mature,' 'more impulsive,' and 'educationally handicapped' in comparison with girls. Moreover, these differences are genetically induced." But is this explanation adequate? Nineteen out of twenty primary teachers are women, and the ratio approaches unity in the lower grades. Whereas American boys lag behind American girls in reading achievement, Preston (1962) has discovered that the reverse is true in German schools, where male teachers are in the majority! There can be little doubt but that boys are more impulsive and physically active than are girls, although whether these behaviors are physically or socially induced is open to question. However, we suspect that these behaviors are less likely to attract attention—be it praise or criticism—in classrooms that are less "feminine" than is typical in America.

Still other findings of interest concern the relationship discovered between teacher expectations and teacher use of praise and criticism. These findings bear directly upon a recent controversy in educational research. The controversy was stimulated by the publication of Rosenthal and Jacobson's *Pygmalion in the Classroom* (1968), which suggested that teachers' expectations of the intellectual ability of pupils are a determinant of intellectual growth in pupils. Rosenthal and Jacobson conducted a study in which teachers of various elementary grade levels were informed that, on the basis of an "intelligence test" administered at the beginning of a school year, some of their pupils would "bloom" intellectually during the year. In fact, the pupils involved were selected randomly and so could be assumed to be no different from the rest of their class. When the classes were retested after several months it appeared that the selected pupils had in fact "bloomed," at least at the first and second-grade levels, for they seemed to have improved in their performance on the intelligence test more than their classmates. Rosenthal and Jacobson claimed that teachers' expectations became, thus, "self-fulfilling prophecies" because teachers behaved differently toward pupils for whom they had high expectations than toward other pupils.

Several critics (Barber and Silver, 1968; Claiborn, 1968; Minor, 1970; Snow, 1969; Thorndike, 1968, 1969; Elashoff and Snow, 1971) have thrown doubt upon the validity of the Pygmalion study. But of more concern to us is the fact that Rosenthal and Jacobson failed to observe classroom behavior and thus failed to discover the process by which teachers might have translated their expectations into differential treatment of pupils.

However, various researchers have been stimulated by the Pygmalion study into doing classroom research involving the use of teacher praise and criticism (see Brophy and Good, 1970; Brophy et al., 1973; Claiborn, 1969; Cornbleth et al., 1972; Dalton, 1969; Evertson et al., 1973; José, 1970; Kranz et al., 1970; Medinnus and Unruh, 1971; Meichenbaum et al., 1969; Rothbart et al., 1971; Rowe, 1973; and Rubovits and Maehr, 1971, 1973).

The work of Brophy and Good (1970) is particularly valuable because it presents an explicit model of the process by which teachers' expectations for pupil achievement may become self-fulfilling prophecies. Their model suggests that

(a) The teacher forms differential expectations for student performance;
(b) He then begins to treat children differently in accordance with his differential expectations;
(c) The children respond differentially to the teacher because they are being treated differently by him;
(d) In responding to the teacher, each child tends to exhibit behavior which complements and reinforces the teacher's particular expectations for him;
(e) As a result, the general academic performance of some children will be enhanced while that of others will be depressed, with changes being in the direction of teacher expectations;
(f) These effects will show up in the achievement tests given at the end of the year, providing support for the "self-fulfilling prophecy" notion. (pp. 365–366)

What evidence have the above studies produced in support of step (b) of the model?

Four of the studies (those of Claiborn, José, Meichenbaum et al., and Rothbart et al.) were experiments wherein a modification of the Rosenthal treatment was tried—unsuccessfully—with naive teachers. They failed to find any effects of induced expectations for pupil achievement upon teacher praise and criticism. Two other experiments (those by Medinnus and Unruh, 1971; and Rubovits and Maehr, 1971) did find a causative relationship between teacher expectations and differential use of praise by teachers. However, only the former found an effect on teacher criticism. Another experiment (Rubovits and Maehr, 1973) found that the effects of induced expectations upon teacher praise and criticism varied according to the race of the pupil. High-expectancy white pupils received more praise than other white pupils, while high-expectancy black pupils received both less praise and more criticism than other black pupils!

Two field surveys (Brophy and Good, 1970; Kranz et al., 1970) found support for the hypothesis that teachers would give more praise to high-expectancy pupils. Three found no difference (Cornbleth et al., 1972; Evertson et al., 1972; and Evertson et al., 1973). Two found quite the opposite—

that teachers gave less praise to high-expectancy pupils (Brophy *et al.*, 1973; and Rowe, 1973). The hypothesis that teachers would give more criticism to low-expectancy pupils was supported by four field surveys (Brophy and Good, 1970; Dalton, 1969; Kranz *et al.*, 1970; and Rowe, 1973), but not by four others (Brophy *et al.*, 1973; Cornbleth *et al.*, 1972; Evertson *et al.*, 1972; and Evertson *et al.*, 1973).

Here again we find significant results involving praise and criticism being unsupported and even contradicted by other studies. Flaws in design and procedures render some studies unfair tests of the Pygmalion hypothesis. In others, contextual variables such as the types of pupils or the time of the school year at which teacher expectancies or behavior were measured might have affected the chances of obtaining significant results. Still others found significant expectancy effects involving behaviors other than praise and criticism. Some findings suggest that expectancy effects may not show up when measures of total praise and criticism are used, but may show up when praise and criticism are analyzed in terms of the categories of pupil behavior to which they are applied. For example, Rowe (1973) found that high-expectancy pupils were praised for correct responses, while low-expectancy pupils were sometimes praised for incorrect responses. Evertson *et al.*, (1972) found that low-expectancy pupils received more criticism for misbehavior than others. Perhaps praise and criticism are significant aspects of teacher behavior, not so much in their total incidence as in the extent to which they are contingent upon particular types of pupil responses.

Finally, it should be emphasized that our review here has looked at evidence of expectancy effects only upon teacher praise and criticism. Several of the studies reviewed found evidence of expectancy effects on other categories of teacher behavior, so that the Pygmalion hypothesis has won considerable support with respect to process variables in general.

The process-product results reported in Boxes 5.3, 5.4, and 5.5 again show that only a minority of studies have found significant relationships between teacher praise, acceptance, and criticism and pupil achievement. The experiment by Hughes (1973) is especially interesting, since it compared the effectiveness of high teacher praise, coupled with low teacher acceptance, applied to correct pupil responses—with the effectiveness of low praise and low acceptance applied to correct pupil responses. The high-praise treatment was clearly more effective than the other, suggesting that praise is a powerful determinant of pupil learning. (Another interesting feature of this experiment was that praise was applied only when pupil responses were correct. This again suggests the importance of investigating the use and effectiveness of praise, acceptance, and criticism in relation to particular types of pupil responses rather than as undifferentiated totals. We return to this issue in the next chapter.)

One other finding concerning pupil achievement stands out. This was the finding that teacher criticism bears a nonlinear relationship with pupil achievement, and that the optimum degree of criticism is higher for more concrete learning tasks than for more abstract learning tasks (Soar, 1968).

The range of affective pupil outcomes explored in these studies is quite wide, and there has been more success in finding significant relationships between teacher praise, acceptance, and criticism and affective outcomes in pupils than with pupil achievement. One interesting and unexpected finding is that teacher praise is negatively related to nonverbal pupil creativity. Another is that teacher criticism is negatively related to pupil anxiety. However, there is no experimental confirmation of any of the above findings. The shortage of experimental studies involving these variables of teacher behavior is worthy of comment, since it probably indicates the great difficulty of experimentally manipulating a single variable of teacher behavior without also changing other teacher behaviors and so confounding the interpretation of results.

Earlier we summarized what we had discovered concerning teacher "indirectness." Let us now attempt a similar summary for praise, acceptance, and criticism. First, they (also) reflect the *Commitment* of progressive education. Second, they are not as conceptually confused as "indirectness." Third, they are usually measured by categorical scores from instruments designed for live-observational use. Fourth, these instruments are reported to be reliable. Fifth, teachers in standard classrooms use relatively little praise, acceptance, and criticism in their communications.[1] Sixth, findings generated for them are also likely to be denied (or even reversed) in other studies. Seventh, significant relationships have been found linking them more often with presage and context variables than with product variables. The *Commitment* is supported to the extent that classrooms have been found affectively neutral. On balance, it would also appear that teachers can be trained to greater acceptance of pupils' ideas. However, only criticism appears related to pupil outcomes, and even for this variable the product evidence is contradictory.

CONCLUSION

As is true for many educators, both of the authors were introduced to the *Commitment* of progressive education and its associated ideologies at an early age, and it gives us not a little anguish to find faults in research that represents this *Commitment*. Nevertheless, much of this research appears flawed.

The biggest problem seems to be that of conceptual confusion. As we have seen, most of the research instruments appear to elide the concepts of *warmth* and *directiveness* in the classroom, processes that appear to operate independently. Again, the categories chosen for research instru-

[1] As Flanders (1960) has suggested, the classroom appears an "affectional desert," and most of its communications are simply "neutral" in terms of warmth.

ments are usually given but minimal definition and little or no explanation as to why they constitute a single facet. Additional problems concern the fact that instruments were designed for live observation and for use with arbitrary time intervals. Finally, confusion has arisen in trying to relate findings from the various research instruments and in constructing derivative measures to indicate the degree of teacher "indirectness."

Within these limitations a number of findings have appeared in our review. Perhaps the most pervasive of these is that many relationships have not only been *supported* in two or more studies but have also been *denied* in two or more studies. One suspects either that the concepts measured by these instruments are invalid, that various instruments are in fact measuring different things, that relationships between these phenomena and other events are curvilinear or are contextually bound, or that more attention needs to be paid to classroom sequences and pupil behavior. (Some evidence is available to support each of these interpretations.) On the positive side, moderate to high reliabilities have been reported for many of these instruments. Teachers in standard classrooms are reported to evidence considerable "directness" and to exhibit praise, acceptance, and criticism for small percentages of the time. Teachers who are "indirect" are associated with—and probably induce—pupils who initiate more. "Indirectness," praise, acceptance, and criticism are all associated with teacher-personality instruments of one kind or another. Evidence has also appeared that teachers can be trained to be more "indirect" and to show greater acceptance of pupils' ideas by training with FIAC.

Do these findings provide a recipe for the "improvement" of education? To validate the *Commitment*, we require three kinds of evidence: (1) evidence that a given teaching practice is characteristic of classrooms today; (2) evidence that it can be changed by appropriate means; and (3) evidence that by so doing we will improve the achievement or attitudes of pupils. Let us review the evidence for both "indirectness" and *warmth*.

Concerning "indirectness" (provided one grants "indirectness" to be a unitary factor), we have seen that classroom teaching *is* mainly "direct." Moreover, teachers can probably be induced to be less "direct" through training. Finally, findings from field surveys appear to show relationships between indirectness and pupil growth, although the evidence is weak, contradictory, and the relations may be curvilinear or contextually bound. However, evidence from experiments is equivocal, suggesting that the apparent relationships found in field surveys are not causative. Thus, the case for "indirectness" is not demonstrated.

Concerning *warmth*, we have seen that the classroom is usually neither "warm" nor "cold," but primarily neutral in tone. Moreover, teachers can probably be induced to use more acceptance through training. Finally, findings from field surveys show some relationships between these categories (particularly criticism) and pupil outcomes, although these effects are almost completely untested experimentally. Thus, the case for warmth is also not yet demonstrated.

Readers are understandably concerned to locate recipes for excellence in teaching. Unfortunately, this research tradition does not offer a simple recipe. Despite scores of published studies, evidence concerning the "improvement" of teaching is simply not yet well established. This has not deterred enthusiasts, however, nor sidetracked those who would advocate the "improvement" of education by training with FIAC or other instruments. As Rosenshine and Furst (1971) have suggested:

> Ideally, we would prefer that research on the validation of teacher behaviors take place *before* these behaviors are disseminated in teacher education programs. But educational practice has been to innovate and to justify the innovations with unsubstantiated "logic" or "theory." Programs that include innovations based on the opinions of educational experts have received much more attention than have programs for research on teacher behaviors. (p. 64)

It seems to us that "improvements" are more likely when supported by both rationale *and* evidence, and we urge readers to join us in reserving *Commitments* until we have established both.

RECOMMENDED ADDITIONAL READING

Amidon, E. J., and Hough, J. B. (eds.). *Interaction Analysis: Theory, Research and Application*. Reading, Mass.: Addison-Wesley Publishing Company, 1967.
A collection of theoretical, methodological, and research articles from the early classical studies to recent applications of FIAC and its modifications in teacher education. Some of the studies reviewed in this chapter are republished in this book.

Brophy, J. E., and Good, T. L. *Teacher-Student Relationships: Causes and Consequences*. New York: Holt, Rinehart and Winston, Inc., 1974.
An excellent summary of the authors' research on the effects of teacher expectations on teacher classroom behavior. Discusses the conditions under which teachers may be expected to treat pupils differentially—and what to do about it.

Flanders, N. A. *Analyzing Teaching Behavior*. Reading, Mass.: Addison-Wesley Publishing Company, 1970.
The most comprehensive statement of the research tradition using FIAC and its derivatives yet to appear. Procedures for applying and modifying FIAC are explained in detail, fundamental theoretical and conceptual issues are discussed, and some of the research reviewed in this chapter is also examined.

Rosenthal, R., and Jacobson, L. *Pygmalion in the Classroom: Teacher Expectation and Pupils' Intellectual Development*. New York: Holt, Rinehart and Winston, Inc., 1968.
One of the most controversial books on education in recent years. Bears directly on the issue of the significance of teacher expectations for pupil growth. Has stimulated observational studies reviewed in this chapter.

VI

MANAGEMENT AND CONTROL

Teacher: And what is the sum of these three angles? . . . Mary?
Mary: Twenty-seven degrees?
Teacher: Peter?
Peter: Thirty-one degrees?
Teacher: Richard?
Richard: Thirty-six degrees?
Teacher: Right! Richard gets a gold star today too. Now let's consider the other side of the figure (pointing to the chalkboard). As you can see, angles G, F, and H also come together at a point. Now, what do you suppose is their sum? Anita?
Anita: Is it 36 degrees too?
Teacher: Arnold? . . . (*Before Arnold can answer, the teacher's attention falls on two boys in the back of the room who are whispering together. The teacher says nothing but merely snaps her fingers—evidently a signal for attention. The two miscreants look up at her, then immediately cease their whispering and sit up "at attention." One or two others in the class look at them and then back at the teacher.*)

Arnold, what is the sum of these three angles?

The concern most often voiced by beginning teachers is the problem of classroom control. How does one manage a room full of energetic and impulsive pupils? How does one keep order and discipline? How is it possible to manage the presentation of subject matter so that each child will learn from it? How can we "turn on" pupils who are both quick and slow, active and passive, interested and bored, hostile and accepting?

This is no minor problem in teaching. As pupils we were all exposed to various managerial styles. Some of our teachers were autocrats, some sensitive and responsive, some masters at fascinating us with the details of knowledge. Each had a managerial style that worked to some degree. But some of our teachers, alas, were less successful managers. Their classrooms were noisy and disorganized or were overcontrolled, or expressions of hostility and challenge from pupils overrode the teacher's attempts to interest pupils in the subject, or pupils spent hours in boredom or even asleep! Although classrooms of these latter kinds provided babysitting services, it is unlikely that pupils learned much in them or developed warm reactions toward the subject matter, other pupils, or the teacher.

Thus, management of classrooms is important. Nor should we be surprised to discover that nearly all texts in the psychology or philosophy of education discuss the problem of control. Treatment of this subject ranges from recommendations for specific control strategies to demands that the teacher provide appropriate "learning environments" or even eschew all attempts to impose control on pupils in the name of classroom democracy or the encouragement of creativity and independence. While we do not want to enter these arguments, it seems to us that adequate management of the classroom environment also forms a necessary condition for cognitive learnings; and if the teacher cannot solve problems in this sphere, we can give the rest of teaching away. We shall not argue that the teacher's job begins and ends with classroom management, but surely this is an important aspect of her task.

We should not be surprised to discover, then, that some of those who have studied classroom teaching have concentrated on issues of management. In this chapter we review three quite different approaches to this topic. The first of these was anticipated in Chapter V. As we saw there, investigators within the classroom-climate tradition have constructed various research instruments which seemed to measure variables relevant to both *warmth* and *directiveness*. Evidence concerning *warmth* variables was reviewed in Chapter V. In this chapter we first turn to scores generated by these same instruments that relate to *directiveness* variables as indicators of classroom control.

We next consider a program of studies that represents a more sophisticated approach to the managerial problem. This is Kounin's research on problems of discipline and the management of class groups. As we shall see, this program offers a wealth of novel concepts for describing teaching as well as findings that help us to understand the processes of better classroom management.

Finally, we review yet another approach to classroom management—research that has reflected the tradition of reinforcement theory and behavior modification. As we shall see, classroom research using reinforcement notions has involved successful control over both pupil discipline and pupil learning.

These three approaches represent sharply different traditions and ideas concerning the management problem. Yet each has something to offer the serious student of teaching. We shall review the three approaches in comparison at the end of the chapter.

DIRECTIVENESS

In Chapter V we discovered a research tradition that has focused on classroom climate. Fundamental to many studies in this tradition has been the idea that teaching examples can be placed along a single continuum or dimension, one end of which is presumed to represent "good" teaching. Moreover, that dimension appears to have been an amalgam of at least two notions—*warmth* and *directiveness*. In the last chapter we reviewed research on *warmth* variables. We now turn to evidence from these same studies that may be interpreted for the dimension of *directiveness*.

Concepts of Classroom Behavior

If *directiveness* is an unidimensional scale along which various styles of classroom teaching may be placed, at one end we would find the autocratic, teacher-dominated classroom. Such a classroom would be characterized by a great deal of teacher talk; by many teacher directions; by lectures, not discussions; and by little pupil talk and even less pupil initiation. At the other end one would find classrooms with a lot of pupil talk, especially pupil initiation; by a teacher who controls unobtrusively; by stimulation rather than demand; by give and take; and by motion, excitement, challenge, and self-direction.

Does all of this sound familiar? It should, for we are still within the traditional ideology of progressive education, and the *Commitment* is to increasing pupil participation, particularly pupil initiation, through reductions in lecturing and direction giving and increases in questioning. But there are problems with these prescriptions. How do we know that all of these kinds of classroom events co-vary together? Can we be sure that pupils will speak up if the teacher stops speaking? Is pupil initiation or response associated with pupil achievement? When the teacher fades into the background is this action accompanied by increases in the excitement, challenge, and self-direction of the classroom? Answers to these questions might warrant reconsideration of some of the assumptions made concerning directiveness. Perhaps directiveness is not merely a matter of opposition of autocratic and democratic styles of teacher control. Perhaps, just perhaps, there are several different ways in which a teacher might control the learning of pupils within the lesson.

In theory it would be feasible to review evidence for the general dimension of *directiveness*. However, given the confusion between this concept and that of *warmth*, such a review would merely recapitulate the findings reported in Chapter V for the amalgamated dimension "indirectness." Instead, we shall consider a number of categorical scores that bear on the directiveness problem.

For convenience these will be defined in terms of FIAC. Let us take one more look at Figure 5.3. Recall that the ten categories of FIAC were designed for live observation with three-second intervals. Thus, if we take the total number of tallies made within any given category and multiply it by three, we have a figure that presumably represents the number of seconds in the lesson during which interaction with the defined characteristic was occurring. By proceeding in such a fashion we can define the following concepts and operations:

Teacher talk—The proportion of lesson time devoted to teacher utterances (frequencies summed for categories 1 through 7);

Teacher questions—The proportion of lesson time devoted to questions asked by the teacher (frequencies for category 4);

Teacher lecturing—The proportion of lesson time devoted to lecturing by the teacher (frequencies for category 5);

Teacher giving directions—The proportion of lesson time devoted to direction giving by the teacher (frequencies for category 6);

Pupil talk—The proportion of lesson time devoted to pupil utterances (frequencies summed for categories 8 and 9);

Pupil responding—The proportion of lesson time devoted to responses by pupils (frequencies for category 8);

Pupil initiation—The proportion of lesson time devoted to initiations by pupils (frequencies for category 9); and

Silence or confusion—The proportion of lesson time during which silence or confusion is taking place (frequencies for category 10).[1]

Classroom Research

Findings for research on *directiveness* variables are given in Box 6.1. About 25 different studies generated the results reported in this box. Without exception these were listed in Box 5.1, and in consequence, Box 6.1 is confined to the review of findings. Of these studies approximately one third were conducted by Flanders using FIAC or related instruments and the remainder by other investigators. Thus, the majority of results are subject to the same difficulties we noted for this research tradition in Chapter V. Most of the studies were field investigations. However, five presage-process experiments are included (Bondi, 1969; Furst, 1967b; Hough and Ober, 1967; Lohman *et al.*, 1967; Traill, 1971). These latter were all concerned with contrasting "standard" teacher training with an "experimental" curriculum that stressed either instruction in the use of FIAC or the advantages of teaching in an "indirect" manner.

Teacher talk Teacher talk is reported to comprise not less than half of all time spent in normal classroom interaction. If this is not exactly what was specified in Flanders' "law of two-thirds," it is still a substantial portion of time and means that individual pupils will speak, on the average, less than 1/30 as often as the teacher. Moreover, according to the

---

[1] This list is presented with some diffidence. Individual studies have concerned themselves with various other concepts that are related to directiveness (for example, see Furst, 1967b). On the other hand, Rosenshine (1971) found sufficient data to provide summaries only for *teacher talk, pupil talk,* and *teacher questions*—and experienced difficulty with even the last concept due to variation in the ways it was measured in various studies.

BOX 6.1   Findings Pertaining to Directiveness

FINDINGS FOR TEACHER TALK

Process Occurrence

6.1-1   *Teacher talk* comprises one half to two thirds of all classroom interaction time (F&A67), (Fu67b), (D&L70).

Context-Process Relationships

None reported.

Presage-Process Relationships

6.1-2   *Greater practice teaching experience* is associated with *less teacher talk* (Kir67).

6.1-3   *Teachers rated "superior"* exhibit *less teacher talk* than do those not so rated (A&G67).

6.1-4   *Experimental treatment* does not produce change in *amount of teacher talk* (Fu67b)E.* *In contradiction*, it is also found that

      6.1-4a   *Experimental treatment* decreases the *amount of teacher talk* (Kir67)E.

Process-Process Relationships

None reported.

Process-Product Relationships

6.1-5   *Amount of teacher talk* is unrelated to *pupil achievement* (Flan3), (Flan4), (Flan5), (Flan6), (Flan7), (Sha66), (W&N70).

6.1-6   *Amount of teacher talk* is unrelated to *pupil attitudes* (Flan4), (Flan5), (Flan6), (Flan7). *In contradiction*, it is also found that

      6.1-6a   *Greater teacher talk* is associated with *more positive pupil attitudes* (Flan3); and also

      6.1-6b   *Greater teacher talk* is associated with *less positive pupil attitudes* (Flan2).

FINDINGS FOR TEACHER QUESTIONS

Process Occurrence

6.1-7   *Teacher questions* represent a tenth to a sixth of all classroom interaction time (D&L70), (F&A67), (Fu67b).

Context-Process Relationships

6.1-8   *Higher grade level* is associated with *less teachers' use of questions* (F&A67).

6.1-9   *Sex of pupil* is unrelated to *teachers' use of questions* (B&G70). *In contradiction*, it is also found that

      6.1-9a   *Boys* receive *more teachers' questions* than girls (Fel70).

Presage-Process Relationships

6.1-10   *Teachers' expectations for pupil achievement* are unrelated to *teachers' use of questions* (B&G70).

6.1-11   *Experimental treatment* is unrelated to *teachers' use of questions* (H&O67)E, (L&a67)E. *In contradiction*, it is also found that

      6.1-11a   *Experimental treatment* increases *teachers' use of questions* (Bon69)E, (Fu67b)E.

---

* Findings generated experimentally are indicated with an E. For description of experimental treatments see Box 5.2.

Process-Process Relationships

None reported.

Process-Product Relationships

6.1-12 *Teachers' use of questions* is unrelated to *pupil achievement* (Flan3), (Flan4), (Flan5), (Flan6), (Flan7), (Wal66). *In contradiction*, it is also found that

    6.1-12a *Higher teachers' use of questions* is associated with *greater pupil achievement* (Wal66).

6.1-13 *Teachers' use of questions* is unrelated to *pupil attitudes* (Flan3), (Flan4), (Flan5), (Flan6), (Flan7). *In contradiction*, it is also found that

    6.1-13a *Higher teachers' use of questions* is associated with *more positive pupil attitudes* (Flan2).

FINDINGS FOR TEACHER LECTURING

Process Occurrence

6.1-14 *Teachers' use of lecturing* comprises a sixth to a fourth of all classroom interaction time (D&L70), (F&A67), (Fu67b).

Context-Process Relationships

6.1-15 *Higher grade levels* are associated with *greater teachers' use of lecturing* (F&A67).

Presage-Process Relationships

6.1-16 *Longer practice teaching experience* is associated with *greater teachers' use of lecturing* (Kir67).

6.1-17 *Teachers rated "superior"* have *shorter lecturing segments* than those not so rated (A&G67).

6.1-18 *Higher teachers' humanistic attitudes to pupils* are associated with *lesser teachers' use of lecturing* (Gol71).

6.1-19 *Experimental treatment* is unrelated to *teachers' use of lecturing* (Car70)E, (Fu67b)E, (H&O67)E. *In contradiction*, it is also found that

    6.1-19a *Experimental treatment* decreases *teachers' use of lecturing* (Bon69)E, (L&a67)E, (Tra71)E.

Process-Process Relationships

None reported.

Process-Product Relationships

6.1-20 *Higher teachers' use of lecturing* is associated with *greater pupil achievement* (Soa66).

FINDINGS FOR TEACHERS' USE OF DIRECTIONS

Process Occurrence

6.1-21 *Teachers' use of directions* occupies 10 percent or less of all classroom interaction time (D&L70), (Fu67b), (Tis70).

Context-Process Relationships

6.1-22 *Higher grade levels* are associated with *lesser teachers' use of directions* (F&A67).

Presage-Process Relationships

6.1-23 *Teachers rated "superior"* exhibit *less teachers' use of directions* than those not so rated (A&G67), (Pan67).

6.1-24 *Experimental treatment* is unrelated to *teachers' use of directions* (Fu67b)E. *In contradiction*, it is also found that

    6.1-24a *Experimental treatment* reduces *teachers' use of directions* (Bon69)E, (H&O67)E, (L&a67)E, (Tra71)E.

(Box 6.1, continued)

Process-Process Relationships
   None reported.
Process-Product Relationships
   None reported.

FINDINGS FOR PUPIL TALK

Process Occurrence

   6.1-25 *Pupil talk* occupies a fifth to a third of all classroom interaction time
      (D&L70), (F&A67), (Fu67b).

Context-Process Relationships

   6.1-26 *Higher grade levels* are associated with *less pupil talk* (F&A67).

Presage-Process Relationships

   6.1-27 *Longer practice teaching experience* of teachers is associated with *greater
      pupil talk* (Kir67).
   6.1-28 *Teachers rated "superior"* have *more pupil talk* than those not so rated
      (A&G67).
   6.1-29 *Teachers' humanistic and custodial attitudes to pupils* are unrelated to
      amount of pupil talk (Gol71).
   6.1-30 *Experimental treatment given to teachers* is associated with *greater
      pupil talk* (Fu67b)E, (Kir67)E.

Process-Process Relationships

   See Boxes 5.2, 5.3, 5.4, and 5.5.

Process-Product Relationships

   6.1-31 *Amount of pupil talk* is unrelated to *pupil achievement* (F&a66), (Fu67a),
      (Sha66), (Soa66), (W&N70).

FINDINGS FOR PUPIL RESPONSES TO TEACHERS' INITIATIONS

Process Occurrence

   6.1-32 *Pupil responses* constitute about 20 percent of all classroom interaction
      time (D&L70), (Fu67b).

Context-Process Relationships
   None reported.

Presage-Process Relationships

   6.1-33 *Teachers rated "superior"* exhibit *more pupil responses* than those not so
      rated (Pan67).
   6.1-34 *Teachers' humanistic and custodial attitudes to pupils* are unrelated to
      amount of pupil responses (Gol71).
   6.1-35 *Experimental treatment given to teachers* is unrelated to *amount of pupil
      responses* (Fu67b)E, (L&a67)E. *In contradiction,* it is also found that
      6.1-35a *Experimental treatment given to teachers* reduces the *amount
         of pupil responses* (Bon69), (H&O67)E, (Tra71)E.

Process-Process Relationships

   See Boxes 5.2, 5.3, 5.4, and 5.5.

Process-Product Relationships

   6.1-36 *Pupil responding* (as compared with nonresponding) is unrelated to
      pupil achievement (HuD73)E.

FINDINGS FOR PUPIL INITIATION

Process Occurrence

6.1-37 *Pupil initiation* comprises less than ten percent of all classroom interaction time (D&L70), (Fu67b).

Context-Process Relationships

6.1-38 *Higher pupil achievement* is associated with *greater amounts of pupil initiation* (G&a73).

6.1-39 *Girls* exhibit *more pupil initiation* than boys (G&a73).

Presage-Process Relationships

6.1-40 *Teachers rated "superior"* exhibit *no more pupil initiation* than those not so rated (Pan67). *In contradiction*, it is also found that
  6.1-40a *Teachers rated "superior"* exhibit *more pupil initiation* than those not so rated (A&G67).

6.1-41 *Higher teachers' humanistic attitudes to pupils* are associated with *greater amounts of pupil initiation* (Gol71).

6.1-42 *Higher teachers' expectations for pupil achievement* are associated with *greater amounts of pupil initiation* (B&G70).

6.1-43 *Experimental treatment given to teachers* is unrelated to the *amount of pupil initiation* (Fu67b)E. *In contradiction*, it is also found that
  6.1-43a *Experimental treatment given to teachers* increases the *amount of pupil initiation* (Bon69)E, (L&a67)E, (Tra71)E.

Process-Process Relationships

See Boxes 5.2, 5.3, 5.4, and 5.5.

Process-Product Relationships

None reported.

FINDINGS FOR SILENCE AND CONFUSION

Process Occurrence

6.1-44 *Silence and confusion* comprise a sixth to a quarter of all classroom interaction time (F&A67), (Fu67b).

Context-Process Relationships

6.1-45 *Grade level* affects the *amount of silence and confusion*. Between grades I and VI, silence and confusion increase with increasing grade level (F&A67).

Presage-Process Relationships

6.1-46 *Teachers rated "superior"* are associated with *less silence and confusion* than those not so rated (A&G67), (Pan 67).

6.1-47 *Experimental training* does not affect the *amount of silence and confusion* (H&O67)E, (L&a67)E. *In contradiction*, it is also reported that
  6.1-47a *Experimental training* reduces the *amount of silence and confusion* (Fu67b)E.

Process-Process Relationships

None reported.

Process-Product Relationships

None reported.

Commitment, such a state of affairs is surely bad and should be corrected What additional evidence can we find to back up the *Commitment?*

Findings within the presage-process category look promising. We are told that student teachers *decrease* the amount of their talking as they gain experience, that teachers who are rated "superior" by others will exhibit less teacher talk than average teachers, and that experimenta training can reduce the amount of teacher talk. So far so good. But we also need to know that reducing teacher talk leads to desired classroom products And here we run into strife. In terms of findings reported, amount of teacher talk is unrelated to pupil achievement. If this were not enough different studies report that amount of teacher talk is *positively, negatively* and *un*related to pupil attitudes! Surprisingly, some researchers remain convinced of the usefulness of reducing teacher talk, despite—or perhap in misunderstanding of—the cited evidence (see Amidon and Giammatteo 1967, for example). However, we suspect (with Rosenshine, 1971) tha teacher talk is simply a weak variable, and those interested in improving the effectiveness of teaching would be better advised to improve the quality (rather than reduce the quantity) of teacher speech.

Teacher questions Teacher questions constitute but one aspect of teacher talk, and it should come as no surprise to discover that they comprise only a sixth or less of total classroom interaction time. Grade leve and pupil sex also appear to affect teacher questions, with fewer questions appearing in the upper grades and being directed to girls. Few presage process findings are reported for this variable, possibly because those sharing the *Commitment* are less certain whether teacher questions are a good or bad thing. Of the four experimental studies two report a significan effect; experimentally trained teachers ask more questions than those no so trained. In contrast, we find that several studies have investigated the relationships between teacher questions and the product variables of pupil achievement and pupil attitudes. Since the great majority of these studies found no significant relationships, we conclude that this too is a weak variable. It may not be the fact of asking questions that is important but rather that the content and format of questions and the occasions upor which they are asked determine their significance.

Teacher lecturing Few findings are reported for teacher lecturing and only one of the process-product variety. We learn that lecturing constitutes another one sixth to one fourth of classroom interaction time and that grade level affects the amount of lecturing. Further, the greater the experience of the student teacher, the more time she spends in lecturing (Recall that her time spent in teacher talk and teacher questioning are both declining.) Teachers with humanistic attitudes toward pupils spend less time lecturing, teachers rated "superior" have shorter lecturing segments, and it is possible, although by no means certain, that we can decrease the amount of time spent in lecturing by means of experimental training. Given the *Commitment,* which suggests that lecturing is a "No-No," it is surprisng that so few process-product findings have yet been reported for this concept. The one we have found indicates that lecturing is associated with greater pupil achievement rather than the opposite.

Teachers' use of directions   Only five findings are reported for teacher giving directions, one of which is contradicted. We learn that teachers give fewer directions at the upper-grade levels. In addition, teachers rated "superior" give fewer directions, and specified experimental programs have the effect of reducing teacher direction-giving behavior. However, there no evidence of the process-process or process-product types dealing with the effects of directions upon pupils. We presume that most behaviors coded in this category are concerned with management, so that when a teacher scores high here she is less likely to be communicating substantive content. We return to this issue in Chapter VII.

Pupil talk   Pupil talk comprises a fifth to a third of all classroom interaction time. It also appears that pupil talk declines as we go up the grade-level ladder, that student teachers will allow more pupil talk when they have had more experience, that teachers who are rated "superior" have more pupil talk in their classrooms, and that experimental training of teachers increases the amount of pupil talk. Process-process findings involving pupil talk were reported in Chapter V and will not be repeated here. Unfortunately for the *Commitment*, pupil talk turns out to be unrelated to pupil achievement. Once again, we suspect that the sheer volume of pupil talk is an unpromising variable for further research. Rather, we should turn to analysis of the forms, content, or occasions for pupil utterances for insights into teaching effectiveness. Pupils, just as teachers, can utter drivel, and when they do so they are not likely to aid themselves or others in the classroom.

Pupil responses to teacher initiations   Pupil responses, as distinct from pupil initiations, are found to account for approximately 20 percent of classroom interaction time. They have been found to occur more in the classrooms of "superior" teachers and yet to be reduced when teachers are exposed to experimental training with FIAC. Again, process-process findings involving pupil responses were discussed in the previous chapter and will not be repeated here. By far the most significant finding was experimentally derived by Hughes (1973), who found that pupils from whom responses were experimentally elicited achieved no better than pupils who were excluded from responding. By inference, therefore, attempts to increase pupil involvement by increasing the mere quantity of pupil responses are unlikely to raise pupil achievement.

Pupil initiation   Normally this category of pupil talk occurs in less than ten percent of classroom interaction time, and part of the *Commitment* is that this should be increased. "Superior" teachers have—and have not—been found to have a higher occurrence of pupil initiation, as have teachers with humanistic attitudes toward pupils and teachers with higher expectations for pupil achievement. Experimental teacher training with FIAC

appears to lead to increased pupil initiation. Process-process findings f(
pupil initiation were reported in Chapter V. Whereas it was earlier reporte
that boys receive more teachers' questions than girls, it appears that gir
respond to that situation by initiating more often than boys. Higher-achie
ing pupils are found to engage in initiation more than others, but there
no evidence that their higher achievement is caused by their more frequel
initiation. Indeed, the absence of process-product findings for this variab
of pupil talk suggests that its increase has been accepted as desirab
without question or as an end in itself.

Silence and confusion If one assumes that orderly, uninterrupted tal
is the best vehicle of learning for pupils, then silence and confusion mu
be bad things in the classroom. However, some questions can be answere
best when adequate time to think is available, thus it may actually be
good thing when silence appears. Not surprisingly, we learn that silenc
and confusion comprise a sixth to a quarter of classroom interaction tim
and that they increase in frequency as the grade level goes up. Howeve
investigators are *Committed* to reducing silence and confusion, thus w
learn that the classrooms of teachers rated "superior" exhibit less of thes
and that experimental training sometimes reduces their amount. Unfort
nately, no process-product relationships are reported for this variable, an
nearly all studies elide the processes of silence and confusion, which w
suspect are quite distinct in their genesis and effects. We suggest that th
too is a weak variable for future research.

Let us now summarize what we know about *directiveness*. First, d
rectiveness also reflects the *Commitment* of progressive education. Secon(
directiveness is not as conceptually confused as "indirectness." It does n(
appear to comprise a single variable, however, but to be reflected in
number of different classroom processes. Third, directiveness variables ar
usually measured by summed categorical scores from instruments that ar
designed for live-observation use. Fourth, these instruments are reporte
to be reliable. Fifth, findings for aspects of directiveness are likely to b
denied or reversed in other studies. Sixth, teachers are likely to talk mor
than half the time and pupils a third of the time in the typical classroom
Seventh, some of the directiveness variables reviewed above can be affecte
by experimental programs of teacher training. Eighth, these variables als
appear to be weak in terms of affecting pupil achievement or attitudes.

Once again, the findings from the classroom-climate tradition are no
impressive. One does not have to look far for an explanation of why thes
findings should be so weak. As we have noted, the instruments used in mos
of these studies represent an *ad hoc* collection of categories that are nc
really logical alternatives. In addition, the concepts we have so far used fo
discussing *directiveness* do not really get at the root of the managemen
problem. To control someone is to maneuver him in such a way that he i
doing what you want him to do, and then you can turn to something else
Thus, management must be an *inter*active phenomenon, and we are unlikel

to discover much about it without looking at the relationships between teacher strategies and pupil responses. FIAC and its progeny are poor tools for such a purpose. Let us now consider studies representing stronger concepts and methods.

DISCIPLINE AND GROUP MANAGEMENT

The next research effort we shall consider is a strikingly original program that has been conducted by Kounin and his associates at Wayne State University during the past 15 years. This program began with research on the problem of classroom discipline. Surely a common problem in many classrooms is the occurrence of pupil deviancy. Pupils are forever speaking out of turn, whispering, not paying attention to the lesson, and occasionally making rude remarks or challenging the teacher. What does the teacher do when these episodes of deviancy occur, and how are her actions related to the subsequent behavior of both those pupils who are deviant and others? Moreover, to what extent can the teacher's managerial success be assigned to her ability to manage deviancy?

These are reasonable questions, and much of Kounin's early research consisted of studies that were attempts to answer them. Some of these studies lie beyond our purview, since they were conductd in university classrooms or summer camps or consisted of experiments in which no classroom observation took place. However, one early study of disciplinary events in kindergarten classrooms (Kounin and Gump, 1958) definitely belongs to our review and is cited here as much for its intriguing concepts as for its findings.

Programmatic research demands a common theme, and for most researchers this means *Commitment* to a limited set of questions, concepts, or methods of investigation. Rare it is to find investigators who will conclude that they have been on the wrong track completely. And yet the more Kounin pursued the question of classroom discipline, the more dissatisfied he became with the answers he was finding in his data. Incidents of pupil deviancy were rare at the upper-grade levels, management of discipline seemed to be ritualized for most teachers, and success in teaching seemed to involve more managerial issues than simply the control of discipline. Kounin's dissatisfactions came to a head in a second study (Kounin *et al.*, 1966) in which five different qualities of teacher-control strategies were found codable. However, *none* of these predicted success even in the immediate episode of deviancy, let alone general levels of pupil involvement and deviancy. As a result of these findings, Kounin concluded that he had been studying the wrong question completely!

Rather than abandon the effort Kounin returned to actual classrooms and to the intensive reanalysis of his videotape data. Over some months he was able to develop a number of concepts relating to larger issues in group management. Most of these are strikingly original, and they figure in significant relationships. As we shall see, Kounin was able to demonstrate relationships between these concepts and pupil-behavior measures, not only in his original videotape data but also in a new and larger sample of classroom videotapes (Kounin, 1970). Moreover, the strength of relationships reported by Kounin is stronger than for most other research programs reviewed. Despite the fact that Kounin's research has not yet been validated with investigations of presage-process and process-product relationships, it would appear that he has many insights to offer us on the problems of management.

Concepts of Teaching Behavior

Discipline Let us turn first to Kounin's early research on the management of deviancy. As can be appreciated, not all occurrences of pupil deviancy are responded to by the teacher. Some deviant acts are engaged in behind the teacher's back, and some the teacher chooses to ignore. However, there comes a time in the life of the teacher when she can no longer ignore the deviant, and a *desist incident* occurs. In Kounin's usage the desist incident begins with an identifiable action on the part of the teacher that is stimulated by pupil deviancy. It may be as simple as a glance or gesture, or the teacher may speak the pupil's name ("John!"), or the deviancy may be spoken of and an alternative behavior suggested. The incident continues as long as the teacher continues to focus on the deviant and his actions, which may be as short as an instant of time or may last for several minutes of challenge and response. Then the classroom returns to its normal pursuits, such as the lesson at hand.

Although the term *desist incident* may be new to us, we recognize the concept to which it refers as a familiar one. Desist incidents are phenomenal units that occur sporadically during the classroom lesson. Kounin reports that observers can spot such incidents with high reliability and has developed a number of different scales or dimensions along which desist incidents can be reliably rated. Let us consider six of these: clarity, firmness, roughness, child treatment, intensity, and focus.

Desist *clarity* "refers to how much information the teacher provided in her desist. A simple 'stop that,' no matter how emphatically uttered, has little clarity. Nothing is specified about who the deviant is, what he did that was wrong, what he should do to correct it, or why he shouldn't do it. Clarity is added by specifying the deviant and/or the deviancy" (Kounin, 1970, pp. 8-9).

Desist *firmness* "refers to the degree to which the teacher packs an 'I-mean-it' and a 'right now!' quality into the desist. If a teacher is explaining traffic lights to a group, casually says 'stop it' to a misbehaving child, and immediately resumes explaining the traffic lights, the desist possesses little firmness. Firmness is added if she has a 'follow-through' and looks at the deviant until he stops; if she walks toward the child during the desist; if she speaks emphatically; if she touches or 'guides' the child to the proper behavior; and the like" (p. 9).

Desist *roughness* "refers to desists in which the teacher expresses anger or exasperation. These consist of desists containing angry looks or remarks, threatened or actual punishments, or physical pressure beyond firmness" (p. 9).

Clarity, firmness, and roughness were originally developed as independent facets for coding desist incidents in Kounin and Gump's (1958) kindergarten study. Clarity and firmness were also coded in Kounin's first videotape study (Kounin *et al.*, 1966). However, in the latter work roughness was no longer found to be codable but was rather replaced by three different facets that were also considered to be independent of clarity and firmness.

Desist *child treatment* refers to "how the child was treated in the desist. Does the child see the teacher as being for or against him in this incident?" (Kounin, 1970, p. 68). Coding alternatives ranged from pro-child (if the teacher was seen as protecting the child, or complimenting, rewarding, or praising him), through neutral, to anti-child (if the teacher expressed anger, sarcasm, or threats and the like).

Desist *intensity* "refers to the intensity of the stimulus quality of the desist: its attention-demanding properties and its potential to intrude into the awareness of audience children" (p. 67). Coding alternatives ranged from low (if the desist signal did not contrast with the background activity), through medium, to high (if the desist was long in duration, or had high stimulus intensity, or contained affect-laden material).

Desist *focus* "refers to what the teacher concentrates upon in her desist order. By inference, if not by explicitly stated content, behavior orders have a *desist* or stop ('stop talking') content and an induction or *begin* ('work on your arithmetic') content. Which is the teacher focusing on? The deviancy part or the induction part? Or both?" (pp. 67–68).

Each of these six concepts is presumed to be an independent quality of teacher behavior and was found by Kounin to be reliably judgable for desist incidents. To the extent that teachers are actually in control of classroom events they may be considered *independent variables*. But what difference does it make if teachers do or do not exhibit them in the classroom? What happens when the teacher is clear, firm, rough, or intense in her desist incidents? Eventually we would hope to seek answers to these questions in pupil products, such as achievements or attitudes. But at least proximal answers can be sought in the *behavioral* responses of pupils to the desist incident. These constitute *dependent variables*, and Kounin has studied several that are directly related to the desist incident.

The simplest of these latter variables is *desist success*. This variable is concerned with the subsequent behavior of the *target* pupil and consists of a seven-point scale ranging from "immediate, quick, eager, and enthusiastic conformity" through "ordinary conformity and obedience" and "resistance shown" to "open defiance" (Kounin, 1970, p. 65). Surprisingly, this simple measure was not coded in the 1958 Kounin and Gump study. Instead, the first study concerned itself with the "ripple effect" of discipline—that is, with the effect of the teacher's choice of desist stategies upon *audience* pupils. In order to study this effect it is necessary to observe the behavior of one or more pupils who are *not* identified by the teacher as deviants before, during, and after the desist incident. Again, a single facet was developed for coding the behavior of audience pupils, although no "dimension" was presumed to underlie the coding categories. The categories used were:

> *no reaction*—the audience child shows no behavior which the coder can interpret as related to the desist incident—if the child was drawing he simply continued his drawing; *behavior disruption*—the child shows anxiety or apprehension, confusion, increased restlessness, decreased involvement in the legitimate ongoing activity; *increased conformance*—the child's behavior was more conforming than it was previous to the desist—he stopped misbehavior of his own, paid closer attention to the lesson, stood or sat even "straighter"; *increased nonconformance*—in this case the audience child engages in a misbehavior of his own following the desist event . . . ; *ambivalence*—this was coded when the child showed increased conformance in one act and increased nonconformance in another act following the desist. (Kounin, 1970, pp. 9–10)

Once again, Kounin reported high reliabilities for these judgments concerning the effects of desist incidents on both target and audience pupil behaviors.

Finally, one additional judgment was asked of coders in the early kindergarten study. Reasoning that the immediate, prior orientation of the audience pupils might have some influence over how they reacted to the desist incident, coders were asked to make a *contextual* judgment. Audience pupils were also judged for whether their immediate, prior behavior was *deviancy-free* (that is, they were engaged in legitimate work) or *deviancy-linked* (that is, they were engaged in misbehavior themselves or else were watching the deviancy) (see Kounin, 1970, p. 11).

Let us now summarize the concepts used by Kounin for studying discipline. All of them are concerned with the appearance of a phenomenal episode wherein the teacher attempts to control deviancy—the *desist incident*. Teacher behavior during the desist incident can be coded for a number of independent qualities, specifically *clarity, firmness, roughness, child treatment, intensity,* and *focus.* Pupil response to the desist incident can also be coded, and Kounin differentiates between response of the *target pupil* (coded as *desist success*) and that of the *audience pupils* (coded for *no reaction, behavior disruption, increased conformance, increased nonconformance,* and *ambivalence*). Finally, coders are also asked to judge whether audience pupils are or are not themselves *deviancy-linked* at the time of the desist incident. As we shall see, these concepts were used both in Kounin's early kindergarten study (Kounin and Gump, 1958) and in the first of his two videotape studies (Kounin *et al.*, 1966).

Group management As we know, Kounin himself has concluded that teacher success in the control of discipline is not overly important in the overall picture of classroom management, and shortly we shall review the evidence that led him to this conclusion. But surely teachers differ from one another in their managerial strategies. How can we discriminate these differences, and what effects do they have on the behaviors of pupils? To answer these questions Kounin developed a series of concepts and coding systems. As we shall see, these latter were based on a number of different phenomenal units for expressing classroom events and would presumably require recordings or transcriptions for their implementation in actual classroom research. Each concept is simple in orientation, however, and has immediate appeal for the teacher.

Let us begin with the *desist-incident* unit. It seems difficult to believe that such episodes are totally without impact on the success of classroom management. Surely the really inept teacher may spend a sizable proportion of the lesson controlling deviancy rather than in instruction, and this by itself would constitute managerial failure. What, then, are the facets of desist incidents that make for success?

Two such facets are defined by Kounin. The first of these is termed *withitness* (believe it or not). A teacher who is "with it" is one who communicates to pupils, by her behavior, that she knows what is going on or has "eyes in the back of her head." Teachers who are "with it" will pick up the first signal of deviancy, will clamp on the proper pupil, will ignore a minor misbehavior in order to stop a major infraction, and so forth. In operational terms, teachers who made few mistakes in their desist incidents were given a high score for withitness. Two kinds were judged by the researchers.

Target mistakes consisted of: 1. The teacher desisted the wrong child for a deviant act, or desisted an onlooker or contagee rather than an initiator. 2. The teacher desisted a less serious deviancy and overlooked a more serious deviancy . . . *Timing mistakes*, or being too late, consisted of: 1. The deviancy *spread* before it was desisted . . . 2. The deviancy *increased in seriousness* before it was desisted. . . . (Kounin, 1970, p. 82)

In contrast with earlier judgments made about desist incidents, withitness is not conceived as a characteristic of each incident. Rather, a single score is constructed indicating the withitness of the teacher during the lesson or classroom day. This score is simply the proportion of desist incidents wherein no mistakes was made—the greater the score, the more "with it" the teacher.

The second facet judged for desist incidents is termed *overlapping-ness* by Kounin. Overlappingness "refers to what the teacher does when she has two matters to deal with at the same time. Does she somehow attend to both issues simultaneously or does she remain or become immersed in one issue only . . ." (p. 85). This quality is judged on an either-or basis. The judgment of *some overlapping* was justified if the teacher evidenced attending to both issues during the event. "As an example: The teacher was listening to Mary read in the reading group, then looked at two boys in the arithmetic seatwork group who were making paper airplanes. *She turned back to Mary, saying: 'Keep on reading.'* Then she got up, walked toward the two boys . . ." (p. 87). The judgment of *no overlapping* was given if the teacher manifested no attention to other ongoing events while dealing with a problem of deviancy.

Overlappingness can be judged for other kinds of units than desist incidents, of course. (Like Shell Oil, the teacher can do more than one thing at once.) In Kounin's research overlappingness is also judged for *child-intrusion incidents.* This second type of phenomenal unit occurs when an individual pupil approaches the teacher during an ongoing activity. For example, a child from the seatwork setting might approach the teacher with a paper in hand to show her while the teacher is working with a reading group. Such incidents also provide potential for judging overlappingness. If the teacher ignores the child, or alternately the reading group while paying attention to the child, *no overlapping* was coded. If the teacher manifested some attention to both stimuli, *some overlapping* was the judgment. As with withitness, a total score for overlappingness was calculated for the entire observation by calculating the proportion of both kinds of incidents in which *some overlapping* was judged.

Kounin's next two concepts were concerned with the problems of lesson flow and time management. The first, *smoothness*, concerns the absence of behaviors initiated by teachers that interfere with the ongoing flow of academic events. A number of such behaviors were noted on a sign basis as they occurred. These included *stimulus-boundedness* (coded when the teacher paid attention to irrelevant or intrusive details rather than the subject at hand); *thrusts* (coded when the teacher burst in on children's activities with an order, statement, or question); *dangles* (coded when the teacher started, or was in, some activity and then left it "hanging in mid-air" only to be resumed after an interval); *truncations* (coded when an activity was left "hanging in mid-air" and was not resumed); and *flip-flops* (coded when the teacher terminated one activity, started another, and then initiated a return to the activity that she had terminated). Teachers were judged to be high on *smoothness* if they had few of such interfering behaviors. In order to make this judgment a score was constructed by noting the number of six-second intervals during the observation period in which one or more of such behaviors occurred, dividing it by the total number of intervals, and subtracting the proportion thus obtained from one.

The second concept concerning lesson flow was termed *momentum*. In general, momentum concerns the absence of teacher behaviors that slow down the pace of the lesson. Two types of "slow-down" behaviors were conceptualized by Kounin: *overdwelling* (coded whenever the teacher overdwelt on pupil behavior, a subpoint rather than the main point, physical props rather than substance, or instructions or details to the point of boredom); and *fragmentation* (coded when teachers dealt with individual pupils one at a time rather than the group, or props one at a time rather than en masse). Nagging is an example of overdwelling, as is endless repetition and elaboration of instructions. The teacher who tells pupils to "Put your pencils away . . . Now put your erasers away . . . Now your workbooks . . . Now hand your papers to me . . ." is engaging in fragmentation. Once again, *momentum* is judged as the absence of such "slow-down" features, and a score for momentum is calculated by noting the number of six-second intervals during the observation period within which one or more such behaviors occurred, dividing it by the total number of intervals, and subtracting the proportion thus obtained from one.

Two additional concepts were set forth to capture the way in which the teacher approached classroom groups. The first, *group alerting*, "refers to the degree to which a teacher attempts to involve nonreciting children in the recitation task, maintain their attention, and keep them 'on their toes' or alerted" (Kounin, 1970, p. 117). This concept was also operationalized by noting signs or "group alerting cues." Among "positive" signs suggested by Kounin were:

1. Any method used to create "suspense" before calling on a child to recite . . . 2. Keeping children in suspense in regard to who will be called on next . . . 3. Teacher calls on different children frequently or . . . asks group for show of hands before selecting a reciter. 4. Teacher alerts nonperformers that they might be called on in connection with what a reciter is doing . . . 5. Teacher presents new, novel, or alluring material in a recitation . . . (pp. 117–118)

"Negative cues" suggested included:

1. The teacher changes the focus of her attention away from the group . . . 2. The teacher prepicks a reciter or performer before the question is even stated. 3. The teacher has reciters perform in a predetermined sequence of turns . . . (p. 118)

A complex system of scoring teachers for *group alerting* was used (based on 30-second intervals), but in general the higher the score, the more positive cues and the fewer negative cues the teacher exhibited during the period of observation.

The second group-management concept, *accountability*, "refers to the degree to which the teacher holds the children accountable and responsible for their task performances during recitation sessions" (p. 119). Once again, a series of signs classified as "accountability cues" were looked for. These included:

> 1. Teacher asks children to hold up their props exposing performances or answers in such a manner as to be readily visible to the teacher. 2. Teacher requires children to recite in unison while the teacher shows signs of actively attending to the recitation. 3. Teacher brings other children into the performance of a child reciting . . . 4. Teacher asks for the raised hands of children who are prepared to demonstrate a performance and requires some of them to demonstrate. 5. Teacher circulates and checks products of nonreciters during a child performance. 6. Teacher requires a child to demonstrate and checks his performance. (pp. 119–120)

As with group alerting, *accountability* was scored in 30-second intervals, but in general those teachers high in this variable exhibited a larger number of "accountability cues" during the observation period.

Finally, two additional concepts were suggested that reflected the teacher's attempts to maintain interest and avoid satiation. The first, *valence and challenge arousal*, concerned direct attempts by the teacher to get the pupils more enthusiastic, involved, or curious about academic affairs. It was coded only at transition points between activities. Those transitions wherein the teacher added something by "(1) showing genuine zest and enthusiasm; (2) making a statement pointing out that the activity possesses special positive valence . . . ; or (3) making a statement pointing out that the activity possesses some special intellectual challenge" (p. 130) were noted. A *valence and challenge arousal* score was then computed by calculating the proportion of transitions that contained one or more such cues. (In contrast with all other concepts for group management, Kounin reports only low observational reliability for valence and challenge arousal.)

The last managerial concept, *variety*, concerned the degree to which activities in the lesson were truly different from one another. In order to code this variable the lesson had to be divided into phenomenal units, *activities* (about which we will have more to say in the next chapter), which could be coded for various features. Altogether, eight different features were coded for each activity: *content, covert behavior mode, teacher's lesson presentation pattern, props, group configuration, child responsibility, overt behavior mode,* and *location*. Separate coding systems were developed for each feature, each system constituting a separate facet. In general, *variety* was scored by noting how many of these activity features changed as one went from each activity to the next during the observational period. A teacher could receive a high score for variety in two ways, by having a lot of slightly different activities or by having a few vastly different activities.

As noted, each of these eight variables that represent some aspect of teacher managerial style was designed to provide a total score for a lesson or classroom day. How, then, are we to tell whether the teachers so scored are or are not successful in managing their classrooms? Once again, an "ideal" answer to this question would involve product measures. However, Kounin provides us with some interesting, albeit proximal, answers by providing two scores for pupil behavior. The first, *work involvement*, involved coding the behaviors of individual pupils every 12 seconds throughout the observation period. A three-category facet was used for this purpose. Pupils were either: "1. *Definitely in* the assigned work . . . 2. *Probably in* the assigned work . . . or 3. *Definitely out* of the assigned work" (Kounin, 1970, pp. 77–78). A total score was computed for each pupil by forming a ratio of those intervals coded as "definitely in" to those coded as "definitely out"; thus a high score indicated observable work involvement.

The second pupil measure, *deviancy*, was also originally coded in terms of a three-facet category with judgments called for each 12 seconds: (1) *not misbehaving,* (2) engaging in *mild misbehavior,* or (3) engaging in *serious misbehavior.* However, few occasions of serious misbehavior were found, and the eventual *deviancy* score computed for pupils was the proportion of 12-second intervals during which any misbehavior occurred.

Kounin presumed that these two measures of pupil behavior, *work involvement* and *deviancy,* are dependent variables. However, their status is less secure than those Kounin used in his research on discipline. In the earlier research scores were calculated for pupil behavior *after each desist incident,* thus there was at least a temporal relationship between teacher behaviors and pupil responses. In the group-management research both teacher and pupil behaviors were eventually scored on a whole-lesson basis, thus the causative effect of teacher behavior upon pupil behavior can only be plausibly argued.

One contextual variable was also used in Kounin's group-management research. In general, Kounin categorized all activities as being either *recitations* or *seatwork,* although the relationships between these judgments and those involved in the code for *variety* are not made clear. As we shall see, scores for pupil *involvement* and *deviancy* are somewhat different in these two contexts, and the pattern of relationships between teacher managerial styles and pupil behaviors is clearly distinct. In addition, Kounin's first videotape study provided two additional contextual variables: *grade level* and *emotional disturbance of pupils.* In fact, one of the major aims of this study was to see whether teachers should treat pupils differently when they were known to be emotionally disturbed. As we shall see, the evidence suggests that advisable teacher behavior is the same for both "disturbed" and "normal" pupils.

In summary, eight different variables are suggested by Kounin for differentiating the group-managerial behaviors of teachers: *withitness, overlappingness, smoothness, momentum, group alerting, accountability, valence and challenge arousal,* and *variety.* These were measured in various ways in Kounin's research, but each teacher was given a single score representing her effectiveness on that variable throughout the observation period. Two "dependent variable" scores were calculated for pupil behaviors: work *involvement* and *deviancy.* Each of the latter also generated a single score representing the observation period, although separate scores were generated for each pupil observed. Activities were also judged for whether they were *recitations* or *seatwork,* and for one study two additional contextual variables were also available, *grade level* and *emotional disturbance of pupils.*

Classroom Research

As has been noted, Kounin and his associates have reported three studies that involved the observation of classrooms. Details and findings of these studies may be found in Box 6.2. As will be seen, the early study by Kounin and Gump was conducted during the first four days of the kindergarten school year and involved data collected by specimen records. This study was confined to investigations of the "ripple effect," thus to discipline concepts and to the effect of teacher desist incidents on audience pupils.

BOX 6.2   Findings for Discipline and Group Management

STUDIES REVIEWED

Kounin and Gump (1958)	(K&G58)
Kounin *et al.* (1966)	(K&a66)
Kounin (1970)	(Kou70)

INSTRUMENT, METHOD OF GATHERING DATA, CODING SYSTEM, UNIT STUDIED, RELIABILITY

Kounin Discipline Concepts, specimen records, multifacet category systems, desist incidents, high reliability (K&G58).

Kounin Group-Management Concepts, videotape recordings and transcripts, multifacet category systems and sign systems, various phenomenal units and time units, high reliability (K&a66), (Kou70).

DESIGN OF STUDY, SUBJECTS, CONTEXTS

Field Surveys

(K&G58) 26 teachers and their pupils; kindergarten; the first four days of the school year.

(K&a66) 30 teachers and their pupils; grades I through VI; one-half day for each classroom.

(Kou70) 49 teachers and their pupils; grades I and II; one full day for each classroom.

FINDINGS

Process Occurrence

None reported.

Context-Process Relationships

6.2-1 *Grade level* affects *pupil work involvement* and *deviancy.* (Involvement increases at upper-grade levels, deviancy decreases) (K&a66).

6.2-2 *Activity format* affects *pupil work involvement* and *deviancy.* (Involvement is greater and deviancy lower in recitation than in seatwork) (K&a66).

6.2-3 *Emotionally disturbed pupils* exhibit *less work involvement* and *more deviancy* than other pupils (K&a66).

6.2-4 *Deviantly linked audience pupils* are more likely to *conform, nonconform,* and *react ambivalently* following a desist episode than are other audience pupils (K&G58).

Presage-Process Relationships

None reported.

Process-Process Relationships

6.2-5 *Teacher desist clarity* is
positively related to *subsequent conformity of audience pupils* (K&G58),[1]
unrelated to *desist success* (K&a66),
unrelated to *pupil work involvement* (K&a66),
unrelated to *pupil deviancy* (K&a66).

6.2-6 *Teacher desist firmness* is
positively related to *subsequent conformity of deviantly linked audience pupils* (K&G58),[1]
negatively related to *subsequent nonconformity of deviantly linked audience pupils* (K&G58),[1]
unrelated to *desist success* (K&a66),
unrelated to *pupil work involvement* (K&a66),
unrelated to *pupil deviancy* (K&a66).

6.2-7 *Teacher desist roughness* is
positively related to *disruption of subsequent audience pupil behavior* (K&G58).[1]

6.2-8 *Teacher desist child treatment* is unrelated to *desist success, pupil work involvement,* and *pupil deviancy* (K&a66).

6.2-9 *Teacher desist intensity* is unrelated to *desist success, pupil work involvement,* and *pupil deviancy* (K&a66).

6.2-10 *Teacher desist focus* is unrelated to *desist success, pupil work involvement,* and *pupil deviancy* (K&a66).

6.2-11 *Teacher desist withitness* is
positively related to *pupil work involvement in recitation* (Kou70),[2,3]
negatively related to *pupil deviancy in recitation* (Kou70),[2,3]
positively related to *pupil work involvement in seatwork* (K&a66), (Kou70),
negatively related to *pupil deviancy in seatwork* (K&a66), (Kou70).[2]

6.2-12 *Teacher desist overlappingness* is
positively related to *pupil work involvement in recitation* (Kou70),[3]
negatively related to *pupil deviancy in recitation* (Kou70),[3]
negatively related to *pupil deviancy in seatwork* (Kou70).[3]

6.2-13 *Teacher transition smoothness* is

(Box 6.2, continued)

---

positively related to *pupil work involvement in recitation* (K&a66), (Kou70),[2]
negatively related to *pupil deviancy in recitation* (K&a66), (Kou70),
positively related to *pupil work involvement in seatwork* (K&a66), (Kou70),
negatively related to *pupil deviancy in seatwork* (Kou70).[3]

6.2-14 *Teacher momentum* is
positively related to *pupil work involvement in recitation* (Kou70),[2]
negatively related to *pupil deviancy in recitation* (Kou70),[2]
negatively related to *pupil deviancy in seatwork* (Kou70).

6.2-15 *Teacher group alerting* is
positively related to *pupil work involvement in recitation* (Kou70),[2]
negatively related to *pupil deviancy in recitation* (Kou70),
negatively related to *pupil deviancy in seatwork* (Kou70).

6.2-16 *Teacher accountability* is
positively related to *pupil work involvement in recitation* (Kou70),
negatively related to *pupil deviancy in recitation* (Kou70).

6.2-17 *Teacher valence and challenge arousal* is
positively related to *pupil work involvement in recitation* (Kou70),
negatively related to *pupil deviancy in recitation* (Kou70),
positively related to *pupil work involvement in seatwork* (Kou70),
negatively related to *pupil deviancy in seatwork* (Kou70).

6.2-18 *Teacher seatwork variety and challenge* is
positively related to *pupil work involvement in seatwork* (K&a66),[4] (Kou70),[2]
negatively related to *pupil deviancy in seatwork* (K&a66),[4] (Kou70).

6.2-19 *Duration of activities* is unrelated to *pupil work involvement* or *deviancy* (K&a66), (Kou70).

Process-Product Relationships

None reported.

---

[1] These results held for the first day of the school year (in kindergarten), but faded on subsequent days—see text.
[2] These results were relatively stronger than others in (Kou70)—see text.
[3] These findings were not obtained in (K&a66)—see text.
[4] These results were found for grades I and II only in (K&a66) and tended to be reversed for grades III through IV—see text.

Both the second and third studies involved videotape recordings and transcripts. The 1966 study concerned a sample of 30 teachers, 15 of whom taught grades I and II and 15 who were from grades III through V. One half of a classroom day was videotaped for each teacher studied, but analysis was confined to interaction during classroom "lessons" only. As has been mentioned, one aim of the first videotape study was to find out whether managerial techniques would work equally for "disturbed" and "normal" pupils, thus classrooms chosen for study contained pupils who were identified in both categories. The 1966 study began with the coding of discipline concepts. After the failure of these concepts to generate relationships with pupil work involvement and deviancy, Kounin began the development of group-management concepts and investigated some of these with the small sample represented in the study. Data for four of the managerial concepts were reported: withitness, overlappingness, smoothness and variety.

Kounin's third study also involved videotapes and transcripts. However, a larger sample of teachers from grades I and II was used, and a full classroom day was videotaped for each ·teacher. In addition, findings were reported for all eight of the group-management concepts. In both videotape studies data for pupil work involvement and deviancy were calculated for several pupils per classroom, and efforts were made to sample pupils randomly within the physical confines of the classroom.

As shown in Box 6.2, Kounin's findings are confined to context-process and process-process relationships. Among the former we learn that pupil work involvement was greater, and deviancy less, in the upper grades and among "normal" rather than "emotionally disturbed" pupils. Surely these findings are requisite if we are to consider *work involvement* and *deviancy* to be valid indicators of managerial success. If classrooms were not better managed at the upper-grade levels and among nondisturbed pupils, teachers' efforts would be futile indeed! It is interesting to note, however, that work involvement is greater and deviancy lower in recitation than in seatwork. This finding will be interpreted along with others concerned with lesson format in Chapter VII. Finally, we also learn that pupils who are deviantly linked are more likely to react to desist incidents than those who are "innocent," although the pattern of their reactions is not all that consistent. (This finding, however, stems from the kindergarten study only.)

Substantive findings favoring discipline concepts all come from the kindergarten study. We learn that *desist clarity* induced greater conformity among audience pupils, that *desist firmness* induced greater conformity among deviantly linked audience pupils (only), and that *desist roughness* induced behavior disruption among audience pupils. (Unfortunately, no attempt to relate these concepts to desist success was reported in this early study.) While these findings are promising, there are flies in the ointment. The authors also reported that the effects obtained were strongest for the *first day* of kindergarten and were weaker on subsequent days. Moreover, they were unable to replicate these "ripple effect" findings in subsequent (albeit nonobservational) studies of upper-grade and high school pupils. Thus, we suspect that though the ripple effect is a valid notion, it accounts for very little of the variance of classroom events at other grade levels.

Other findings reported for the discipline concepts are unpromising, to say the least. Desist *clarity, firmness, child treatment, intensity,* and *focus* were simply unrelated to desist success, pupil work involvement, or pupil deviancy. Given these findings, it is not surprising that Kounin chose another tack to pursue, although more power to him for his honesty and subsequent ingenuity in solving the problem.

Findings for the group-management concepts are far more promising. *Each* of the eight concepts turned out to be related to pupil behaviors in at least two of the four criterion measures used. Altogether, thirteen findings are reported for the second videotape study for which equivalent findings might have been generated in the first. Of these thirteen, seven were replicated in the first study, none reversed, and six not confirmed (presumably because of poorer data). Moreover, many of the relationships reported are strong ones. Findings of correlations greater than ± .50 are not often found in the social sciences, and yet Kounin reports several correlations of this magnitude. For convenience these are noted in Box 6.2. In addition, readers might be interested in seeing Kounin's actual correlations, which are reproduced as Table 6.1.

Not all of Kounin's variables were equally effective in predicting

Table 6.1   Correlations between Teacher Style and Children's Behavior in Recitation and Seatwork Settings
$N = 49$ classrooms (r of .276 significant at $p < .05$)

	RECITATION		SEATWORK	
	Work Involvement	*Freedom from Deviancy*	*Work Involvement*	*Freedom from Deviancy*
Momentum (Freedom from slowdowns)	.656[1]	.641	.198	.490
Withitness	.615	.531	.307	.509
Smoothness (Freedom from thrusts, dangles, stimulus-boundedness)	.601	.489	.382	.421
Group alerting	.603	.442	.234	.290
Accountability	.494	.385	.002	−.035
Overlappingness	.460	.362	.259	.379
Valence and challenge arousal	.372	.325	.308	.371
Seatwork variety and challenge	.061	.033	.516	.276
Recitation variety and challenge	.238	.162		
Overall variety and challenge	.217	.099	.449	.194
Average duration of seatwork activities ("attention span")			.231	.005
Class size (range 21–39)	−.279	−.258	−.152	−.249
Boy-girl ratio	−.132	−.097	−.197	−.171
Maximum multiple *r*'s	.812	.720	.686	.741

Adapted from Kounin, 1970, p. 169.
[1] Significant coefficients are shown in italics.

work involvement and deviancy, of course. Moreover, the relationships found were somewhat different for the recitation and seatwork settings. For ease of interpretation the relationships found are recast slightly below.

	Findings for Recitation	Findings for Seatwork
Findings for Work Involvement	*Withitness* *Smoothness* *Momentum* *Group Alerting* Overlappingness Accountability Valence	*Variety* Withitness Smoothness Valence
Findings for Deviancy	*Withitness* *Momentum* Overlappingness Smoothness Group Alerting Accountability Valence	*Withitness* Overlappingness Smoothness Momentum Group Alerting Valence Variety

For convenience those variables generating strong relationships are given in italics. As can be seen, *withitness* was the strongest of the group-management variables, predicting strongly to three of the four criterion measures. *Momentum* was also a strong variable in the *recitation* setting. (It appeared to make less difference in seatwork.) *Smoothness* and *group alerting* also were strong for work involvement in the recitation setting, while *variety* predicted work involvement in seatwork. (In fact, it is worthwhile noting that variety bore no apparent relationship with either work involvement or deviancy in the recitation setting, while *accountability* proved equally useless in generating results for seatwork.) Of the four criterion measures Kounin's variables predicted *work involvement in the recitation setting* most effectively, *work involvement in the seatwork setting* least effectively. Plausible explanations can be advanced for many of these findings, and readers might feel challenged to construct a *theory of classroom management* to accommodate them. (For example, Kounin et al., 1966, speculated about the fact that withitness was a stronger predictor than overlappingness and suggested that pupils were able to perceive the teacher who was "with it" but not the teacher who was "overlapping.")

At the same time, the fact that findings are reported for so many of these variables should raise questions in our minds about the independence of these effects. Are not these eight managerial variables correlated with one another, and if so, are we not in fact reporting the same "finding" several times in Box 6.2? Indeed, the eight managerial variables *are* correlated, as we see in Table 6.2, although the correlations are not particularly great in the main. However, Kounin was concerned with the possibility that some of his effects were spurious and took statistical pains

Table 6.2   Intercorrelations among Teacher Style Measures

	MOMENTUM	WITHITNESS	SMOOTHNESS	GROUP ALERTING	ACCOUNTABILITY	OVERLAPPINGNESS	VALENCE AND CHALLENGE AROUSAL	SEATWORK VARIETY AND CHALLENGE	CLASS SIZE
Momentum		.499	.745	.294	.385	.404	.268	-.091	-.160
Withitness			.479	.474	.370	.598	.271	.224	-.097
Smoothness				.420	.289	.482	.259	-.037	-.069
Group alerting					.494	.416	.347	.080	-.145
Accountability						.275	.161	.084	-.076
Overlappingness							.067	.039	-.136
Valence and challenge arousal								.325	-.084
Seatwork variety and challenge									-.206
Class size									

Adapted from Kounin, 1970, p. 170.

to see whether they "held up" while other managerial variables were held constant. Without exception, those findings indicated as strong ones in Box 6.2 were found to hold up, although some of the weaker relationships were found to be questionable (see Kounin, 1970, pp. 171–174).

It would be difficult to provide a more concise summary of Kounin's many findings than has already been given above. However, it is worthwhile that we summarize briefly the strengths and weaknesses of these studies. Among strengths: the concepts used are striking and original; the methods employed for classroom observation were sophisticated; reliability for coding judgments was high; and, above all, the relationships found between teacher and pupil variables were strong. Among weaknesses: the methods used for operationalizing concepts in research were complex; classrooms studied have so far been confined to the lower grades; and so far Kounin has not chosen to study, or at least to report findings for, process occurrence or presage-process or process-product relationships. Thus we cannot know yet whether Kounin's variables are related to such outcomes as pupil achievement or attitudes or whether teachers can be taught to recognize, change, or "improve" their managerial skills. (We suspect that both kinds of relationships *can* be discovered, but the evidence is simply not yet in to check our suspicions.) Apart from a general desire to unearth teacher managerial skills that work, Kounin's research appears reasonably free from *Commitments*. Indeed, we have seen that he was willing to abandon an early set of concepts and questions when evidence appeared to suggest their fruitlessness. Although we should want to refrain from giving our *Commitment* to the positive ends of Kounin's managerial-style dimensions until presage and product evidence is in, we suspect that Kounin's research holds considerable promise for the eventual improvement of classroom teaching. We should like to see whether these managerial concepts apply as well to secondary classrooms as they appear to apply at the primary level. We suspect they might need some modification.

REINFORCEMENT AND BEHAVIOR MODIFICATION

The third and last perspective on classroom management we shall review has its roots in animal experimental psychology. As is well known, it is possible to train animals by means of systematic reinforcement to perform almost any kind of behavior for which their bodies are physically equipped. In such training the animal is either rewarded for performing as the investigator wishes or is punished for behavior that is not desired. In time, the animal learns to behave appropriately: thus dogs and cats learn to defecate elsewhere than on the carpet; horses, elephants, and working dogs learn to "earn their keep"; and dozens of different kinds of animals learn the tricks that so entertain us at the circus.

Children also learn by reinforcement, as is well understood by the mother who spanks or the father who provides a special weekend trip when his children have been "good." Teachers also use reinforcement, of course. Praise, smiles, and gold stars are used to reward pupil behavior of which the teacher approves, while frowns, statements of disapproval, and occasionally punishments appear when the pupil engages in deviancy or does not know the lesson. Much of this latter is applied in a nonsystematic fashion, however (a fact which might underlie the inconsistent results reported for teacher praise, acceptance, and criticism in Chapter V). In Chapter IX we shall review evidence that many pupil responses to teacher questions pass without a reactive comment from the teacher. In addition, resources available to the teacher for reinforcing pupils are mainly verbal ones, and statements appropriate for rewarding middle-class pupils may be quite inappropriate for rewarding pupils who are lower class, disturbed, or from some ethnic minorities. Finally, it is difficult to administer systematic reinforcement to the individual pupil in the typical, multipupil classroom. Most pupils have to be content with watching the teacher apply reinforcements to others, not themselves.

For these reasons, among others, those familiar with reinforcement have for some time advocated the improvement of teaching by training teachers to be more systematic in their application of rewards or punishments to pupils. At an earlier date it was claimed that reinforcement could be used by teachers in the classroom as a means of increasing pupil achievements. When this proved difficult advocacy has taken the route of promoting the use of teaching machines, computer-assisted instruction, or other educative programs in which instruction can be individualized for pupils. Most recently, those sharing the reinforcement *Commitment* have turned to the use of reinforcement for control of observable classroom behaviors of pupils, and it is to this latter research that we now turn.

The innovations suggested by reinforcement enthusiasts are among the more exciting in contemporary education. At the same time, reinforcement notions have also generated hostility among other educators. For one thing, learning theorists will sometimes use an obscure jargon to express quite simple ideas. For another, many of their theoretical notions are derived from animal studies in which the investigator cannot converse with his subjects. At the very least, this leaves those who advocate reinforcement in some difficulty as they try to accommodate the fact that teachers can warn pupils of consequences even more easily than they can provide those consequences personally. (To the best of our knowledge no study has yet been published in which the investigator attempted to explain to a rat the consequences of learning to press a bar!) However, in the hands of some reinforcement theorists this "shortcoming" becomes a major philosophical tenet, and we are asked to eschew such odd "mentalistic" notions as the idea that our pupils might possibly think as well as act (see, for example, Skinner, 1971). Needless to say, to argue such a position is to wave a red flag at most teachers. Finally, many progressive educators believe that the teacher should avoid being a personal source of rewards and that pupils should be stimulated by their own love of the subject and desires to avoid unacceptable behavior.

Not surprisingly, reinforcement techniques have more often been applied to difficult or "hopeless" human problems, such as alcoholism, sexual deviation, schizophrenia, or the education of "problem children." After all, if conventional methods of socializing have failed, what have we to lose in trying reinforcement? Moreover, programs stressing reinforcement have aimed at the modification of unacceptable *behaviors* rather than at the restructuring of thought processes. Such an emphasis on *behavior modification* may be contrasted with more conventional forms of education or psychotherapy which presume to control the future behavior of the pupil or client by giving him information or understanding. To the extent that proponents of reinforcement care at all about what the client thinks, it is claimed that thoughts will modify themselves to accommodate the changed patterns of behavior that have been induced through reinforcement. Thus, school psychologists, social workers, and others who practice psychotherapy are the "enemy," and behavior modification is seen as a vastly powerful tool that can replace their ineffective efforts.

As a sample of this latter thinking, the following was appended as a sequel to an article reporting successful behaviorial control over tantrums in an eight-year-old black girl:

> In the fall Diane was moved to another school. With the changed situation, tantrums re-occurred. They were handled by sending Diane to the principal's office. This often required the principal to remain in the office through lunch until he could return her to class. In the middle of the year, Diane was "staffed" at the new school. Mrs. C. attended the staffing and described the procedures used to control Diane the previous year. Both the principal and the new teacher were convinced that some "deep-down disturbance" was causing the tantrums and that talking about "how she feels" would help. They could not see the behavior as being maintained by the attention it received or by escape from the classroom. An attempt was made to place Diane in a special research classroom for emotionally disturbed children, but she was not accepted. She was placed on daily tranquilizers. A report from the school social worker in April, 1967 indicated that Diane's behavior had "deteriorated to a level worse than it had ever been the previous year". Diane was re-staffed and was scheduled to enter the special research class for emotionally disturbed children in September. . . . (Carlson *et al.*, 1968)

We should not like to get embroiled in this larger, emotionally laden issue. As we shall see, considerable evidence has been amassed which indicates that teachers can control some aspects of pupil classroom behaviors through reinforcement. But this research is not without flaw and surely does not answer a number of key questions we would like to ask of it. Thus, we are less than convinced that it offers evidence suggesting the inherent ineffectiveness of other classroom control procedures or of school psychologists.

Concepts of Teaching Behavior

To control someone's behavior by means of reinforcement seems a simple matter. All that is required is to provide him rewards when he does something you want him to do or punish him when he does something you dislike. For example, let us assume that we want a pupil to stop whispering to his neighbors and to concentrate on his studies. We wait until he is whispering and then frown at him. As soon as he returns to his studies we give him an encouraging smile. We keep this up each time he whispers or studies, and in time he learns to behave appropriately. We can tell that he has really learned when it is no longer necessary to frown or to smile at him in order to keep him studying and free from whispers.

In formal terms the behavior of the pupil is termed a *response* and the teacher's behavior a *stimulus* or *reinforcement*. A reward is termed a *positive* stimulus, a punishment a *negative* stimulus. The game of reinforcement, then, involves a small sequence of events. First, we find the pupil engaging in a behavior we wish to encourage or discourage (response). Next, we apply a positive or negative stimulus to him in order to encourage or discourage the response. Finally, we look to see whether our stimulus is having an effect, thus checking for evidence that the pupil's behavior has changed (response$_2$).

Actually, it isn't quite this simple. For one thing, to define positive and negative stimuli (or reinforcements) in terms of rewards and punishments is cheating, so to speak. How do we know that a given stimulus is a reward? The simple answer is to say that rewards are pleasant experiences while punishments cause distress. But this would require that we interview subjects to find out what pleases or distresses them, which violates the stipulation that we stay at the behavorial level. This problem may be solved in at least two ways. The less formal is to define reinforcements in terms of recognition responses. Thus, positive stimuli are those which usually elicit signs of pleasure, such as smiles, laughter, or eager acceptance. Negative stimuli normally elicit frowns, "ouch," or outright avoidance on the part of subjects. Such responses need not appear on all occasions. Once we have encountered them with reasonable frequency we conclude that the stimuli that elicit them will work universally. More formally, a positive stimulus may be defined, relative to others, as any behavorial experience which the subject chooses over others (see Premack, 1965). Whichever way we proceed, positive and negative stimuli are presumed to be context free. Thus, candy, praise, and money are presumed always to be positive; frowns, criticism, and corporal punishment are universally negative.

But are positive and negative reinforcements really universal in their application? Will candy work for the child who is sated, praise for the jaded sophisticate, or corporal punishment for the tough youth who wants to prove he can take it? If we take these examples seriously, it appears that choice of stimulus would have to be adjusted to the personality of the subject pupil. Stimuli must also be chosen to fit the context. To illustrate this, consider the different kinds of exchange that take place in a business encounter and between two young people in love. In the former context it is quite appropriate to offer the other money for services, in the latter it would be considered an affront (at least)! Each kind of context has its list of appropriate and inappropriate stimuli that can be used, and at least part of the objections voiced by educators to the use of reinforcement in classrooms have been generated by the poor choice of stimuli used in demonstrations—such as candy. (For a general discussion of the relationships between contexts and stimuli, see Foa and Foa, in press.)

A number of different kinds of reinforcements have been examined for use by teachers in the classroom. For convenience we shall sort these into several classes. Perhaps the most often studied, and certainly the simplest for the teacher to use, is *teacher praise,* which is always presumed to be a positive stimulus. At the same level, *teacher criticism* is also studied, but presumed to be negative. Another group of studies has made use of *material incentives* such as candy, small toys, school supplies, or other consumables presumed to have positive valence for pupils. Praise, criticism, and material incentives are all presumed to be "primary reinforcers" in that they represent contingencies that were established long before the pupil entered the classroom. Each class is not without difficulties, however. Praise is assumed to be a weak stimulus, criticism simply does not work reliably, as we shall see, while the teacher soon runs out of material incentives. Thus, another group of studies have begun using secondary reinforcers whose value must be learned by the pupil as part of the reinforcement game. We shall refer to these kinds of reinforcements as *tokens,* although the actual symbols used by the teacher may range from poker chips through check marks to gold stars and badges to wear to scrip or actual money. Such tokens have little value in and of themselves; rather, they must be exchanged for commodities valued by the pupil. Following a distinction suggested by O'Leary and O'Leary (1971), we shall distinguish between *extrinsic tokens*—those that are backed up by commodities not normally found in the classrooms, such as material incentives; and *intrinsic tokens*—those that are backed up by commodities or experiences usually present, such as access to free time, movies, or a story hour.

This brings up yet another class of reinforcers. For some time it has been known that experimental animals will learn to "work" in order to earn the right to "play" (again, see Premack, 1965). In technical terms this involves *response manipulation*. The teacher first determines what his pupils prefer to do by watching those things they most often choose to do and then sets up sevents so that the pupil cannot do his preferred thing until he has *first* done what the teacher wants him to do. For example, pupils can earn the right to an extra long recess through academic achievement, or the privilege of studying a desired subject can be made contingent on the mastering of a boring spelling list.

Still another form of reinforcement is *peer manipulation*. In the typical study using this technique reinforcement is not applied to the individual pupil but rather to a group or team of pupils who are rewarded or punished in concert. Through such means, it is argued, the efforts of the teacher are multiplied, for she then recruits a number of willing co-reinforcers who will bring pressure to bear on pupils to "shape up" so that their team gains access to rewards or avoids punishments.

Finally, we shall also review a handful of studies wherein *vicarious reinforcement* was at issue. As we have already noted, pupils are more likely to witness classroom reinforcement than they are to experience it personally. Most teachers and reinforcement enthusiasts assume that those who witness reinforcement will also be positively affected by it—or at least will suffer no negative effects. And yet this assumption is rarely studied. In those few cases where the investigator looks at the comparative effects of reinforcement on both target and nontarget pupils, we shall refer to the latter as the recipients of vicarious reinforcement.

Vicarious reinforcement is sometimes confused with yet another concept popular with behavior modifiers—*modeling*. As we shall use the term here, modeling refers to instances in which pupils are found to pattern their behavior after the behavior exhibited by another in the classroom. Surely this is an important process in the classroom. Teachers serve as models for decorum and adult behavior as well as exhibit attitudes toward the subject and pupils. Other pupils will serve as models, too—as laughter, enthusiasm for the subject, or challenge and deviancy can all spread about the classroom on occasion. Excellent experimental studies of modeling have been reported (see, especially, Bandura, 1969). It comes as a surprise, then, to discover that practically no research has yet been conducted on modeling in the classroom context.

Classroom reinforcement is subject to a number of problems, and it is wise that we consider some of these briefly. One concerns the complex relationship between the reinforcement schedule, learning, and subsequent retention of the learned response. Considerable research supports the general contention that learning is most rapid when the subject receives an invariant schedule; that is, when the stimulus is applied on each and every occasion in which an appropriate response has appeared. On the other hand, responses learned with an invariant schedule of reinforcement are likely to disappear when the reinforcing stimulus is taken away.

Responses learned with a random, irregular schedule of reinforcement take longer to acquire but are more likely to be retained when the stimulus is withdrawn (which is one reason why fishing is so popular). However, not much is yet known about schedules of reinforcement in the classroom. Worse, most investigators seem satisfied to have achieved behavioral control over pupils by the reinforcement means reported and appear unconcerned whether pupils have or have not retained their new habits over an extended period of subsequent time. As was suggested by Lipe and Jung, "a long range goal of incentive manipulation is that learning will eventually provide intrinsic rewards, and thus students will learn how to motivate themselves to complete boring but necessary learning tasks" (1971, p. 261). Unfortunately, we can find no classroom research bearing on this laudable goal.

Another problem concerns the differential usefulness of positive and negative reinforcements. As Skinner has often noted, positive reinforcement is a more humane, moral, and generally effective method of controlling others than is negative reinforcement. When rewards are offered the subject has the choice of performing, thus earning the reward, or not performing, and perhaps obtaining other benefits from elsewhere. Thus, freedom of choice is maintained—at least in theory. When punishments are employed the subject is bound to "lose," for he will either be punished or must perform as he would not normally choose. In addition, as we shall see, positive reinforcement is simply more effective in the classroom than is negative reinforcement. Reprimands or scolding may, in fact, serve to stimulate additional deviancy on the part of pupils for whom any recognition is better than none—and thus operate as positive reinforcers in violation of the teacher's intention.

The only difficulty with this argument is that we may have to wait a long time for some pupils to evidence the response we would like to reinforce positively. Whereas bar pressing is a type of random behavior that often occurs in rats that are placed in a Skinner Box, the correct pronunciation of German words may never occur spontaneously among pupils in the classroom. To stimulate at least one instance of the desired behavior to reinforce—in this case a correct pronunciation—the teacher is tempted to "cheat" on the reinforcement paradigm by pronouncing the word herself, explaining how the tongue is placed in the mouth to get the proper sound, or suggesting another word that rhymes with the pronunciation desired. In such instances reinforcement is supplemented by other educative strategies, such as modeling, the provision of symbolic information, or cognitive restructuring. And if the pupil learns in such a context we cannot tell whether he learned because of reinforcement, the other strategies used, or a combination of both. As we shall see, much of the research presumably conducted on classroom reinforcement cheats in this way.

A final problem, and perhaps the most serious, is the difficulty of applying reinforcement appropriately to 30 or more pupils in the mass classroom. Obviously, some pupils learn more quickly than others, while some have habits or impulses not shared by the rest of the group. Clearly, an appropriate schedule of reinforcement for Billy may not be appropriate for Susie. As we shall see, most studies of classroom reinforcement have concentrated on the control of but one or two "problem" pupils in the mass classroom or have made use of small artificial classrooms wherein pupils with similar problems are concentrated. Such studies have unknown applicability to the problems of mass classroom control.

Clearly, these problems limit the usefulness of applying reinforcement notions in classroom teaching. Whether they are sufficient to cause us to ignore the claims of advocates is not yet clear. We suspect, with Bandura, that reinforcement is only one of a catalogue of strategies open to the teacher and must be supplemented with others to accomplish effective management of the classroom. Let us, however, look at the evidence.

Classroom Research

It would require much space to review the literally hundreds of studies wherein reinforcement has been used with children. Most of these would be beyond our interest anyway, since they do not involve the teacher and a classroom context. Others concern the use of teaching machines or programs of computer-assisted instruction, thus making use of resources that are not available to the typical teacher. Rather than review these we confine our attention here to studies wherein teachers have attempted to control pupil classroom behavior by direct means of behavior modification. Actually, even this limited task is not easy. For one thing, a substantial number of studies have been reported. For another, many studies have used somewhat artificial "classrooms" that were assembled for other purposes than programs of instruction. Thus, the line between studies that should fall into our review and those that should not is hard to draw. In constructing our review we have concentrated on studies reported in the last decade and have depended on such review sources as Hanley (1970), Lipe and Jung (1971), O'Leary and Drabman (1971), and O'Leary and O'Leary (1971).

Studies reviewed may be found in Box 6.3. As will be seen, without exception these are *all* experimental in nature. They all have concerned the contrasting of various schedules of teacher reinforcement. In most cases the dependent variable has been pupil classroom behavior. In a few cases product variables have also been studied. While such a research tradition has its strengths, it also leaves unanswered a number of vital questions. For one, we are provided no information concerning process occurrence. Perhaps teachers already provide a great deal of reinforcement to pupils in the classroom and thus need no further encouragement along this line! Who knows? Nor have any studies that we can discover yet concerned themselves with presage or contextual variables. We are not told whether it is easy, or

---

BOX 6.3   Findings for Behavior Modification

STUDIES REVIEWED

Barrish *et al.* (1969)	(Ba&69)
Becker *et al.* (1967)	(Be&67)
Benowitz and Busse (1970)	(B&B70)
Birnbrauer *et al.* (1965)	(Bi&65)
Broden, Bruce *et al.* (1970)	(B&70a)
Broden, Hall *et al.* (1970)	(B&70b)
Bushell, *et al.* (1968)	(Bu&68)
Chadwick and Day (1970); also	
Day and Chadwick (1970)	(C&D70)
Evans and Oswalt (1968)	(E&O68)
Hall *et al.* (1971)	(Ha&71)
Hewett *et al.* (1969)	(He&69)
Homme (1966)	(Hom66)
Madsen *et al.* (1968)	(Ma&68)
McAllister *et al.* (1969)	(Mc&69)
McKenzie *et al.* (1968)	(Mc&68)
O'Leary and Becker (1967)	(O&B67)
O'Leary and Becker (1969)	(O&B69)
O'Leary *et al.* (1969)	(Ol&69)
O'Leary *et al.* (1970)	(Ol&70)
Osborne (1969)	(Osb69)
Packard (1970)	(Pac70)
Risley and Hart (1968)	(R&H68)
Van Wagenen and Travers (1963)	(V&T63)
Ward and Baker (1968)	(W&B68)
Wasik *et al.* (1969)	(W&a69)
Wolf *et al.* (1968)	(Wo&68)

INSTRUMENT, METHOD OF GATHERING DATA, CODING SYSTEM, UNIT STUDIED, RELIABILITY

O'Leary Instrument, live observation, sign system, various types of deviant behavior, high reliability (O&B67), (O&B69), (Ol&69), (Ol&70).

Various Instruments, mostly live observation; sign systems; deviant behavior, involvement, or classroom performance; reliability usually ignored (Ba&69), (Be&67), (B&B70), (Bi&65), (B&70a), (B&70b), (Bu&68), (C&D70), (E&O68), (Ha&71), (Hom66), (Ma&68), (Mc&69), (Mc&68), (Osb69), (Pac70), (R&H68), (W&B68), (W&a69), (Wo&68).

No Classroom Observation (V&T63).

DESIGN OF STUDY, SUBJECTS, CONTEXTS

Process-Process Experiments

(Ba&69)	1 teacher and pupils; grade IV
(Be&67)	5 teachers and pupils (2 target pupils, small classes); primary; pupils with behavior problems
(B&B70)	4 teachers and pupils; grade IV; black, ghetto classrooms
(Bi&65)	1 teacher and pupils; primary; retarded pupils
(B&70a)	1 teacher and pupils (2 target pupils); grade II
(B&70b)	1 teacher and pupils (small class); grades VII and VIII; pupils at least one year behind in school work

(Box 6.3, continued)

(Bu&68)　　1 teacher and pupils (small class); preschool

(C&D70)　　1 teacher and pupils primary; black and Mexican-American pupils with "severe behavior problems"

(E&O68)　　**4** teachers and pupils (1 target pupil); grades IV and VI

(Ha&71)　　3 teachers and pupils (1 target, 1 target, 10 target pupils); primary; pupils with behavior problems

(Hom66)　　? teachers and pupils; secondary; drop-outs and potential drop-outs

(Ma&68)　　2 teachers and pupils (1 target, 2 target pupils); primary; pupils with behavior problems

(Mc&69)　　1 teacher and pupils; junior high; English

(Mc&68)　　1 teacher and pupils (small class); primary; pupils with "learning disabilities"

(O&B67)　　1 teacher and pupils (small class); grade III; pupils with behavior problems

(O&B69)　　1 teacher and pupils; grade I; rest period

(Ol&69)　　1 teacher and pupils (7 target pupils); grade II

(Ol&70)　　5 teachers and pupils (2 target pupils); grades II and III

(Osb69)　　1 teacher and pupils (small class); primary; pupils with low IQ's or deaf

(Pac70)　　3 teachers and pupils; grades III, V, VI

(R&H68)　　2 teachers and pupils; preschool; black, ghetto classroom

(W&B68)　　3 teachers and pupils (4 target pupils, 4 nontarget pupils); grade I: pupils with behavior problems

(W&a69)　　1 teacher and pupils (2 target pupils); grade II

Process-Product Experiments

(He&69)　　6 teachers and pupils (small classes); grades II–VI; special classes for emotionally disturbed pupils

(V&T63)　　12 teachers and pupils (small classes, 4 target and 4 nontarget pupils in each); grades IV, V, VI; artificial classrooms assembled for the experiment

(Wo&68)　　1 teacher and pupils (15 target pupils); grades V and VI; special remedial class in urban poverty area

FINDINGS

Process Occurrence

None reported.

Context-Process Relationships

None reported.

Presage-Process Relationships

None reported.

Process-Process Relationships

6.3-1　*Teacher praise* (as a positive reinforcer of acceptable behavior) reduces the *amount of pupil deviancy* (Be&67)E,* (Ma&68)E, (W&B68)E, (O&B69)E, (Mc&69)E, (W&a69)E.

6.3-2　*Teacher criticism* (as a negative reinforcer of deviant behavior) does not affect the *amount of pupil deviancy* (O&B69)E, (Mc&69)E, (W&a69)E. *In contradiction*, it is also found that

---

* Findings generated experimentally are indicated with an E.

6.3-2a *Teacher criticism* (as a negative reinforcer of deviant behavior) reduces the *amount of pupil deviancy* (Ha&71) E; and also

6.3-2b *Quietly delivered teacher criticism* (as a negative reinforcer of deviant behavior) reduces the *amount of pupil deviancy* (Ol&70)E.

6.3-3 *Teacher use of material incentives* (as a positive reinforcer of acceptable behavior) decreases the *amount of pupil deviancy* (R&H68)E, (C&D70)E.

6.3-4 *Teacher use of material incentives* (as a positive reinforcer of correct responses) increases *proportion of correct responses* (B&B70)E.

6.3-5 *Teacher use of extrinsic tokens* (as a positive reinforcer of acceptable behavior) reduces the *amount of pupil deviancy* (O&B67)E, (Ol&69)E.

6.3-6 *Teacher use of extrinsic tokens* (as a positive reinforcer of acceptable behavior) increases *pupil attendance* (Ol&69)E.

6.3-7 *Teacher use of extrinsic tokens* (as a positive reinforcer of correct responses) increases *proportion of correct responses* (Bi&65)E.

6.3-8 *Teacher use of intrinsic tokens* (as a positive reinforcer of acceptable behavior) increases the *amount of pupil task involvement* (Bu&68)E, (Mc68)E, (B&70b)E.

6.3-9 *Teacher use of response manipulation* (as a positive reinforcer of acceptable behavior) increases the *amount of pupil task involvement* (Osb69)E, (Hom66)E, (Pac70)E.

6.3-10 *Teacher use of response manipulation* (as a positive reinforcer of acceptable behavior) decreases the *amount of pupil deviancy* (Osb69)E.

6.3-11 *Teacher use of peer manipulation* (as a positive reinforcer of acceptable behavior) decreases the *amount of pupil deviancy* (E&O68)E, (Ba&69)E.

6.3-12 *Teacher use of vicarious reinforcement* (as a positive reinforcer of acceptable behavior) had no effect on *nontarget pupil deviancy* (W&B68)E. *In contradiction*, it is also found that

6.3-12a *Teacher use of vicarious reinforcement* (as a positive reinforcer of acceptable behavior) decreases the *amount of nontarget pupil deviancy* (but not as much as that seen for target pupil deviancy) (B&70a)E.

Process-Product Relationships

6.2-13 *Teacher use of extrinsic tokens* (as a positive reinforcer of acceptable behavior) increases *pupil achievement* (Wo&68)E, (He&69)E.

6.3-14 *Teacher use of vicarious reinforcement* (as a positive reinforcer of correct responses) increases the *achievement of nontarget pupils* (but not quite as much as it does for target pupils) (V&T63)E.

---

indeed even possible, to train teachers to use reinforcement more consistently. Nor are we provided information concerning the effects of subject matter, grade level, or pupil population on reinforcement. As can also be seen in Box 6.3, most of the evidence so far collected concerns "problem" pupils at the primary level, and we suspect that behavior modification is either more difficult or less useful at the secondary level—but we cannot tell from these studies whether this is true or not. Finally, as is true whenever research is pursued solely by a program of isolated, experimental studies, we cannot be sure how often the effects claimed are actually obtained.

Clearly, failures are not publishable, but the *Committed* investigator wi pursue matters until he has achieved success. Thus, we cannot tell how ofte behavior modification works versus how often it does not work in the clas room. As O'Leary and Drabman suggest: "almost any researcher workir with token programs can cite at least one example of a token progra' which failed in one way or another. . . . Unless studies are extremely we designed, it is difficult to draw conclusions from studies which show no di ferences between groups, and as a result failures are infrequently pul lished" (1971, p. 385).

The above comments would apply regardless of the type of exper mental method used. However, many of the studies exhibit additional prol lems of methodology that should be borne in mind when reviewing the findings. First, many of them have involved very small numbers of subject often but one classroom, and in some instances but one target pupil! Secon most (but not all) studies reported time-sequence data for experiment; classrooms only and made no use of control classrooms. Third, most studi(collected data concerning pupil behavior by means of live observation wit primitive sign instruments that focused on only selected aspects of pup behavior. In about half of those studies reviewed little concern was give to the ("obvious") process of observing pupil behavior, but when invest gators chose to discuss the problem they usually reported high reliability fc their observational instruments.

Fourth, most studies did not bother to observe either the behavior c nontarget pupils or the behavior of the teacher who was responsible for pr(viding the experimental treatment. Thus, we are provided little informatio concerning what happened to the other pupils when target pupils wer being controlled, nor even whether teachers actually followed the invest gator's instructions in presenting reinforcement.

This latter matter relates to a fifth and really serious problem. Fro) anecdotal evidence provided by investigators it would appear that in mo; of these studies the experimental treatment was confounded. Instead (providing reinforcement alone, teachers provided it together with explana tions, encouragement, modeling, and various other supportive stimuli, s; we cannot be really sure that the results reported are due to reinforcemen; Taken at its worst, this suggests that much of the results apparently gen erated may have been due to the *Hawthorne Effect*, in which the targe pupil's behavior is modified simply because the teacher is paying enthusiasti attention to him. In an unintentionally revealing statement O'Leary an(Drabman note that: "Several anecdotal examples suggest that where teacher does not believe that a token system will be effective, her succes will be minimized" (1971, p. 386). Thus, reinforcement effects may have beei generated entirely by True Believers!

Finally, sixth, most of the studies were concerned with but smal groups of problem pupils; thus, they may or may not tell us much abou how to control larger numbers of pupils in the mass classroom. Worse, w(have been unable to find any evidence in these studies suggesting long term effects. Most studies have ignored the problem of retention of learned behaviors. Where this problem was engaged it was studied in some sort of a time-sequential design in which it was shown that pupil misbehavior (or whatever) reoccurred when the reinforcing stimuli were withdrawn. Thus, one gains the impression that we are here reviewing strategies for teacher survival in difficult classroom situations rather than for teacher induction of desired changes in pupil behavior on a permanent basis.

Within the context of these limitations, however, the findings generated by these studies are remarkably clear and consistent. As can be seen, the amount of pupil deviancy can be reduced by various types of stimuli if employed in programs of consistent reinforcement—including praise, material incentives, extrinsic tokens, response manipulation, and peer manipulation. (Of these, surely *praise* is the easiest for teachers to offer in the typical classroom situation.) Material incentives, extrinsic tokens, intrinsic tokens, and response manipulation have also been found useful for controlling pupil task involvement or proportion of correct responses on subject tasks. Moreover, tokens are also reported to be useful for increasing pupil achievement.

All of these findings concern positive reinforcement, of course. When we turn to negative reinforcement (via teacher criticism) the picture is not nearly so clear. Most studies report no effects, or even negative effects, for criticism, although one study reports success with this method of reinforcement, and another notes that quietly delivered criticism can be more effective than public criticism. Evidently, it is more useful to concentrate on pupils' successes than to dwell on their failures; moreover, this practice makes for a generally happier classroom.

Findings for vicarious reinforcement are also problematic. One study reported that teacher reinforcement had no effects on nontarget pupil deviancy, while another study reported effects that were in the same direction but weaker than those for the target pupil. Altogether, these results provide little information concerning the process effects of reinforcement on nontarget pupils. However, in perhaps the best-designed of all the studies reviewed, Van Wagenen and Travers (1963) have reported that pupils subjected to vicarious reinforcement learned nearly as much (German language vocabulary) as those provided direct reinforcement—or those taught by teaching machines, for that matter. If we take this one study to indicate research to come, it would appear that positive benefits can also be induced in nontarget pupils by means of reinforcement.

Let us now summarize what is known about reinforcement and behavior modification in the classroom. First, research within this tradition reflects a *Commitment* that stems from learning theory and animal research. This *Commitment* stresses that control over pupil behavior may be obtained by systematic applications of reinforcement, and that concern for pupils' internal states should be ignored. Second, studies reflecting this tradition have been experimental in nature and have ignored process occurrence and presage-process and context-process phenomena. Third, most of these studies have concerned "problem" pupils. Fourth, most have concerned either one or two target pupils within a mass classroom or small classes of pupils who were known to have similar problems. Fifth, most studies were flawed by poor design features such as poor observational instruments, lack of control groups, or confounded treatments. Sixth, within these limitations positive reinforcement has been shown to work in reducing pupil deviancy and increasing pupil task involvement and even achievement. Seventh, findings for negative reinforcement are more equivocal. Eighth, findings for vicarious reinforcement indicate that desired effects will spread from target to nontarget pupils. Ninth, little evidence has been advanced to show that pupil effects obtained will persist after the reinforcing stimuli have been removed.

Although research within the reinforcement tradition is limited by methodological shortcomings, it is considerably clearer in conceptualization than is research representing the classroom-climate tradition. We find the notions of positive and negative reinforcement reasonably clear and the reinforcement paradigm simple to understand. Moreover, we suspect that reinforcement *can* be used by teachers to obtain control over difficult pupils who persist in imposing behavior problems on the classroom, and that *praise* is probably the best form of reinforcement to use on balance. At the same time, we doubt that this tradition has much to say about the larger problems of classroom management, nor has much information yet been provided that tells the teacher how to encourage self-control in problem pupils.

CONCLUSION

Three different research traditions have been reviewed that bear on the subject of classroom management and control. We first considered that classroom-climate tradition that appears to conceive management a matter of *directiveness,* for which a single dimension is presumed to obtain running from the teacher-controlled to the pupil-controlled classroom. As we have seen, this tradition has generated a good deal of research and a number of impressive findings of the context-process and presage-process varieties. However, the process-product findings are weak, and on balance it appears that the concepts and methods of this tradition are inadequate.

We next took up Kounin's research on discipline and classroom group management. This research actually represents two different conceptualizations of the control problem. The first concerns discipline, or the direct management of deviancy. Whereas this orientation was found to have some usefulness in describing management at the kindergarten level, it was found less useful for higher grades. The second concerns the management of classroom groups by teachers, and a host of provocative concepts was advanced and validated with observational research in which pupil deviancy and pupil task involvement were the dependent variables. This research has yet to be tied to presage or product variables, however, and has so far been confined to the primary level.

We finally considered research representing the traditions of reinforcement and behavior modification. In this tradition control is viewed as a matter of teacher provision of reinforcements following the appearance of pupil behaviors that are to be encouraged or discouraged. Research using reinforcement notions has been exclusively experimental, and the experiments reported are largely flawed. However, the evidence available suggests that reinforcement may indeed be used to control the behavior of "problem" pupils in the classroom, at least at the primary level.

Taken together, these three traditions provide a wealth of concepts for examining the problems of classroom management. We suspect also that teachers can obtain useful information concerning classroom control from both the Kounin and reinforcement research efforts—although we should like to see both explored with a wider variety of methods and more product variables, particularly at the secondary level.

RECOMMENDED ADDITIONAL READING

Bandura, A. *Principles of Behavior Modification.* New York: Holt, Rinehart and Winston, Inc., 1969.
One of the key works in the tradition of behavior modification. The author considers such diverse topics as modeling, rewards, aversive control, extinction, desensitizing, counterconditioning, and symbolic control. He also concerns himself with issues of value and the philosophical implications of reinforcement.

Clarizio, H. F. *Toward Positive Classroom Discipline.* New York: John Wiley & Sons, Inc., 1971.
A persuasive introduction to the use of behavior modification in classrooms. The author takes up many topics—rewards, punishments, modeling, densitization, and others. Not particularly concerned with research, this work simply provides readers with plausible arguments concerning why behavior modification ought to work in classrooms and offers a number of suggestions for making it more effective.

Kounin, J. S. *Discipline and Group Management in Classrooms.* New York: Holt, Rinehart and Winston, Inc., 1970.
A well-written description of Kounin's pursuit of the classroom-management problem. The author begins with his early research on discipline. He then discusses the evidence that caused him to abandon the study of discipline in favor of group management. Concepts for group management are then defined and illustrated. Research findings are also supplied.

O'Leary, K.D., and O'Leary, S. G. (eds.) *Classroom Management: The Successful Use of Behavior Modification.* New York: Pergamon Press, 1971.
A collection of research studies representing the reinforcement tradition. The editors provide a clear introductory essay on behavior modification together with summary statements for each section. Topics discussed include those considered in this chapter, as well as modeling, teaching machines, the use of paraprofessionals in classroom management, and self-management.

VII
THE CLASSROOM AS
A SOCIAL SYSTEM

Teacher: All right class, we've done enough arithmetic for the morning. Let's put our workbooks and pencils away . . .
Not now, John . . .
Susan, what's the matter? Aren't you feeling well? . . .
Now, class, we're going to work on our reading assignments. I want the "Bluebirds" to take out their books and begin reading on page 73 . . . Did you get that? Page 73. The story about the three foxes . . . OK. Now I want the "Red Chiefs" to take these sheets of paper and try to figure out what each of the words on it means. If you know what it means, write down the definition on the sheet. If you don't know, guess. Mike, will you come up and get the sheets? . . . Now does everyone understand? . . . The rest, those who are in the "Outlaw" group, will you come up to my desk now . . . QUIETLY . . . I want to hear you read to me aloud.

Terminating some activities and structuring new ones, organizing pupils into one large group or several smaller ones, individualizing instruction, determining group membership and procedures, allowing participation by some but not others—these are some of the tasks performed by the teacher in the classroom. What do we know about classroom activities, teacher and pupil roles, grouping practices, and the like? What are they? How often do they occur? What are their interrelationships? What are their effects? Systematic observation of classrooms has produced considerable evidence pertinent to these questions, and it is with that evidence that this chapter is concerned.

The majority of research on teaching has been generated by a desire to improve it. Most researchers in this field are educators themselves, and they have tended to use concepts and insights from their own training in the formal study of classroom events. Moreover, their operations, and to some extent their judgments, have been colored by their *Commitments* to improvement. However, the research tradition we now take up has sprung more from a desire first to describe, rather than immediately to improve, teaching. To understand these descriptive studies let us put aside all that we have learned concerning educational ideology and begin simply by taking a long, hard look at classroom events. To use a grossly overworked example, let us become men from Mars who have grown up in a society that does not feature the processes of formal education (see Adams and Biddle, 1970, p. 8). To such an observer each feature of classroom teaching is problematic, a curiosity. Let us focus not on what classroom education should be or should accomplish but rather upon what it *is* and *does* accomplish. What, then, do we see?

Perhaps we are first and most permanently impressed by the *systematic* features of this phenomenon. Classrooms everywhere feature a score or more of immature pupils and usually one teacher. Moreover, the behaviors of these persons seem highly structured and predictable. The teacher talks much of the time, strides back and forth, gestures, writes on the chalkboard. The pupils sit in docile rows, usually speak only when nominated, wave their hands frantically for attention. Moreover, when these systematic behavior forms change they are likely to change in organized and predictable ways. Sometimes the entire group stands to attention and sings or chants in unison. Sometimes it sits in a circle and listens to the teacher read or share experiences. Sometimes it lines up, two by two, before going out of the door. Sometimes it takes out paper, pencil, and workbooks and does assignments at its desks. Quite apart from individual departures from these patterns, our overall impression is one of *organization*.

The classroom, then, is an organized social system, and it is reasonable to presume that its members are affected by the forms of that organization. To put it another way, it is reasonable to presume that teaching, and teaching effectiveness, will be influenced by the structured forms of classroom interaction. One style of teaching is possible when the classroom is a single group, another becomes possible when several groups are present. When the classroom is excited and noisy the teacher is likely to behave in quite a different way than when it is stolid and silent. Again, teaching is probably affected by the presence or absence of classroom artifacts—chalkboards, goldfish, new textbooks, teaching machines, television sets, all have potential effects on the ways in which teachers and pupils behave, and ultimately on the effectiveness of instruction.

Let us begin, then, with the systematic aspects of classroom behavior. What makes the classroom a social system, what kinds of research are possible concerning the classroom as a system, and what do we now know about the effects of the system's properties on teaching and learning?

BACKGROUND

For years educators have understood in a general way that classrooms are miniature social systems. However, most contemporary discussions of this fact begin with Willard Waller's (1932) publication, *The Sociology of Teaching*. This remarkable work set forth many of the most significant topics of research that are pursued in the sociology of education to this day.

Moreover, Waller suggested a number of concepts for viewing the class room and propositions concerning teaching that are as insightful and fresh today as if they had appeared in contemporary journals.

Defining the school as a "place where people meet for the purpose of giving and receiving instruction," Waller viewed classrooms as conven tionalized settings in which standardized and rule-bound interaction take place between teachers and pupils. A number of factors serve to constrai the forms of classroom interaction, among them the curriculum, the physica artifacts of the room, the beliefs and values of the community, the impulse of pupils, and the customs governing the ways classrooms have been con ducted in the past. These constraints mean that only certain varieties of classroom activities, or lesson formats, are likely.

Lesson formats, in turn, may be analyzed as systems of *roles*. As used i such a discussion, a role consists of a pattern of behavior that is character istic of one or more persons in the context we are studying. For exampl one aspect of the teacher's role involves question asking, while the pupil role features question answering. But each of these roles is tied to th other; teachers will not normally persist in asking questions unless pupil are willing to answer; pupils will not normally offer answers unless a ques tion has been asked. Thus, classroom roles are also assembled into charac teristic *activities*. Moreover, these activities are not only recognized b educators but are enjoined in educational ideology and tradition and ar sometimes specified in curriculum guides. Finally, if successful, we presum (or hope) that classroom activities will lead to understanding on the part o pupils.

Actually, the classroom is more complex than this discussion suggest For one thing, the activities of the classroom may differ greatly, dependin on subject matter. We might expect a more formalized lesson in mathe matics, more variability in social studies, and a wholly distinct activity fo mat in the physics laboratory. For another, roles will vary depending on th background, ability, and needs of classroom participants. The lively, wel informed teacher performs quite differently in the classroom than does th dull ignoramus. Each has a characteristic style; each is likely to provok different activity formats. Different roles are performed by different pupil too—by boys and girls, by the dull and bright, by the shy, boisterous, pr cocious, and hostile.

In addition, teachers and pupils may not be equally motivated to pla the "classroom game." Given the fact that teachers are to give, and pupil to receive, instruction, teachers are likely to enjoy the typical classroo more than are pupils. For teachers instruction may provide an excuse fo power, an ego trip, or an opportunity to exercise moral commitment. Fo pupils all too often it provides merely boredom, the restriction of physica impulses, and lock-step instructional practices. Because they are coerce into classrooms, some pupils are likely to adopt roles that interfere wit instruction. These, too, form part of the activity context of classroom educa tion—although we are not likely to think of them as "successful" examples of teaching.

A second source of insights for analysis of the systemic aspects of classroom interaction has undoubtedly been the work of social psychologists focusing on the small group. As an early example of this effort let us consider the contributions of Moreno (1953). It was Moreno who first suggested the method of *sociometry*, which provides us a convenient means of discriminating the lasting social groupings of a classroom. In using sociometric methods the investigator asks subjects to indicate who, for example, are their best friends among the group members. A sociometric "map" of the classroom is then drawn indicating the groups of subjects who choose one another. Such a map is exemplified in Figure 7.1, which indicates the sociometric choices for a fifth-grade classroom. Note that the groups indicated for this classroom exhibit few cases involving both boys and girls,

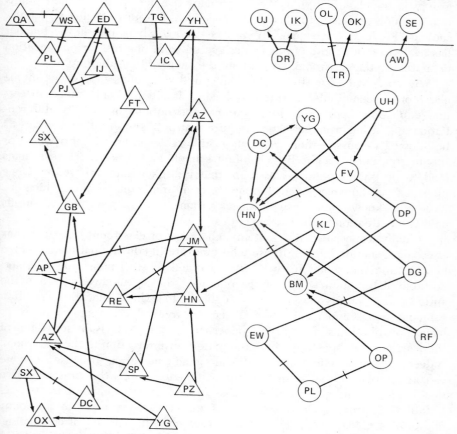

Figure 7.1   Sociometric class structure, grade V. Boys are indicated by triangles, girls by circles; arrows indicate a nonreciprocated choice; chosen pupils from other classrooms appear above the solid line. (Adapted from Moreno 1953, p. 158)

perhaps indicating that pupils at this grade level are generally not attracted by members of the other sex.

For some time teachers have been taught to make sociometric maps of this sort of their classrooms as an aid to discovering who the popular pupils are in their classrooms and who the isolates are. Armed with this information, it is argued, the teacher is in a better position to control the classroom and to plan individualized instruction to bring out isolated pupils.

But classroom groups may be defined in other ways than by choice of best friends. One obvious way to define groups is simply by noting which pupils talk to each other. If Johnny and Billy have their heads together at the back of the room, they can be considered a subgroup within the classroom. Moreover, teachers are often concerned about such subgroups, for when Johnny and Billy are whispering together they are unlikely to be paying attention to the course of the lesson. Teachers will often create subgroups in the classroom, too. We know many teachers who sort their pupils into learning groups with special abilities. These groups often have names, such as "Eagles," "Spacemen," "Wowsers," and the like, and all the teacher has to do to move those pupils so designated from one task or one location to another in the classroom is to call out the name of the subgroup.

By now, of course, the notion that pupil subgroups may occur in the classroom is commonly accepted. Indeed, it is often recommended in certain educational curricula. For example, the notions of activity differentiation and of intrinsic motivation require that pupils with different interests be allowed to pursue those interests in different corners of the room. For this reason, curricula for British infant schools and American free schools tend to be built around a classroom that is broken into subgroups. Once upon a time, however, such notions were an anathema to most educators. Everyone "knew" that the well-run classroom was one in which all pupils paid strict attention to the teacher.

Finally, concern for the systemic character of classroom education has also been generated among those who innovate in educational media. Once upon a time classrooms featured such artifacts as steel pens, inkwells, and portable slates upon which pupils practiced their penmanship. When the authors were pupils classrooms were likely to exhibit blackboards, filing cabinets, maps, and fixed desks. Today the typical classroom is likely to have movable desks, a library of paperbacks, and a television set. Each of these artifacts will possibly affect the pattern of interaction in the classroom. Indeed, most innovations in educational media come about because someone can argue plausibly that instruction will benefit from the presence of a new device in the classroom. Needless to say, not all innovations are successful in improving classroom instruction. To explore in depth the many effects of a given innovation requires research, which is too often missing. Interested readers might want to consult Rossi and Biddle (1966) for a discussion of the problem of media impact on American education and the wider society.

CONCEPTS OF CLASSROOM BEHAVIOR

The discussion above suggests a wide variety of concepts for the study of classrooms as social systems. Some of these concepts are unmanageable, others might be used for research purposes, although investigators have not yet done so, and still others have already begun to generate research and findings for educators. Let us consider a selection of the latter.

Lesson Format

The idea that one might have different ways or strategies for presenting a given topic is immediately attractive to educators. After all, some of our educational vocabulary refers specifically to such matters. To *lecture*, for example, presumably means to hold forth without much interruption, while to conduct a *discussion* suggests a good deal of give and take. These are examples of different *lesson formats*, by which we mean the standing or characteristic ways of conducting classroom interaction.

Educational ideology suggests that lesson formats are of great importance. If we are to believe almost any advocate, it makes a vast difference whether pupils are to be treated in the mass or individually, whether they are to be constrained to sit quietly or are allowed to move about, whether the teacher is to talk a great deal or very little, whether pupils must only answer or can also initiate content. And yet we have not been able to locate even one study that has surveyed a substantial number of classrooms to discover the formats that are habitually used in education. Furthermore, it would appear that there is no standardized vocabulary with which lesson formats are discussed by educators.

Consider the term "discussion." Does this term encompass those formats in which the teacher questions and pupils are allowed merely to answer, or is it confined to situations in which pupils are allowed free-and-open exchange, and if the latter, is the teacher allowed to participate at all? The answer to this question will vary, depending upon which authority one reads. It would appear difficult even to think about lesson-format differences constructively, let alone to conduct research on their frequencies of occurrence, without an agreed-upon vocabulary.

An interesting discussion of this problem may be found in Herbert's (1967) *A System for Analyzing Lessons*. Herbert's method for viewing formats is diagrammed neatly in a single figure, which we have reproduced as Figure 7.2. In general, to tell what kind of a format is being used, Herbert suggests that three kinds of decisions are necessary. First, one must decide whether the teacher (alone) is working on the subject matter, whether the teacher and pupils (together) are working on it, or whether the pupils (alone) are involved. Decisions at the second and third levels vary depending on which of the three branches of the diagram one enters. If the teacher is alone, one must then decide whether the teacher is using verbal

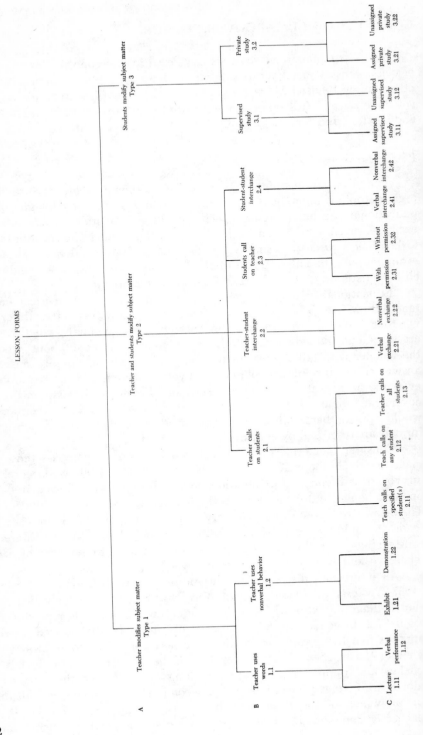

Figure 7.2 Herbert's scheme for classifying lesson formats. (Adapted from Herbert, 1967, p. 39)

182

or nonverbal materials. If teacher-pupil interaction is taking place, one looks at the pattern of that exchange. If pupils are alone, one turns to analysis of the role that the teacher is playing *vis-à-vis* the pupils.

At least two other approaches have been made to the problem of classifying lesson formats, however, and both have led to research and findings. One approach is to define lesson formats "off the top of the head," using common sense words and ignoring the issue of whether definitions overlap or not. Perhaps the best example of this approach is that of Perkins (1964, 1965), in which six categories are offered for the classification of formats: *large-group discussion, class recitation, individual work or project, seat work, small-group or committee work,* and *oral report.* Definitions of these categories are given in Figure 7.3. (Note that Perkins' category system deals with four different facets of classroom events. His categories for lesson format are found in the lower left-hand quadrant of the figure and are headed "group structure." We shall return to the other concepts used by Perkins shortly.)

Perkins' classification is based on the idea that formats should be classified in terms of pupil activity rather than teacher activity. Thus, teachers might have been remarkably active or completely silent during a large-group discussion; for Perkins the teacher's role is not involved in the format decision. Perkins reports moderate reliability for judgments made using this system.

Another classification system is reported by Flanders (1964). Once again, six categories are provided:

(1) *routine* administration—such as taking roll, distributing or collecting materials, and so forth; (2) *evaluation* of the products of learning—such as discussion of homework, test results, or student reports; (3) introducing *new material*—such as a class discussion of a new formula (or new facts about a country); (4) *general discussion* of old material or current problems; (5) *supervision of seat work*—periods when students were busy doing homework or projects . . . ; (6) *teacher-pupil planning*—or class discussions about the organization of work. (p. 211)

These categories could be "clearly identified by the observer," according to Flanders.

Yet another *ad hoc* system was developed by Lundgren (1972) through the study of eleventh-grade mathematics lessons. Lundgren used the term "themes" to apply to his concepts, but to us they seem like format terms. These included: *going through theory, going through type examples, working with exercises, examination and control of homework or written test, classroom management,* and *not subject relevant and not relevant to the tasks of the teacher.*

The difficulty with *ad hoc* approaches such as those used by Perkins, Flanders, and Lundgren is that one doesn't really know how to appose

FIGURE 7.3   Definitions for categories in Perkins' code. (Adapted from Perkins, 1965, p. 2)

	Student Categories		*Teacher Categories*	
	LISWAT	Interested in ongoing work: listening and watching—passive.	1.	Does not accept student's idea, corrects it: rejection or correction of student's response.
	REWR	Reading or writing: working in assigned area—active.	2.	Praises or encourages student or behavior: enthusiastic acceptance of student's response.
	HIAC	High activity or involvement: reciting or using large muscles—positive feeling.	2A.	Listens to, helps, supports, nurtures student: accepting, helping response; also listening to recitation.
	WOA	Intent on work of nonacademic type: pre-school activity not assigned to be done right then.	3.	Accepts or uses student's answer or idea.
Actual Pupil Role	WNA	Intent on work of nonacademic type: preparing for work assignment, cleaning out desk, etc.	4.	Asks questions about content (what? where? when?): wants to find out whether student knows and understands material.
	SWP	Social, work-oriented—PEER: discussing some aspect of schoolwork with classmate.	4A.	Asks questions that stimulate thinking (why? how?): encourages student to seek explanations, to reason, to solve problems.
	SWT	Social, work-oriented—TEACHER: discussing some phase of work with teacher.	5.	Lectures, gives facts or opinions about content: gives information in discussion, recitation, or committee meeting.
	SF	Social, friendly: talking to peer on subject unrelated to schoolwork.	6.	Gives directions, commands, or orders with

Actual Teacher Role

Student Categories

WDL   Withdrawal: detached, out of contact with people, ideas, classroom situation; day-dreaming.

DISC   Large-group discussion: entire class discusses an issue or evaluates an oral report.

REC   Class recitation: teacher questions, student answers—entire class or portion of it participating.

IND   Individual work or project: student is working alone on task that is not a common assignment.

Group Structure

SEAT   Seat work, reading or writing, common assignment.

GRP   Small-group or committee work: student is part of group or committee working on assignment.

REP   Oral reports—individual or group: student is orally reporting on book, current events, or research.

Teacher Categories

7. Criticizes or justifies authority: disapproves of conduct or work of student or group of students.

10. Is not participating in class activities: is giving test or is out of room—class silent or in confusion.

LDR   Leader-director—teacher initiative—active: conducts recitation or discussion, lectures, works with small groups.

RES   Resource person—student-centered, lesser role than leader: helps group or committee, brings material, suggests.

SUPV   Supervisor—teacher initiative, passive role during seatwork: circulates to observe and help.

SOC   Socialization agent: points to and reinforces social expectancies and rules; criticizes behavior.

EVL   Evaluator: listens and gives mark for oral report, individual or group; asks, "How many did you get right?"

Ideal Teacher Role

results reported for the several systems. It would appear, for example, that Perkins' category "seat work" and Flanders' category "supervision of seat work" cover much of the same material. But how does Flanders handle Perkins' category of "small-group or committee work," and how does Lundgren accommodate Flanders' "teacher-pupil planning"? Such problems cannot be answered until investigators are willing to conceptualize on more explicit grounds.

A somewhat different approach is represented by two somewhat different major research projects. The first, conducted by Gump (1967), attempted to analyze lesson formats in terms of five independent facets: *lesson concern, teacher leadership pattern, group quality, pupil activity demand,* and *action sequencing. Lesson concern* was basically a subject-matter code, although Gump also included within it such categories as "milk and story," "rest," "transition-in," and "transition-out" as recognizable events within the (third-grade) classroom day. *Teacher leadership pattern* concerns "the basic, persistent pattern of the teacher's relationship to the maintenance of the [format]." *Group quality* deals with the subgroup structure of the format. *Pupil activity demand* concerns what it is that pupils are expected to be doing during the format. *Action sequencing* provides categories for judging whether pupils are managed or manage themselves, and whether they engage in mass performance, "take turns," and the like.

For Gump, then, the lesson format may be conceptualized as having at least these five independently defined components. Moreover, Gump reports high reliability figures for judgments made in terms of these facets. These figures were obtained for judgments made for a "segment" of the classroom day. In general, segments were lengthy units of time during which there were no changes in the prescribed *lesson concern* or "activity format," the latter being defined in a somewhat vague fashion. For our purposes, segments may be considered units of time during which no major changes in prescribed lesson format occur. One particularly exciting aspect of Gump's work is that having isolated these five independently defined components of lesson format, he then proceeded to put them back together to show us which formats are most likely to occur. In Table 7.1, for example, we find the seven most common "action structures" Gump found in third-grade classrooms—that is, formats that are defined in terms of four out of the five facets studied by Gump (omitting only *lesson concern*).

Gump's approach describes lessons as ideal types. Lesson formats are described in terms of the "steady states" to which they presumably return rather than in terms of those events that actually occur when they are taking place. Thus, Gump is no more able to make format distinctions that reflect pupil initiation than were Herbert, Perkins, or Flanders. Rather, the *actual* behaviors of teachers and pupils are considered to be potential dependent variables that might or might not reflect activity-format differences.

In this respect the second study we shall review (Adams and Biddle,

Teacher Leadership	Pupil Activity	Action Sequencing	Grouping Arrangements	Number of Segments	Total Occupancy (Minutes)	Total Occupancy (Percent)	Descriptions in Common Terms
1 Not in Segment	Work with Own Materials, Task	Self Pace	Group/Private	14	20,588	21%	"Isolated Seatwork"
2 Watcher-Helper	Work with Own Materials, Task	Self Pace	Class/Private	13	7,901	8%	"Supervised Study"
3a Action Director or Recitation Leader	Attend to Class Events	External Pace/Serial Perform	Class/Interdependent	55	19,135	19%	"Whole-class Recitation"
3b Action Director or Recitation Leader	Attend to Class Events	External Pace/Serial Perform	Group/Interdependent	90	9,778	10%	"Reading Circle"
3c Action Director or Recitation Leader	Attend to Class Events, Task	External Pace/Serial Perform	Class/Interdependent	7	3,961	4%	"Whole-class Recitation and Seatwork"
4 Instructor or Reader	Attend to Class Events	External Pace/No Perform	Class/Interdependent	17	3,845	4%	"Teacher Reading"
5 Action Director	Readying	External Pace/No Perform	Class/Neither Interdependent nor Private	54	8,032	8%	"Getting Ready"
			Sum	250	73,240		
			Percent of all data	67	73		

Adapted from Gump, 1967, p. 50.

1970; see also Biddle and Adams, 1967) represents a different approach. Instead of describing format prescriptively, the authors attempt to set forth what actually happens. For Adams and Biddle the classroom consists of one or more ongoing groups. Each group has both a *structure* and a *function*, either of which may change rapidly over time. Among those aspects of *structure* considered are the number and size of groups, the composition of groups, and the communicatory roles played by group members. Among aspects of *function* Adams and Biddle study the content and mode of their concerns (the former, what it is that groups are considering; the latter, how they are considering it). In addition, groups are also coded for their *location* within the physical confines of the classroom.

For Adams and Biddle, then, no less than for Gump, the lesson format consists of an entity that can be broken into a number of independently defined components. Moreover, Adams and Biddle also report high reliabilities for their categorical systems, basing judgments upon videotape recordings of classroom events and "episodes" during which no (coded) aspect of the lesson format changed. In addition, some of the categories used by Gump overlap those used by Adams and Biddle, as we shall see below. However, the basic problem of whether we are to consider lesson formats ideally or descriptively separates these two studies. For Gump the format is an ideal type, and it is reasonable to ask how a given format affects the behaviors of teachers and pupils. For Adams and Biddle the format is descriptive and is made up of teacher and pupil behaviors, among other things.

Let us now take a closer look at structural and functional components of lesson formats, using concepts set out by Gump, Adams and Biddle, and others.

Group structure   By *group structure* we mean whether the classroom is a total communicating group or is fractioned into subgroups (and if the latter, into how many), who the members of those groups might be, and what kinds of roles they might be playing with regard to the communicative pattern in those groups. To give examples, a classroom that is composed of a lecturer and an audience has a different structure from one wherein the information source is a television set. Both are different from a classroom broken into two or more learning groups. A group containing a speaker and an audience is distinct from one containing two interactors and an audience, and so on.

Two systems of concepts have been suggested for classifying group structure, one ideal, the other descriptive. Gump suggests a facet of seven ideal categories: *class/interdependent, class/private, class/neither interdependent nor private, class/sectioned, group/interdependent, group/private,* and *group/neither interdependent nor private.* Definitions of these terms are given in Figure 7.4. In general, this classification is based more on pupil roles than on teacher roles, for in none of Gump's classifications are we given more than a hint of what the teacher is supposed to be doing.

FIGURE 7.4   Definitions for Gump's group-structure categories. (Adapted from Gump, 1967, p. 28)

		Group Quality
Total Group	1. Class/Interdependent	Pupils listen to and respond to the actions of one another, e.g., recitation, singing, listening together to story.
	2. Class/Private	Pupils attend to own affairs; not observe or respond to behavior of one another. En masse testing, rest, and seatwork are often of this type. Nonawareness of, nonreaction to the other person is the most suitable orientation.
	3. Class/Neither Interdependent nor Private	Pupils do a number of different things. Neither "togetherness" nor privacy is clearly the action relationship built into the segment, e.g., getting ready to go home or getting ready to start day.
Subgroup	4. Class/Sectioned	Pupils divided into groups but total class is run by T as unit, e.g., four groups of students around four tables of equipment—but all do same thing, all are parts of total class lesson.
	5. Group/Interdependent	Pupils in a group of face-to-face size. They are to listen to and respond to the action of one another, e.g., reading circle group.
	6. Group/Private	Pupils' group less than class size but are to work together, e.g., some seatwork segments.
	7. Group/Neither Interdependent nor Private	Pupils' groups less than class size but are not supposed to be especially private or other-oriented.

(And clearly, the teacher might be doing various things.) In addition, it is possible that the system is somewhat constrained because of the third-grade classrooms studied.

Another way of handling the problem is suggested in the concepts put forth by Adams and Biddle. For these authors the problem of group structure is, again, fractionable into component facets. The first of these facets is *communication structure*, which refers to the number and configuration of communicating groups one finds in the classroom at a given moment. As suggested by Adams and Biddle (1970):

> Theoretically the number of classroom members involved in any one communication exchange could range from two to everybody in the group. During certain kinds of exchanges, however, some members may not be involved in the communication network at all; these are the *disengaged* [or noninvolved]. At other times no communication of any kind may be in evidence. . . . [However] when more than fifty percent of the class are attending

to a single communication, this is called a *central group*. A group with fewer than fifty percent has been called a *peripheral group*. . . . Taken together, the various groups within a classroom form a communication structure, a pattern that may give evidence of considerable change and variation over time. (p. 16)

In addition to discriminating the communication structure of the classroom, Adams and Biddle also studied the *allocation of communicating roles* within each classroom group. This was done by discovering which group members perform the activities of *emitter, target,* and *audience* within each group. As defined by the investigators, all group members must belong to one of these categories. Thus,

> An *emitter* is the person who speaks first when a communication group is set up. The *target* is a person or group to whom the emitter addresses himself. The *audience* consists of those members who are attending to the communication. (p. 17)

Although it would be theoretically possible to discover which of the classroom members performed which of these roles at any moment in time (thus to discover, for example, whether Johnny was more likely to appear as an emitter or target than was Janie), Adams and Biddle confined their analysis of role allocation to the positional categories of teacher and pupils, and if the latter, to designating the number of pupils who were so classified. Thus, we might discover that a given peripheral group was composed of a teacher-emitter, a single-pupil target, and a single-pupil audience. Or again, another peripheral group might have no audience but consist of a single-pupil emitter and a single-pupil target.

In contrast to Gump's categories, those used by Adams and Biddle are based upon teacher as well as pupil behavior. They are also designed for application to secondary as well as to primary classrooms. Finally, they are descriptive rather than ideal in orientation. For this reason they are capable of generating information not only about group structure but also about (actual) teacher and pupil roles.

Group function By group function we mean what classroom groups are up to. For example, some groups are concerned with the subject matter, some with the organizing of classroom effort, some with irrelevancies. Again, some groups are engaged in ritual while others are discussing ideas in some depth.

Two systems for classifying *group function* are available, one each from the Gump and the Adams and Biddle studies. Both of these systems are descriptive in orientation, and of the two the Adams and Biddle classification is the clearer. For Adams and Biddle group function is to be analyzed into two independent facets: *content* and *mode*. Content concerns what it is that the group is talking about, and four content classifications are offered: *scheduled subject matter, nonscheduled subject matter, sociation,* and *organization. Scheduled subject matter* refers to contents of communications that directly relate to the kind of lesson taking place at the time. For example, in an arithmetic lesson scheduled subject matter means communications about arithmetic. *Nonscheduled subject matter* means other academic concerns, such as "excursions into social studies, biology, literature, and the like." *Sociation* concerns transactions "where content either focuses on the process of being sociable or clearly represents recognized social conventions. 'Good morning class,' and 'How do you do,' are communications of the latter kind." In the case of the former, concerns expressed for the welfare of another and exhortations to "be well mannered" are appropriate examples. *Organization* involves "matters that directly involve the administration of the classroom" (Adams and Biddle, 1970, p. 13).

The second facet used by Adams and Biddle, *mode,* deals with how the group proceeded with the content they were considering, or more accurately, with the level of sophistication of its proceedings. Three categories are provided: *operation, information dissemination,* and *intellectualization.* Operations represent "doings" and are exemplified by penmanship practice, group singing, and rituals. *Information disseminations* are "knowings" and are exemplified by the transmission of facts, dates, or definitions from one person to another. *Intellectualization* is characterized by "understanding" and is exemplified by attempts to explain, to account for, or to deduce by formal logic.

Although Adams and Biddle actually studied content and mode separately, most of their findings suggested that these two aspects of function were interrelated. Thus, "information dissemination about scheduled subject matter" was quite a different sort of function from "information dissemination about organization." These two types of functions appeared under quite different circumstances, were utilized differentially by teachers and pupils, were unequally characteristic of different grade levels, and so forth. For this reason the Adams and Biddle study reported findings for twelve different functional categories, created when one considers all possible combinations of the content and mode.

In contrast with concepts from Gump's study already reviewed, Gump considers *function* to be an aspect of the actual teacher's role rather than an ideal characteristic of the lesson format. Thus, *function* (which Gump calls "content") is viewed as a dependent variable, a phenomenon that can be affected by, but is not likely to affect, the format of the lesson.

Function was coded by Gump in two stages. First, teacher "acts" were sorted into a large number of functional categories, for which moderate reliability was obtained. These were then re-sorted into broader categories, which increased reliability. Altogether, four major categories were used, each of which was subdivided into smaller categories. These were (1) *teaching*—which includes *recitation question, feedback* (contributions correct, incorrect), *imparting knowledge and appreciation,* and *work status questions;* (2) *structuring the behavior and behavior object pattern*—which includes *movement* of behavior objects and pupils, *structure* (task assignment, orientation), *attention changes* (and action starts and stops), and *information seeking* (regarding activity and role desires); (3) *dealing with deviating behavior*—which includes *stance and energy improvement, countering*, and *permission*; and (4) *other acts*—which includes *individual problems* and *amenities and miscellaneous*. The genesis of this particular category scheme is not clear to us, nor does Gump define these categories formally. In general, we presume that his "teaching" category represents the two *subject-matter* categories of Adams and Biddle, while "structuring the behavior . . ." is presumably a matter of *organization*. Adams and Biddle's category of *sociation* is not represented, and it is not clear why Gump chooses to set up a separate category of "dealing with deviating behavior."

Teacher roles Some of the concepts presented by Gump and Adams and Biddle could easily have been discussed as teacher roles in this section. However, Gump gave separate consideration to what he termed "teacher leadership pattern," within which he developed eight categories that might better be viewed as teacher roles. These are *not in segment, watcher-helper, participator, action director, recitation leader, instructor, reader, tester*. Definitions of these categories are provided in Figure 7.5.

Other lists of teacher roles also appear in works by Perkins (1964, 1965), Amidon and Hunter (1967), and Lundgren (1972). The reader will

FIGURE 7.5 Definitions for Gump's teacher-role categories. (Adapted from Gump, 1967, p. 27)

Teacher Leadership Pattern (Teacher = T)

1. Not in Segment	T not helping, not clearly and consistently attending to segment. T not key to pupil action. T usually busy in another segment.
2. Watcher-Helper	T is with this working group; clearly watching over them or helping them. May circulate, stand at back; may even be at desk, but if at desk, is at least periodically involved in segment affairs.
3. Participator	T may sing with, salute with. Code when T is not leading but participates along with students.
4. Action Director	T gives directions for cleanup, orders to manage activity, leads a song, acts as master of ceremonies. T is key to action, is making demands for doing, but she is not supplying the core action.
5. Recitation Leader	T asks for reciters, comments on answers, may quiz.
6. Instructor	T tells pupils how to make something, what facts are, etc. Does not use recitation format to do this. Does not ask for contributions from pupils to any degree. May answer pupil questions; may question pupils briefly to check them out, but this is clearly less than half her effort.
7. Reader	T reads to pupils.
8. Tester	Usually T will give questions orally, but she doesn't have to do this. Could point children to a test they have on their desk. T could give test and function like a proctor. Logically this last should be coded "Watch," but to keep all testing together, T-supervised testing is coded "Tester."

find Perkins' set of teacher-role categories given in the lower right-hand quadrant of Figure 7.3; these include *leader-director, resource person, supervisor, socialization agent*, and *evaluator*. Lundgren used a set of categories that was suggested by Amidon and Hunter (1967): *motivating, planning, informing, leading discussion, disciplining, counseling*, and *evaluating*. Once again, it is intriguing to note that these lists do not quite correspond to each other or to the one set forth by Gump. (We are unsure, for example, what Gump would make of Perkins' category *socialization agent*, or what Lundgren would do with Gump's *reader* or *tester*.) We are forced to conclude that these lists are also constructed on an *ad hoc* basis, and that the underlying dimensions along which the teacher's role might be organized are not made clear in any of the studies.

The three categorical lists are stated in terms of observable teacher activities, however, rather than in terms of tasks the teacher might accomplish. These lists, thus, contrast with lists of teacher roles found in some studies of teacher-role expectations. To take but one example of such a study, Fishburn (1962, 1966) proposes six categories for classifying the teacher's role that are based on tasks. These include *director of learning, counseling and guidance person, mediator of culture, member of the school and community, link between school and community*, and *member of the profession*. Although some of these latter categories involve teacher activities outside the classroom, most apply to the classroom too. The list is far different from those suggested by Gump, Amidon and Hunter, and Perkins, however, for teachers' activities identified by the latter might contribute to two or more of the tasks suggested by Fishburn. We presume that role categories of the task variety are difficult to apply in the observation of teacher or pupil behavior.

Pupil roles Gump also offered a classification system for the ideal activities of pupils within a lesson format. This classification involves nine categories: *rest; attend to own materials; work with own materials; attend to class events; work with class events; draw/make; sing, chant, or play instruments; large-muscle activity*; and *reading*. A contrasting system was suggested by Perkins for classifying the actual activities of pupils (see Figure 7.3).

These systems for coding pupil roles appear no less *ad hoc* than those Gump offered for teacher roles. Categories suggested for pupils stress passivity more than those suggested for teachers. In addition, the lists seem somewhat restrictive until we remember that they were made up for primary pupils. If we were to assemble a list for secondary pupils, we might have to add such categories as "laboratory manipulation," "debating," "monitoring others' work," and the like.

Moves in the Classroom Game

We now turn to a research effort that has focused more strongly on the roles and activities of classroom participants than it has on other components of lessons. It can readily be appreciated that the concepts of teacher and pupil roles are broad umbrellas that might be extended to cover nearly the entire content of this book. And yet, as readers may have detected by now, some disagreement exists among educators as to the most fruitful means for conceptualizing and studying those roles. Most investigators have chosen to focus on one or two facets of classroom roles. In contrast, the research we will now consider provides concepts for a wide range of teacher and pupil role behaviors, albeit within a simple framework for viewing classroom inter- action. The original study in this effort was that of Bellack and his associates (1966), and to this interesting effort we now turn.

In general, Bellack *et al.* consider classroom activities to constitute a "game" whose rules are well understood by classroom participants but are not often enunciated. Citing Wittgenstein (1958), they consider the most important aspects of that game to be concerned with language and confine their analysis to the study of units of verbal interaction. In general, these units are termed *moves*, which consist of one or more sentences uttered by a given speaker that have a common content and purpose. The teacher who asks a question of a pupil is making a move. The pupil who answers is mak- ing another one, as is the teacher when she says "Right!" Much of the class- room "game" consists of exchanges of quite short moves among the teacher and her pupils. But even the longer periods of time when the teacher or a pupil "holds forth" can generally, and reliably, be broken into move units for purposes of analysis.

In general, the Bellack group coded all moves into one of four basic types. *Structuring* moves set the stage, *soliciting* moves are designed to elicit a response from others, *responding* moves occur only as a function of solicita- tion and are stimulated by them, and *reacting* moves comment upon other moves. In terms of formal definition:

> Structuring moves serve the pedagogical function of setting the context for subsequent behavior by either launching or halting-excluding interaction between students and teachers. For example, teachers frequently launch a class period with a structuring move in which they focus attention on the topic or problem to be discussed during that session. . . .
>
> [Soliciting moves] are designed to elicit a verbal response, to encourage persons addressed to attend to something, or to elicit a physical response. All questions are solicitations, as are commands, imperatives, and requests. . . .
>
> [Responding] moves bear a reciprocal relationship to soliciting moves and occur only in relation to them. Their pedagogical function is to fulfill the expectation of soliciting moves; thus students' answers to teachers' questions are classified as responding moves. . . .
>
> [Reacting] moves are occasioned by a structuring, soliciting, responding, or prior reacting move, but are not directly elicited by them. Pedagogically, these moves serve to modify (by clarifying, synthesizing, or expanding) and/or to rate (positively or negatively) what has been said previously. Reacting moves differ from responding moves: while a responding move is always directly elicited by a solicitation, preceding moves serve only as the occasion for reactions. Rating by a teacher of a student's response, for exam- ple, is designated as a reacting move. (Bellack et al., 1966, p. 4)

Clearly, it is the intent of the Bellack team that these four categories form a facet, and they report high reliability for the operation of sorting classroom moves into the category set. It seems to us that the classification is based on a set of complex assumptions concerning the classroom that is not really made clear, and one can imagine other classroom moves that would not fit into the system—for example, verbal reactions to nonverbal events, or the telling of jokes. On the other hand, the authors make quite clear that judgments concerning the classification of moves must be done within context; thus a given remark might be judged a structuring, soliciting responding, or reacting move depending on its function within the discourse record. Indeed, as we shall see in Chapter X, each move is conceived to be embedded within a sequence of interaction—termed a *teaching cycle*—which may, in turn, begin only with a structuring or soliciting move.

As interesting as these basic notions may be, concepts suggested by the Bellack group do not stop with them. In addition to classifying moves for their basic *type*, each move is coded for its *speaker* (or other source), its *length* (in terms of lines of text in a discourse transcription), its *substantive meaning* (or reference to subject-matter topic), its *instructional meaning* (or reference to factors related to classroom management), and its *logical meanings* (or reference to cognitive processes involved in dealing with subject matter and management). *Speaker* and *length* are self-explanatory notions. *Substantive meanings* concern the topic of the lesson, and for these the investigators provided a content code based on the topics that should have appeared among the classrooms studied (all of which had been provided a standard curriculum). Codes for *instructional meanings* included categories for assignments, materials, persons, procedures, statements, logical processes, actions (subcategorized into actions-general, -vocal, -physical, -cognitive, and -emotional), and language mechanics. Depending on what was said, a given move might or might not have a substantive meaning and/ or an instructional meaning. (As we shall see, most moves had substantive meanings; however, only about half of all moves could be coded for instructional meaning.) A complex code was also provided for *logical meanings*, which we shall not consider here because it fits nicely with other research using logical models that is reviewed in Chapter IX.

Each of the codes described in the above paragraph could be applied to *all four* of the basic types of moves. In addition to these, the Bellack group also provided an additional coding system that was used for *reacting* moves alone. In general, the system differentiated between reacting moves that were *substantive*, those that *rated* the response, and several other types. When ratings were considered the authors differentiated between reactions that were positive, neutral, and negative in tone. (Recall that in Chapter VI we reviewed a research tradition that would seek to increase the use of positive reinforcement by teachers. We noted that the experimental studies conducted by this group provided no information on whether the "natural" state of teacher reinforcement was positive or negative. Obviously, the Bellack tradition offers just such information.) Other authors

(Zahorik, 1968, 1970; Hawkins and Taylor, 1972; Hughes, 1973) have also taken up the problem of classifying teacher reactions, and we have reproduced their categories as Figures 7.6, 7.7, and 7.8. Once again, the relationship among these several codes is not clear at this time, although there is obvious overlap among them.

As the above paragraph would indicate, Bellack's research has already had an impact on other investigators. Altogether we review six additional studies that reveal this impact directly. The conceptualization of moves in classroom verbal behavior is, however, not unique to the Bellack group. In fact, there is reason to believe that Bellack himself was influenced in this regard by the work of others, such as that of B. O. Smith and his associates (Smith and Meux, 1962). The pioneering study by Smith and Meux focused

FIGURE 7.6   Zahorik categories for coding teacher reactions. (Adapted from Zahorik, 1968, p. 148)

1.0 Praise-confirmation
    1.1 Simple praise-confirmation
    1.2 Elaborate praise
    1.3 Elaborate confirmation
2.0 Reproof-denial
    2.1 Simple reproof-denial
    2.2 Elaborate reproof
    2.3 Elaborate denial
3.0 Praise-confirmation and reproof-denial
4.0 Positive answer
5.0 Negative answer
    5.1 Negative-answer repetition
    5.2 Statement of correct answer
6.0 Positive answer and negative answer
7.0 Positive explanation
8.0 Negative explanation
9.0 Response extension: development
    9.1 Response-development solicitation without clues
    9.2 Response-development solicitation with clues
    9.3 Response-development statement
10.0 Response extension: improvement
    10.1 Response-improvement solicitation without clues
    10.2 Response-improvement solicitation with clues
    10.3 Response-improvement statement
11.0 Solicitation repetition: several answers
    11.1 Several-answers solicitation without clues
    11.2 Several-answers solicitation with clues
12.0 Solicitation repetition: one answer
    12.1 One-answer solicitation without clues
    12.2 One-answer solicitation with clues
13.0 Lesson progression: different topic
14.0 Miscellaneous feedback

upon the logic of classroom discourse and so is reviewed more fully in Chapter IX. However, these authors also recognized the existence of such moves as soliciting, structuring, responding, and reacting, although they did not use those exact terms. Nuthall and Lawrence (1965)—from the University of Canterbury in Christchurch, New Zealand—elaborated further upon the Smith concept of verbal moves. Subsequently, the Canterbury group has contributed a series of studies progressing from an excellent field survey (Wright and Nuthall, 1970) to a number of experiments (Nuthall and Church, 1971; Hughes, 1973).

A full list of moves investigated by Wright and Nuthall, grouped in the manner of Bellack, is provided in Figure 7.9. Note that responding moves were not included in this study but that additional concepts to those of Bellack were included. In particular, Wright and Nuthall contributed the notion that structuring might occur at the end of an episode of verbal interaction, as well as at its beginning. As we shall see, this is an important insight (and one that also appeared in Lundgren, 1972). Further attention by Wright and Nuthall to the potential importance of the placement of struc-

FIGURE 7.7 **Hawkins and Taylor categories for coding teacher reactions. (Adapted from Hawkins and Taylor, 1972)**

1. No Comment—where the teacher does not verbally react to the pupil response.

2. Probing —where the teacher responds with further clarifying questions in an attempt to obtain a more correct or more adequate pupil response.

3. Comment —where the correctness or adequacy of the pupil response is indicated.

   a. *Confirmation:* a comment which indicates the correctness or adequacy of a pupil response, but which does not express findings or give additional information. Repetition is included here.

   b. *Extension:* a comment in which information is given by the teacher so that the pupils' correct answer is extended, modified, or applied.

   c. *Positive Personal Judgment:* a comment which expresses positive feelings toward the pupil rather than informational context.

   d. *Negative Personal Judgment:* a comment which expresses unfavorable feeling toward the pupil, but says nothing about his work.

   e. *Correction:* a comment which indicates that a response was incorrect or inadequate, but gives no reasons. It does not comment on the pupil personally, nor is information concerning the correct answer given.

   f. *Corrective Information:* a comment which follows an incorrect response, and which provides information about the correct answer, or which explains why the response was inadequate.

   g. *Noncommittal:* a comment which does not provide clear information about the correctness or adequacy of a pupil's response.

FIGURE 7.8   Hughes' categories for coding teacher reactions and their reported use in experimental groups. (Adapted from Hughes, 1973, p. 34)

	PERCENT TOTAL TEACHER REACTING STATEMENTS	
	Reacting Group	No Reacting Group
A. Reactions to correct responses		
1. *Praise.* This category included such reactions as "Good," "Very Good," "Very good indeed," "That's right, well done," "That's a very full answer," "That's exactly what I was looking for," etc., followed by a statement of the correct answer.	30.50[a]	0.00
2. *Confirmation.* This category included such reactions as "Yes," "Correct," "Right," "Thank you," "I agree," etc. As with the praise reactions, each confirmation reaction was followed by a statement of the correct answer.	3.50	9.00
3. *Positive answer statement.* This category contained a statement of the correct response and nothing more.	1.50	27.50
B. Reactions to incorrect responses		
4. *Supportive denial.* This category included reactions such as "That was a good try but it's not correct, I'm afraid." "Not a bad effort but . . .," "On the right lines but . . .," "I won't say you're wrong but . . .," etc., followed by a statement of the correct answer.	5.00	1.00
5. *Denial.* This category included reactions such as "No," "That's not right," "That's incorrect," "That's wrong," "I disagree," etc., followed by a statement of the correct answer.	1.50	2.50
6. *Negative answer statement.* This category contained a statement of the correct answer and nothing more.	2.00	4.00
C. Reactions to don't-know responses		
7. *Urging-Reproof.* This category included reactions such as "Are you sure you don't know?," "Would you like to have a try?," "Haven't you got any ideas?," "Are you dreaming?," "Aren't you paying attention?," "Weren't you listening to the question?," etc. This category was used sparingly, especially the reproving statements. The particular statement used was fitted to the behavior of the pupil involved. For example, "Aren't you paying attention?" was used only when the pupil showed clear evidence of not paying attention.	1.50	0.00
8. *Answer statement.* This category contained only a statement of the correct answer.	4.00	6.00

[a] All figures subject to rounding errors.

FIGURE 7.9   Moves investigated by Wright and Nuthall. (Adapted from Wright and Nuthall, 1970)

Structuring
1. Structuring (total)
2. Teacher information following a question
3. Terminal structuring (structuring at the end of an episode of teacher-pupil interaction)
4. Prequestion structuring as a percent of total structuring
5. Postquestion structuring as a percent of total structuring
6. Terminal structuring as a percent of total structuring

Soliciting
7. Teacher utterances with one question
8. Teacher utterances with two questions
9. Teacher utterances with more than two questions
10. Closed questions
11. Open questions
12. Alternative subsequent question
13. Percent of questions leading to pupil response
14. Percent of questions: closed
15. Percent of questions: open

Reacting
16. Redirects question (to another pupil)
17. Reciprocates to extend (pupil thought at the same level)
18. Reciprocates to lift (pupil thought at a higher level)
19. Affirmative and negative
20. Indefinite and complex
21. Thanks and praise
22. Managerial comment
23. Challenging comment
24. Repetition of response

Monologue
25. Monologues
26. Recapitulation at the beginning of a subsequent lesson
27. Revision at the end of a lesson
28. Total lines of recapitulation as percent of total lines (of transcript)
29. Total lines of revision as percent of total lines (of transcript)
30. Total lines of recapitulation plus revision as percent of total lines (of transcript)

turing is to be seen under the heading of monologues in the variables termed *revision* (at the end of a lesson) and *recapitulation* (at the beginning of subsequent lessons).

Location and Other Ecological Features

For our last format variable we turn to a problem that many educators have thought about although few have studied. Clearly, the physical environment of the classroom affects the behavior of classroom members. Pupils at the back of the room are likely to be treated somewhat differently by the teachers and to behave differently than those in front. Doors, pencil sharpeners, the teacher's desk, cloak rooms, library shelves, maps, goldfish bowls—all potentially attract a unique pattern of pupil behaviors in their environments. Sunlight and bright colors are likely to encourage a lively classroom, while carpeting on the floor probably deadens sound, increases attention span, and reduces fatigue.

Though possibly all of these assertions are true, almost none has yet been tested with studies of classroom interaction. We review here several approaches that have contributed to our knowledge of ecological impact on the classroom. The first is represented by the Adams and Biddle study, in which an effort was made to locate classroom subgroups (and actors) within the physical space of the classroom. The coding system adopted by Adams and Biddle was based upon a 25-cell grid that was imposed by the investigators on each of the classrooms studied. This grid was oriented through knowledge of how the majority of pupils' desks faced in the room (recall that Adams and Biddle used videotapes for their data). It enabled the investigators to study where classroom subgroups, emitters, targets, and audiences were located and also to follow the teacher as she moved about the classroom. It did not, unfortunately, provide information concerning the layout of features in the various classrooms of the study, nor how teacher (and pupil) movement or other behaviors were affected by environmental features.

To some extent these shortcomings were engaged by two unrelated studies we shall also review. Like the Adams-Biddle research, these latter also made use of videotapes. In both cases, however, the study of ecology and movement were smaller parts of a larger effort. In the case of the study reported by Neujahr (1970), stress was given to the examination of classroom activities by means of concepts first suggested by Bellack et al. (1966). However, Neujahr also chose to study classroom locations of actors in terms of a number of features found in standard classrooms. The categories used for coding included *classroom-as-a-whole*, the *teacher's desk*, *pupils' desks*, *media* (chalkboard and apparatus), *other locations*, and *teacher-pupil separated*. As we shall see, Neujahr reports that the functions of communication appear to vary among these locations. Rosenshine's (1968) study grew out of programmatic research on "explaining" (see Chapter IX). Among other variables studied, however, was the presence of "gesture and movement" by teachers.

We also review a fourth study (Hill and Furst, 1969) concerned with the impact of educational media on classroom interaction. As readers may be aware, a sizable group of studies has now appeared concerned with the impact of new devices for communicating with the pupil on pupil learning. Television, teaching machines, and language laboratories have all been studied for their effects. Unfortunately, most of this research has neglected the processes of the classroom, thus we have as yet little knowledge concerning how the new medium was actually used in teaching. Hill and Furst (1969), however, have studied the impact of a new medium—in this case a device for computer-assisted instruction—on classroom events. The focus of their study was not upon the problem of conceptualizing the classroom but rather upon the effects of a given innovation. Moreover, the medium was introduced together with a new curriculum for its use, so that findings of the study may have been produced by the medium or by curriculum innovation. Nevertheless, the results of the study are instructive.

Finally, we review research by Keeves (1972), which included systematic observational study of the effects of classroom materials and equipment. Keeves employed a variable termed *stimulation*, which had earlier been used by Anthony (1967). Anthony used the term to refer to a factor on which loaded ratings of such items as the variety of objects handled by pupils, the variety in observed teaching devices, and the number of three-dimensional displays in the classroom. Keeves used the term for a variable identified through cluster analysis. The items of the cluster included frequency counts, as distinct from ratings, but differed slightly from mathematics to science classrooms. For mathematics classrooms the cluster was made up of the number of assignments involving an individual choice, distinct changes in student and teacher activity, the number of items of teaching equipment in the room, and the total number of displays and exhibit items. For science classrooms the list was the number of assignments involving an individual choice, the use made by the teacher of slides and similar visual aids, the number of items of teaching equipment in the room, and the number of display and exhibit items on an academic work. As used by Keeves, then, *stimulation* is a measure of the stimulus density of classroom objects used in teaching.

CLASSROOM RESEARCH

As in Chapter V, the large number of findings reported in this chapter forces us to separate the review of studies from findings. Studies and their design details appear in Box 7.1. Box 7.2 takes up findings concerned with lesson format, 7.3 concerns itself with group structure, 7.4 with group function, 7.5 with teacher roles, 7.6 with pupil roles, 7.7 with moves in the classroom game, and 7.8 with ecology and movement. In contrast with Chapter V, however, most of the findings reported in Boxes 7.2 through 7.8 were generated in isolated, complex, and expensive, multifaceted programs of research that have yet to be replicated. As a result, this chapter is rich in findings, but most of the results tabulated are based on only single samples of classrooms.

Several of the studies cited represent exceptions to the above generalizations. Two of Flanders' studies first reported in Chapter V (Flanders, Projects 3 and 4; see also Flanders, 1964) made use of a supplementary

BOX 7.1   Studies of the Classroom as a Social System

STUDIES REVIEWED

Abraham *et al.* (1971; Reynolds *et al.*, 1971; Nelson *et al.*, 1971)	(Abr71)
Adams and Biddle (1970; Biddle and Adams, 1967)	(A&B70)
Bellack *et al.* (1966)	(Bel66)
Flanders (1964, Projects 3 and 4)	(Flan3)
Furst (1967c)	(Fur67)
Gump (1967)	(Gum67)
Hawkins and Taylor (1972)	(H&T72)
Hill and Furst (1969)	(H&F69)
Hogan (1973)	(Hog73)
Hughes (1973)	(HuD73)
Keeves (1972)	(Kee72)
Kounin *et al.* (1966)	(K&a66)
Kounin (1970)	(Kou70)
Lundgren (1972)	(Lun72)
Neujahr (1970)	(Neu70)
Perkins (1964, 1965)	(Per64)
Power (1971)	(Pow71)
Resnick (1971)	(Res71)
Rosenshine (1968)	(Ros68)
Wright and Nuthall (1970)	(W&N70)
Zahorik (1968)	(Zah68)
Zahorik (1970)	(Zah70)

INSTRUMENT, METHOD OF GATHERING DATA, CODING SYSTEM, UNIT STUDIED, RELIABILITY

Adams and Biddle Instrument, videotape recordings, multifacet category system, "episodes" during which no codable change is noted (see text), high reliability (A&B70).

Canterbury Instrument, transcripts, multifacet category system, T and P verbal moves, reliability not reported (W&N70), (HuD73).

Columbia Instrument, audiotapes and transcripts, multifacet category system, T and P verbal moves, moderate reliability (Bel66), (Fur67),(Pow71), (Lun72).

COR, live observation, single-facet system, T and P moves, moderate to high reliability (Abr71).

FIAC, live observation, single-facet category system (supplemented by judgments about lesson format), T and P utterances in three-second intervals, moderate to high reliability (Flan3).

Gump Instrument, specimen records and time-lapse photographs, multifacet category system, "segments" of the classroom day plus T and P "acts" (see text), high reliability (Gum67).

Hawkins and Taylor Instrument, transcripts, multifacet category system, "activity unit," i.e., "unit of interaction which contains within its boundaries one set of persons who share continuous semantic content"; moderate to high reliability (H&T72).

Hill and Furst Instrument (modified FIAC), live observation plus questionnaire, single-facet category system, T and P utterances, moderate to high reliability (H&F69).

Hogan Instrument, audiotapes and transcripts, multifacet category system, "segments" of the classroom, teaching episodes, and "performer units"; high reliability (Hog73).

Hughes Instrument, transcripts; single-facet category system, teacher reacting moves, reliability not reported (HuD73).

Keeves Instrument, live observation, multifacet sign and category system, units are not clear but included items of equipment and materials, moderate reliability (Kee72).

Kounin Group-Management Concepts, videotape records and transcripts, multifacet category systems and sign systems, various phenomenal units and time units, high reliability (K&a66), (Kou70).

Neujahr Instruments, videotapes and transcripts, multifacet category system, T and P verbal moves, high reliability (Neu70).

Perkins Instrument, live observation plus Bales-Gerbrands recorder, two multifacet category systems, "behaviors" observed during two-minute time periods, moderate reliability (Per64).

Resnick Instrument, live observation, single-facet category system, T utterances during three-minute intervals, high reliability (Res71).

Rosenshine Explaining Instrument, videotapes and transcripts, multifacet category system, words, phrases, clauses, sentences, movements, gestures; reliability not reported (Ros68).

Zahorik Instrument, audiotapes and transcripts, single-facet category system, teacher feedback (reaction) behavior, high reliability (Zah68), (Zah70).

DESIGN OF STUDY, SUBJECTS, CONTEXTS

Field Surveys

(A&B70) 32 teachers and their pupils, grades I, VI, and XI; social studies and mathematics; male and female teachers, older (>45) and younger (<30) teachers

(Bel66) 15 teachers and pupils, grades X and XII; economics; 4 lessons for each teacher; New York

(Flan3) 31 teachers and pupils, 16 of them grade VIII, mathematics, 15 of them grade VII, social studies

(Fur67) As for (Bel66)

(Gum67) 6 teachers and their pupils, grade III; two complete classroom days studied per teacher

(H&T72) 2 teachers and pupils, one classroom containing 37, the other 61, pupils, grade IV; five complete classroom days per teacher: Queensland (Australia)

(Hog73) 9 teachers and their pupils, 3 from single-grade classrooms (grades I, IV, and VII), 3 from composite-grade classrooms (I–II, III–V, VI–VII), 3 from one-teacher schools; one full day for each classroom; Queensland (Australia)

(Kee72) 215 pupils in 72 grade VII mathematics and science classrooms; about 4 sessions each; Canberra (Australia)

(K&a66) 30 teachers and their pupils; grades I through V; one-half day for each classroom

(Kou70) 49 teachers and their pupils, grades I and II; one full day for each classroom

(Lun72) 9 teachers and pupils, grade XI, mathematics; 1–10 sessions each; Göteborg (Sweden)

(Neu70) 3 teachers (1 each for mathematics, science, and social studies) instructing the same 4 classroom groups, grade VI; one week of lessons observed for each teacher and group; lessons "individualized"

(Box 7.1, continued)

(Per64)	27 teachers and their pupils; grade V; language arts, arithmetic, social studies, and science; 72 pupils observed in all (36 "achievers" matched with 36 "underachievers" for sex and ability); each pupil observed together with his or her teacher for various two-minute periods
(Pow71)	4 teachers and their pupils; grade VIII; science; 5 lessons for each teacher; Queensland (Australia)
(Res71)	4 teachers and their pupils; self-directed (British) infant classrooms (grade I); both morning and afternoon sessions
(Ros68)	43 teachers and pupils, grade XII, social studies; two 15-minute lessons each on Yugoslavia and Thailand (analysis confined to 15 most, 15 least effective teachers)
(W&N70)	17 teachers and pupils, grade III; three nature study lessons, standardized content; Christchurch (New Zealand)
(Zah68)	15 teachers and their pupils, grades III and VI; one social studies "discussion" lesson based on the same issue in current events per teacher
(Zah70)	As for (Zah68)

Context-Process Experiment

(H&F69)	6 teachers and their pupils; high school, biology (4 teachers) and reading (2 teachers); two lessons observed per teacher, one conventional, one taught by computer-assisted instruction

Process-Product Experiments

(Abr71)	2 teachers each conducting four different classes, grade VI; black ghetto and white suburban schools; "probing" and "nonprobing" discussion strategies
(HuD73)	1 role-playing teacher, grade VII; 3 nature-study lessons; Christchurch (New Zealand)

Experiment I:	9 classes, each received either a random, a systematic or a self-selected responding treatment
Experiment II:	2 classes; about 50 percent of each received a responding treatment, the rest a no-responding treatment
Experiment III:	2 classes; about 50 percent each received a positive reacting treatment, the rest a minimal reacting treatment

code for lesson format, and findings from them have been reported here as well as in Chapter V. Needless to say, these studies made use of FIAC and live observation. A third study (Hill and Furst, 1969) also used live observation and a modification of FIAC. As was suggested above, the latter authors' concern was with the impact of computer-assisted instruction on classroom interaction, and they used a neat design for the purpose. Traditional lessons taught by six teachers were studied, and then these same teachers were also studied as they taught lessons using CAI.

Another study that also made use of live observation (Resnick, 1971) is unique among all the studies reported in this text in that it took up classroom interaction in self-directed (British infant) schools. The author used an observational instrument similar to FIAC, but did not observe a comparison group of traditional classrooms, so we can not really tell how "different" the classrooms he observed were from traditional ones. Fortunately for our purposes the concept of communication *function* was employed. The (single-facet) coding system used was designed to deal with teacher behaviors only. Teacher "moves" were first broken into *questions, directions, information (giving), praising, writing or reading, giving* (or *withholding*) *permission,* and *unclassifiable moves.* Within most of these categories a further breakdown was then provided between those moves concerned with *management, personal,* and *substantive* issues—which appears to parallel the Adams and Biddle distinctions. Classrooms for four different teachers were observed.

Perkins (1964, 1965) also made use of live observation, but his methodology was more complex than that traditionally used for FIAC studies. Instead of placing a single observer in the classroom, *two* observers were used—one to watch the teacher, the other to watch a pupil. Recordings were made using a Bales-Gerbrand (1943) recorder, "an electrically powered machine that moves tape (paper on which categorizations are recorded) at a constant speed, thereby enabling the duration of each behavioral response to be accurately measured" (1965, p. 5). Each observer was given the task of making two independent judgments. As indicated in Figure 7.3, one observer coded *actual pupil role* and *group structure,* the other coded *actual teacher role* and *ideal teacher role.* Perkins' categories for group structure and ideal teacher role have already been discussed, while those for actual teacher role were a modification of FIAC. Some 27 fifth-grade classrooms were studied, but Perkins did not study the interaction of all pupils in those settings. Rather, he focused on 36 underachievers who were matched with an equal number of achievers for sex and ability. Paired observations of the teacher and one of these 72 pupils were made by two live observers for two-minute intervals, and some 2,410 two-minute observations were made in all.

Finally, Keeves' (1972) study also represented a complex application of live-observation methodology. The study was a massive one concerned with the relationships between home, peer-group, and classroom variables upon pupil attitudes and achievement in mathematics and science. Keeves took a random sample of grade VI children in Canberra, Australia, and followed them through to secondary school at the grade VII level. We review only that part of his study involving the classrooms of children in his sample. Seventy-two classrooms were observed in all, and an average of four sessions were observed for each classroom.

The study by Gump (1967) represents a sharp departure from the live-observation methodology. It is, in fact, the major study we review in this text that depended on specimen records for its basic data. To recapitulate, specimen records are running accounts of a complex interaction situation (in this case, classrooms, of course) that are dictated by an observer into a stenomask. These accounts are then typed in a standard format, and coding is done from the transcription. In addition to specimen records, Gump also worked from time-lapse photographs, which provided him information about what pupils were doing throughout the classroom. Gump's study was also different from most others we are reporting in that he dealt with the entire classroom day rather than with selected lessons. Six grade III teachers were studied, and two complete classroom days were converted into specimen records for each teacher. Thus Gump provides unique data concerning the other things a primary teacher does in addition to conducting lessons. As previously indicated, Gump used a long prescriptive unit (called the "segment") for making judgments about lesson format. In addition, he also coded the individual acts of teachers and pupils. High reliability for coding categories was reported, but it must be remembered that this assessment was made against specimen records that possibly have a certain amount of built-in bias.

Gump's work has already had an impact on other investigators. For example, Hogan (1973) also used segments in the study of classrooms from Queensland (Australia). Nine classrooms were studied—three representing single-grade classrooms (grades I, IV, and VII), three multigrade classrooms (I-II, III-V, VI-VII), and three classrooms from isolated one-teacher schools that represented all primary grades. This study is the only one we know of so far that has studied multigraded classrooms. Two-track audiotapes were used, and the coding system involved not only the study of segments, but also teaching episodes and "performer units."

Gump's research also made use of some concepts that were similar to those of Kounin (1970; Kounin et al., 1966). Although our major review of Kounin's research program was given in Chapter VI, one or two of his findings relate to systemic properties of the classroom and are included in this chapter. As will be recalled, the two Kounin studies made use of videotapes transcriptions, and complex multifaceted codes.

The study of Adams and Biddle (1970) represents another complex videotape methodology. Like Kounin, these investigators used two video cameras, a broadcasting microphone for the teacher, supplementary microphones for the rest of the classroom, and a truck full of complex equipment. Data for the study were taken from middle-class white suburban schools. In order to minimize the potential effects of electronic gear in the classrooms, the authors report that they set up equipment several days prior to collecting recordings. In all, more than 100 hours of recordings were made initially, from which 32 lessons were chosen for analysis. The sample included both male and female teachers, half of whom were age 45 or older and the others under age 30. Two traditional subjects were studied (mathematics and social studies) as well as three different grade levels (grades I, VI, and XI). Coders worked directly from videotapes, without transcriptions. In general, new coding decisions were made whenever a codable feature of the lesson format changed. High reliability for coding categories is reported by the authors.

All but one of the remaining studies reflected the concepts and research designs used by Bellack or B. O. Smith. In the original Bellack study (Bellack et al., 1966) fifteen high school teachers were studied, each of whom was given the task of presenting four lessons on international economic problems using standardized materials. (Despite this attempt at standardization, the authors reported great variability in the selection of topics for discussion by the teachers!) Methods used in the study included the use of audiotape recordings and lesson transcripts. As we have noted, classroom moves were coded for both teachers and pupils, and the code used involved a number of different facets of judgment. Finally, a number of product measures were also obtained from pupils, including a test of subject-matter knowledge and an attitude scale. (Findings presented in the original report for these latter were generally inconclusive. However, here and in Chapter IX we review some product results that were generated for Bellack's categories in a subsequent analysis by Furst, 1967c).

Six other studies are also reviewed that made use of Bellack's conceptual tools. In three of these field studies were conducted in another national context, and the authors sought to compare and contrast their findings with those obtained in the original Bellack study. Power (1971a) studied classroom interaction in grade VIII science lessons in Queensland (Australia). Four different teachers were studied, each of whom taught five lessons. Hawkins and Taylor (1972) also studied teaching in Queensland, this time at the grade IV level. Two classrooms were contrasted, one having 37 pupils, the other 61. In contrast, Lundgren (1972) conducted research in Göteborg (Sweden) involving nine grade XI mathematics classes.

In the other three studies substantial modifications were made in the original Bellack coding system. Abraham et al. (1971) (Reynolds et al., 1971; Nelson et al., 1971) sought to examine the processes and products that characterized "probing" and "nonprobing" lessons. In an unusual experimental design, two teachers were trained to conduct discussions using these two contrasting strategies. They then conducted discussions in eight different grade VI classrooms, four of which were placed in white suburban schools, the other four in black ghetto schools. An original instrument was developed by the authors for live observation entitled the Classroom Observational Record (COR), but teacher and pupil moves were, in fact, coded, and we would judge that the system reflected Bellack's concepts in the main. The authors also developed measures for product variables, each of them "cognitive skills" that might be influenced by "probing" versus "nonprobing" discussions. These were entitled "Observation—the ability to gather data through the use of the five senses; Inference—the ability to project into an unexplored area from observations . . . ; Verification—the ability to test the validity of an inference; [and] Classification—the ability to form group having some common specified observed property" (Abraham *et al.*, 197 p. 8).

Neujahr (1970) has also applied Bellack's concepts, in modified form in a field study that made use of videotapes and transcripts. Twelve grad VI classroom situations were studied in all: four different groups of pupil were taught by the same three teachers, one teaching mathematics, on science, and one social studies. (Unfortunately, only one teacher was the available for each subject taught.) Each of these twelve teaching situation was studied for several different lessons. In most cases teachers claimed the lessons were "individualized," and the author offers evidence contrastin his "individualized" lessons with those studied by Bellack *et al.* (1966), a well as with several lessons from his own sample that were not "individua ized." In addition to coding the moves of teachers and pupils, Neujahr als studied the classroom locations of actors using the concepts describe earlier, and his findings offer evidence concerning the relation betwee classroom moves and ecology.

Zahorik (1968, 1970) also developed additional instrumentation to stud teacher reaction. Fifteen teachers were studied, at grades III and VI, eac teaching a single social studies lesson based on current events. Audiotape and transcripts were used.

The Canterbury studies (Wright and Nuthall, 1970; Hughes, 1973 were conducted in Christchurch, New Zealand. Both made use of transcript: The Wright and Nuthall research was a field study at the third-grade leve Seventeen teachers, some of whom were very experienced while others wer student teachers, taught three lessons on a standardized unit in nature study These lessons were audiotaped and transcribed for analysis. A substantia number of different teaching variables were coded, and both factor analysi and multiple-regression analysis were used to establish process-process and process-product relationships. In fact, given the eclectic character of the study, we have chosen to report some of Wright and Nuthall's findings in this chapter, while others appear in Chapters V, VIII, and X. Hughes' (1973 experiments involved a single experimenter-teacher applying treatment involving manipulation of soliciting, responding, and reacting moves. Three nature-study lessons were given to pupils in thirteen grade VII classrooms Transcripts were used to check on the validity of the experimental treat ments.

The last study reviewed (Rosenshine, 1968) also made use of video tapes and transcripts. This study grew out of programmatic research on the subject of "explaining" and is dealt with in greater detail in Chapter IX. The study involved analysis of some 30 different lessons—15 of them conducted by relatively "effective" and 15 by relatively "ineffective" teachers. Each teacher conducted two 15-minute lessons, one on Yugoslavia and one on Thailand. A substantial number of different variables were studied, most of them linguistic in orientation. Nevertheless, one of the variables concerned "teacher gesture and movement," which causes us to review the study in this chapter.

Findings for Lesson Format

We now turn to findings generated by these studies and are struck by the complexity and richness of the results offered. More than 100 findings are listed in Boxes 7.2 through 7.8. For convenience each finding is listed but once, although citations appear within each box concerning other related findings to which the reader may wish to turn.

Findings for *lesson format* appear in Box 7.2. Findings from both Perkins and Gump suggest that primary classrooms spend most of their time in *seatwork* and *class recitation*, while Adams and Biddle report substantial time committed to "lecturing," "response," and "questions and directives." Not surprisingly, subject matter is found to affect the lesson format, with mathematics featuring a closer, more formal relationship between group function and structure than social studies. (Moreover, grade level also affects format, although findings pertaining to the latter are tabulated in subsequent boxes). However, it might come as a surprise to discover that teacher *age* and *sex* also affect format. Lessons taught by younger teachers exhibit a closer relationship between *structure* and *function* than do those taught by older teachers, while female teachers similarly generate a closer relationship than do men.

BOX 7.2   Findings for Lesson Format

Process Occurrence

7.2-1   In (grade V) lessons most time is devoted to *seatwork* and *class recitation*. Little time is spent in *individual work, small-group work, large-group discussion,* or *oral reports* (Per64).

7.2-2   Most of the (grade III) classroom day is spent in *isolated seatwork, whole-class recitation,* and *reading circle.* Somewhat less time is spent in *supervised study, getting ready, whole-class recitation and seatwork,* and *teacher reading*—with other activities receiving even less emphasis (Gum67).

7.2-3   Most lessons are dominated by a central group that spends its time in three traditional patterns of role allocation: (1) *teacher-emitter with a quorum audience* ("lecturing"); (2) *single-pupil emitter, teacher target, quorum audience* ("response"); and (3) *teacher-emitter, single-pupil target, quorum audience* ("questions and directives") (A&B70).

Context-Process Relationships

7.2-4   *Subject matter* affects the *lesson format.* (For example, mathematics les-

---

* Findings generated experimentally are indicated with an E.

(Box 7.2, continued)

sons exhibit a closer relationship between *group structure* and *group function* than do social studies lessons) (A&B70), (Res71).

Presage-Process Relationships

7.2-5   *Teacher age* affects *lesson format.* Lessons taught by *younger* teachers exhibit a closer relationship between *group structure* and *group function* than do *older* teachers' lessons (A&B70).

7.2-6   *Teacher sex* affects *lesson format. Female* teachers' lessons exhibit a closer relationship between *group structure* and *group function* than do *male* teachers' lessons (A&B70).

Process-Process Relationships

7.2-7   *Lesson format* affects *group function.* For example, *whole-class recitation* and *reading circle* exhibit moves concerned with *subject matter, music* exhibits *structuring, supervised study* generates *deviancy control* (Gum67).

7.2-8   *Lesson format* affects *type of moves* emitted in teaching. *Individualized lessons* feature more *structuring, soliciting,* and *reacting; standard lessons* more *responding* moves (Neu70).

7.2-9   *Lesson format* affects *rate of teacher emission of moves.* For example, the following rates of emission of moves per minute are found (for grade III): *whole-class recitation* (6), *reading circle* (4), *music* (3.5), *supervised study* (2), and *isolated seatwork* (0.2) (Gum67).

7.2-10   *Lesson format* affects *teachers'* "indirectness." *Planning, introducing new material,* and *general discussion* are more likely to involve "indirect" teaching; *seatwork, evaluation,* and *routine administration* less likely (Flan3). Again, "indirect" teaching is less likely during *not-relevant* and *giving-homework* lesson themes (Lun72).

7.2-11   *Lesson format* affects *teacher role.* For example, *going through* and *preparation of homework or written tests* involve more teacher *informing* and less teacher *leading discussion* than other lesson themes (Lun72).

7.2-12   *Lesson format* is unrelated to *pupil involvement* (Kou70). In contradiction, it is also found that

7.2-12a *Lesson format* affects *pupil involvement. Pupil involvement* is highest for *reading circle,* less high for *tests, instruction,* and *whole-class recitation,* and lower for *supervised study, isolated seatwork,* and *pupil presentations* (Gum67).

7.2-13   *Lesson format* is unrelated to *pupil deviancy* (Kou70).

7.2-14   *Lesson format* affects *pupil self-touching behavior.* (*Self-touching* is particularly high during "passive" formats such as *teacher reading, whole-class recitation, instruction,* or *pupil presentation* and low for *reading circle* (Gum67).

7.2-15   *Duration of lesson* is unrelated to *pupil involvement* (Kou66), (Kou70).

7.2-16   *Duration of lesson* is unrelated to *pupil deviancy* (K&a66), (Kou70). (Also see 7.7-25.)

Process-Product Relationships

7.2-17   *Probing lessons* induce more *pupil inferences* and more *accurate pupil inferences* (concerning subject matter) than do nonprobing lessons (Abr71)E.*

7.2-18   *Nonprobing lessons* induce more *pupil observations* (concerning subject matter) than probing lessons in *black ghetto classrooms; probing lessons* induce *more observations* in *white suburban classrooms* (Abr71)E.

All well and good, but does format make a difference? Two kinds of answers may be sought for this question. On the one hand, when a separate ideal-type code is provided for format, process-process relationships may be sought between format conditions and other systemic properties of the classroom. Thus, we find that format is reported to affect *group function* (Gump), *classroom moves* (Neujahr), *rate of move emission* (Gump), *teacher "indirectness"* (Flanders), and *teacher role* (Lundgren). Moreover, format is also reported (by Gump) to affect *pupil involvement* and *pupil self-touching behavior*. The former is denied by Kounin, who reports that format is unrelated to *pupil deviancy*. (We are not quite sure what to make of these contradictory findings, nor are they commented upon by either Gump or Kounin.) Finally, Kounin also reports that duration of the lesson is unrelated to *pupil involvement* and *deviancy* (thus contradicting some common notions concerning pupil satiation).

What do these findings signify? To the extent that the low-inference evidence used by investigators for judging lesson format was in fact independent of that used to judge group function, classroom moves, and so on, we suspect that little has been told us other than the fact that different types of lessons are, indeed, "different." We surely have not yet seen much evidence that lesson format affects pupil behavior in a significant way.

On the other hand, a second kind of evidence concerning format may be sought in process-product research. If formats make a difference, then pupils should be found to respond differentially to them in achievement or attitudes. As can be seen in Box 7.2, none of the format distinctions appearing in earlier findings has yet been applied in process-product research, nor are we convinced that it is meaningful or even possible to make such applications. Instead, we find two intriguing findings from Abraham *et al.* (1971) that concern the use of "probing" in classroom discussions. Probing lessons are found to induce more pupil "inferences" than nonprobing lessons. This finding is reported to hold in both white suburban and black ghetto schools. In contrast, it is also reported that *non*probing lessons are more successful in inducing pupil "observations" in the black ghetto context, while probing lessons are more successful with observations in the white suburban setting. Now this is worth contemplation! If the investigators' notion of observation may be equated with fact acquisition, what they are telling us is that pupils from disadvantaged schools will actually do better with standardized achievement tests when instructed in lessons that are carefully structured and constrained.

Findings for Group Structure

Findings for group structure appear in Box 7.3. If there were ever a "dry and unpromising" variable for classroom research, surely it is group structure! After all, what difference can it possibly make if the lesson is conducted in large or small groups? Read on and see.

BOX 7.3   Findings for Group Structure

Process Occurrence

7.3-1   Most of the (grade III) classroom day is spent in *class-independent* ("whole-class"—30 percent) and *group-private* ("seatwork"—25 percent) activities. Less time is spent in *class-intermediate, class-private, group-interdependent, group-intermediate,* or *class-sectioned* activities (Gum67).

7.3-2   During most (85 percent) of the lesson time a *central group* exists in the classroom. *Peripheral groups* appear less often (20 percent), as do *noninvolved persons* (25 percent) (A&B70).

7.3-3   Incidents involving *peripheral groups* and *noninvolved persons* last for less time than incidents involving the *central group* (A&B70). (Also see 7.2-3.)

Context-Process Relationships

7.3-4   *Subject matter* affects *group structure. Social studies* lessons exhibit more *peripheral groups* and more *noninvolved* persons than do *mathematics lessons* (A&B70).

7.3-5   *Grade level* affects *group structure. Grade I* lessons exhibit more *peripheral groups* and more *group emitting* ("chanting in unison"). *Grade VI* lessons are less likely to feature *central groups. Grade XI* lessons are less likely to feature *noninvolved persons* and are more likely to be *structurally organized* (A&B70).

7.3-6   *Educational media* affect *group structure.* Classrooms involving *computer-assisted instruction* exhibit more *teacher interaction with individual pupils* than standard classrooms (H&F69)E.*

7.3-7   *Multigradedness* affects *group structure. Multigraded classrooms* exhibit more *independent subgroups* than do standard classrooms (Hog73).

Presage-Process Relationships

7.3-8   *Teacher age* affects *group structure. Older teachers'* lessons exhibit more *noninvolved persons* and fewer *peripheral groups* than do lessons of *younger teachers* (A&B70).

7.3-9   *Teacher sex* affects *group structure. Male teachers'* lessons exhibit more *noninvolved persons* and more *audience only central groups* than do lessons of *female teachers* (A&B70).

Process-Process Relationships

7.3-10   *Group structure* affects *pupil involvement.* Small groups are associated with *higher pupil involvement* than is the total classroom group (Gum67).

7.3-11   *Group structure* affects *group function.* Incidents involving *intellectualization* last longer in *peripheral groups* than in the *central group.* In addition, *peripheral groups* are more often involved with *nonrelevant subject matter* than is the *central group* (A&B70). (Also see 7.4-12.)

Process-Product Relationships

None reported.

---

* Findings generated experimentally are indicated with an E.

Not surprisingly, we learn that much of the classroom day is spent in *whole-class activities*, while a *central group* exists during the preponderance of time in the classroom lesson. Evidently, most classrooms are not yet the pupil-self-directed entities that some critics wish they were. In addition, we learn that subject matter affects group structure, with more *peripheral groups* and *noninvolved persons* appearing in social studies than in mathematics. Furthermore, classrooms are more likely to become group organized as one goes up the grade-level ladder. Classrooms involving computer-assisted instruction involve more teacher *interaction with individual pupils*. Moreover, the age and sex of teachers both appear to influence group structure. Finally, multigraded classrooms involve more independent subgroups than do standard classrooms.

When we turn to process-process relationships some surprises await us, however. Therein we find that pupils are more likely to be *involved* in small groups than in the total classroom, that *intellectualization* is more likely in peripheral groups, but that peripheral groups are also more likely to be involved with *nonrelevant subject matter*. These findings, taken together with finding 7.6-11, suggest that the ideal teaching situation is neither that of pupils in isolation or the class as a whole but rather that of small, supervised groups. We also suspect that variety is the spice of successful classroom life, and that whereas unmitigated whole-class activities are a bore, un-alloyed experiences where pupils study in isolation are equally undesirable. If true, such facts would provide natural limits to the effectiveness of attempts to "individualize" education—and particularly to computer-assisted instruction.

Once again, however, we find little evidence that group-structure variables have yet been investigated for their impact on product variables. Surely these are also worthy of additional investigation.

Findings for Group Function

Findings for group function are complex and wordy (see Box 7.4). Gump finds that most of the classroom day is taken up with *academic lessons* and that teachers are more likely to be *teaching* than to be doing other things such as *structuring, controlling deviancy*, and so forth. Adams and Biddle report that classrooms spend most of their time in *information dissemination* and much of it concerned with *relevant subject matter*. Finally, both Adams and Biddle and Resnick report that longer incidents in the classroom are more likely to concern *relevant subject matter*, while shorter ones take up such issues as *organization* and *sociation*. All of this suggests that classrooms are businesslike places, even if their level of discourse leaves something to be desired.

Group function is also reported to vary with subject matter and grade level, as well as with teacher age and sex and with computer-assisted instruction. Social studies lessons exhibit more *information dissemination* about

BOX 7.4   Findings for Group Function

Process Occurrence

7.4-1   Most of the (grade III) classroom day is taken up with *academic lessons* (75 percent), followed by *procedural, relaxation,* and *artistic* emphases (Gum67).

7.4-2   Teachers' activities are more likely to concern *teaching* (50 percent) than they are *structuring* (25 percent), *deviancy control,* or *other matters* (Gum67).

7.4-3   Classroom groups spend most (75 percent) of their time in *information dissemination,* little time (20 percent) in *intellectualization,* and almost no time in *operations* (A&B70).

7.4-4   Classroom groups spend most (50 percent) of their time on *relevant subject matter* (one half), less on *organization* (20 percent) and *nonrelevant subject matter* (20 percent), and little on *sociation* (A&B70), (Res71).

7.4-5   *Longer incidents* (exchanges) are more likely to concern *relevant subject matter;* shorter incidents (exchanges) are more likely to concern *organization and sociation* (A&B70), (Res71). (Also see 7.7-5, 7.7-6.)

Context-Process Relationships

7.4-6   *Subject matter* affects *group function. Social studies* lessons exhibit more *information dissemination about relevant subject matter, information dissemination about nonrelevant subject matter,* and *intellectualization about organization* than do *mathematics* lessons. Mathematics lessons are higher on *information dissemination about sociation* (A&B70).

7.4-7   *Grade level* affects *group function. Grade I* lessons exhibit more *operation with relevant subject matter, information dissemination about sociation,* and *intellectualization about organization. Grade XI* lessons exhibit more *information dissemination about relevant subject matter* and *intellectualization about relevant subject matter* (A&B70).

7.4-8   *Educational media* affect *group functions.* Classrooms involving *computer-assisted instruction* exhibit more interaction concerning *organization* than standard classrooms (H&F69)E.* (Also see 7.8-5.)

7.4-9   *Multigradedness* does not affect *group function. Multigraded classrooms* are not different from standard classrooms in time spent in *organization* (Hog73).

Presage-Process Relationships

7.4-10 *Teacher age* affects *group function. Older teachers'* lessons exhibit more *information dissemination about relevant subject matter* than do *younger teachers'* lessons. Those of younger teachers show more *intellectualization about relevant subject matter, information dissemination about nonrelevant subject matter,* and *information dissemination about sociation* (A&B70).

7.4-11 *Teacher sex* affects *group function. Male teachers'* lessons exhibit more *information dissemination about relevant subject matter* and *information dissemination about sociation* than do those of *female tecahers.* Women's lessons exhibit more *intellectualization about organization.* (A&B70).

---

* Findings generated experimentally are indicated with an E.

Process-Process Relationships

7.4-12 *Group function* affects *group structure*. For example, *information dissemination about relevant subject matter*, *information dissemination about organization*, and *intellectualization about organization* are all likely to provoke *teacher emitter and quorum audience* (that is, "lecturing") (A&B70).

7.4-13 *Group function* affects *pupil involvement*. Disappearance of the *central group function* is positively associated with *pupil noninvolvement* (Gum67).

(Also see 7.2-7, 7.4-8, 7.5-12, 7.6-7, 7.8-10.)

Process-Product Relationships

None reported.

---

both *relevant* and *nonrelevant subject matter*, as well as *intellectualization about organization*. Grade I spends more time in *operations*. It also *disseminates information about organization*, while grade VI *intellectualizes about organization*. At the grade XI level *organizational* matters are no longer an issue at all; however, *information dissemination* and *intellectualization* about *relevant subject matter* are both high. Older teachers are higher on *information dissemination*, younger teachers on *intellectualization* concerning *relevant subject matter*, but younger teachers also consider *nonrelevant* materials more. Male teachers *disseminate more information about relevant subject matters* and *sociation*; women *intellectualize about organization*. Finally, the presence of computer-assisted instruction appears to induce more time spent in *organization* than is true for standard classrooms.

Group function also turns out to be related to lesson format, teacher role, group structure, and ecological features of the classroom. (See the other boxes in this chapter for details.) Surprisingly, only one finding is reported wherein group function relates to pupil role—Gump reports that *involvement* decreases when the central group function disappears—and no studies have yet appeared to take up the relationships between group functions and product variables.

Findings for Teacher Roles

Another component of lesson format is teacher role, and immediately we encounter an enigma. As readers will appreciate, any study that concerns the behavior of teachers is, in effect, a study of teacher roles, thus the findings reviewed in Box 7.5 are but a selection of results that could have been tabulated under a teacher-role heading. In general, those appearing in Box 7.5 used an explicit role terminology in describing the teacher.

Findings presented are nearly all of the process-occurrence, context-process, and presage-process variety. We learn that teachers spend most of their time as recitation or discussion leaders, supervisors of action, and

BOX 7.5   Findings for Teacher Roles

Process Occurrence

7.5-1   (Grade V) teachers spend most of their time in lessons as a *leader-director* (50 percent) and as a *supervisor* (30 percent). Little time is spent as a *resource person, evaluator,* or *socializing agent* (Per64).

7.5-2   (Grade III) teachers spend most of their time during the classroom day as a *recitation leader* (25 percent), *action director* (25 percent), *not directly involved* (25 percent), and as a *watcher-helper* (16 percent). Little time is spent as an *instructor, reader, tester,* or *participator* (Gum67).

7.5-3   (Grade XI) teachers spend most of their time in lessons as *discussion leaders* (40 percent), *informers* (30 percent), *evaluators* (20 percent), and *planners* (10 percent). Little time is spent as *motivators, discipliners,* or *counselors* (Lun72).

7.5-4   Teachers address *individual pupils* slightly more often than they address *pupil groups* (Gum67).

7.5-5   Most teacher *solicitations* are directed to *specified pupils* (50 percent), fewer to *any pupil* (25 percent) or *selected pupils,* and fewer yet to *all pupils* (Bel66).

7.5-6   During much of the lesson time teachers appear as *emitters* (50 percent), less often as *targets* (25 percent), and but rarely as members of the *audience* or *uninvolved* (A&B70). (Grade XI) teachers are *emitters* in about 60 percent of all verbal moves and targets in about 40 percent (Lun72).

7.5-7   Teachers spend most of their time in the *central group* of the classrooms (eight tenths) (A&B70).

7.5-8   Most *teacher utterances* (in the self-directed classroom) are *questions* (Res71).

7.5-9   The majority of all *teacher reacting* moves are (at least somewhat) *positive* in tone (Bel66).
(Also see 7.4-8, 7.7-1, 7.7-2, 7.7-3, 7.8-1, 7.8-2.)

Context-Process Relationships

7.5-10   *Subject matter* affects *teacher role.* Teachers are more likely to be *emitters* in *mathematics* than in *social studies* (A&B70).

7.5-11   *Subject matter* affects *teacher group-involvement role.* Teachers are more likely to be involved in the *central group* in *social studies;* in *mathematics* they are more likely to be in *peripheral groups* or to be *noninvolved* (A&B70).

7.5-12   *Average I.Q.* of *"steering-group"* pupils varies inversely with amount of teacher *informing* and *disciplining;* co-varies directly with amount of teacher *leading-discussion;* is unrelated to amount of teacher *motivating, planning,* and *evaluating* (Lun72).

7.5-13   *Grade level* affects *teacher role. Grade I* teachers are more likely to be *emitters* or *targets* in the *central group* than are *grade VI* or *grade XI* teachers (A&B70).

7.5-14   *Educational media* affect *teachers' roles.* Classrooms involving *computer-assisted instruction* exhibit less *teacher corrective feedback* and more *teacher silence* than standard classrooms (H&F69)E.*

7.5-15   *Multigradedness* affects *teacher role. Multigraded classrooms* exhibit

* Findings generated experimentally are indicated with an E.

more teacher effort spent on *new work* and less on *revision* and *review* than standard classrooms (Hog73).
(Also see 7.3-6, 7.7-22.)

Presage-Process Relationships

7.5-16 *Teacher age* affects *teacher role.* *Younger teachers* are more likely to be *emitters* and *targets* (and less likely to be in the *audience*) of the *central group* than are *older teachers* (A&B70). They are also more likely to *speak privately* with pupils and to be *noninvolved* than are older teachers (A&B70).

7.5-17 *Teacher age* affects *teacher group-involvement role.* *Older teachers* are more likely to generate *peripheral groups of which they are not a member* (A&B70).

7.5-18 *Teacher sex* affects *teacher role.* *Male teachers* are more likely to be *emitters* than are *female teachers* (A&B70).

Process-Process Relationships

7.5-19 *Teacher role* affects *pupil involvement.* Centrality of teacher role is associated with higher pupil involvement; that is, involvement is greater when the teacher is an *action director, recitation leader, instructor,* and *tester* (Gum67).

7.5-20 *Teacher role* affects *group function.* Group functions tend to disappear when the teacher is not "in charge"; that is, when she is *out of the group,* a *target,* a member of the *audience,* or *noninvolved* (A&B70).
(Also see 7.2-8, 7.2-9, 7.2-10, 7.5-14, 7.7-26.)

Process-Product Relationships
(See 7.7-29, 7.7-30, 7.7-34.)

informers, or are not directly involved in classroom events. About half the time teachers are emitters (suggesting that teachers are actually talking for several *hours* during the typical school day), and during most of the time teachers are members of the central classroom group.

Nearly all contextual and presage variables examined are found to affect teacher role in some way. Teachers are more likely to be emitters and to be in peripheral groups in mathematics than in social studies. Grade I teachers are more likely to be emitters or targets in the central group than are grade VI or XI teachers. The same finding also holds for younger teachers, while older teachers are more likely to generate peripheral groups of which they are not a member. Male teachers are more likely to be emitters than are female teachers (that is, men talk more!). Teachers involved with computer-assisted instruction are more likely to exhibit *silence* and less likely to offer *corrective feedback.* Teachers in multigraded classrooms spend more time on *new work* and less on *revision* and *review* than do teachers in standard classrooms.

Perhaps the most intriguing finding in this set involves the notion of "steering group" used by Lundgren. Lundgren hypothesized that teachers were likely to conduct their teaching so as to "reach" pupils toward the lower end of the ability continuum of the classroom. Accordingly, he defined as the steering group those pupils whose I.Q. was between the tenth and twenty-fifth percentiles for their class. In finding 7.5-12 we see evidence of the validity of the notion in that the average I.Q. of the steering group is positively related to the amount of *leading discussion* and negatively related to the amount of *informing* and *disciplining* done by teachers. (Additional findings concerning the steering group appear in Box 7.7.)

Teacher role is also found to affect, or to be affected by, a wide variety of other events in the classroom, including *lesson format, group function* and *classroom location*. However, evidence that teacher role "makes a difference" in the lives of pupils is scanty. Gump reports that pupils are more likely to be "involved" when the teacher is "central" to classroom activities but as yet no evidence has been advanced to suggest that teacher role (conceived as in Box 7.5) affects pupil achievement or attitudes. (Contrast this picture with that of Box 7.7.) Altogether, findings for teacher role are more suggestive than those for lesson format, but we have even less evidence of their usefulness in predicting the effectiveness of teaching.

Findings for Pupil Roles

Results concerning pupil roles are tabulated in Box 7.6. Once again readers are reminded that the pupil-role concepts encountered in this chapter are but a selection from the larger universe of concepts that have been found useful for describing pupil classroom behavior. In addition, findings presented in Box 7.6 have a somewhat different relationship to the problem of analyzing teaching than those of the other boxes in this chapter. Lesson format, teacher role, group structure, and the like, are conceived as *independent* variables whose effects on pupil behavior and pupil learning are to be studied; pupil roles are potential *dependent* variables and may serve as a criterion by which we can judge the effectiveness of teaching directly— although the authors' bias suggests that we must ultimately judge the success of teaching in terms of product variables.

Among process findings in Box 7.6 we learn that the pupil role is considerably more passive than the teacher role. Pupils spend most of their time in *listening* and *watching* and in *reading* and *writing*. Less time is spent in any activities that involve gross muscular effort or expressiveness or in talking with others. And when pupils speak at all, it is likely that they are addressing the teacher. All of these findings constitute grist for critics who would find the classroom a dull, teacher-dominated environment, although whether pupils actually "suffer" from such practices or whether it would be possible to run a multipupil classroom effectively by other techniques is not yet established. Finding 7.6-9 suggests that computer-assisted instruction might be one technique for improving matters.

Among context-process relationships reported we find some interesting findings concerning pupil sex. Boys are reported to spend more time in *high activity, work in another academic area,* and *withdrawal* than girls. We also learn (from Box 7.7) that girls *emit more moves* than boys and

---

BOX 7.6   Findings for Pupil Roles

Process Occurrence

7.6-1   (Grade V) pupils spend most of their time in the lesson *listening and watching* (30 percent) and *reading and writing* (30 percent). Less time is spent in *withdrawal, high activity or involvement, nonacademic work, specializing, discussing work with peers, work in another area,* or *discussing work with teacher* (Per64).

7.6-2   During most of the (grade III) classroom day pupils *attend class events* (30 percent) and *work with their own materials* (30 percent). Less often they *work with class events; prepare; sing, chant,* or *play an instrument; draw or make; engage in large-muscle activities; rest;* or *attend to own materials* (Gum67).

7.6-3   Grade XI pupils are *emitters* in 40 percent, and *targets* in 60 percent, of *all verbal moves* (Lun72).

7.6-4   Most pupil solicitations (85 percent) are directed to the *teacher.* Of the rest, most go to *specified pupils* or to *any pupil* (Bel66).
        (Also see 7.5-5, 7.7-2, 7.7-3, 7.8-2.)

Context-Process Relationships

7.6-5   *Boys* spend more time in *high activity or involvement, work in another academic area,* and *withdrawal* than do *girls. Girls* spend more time in *reading or writing, discussing work with peers,* and *nonacademic work* (Per64).

7.6-6   *Underachieving pupils* spend more time in *withdrawal, nonacademic work,* and *work in another academic area* than do *achieving pupils* (Per64).

7.6-7   *Underachieving girls* (only) spend more time in *discussing work* with *peers* than do *achieving girls* (Per64).

7.6-8   Pupils who are members of the "steering group" are *emitters* and *targets* more often than are other pupils (Lun72).

7.6-9   *Educational media* affect *pupil's roles.* Classrooms involving *computer-assisted instruction* exhibit more *pupil initiations* and more *pupil independence* than standard classrooms (H&F69)E.*
        (Also see 7.7-14, 7.7-15.)

Presage-Process Relationships

7.6-10 *Multigradedness* affects *pupil role. Multigraded classrooms* exhibit more *pupil seatwork* than do standard classrooms (Hog73).
        (Also see 7.7-31, 7.7-32, 7.7-33.)

Process-Process Relationships

7.6-11 *Pupil role* affects *pupil involvement.* Activities wherein pupils *work with their own materials* and *pace themselves* are associated with *lower pupil involvement* than other activities (Gum67).

7.6-12 *Pupil role* affects *pupil self-touching behavior.* Pupils who are *resting* are more likely to *touch themselves* than those who are not (Gum67).
        (Also see 7.2-11, 7.2-12, 7.2-13, 7.2-15, 7.2-16, 7.4-13, 7.5-19, 7.6-9, 7.7-25.)

Process-Product Relationships

None reported.

---

* Findings generated experimentally are indicated with an E.

that the moves they exhibit are more likely to be *structuring, soliciting,* and *reacting*—while boys emit responding moves. On the other hand, under-achieving girls are more likely to "waste" time in gossip with other girls. And underachieving pupils of both sexes are more likely to engage in *withdrawal, nonacademic work,* and *work in another academic area.* These findings suggest that pupils will exhibit behavioral cues when they are doing poorly or when they are uninterested in the material, but they do not tell us what to do about the situation as teachers. While pupils generally are targets more often than emitters, their chances of performing both these roles seem to be increased if they are members of the "steering group." Finally, educational media and multigradedness both appear to affect pupil role. Computer-assisted instruction is reported to increase pupil *initiations* and *independence,* while multigraded classrooms exhibit more *seatwork* by pupils.

Roughly a dozen findings report relationships between other kinds of classroom events and pupil roles. Most of these appear in other boxes, and we shall take them up as they appear there. However, two findings by Gump tell us that pupil role conceived in ideal-type terms is likely to affect pupil classroom behavior. Pupils who are (supposed to be) resting are more likely to *touch themselves,* while pupils who are (supposed to be) working with their own materials and pacing themselves are *less involved* than those who are told what to do by the teacher. This finding fits together with findings 7.3-8 and 7.3-9, and we delay its discussion for a paragraph or two.

Although suggestive, these findings are—once again—as yet unvalidated by process-product research. It is one thing to know that pupil roles can be differentiated in the classroom and quite another to have established that role behavior in the classroom relates to pupil learning or attitudes. We suspect that findings of this latter sort could be established. Moreover, they would have obvious and immediate usefulness for teachers. Here, indeed, is a fruitful area for additional research!

Findings for Moves of the Classroom Game

The most productive area of research reviewed in this chapter has utilized the concept of verbal moves in investigating classrooms.

We learn from Box 7.7 that 30 percent of all moves in the lesson are *solicitations,* 30 percent *responses,* 30 percent *reactions,* and only 10 percent *structuring.* These moves are also unequally distributed between teachers and pupils. Teachers utter most of the moves and are more likely to be found *soliciting, structuring,* and *reacting* than pupils. Pupils utter less than half of the moves, and most of their utterances are *responses.* About 90 percent of all moves are concerned with *substantive meaning,* that is, relevant subject matter. About 50 percent are concerned with *instructional meaning,* that is, organizational matters and sociation. Interestingly, these findings do not appear to vary as one goes from one national context to another, for

---

BOX 7.7   Findings for Moves of the Classroom Game

Process Occurrence

7.7-1   Approximately 30 percent of all *moves* in the lesson are *soliciting*, 30 percent *responding*, 30 percent *reacting*, and only 10 percent *structuring* (Bel66), (Pow71), (Lun72).

7.7-2   *Teachers* tend to utter about 60 percent of the *moves* in the lesson, *pupils* about 40 percent of the *moves* (Bel66), (Pow71), (Lun72).

7.7-3   *Teachers* utter most of the *soliciting* (85 percent), *structuring* (90 percent), and *reacting* (70–80 percent) *moves*, but only few (10 percent) of the *responding moves* in the lesson. *Pupils* utter most (90 percent) of the *responding moves*, but only a few of the *soliciting* (15 percent), *structuring* (10 per cent), or *reacting* (20–30 percent) *moves* (Bel66), (Pow71), (Lun72).

7.7-4   Most *reacting moves* are *positive* or *neutral* in tone. Reactions that are *negative* in tone seldom appear (Bel66), (Zah68), (Lun72).

7.7-5   The majority of *moves* (90 percent) are concerned with *substantive meaning* in some way (Bel66), (Pow71), (Lun72).

7.7-6   About 50 percent of all *moves* are concerned with *instructional meanings* in some way. Of these, nearly 50 percent consider *verbal utterances*, and another 20 percent concern the *physical qualities of vocal action* (Bel66), (Pow71).

7.7-7   *Pupils in the "steering group"* emit fewer *soliciting* and *reacting moves* but more *responding moves* than do other pupils (Lun72). They also receive fewer *structuring* and more *reacting moves* from the teacher than do other pupils (Lun72).
         (Also see 7.5-5, 7.5-8, 7.5-9, 7.6-4.)

7.7-8   *Pupils in the "steering group"* receive fewer *positive* and more *negative reactions* from the teacher than do other pupils (Lun72).

Context-Process Relationships

(a) *Findings for Pupil I.Q.*

7.7-9   *Average I.Q. of the class* is unrelated to *number of verbal moves per lesson* (Lun72). In addition:

   7.7-9a   *Average I.Q. of "steering-group" pupils* co-varies directly with *number of verbal moves per lesson* (Lun72). Furthermore:

   7.7-9b   *Average I.Q. in the class* varies inversely with *number of verbal moves per lesson* (Lun72).

7.7-10   *Average I.Q. of "steering-group" pupils* co-varies directly with *number of responding moves per lesson* (Lun72).

7.7-11   *Average I.Q. of "steering-group" pupils* varies inversely with *number of reacting moves that structure* (Lun72).

7.7-12   *Average I.Q. of "steering-group" pupils* co-varies directly with *number of reacting moves that are positive* (and varies inversely with *number of reacting moves that are negative*) (Lun72).

7.7-13   *Average I.Q. of "steering-group" pupils* co-varies directly with *proportion of moves that concern substantive meaning* (Lun72).

7.7-14   *Average I.Q. of "steering-group" pupils* varies inversely with *initiation of verbal moves by pupils* (Lun72).

(b) *Findings for Pupil Sex*

7.7-15   *Pupil sex* affects the *number of pupil moves*. *Girls* emit more *moves* than do *boys* (Neu70).

(Box 7.7, continued)

7.7-16 *Pupil sex* affects *type of pupil moves. Girls* utter proportionately more *structuring, soliciting,* and *reacting moves; boys* more *responding moves* (Neu70).

(c) *Findings for Pupil Properties*

7.7-17 *Pupil desire to receive teacher solicitations* co-varies directly with *number of pupil self-controlled responses* (HuD73).

(d) *Findings for Grade Level*

7.7-18 *Grade level* affects *type of reacting move. Simple praise* and *moving on to a new topic* are more likely at *grade III, answer repetition* and *answer solicitation* are more likely at *grade VI* (Zah68).

(e) *Findings for Class Size*

7.7-19 *Class size* co-varies directly with *teacher use of negative personal judgment* and varies inversely with *use of corrective information and correction in reactions* (H&T72).

7.7-20 *Class size* varies inversely with *learning potential of teacher reactions* (H&T72).

(f) *Findings for Subject Matter*

7.7-21 *Subject matter* affects *type of reacting move. Social studies* lessons exhibit more *extension* and less *corrective information. Mathematics* exhibits the most *probing, English* somewhat less *probing, social studies* the least *probing* (H&T72).

(g) *Findings for Multigradedness*

7.7-22 *Multigraded classrooms* are less likely to involve *interactions between teacher and individual pupils* than are standard classrooms (Hog73).

Presage-Process Relationships

7.7-23 *Teachers' familiarity with pupils' names* co-varies directly with *number of moves emitted* by and *addressed* to *pupils* (Lun72).

7.7-24 *Teachers' familiarity with pupils' names* co-varies directly with *number of solicitations addressed to, reactions obtained from,* and *responses given to pupils* (Lun72).

Process-Process Relationships

7.7-25 *Lesson format* affects *type of pupil moves.* In *"individualized"* lessons pupils emit more *structuring, reacting,* and *soliciting moves;* in *standard* lessons they make more *responding moves* (Neu70).

7.7-26 *Group function* affects *type* and *focus of teacher moves.* Teacher solicitations concerned with *substantive meaning* are more likely to be addressed to *selected pupils; managerial* solicitations are more likely to be addressed to *specific pupils* (Bel66).

7.7-27 *Type of teacher solicitation* affects *number of pupil responses. Closed solicitations* are more likely to be followed by *pupil responses* than are *open solicitations* (W&N70).

7.7-28 *Form of expression of pupil response* affects *type of teacher reaction. Written* pupil responses are more likely to be followed by teacher use of *corrective information* and *probing; oral* responses are more likely to provoke *confirmation* (H&T72).
(Also see 7.2-14.)

Process-Product Relationships

7.7-29 *Amount of teacher structuring* is unrelated to *pupil achievement* (W&N70). *In contradiction,* it is also reported that

---

7.7-29a *Moderate use of teacher structuring* co-varies directly with *pupil achievement* (Fur67).

7.7-30 *Frequency of teacher solicitations* co-varies directly with *pupils' perceived frequency of solicitations directed to them* (HuD73).

7.7-31 *Amount of pupil responding* is unrelated to *pupil achievement* (HuD73)E.*

7.7-32 *Pupil opportunity to predict and control their responding* is unrelated to *pupil achievement* (HuD73)E.*

7.7-33 *Achievement test-item relevance of pupil responses* is unrelated to *pupil achievement* (HuD73).

7.7-34 *Type of teacher reaction* affects *pupil achievement. Teacher use of thanks and praise* in reactions co-varies directly with *pupil achievement*. Other reaction types (*simple affirmation* or *negation, reflection, challenge, repetition, redirection,* and so on) are unrelated to *pupil achievement* (W&N70), (HuD73)E.

*Findings generated experimentally are indicated with an E.

they have been replicated in both Sweden and Australia. (In Chapters IX and X we take up again the question of international similarities and differences.)

Finding 7.7-4 is particularly interesting because it provides evidence that teachers' reacting style is predominantly, if not ritualistically, positive in tone. As a matter of fact, we shall consider information in Chapter IX suggesting that reactions are no less positive when the pupil produces incongruent or inadequate responses. Apparently the "natural state" of contemporary teaching involves considerable positive reinforcement!

Lundgren's study produced an interesting series of results involving the "steering group" of pupils. Members of the steering group emit fewer *soliciting* and *reacting* (and more *responding*) *moves* than do other pupils, while they also receive fewer *positive* and more *negative* reactions from teachers than do other pupils. These findings are complemented by context-process findings concerning the relationships between pupil I.Q. and classroom moves. As reported by Lundgren, average I.Q. of the class is unrelated to the *number of verbal moves* per lesson. Number of verbal moves *is* related, however, to the average I.Q. of steering-group pupils—the greater the I.Q. of the steering group, the more the moves. This finding is closely tied in with that of finding 7.7-9b wherein we learn that classes with great variability in I.Q. are likely to exhibit fewer moves in the lesson. We also learn from Lundgren that classrooms involving steering groups of low intelligence will exhibit fewer *responding moves,* more *reacting moves that structure,* fewer *reacting moves* that are *positive,* more *reacting moves* that are *negative,* fewer moves that concern *substantive meaning,* and more *initiation of verbal moves* by pupils. Taken together, we suspect that these findings provide a view of the problems faced by the teacher who must contend with classrooms involving below-average pupils. They also validate Lundgren's original insight that teaching is, at least in part, addressed to pupils toward the bottom end of the ability continuum. It would be interesting to know whether pupils at the high end of the continuum also exert influence on the style of teaching. This problem was not addressed by Lundgren, however.

Other studies have found that grade level, class size, and subject matter provide contexts that affect the types of reacting moves performed by teachers. Multigraded classrooms are also less likely to involve individual teacher-pupil interaction. Especially interesting are findings concerning the effects of class size upon reactions. Hawkins and Taylor argue, on the basis of previous research and theory, that some types of teacher reactions were of "higher learning potential" than others. Reactions that probe pupils for more adequate responses, that inform the pupil as to the correctness of his response, or that cause pupils to extend their responses were thought to have high learning potential. Hawkins and Taylor found that the incidence of high-learning-potential teacher reactions was significantly higher in a class of 37 pupils than in a class of 61 pupils. There was also greater use of negative personal judgments and less use of corrective information and simple corrections by the teacher in the larger class. Since only two classes were used in the study, the authors advocated caution in generalizing these results. It would be interesting to see whether such differences exist between classes of about 35 pupils, which we suggest is a more normal class size, and classes of about 20 pupils, which are more likely to be sought these days by teachers' unions and the like.

Among the context-process findings are two suggesting that girls and boys behave differently in the classroom. Apparently, when pupils do make their few incursions into structuring, soliciting, and reacting they are more likely to be girls than boys. There can be little surprise in the finding that when pupils are permitted to choose when they will respond, their frequency of responding is positively related to their previously expressed desires to respond. This might simply mean that when teachers permit them, pupils do as they like!

Findings 7.7-23 and 7.7-24 are in need of further explanation. Lundgren discovered that when in an interview situation teachers were asked to recall the names of their pupils, they tended to recall a block of about a half-dozen names, pause, then recall another block of names, and so on. This and teachers' attempts to explain the phenomenon suggested that teachers have "cognitive groupings" of pupils that tend to be based on teachers' expectations or perceptions of pupil ability. Differences in the number and types of moves emitted and received by these groups were found by Lundgren, suggesting the presence of the Pygmalion effect discussed more fully in Chapter V.

Advocates of individualized instruction will be interested in finding 7.7-25 that pupils do more structuring, soliciting, and reacting under those conditions. Finding 7.7-27, concerning closed versus open solicitations, is one

THE CLASSROOM AS A SOCIAL SYSTEM

we will return to below. Meanwhile, it is rare to find a study that investigated written as well as oral pupil responses. Yet Hawkins and Taylor found that teachers' reactions varied according to the medium of pupils' responses. Teachers were found to use more *probing* and *corrective information* and less *confirmation* in reacting to written responses.

Finally, we come to process-product findings, all but one of which came from the Canterbury studies by Wright and Nuthall and by Hughes. The exception came from Furst's reanalysis of the data collected by Bellack *et al.* (1966). Furst found that moderate rather than high or low use of teacher structuring was optimal in relation to pupil achievement. Thus, we have further evidence that simple linear relations between teacher behavior and pupil achievement are not always the nature of reality. On this point it should also be borne in mind that Wright and Nuthall found no significant linear relationship between amount of teacher structuring and pupil achievement.

Of the remaining findings only two report success in obtaining relationships with product variables. Interestingly, lack of success in the studies reported by Hughes (1973) appears to be educationally significant. As we noted earlier, the Wright and Nuthall (1970) study did not include measures of pupil responding, but these were explicitly studied in Hughes' research. Two carefully designed and implemented experiments were conducted to contrast different opportunity patterns for responding. (A third experiment contrasted types of reactions—see below.) The first experiment involved teachers asking questions in such a way that pupils either had no opportunity to predict when they would be called upon, or had full opportunity to predict, or could, in fact, control whether or not they would be called upon. The second experiment did not permit pupils either to predict or control but simply involved the exclusion of some pupils from responding and a random distribution of questions to the rest. *None* of these treatments produced significant differences in pupil achievement, although pupils *were* able to perceive differences in solicitation patterns. This suggests that opportunities to respond are not particularly influential in predicting achievement. Perhaps it is just as beneficial for pupils to be involved through listening as through overtly responding during lessons, although evidence presented in Chapter VI questioned this conclusion.

The remaining finding appears significant for those who would improve teaching. Readers will recall that we have already reviewed evidence suggesting that most teacher reactions are predominantly, if not ritualistically, positive in tone. To supplement this finding both Wright and Nuthall and Hughes report that teachers who use *thanks* and *praise* are more likely to induce high pupil achievement than those who use other types of reaction. (Hughes' results were generated experimentally.) Apparently, it is not sufficient to be merely ritualistically positive in reacting; rather, the successful teacher needs to add emphasis to her reactions. We suspect that this finding complements those obtained (also in Chapter VI) in the behavior-modification research and suggests, once again, that positive reinforcement can be used to good effect in classroom teaching.

Findings for Location and Other Ecological Features

Box 7.8 constitutes more of a rag bag than the other boxes of this chapter, since investigators are not in complete agreement on how to conceptualize the physical environment of the classroom. Of the findings reported, perhaps the most significant is Adams and Biddle's discovery that the majority of both *emitters* and *targets*—whether they be teachers or pupils —are located front and center in the classroom. Thus, pupils who are located around the periphery of the classroom are more likely to be spectators than actors in the classroom drama. It could be, then, that if the teacher wants to encourage participation on the part of a quiet pupil, or silence on the part of someone who is noisy, she need merely move the pupil to another location in the room!

Interestingly enough, this finding was not original with Adams and Biddle (see Dawe, 1934). Its implications for product variables are not completely clear. For many years it has been known that pupils who achieved well were more likely to be sitting front and center in the classroom (see Farnsworth, 1933; or Griffith, 1921), but this has usually been interpreted to be a matter of seat preference. It may be that pupils who are more actively involved in classroom communication will—thereby—learn more or form more positive attitudes. But, as we have seen in this chapter and in Chapter VI, the evidence contrasting experienced with witnessed learning is not overwhelming.

Among context-process findings subject matter and grade level are both found (by Adams and Biddle) to affect group location. Emitters and targets are more likely to be *diffusely* located in social studies lessons and at the grade I level. Grade VI teachers *move* around the classroom more. In addition, Neujahr reports that substantive meanings are more likely to occur at the *teacher's desk* in mathematics classes, at *pupils' desks* in social studies, and at *media locations* in science lessons. (This finding is questionable, however, since the investigator observed but a single teacher for each subject matter studied.) Adams and Biddle also found that teacher age (but not teacher sex) affects the classroom ecology. Older teachers are more likely to be *front and center* and to have a diffuse audience than are younger teachers.

Next we take up Keeves' (1972) study of 215 seventh-grade pupils in seventy-two mathematics and science classrooms in Canberra, Australia. As we know, this study concerned the effects of a number of different factors on pupil achievement, including the "*stimulation*" potential of classroom artifacts. Keeves' *stimulation* variable was defined slightly differently in mathematics classrooms than in science classrooms, and in both definitions *stimulation* involved both artifacts and their use. Keeves found *stimulation*

BOX 7.8   Findings for Location and Other Ecological Features

Process Occurrence

7.8-1   Teachers spend most of their time at the *front* of the classroom (seven tenths) with the rest split between *walking around* and *visiting center locations* (A&B70).

7.8-2   Most *emitters* (both teachers and pupils) and most *targets* (both teachers and pupils) are located at *center front* and *down the middle* of the classroom. However, most *audiences* are *diffusely* located (A&B70).

Context-Process Relationships

7.8-3   *Subject matter* affects *group location*. Emitters and audiences are both more likely to be *diffusely located* in social studies than in mathematics lessons (A&B70).

7.8-4   *Grade level* affects *group location*. Emitters and targets are both more likely to be *diffusely located in grade I* lessons than in *grade VI* or *XI* lessons. Emitters, targets, and audiences are more likely to be located at specific locations around the classroom at *grade VI*. Emitters are more likely to be *front and center* in *grade XI* (A&B70).

7.8-5   *Subject matter* affects *the relationship between location and communication function*. Substantive meanings are more likely in *mathematics* at the *teacher's desk* and at *media* locations; in *social studies* at *pupils' desks* and *other* locations; *in science* at *media* locations (Neu70).

7.8-6   *Grade level* affects *teacher location*. *Grade VI* teachers are more likely to *move around* the classroom; *grade XI* teachers are more likely to be *front and center* than are *grade I* teachers (A&B70).

Presage-Process Relationships

7.8-7   *Teacher age* affects *group location*. Emitters and targets of *older teachers* are more likely to be *front and center*, audiences of *older teachers* are more likely to be *diffusely located* (A&B70).

7.8-8   *Teacher age* affects *teacher location*. *Older teachers* are more likely to be located *front and center* than are *younger teachers* (A&B70).

Process-Process Relationships

7.8-9   *Educational materials* affect *pupil attentiveness*. "*Stimulation*" is positively related to *pupil attentiveness* in mathematics, but is unrelated to *pupil attentiveness* in science (Kee72).

Process-Product Relationships

7.8-10   *Teacher use of gesture and movement* is positively associated with *pupil achievement* (Ros68).

7.8-11   *Educational materials* affect *pupil achievement*. "*Stimulation*" is positively related to *pupil achievement* in mathematics but is unrelated to *pupil achievement* in science (Kee72).

7.8-12   *Educational materials* do not affect *pupil attitudes*. "*Stimulation*" is unrelated to *pupil liking for mathematics and science* (Kee72).

to relate to *pupil attentiveness* in mathematics but not in science. He also found that *stimulation* was weakly related to measures of *achievement* in mathematics and science when uncontrolled for prior achievement. However, when these achievement measures were controlled for prior achievement, a significant, though very slight, positive relationship was found only in mathematics. *Stimulation* was unrelated to *pupil liking* for mathematics and science.

Finally, we take up the interesting finding reported by Rosenshine that teacher use of gesture and movement is positively associated with pupil achievement. If we take Rosenshine seriously, teachers who are less likely to move about are going to be less effective. We should also like to see his finding confirmed with additional research, however, along with other studies of the product effects of ecological features.

CONCLUSION

The difficulty with many of the findings reported in this chapter is that we are not yet certain of their implications for pupils. Plausible arguments may be made for the significance of various lesson formats in the classroom —indeed, many innovations in curriculum are clothed in just such arguments. And yet this text will present any number of seemingly plausible arguments that have failed to generate supporting data in classroom research. We would certainly advocate that attention now be given to further experimental studies in which the effects of various lesson formats, teacher roles, group structures and functions, and patterns of moves be explored with a variety of product variables.

At the same time, the research reported here is rich with concepts and findings that might be useful for teachers. Taking the latter first, to know that subject matter, teacher age, teacher sex, and other contextual and presage variables affect the format of the lesson is to help the administrator to plan educational experiences for his pupils. If older teachers are businesslike, then perhaps we should encourage older teachers to take on secondary classrooms where their skills might be more appropriate. Again, to discover that pupils are more likely to be involved if they are front and center in the classroom should enable the teacher to plan appropriate experiences for pupils whom she would like to encourage or "calm down."

In our view the most significant findings have been yielded by research into the verbal moves performed in the classroom. The concepts, research designs, and findings belonging to this body of research illustrate many of the promises held out for classroom interaction research. The studies conducted at the University of Canterbury in New Zealand provide a model for long-term research—beginning with an exploratory investigation of classrooms to test and develop concepts of behavior, progressing to a field survey in which relationships between those behavioral variables and pupil achievement are investigated, and leading eventually to experiments which allow the question of causation to be studied.

Other studies reviewed in this chapter are also of interest for concepts that we may apply when thinking about the events that are going on in our classrooms. Often we think of instruction as a process involving only the teacher and a single pupil. Or if we think about lesson format at all, it is with such unclear words as "lecture" or "discussion." The fact is that *all* classrooms are social systems. They have their characteristic ways of behaving, their problems, their customs, their beliefs, their advantages and shortcomings. A teacher may affect the learning of pupils quite as much by creating a classroom environment in which learning is encouraged as by working directly with the pupil herself. (As a matter of fact, some of the strategies for creating such an environment are intimated in the findings of this chapter. If peripheral groups are more likely to intellectualize, if pupil involvement is greater in peripheral groups than when the classroom is a single group, then maybe we need more subgroup formats.)

Teachers sometimes feel that classrooms provide them more than they bargained for. Most teachers have an interest in guiding and instructing the young. Most texts in teacher education suggest that guiding and instructing is what the teacher will be doing. But often the teacher finds out that her job is more managerial than instructional—that it may be more akin to that of the lion tamer or the manager of a three-ring circus. But success in the management of some 30 or more pupils is part of the classroom game. Maybe the truly wise teacher is one who views the classroom social system as an asset rather than a hindrance, for manipulation of lesson format is as important to the effectiveness of teaching as is skill in lecturing, knowledge of the subject or, for that matter, "guiding and instructing."

RECOMMENDED ADDITIONAL READING

Adams, R. S., and Biddle, B. J. *Realities of Teaching: Explorations with Videotape.* New York: Holt, Rinehart and Winston, Inc., 1970.

A short, popularized account of the Adams-Biddle research project. Major concepts are defined and illustrated, and some of the most important findings are discussed.

Bellack, A. A., Kliebard, H. M., Hyman, R. T., and Smith, F. L., Jr. *The Language of the Classroom.* New York: Teachers College Press, Columbia University, 1966.

The major report of the Bellack research program. Detailed and sometimes difficult to read, it nevertheless contains a splendid and provocative set of Rules for the Classroom Game (in its last chapter).

Herbert, J. *A System for Analyzing Lessons.* New York: Teachers College Press, Columbia University, 1967.

A brief, clear description of Herbert's system for classifying the lessons of classrooms.

Jackson, P. W. *Life in Classrooms.* New York: Holt, Rinehart and Winston, Inc., 1968.
A thoughtful and provocative description of some of the systemic features of classrooms and how these affect the lives of pupils. Makes use of data from a number of original studies.

Smith, L. M., and Geoffrey, W. *The Complexities of an Urban Classroom: An Analysis Toward a General Theory of Teaching.* New York: Holt, Rinehart and Winston, Inc., 1968.
A sensitive, insightful, often painful account of the practices and problems of one junior high teacher in a slum school. Probably the best study yet reported in which participant observation is applied to classroom events. Contains numerous concepts and insights concerning teacher and pupil roles and examines how the lives of classroom members are influenced by their joint social environment.

VIII
KNOWLEDGE AND INTELLECT

Teacher: Who can tell me why when it's summer in the northern hemisphere it's winter in the southern hemisphere? . . . Yes, Julie.

Julie: Because when it's hot in the north, it's cold in the south.

Teacher: Well, yes Julie, that's true, but why? Why is it cold in the southern hemisphere when it's warm in the northern hemisphere? . . . Anyone? . . . O.K. Well, let's see. John, where does the earth get its warmth from?

John: From the sun.

Teacher: Right. Mary, does the sun shine on all parts of the earth with equal directness?

Mary: No. It shines more directly down at the equator.

Teacher: O.K. That tells us it might be warmer at the equator than at the poles, but it doesn't tell us why it's winter in Australia when it's summer in America. Tom, is the sunshine at noon always at the same angle in New York?

Tom: No. In summer the sun's higher in the sky.

Teacher: Right. And what about Sydney? Is the sun always at the same angle here, Cathy?

Cathy: It's higher in the summer here, too.

Teacher: Good. That's right. And when it's winter in Sydney the sun appears lower in the sky. Now, when places in the northern hemisphere have the sun more directly overhead, what do you know about places in the southern hemisphere? Julie?

Julie: The sun is lower in the sky?

Teacher: Yes. Good girl. Now, can anyone tell me why the angle of the sun should be important? Yes, Julie, we'll give you another chance.

Julie: Because we heat up more when the sun is directly overhead.

Teacher: Great. Yes, that's the reason. Does everybody understand that? . . . Good . . . Now, why is it that the sun should be directly overhead at some times during the year and lower down in the sky at others? . . .

We have chosen the above segment of classroom interaction as a beginning for this chapter because it exemplifies the way in which the teacher uses verbal moves, especially questions, to guide thought processes. The segment begins with the teacher's seeking a cause for seasonal differences between the northern and southern hemispheres. Initial pupil responses do not provide an adequate explanation, so the teacher launches upon a carefully sequenced series of questions designed to elicit salient facts until, finally, he returns to the initial question and gets the explanation he wants. But what is the place of these different types of thought processes in classrooms? How often are more complex processes such as causal explanations sought? What types of thinking predominate? Are there too many facts and not enough causes? This is a sample of the questions, and it is with these types of issues that this chapter and the next are concerned.

Given the importance attached to the intellectual aspects of schooling, one might expect that research on cognitive processes in classrooms would be at least as prominent as research on social-emotional characteristics. Such is not the case, however. The 1963 edition of the *Handbook of Research on Teaching* (Gage, 1963a) contained chapters on the personality of teachers, the measurement of noncognitive variables in research on teaching, social interaction in the classroom, and the social background of teachers—but none on cognitive aspects of teaching. Indeed, there was only *one* entry pertinent to this topic in the entire lengthy index of the handbook!

Since 1963, however, studies of the cognitive aspects of classroom behavior have begun to appear. We have found that this literature reflects several distinct orientations. The first constitutes the interest of psychologists concerned with the nature of intelligence and with the identification of intellectual skills and abilities. The second is the stance of the logician interested in the extent to which classroom behavior is "logical." The third is that of the linguist who seeks understanding of classroom behavior by studying the words and word sequences of communications among the teacher and her pupils. For convenience, we have grouped these orientations into two chapters. This chapter reports studies reflecting psychological concerns, while Chapter IX deals with the application of logical and linguistic concepts.

STUDIES REFLECTING BLOOM'S TAXONOMY

Given the historical contribution of psychologists to the ways we think about education, it is not surprising that studies of classroom processes should be influenced by psychological concepts. In general, these studies seem to have been generated by three major systems for viewing the cognitive aspects of behavior. The first is the Taxonomy of Educational Objectives assembled by Bloom and his associates (1956). The second is the system for viewing intelligence proposed by J. P. Guilford (1956). The third is reflected in the work of Hilda Taba and her colleagues (1964, 1966). We review each of these conceptual systems in turn, as well as the classroom studies that have used them.

In 1956 Benjamin Bloom *et al.* published their now famous *Taxonomy of Educational Objectives: Handbook I—The Cognitive Domain.* As originally formulated, the taxonomy was concerned with educational *objectives* rather than with classroom processes. In general, it was stimulated by an awareness that many discussions about curricula and evaluation are ineffective because of the ambiguity and vagueness of concepts concerning the objectives of teaching. Furthermore, the authors hoped that the taxonomy would aid in the development of curriculum activities and materials appropriate to a *range* of cognitive objectives, and the evolution of tests to evaluate attainment of them. The taxonomy was designed as a classification of pupil behaviors in terms of the intended cognitive outcomes of schooling. Presumably, such a classification does *not* include all cognitive behaviors that occur in the classroom or actually result from classroom education. (Pupils probably learn some things from our classrooms that we did not intend!)

Publication of the taxonomy has had a considerable impact on educational thought. This source provides educators with a ready-made hierarchy of categories with which to think about the presumed cognitive outcomes of classroom teaching. Not surprisingly, it has stimulated various kinds of research on teaching, as well as efforts of educational philosophers and textbook writers. We shall, of course, limit our discussion to applications of the taxonomy in research on classroom behavior.

Concepts

After an exhaustive review of statements concerning educational objectives about knowledge and intellectual abilities and skills, Bloom and his associates listed these objectives in terms of the complexity of behavior specified and arrived at a hierarchy containing six major classes. Their classification is given in Figure 8.1.

Each of the six major classes was defined in such a way that the intended behaviors in one class are likely to make use of and be based on the intended behaviors in the preceding classes. Thus, the six major categories of the system are presumed to form a hierarchy.

A distinction is made in the taxonomy between *knowledge* and the higher levels of intellectual skills and abilities.

Knowledge is defined in the following way:

> By knowledge, we mean that the student can give evidence that he remembers, either by recalling or by recognizing, some idea or phenomenon with which he has had experience in the educational process. For our taxonomy purposes, we are defining knowledge as little more than the remembering of the idea or phenomenon in a form very close to that in which it was originally encountered. (Bloom *et al.*, 1956, pp. 28–29)

The authors saw fit to point out, however, that while the objective—knowledge—emphasizes most the processes of remembering, it may also involve more complex processes such as relating and judging. For example, a subject who encounters a test item designed to tap his knowledge has to make judgments about what it is that is being sought in the item, and then relate

FIGURE 8.1   The taxonomy of educational objectives in the cognitive domain (Adapted from Bloom et al., 1956, pp. 201–207)

1.00 Knowledge
    1.10 Knowledge of specifics
    1.20 Knowledge of ways and means of dealing with specifics
    1.30 Knowledge of the universals and abstractions in a field
2.00 Comprehension
    2.10 Translation
    2.20 Interpretation
    2.30 Extrapolation
3.00 Application
4.00 Analysis
    4.10 Analysis of elements
    4.20 Analysis of relationships
    4.30 Analysis of organizational principles
5.00 Synthesis
    5.10 Production of a unique communication
    5.20 Production of a plan, or proposed set of operations
    5.30 Derivation of a set of abstract relations
6.00 Evaluation
    6.10 Judgments in terms of internal evidence
    6.20 Judgments in terms of external criteria

his knowledge to it. It is possible that the required knowledge is stored in his memory, but that he fails to reproduce it because he has not understood the question or because he has not been able to reorganize the problem to provide appropriate cues for the knowledge he possesses. However the most distinctive characteristic of the knowledge objective seems to be its emphasis upon the psychological process of remembering.

In contrast to knowledge, intellectual skills and abilities require more than remembering. They require that remembered knowledge be put to use in reaching more difficult outcomes through processes of organization and reorganization. The authors of the taxonomy suggest that:

> The most general operational definition of these abilities and skills is that the individual can find appropriate information and techniques in his previous experience to bring to bear on new problems and situations. This requires some analysis or understanding of the new situation; it requires a background of knowledge or methods which can be readily utilized; and it also requires some facility in discerning the appropriate relations between previous experience and the new situation. (p. 38)

An attempt was also made to distinguish between intellectual *skills* and intellectual *abilities*, though the authors did not consider the distinction vital to their purposes in constructing the taxonomy. The distinction seems to be that intellectual skills require competence in applying a generalized technique or method in coping with a new situation or problem, but they do not require specialized knowledge. Intellectual abilities, however, require both competence of technique and specialized knowledge.

As we shall see presently, the taxonomy has been used as a basis for making distinctions between *lower-level* and *higher-level* thinking in the classroom. The foundation of this dichotomy seems to be the hierarchical arrangement in the taxonomy of objectives according to their position on the dimension ranging from simple to complex or easy to difficult. The assumption is that problems involving behaviors at the beginning of the list can be solved more readily than those requiring behaviors later in the list. The committee comments on this hypothesis as follows:

> We have studied a large number of problems occurring in our comprehensive examinations and have found some evidence to support this hypothesis. Thus, problems requiring knowledge of specific facts are generally answered correctly more frequently than problems requiring a knowledge of the universals and abstractions in a field. Problems requiring knowledge of principles and concepts are correctly answered more frequently than problems requiring both knowledge of the principle and some ability to apply it in new situations. Problems requiring analysis and synthesis are more difficult than problems requiring comprehension. (pp. 18–19)

Bloom and his associates saw reasons for stressing both knowledge and intellectual abilities and skills in education. Regarding knowledge they argue:

1. One's acquaintance with reality is developed with increase in knowledge or information, but in fields where knowledge is in rapid transition its acquisition can be justified only in relation to other educational objectives;
2. Knowledge is basic to other goals of education, such as critical thinking and the development of attitudes. Even tentative knowledge is important as a basis for learning the methodology and solving the problems of a new field of inquiry; and
3. American culture places great emphasis upon the acquisition of knowledge.

Nevertheless:

4. "Because of the simplicity of teaching and evaluating knowledge, it is frequently emphasized as an educational objective out of all proportion to its usefulness or its relevance for the development of the individual" (p. 34); and
5. Sometimes knowledge is emphasized on the grounds that its full value will be realized in an occupational setting in later life. However, requiring a pupil to learn such knowledge assumes that his future occupation can be predicted.

Regarding intellectual skills and abilities, the authors argued:

1. In an open and changing society where solutions at one time ma
   not be adequate at another and where there is inconsistency in th
   types of problems encountered, much emphasis needs to be place
   on the development of problem-solving strategies and the applicatio
   of knowledge to new situations. These objectives are vital to secur
   the successful personal adjustment of individuals and their effectiv
   participation as citizens in a democracy;
2. Intellectual skills and abilities are more widely applicable tha
   knowledge; and
3. Educational outcomes which can be generalized and applied in
   variety of situations during schooling are likely to be retained longe
   than specific, infrequently encountered outcomes.

These arguments suggest the *Commitment* made by researchers wh
have used insights from the Bloom taxonomy. Presuming that most class
room education is concerned with little but facts and knowledge, they hav
sought to "improve" matters by training teachers to stress intellectual skill
and abilities. This *Commitment* is reflected in the terms chosen to represen
the underlying dimension of the taxonomy. Thus, it is commonly argue
that too much of current education is conducted using "*lower-level*" think
ing. To improve classroom teaching we must encourage teachers to stres
"*higher-level*" processes. However attractive this argument may appear, i
rests ultimately on three assumptions that can be checked through research

1. that current classroom practice stresses lower-level thought (that is
   facts and knowledge);
2. that teachers (or teacher trainees) can be taught to place more stres
   on higher-level thought (that is, intellectual skills and abilities); an
3. that pupils will benefit from greater stress on higher-level thought.

Let us see if the research evidence supports these assumptions.

Research on Classroom Behavior

Since the Bloom taxonomy was designed to express educational objec
tives, not surprisingly it has had extensive application in discussion of cur
ricula and tests. Implications of the taxonomy for the guidance of question
ing by teachers in interaction with their pupils were suggested by Sander
(1966), but formal applications to classroom research were not, as far a
we know, reported until 1968. Two major observational systems have ap
peared that are based on the taxonomy, as well as modifications and othe
applications.

The first of these is the *Teacher-Pupil Question Inventory* (TPQI)
(Davis and Tinsley, 1968), which is reproduced in Figure 8.2.

FIGURE 8.2   Categories of the Teacher-Pupil Question Inventory (TPQI). (Adapted from Davis and Tinsley, 1968, p. 141)

1. *Memory*—The one questioned recalls or recognizes information (facts, generalizations, etc.);
2. *Translation*—The one questioned changes information into a different form (linguistic, symbolic, image, etc.);
3. *Interpretation*—The one questioned states relationships between various types of data;
4. *Application*—The one questioned solves a realistic problem requiring the identification of the crucial issue or points and the selection and use of appropriate knowledge and skills;
5. *Analysis*—The one questioned answers with explicit attention to the relationship(s) between the ideas expressed and with obvious awareness of the process employed in the reasoning;
6. *Synthesis*—The one questioned suggests answers to a problem that is original, speculative, or creative;
7. *Evaluation*—The one questioned makes a judgment according to explicit criteria (external or internal);
8. *Affectivity*—The one questioned responds with a statement of feeling, emotion, or opinion without a standard of appraisal;
9. *Procedure*—The question relates to classroom organization, student behavior, or instructional management.

NOTE: Each question asked by the teacher or a pupil is to be scored in but a single category.

The other is the *Florida Taxonomy of Cognitive Behavior* (FTCB) (Brown *et al.*, 1968), shown in Figure 8.3.

Several differences should be noted between these two instruments. First, the TPQI was designed to be applied to information and ideas *asked for* in the classroom by both teachers and pupils, although the definitions of the categories given in Figure 8.2 suggest that responses were the main object of inquiry, whereas the FTCB was designed to be applied to information and ideas *given*. Second, the TPQI is a *category* system whereas the FTCB is a *sign* system. While a score is generated for the TPQI for each question asked, rules stated for the FTCB stress that but one checkmark can be entered for any given type of behavior encountered during a six-minute observational period, regardless of however many occurrences of that behavior type appeared. Thus, the range of scores for each behavioral class of the FTCB over a total period of observation of 30 minutes can be only from zero to five. Theoretically, there is no upper limit to the range of scores for each category of the TPQI. Third, whereas the TPQI collapses into one broad category labeled "Memory" the distinctions originally made in the Bloom taxonomy between three classes of knowledge, the FTCB retains these distinctions. Fourth, the TPQI allows for the separate coding of questions not directly concerned with cognitive learning tasks by the inclusion of procedural and affectivity categories. Fifth, the behavioral definitions provided for the TPQI are less specific than those provided for the FTCB.

FIGURE 8.3 Classes of the Florida Taxonomy of Cognitive Behavior (FTCB). (Adapted from Brown et al., 1968)

1.10 Knowledge of Specifics
  1. Reads
  2. Spells
  3. Identifies something by name
  4. Defines meaning of term
  5. Gives a specific fact
  6. Tells about an event
1.20 Knowledge of Ways and Means of Dealing with Specifics
  7. Recognizes symbol
  8. Cites rule
  9. Gives chronological sequences
  10. Gives steps of process, describes method
  11. Cites trend
  12. Names classification system or standard
  13. Names what fits given system or standard
1.30 Knowledge of Universals and Abstractions
  14. States generalized concept or idea
  15. States a principle, law, theory
  16. Tells about organization or structure
  17. Recalls name of principle, law, theory
2.00 Translation
  18. Restates in own words or briefer terms
  19. Gives concrete example of an abstract idea
  20. Verbalizes from a graphic representation
  21. Translates verbalization into graphic form
  22. Translates figure statements to literature statements, or vice versa
  23. Translates foreign language to English, or vice versa
3.00 Interpretation
  24. Gives reason (tells why)
  25. Shows similarities, differences
  26. Summarizes or concludes from objects of evidence
  27. Shows cause and effect relationships
  28. Gives analogy, simile, metaphor
  29. Performs a directed task or process
4.00 Application
  30. Applies previous learning to new situations
  31. Applies principle to new situation
  32. Applies abstract knowledge in a practical situation
  33. Identifies, selects, and carries out processes
5.00 Analysis
  34. Distinguishes fact from opinion
  35. Distinguishes fact from hypothesis
  36. Distinguishes conclusions from statements which support it
  37. Points out unstated assumption
  38. Shows interaction or relationship elements
  39. Points out particulars to justify conclusions
  40. Checks hypotheses with given information

41. Distinguishes relevant from irrelevant statements
42. Detects error in thinking
43. Infers purposes, points of view, thoughts, feelings
44. Recognizes bias or propaganda

6.00 *Synthesis (Creativity)*

45. Reorganizes ideas, materials, process
46. Produces unique communication, divergent idea
47. Produces a plan, proposed set of opportunities
48. Designs an apparatus
49. Designs a structure
50. Devises scheme for classifying information
51. Formulates hypothesis, intelligent guess
52. Makes deductions from abstract symbols, propositions
53. Draws inductive generalization from specifications

7.00 *Evaluation*

54. Evaluates something from evidence
55. Evaluates something from criteria

NOTE: Each of the 55 classes of behavior is to be checked for *teacher* and/or *pupil* occurrence if behavior falling into that class appears during a six-minute observational period.

Finally, it is worth noting that neither system includes the comprehension subcategory of *extrapolation* used in the Bloom taxonomy. It is possible, of course, that this type of behavior occurs so rarely in the classroom that it is not worth coding. Alternatively, extrapolation in the classroom may be indistinguishable from the other categories suggested in the taxonomy.

Box 8.1 reports details of studies using categories based on the Bloom taxonomy. Both field surveys and presage-process experiments are reported, although still only a few of each. All grade levels are represented, from K through XII, and a variety of subjects. What, then, have the studies found?

BOX 8.1   Research Using Bloom's Categories

STUDIES REVIEWED

Borg *et al.* (1970)	(Bor70)
Bruce (1971)	(Bru71)
Davis and Tinsley (1968)	(D&T68)
Mood (1972)	(Moo72)
Murray and Williams (1971)	(M&W71)
Ragosta *et al.* (1971)	(Rag71)
Rogers and Davis (1970)	(R&D70)
Solomon and Wood (1970)	(S&W70)
Tinsley *et al.* (1970)	(Tin70)
Williams (1970)	(Wil70)
Wilson (1969)	(Wis69)
Wood (1970)	(Woo70)

Box 8.1 (continued)

INSTRUMENT, METHOD OF GATHERING DATA, CODING SYSTEM, UNIT STUDIED, RELIABILITY

TPQI, live observation, single-facet category system, T and P questions, "almost unanimous" agreement reported (D&T68), (Tin70).

Teacher Oral Question Observation Schedule, live observation, single-facet category system, T and P questions, moderate reliability (R&D70).

FTCB, live observation, sign system, "items of behavior" within six-minute periods, moderate reliability (M&W71), (S&W70), (Wil70), (Woo70).

FTCB (K-1 Form), audiotapes, sign system and single-facet category system, "items of behavior" within five-minute period for sign system, unit not defined within three-second interval for category system, reliability not specified (Rag71).

Borg Categories, videotapes, single-facet category system, T and P questions, high reliability (Bor70).

FIAC, subscripted within categories 4, 5, 8, and 9 on the basis of Bloom's taxonomy; live observation, teacher and pupil talk, moderate reliability (Moo72).

Teacher Question Inventory, audiotapes, single-facet category system, T questions, reliability not specified (Bru71), (Wis69).

DESIGN OF STUDY, SUBJECTS, CONTEXTS

Field Surveys

(Bru71)	33 female teachers trained in SCIS science approach, elementary, science
(D&T68)	44 student teachers and pupils, secondary, social studies
(Moo72)	15 teachers and pupils, grade II
(Rag71)	70 teachers and pupils, grades K–1, experimental program
(S&W70)	71 student teachers, primary and secondary
(Tin70)	10 teachers (half judged to be "content-oriented," half "process-oriented") and pupils, grades I-XII; several subjects
(Wis69)	15 teachers trained in SCIS science approach and 15 "traditional" teachers, elementary, science
(Woo70)	117 teachers and pupils, grades I–XII; several subjects

Presage-Process Experiments

(Bor70)	74 teachers and pupils, also 19 teachers and pupils, secondary, several subjects
(M&W71)	26 student teachers and pupils, secondary, English
(R&D70)	20 student teachers, grade V, social studies
(Wil70)	60 student teachers and pupils, secondary, social studies and English

FINDINGS

Process Occurrence

8.1-1   Many more units coded for *knowledge* than for any other category (Bor70), (D&T68), (Moo72), (M&W71), (Tin70), (Wil70), (Wis69), (Woo70).

Context-Process Relationships

8.1-2   *Grade level* affects *teacher use of categories*. (Junior high student teachers use more translation and evaluation questions than do senior high student teachers) (D&T68).

8.1-3   *"Process" versus "content" orientation of classes* is unrelated to *teacher use of categories* (Tin70).

8.1-4   *Subject matter* (social studies versus English) is unrelated to effect of training on *teachers' use of "higher-level" categories* (M&W71), (Wil70).

Presage-Process Relationships

8.1-5   *Teacher scores on MTAI* are unrelated to *teacher use of "higher-level" categories* (Bru71).

8.1-6   *Teacher length of experience* co-varies inversely with *teacher use of "higher-level" categories after training* in SCIS science approach (Bru71).

8.1-7   *Teacher age* co-varies inversely with *teacher use of "higher-level" categories* (Bru71).

8.1-8   *Teacher academic background in science* is unrelated to *teacher use of "higher-level" categories* (Bru71).

8.1-9   *Teacher training in use of the taxonomy* lowers *teacher use of knowledge* and raises *teacher use of "higher-level" categories* (M&W71)E,* (R&D70)E, (Wil70)E.

8.1-10 *Teacher training in use of the taxonomy* lowers *pupil use of knowledge* and raises *pupil use of "higher-level" categories* (M&W71)E, (R&D70)E, (Wil70)E.

8.1-11 *Teacher training in SCIS science approach* lowers *teacher use of knowledge* and raises *teacher use of "higher-level" categories* (Bru71), (Wil70).

Process-Process Relationships

8.1-12 *Teacher use of categories* co-varies directly with *pupil use of categories* (D&T68), (Moo72), (M&W71), (Wil70), (Woo70). *In addition*, it is also found that

> *Pupil use of "lower-level" categories* co-varies directly with *teacher use of "lower-level" categories*, but *pupil use of "higher-level" categories* co-varies with *other pupil behaviors* (D&T68).

8.1-13 *Teacher use of synthesis and evaluation categories* co-varies directly with *teacher use of concrete content* and inversely with *teacher use of abstract content* (S&W70).

8.1-14 *Teacher "indirectness"* co-varies directly with teacher use of *"higher-level" categories* but is unrelated to *pupil use of "higher-level" responses.* (Moo72)

Process-Product Relationships

8.1-15 *Teacher use of "higher-level" categories* (by student teachers) is unrelated to *pupil achievement* (R&D70)E. *In contradiction*, it is also found that

> 8.1-15a *Teacher use of "lower-level" categories* (in grade I classrooms of disadvantaged pupils) co-varies directly with *abstract-complex pupil growth;* teacher use of *"higher-level" categories* co-varies inversely with *abstract-complex pupil growth* (Rag71).

* Findings generated experimentally are indicated with an E.

First, most of the studies report acceptable levels of reliability for their instruments, but this does not necessarily mean that their attempts are valid operationalizations of Bloom's original concepts, or indeed for the same concepts as those studied by other instruments. The fact is that all of these systems require fairly high-inference judgments, thus exactly what content will go into each category cannot be ascertained. Within these limitations the fact that meaningful findings were generated with these instruments suggests their general validity.

Second, those classrooms studied have indeed shown a higher frequenc of questions thought to require lower-level cognitive processes and e changes involving knowledge in particular. (This finding supports the fir: assumption needed to support the *Commitment*.) As the investigators an many others have presumed, the classrooms studied were oriented towar facts rather than toward explanation or understanding.

Third, only minimal information is provided concerning contextu: variables that might affect cognitive process in the classroom. One pr(sumes that sharp differences in the use of taxonomic categories would a[pear for such subjects as mathematics or the sciences, or even within subje(areas, or between student teachers and experienced teachers, but thes propositions have yet to be researched.

Fourth, only one study (Bruce, 1971) has investigated relationshi[between such teacher presage variables as attitudes, experience, age, an academic background and their use of these cognitive categories. The su(cess of this study in identifying statistically significant relations involvin these variables should encourage further research into presage-process rel; tionships of these types.

Fifth, teachers who are trained in the Bloom taxonomy can be induce to greater use of higher-level categories. (This finding verifies the secon assumption needed to support the *Commitment*.) Moreover, pupils of teacl ers so trained also seem more likely to use higher-level categories in the classroom contributions, although the evidence is not as strong. Evidenc supporting any particular type of training program is weaker still, althoug the use of model lessons, particularly those which exemplify only positiv instances of higher-level questioning, appears promising. To the extent, the: that classroom education can be improved by raising the level of discours the research suggests means for doing just this.

Sixth, the most pervasive process finding reported is that pupil use (categories varies with teacher use. Thus, if teachers use lower-level cat(gories, pupils will do so too. Most of the studies have presumed that th relationship was causative, with teacher behavior the independent variabl(However, this causative interpretation has been questioned by one stud (Wood, 1970), which found that use of higher-level categories by pupils cc varied with other pupils' behavior rather than with teacher behavior. In h discussion of these findings Wood says:

> It is clear that teachers should not remain fixed at the two lowest cognitiv levels (1.00 knowledge, 2.00 translation) if they seek to facilitate high(level student cognition. Neither should they simply move up the cognitiv hierarchy. Rather, higher levels of student cognition appear to be facilitate when the teacher recedes to the "field" and students become "figure" . . .
>
> [It appears] that peer group relationships are crucial in the facilitatio of high levels of student cognition. In some measure, this implication calls f(more training which casts the teacher in the role of a catalyst helping t channel and direct classroom discussion activities without dominating (directly controlling. (p. 92)

Seventh, but does "raising the level of discourse" result in pupil growth? Frankly, evidence concerning this last, vital question is weak. Only two studies have attempted to answer it in terms of the Bloom taxonomy. One found no significant overall relationship (Rogers and Davis, 1970), but a significant negative relationship between higher-level questioning and pupil performance on test items of the analysis type. The other found that for disadvantaged first-grade children the use of lower-level categories was positively associated with higher amounts of abstract-complex pupil growth, and the latter tended to be negatively associated with the use of higher-level categories (Ragosta *et al.*, 1971). Thus, while to adherents to the *Commitment* it appears self-evident that teachers should place more stress upon such higher-level processes as *synthesis* and *evaluation*, no evidence has appeared to date suggesting that this stress will give desired *product* effects. (In other words, the third assumption underlying the *Commitment* has not yet been supported.)

Finally, a problem has arisen concerning the presumed unidimensionality of the categories of the taxonomy. The assumption usually made by researchers is that there is but a single dimension underlying the taxonomy, running from simple to complex cognitive operations. The study by Solomon and Wood (1970) is especially interesting in that it researched the notion that interaction in classrooms varies along two cognitive dimensions rather than one. These two dimensions are *simple-versus-complex* and *concrete-versus-abstract*. *Simple* tasks involve knowledge or comprehension, while synthesis or evaluation should be considered more *complex*. *Concreteness*, on the other hand, involves the use of low-order constructs such as "cow," "seven," or "Chicago," while in abstract tasks one finds such class-inclusive terms as "mammal," "integer," or "metropolis." Some discussion of these two dimensions was provided in the Bloom taxonomy, where it was thought that the subcategories of knowledge objectives could be viewed as varying from concrete to abstract in parallel with variations from simple to complex. But what might the relation be in the upper levels of the Bloom categories? Solomon and Wood applied the FTCB and an instrument called the *Taxonomy of Image Provocation Profile* to their sample of student teachers and found a *negative* relationship between the higher levels of the simple-complex dimension or, as Solomon (1970) reports it:

It is interesting to note . . . that the highest levels of teacher cognition (synthesis and evaluation) are positively related to concrete classroom experiences . . . and negatively related to abstract classroom experiences. . . . (p. 59)

Why should such a relationship appear? Possibly because classroom participants have difficulty dealing simultaneously with processes that are complex and content that is abstract. But whatever the interpretation, this finding poses problems for the *Commitment*, since the ability to handle abstract content and that concerned with complex thinking would both appear advantageous. But when should one be stressed and when the other?

This suggestion that classroom discourse should be conceived an analyzed along the two dimensions of simple-complex and concrete-abstrac appears promising. As we shall see in the rest of this chapter, the distinctio between these two dimensions is also made in other systems for conceptua izing cognitive aspects of classroom behavior, but in none of the researc traditions is the distinction pursued fully.

STUDIES REFLECTING GUILFORD'S MODEL

The second source of categories employed by students of classroor behavior in the cognitive domain has been the work of J. P. Guilford. Fc years psychologists have debated the nature of intelligence. After reviewin prior theories and research Guilford (1956) hypothesized a three-dimension; structure for intelligence consisting of *operations, contents,* and *products.* I his view an intellectual ability consists of performing a particular type c cognitive *operation,* upon a particular type of *content,* to produce a partic ular type of *product.* He conceived five types of *operations*: cognition, men ory, divergent production, convergent production, and evaluation; fou types of content: figural, symbolic, semantic, and behavioral; and six types c *products*: units, classes, relations, systems, transformations, and implication. Thus, his theory suggests 5 x 4 x 6, or 120, unique intellectual abilities, a represented by the cells of the cube in Figure 8.4.

Guilford has claimed recently (1970) that of the 120 hypothesize abilities 23, 14, 16, 13, and 13 abilities have been identified, respectively, fc cognition, memory, divergent production, convergent production, and eva' uation. A particular value of the model, according to Guilford, is not onl its systematization of already demonstrated abilities but its capacity fc suggesting where to look for still undemonstrated abilities.

Already, however, a basis for elaborating the model has been suggeste by the discovery of more than one ability within some cells. Apparentl these proliferations arise from variations in the sensory modalities involvec Thus, when researchers go beyond testing situations that appeal principall to the visual sense to those that appeal to the auditory, kinesthetic, and pe haps even the olfactory and gustatory senses, more abilities might b identified.

Concepts

It is not our intention to go into a detailed exposition of all the concept involved in Guilford's three-dimensional model. We will deal only briefl with the types of *content* and *products* he suggests and then dwell on *oper ations,* which have proved to be the most attractive of the three dimension for research in the classroom.

Content   Figural content includes nonverbal concrete forms and spatia

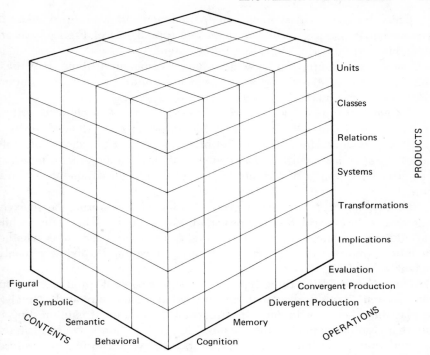

Figure 8.4   Guilford's theoretical model for the "structure of intellect." (From Gallagher, 1965, p. 23)

relationships. When a child is asked to manipulate triangular, square, and various other-shaped pieces of wood to fit cutouts in a form board, or to identify missing objects in a picture, or to build a "staircase" with Cuisenaire rods, he is asked to operate upon figural content.

Semantic content involves verbal concepts and meanings. Answering questions concerning the meaning of a paragraph of prose, defining a term, or evaluating the logic of an argument are common examples of operations performed upon semantic content.

Symbolic content includes nonverbal symbols, numbers, or letters. The arithmetic processes of addition, subtraction, multiplication, and division are usually performed with numbers which are examples of symbolic content. Similarly, map reading, spelling, and musical notation involve symbolic content.

Behaviorial content refers to the behavior, thoughts, attitudes, and feelings of a social object. Anticipating the reactions of others to a particular event and interpreting the feelings of another are possible examples of activities involving behavioral content.

Products   In considering products we will illustrate our discussion with semantic content.

Units are the smallest identifiable components of a group or class of phenomena. If you ask a child to name the capital city of France, you are asking him to produce a unit of semantic content.

Classes are groups of units which share a common attribute. If you ask a child to group all the nouns in a page of prose into various types, you are asking for the production of classes.

Systems are organized structures of units. If you ask a child to write a sentence about London, you are asking him to produce a system of words.

Transformations involve any kind of change or rearrangement of units, classes, or systems. Translating a sentence about London from English to French is an example of the production of a transformation of semantic content.

Finally, *implications* are involved in using given information to come to some conclusion which is not provided. For example, if one tells a child that all men are human and that Socrates is a man and then asks whether Socrates is human, one is asking for an implication involving semantic content.

Operations   Of the three types of concepts—content, products and operations—only those dealing with operations have been employed in analyzing classroom behavior to date. In discussing these latter it is interesting to note that Guilford is more explicit concerning the relation between abstractness and complexity than was the Bloom taxonomy. According to Guilford, variations in abstractness are to be found in content, while variations in complexity apply particularly to products and operations. Thus, it would seem that abstractness of content is conceptually independent of complexity of product and operations. The arrangement of categories of operations along the simple-complex dimension will become clear in the discussion to follow.

By *cognition*, the first category within operations, Guilford means the processes involved in "the discovery of information and the rediscovery or recognition of information" (Guilford, 1959, p. 359). An example involving semantic content and class product is provided by Guilford (1970) in the following:

> Given the set of words *footstool, lamp, rocker, television,* can the examinee grasp the essence of the nature of the class, as shown by his naming the class, by putting another word or two into it, or by recognizing its name among four alternatives? The ability pertains to discovery or recognition of a class concept. (p. 355)

The *memory* operation involves the retention of material or information and is evidenced in the individual's reproducing or recalling previously acquired knowledge. This category has essentially the same meaning for Guilford as "knowledge" had for Bloom *et al.*, and we shall not elaborate on it here.

Convergent production, or convergent thinking as it is sometimes called, "proceeds toward one right answer, that is to say, a determined or a conventional answer" (Guilford, 1959, p. 359). Gallagher (1965) provides some examples of convergent thinking in the following:

> T: If I had 29¢ and gave John 7¢, how much money would I have left?
> Bob: Twenty-two cents.

> T: Can you sum up in one sentence what you think was the main idea in Paton's novel, *Cry the Beloved Country?*
> Pete: That the problem of the blacks and whites in Africa can only be solved by brotherly love; there is no other way.

Thus, convergent thinking may be involved in the solving of a problem, in the summarizing of a body of material, or in the establishment of a logical sequence of ideas or premises—as, for example, in reporting the way in which a machine works, or in describing the sequence of steps by which the passage of a bill through Congress is accomplished. (p. 25)

Divergent production, or divergent thinking, is defined by Guilford (1959) as "the kind that goes off in different directions. It makes possible changes of direction in problem solving and also leads to a diversity of answers, where more than one answer may be acceptable" (p. 381). Gallagher (1965) gives the following examples, from classroom discourse, of divergent thinking:

> T: Suppose Spain had not been defeated when the Armada was destroyed in 1588 but that, instead, Spain had conquered England. What would the world be like today if that had happened?
> Sam: Well, we would all be speaking Spanish.
> Peg: We might have fought a revolutionary war against Spain instead of England.
> Tom: We might have a state religion in this country. (pp. 25–26)

Evaluation in Guilford's model is similar in definition to the evaluation category of the Bloom taxonomy. According to Guilford (1959), "evaluative abilities have to do with testing information and conclusions as to their suitability, acceptability, goodness, or correctness. This involves the question of standards or criteria. The evaluative factors differ in terms of criteria of judgment as well as in terms of the usual three content categories . . ." (pp. 390–391). Gallagher (1965) gives the following examples and comments on this type of thinking as revealed in classroom discourse:

> T: What do you think of Captain Ahab as a heroic figure in Moby Dick?
> Bob: Well, he was sure brave, but I think he was kind of mean the way

he drove the men just because he had this crazy notion of getting back at Moby Dick.

T: Is it likely that we will have a hard winter?
Mary: Well, I think that the pattern of high pressure areas suggests that we will.

T: Who was the stronger President, Jackson or Adams?
Mike: Adams.

In the first of the above examples, the student is asked to construct a value dimension of his own in terms of what he considers "heroic," and then to make a judgment as to where on this value dimension he would place Captain Ahab. In the second response, the student is asked to make an estimate or to give a speculative opinion or assessment of probability. A third possibility, not illustrated here, involves entering a qualification of disagreement, wherein the respondent would offer a modification of a prior judgment of another student; or he may state a counter-judgment, in which he declares direct opposition to the statement of the previous speaker. (pp. 26–27)

In summary, although Guilford's concepts of *content* and *product* might also be used for observational research in the classroom, the research we review focused solely on operations. Five classes of operations were suggested by Guilford: *cognition, memory, convergent production* (or thinking), *divergent production* (or thinking), and *evaluation.* It would appear from examining these categories, and to some extent from reading Guilford, that these, like the Bloom categories, lie along a dimension ranging from simple to complex cognitive processes. Thus cognition and memory are "simple" or "low-level" processes. Moreover, if we assume that contemporary classroom education is surely conducted at too low a level, we arrive at a *Commitment* that is similar to the one held by those influenced by the Bloom taxonomy: Teachers should be encouraged to stress more complex processes in their teaching.

Some educational theorists have gone further, however, and have seen in Guilford's concepts of convergent and divergent thinking a formal means for approaching the emotion-laden issue of creativity. Thus, teachers who stress convergent thinking are demanding conformity of their pupils, while those who stress divergent thinking are fostering creativity—thus a further, or more restricted, *Commitment*: Teachers should be encouraged to stress divergent production in the classroom. Let us see what evidence there is, if any, for either of these *Commitments* in classroom research.

Research on Classroom Behavior

The main attempt to translate Guilford's notion for use in classroom research has been the *Aschner-Gallagher Classification System* (Aschner *et al.*, 1965), an abbreviated version of which is presented in Figure 8.5.

FIGURE 8.5   Aschner-Gallagher Classification System. (Adapted from Gallagher, 1965, pp. 28–31)

I. Routine (R)

This category includes routine classroom procedural matters such as management of the classroom, the structuring of class discussion, and approval or disapproval of the idea or the person.

Management

Mq—*Question:* Requests or invitations to speak; calling for questions, as in "Anybody have a question?"

Mp—*Procedure:* Announcements or procedural instructions, given or requested for individuals or the group as a whole.

Ma—*Aside:* Incidental or parenthetical comment; gratuitous content.

Mnc—*Nose-Counting:* Calling for or responding with a show of hands for a tally or canvas.

Mfb—*Feedback:* Request for or response with signs from group as to whether or not the speaker's actions or remarks are clearly understood.

Mw—*Work:* Nonverbal actions or seatwork going on in connection with current discussion or class proceedings.

X—Unclassifiable response primarily due to technical recording difficulties.

Structuring

Sts—*Self-Structuring:* Conventional prefatory move to signal content and purpose of one's own next remarks or behavior.

Sto—*Structuring Other(s):* Engineering next speech or actions of other(s). Monitoring other's performance. Pump-priming to keep discussion going on a point already before the class.

Stf—*Future Structuring:* Forecast of future activity, study, learning, etc. beyond this particular class session.

Stc—*Class Structuring:* Focusing class attention on point to be emphasized or taken up; laying groundwork for question or problem; probing, pushing, adding data for bogged-down class (teacher only).

Verdict

Ver—*Verdict:* (+ or −) Impersonal praise or reproach on quality of *academic* performance of individual or group.

Verp—*Personal Verdict:* (+ or −) Personal praise or reproach of individual. (Occasionally by T on whole class.) Negative Verp generally on deportment.

Agr—*Agreement:* (+ or −) Acceptance or rejection of content; conceding a point; *not* permission-giving nor procedural.

S—*Self Reference:* Speaker's personal report or comment upon or about self. Often conventional device; cautionary tactic.

Du—*Dunno:* Explicit indication that one does not know.

Mu—*Muddled:* Speaker confused, mixed up, flustered.

Hu—*Humor:* Remark of evident witty, humorous, or comic intent; response (usually laughter) to same.

Figure 8.5 (continued)

II. Cognitive-Memory (C-M)

C-M operations represent the simple reproduction of facts, formulas and other items of remembered content through use of such processes as recognition, rote memory and selective recall.

Scr—*Scribe:* Giving a spoken or written spelling or exemplification of a word or expression.

Recapitulation

Req—*Quoting:* Rote recitation or literal reading from text, paper or notes in hand.

Rep—*Repetition:* Literal or nearly verbatim restatement of something just said.

Rec—*Recounting:* Narration of past extra-class occurrence.

Rev—*Review:* Recitation of material which occurred or was discussed in current or past class session.

Clarification

Clm—*Clarifying Meaning:* Rendering a previous statement more intelligible either by (a) restating or rephrasing or (b) adding informative details.

Clq—*Clarifying Qualification:* Render a previous statement more accurate either by (a) "Entering a rider" upon the remark or (b) entering an explicit correction.

Factual

Rs—*Fact Stating:* Requests for and recitations of items taken to be matters of fact.

Fd—*Fact Detailing:* Spinning out further a prior assertion of fact or other statements (As, Exr) in which factual items were mentioned.

Fm—*Factual Monologue:* Reporting of factual material in the form of a monologue during which verbal exchange is conventionally excluded.

III. Convergent Thinking (CT)

Convergent thinking is thought operation involving the analysis and integration of given or remembered data. It leads to one expected result because of the tightly structured framework which limits it.

Translation

Tr—*Translation:* Shift of conceptual material from symbolic or figural content to semantic, or vice versa.

Association

As—*Association:* Involving likenesses and differences; degrees of comparison; and relationships of direction, spatial position and/or classification, etc.

Explanation

Exr—*Rational Explanation:* Asking or telling why X is the case; why Y caused X, etc. Substantiating a claim or conclusion by citing evidence.

Exv—*Value Explanation:* Asking or telling why X is good, bad, useful, important, etc. Justifying a rating, viewpoint, or value-based judgment by giving reasons why.

Exn—*Narrative Explanation:* Step-by-step account of how something is done, how a mechanism works, or of what led up to an event or given outcome.

Conclusion

Gen—*Generalization:* Integration of prior remarks by slightly more general reformulation.

Cons—*Summary Conclusion:* Summary reformulation, often serial or enumerative, or material treated in discussion or reading.

Conl—*Logical Conclusion:* Calling for a deductively drawn implication from material presented.

IV. Evaluative Thinking (ET)

Evaluative thinking deals with matters of value rather than matters of fact and is characterized in verbal performance by its judgmental character.

Unstructured

Ura—*Unstructured Rating:* A value judgment produced or requested on some idea or item in terms of a scale of values provided by the respondent.

Uju—*Unstructured Judgment:* A value judgment produced or requested on some idea or item wherein the value dimension has already been provided.

Structured

Svp—*Structured Probability:* An estimate or speculative opinion is given or requested as to the likelihood of some occurrence or situation.

Svc—*Structured Choice:* Speaker calls for or declares his position as a choice between alternatives (not between *Yes or No* answers).

Qualification

Qj—*Qualified Judgment:* An offer or request for a rider or modification to a prior value judgment. Also, attempts to make more precise the value dimension discussed.

Qc—*Counter Judgment:* Speaker declares a directly opposed position with respect to value statement of a previous classroom speaker.

V. Divergent Thinking (DT)

In a divergent thinking sequence, individuals are free to independently generate their own ideas within a data-poor situation, often taking a new direction or perspective.

El—*Elaboration:* Structured or free (s or f). Building upon a point already made; filling out or developing a point, but not shifting to a new point. often by concocting instances or examples.

Ad—*Divergent Association:* (s or f) Constructing a relationship between ideas, casting the central idea into sharper and often unexpected perspective, by comparisons, analogies, etc.

Figure 8.5 (continued)

> Imp—*Implication:* (s or f) Extrapolation beyond the given, projection from given data—typically by antecedent-consequent or hypothetical construction—to new point(s) of possibility.
>
> Syn—*Synthesis:* Spontaneous performance, tying in, integrating the current central idea with an entirely new point or frame of reference. May be a variation or reversal of a previous conclusion.
>
> *Double Paired Ratings:* The complex nature of verbal classroom interaction often requires the combination of more than one of the above described categories.

In this system the cognition and memory operations were combined into a single *cognitive-memory* category because of difficulty reported by the investigators in distinguishing these two in classroom interaction, and because both were considered to represent nonproductive thinking operations. In addition, a broad classification of classroom *routine* was included so that noncognitive aspects of classroom interaction might be coded.

Use of the two categories of convergent thinking and divergent thinking was also made by Medley and his colleagues (1966) through application of their OScAR 4V, a version of their Observational Schedule and Record instrument. Among the 42 items of OScAR 4V, 24 items are used to code *interchanges,* which are units of teacher-pupil verbal interaction. Four kinds of *entries* to interchanges are recognized. One of these applies to interchanges that are initiated by pupils, the other three to teacher-initiated interchanges:

> If a pupil addresses the teacher with a question or statement, the interchange is coded as Pupil Initiated. If the teacher asks a question which relates to the answer made to a preceding question, the interchange is coded as *Elaborating.* If the teacher asks a question not relating to the preceding question to which there is apparently only one "right" answer, the interchange is coded as *Convergent;* if the teacher asks a question not related to a preceding question to which there are apparently two or more "right" or acceptable answers, the interchange is coded as *Divergent.* (Medley, 1967, pp. 7–8)

Thus, the Guilford-inspired distinction between convergent and divergent production is applied only to teacher-initiated questions.

Unfortunately, the only published report of a third instrument that presumably uses concepts from Guilford (Thompson and Bowers, 1968) does not include definitions or examples of the use of divergent and convergent categories in analyzing questions, so we must assume that they were consistent with Guilford's definitions.

Details of the few studies that have used Guilford's concepts to date are reported in Box 8.2. The information supplied in Box 8.2 raises a serious question concerning the reliability of Guilford's concepts when applied to classroom behavior. OScAR 4V was found to have low reliability, and although we have seen fit to rate the AGCS as of moderate reliability, Gallagher's own comments cast doubt upon the matter.

BOX 8.2 Applications of Guilford's Categories

STUDIES REVIEWED

Gallagher (1965)	(Gal65)
Hudgins and Ahlbrand (1967)	(H&A67)
Medley *et al.* (1966)	(Med66)
Thompson and Bowers (1968)	(T&B68)

INSTRUMENT, METHOD OF GATHERING DATA, CODING SYSTEM, UNIT STUDIED, RELIABILITY

AGCS, transcripts, multifacet category system, T and P utterances, moderate reliability (Gal65), (H&A67).

OScAR 4V, live observation, multifacet category system, T initiations and reactions, low reliability (Med66).

Thompson & Bowers Instrument, unknown, unknown, T questions, reliability not discussed (T&B68).

DESIGN OF STUDY, SUBJECTS, CONTEXTS

Field Studies

(Gal65)	5 experienced teachers, 10 groups of "academically talented" pupils junior high, social studies, English, science.
(H&A67)	9 experienced teachers and pupils, junior high, English
(Med66)	70 student teachers and pupils, secondary, several subjects
(T&B68)	15 experienced teachers, grade IV

FINDINGS

Process Occurrence

8.2-1 Teachers use *more cognitive memory* than they do others (Gal65), (H&A67).

8.2-2 More classroom exchanges are *convergent* than *divergent* (Med66).

Context-Process Relationships

8.2-3 *Pupil sex* affects *pupil use of categories.* (Boys are *more expressive* than girls.) (Gal65).

8.2-4 *Pupil group and session* affect *teacher use of categories for questions* (but not for teacher statements) (Gal65).

8.2-5 *Pupil group and session* are unrelated to *pupil use of categories* (Gal65).

8.2-6 *Phase of the lesson* affects *teacher use of categories.* (Over time, teachers tend more to encourage pupil answers and reject inaccurate answers to all questions that are *not* divergent.) (Med66).

Presage-Process Relationships

None reported.

Process-Process Relationships

8.2-7 *Teacher use of categories in questions* co-varies directly with *pupil use of categories in responses* (Gal65), (H&A67).

8.2-8 *Teacher use of categories in questions* is unrelated *to teacher use of categories in statements* (Gal65).

8.2-9 *(Student) teacher reactions* are unrelated to whether interchange is *convergent* or *divergent* (most reactions are "positive") (Med66).

Box 8.2 (continued)

Process-Product Relationships

8.2-10 *Moderate teacher use of convergent questions* co-varies directly with *pupil growth of vocabulary*; *high* and *low* use of *convergent questions* is associated with *less pupil vocabulary growth* (finding does not hold for social studies) (T&B68).

8.2-11 *Teacher use of convergent questions* co-varies directly with *pupil achievement.* (*Teacher use of divergent questions* is not related to *pupil achievement.*) (W&N70).

In his report on this research Gallagher (1965) discusses the evolution of the instrument. The investigators began by trying to operationalize Guilford's model, then shifted to one where cognitive memory was seen to underlie others and finally to one where all types of operations were seen to be interrelated. The type of classroom occurrence which led to this third view is exemplified by Gallagher in the following:

For instance, one type of evaluative question could be, "Do you consider Communist China a major threat to the United States?" The answer of the student would be an evaluative one in the sense that the student is required to construct a value dimension ranging from threat to nonthreat and then to make a judgment as to where on this continuum to place Communist China.

But, if one examines how a student arrived at such an evaluative statement it can readily be seen that he had to do convergent thinking to develop a closely reasoned and logical process leading to his conclusion; or he had to produce examples constructed from his experience or imagination which would justify or illustrate the particular value judgment he finally makes. (pp. 40–41)

Furthermore, Gallagher reports difficulty in obtaining agreement between judges on distinctions between convergent and divergent thinking in the classroom. This led him to doubt that these two categories, as well as evaluative thinking, did actually involve distinct cognitive operations. At root they all seemed to involve similar syllogistic thinking of the if-then type:

Viewing the problem from the standpoint of mental operation, the differences between the process followed by the student was often hardly distinguishable from divergent to convergent. The difference lies in the style of question and in strategy of selection of one answer from a number of alternatives in the divergent thinking problem. . . .

Once this particular line of thought was established it became clear that the distinction between the operation of evaluative and convergent or divergent thinking also became dubious. . . . The question then seemed to be, *was the difference mainly in how the problem was posed,* rather than in the mental operation that was followed? (p. 43)

To take Gallagher's doubts seriously is to question the efficacy of attempting to study classroom events in terms of Guilford's and Bloom's concepts. Rather, Gallagher appears to be arguing for the logical or semantic analysis of classroom discourse—concepts for which are taken up in the next chapter.

The issues of reliability and validity were not engaged in the remaining studies reported in Box 8.2. On the whole, then, evidence concerning the question of reliability is less impressive than for systems based on the Bloom taxonomy.

Given this problem of reliability, what findings have emerged from applications of the Guilford categories to classroom behavior?

First, as was true for studies based on the Bloom taxonomy, the Guilford-based studies have also found that classrooms stressed simple cognitive processes and tended to avoid divergent and evaluative thinking. A single study also reports greater use of convergent than divergent productions in normal secondary school classrooms (Medley *et al.*, 1966).

Second, several contextual variables were studied. Boys were found to be more expressive than girls. Pupil group and session were found to affect teacher questioning behavior, but not teacher stating behavior or pupil questions or pupil statements (Gallagher, 1965). As the semester progressed teachers were found to provide more encouragement for pupil responses and greater rejection of inaccurate pupil responses for all but divergent questions (Medley *et al.*, 1966).

Third, no findings can be reported for presage-process relationships. The problem simply was not investigated in these studies.

Fourth, as found in studies based on Bloom, again it is reported that type of category stressed by teachers co-varies with type of category stressed by pupils—and again this finding was interpreted as reflecting teacher control of the cognitive processes in classroom discourse. However, the category stressed in teacher *questions* appeared unrelated to stress given in teacher *statements* (Gallagher, 1965), and type of teacher response was independent of whether teacher-pupil interchange was convergent or divergent (both were approved) (Medley *et al.*, 1966).

Fifth, again as was true for studies reflecting the Bloom taxonomy, evidence concerning the relationship between cognitive processes in the classroom and pupil growth is weak. Only one grade IV field survey (Thompson and Bowers, 1968) looked at the question at all. This study found that teachers who were given *moderate* scores on a convergence-divergence continuum were associated with greater pupil vocabulary growth than those who scored either *high* or *low*. Once again, it seems "self-evident" to some educators that classrooms high in divergent thinking will have better effects on pupils than those stressing convergent thinking or rote memory. However attractive this argument, the evidence is simply not yet available, and what little evidence there is suggests that the relationship between these two phenomena may be nonlinear. This does not mean that the

Commitment is wrong. But evidence concerning the effects of divergent production is weak. Furthermore, evidence that teachers can be trained to seek divergent production is missing in research to date.

STUDIES USING TABA'S CATEGORIES

The third research tradition we shall review in this chapter is especially interesting because it represents one of the few attempts we have found in which research on teaching behavior has been used to aid the development of a new curriculum. This is the research program conducted at San Francisco State College by Hilda Taba and her associates. This program has made a number of contributions that lie beyond the sphere of our review. However, two major studies of classroom behavior were built into the program (Taba *et al.*, 1964; Taba, 1966), and to the reports of these studies we now turn.

In general, Taba and her colleagues sought to improve teaching by developing and applying concepts for classroom behavior that were based on knowledge concerning cognitive development in children. They also presumed that teaching strategies should be adjusted and matched to specific learning objectives rather than be considered global processes serving any and all educational objectives. Teaching strategies, they argued, need to be devised on the basis of a theoretical framework which takes in both the *principles of learning* and the *structure of the content and tasks* to be achieved.

Stress was given to a number of principles that the research team found in theories of cognitive development.

1. Cognitive processes are subject to training;
2. Thought follows certain developmental sequences, in which mastery of each preceding step is a prerequisite to the mastery of the next; and
3. Thought matures through the continuous organization and reorganization of conceptual structures involving the processes of assimilation and accommodation.

The implications of these principles for education were seen to be many, but especially the following:

a. Learning tasks proceed in cycles in which the simpler concrete cognitive operations precede the more complex abstract operations;
b. Development of thought is not a short-term goal but requires time, practice in relation to a curriculum, and teaching strategies that include both an "upward spiraling" in the content and demands for cognitive functioning;

c. Learning tasks should be rotated systematically, thus avoiding both a prolonged exposure to facts without reshaping of conceptual schemes and premature leaps to more complex types of thought;

d. Conceptual reorganization cannot be *given* to pupils. Rather, they must be *led* to discover ideas and conceptual structures of their own;

e. Individual differences exist in the amount of concrete thinking required before formal or abstract thought can emerge.

In more concrete terms Taba and her colleagues saw cognitive operations as composed of three major tasks: *concept formation, inference,* and *application of principles.* These tasks were presumed to be related logically to one another so that concepts must be formed before inferences can be made, and inferences must be made before principles can be applied. In addition, the investigators also conceived logical sequences involving elements within each task. Thus, within the task of concept formation appear a number of skills that must be mastered in sequence: (1) differentiation, (2) grouping, and (3) labeling. Within the task of making inferences, there is a necessary sequence which involves (1) assembling concrete information, (2) identifying and discriminating the various points of this information, (3) establishing relationships between the points, (4) comparing and contrasting, and (5) generalizing.

Major implications of these principles were seen to be:

1. The teacher must have two cognitive maps—one of the logic of the content and one of the psychology of the cognitive processes involved in learning the content;

2. In order to promote cognitive development the teacher must make careful decisions about the appropriate pacing of each teaching step, when to maintain or shift the focus, when to "lift the level of thought";

3. The teacher must place more emphasis upon "seeking" than upon "giving," and "seeking" should emphasize divergent rather than convergent thinking.

Finally, the Taba team emphasized that effective teaching depends not upon the performance of specific categories of behavior but in the way in which these are combined to form strategies.

The impact of teaching lies not alone in its single acts, but in the manner in which these acts are combined into a pattern; the particular combination of focusing, extending, and lifting; the length of time spent on a particular operation in preparation for another level; how the functions of "giving" and "seeking" are distributed; and the way in which the intake of information is alternated with processing, transforming, and synthesizing the information. (Taba *et al.*, 1964, p. 55)

Concepts

Concepts advanced in Taba's two studies were similar, although not identical. Both used the same unit of analysis, *thought unit,* defined to be "a remark or series of remarks which expresses a more or less complete idea, serves a specified function, and can be classified by a level of thought" (Taba *et al.,* 1964, p. 115). A thought unit, thus defined, could consist of utterances ranging from single words to complete paragraphs. We take it that Taba's thought unit can be no larger than one of Bellack's "moves." However, a given move might involve two or more thought units if the latter had different content, though the same interactive function.

Each thought unit was first coded according to its *designation:* that is, whether it emanated from the *teacher* ("T") or a *pupil* ("C"), and whether the emitter was *giving* ("G") or *seeking* ("S") information. Thus, four coding categories were possible: TG, TS, CG, and CS. Next, a distinction was made between two broad types of teaching or *pedagogical functions,* those which are substantive or content related and those which are performed independently of any particular content and which are primarily managerial. (We shall ignore these latter in our discussion here.) Finally, the investigators also set forth a set of categories pertaining to levels of thought and the logic of content. The categories used in the first study are presented in Figure 8.6. Those used in the second study are presented in Figure 8.7. Categories for judging thought level were organized under major headings intended to reflect the three cognitive tasks of concept formation, inference, and application of the principles we discussed earlier.

FIGURE 8.6   Thought-level codes of the first Taba study. (Adapted from Taba et al., 1964, pp. 199–201)

Cognitive task: Grouping and labeling (giving or seeking)

10	specific or general information outside of focus
11	specific or general information within focus
12	specific or general information with qualifications
30	grouping information without basis
31	grouping information with implicit basis
32	grouping information with explicit basis
40	categorizing information without basis
41	categorizing information with implicit relationships between items
42	categorizing information with explicit relationships between them

Cognitive task: Interpreting information and making inferences (giving or seeking)

10	specific or general information outside of focus
11	specific or general information within focus

12	specific or general information with qualifications and relationships
50	specific reason or explanation that does not relate to the information
51	specific reason or explanation that relates or organizes the information
52	specific reason or explanation that states how it relates or organizes the information
60	irrelevant or incorrect inference which is derived from information
61	relevant inference which is derived from information
62	relevant inference which is derived from information and expresses a cause and effect relationship, explanation, consequence, or contrast
70	relationship between information which implies an irrelevant or incorrect principle or generalization
71	relationship between information which implies a principle or generalization
72	principle or generalization which is derived from information

Cognitive task: Predicting consequences (giving or seeking)

90	correcting the cause or condition

Establishing parameters of information

100	relevant information
101	relevant information for establishing the parameter for a particular hypothesis or prediction
102	relevant information for the parameter or any particular prediction with appropriate explanation

Establishing parameters of conditions

110	irrelevant or untenable condition for the logical parameter (if-then) or for the particular prediction or hypothesis
111	relevant condition without connecting it with relevant information
112	relevant condition and information and establishing logical connection between them

Prediction: Level one (100), immediate consequences
Level two (200), remote consequences

120–220	incorrect or out of focus prediction
121–221	prediction with no elaboration
122–222	prediction accompanied by explanation, qualification, differentiation, comparison, or contrast
123–223	prediction accompanied by a stated or implied principle

Throughout Taba's writing considerable importance is attached to *thought levels,* and teachers are encouraged to "lift the level of thought" as often as may be appropriate. Moreover, in the first study Taba attempted to study the occasions on which teachers in fact "lifted the level of thought" in their classrooms and provided a separate code for such occasions.

FIGURE 8.7   Categories for thought levels in the second Taba study. (Adapted from Taba, 1966, pp. 140–150)

COGNITIVE TASK 1: CONCEPT FORMATION

I Enumeration

TS I	Teacher seeks enumeration
10	Incorrect enumeration of specifics
11	Correct enumeration of specifics
12	Correct enumeration of specifics with clarification, amplification, and/or giving comparative data without making an inference
13	Correct enumeration with reason or explanation

II Grouping

TS II	Teacher seeks grouping
20	Incorrect grouping
21	Correct grouping
22	Correct grouping with clarification, amplification, and/or giving comparative data without making an inference
23	Correct grouping with reason or explanation

III Labeling (Categorizing) and Subsuming on a Single Basis or on a Multiple Basis

TS III	Teacher seeks categorization (labels for groups)
30	Incorrect subsuming
31	Correct subsuming
32	Correct subsuming with clarification, amplification, and/or giving comparative data without making an inference
33	Correct subsuming with reason or explanation
40	Incorrect categorizing of a single item in more than one category
41	Correct categorizing of a single item in more than one category
42	Correct categorizing of a single item on multiple bases, with amplification, and/or giving comparative data
43	Correct categorizing of a single item on multiple bases, with reason or explanation

COGNITIVE TASK 2: INFERRING AND GENERALIZING

I Identifying Points, Giving Information

TS I	Teacher seeks information, without specifying the level
0	Incorrect information in the thought unit
1	Giving specific units of data
2	Relating, comparing, contrasting units of data

II Explaining

TS II	Teacher seeks explanation (without specifying whether factual or inferential)
3	Providing a factual explanation
5	Providing an inferential explanation

III Making Inferences, Generalizing

TS III	Teacher seeks inference, generalization, or principle without specifying a particular level
4	Giving inference from units of data
6	Giving an inference that is a generalization upon generalizations drawing analogies
7	Giving the logical relationship between inferences

COGNITIVE TASK 3: APPLICATION OF PRINCIPLES

I Predicting

4P	A prediction based upon simple inference, that is, at thought level 4
6P	A prediction based upon compound inference, that is, at thought level 6
1Cp	Changing the given parameters or giving hypothetical and/or irrelevant parameters at thought level 1
2Cp	Changing the given parameters or giving hypothetical and/or irrelevant parameters at thought level 2
3Cp	Changing the given parameters or giving hypothetical and/or irrelevant parameters at thought level 3
$4P_2$	A prediction, generated by a Cp based upon simple inference, that is, at thought level 4
$6P_2$	A prediction, generated by a Cp, based upon compound inference, that is, at thought level 6

II Explaining and Supporting Predictions

IF, 2F, 3F	Factual support for a prediction at thought level 1, 2, or 3
5I, 6I	Inferential support for a prediction at thought level 5 or 6

III Verifying the Predictions by Logical Inference

1LO, 2LO, 4LO, 6LO	Logical conditional support on thought level 1, 2, 4, or 6

An example of this type of "thought lifting" is provided by Taba in the first study:

1) T	Does anyone remember how the women carried things?	TS 11 FC
2) C	On their heads.	CG 11
3) T	Well, now, how do you suppose they carried these things on their heads? Everybody stop and think— why, as they went to market, were they all carrying things on their heads?	TS 51 L
4) C	Their hands get tired.	CG 51 L
5) T	Yes, their hands might get tired, but there are other reasons, too. Can you think of any other reasons?	TGR
6) C	Baskets might be heavy.	CG 51
7) T	Yes, any other reasons?	
8) C	They don't have any bags.	CG 51

9) T They didn't seem to have any bags. Didn't see any,   TGR
did we? Any other reasons?
10) C They had so many things—they can get that on their   CG 51
head and carry them in their hands.

The teacher's inquiry on line 3 seeks to lift the level of thought from
the informational level (11) to the reason level (51) and therefore receives
the function coding L. (Taba et al., 1964, pp. 205–206)

Interestingly enough, the concept of thought level was somewhat different in each study. In the first study, as shown in Figure 8.8, thought
levels were defined independently for each cognitive task, so that the same
type of thinking, for example, labeling, might be rated as high level in
relation to concept formation but low level in relation to inferring and
generalizing. However, in the second study the same set of categories was
used in coding thought levels for the two cognitive tasks of inferring and
generalizing and application of principles. These categories are shown in
Figure 8.9.

A further elaboration in the second study was the use of the categories
contained in Figure 8.9 to operationalize notions of concreteness and
abstractness of thought. The authors of that study seem to have discovered
for themselves the idea we suggested earlier in this chapter—that the

FIGURE 8.8   Definition of thought levels in the first Taba study.
(Adapted from Taba et al., 1964, p. 153)

COGNITIVE TASK	LEVEL I	LEVEL II	LEVEL III
Grouping and labeling (Discussion 1)	11–22 Enumerating specific and general information	31–32 Grouping information	41+ Categorizing and labeling information
Interpreting information and making inferences (Discussion 2 and 3)	11–42 Enumerating, grouping and categorizing	51–61 Giving reasons or making inferences	62+ Making inferences and stating cause-and-effect relationships. Stating principles
Predicting consequences and explaining new phenomema (Discussion 4)	121 and 221 Predicting and explaining without rationale	101–102, 201–202, 111 and 211, 122 and 222 Giving information that establishes parameters. Giving conditions. Predicting or explaining with reasons, etc.	112 and 212, 123 and 223 Stating conditions and establishing logical connections. Predicting accompanied by stated or implied principles

. **FIGURE 8.9** Categories, levels of thought, and the concrete-abstract dimension in the second Taba study. (Adapted from Taba, 1966)

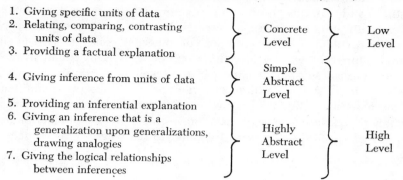

1. Giving specific units of data
2. Relating, comparing, contrasting units of data
3. Providing a factual explanation

4. Giving inference from units of data

5. Providing an inferential explanation
6. Giving an inference that is a generalization upon generalizations, drawing analogies
7. Giving the logical relationships between inferences

Concrete Level
Simple Abstract Level
Highly Abstract Level

Low Level

High Level

dimensions of logical complexity and abstractness may vary independently —for they suggest that the same logically complex process of explaining is *concrete* if it is factual, but *abstract* if it is inferential. Indeed, from Figure 8.9 it might be possible to argue that the distinctions among thought levels in the Taba studies are based more on the concrete-abstract dimension than on the logical-complexity dimension.

In addition to concerns for "lifting the level of thought," the first Taba study also included a related process, "extending thought on the same level." This latter concept refers to the addition of logically related information that represents no shift in level of complexity or of abstraction. For example, the teacher might solicit further details concerning some matter from pupils, or pupils might volunteer a second, third, or fourth explanation that was at the same thought level as the first explanation given. When examples of thought extension were encountered in the thought units of the lesson, these too were noted.

Like those influenced by Bloom *et al.* or Guilford, Taba and her associates appear strongly *Committed* to the improvement of education by encouraging "higher levels" of thought in the classroom. In operational terms, they too would appear to believe that too many thought units are at a "low level" in the typical classroom; teachers may be encouraged to use more "high-level" units through training; and pupils will benefit from the greater use of "high-level" units. In addition, the Taba group appears *Committed* to teacher *seeking* rather than giving; teacher thought units that seek to "*lift the level of thought*"; and, to a lesser extent, teacher thought units that "*extend thought*." Each of these types of teacher behavior should also be encouraged and will be found to have salubrious effects. (Indeed, so strong are these latter *Commitments* that no coding categories are provided for instances wherein teachers might have "lowered" or "depressed" the level of thought, or perhaps prevented thought extension from occurring!)

The Taba studies differ from those reviewed earlier, however, in that it is recognized that attempts to solicit high thought levels can be premature and that unless timed carefully these attempts can even retard cognitive growth. In addition, this group of investigators has promoted their *Commit ment* not only through classroom research but also with an extensive pro gram of curriculum development based on the same concepts used in their research. Moreover, we would judge that the Taba curriculum material have already had substantial impact in the teaching of social science. Bu to repeat our oft-stated position, in order for us to accept *Commitment* such as those of the Taba group we must find that they are at least sup ported by process-occurrence, presage-process, and process-product findings Let us now look at Taba's reported findings to see whether the evidence i there.

Research on Classroom Behavior

The main objectives of both Taba studies were to examine the develop ment of thought under optimum training conditions defined as:

1. A curriculum designed for the development of thinking;
2. Teaching strategies designed to emphasize the mastery of the essen tial cognitive skills; and
3. A sufficient time span to allow for developmental sequences in training.

For these reasons data were collected in experimental classrooms involving a social studies curriculum that was organized to give emphasis to basic ideas and details rather than to the coverage of broad areas of content. Moreover, the curriculum contained a careful sequencing of learning experi ences to reflect the principles of sequence, rotation of assimilation and accommodation, and encouragement of autonomy discussed earlier.

The teachers of the experimental classrooms each received a special training program of ten days' duration divided into two major areas: analy sis of the structure and rationale of the curriculum, and training in the teaching strategies for the development of skills involved in the three cogni tive tasks. Training with respect to the curriculum involved the examina tion of the sources of criteria for curriculum decisions, a range of behavioral objectives, the selection and organization of content, and the structure and sequence of learning experiences. Training in teaching strategies for the development of cognitive skills was described as follows:

> The work on each cognitive task involved at least three steps, accomplished in two or three sessions. First there was a presentation of the structure of the process and of the progressive steps in mastering it. This presentation was accompanied by such illustrations as were available. The second step con sisted of a "scoring" of one tapescript of a discussion involving the task in question, followed by an analysis of the particular patterns by which the

discussion was managed, what successes were evident, what errors were committed, and what the consequences of these errors were. Third, each teacher received the tapescript of discussions he had held with his own class, with an assignment to analyze it on his own for successes, errors, and problems. (Taba et al., 1964, p. 67)

The two studies differed in some important ways. Whereas the first study included classes from grades II through VI, the second study featured only grades IV through VI. In addition, the first study involved only teachers trained in the program described above, whereas the second involved four groups of teachers. The first group consisted of teachers who received the special training and of pupils who had had one or more years of exposure to the special curriculum. The second group constituted teachers who would receive the special training during the study and of pupils who were recently introduced to the special curriculum. The third involved teachers who received no special training and of pupils who were recently introduced to the special curriculum. The fourth consisted of teachers who received no special training and of pupils who had had no exposure to the special curriculum.

The classroom behavior data for both studies were derived from typescripts of audiotapes of *four* recorded classroom discussions spaced throughout one school year. The first discussion was directed toward the cognitive task of grouping and labeling, the second and third to interpreting data, and the fourth to predicting consequences. Reliability data are presented for the first study only, but they indicate that the coding system works well.

Other details of the two studies are included in Box 8.3. Before discussing the results presented in Box 8.3, some explanation of the ways in which we arrived at the findings reported there is needed.

Since most of the findings reported in the Taba studies were not subjected to tests of statistical significance, we have had to rely on our own "eyeball" analysis of trends in preparing Box 8.3. We have done so with some diffidence.

No *process-occurrence* findings are reported in Box 8.3, since variations from one cognitive task to another were so great as to make generalizations across them misleading.

Where *experimental curriculum* is used as a *context* variable in Box 8.3, the findings were gleaned by comparing teachers who received no special training but whose pupils were newly introduced to the special curriculum with the control teachers who also received no special training but whose pupils were not exposed to the experimental curriculum. This comparison would allow for some control of teacher training, so that any differences could more confidently be attributed to the experimental curriculum.

Where presage-process findings for *teacher training* are reported, these were obtained from the second study by comparing the group of teachers who received special training during the study and whose pupils were newly introduced to the special curriculum with the group of teachers who received no special training but whose pupils were also newly introduced to the special curriculum. It was thought that control for experience of the new curriculum could be assumed in comparisons between these two groups only and that, accordingly, any differences could more validly be attributed to special teacher training.

All other findings obtained from the second study are based on the total sample of teachers and classes. In addition, data on thought levels for the cognitive task of concept formation were not reported in the second Taba study and so could not be included in any of the findings in Box 8.3.

Finally, the design of the two studies made it impossible to extricate the nature of the cognitive task from the time of the year as independent variables. Thus, it is also possible that findings we have attributed to the nature of the cognitive task are partly, if not wholly, attributable to normal changes occurring over the period of the school year.

In addition to these problems, the authors experienced unusual difficulty in attempting to extract findings from the two Taba studies. As we have seen, there was a certain amount of conceptual confusion in the inception of the research. Operational definitions were not always clearly spelled out, and the investigators tended to use multiple terms for the same operation or somewhat different measurements for an identically designated concept. Furthermore, at numerous points we were frustrated by the nearly certain knowledge that findings of interest must have been available to the investigators, only they did not report them to others. Finally, the criterion tests of pupil achievement had such low reliability coefficients that little confidence can be placed in findings involving them. Bearing these problems in mind, what do the findings show?

BOX 8.3   Research Using Taba's Categories

STUDIES REVIEWED

Taba et al., (1964)	(Tab64)
Taba (1966)	(Tab66)
Wright and Nuthall (1970)	(W&N70)

INSTRUMENT, METHOD OF GATHERING DATA, CODING SYSTEM, UNIT STUDIED, RELIABILITY

Taba Instrument, transcripts, multifacet category system, thought units, high reliability (Tab64).

Modified Taba Instrument, transcripts, multifacet category system, thought units, reliability not reported (Tab66).

Canterbury Instrument, transcripts, multifacet category system, T and P verbal moves, moderate reliability (W&N70).

DESIGN OF STUDY, SUBJECTS, CONTEXTS

Field Survey

(Tab64)   20 teachers (all psecially trained) and pupils, grades II-VI, social studies

(W&N70)   17 teachers and pupils, grade III, three nature-study lessons, standardized content; Christchurch (New Zealand)

Presage-Process Experiments

(Tab66)   24 teachers and pupils, grades IV-VI, social tsudies

FINDINGS

Process Occurrence

None reported.

Context-Process Relationships

8.3-1   *Experimental curriculum* is unrelated to:
substantive teacher use of "seeks information" (categories 1 and 2, Fig. 8.9); *substantive pupil use of "gives information"*;
substantive teacher use of "seeks explanation" (categories 3 and 5, Fig. 8.9); *substantive pupil use of "gives explanation"*;
substantive teacher use of "seeks generalization"; (categories 4, 6, and 7, Fig. 8.9);
substantive pupil use of "gives generalization";
total pupil use of "concrete" thought units (see Fig. 8.9);
total pupil use of "simple abstract" thought units (see Fig. 8.9);
total pupil use of "highly abstract" thought units (see Fig. 8.9) (Tab66)E.*

8.3-2   *Nature of the cognitive task:*
affects *substantive teacher use of "seeks information"*;
affects *substantive pupil use of "gives information"*;
affects *substantive teacher use of "seeks explanation"*;
is unrelated to *substantive pupil use of "gives explanation"*;
affects *substantive teacher use of "seeks generalization"*;
affects *substantive pupil use of "gives generalization"*;
affects *total pupil use of "concrete" thought units*;
affects *total pupil use of "simple abstract" thought units*;
is unrelated to *total pupil use of "highly abstract" thought units.*
(*Inferring* and *generalizing* involve: more information, more explanation, less generalization, more concreteness, and less abstractness than does *application of principles.*) (Tab66).

8.3-3   *Grade level* affects *pupil thought level:*
For first cognitive tasks (grouping and labeling), grades III, IV, and V stressed thought level I; grades II and II thought level II; and grades V and VI thought level III.
For second cognitive task (interpreting and making inferences), grades II, III, and IV stressed thought level I; grade V stressed thought level II (Tab64).

Presage-Process Relationships

8.3-4   *Special training of teachers:*
decreases *substantive teacher use of "seeks information"*:

---

* Findings generated experimentally are indicated with an E.

Box 8.3 *(continued)*

decreases *substantive pupil use of "gives information"*;
increases *substantive teacher use of "seeks explanation"*;
is unrelated to *substantive pupil use of "gives explanation"*;
increases *substantive teacher use of "seeks generalization"*;
increases *substantive pupil use of "gives generalization"*;
decreases *total pupil use of "concrete" thought units*;
increases *total pupil use of "simple abstract" thought units*;
increases *total pupil use of "highly abstract" thought units* (Tab66)E.

8.3-5   *Pupil I.Q. is unrelated to total pupil use of "high-level" thought units* (Tab64), (Tab66).

Process-Process Relationships

8.3-6   *Pupil use of high-level thought units* is positively related to *total number of thought units uttered by pupil* (Tab64), (Tab66).

8.3-7   *Pupil use of high-level thought units* is positively related to *teacher use of high-level thought units* (Tab64), (Tab66).

8.3-8   *Teacher use of units seeking to lift level of pupil thought is* followed by *pupil higher-level thought units* about three-quarters of the time. (On the other hand, about half of pupil use of higher-level thought units are not solicited by teacher.) (Tab64).

8.3-9   *Teacher use of units seeking extension of thought on the same level* is followed by *pupil thought units at the same level* about 7/10 of the time. (On the other hand, about one-third of pupil use of units at the same level are not solicited by teacher.) (Tab64).

Process-Product Relationships

8.3-10   *Pupil use of high-level thought units for first cognitive task* (grouping and labeling) is unrelated to *inference, discrimination, overgeneralization,* and *caution* (posttest scales of Social Studies Inference Test—SSIT) (Tab64).

8.3-11   *Pupil use of high-level thought units for second cognitive task* (interpreting and making inferences) is unrelated to *caution* and *overgeneralization* (SSIT). Pupils using high-level thought and also participating highly in second cognitive task·have higher scores on *inference* and *discrimination* (SSIT) (Tab64).

8.3-12   *Pupil use of high-level thought units for third cognitive task* (predicting consequences) is unrelated to *inference, discrimination,* and *overgeneralization* (SSIT). Pupils using low-level thought and also participating highly in third cognitive task have higher scores on *caution* (SSIT) (Tab64).

8.3-13   *Pupil use of high-level thought units* is unrelated to *pupil achievement* (STEP Social Studies Test) (Tab66).

8.3-14   *Teacher requests to lift thought level* are unrelated to *pupil achievement* (W&N70).

8.3-15   *Teacher requests to extend thought on the same level* are unrelated to *pupil achievement* (W&N70).

First, and perhaps most important, we learn that the implementation of the specially designed curriculum, of itself, appeared to make little or no difference to the quality of the thought expressed in the classroom. However, we also learn that the special program of teacher training was a very powerful influence on these process variables. Thus, it seems that curriculum change may be of little benefit in the attainment of process objectives unless it is complemented by carefully devised and implemented teacher training.

Second, the types of thought processes exhibited in classrooms appear to be very dependent upon the nature of the cognitive task focused upon. Thus, in the control group of the second study the incidence of low-level thought among pupils varied from as much as 69 percent of thought units given in one lesson to as little as 25 percent in another lesson where the cognitive task was different. Unless we assume that teachers normally do not often vary the nature of the cognitive task, it seems that the global figures on the incidence of low-level thought provided by studies using the Bloom and Guilford categories may be of little value.

Third, it appears that there is no simple relationship between grade level and level of thought, though there is evidence of a trend for the higher grade levels to exceed chance in the incidence of higher thought levels.

Fourth, pupil intelligence is found unrelated to the use of higher-level thought units by pupils. This finding seems surprising in view of the trend mentioned above toward a positive relationship between grade level and the use of higher thought levels by pupils.

Fifth, considerable evidence is also advanced to show that teachers can influence pupils in the latters' classroom behavior. When teachers seek higher levels of thought pupils are likely to respond. When teachers seek to raise the level of thought pupils acquiesce. When teachers seek to extend thought pupils also respond. If we should consider these pupil behaviors to indicate "success" in teaching (in the manner of Kounin, for example), then strong evidence has been advanced favoring the *Commitment*. But Taba and her associates chose to validate their claims against pupil product variables—as do we—so these findings are merely of proximal interest. They do show, however, that teachers generally achieve what they seek from pupils in the immediate classroom context.

Sixth, both studies provided further evidence that the degree of pupil participation in discussions is positively related to the levels of thought communicated by pupils. We still, however, do not know whether the higher-level thought occurs by virtue of increased participation or whether this finding simply indicates that pupils who are more capable of engaging in higher-level thought are thereby induced to participate more than others.

Seventh, unfortunately, in neither Taba study were relationships between teacher behavior variables and pupil achievement explored. Instead, only pupil variables were used in the study of process-product relationships. In the first study these relationships had to be explored independently for the different cognitive tasks, since the meaning of higher and lower thought levels varied according to the cognitive task. Unfortunately, too, for our purposes, the first study explored relationships between pupil use of high and low thought levels and pupil achievement only within levels of pupil participation in the lessons. From the first study we learn that high-participating pupils who exhibit high thought levels in relation to the cognitive task of interpreting information and making inferences perform better than others on tests of inference and discrimination. We learn, too, that high-participating pupils who exhibit low levels of thought in relation to the cognitive task of predicting consequences and explaining new phenomena are more cautious than others in going beyond given data to make inferences.

In the second Taba study measures of thought levels were common across different cognitive tasks, and so it was possible to explore general relationships between thought level and achievement. There was little sign of a significant general relationship between levels of thought uttered by pupils and achievement in social studies as measured in that study.

Finally,. Wright and Nuthall (1970) also explored Taba's concepts of teachers' seeking to lift and extend thought in their eclectic study. Neither concept was found to relate to pupil achievement.

In summary, the Taba studies together provide no evidence concerning the contention that the level of thought in classrooms is normally "too low." They do, however, fulfill the second evidential requirement for the *Commitment,* providing support for the notion that teacher behavior *can* be influenced by appropriate training and, furthermore, that such training produces change in pupil behavior. The third requirement, that such change will result in enhanced pupil achievement, is, however, given only weak support. Finally, despite the best intentions of the investigators, we can find no evidence that the Taba curriculum, of itself, leads to hoped-for pupil growth. (Lack of confirming evidence has not deterred advocacy by the Taba group, that we can detect, nor has it noticeably affected the enthusiasm of educators who have adopted the Taba curricula.) We will return to other ideas in the second Taba study in Chapter X.

CONCLUSION

In this chapter we have reviewed three systems used for viewing cognitive processes in the classroom. The first was the Taxonomy of Educational Objectives in the Cognitive Domain of Bloom and his associates. Studies using this system have included both field investigations and presage-process experiments. The second, Guilford's system for viewing the operations of the intellect, has generated less classroom research, all of it field investigations. Third, there is the Taba system that was used fully, to our knowledge, in only two studies.

Several conclusions appear to be warranted:

1. The categories of behavior suggested can be recognized in classroom processes with reasonable degrees of reliability, but there are still problems in their application;

2. The classrooms studied have tended to emphasize lower-level cognitive processes;

3. Teacher cognitive behaviors appear to be related to (and probably to influence) pupil cognitive behavior, although the latter also reflects other contextual factors, too;

4. Pupils who are more expressive tend to participate at higher cognitive levels than others;

5. Cognitive behavior varies in relation to contextual variables, such as the tasks to be performed, the sex of the pupils, and grade level;

6. Teachers can be taught to raise the level of cognitive operations in the classroom, although this conclusion has not been researched with respect to the Guilford categories.

Moreover, we have discovered a *Commitment* in much of this research to improving education by means of "raising" the level of classroom cognition. This *Commitment* is based on the assumption that higher-level classroom processes will have salubrious effects on pupil growth. However, the evidence either challenges this assumption or is missing. This does not mean that raising the level of classroom discourse is fruitless. On the contrary, we (also) presume that too much classroom discourse is stodgy, dull, and centered on facts and memory. To this extent the proponents of instruments and training programs designed to raise the level of cognitive discourse are presumably "on to something," and research should eventually show pupil growth to be associated with this enterprise. But there are several difficulties with the argument and with its associated research to date.

For one thing, contextual variables need to be considered much more than they have been so far. It would appear that the observer needs to have knowledge of the prior learnings of pupils and the nature of the cognitive task focused upon before confident judgments can be made as to whether a unit of behavior should be classified in one category or in another. Therefore, he needs to familiarize himself with the prior activities of the classroom in order to minimize the number of possibly unwarranted inferences made when these observational categories are formally applied. Furthermore, it would seem that units of behavior have limited meaning in themselves and must be judged in relationship to prior and succeeding units of behavior. The finding that as much as 60 percent of questions and responses are of the lower-level types has distressed some researchers, who have concluded that the intellectual climate of these classrooms was therefore meager. But a more careful analysis might have revealed that some of these acts of memory were essential for later engagement of higher-level activities. Such a possibility can be studied only through analysis of the structure and sequence of classroom activities. While most of the research reviewed in this chapter has ignored this point, the Taba studies, particularly the second one, included this type of analysis, as we shall see in Chapter X.

Future research also needs to take much more notice of the importance of pupil variables, such as their sex, home background, and current stat of cognitive development. If it is true that disadvantaged first-grade childrei benefit in some respects more from lower-level than higher-level teachin; behavior, is this also true for children from different backgrounds and a different grade levels?

The classroom context is an especially important consideration in re search which seeks the effects of modifying teaching behavior througl training in the use of higher-level thought. It needs to be realized tha pupils are probably used to participating, or not participating, in a settin; in which lower-level thinking is more typical. Thus, significant effects o» pupil learning of changes in the prevailing climate of the classroom ar« unlikely to be found in the short term.

Finally, we have also questioned the dimensionality of the low-level- high-level dichotomy in cognitive processes. Bloom, Guilford, and Taba al gave some recognition to the separate existence of simple-versus-comple» and concrete-versus-abstract dimensions, but their explorations were limited The Guilford and Taba approaches to conceptualizing the two dimension» suggest that complexity applies more to cognitive processes and product and that abstractness applies particularly to content. Thus, the evidence tha there is a negative relationship between abstractness and high degrees o complexity might indicate that while teachers can manage both simple anc complex processes with concrete material, or concrete and abstract conten» with simple processes, they experience difficulty when both complex pro» cesses and abstract content are involved.

Perhaps, too, some of these combinations are more effective in promot ing certain types of pupil growth than others. A possible explanation fo the finding of a positive relation between simplicity of processes and highe cognitive pupil growth might be that pupils were more likely to encounte. abstract content when teachers emphasized simpler processes.

RECOMMENDED ADDITIONAL READING

Bloom, B., et al. (ed.). Taxonomy of Educational Objectives, Handbook I: Th(Cognitive Domain. New York: David McKay Company, Inc., 1956.
  Apart from providing the full details of the categories of the cognitive tax onomy, this work describes procedures adopted in the development of th(system, discusses the value of the various types of cognitive objectives, anc gives many examples of test items corresponding to the categories of th« taxonomy.

Hudgins, B. B. The Instructional Process. Chicago: Rand McNally & Company 1971.
  A valuable introductory text on classroom interaction research. It also contain several chapters on cognitive processes in the classroom. Several researcl studies reviewed in this chapter are also reviewed by Hudgins.

Hyman, R. T. (ed.). *Teaching: Vantage Points for Study.* Philadelphia: J. B. Lippincott Company, 1968.

A book of readings grouped into sections corresponding to the organization of this book. Some of the sections present research studies reviewed in this chapter.

Nelson, Lois H. (ed.). *The Nature of Teaching: A Collection of Readings.* Waltham, Mass.: Blaisdell Publishing Company, 1969.

A book of readings similar in content to Hyman's collection. Several of the research studies we have reviewed in this chapter are contained in Nelson's book.

Rosenshine, B., and Furst, N. "Research in teacher performance criteria." In B. Othanel Smith (ed.), *Research in Teacher Education: A Symposium.* Englewood Cliffs, N.J.: Prentice-Hall, Inc., 1971.

This chapter is a comprehensive review of process-product research on teaching, including several studies employing the Bloom and Guilford categories in coding classroom behavior.

Sanders, N. M. *Classroom Questions: What Kinds?* New York: Harper & Row, Publishers, Inc., 1966.

This book is one of the earliest attempts to translate the Bloom taxonomy for use by teachers in verbal interaction with pupils. Many examples of classroom questions corresponding to the ideals of the taxonomy are provided.

IX

LOGIC AND LINGUISTICS

Teacher: Now ... uh ... so far we've done quite a bit of work on Greece and other countries like that in ... uh ... that part of the world, but we haven't done much lately on Asian ... uh ... countries in Asia.

So, let's go on now to talk about India.

India has a very large population like ... uh ... China. It is a pretty poor place ... uh ... country, too, and lots of people starve there every day from lack of food and stuff. You can see it on the map there sticking out into the ... uh ... Indian Ocean. It's one of the biggest countries in Asia, too, but it's not as big as the United States or some other places.

Years ago India was ... uh ... one country and was part of the British Empire. Not long after the Second World War it ... uh ... became independent and it was ... uh ... split into two countries. Who can tell me what those two countries are called?

Susan: Pakistan?

Jim: Bangla Desh used to be part of Pakistan.

Teacher: That's right, Jim. It used to be part of India once, too. Mary, do you know why they wanted to become ... uh ... independent?

Mary: England wasn't looking after them properly during the war.

Teacher: O.K. Well, they probably thought that anyway. Now, who can tell me some ... uh ... things that are different there? Some ways that India is different from Pakistan?

In the above segment we again encounter the teacher attempting to communicate with pupils about substantive material. However, unlike the fluent, closely reasoned line of questioning contained in the introduction to Chapter VIII, here we find hesitancy, vagueness, and acceptance of an inadequate pupil response. What do pupils make of phrases like "very large," "pretty poor," "one of the biggest," "some other places," and so on? Why did the teacher not pursue further the reasons underlying Indian independence? What are the implications of the teacher's having to rephrase his final question? These questions raise issues about the logic and linguistics of classroom discourse that are the focus of research reviewed in this chapter. As we shall see, this research has not only generated its own findings but its concepts also shed light on some of the problems we have considered in former chapters.

The idea that teaching might be analyzed for its logical character has deep roots in educational philosophy. Surely Socrates provides us a model for the use of logic in instruction. Other logical models were advocated by Dewey, Kilpatrick, and more recently Piaget and Bruner—among others. Moreover, logical methods are also suggested to underlie a number of psychological theories in education. Such an observation has been made of Guilford's theories by Meux and Smith (1964), while we have already seen that when Gallagher (1965) attempted to operationalize the distinction between *convergent, divergent,* and *evaluative* thinking he felt that the task required a more formal, syllogistic analysis.

Despite such suggestions, the actual study of classroom logic is barely a decade old. As we shall see, two major instruments have been developed for this task. Although developed independently, these two systems share various features and have generated similar findings. And despite the fact that they have been applied as yet in only a handful of studies, both systems have had an impact on recent theories and texts in education.

The idea that teaching might also be analyzed as a form of linguistic activity is less familiar to educators. We are apt to think of education in terms of the exchange of "ideas" rather than in terms of the symbols with which those ideas are conveyed. And yet, teaching activities are linguistic in at least two senses: for one, most of the information exchanged in the classroom is verbal; for another, much of the *content* of instruction concerns verbal matters. When a teacher is doing her job, she is often both using and speaking about *words* or other linguistic symbols.

Not surprisingly, then, research on teaching has also begun to reflect the insights of formal linguistic analysis. This latter effort is even newer than research using logical models. Nevertheless, it too has promise for making a major impact on education.

STUDIES USING CONCEPTS OF LOGIC

The effective use of logic has long been regarded as a criterion of educational excellence, for one of the marks of a civilized man has been his ability to evaluate and withstand the emotionally laden illogic of demagogues, advertisers, and charlatans. This type of critical or reflective thinking involves the ability to identify assumptions, to bring facts to bear upon their evaluation, to compare alternatives and make rational choices on the basis of the comparison. Rationality is one of the hallmarks that distinguishes expertise from something less.

But logic has been valued not only because it assists man in this reflective or passive sense. The advance of civilization has not been achieved merely by resisting deleterious pressures. Man has had problems which he has had to solve actively. He has had to generate hypotheses, choose sources of data, and test his assumptions. He has had to act upon his environment rather than let it act upon him. Productive thinking makes no less heavy demands upon reason than reflective thinking. Thus, the application of logic has involved both the practice of asking "authorities" for their credentials and acquiring credentials of one's own.

These arguments have been directed specifically to the role of the teacher by Smith and Meux (1962), who write:

> The teacher's authority for saying that a student's response is either correct or incorrect has traditionally rested largely upon what the textbook says. This practice has been decried as enslaving the student and the teacher intellectually, as thwarting initiative and creativity, and as emphasizing memorization in learning. If this practice is to be abandoned, it would seem that the teacher must learn to understand and control the logical operations which he and his students perform. The responses given by the student are correct because of what the book says or they are correct on logical grounds. Of course, they may be correct on both counts. But the teacher who is able to move about logically in a network of ideas and to monitor the performance of logical operations would appear to be free, in large measure, from enslavement to the text. To monitor such performance the teacher must have recourse to the rules by which logical operations may be evaluated. (p. 60)

Smith and Meux also provide a concise historical overview of the status of logic in the development of psychological approaches to the study of teaching. They point out that when psychology was in a prescientific stage of development during the nineteenth century, logic had a central place in thinking about teaching. Since the laws of logic were accepted as the laws of thought, psychology and logic were presumed to cover much of the same ground.

This presumption was eroded as psychology began to develop a data base. For one thing, it became clear that verbal behavior was seldom similar to formal logical structures. That people communicated messages to one another was evident, but the content of those messages seemed as much carried by emotions, gestures, or tone of voice as by the logic of the argument, narrowly conceived. For another, psychoanalysts focused our attention on the unconscious and other nonlogical sources for explaining behavior. But perhaps the most severe blow to logic was dealt by the behavioristic theories of Thorndike, who reduced thinking to a series of stimulus-response connections in which covert mental processes seemed to play no significant part. Why study logic at all if behaviors of the pupil can be controlled by proper presentation of stimuli?

However, interest in logic is being rekindled as educators discover the limitations of these viewpoints. Smith and Meux suggest that contemporary interest in logic reflects at least two different postures. The first stems from the reconstruction of logic by John Dewey, who argued that the rules of *successful* inquiry are, in fact, the rules of logic. Following Dewey's lead, educational psychologists have begun to turn their attention to problem solving, but with stress on the psychological rather than the logical elements of Dewey's theory. Smith and Meux see the current emphasis upon inquiry and discovery methods in education as manifestations of this trend and point out: "In this version of inquiry and teaching, there is no distinction between valid and invalid thinking, for such distinction cannot be made within this kind of psychological analysis of problem-solving" (p. 7).

The second posture begins with the assumption that logical elements do indeed appear in both thought and communication, only we have had too narrow a view of the types of logical processes that might be involved. A major proponent of this viewpoint would be Piaget, who has studied the development of logic in the behavior of children. Smith and Meux view this latter posture as an emphasis of the future and conclude:

> We thus see that there is a tendency in current psychology to investigate and describe the operations which logicians are concerned to evaluate in terms of the rules of logic. . . . It could be said that when we are looking at the performance of the [instructional] operation we are studying teaching behavior from a psychological standpoint. [But] when we are examining the operation from the standpoint of its structure and the rules by which it is evaluated, we are looking at teaching behavior logically. (p. 8)

We would judge the studies reviewed in this section of the chapter to exhibit this latter posture.

Concepts

The Illinois Instrument　Concepts for analyzing instructional logic have been developed in two major programs of research, one at the University of Illinois, the other at Teachers College, Columbia University. The Illinois group was led by the educational philosopher B. Othanel Smith and has produced two separate studies that are sometimes confused with one another. Our concern in this chapter is with the first of these, *A Study of the Logic of Teaching* (Smith and Meux, 1962). In Chapter X we shall consider the second study of the Illinois group, *A Study of the Strategies of Teaching* (Smith *et al.*, 1967).

In attempting to think about the logical characteristics of instruction Smith and Meux differentiated between two broad classes of classroom events: *monologues* and *episodes*. In general, monologues occur whenever a single speaker holds forth for an extended period of time, while episodes are characterized by exchange or interaction between two or more speakers. In the authors' words: "The episode is a multi-speaker unit; it consists in the one or more exchanges which comprise a completed verbal transaction between two or more speakers. The monolog, a single-speaker unit, is the solo performance of an individual addressing the classroom group" (p. 13). Although both monologues and episodes can be analyzed for their logical characteristics, Smith and Meux chose to concentrate on the latter unit, or on the logic of classroom *inter*action.

In general, an episode consists of a series of utterances by teacher and pupils that have a common topic and logical structure. This sounds like a rather vague notion, but Smith and Meux found it easy to identify episodes of interaction. To illustrate this concept three example episodes are provided in Figure 9.1.

FIGURE 9.1   Three example episodes. Note that entries are in italics. (Adapted from Smith and Meux, 1962, pp. 15 ff. and 179)

Episode 1

T: *Now who do you know who was the first person who discovered the Hawaiian Islands? Steve?*
Steve: Was it Captain Cook?
T: That's right.

Episode 2

T: *Well, is democracy necessarily opposed to imperialism?*
Sam: No, they're not opposed to imperialism necessarily, but it's the way that Russia goes about getting her countries that a democracy does not like. Because she takes all . . .
T: All right. It's all right, then to have—it's democratic to have subject peoples, but it's just the way you get them to be subject? It that what you're saying?
Sam: No, like the United States has countries under her, but she has them— she gives them freedoms and things, but Russia—she doesn't have their— they don't have any voice in the government or anything, and the United States' colonies do.
T: In other words, it's all right to have people under you if you are kind to them? It's all right to treat people as second class beings if you are kind to them—just like you are kind to your little dog, or something?
Sam: No.
T: Feed him regular, pet him a little bit?
Sam: You're twisting around what I said, though, I said . . . You've got me all confused.

Episode 3

T: All right, now, as Carol pointed out, Alan Paton is pleading for the alternative solution—that of brotherly love or peaceful co-existence between the races. *Now, what do you think of a novelist who tries to preach a lesson or to promote his point of view through the medium of fiction?* You think of that. Mary?
Mary: I was just going to say that I think it's the type of the novel. I mean it's the way that it is presented that moves us. He could present it in different ways if he wanted to. Not necessarily the—the novel or—oh, something that teaches you a moral lesson.
T: All right, just as we discussed, it's a short story. Some stories do have a moral lesson to preach and then they become parables rather than just generalized short stories. And others simply are entertaining. Denny?

Denny: Well, I think that more people would be interested in the fiction form of the novel than in just a pamphlet giving specific reasons why the two races should live together in brotherhood. I think it would attract more attention and be more interesting.

Judy: Well, since it's—when people read it, it's more parallel to everyday life. You might be able to understand it a lot better in a novel and so on. Otherwise, you just see these facts and you wouldn't associate yourself and how you would feel and react to it.

T: All right.

As can be seen, the episode has a sequential character, and Smith and Meux developed a number of concepts to express aspects of that sequence. Typically, an episode was found to begin with a teacher question as an initiating or opening move, called the *entry*. It would then be continued by one or more pupil responses, culminating in a reaction by the teacher to close the episode. In general, episodes were found to occur in three forms: *simple episodes* in which a single pupil spoke but once, *reciprocating episodes* in which a given pupil was found to respond on a given subject several times, and *coordinate episodes* in which a number of pupils responded in succession to the initial teacher question. (The three episodes given in Figure 9.1 exemplify simple, reciprocating, and coordinate forms, respectively.)

Smith and Meux considered a number of ways of analyzing the logic of episodes. Initially they attempted to classify episodes into traditional categories of logic. This was abandoned because of "the great variety and complexity of symbolic operations demanded by teachers" (p. 30). In addition, it was discovered that whereas teachers would sometimes "call for" a given type of logical response on the part of pupils, pupils would respond with quite different types of information.

Eventually the authors decided to classify episodes in terms of the *ideal response* demanded by its *entry*. The ideal response need not be the one actually given by a pupil, nor in fact need it be the one expected by the teacher. Rather, it is the response which would appear to be the most appropriate logical form to complete the sense of the entry. Altogether twelve logical types of entries were finally identified, together with a thirteenth category for entries that were not to be coded for logic. Definitions and examples of these thirteen categories are given in Figure 9.2. These thirteen categories were presumed by Smith and Meux to form a facet for the coding of episodes. Thus, *all* classroom episodes were presumed to be classifiable by reference to their entries in terms of one of these categories. Moreover, most results reported by Smith and Meux concern occurrences of episodes that were thus coded.

These categories, however, formed only part of the conceptual effort of the Illinois team. As Figure 9.2 indicates, some of the basic logical categories were in turn subdivided. In addition, the Illinois team was concerned with subsequent characteristics of the episode; that is, with those moves that

FIGURE 9.2   Entry categories of the Illinois logic instrument. (Adapted from Smith and Meux, 1962, pp. 36 ff and Appendix 3, and from Nuthall and Lawrence, 1965, p. 6)

DEFINING: The meaning of words or terms is asked for, implicitly or explicitly; e.g., "What is the definition of 'felony'?" "What is a cablegram?" "What does this mean?"

DESCRIBING: An account of something which has been mentioned or suggested is required; e.g., "Can you tell us something about the schools of New Zealand?" "Where is Singapore?" "What do you notice about the fish in the aquarium?"

DESIGNATING: Something has to be identified by name—a word or a symbol; e.g., "Give an example of a substance which dissolves in water." "Can you recall the name of the hero?" "Which word is to be modified?"

STATING: Names, descriptions, etc., are not asked for, but statements of issues, steps in a proof, rules, conclusions, or a state of affairs. For example, the question, "What is the conclusion?" asks for a statement of some sort; it can seldom be answered satisfactorily merely by naming. "What is the next thing to do in solving the problem?" "What is the formula for the area of a square?" "What answer did you get?"

REPORTING: A request is made for a report to be given on information contained in some source such as a textbook, or for a review or summary of this information; e.g., "Did your book say anything about the Indians?"

SUBSTITUTING: The student is asked to perform a symbolic operation, usually of a mathematical nature; e.g., "Multiply it." "Simplify this equation."

EVALUATING: An evaluation of an object, person, expression, event, action, or state of affairs is required; e.g., "Was the strike a sensible thing?" "Do you think that silicon is very valuable in industry?" "Is it a good book?"

OPINING: The student is required to express his belief or opinion about what is possible, what might have been the case, what could be in the future, etc. He makes an inference from evidence rather than a report of a single fact; e.g., "Do you think Napoleon would favour present French foreign policies?" "Does a fish have to live in water?" "What will the next generation think about our methods of transport?"

CLASSIFYING: Explicit reference is made to an instance or class (type, sort, group, set, kind) of things or both. A given instance is to be put in the class to which it belongs, or a given class is to be placed in a larger class; e.g., "What special type of triangle is this?" "What group of animals does the jellyfish belong to?"

COMPARING AND CONTRASTING: This type of initiating statement is usually marked by the presence of such words as "difference between," "differ from," "be different," "compare," "like," "correspond"; e.g., "What do they (words on the board) have in common?" "Is the state the same as the government?" "Would a quail be something like a partridge?"

CONDITIONAL INFERRING: A prior condition is given and a consequence is asked for, or both the prior condition and the consequence are given and the student is asked to affirm or deny the prior condition; e.g., "If they (two lines) are parallel, then what is the altitude of the two triangles?" "If you have a car and do fifty miles an hour for three hours, how far do you go?" "Is he a good judge if he sentences the man to hanging?" (within the context of the story).

EXPLAINING: Initiating statements in this category give a consequence of some kind and require that the appropriate prior condition be given, or they require that some general rule or set of conditions be given which explains why a certain prior condition is followed by a certain consequence. There are six subcategories:

MECHANICAL EXPLAINING: An event or action is to be accounted for by describing the way the parts of a structure fit together; e.g., "How do fish make a sound?"

CAUSAL EXPLAINING: An event, situation, or state is to be accounted for by citing another event (situation, or state) as its cause; e.g., "What makes a person's muscles sort of twitch-like?"

SEQUENT EXPLAINING: A sequence of events is to be cited of which a given event is the sequel; e.g., "How did McKinley happen to be killed?"

PROCEDURAL EXPLAINING: Steps or operations by which a given result or end is attained are to be described; e.g., "How did you get 72 for an answer?"

TELEOLOGICAL EXPLAINING: Actions, decisions, states of affairs, or values are to be justified by reference to purposes, functions, or goals; e.g., "Why are you doing those problems?"

NORMATIVE EXPLAINING: Actions, decisions, or choices are to be justified by citing a definition, a characteristic, or rule; e.g., "Why do we call them the Chordata animal group?" "Why do we use shorter pencils?"

DIRECTING AND MANAGING CLASSROOM: Many entries have little or no logical significance. They are designed not to evoke thought but to keep the classroom activities moving along.

came after the entry. In order to analyze the latter the team drew up models for what each of the types of episodes would look like *in its ideal state*. This model was then expressed as a set of rules that would govern the verbal activities of teacher and pupils once the episode was underway, if participants behaved logically. Of course, participants do not always behave in such a manner, so the Illinois group was also concerned with the development of concepts for expressing the ways in which pupils and teachers deviated from the idealistic form of the episode as suggested by its entry. Most of these latter concepts were stated only tentatively in the original (1962) report, however, and developments along this line appear to have been superseded by the second Illinois study, to be reviewed in Chapter X.

Three additional studies have appeared in which the Illinois concepts were applied and extended. In the first of these Nuthall and Lawrence (1965) attempted not only to apply the Illinois concepts to classroom interaction in another country (New Zealand) but also to extend the analysis to consider other aspects of the episode. This was done in several ways. For one, Nuthall and Lawrence observed that in typical reciprocating and coordinate episodes the teacher asked not only an *initiatory question* (or entry) but also a series of *continuant questions* that had some properties in common with the entry. This led them to suggest that the entire episode could be viewed as a series of moves by the teacher and pupils, and that classificatory codes might be provided that would enable the formal analysis of move sequences. (For these concepts see Chapters VII and X.)

Of more immediate interest to us here, Nuthall and Lawrence were able to extend the system of logical analysis proposed by the Illinois group in two ways. First, the categories originally developed for classification of entries were shown to apply also to continuant questions asked by the teacher. Second, Nuthall and Lawrence were able to study the adequacy of pupil's responses to teacher questions using a modification of the Illinois category system. This latter was done for explanatory episodes only. As was suggested in Figure 9.2, explanatory episodes can be subcategorized into *mechanical, causal, sequent, procedural, teleological,* and *normative* forms. Each of these types of entry calls for different types of information as a response. For example, a normative question would appear to call for the citing of a rule, a causal question would require a statement of a cause-effect relationship, a teleological question would call for a discussion of purpose or aim, and so on. Proceeding in this fashion, Nuthall and Lawrence were able to devise categories for *pupil responses* that paralleled the ones originally proposed by the Illinois group for teacher entries, and thus to study the logical relationship between question and response.

Two other applications appear in the work of Tisher (1970) and Wright and Nuthall (1970). The former study constitutes not only an application of the Illinois logic categories in yet another society (Queensland, Australia), but Tisher also attempted to relate use of various logical categories to pupil achievement. In order to do this Tisher suggested that the categories be grouped into two sets—those that made high-level cognitive demands on pupils and those that did not. Categories making high-level demands included evaluating, opining, substituting, classifying, comparing and contrasting, conditional inferring, and explaining. Wright and Nuthall (1970) made a similar distinction, but where Tisher used the terms "higher" and "lower level," they used the terms "open" and "closed" to refer to teachers' questions. Although this classification appears somewhat arbitrary, the underlying concept Tisher and Wright and Nuthall were working for seems to be similar to that of "cognitive level" we reviewed in Chapter VIII. In other words, when the teacher initiates an episode that requires pupils to participate in evaluating, for example, he is asking for a higher level of cognitive participation than when he merely requires defining or describing. Given these concepts, we would expect Tisher's and Wright and Nuthall's findings to be similar to those reported for cognitive level in Chapter VIII. (We return to evidence for this expectation shortly.)

The Columbia Instrument   The second major program to develop concepts for the logical analysis of instruction was the work of Arno Bellack and his associates at Teachers College, Columbia University. As noted in

Chapter VII, the major report of this project, *The Language of the Classroom* (Bellack *et al.*, 1966), reveals a complex project having many types of concepts and findings for educators. In Chapter VII we considered Bellack's description of the "game" of classroom interaction. Here we take up contributions of this research of the study of logic. Still other concepts from this project pertain to the sequential nature of classroom events and are reviewed in Chapter X.

We begin by recapitulating some distinctions that were made in Chapter VII. According to Bellack and his colleagues, the instructional process can be analyzed as a series of *moves* made by the teacher and pupils. Each move consists of one or more sentences uttered by a given speaker that have a common content and purpose, and each may be classified as being either a structuring, a soliciting, a responding, or a reacting move. *Structuring* moves set the stage, *soliciting* moves are designed to elicit a verbal response, *responding* moves occur only as a function of solicitations and are stimulated by them, while *reacting* moves comment mainly upon the response.

Certain differences are apparent between the Illinois and Columbia approaches to the analysis of logic. For one, whereas the Illinois categories were designed for the coding of initiatory acts, usually solicitations, the Columbia categories are coded for moves of any type. Thus, coders were given the task of judging not only solicitations for their logical character but also structuring, responding, and reacting moves as well. This latter strategy has the advantage of making it possible to judge whether or not a pupil response matches a teacher solicitation—a phenomenon that is termed *congruence* by the Columbia group. (For example, if the teacher should ask for a definition and the pupil gives one, their two moves would be termed congruent. If a definition were called for and the pupil volunteered an opinion or an explanation, the two moves would be judged incongruent.) On the negative side the logical categories provided by the Columbia group are somewhat more molar than those suggested by the Illinois team.

Another difference concerns the content of subject matter for which the logical operations are judged. Whereas the Illinois group used only one set of logical categories, the Columbia group judged logical usage somewhat differently for *substantive* and *instructional* matters. Using their concepts, substantive matters are those germane to the content of the lesson while instructional matters concern lesson management. Many of these latter were coded as "directing and managing classroom" by the Illinois team and thus were ignored for purposes of logical analysis. Within the Columbia research a basic set of logical categories was advanced for substantive matters, and then this same set was expanded with additional paralogical categories for the analysis of instructional matters. Since results from the latter analysis were less numerous, are not comparable with the Illinois results, and were largely ignored by the Columbia team in their report, we shall ignore them here too.

The nine basic categories used by Bellack *et al.* are given and defined in Figure 9.3. They are broken into three broad processes and a residual category. *Analytic process* moves are those concerned with the use of language. They "are true by virtue of the meaning of the words of which they are composed. They depend for their truth on an agreed-upon set of rules and follow logically from accepted definitions" (p. 22). Two types of analytic moves were recognized: *defining* and *interpreting*, and the former were also subcategorized into three subtypes. Next, *empirical process* moves "give information about the world, based on one's experience of it. The distinguishing mark of empirical statements is that they are verified by tests conducted in terms of one's experience" (p. 24). Again, two types of empirical moves were recognized: *fact-stating* and *explaining*, the latter including both inferring and comparing or contrasting. *Evaluative process* moves "are verified by reference to a set of criteria or principles of judgment" (p. 25). Once again, two types of evaluative moves were recognized: *opining* and *justifying*. The residual or basket category is termed *logical process not clear*, and (as was also true for the Illinois instrument) the nine categories are presumed by Bellack *et al.* to form a facet for the coding of logical events.

FIGURE 9.3 Categories for substantive logic in the Columbia Instrument. (Adapted from Bellack et al., 1966, p. 22 ff)

2.1 *Analytic Process.* Analytic statements are statements about the proposed use of language. They are true by virtue of the meaning of the words of which they are composed.

    2.11 *Defining—General* (DEF). To define in a general manner is to give a specific example of an item within the class. DEF is also coded when the type of definition asked for or given is not clear. Example: T: What is a barrier? P: It's something that hinders trade, like a tariff.

    2.111 *Defining—Denotative* (DED). To define denotatively is to refer to the objects (abstract or concrete) to which the term is applicable. Example: T: What are public utilities? P: Light, power, gas, water.

    2.112 *Defining—Connotative* (DEC). To definite connotatively is to give the set of properties or characteristics that an object (abstract or concrete) must have for the term to be applicable. DEC thus refers to the defining characteristics of a given term. Example: T: Now what do we mean by quotas? P: The government sets a special amount of things that can come into the country in one year, and no more can come in.

    2.12 *Interpreting* (INT). To interpret a statement is to give its verbal equivalent, usually for the purpose of rendering its meaning clear. Example: T: What does President Kennedy mean when he says, "We must trade or fade?"

2.2 *Empirical Process.* Empirical statements give information about the world, based on one's experience of it. The distinguishing mark of empirical statements is that they are verified by tests conducted in terms of one's experience.

2.21   *Fact-Stating* (FAC). Fact stating is giving an account, description, or report of an event or state of affairs. To state a fact is to state what is, what was in the past, or what will be in the future. Example: T: Now in 1934 . . . in 1934 . . . who was President? P: Roosevelt.

2.22   *Explaining* (XPL). To explain is to relate an object, event, action, or state of affairs to some other object, event, action, or state of affairs; or to show the relation between an event or state of affairs and a principle or generalization; or to state the relationships between principles or generalizations. Example: T: Why do industrialized countries trade the most? P: Because they have more . . . more to offer each other.

2.3   *Evaluative Process.* Evaluative statements are statements that grade, praise, blame, commend, or criticize something. Evaluative statements are verified by reference to a set of criteria or principles of judgment.

2.31   *Opining* (OPN). To opine is to make statements in which the speaker gives his own valuation regarding (a) what should or ought to be done, or (b) fairness, worth, importance, or quality of an action, event, person, idea, plan, or policy. Example: P: I think the farmer is being exploited.

2.32   *Justifying* (JUS). To justify is to give *reasons* for holding an opinion regarding (a) what should or ought to be done, or (b) fairness, worth, importance, or quality of an action, event, policy, idea, plan, or thing. Example: P: I feel that the reason why the United States should not and probably will not in a number of years join the Common Market is that because the Latin countries with which we are associated would feel that we are no longer interested in their opinion.

2.4   *Not Clear* (NCL). When the wording or sense of a statement is ambiguous and the substantive-logical meaning cannot be determined, the logical process is coded NCL.

One has the intuitive feeling that there ought to be a simple relationship between the categories of the Illinois and Columbia projects. They use much of the same vocabulary and appear to be addressing roughly the same questions. Moreover, as we shall see shortly, some of the findings from the two research programs are similar. And yet no person from either group has yet attempted to amalgamate the two systems to our knowledge. Figure 9.4 represents our own attempt at an amalgamation—and may reveal only the depths of our own misunderstanding.[1]

In Figure 9.4 the central columns represent the categories of the Illinois and Columbia instruments, somewhat reordered. The outside columns of the figure represent collapsed forms of each instrument—to the left the

[1] Thanks are due to Nuthall, however, who suggested modifications for the first draft of Figure 9.4.

distinction between lower cognitive and higher cognitive demands made by Tisher, to the right the distinction among analytic, empirical, and evaluative processes made by Bellack *et al.* (and subsequently explored by Furst, 1967c). For the most part the categories of the Illinois instrument provide greater detail than those of the Columbia instrument, although the latter provides differentiation within the realm of definition not offered by the former. Moreover, despite verbal similarity, it appears that there is only *one* instance (opining) of a direct correspondence between the categories of the two systems! This leads us to suspect that *both* systems represent but a partial representation of logical distinctions that can be recognized in instructional discourse. We presume that other investigators will shortly pick up the challenge of proposing a set of logical distinctions sufficient to generate both of these systems, perhaps using some of the insights of linguistics, as we shall suggest in the second half of the chapter.

One additional conceptual problem should be discussed before making a concluding observation concerning both systems. Efforts have been made to explore process-product relationships with both systems, thus to study the effects of utilization of logical categories on the achievement of pupils. In the original report of the Columbia project (Bellack *et al.*, 1966) few relationships of this sort were discernable. However, in a reanalysis of the Columbia

FIGURE 9.4   Proposed relationships among categories of the Illinois and Columbia instruments.

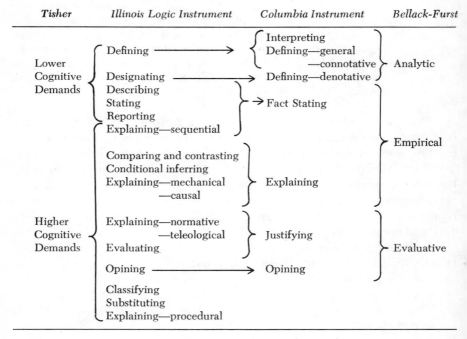

lata Furst (1967c) was able to demonstrate a strong relationship using the concept of *logical variety* (more analytic and evaluative usage in comparison with empirical usage). Since the typical lesson was found to exhibit a preponderance of *empirical process* moves, Furst reasoned that lessons exhibiting *logical variety* would be relatively higher in the proportion of moves that were coded under the *analytic* or *evaluative* aegis. Thus, whereas in the Fisher and Wright and Nuthall studies relationships were sought between the appearance of higher cognitive demands and pupil achievement, in Furst's analysis the predictive concept used was logical variety. Figure 9.4 shows that these two derivative concepts are largely independent of one another.

Apart from the excitement that may be generated by the notion of analyzing classroom logic, the Illinois and Columbia projects share another noteworthy feature. Both have been relatively free of the effects of *Commitment* on the design of their research. This does not mean that the protagonists have not had a desire to improve education or that they are unconvinced of the importance of improving the logical ability of teachers. But, despite this, both research groups have begun their research efforts with an attempt to describe instruction as they find it, to separate description and prescription, and to let exhortation flow from empirical findings rather than from data-free assumptions.

Research on Classroom Behavior

Our review focuses on nine studies representing investigations of logical processes in instruction. Details of these studies are given in Box 9.1, together with their major findings relevant to this chapter. All studies made use of lesson transcripts that were prepared from recordings, and all except Zahorik concentrated on secondary classroom lessons. Reliability figures are reported for all instruments. Not surprisingly, these are somewhat higher for the Columbia instrument, which uses more molar categories than does the Illinois instrument. Taken together, however, these studies suggest that t *is* possible to judge the logic of instruction.

BOX 9.1   Applications for Logic Categories

STUDIES REVIEWED

Bellack *et al.* (1966)	(Bel66)
Furst (1967c)	(Fur67)
Lundgren (1972)	(Lun72)
Nuthall and Lawrence (1965)	(N&L65)
Power (1971)	(Pow71)
Smith and Meux (1962)	(S&M62)
Tisher (1970)	(Tis70)
Wright and Nuthall (1970)	(W&N70)
Zahorik (1968, 1970)	(Zah68)

Box 9.1 (continued)

INSTRUMENT, METHOD OF GATHERING DATA, CODING SYSTEM, UNITS STUDIED, RELIABILITY

Illinois Logic Instrument, transcripts, single-facet category system, T and P moves, moderate reliability (N&L65), (S&M62), (Tis70).

Columbia Instrument, transcripts, multifacet category system, T and P moves, high reliability (Bel66), (Fur67), (Lun72), (Pow71).

Canterbury Instrument, audiotapes and transcripts, multifacet category system, T and P moves, moderate reliability (W&N70).

Zahorik Instrument, audiotapes and transcripts, single-facet category system, teacher feedback (reaction) behavior, high reliability (Zah68).

DESIGN OF STUDY, SUBJECTS, CONTEXTS

Field Surveys

(Bel66)	15 teachers and pupils, grades X and XII; economics; 4 lessons for each teacher; New York
(Fur67)	Same as that of (Bel66)
(Lun72)	9 teachers and pupils, grade IX mathematics; Göteborg (Seweden)
(N&L65)	8 teachers and pupils, junior secondary, several subjects; 18 lessons in all; Christchurch (New Zealand)
(Pow71)	4 teachers and pupils, grade VIII; science; 5 lessons for each teacher; Queensland (Australia)
(S&M62)	14 teachers and pupils, grades IX–XII, several subjects; 5 lessons for each teacher; Illinois
(Tis70)	9 teachers and pupils; grade VIII, science; 6 lessons for each teacher; Queensland (Australia)
(W&N70)	17 teachers and pupils, grade III; three nature-study lessons, standardized content; Christchurch (New Zealand)
(Zah68)	15 teachers and their pupils, grades III and VI; one social studies "discussion" lesson based on the same issue in current events per teacher

FINDINGS

Process Occurrence

9.1-1   More episodes (approximately one fourth) are concerned with *describing* than with any other logical category, followed by *designating, stating, conditional inferring,* and *explaining* (N&L65), (S&M62), (Tis70).

9.1-2   *Continuant questions* are similar in their logical emphases to *initiatory questions* (or entries) (N&L65).

9.1-3   About 80 percent of the teachers' solicitations are concerned with *empirical process,* and slightly more with *explaining* than with *fact-stating* (Bel66).

9.1-4   About a half (50–60 percent) of all moves are devoted to *empirical process,* less than 10 percent to *analytical process,* and less than 10 percent to *evaluative process* (Bel66), (Lun72), (Pow71).

Context-Process Relationships

9.1-5   *Subject matter* affects the use of *logical categories* (N&L65), (S&M62). In particular.

    Geometry exhibits more *stating* and less *evaluating;*
    Science exhibits more *defining* and *describing* and less *directing* and *managing;*

Social studies exhibits more *opining* and less *classifying*;
English exhibits more *stating* and *evaluating* and less *describing*;
Core exhibits more *describing, reporting,* and *directing and managing* and less *defining, comparing and contrasting,* and *explaining* than other subjects.

9.1-6 *Nationality* affects the use of *logical categories* (N&L65), (S&M62), (Tis70), (Pow71). In particular,
Queensland exhibits more *designating* and *stating*;
New Zealand exhibits more *stating, defining,* and *conditional inferring*;
United States exhibits more *reporting, evaluating, opining,* and *comparing and contrasting* (Tis70).
Also, *Queensland* exhibits more *fact-stating*;
while *United States* exhibits more *explaining* (Pow71).

Presage-Process Relationships

9.1-7 *Length of teaching experience* co-varies with teacher's use of *higher cognitive demands* (W&N70).

Process-Process Relationships

9.1-8 More than 85 percent of *teachers' solicitations* and *pupils' responses* are *congruent* with one another (Bel66).

9.1-9 *Congruency* (or its absence) is unrelated to *teachers' immediate reactions to pupils' responses* (Bel66), (Zah68).
In addition, it is also reported that
9.1-9a *Adequacy of pupil response* affects *teacher reaction. Adequate* answers generate more *simple praise and repetition*; poor answers generate *solicitations for additional response* (Zah68).

9.1-10 *Teachers' solicitations requesting sequential* or *procedural explaining* tend to induce *appropriate pupil responses* (N&L65).

9.1-11 *Teachers' solicitations requesting causal, teleological,* or *normative explaining* tend to induce *inappropriate pupil responses* (N&L65), (Tis70).

Process-Product Relationships

9.1-12 *Moderate use of higher cognitive demands* co-varies directly with *growth of understanding* for pupils of *high ability, high prior knowledge,* and *high-achievement orientation.* High- and low-level use of higher cognitive demands is associated with less growth of understanding (Tis70).

9.1-13 *Low-level use of higher cognitive demands* co-varies directly with *growth of understanding* for pupils of low ability (Tis70).

9.1-14 *Teacher's use of lower cognitive demands* co-varies directly with *pupil achievement.* (Teacher's use of higher cognitive demands is unrelated to pupil achievement) (W&N70).

9.1-15 *High-level ratio of analytic and evaluative to empirical categories* co-varies directly with *pupil achievement* (Fur67).

Most of the findings of the Illinois study concern process occurrence and context-process relationships. Of these the strongest findings (also supported by both Nuthall and Lawrence and by Tisher) was that lessons are dominated by *describing*. Regardless of subject matter or national context, approximately one quarter of the episodes of the lesson fall into this category. *Designating* and *explaining* episodes are also popular, although frequencies for these latter vary depending on context. Some rather striking differences also appeared within the Illinois data in the logical categories stressed in different subject areas. Geometry lessons stressed *stating* and deemphasized *evaluating*; science lessons utilized *defining* and *describing* more often and *directing* and *managing* less often; social studies lessons were high on *opining* and low on *classifying*; English lessons exhibited more *stating* and *evaluating* and less *describing*; core lessons stressed *describing*, *reporting*, and *directing and managing* and deemphasized *defining, comparing and contrasting*, and *explaining*. (The numbers and percentages of episodes coded in each of these categories are given in Table 9.1, which is adapted from the Illinois report.)

One of the findings in the Nuthall and Lawrence study was that continuant and initiatory questions were strikingly alike in their logical emphases. (This finding offered little encouragement to the notion that teacher would use more simple logical processes while in the middle of an episode Rather, it seemed that teachers were quite as likely to request classification or an explanation in the middle of an episode as at the beginning.) Another finding concerned the relationship between the logical categorization demanded by the teacher and that actually given in response by pupils. As suggested earlier, this phenomenon was examined for explanatory episodes only, but the results obtained were striking. Whereas approximately 90 percent of all requests for *sequential* or *procedural explaining* were acceded to by pupils, requests for *causal, teleological*, and *normative explanations* did not, in general, generate congruent pupil responses. Several explanations were entertained by the investigators for this result, among them the fact that procedural and sequential questions were more often asked and that pupils (and teachers?) were often confused by the vague language in which causal, teleological, or normative questions were asked. In fact, much of the subsequent response by teachers to "errors" made by pupils consisted of attempts to clarify the nature of the question they had asked in the first place. Whatever the reason, it would appear that questions of the causal, teleological, or normative sort are difficult for pupils to handle at the junior high level.

Three types of results were presented by Tisher that are particularly noteworthy. First, Tisher was able to appose his own results with those of Smith and Meux and Nuthall and Lawrence so as to suggest possible national differences in logical emphases (see Table 9.2). For example, the findings presented by Tisher suggest that science teachers from Queensland exhibit more *designating* and *stating* than science teachers from Illinois, though these might merely be grade-level differences. Note, however, that Tisher's results were also supported by Power (1971), who used concepts from the Columbia research group. (Those unfamiliar with differences in educational emphases among the various English-speaking countries may be referred to a symposium edited by Adams, 1970. In comparison, current Queensland classroom practices would appear to stress fact and rote memorization, while

Table 9.1 Distribution of Logical Categories by Subject Areas in the Illinois Study

	Geometry [5]*	Science [20]	Social Studies [25]	English [15]	Core [5]	Totals for All Subjects
1. Defining	9(2.5)**	57(6.1)	39(4.0)	33(3.7)	1(0.4)	139(4.1)
2. Describing	97(27.2)	294(31.4)	218(22.4)	175(19.4)	77(33.5)	861(25.3)
3. Designating	36(10.1)	159(17.0)	163(16.8)	125(13.8)	21(9.1)	504(14.8)
4. Stating	58(16.3)	29(3.1)	36(3.7)	103(11.4)	4(1.8)	230(6.8)
5. Reporting	6(1.7)	30(3.2)	33(3.4)	12(1.3)	18(7.8)	99(2.9)
6. Substituting	4(1.1)	4(0.4)	2(0.2)	0(0.0)	0(0.0)	10(0.3)
7. Evaluating	2(0.6)	22(2.4)	53(5.4)	70(7.8)	9(3.9)	156(4.6)
8. Opining	6(1.7)	21(2.3)	89(9.1)	51(5.6)	12(5.2)	179(5.3)
9. Classifying	11(3.1)	30(3.2)	11(1.1)	44(4.9)	7(3.1)	103(3.0)
10. Comparing and contrasting	11(3.1)	43(4.6)	27(2.8)	29(3.2)	2(0.9)	112(3.3)
11. Conditional inferring	37(10.4)	82(8.8)	64(6.6)	50(5.5)	15(6.5)	248(7.3)
12. Explaining	40(11.2)	113(12.1)	136(14.0)	134(14.8)	15(6.5)	438(12.9)
13. Directing and managing	39(11.0)	50(5.4)	102(10.5)	78(8.6)	49(21.3)	318(9.4)
Totals	356	934	973	904	230	3397

* Numbers in brackets refer to numbers of lessons analyzed in each area.
** Numbers in parentheses provide percentages of total entries.
Adapted from Smith and Meux, 1962, p. 54.

American classrooms would stress the use of discovery methods and class
room democracy.) Second, Tisher found that one third of pupils' response:
to questions demanding explanation were logically inappropriate and tha
a fifth of the responses accepted by teachers were logically incongruen
with the process of explaining demanded by their questions. Third, Tishe:
examined the relation between use of higher cognitive demands by teacher
and pupil achievement. He found that lower use of such demands wa:
associated with higher achievement for pupils of low ability, while moderat
use of higher cognitive demands was associated with gains for high-abilit
pupils.

Two findings were also available in Wright and Nuthall's (1970) stud
concerning the variable referred to by Tisher as "cognitive demand." Earlie:
we noted that Wright and Nuthall used the terms "open" and "closed" ques
tions to refer to this variable. They report, first, that use of "open" question:
(that is, higher cognitive demand) is greater among teachers who have mor
experience and, second, that use of "closed" questions (lower cognitive de
mand) is associated with greater pupil achievement.

Table 9.2   Distribution of Logical Operations in Initiating
Statements for Three Studies (Percentages)

| | Smith and Meux | | Nuthall and Lawrence Transcripts (New Zealand) | Tisher Science Transcripts (Queensland |
Operation	All Transcripts (Illinois)	Science Transcripts (Illinois)		
1. Describing	25.3	31.4	20	27.2
2. Designating	14.8	17.0	11	26.2
3. Stating	6.8	3.2	15	11.6
4. Reporting	2.9	3.2	2	0.0
5. Defining	4.1	6.1	8	2.4
6. Substituting	0.3	0.4	2	0.3
7. Evaluating	4.6	2.4	2	0.5
8. Opining	5.3	2.2	2	1.0
9. Classifying	3.0	3.2	3	1.0
10. Comparing and contrasting	3.3	4.6	4	2.8
11. Conditional inferring	7.3	8.8	13	7.9
12. Explaining	12.9	12.1	11	12.2
13. Classroom management	9.4	5.4	4	6.9
14. Unclassified	—	—	3	—
	100	100	100	100
Total number of statements	3,397	935	395	2,422

Adapted from Tisher, 1970, p. 384.

These process-product findings by Tisher and by Wright and Nuthall are surprisingly similar to those of Ragosta *et al.* (see Box 8.1) and Thompson and Bowers (see Box 8.2) reported in Chapter VIII. Once again, it would appear that higher-level questioning is less productive of pupil achievement than is often supposed. However, it may not be the higher-level quality, as such, that is the problem. As we saw above, one fault noticed by Nuthall and Lawrence (1965) and Tisher with high-level, explaining-type questions is that they were often vaguely expressed. Could it be, then, that when teachers ask higher-level questions vagueness often enters and interferes with the communication to pupils? Wright and Nuthall provided some support for this possibility when they found a high positive correlation (r = +.75) between frequency of closed (lower-level) questions and teachers' avoiding the repetition of questions. The explanation for this finding might be that lower-level questions can be phrased with less vagueness and, therefore, with less need for repetition. There is, however, more direct evidence concerning vagueness, as we shall see in our discussion of linguistic analyses below.

Several types of findings appeared in the Columbia report. Although coders were asked to judge *each* instructional move for its logical character, most of the logical results reported by Bellack *et al.* concern the logic of teacher *solicitations,* and thus are comparable with results reported in the Illinois research for teacher entries or questions. As previously suggested, about 80 percent of all solicitations were found to be concerned with empirical processes, and slightly more of these with *explaining* than with *fact-stating.* Relevant data for these findings appear in Table 9.3. (Recall that the Columbia data were collected for economics lessons. If we compare the results of Table 9.3 with those of the social studies lessons reported in Table 9.1, frequencies appear to be reasonably similar.)

Another finding concerns *congruence* between the logical categories of teachers' solicitations and pupils' responses. The Columbia group found these two elements logically congruent more than 85 percent of the time. Although this finding appears to run counter to those of Nuthall and Lawrence and of Tisher (in which, it will be recalled, substantial mismatch was discovered between the logical classifications of teachers' questions and pupils' responses in explaining) it should be understood that the Columbia finding is based upon more molar categories of logic, applies to all logic categories, not just explaining, and that the sample consisted of tenth and twelfth graders who might be expected to cope more effectively with more difficult logical processes.

Related to this second finding is a third, also concerned with congruence. As we know from Chapter VII, Bellack *et al.* found that the majority of all teacher reactions were positive in tone. One might presume that teachers would be somewhat *less* positive in reacting to *in*congruent pupil responses. Interestingly, this was not the case, for teacher reactions to such occurrences were also often positive. We suspect that this finding simply reflects a Rule

Table 9.3   Distribution of Substantive Soliciting Moves for the
Columbia Study by Speaker

| | SUBSTANTIVE TASK | | | | | |
| | Total | | Teacher | | Pupil | |
Logical Process	Percent	Moves	Percent	Moves	Percent	Moves
Total	100.0	3335	100.0	2889	100.0	446
Analytic	14.4	483	15.7	454	6.5	29
DEF	13.1	438	14.2	411	6.1	27
INT	1.3	45	1.5	43	.4	2
Empirical	80.2	2674	79.5	2298	84.3	376
FAC	37.0	1235	36.1	1044	42.8	191
XPL	43.2	1439	43.4	1254	41.5	185
Evaluative	5.2	172	4.7	135	8.3	37
OPN	3.7	123	3.5	100	5.2	23
JUS	1.5	49	1.2	35	3.1	14
NCL	0.2	6	0.1	2	0.9	4

Adapted from Bellack et al., 1966, p. 112.

of The Classroom Game ("teachers should react positively to pupil response regardless of their substance"). On the other hand, the fact that reactions were positive does not mean they were undifferentiated. Zahorik found that adequacy of pupil response *did* affect teacher reaction. In general, adequate answers provoked simple *praise* and *repetition*. Poor answers generated *solicitations* for additional response. (To obtain this finding Zahorik sought supplementary ratings of each pupil response from those teachers whose lessons had been recorded.)

Finally, we consider one more finding from the Columbia data. Although Bellack et al. were able to find only weak relationships between choice of logical categories by teachers and pupil achievement, Furst (1967c was able to show that teachers who showed greater *logical variety*—that is more *analytic* and *evaluative* usage in comparison with the concentration on *empirical* usage—were associated with greater pupil achievement.

Although suggestive, these findings leave a lot of territory uncovered For one thing, it is not really clear how the two logical systems fit together or what underlying logical notions are going to prove of value in understanding instruction. For another, presage-process relationships have yet to be investigated, thus we cannot be certain that teachers can be trained to be "more logical" in their instruction. Nor is it clear what the effects would be on pupil behavior or learning if teachers were to "improve" their instructional logic.

Several other interesting questions are raised by these findings. For one both the Nuthall and Lawrence and Tisher findings suggest that pupils frequently have difficulty in responding to teachers' demands for explanations This might be because of pupil inadequacies or because teachers sometimes ask ambiguous questions. Findings by Nuthall and Lawrence, Tisher, and Bellack *et al.* suggest that teachers' reactions to incongruent pupil responses might often be inappropriate. Whether this is because teachers are not primarily concerned with logic or are unable to identify incongruencies or are stifled by inappropriate psychological theories or classroom rules is not clear. What seems to be needed to clarify these issues is research on the immediate objectives to which teachers direct their attention and the assumptions about learning to which they subscribe. As Nuthall (1970) has written:

> As far as this writer is aware, no one has attempted to make explicit the concepts of learning which the skilled teacher uses as he manipulates the discussions that enliven the work in his classroom. How is he interpreting the responses from his pupils? What are the signs he makes use of in determining the course of his actions? It is in the answers to these questions that the explanation of cause and effect in classroom discussion must lie. (p. 28)

To provide answers to questions of this sort will require that we analyze the *sequence* of classroom events rather than simply the presence or absence of certain classes of logic (see Chapter X). Nevertheless, the idea that instruction can be studied for its logical properties—indeed, that teaching *is* logical and that categories can be stated in which various forms of logic can be discriminated—is important. If teachers could be better taught, and pupils in turn to respect, the use of logic and reason, one of the age-old goals of education would surely be within reach.

STUDIES USING LINGUISTIC CONCEPTS

Above all the classroom is a linguistic context. As readers know, teachers and pupils emit words at a fast and furious pace. Much, if not most, of the information transmitted in the classroom is verbal in mode, and teachers often feel uncomfortable whenever the flow of classroom discourse is interrupted, if only for a few seconds. Moreover, words constitute not only the form of classroom activity but also a good portion of its focus or content. Teachers are often concerned with the way in which pupils use language, with their grammar, pronunciation, vocabulary, and definitions, and with pupils' ability to transform verbal utterances into written symbols, and vice versa. So important is language in the classroom that courses, curricula, national debates, and even laws are written to enforce specific methods of teaching language to pupils, for training in use of the common tongue is one of the foremost tasks of any educational system.

When judgments are made that teachers are "responding," are "indirect," or are "being logical," surely most of the cues by which we make such judgments are to be found in the linguistic behaviors of the teachers observed. But what are those cues? Unfortunately, most systems for analyzing classroom behavior do not answer this question. On the one hand we can listen to, or make recordings for later study of, the verbal events of a classroom. On the other we are asked to discriminate when a teacher is "responding," rather than "reacting," or whether her presentation is "logical," "forceful," or "humorous" without being given clear rules that enable us to make these judgments from the verbal events to which they pertain.

The fact is that most of those who study classroom interaction have yet to take seriously the idea that there might be an *absolute* relationship between classroom discourse and the judgments these investigators wish to make concerning teaching. One reason for this attitude is the traditional isolation of linguistic research from the mainstream of investigations in education and the other social sciences. For years linguists concerned themselves primarily with phonemic analysis, the study of accents, and the historical development of language groups. Most of this research was ethnographic in orientation and of little use to educators. More recently linguistics has been influenced by the transformational grammarians. Beginning with the contributions of Chomsky (1965) and his students, concern turned from a preoccupation with phonology to syntax, from pronunciation *per se* to the rules of grammar and the study of verbal forms and sequences. This was surely a step forward, for the transformationalists viewed language as a rule-governed form of behavior and saw their task as the establishment of those rules governing the language they chose to study (or possibly, *all* languages).

More recently linguists have begun the serious study of semantics, or the relationship between language forms, users, and meaning (see Hymes, 1964; and Greenberg, 1957), and in so doing have begun to generate concepts of use in education and the analysis of classroom discourse. Let us consider some of these.

Concepts

In general, any Western language offers us a sequence of unit utterances, called *words*, that are strung together into longer units, called *sentences*. In turn, sentences are also strung together to form *discourses*, which may either be solo performances or involve interaction among two or more speakers. If the latter, the uninterrupted section of discourse spoken by a single speaker may be termed an *utterance*.

Words consist of a set of verbal sounds called phonemes that appear in short, invariant sequences. Although a given word may appear at the beginning, middle, or end of any given sentence, the phonemes of which it is made up always occur in the same order. (In literate cultures we learn also to recognize words by association between the phonemes and a conventionalized spelling, and words can then be recognized in either their spoken or written forms.) In its simplest form the sentence is *propositional* in format. That is, it provides information about some relationship among the words that are included within it. And in simple form the words of the sentence may be divided into those that tell what is done (*verbs*) and those that tell to whom or what it happens (*nouns*). For example, in the sentence "John hits Mary," the verb "hits" asserts a relationship between the two nouns "John" and "Mary." In like manner discourses feature sequences of sentences whose propositions form *arguments*. However, a discourse often features more than one argument.

To analyze such a sentence is relatively simple, although not quite as simple as one might believe at the outset. First, the sentence contains *lexical* features, or a choice of vocabulary. (To have said "Peter hits Mary" would have changed the meaning of the sentence.) Second, the sentence is constructed according to *syntactic* conventions (Chomsky, 1965), or rules concerning the order of enunciation of words. (To have said "Mary hits Peter" would again have changed the meaning, while "Peter Mary hits" is not a sentence at all.) Moreover, had all sentences a simple format such as this, the analysis of arguments would be a simple matter of noting the propositions uttered and sorting out the logic of their coverage, if any.

However, sentences are rarely so simple. For one thing, many propositions in our speech have been reduced to fragments of speech, so that it is possible to convey a number of "ideas" or propositions in a given sentence. Consider the problem of modification. To say that "Mean John hits Mary" is to add the notion that "John is mean" to our original sentence, thus a second proposition. In general, such sentences are said to have *embedded* information in them (Chomsky, 1965; Koutsoudas, 1966), and various kinds of embedding can be recognized, such as adjectives, adverbs, prepositional phrases, and the like. Another way to make sentences complex is to *conjoin* them together ("John hits Mary, and Mary cries"). Still another is to *adjoin* them so as to indicate a logical relationship between the constituent propositions ("John hits Mary, and as a result Mary cries").

Another form of complexity concerns the fact that words may be declined, and thus fall into a *case classification* (see Fillmore, 1968). There is a significant difference in the meaning of the sentences "Peter hits Mary," "Peter hit Mary," and "Peter will hit Mary." Nouns may also be declined, as, for example, when we distinguish between "Peter" and "Peter's." As in the case of embedding, the forms of declension also form a shorthand way of enunciating complex information. Interestingly, much of this information can be conveyed either by the *order* of word utterance or by *declension*. Thus, languages that are rich in declension forms (such as German) tend to have less rigid rules for order than languages wherein declension is less relied upon (as in English). For example, a "house cat" is clearly something different from a "cat house" (!), and it is the order of presentation that tells us which of the two words is the noun and which the adjective. On the other hand, the phrases "running man" and "man running" mean the same thing, because one of the words is declined in such a way that it can be nothing but a modifier.

Still another source of complexity stems from the referential character of language. As is well known, words and sentences are symbols that reference classes of objects or events. Among the latter are included the speaker and other persons, physical objects, behaviors, events that are presumed to happen elsewhere, unobservable states such as someone's "thoughts" or "feelings," historical or possible events, and transcendentals such as ghosts or God. Also included are references to other parts of language, and here also we encounter rules for reference and shorthand forms of expression. Consider pronouns. The speaker might say, "John hit Mary, and then he kicked her." In such a sentence the words "he" and "her" are pronominal substitutes for "John" and "Mary." In like manner it is possible to find other proforms that are being substituted for nouns, verbs, propositions, or indeed for arguments in discourse. Words such as "that" or "it" are often used for proform substitution, and when they appear it is necessary for the listener to figure out those sections of the discourse to which they refer in order to appreciate the speaker's meaning. Interestingly, this task seems to be performed with ease by most listeners, or perhaps most of us have learned to live with a certain amount of referential unclarity in spoken discourse.

Nor does this exhaust the problem of referential complexity. The fact is that some parts of the argument may be left out altogether, either because they can be filled in by the listener from past information exchanged or because they are supplied by gesture or context. Consider the sentence "John and Bill flew the kite." In this statement "John flew the kite," *and* "Bill flew the kite (too)." Two kite flyings have actually occurred, although only one is mentioned in the sentence spoken. The other is filled in by the listener. Or examine the common sequence of events occurring in classroom discourse. The teacher asks a question of one pupil; that pupil does not answer, whereupon the teacher nominates another pupil to speak without repeating the question. Apparently all concerned "understand" that the question has been reasked of the second pupil. Or consider the teacher who spots a pupil who is tormenting another pupil at the back of the classroom. The teacher glares at the offender and says in a stern voice, "Stop!" Her sentence is actually reduced to a mere verbal fragment, although context and gesture make it quite clear who is to do the stopping and what it is that is to be stopped.

So far so good. Although the task is a complex one, in theory it should be possible to disentangle the argument being presented in a sample of discourse. All we need to do is to make explicit the propositions that appear in the sentences of speakers and the structure of their ideational exchange should become clear. But even this may be insufficient for language analysis. Sometimes, perhaps more often than we are willing to admit, language is not really used for propositional enunciation at all. For example, language may be used for emotional expression—for stating delight, love, or a cry for help, or for generating excitement, hatred, or patriotism in the listener. The language of the lover, politician, or preacher may make no sense in logical terms. But if we listen to it analytically we become aware of the innuendos of lexical choice, syntactical rules honored and violated, or tone of voice by which the speaker conveys his "real" message. Again, since words are expressed phonemically, sometimes language is intended to be enjoyed for its rhythm or rhyme rather than for its message. This is particularly true in poetry, of course, but some public speakers—and teachers—design their presentations with sonority in mind. Or language may be used to generate humor. Thus, by appropriate lexical choice or slight distortion of form the punster can suggest a second meaning in his apparently innocent sentence. These latter characteristics of language can also be referenced by speakers, and such references are actually characteristic of certain teachers. Thus, teacher A will interrupt the science lesson to criticize pupil's pronunciation, while teacher B will respond to the pupil's emotional tone rather than to the content of the pupil's response.

Lexical choice So much for the broad outline of linguistic concepts. Now how can such a complex field contribute to our understanding of the teaching process? Perhaps the simplest way is to make use of the information provided by those words chosen by classroom speakers. Should we know, for example, that a classroom discourse contains many examples of words such as "points," "lines," "angles," and the like, we are probably in a geometry lesson, while English lessons are more likely to involve references to language features, history lessons to exhibit dates of battles, chemistry lessons to display the names of elements and compounds. Some aspects of style are also likely to be represented with lexical information. An emphatic teaching style is likely to feature absolutes or superlatives, a mushy style to exhibit words indicating lack of assurance, and so forth. As a general proposition, then, it is likely that certain aspects of teaching will be associated with lexical choice and that teachers who are effective will prove somewhat different from teachers who are ineffective in the words with which they express themselves.

Formal analysis of lexical choice has been around for some time. Early examples of it may be found in the works of Freud (1910) or Thomas and Znaniecki (1927). During World War II somebody discovered that German propagandists were likely to increase their proportion of references to a neighboring country shortly before launching a military attack on that country, and as a result the Allies set up complex programs for the "content analysis" of enemy propaganda. More recently the task of lexical analysis has been computerized. If one enters a discourse text into the computer as a sequence of alphabetic symbols, the computer is quite capable of searching that text for the frequency of occurrence of any words the investigator nominates for search (see Stone *et al.*, 1966).

There are several difficulties inherent in lexical analysis. For one, the meaning of many words varies depending on the context in which they are uttered. (This problem alone has proven of such magnitude as to ruin most attempts to use computers for making translations from one language to another.) For another, after the first reference to a concept the word designating that concept may be replaced by proforms that reference it. In such cases to count merely the cases where the word itself appears is to underestimate seriously the density of focus on the concept in which we are interested. But primarily lexical analysis depends on the establishment of categories into which words can be sorted for purposes of analysis, and these categories will vary somewhat depending on context. For detecting an impending German attack upon the Low countries we may want to lump together "Holland," "Belgium," "Flemish," "Walloon," "Benelux," and so forth. In other contexts we may want to keep these words separated. Several general strategies for sorting items in lexical analysis have been suggested (see Weinreigh, 1966; or Bendix, 1966), but most of the solutions available to date have consisted of dictionaries that are arbitrary and context generated.

Perhaps the best application of lexical concepts to classroom events to date is that of Hiller, Fisher, and Kaess (1969; see also Hiller, 1971). This work formed part of a larger project at Stanford University headed by N. L. Gage in which the verbal processes of *explaining* were examined. In attempting to find behavioral correlates of skill in explaining, Hiller *et al.* first set forth 35 categories of classes in which linguistic phenomena, drawn from classroom discourse, could be sorted. These were eventually sorted into five broader classes:

1. *Verbal fluency*—indicated by average sentence length, proportion of commas, and proportion of "uhs," "ahs," etc.;
2. *Optimal information amount*—indicated by number of words, cues to items on a criterion test, number of adjectives, illustrations, exaggerations, and details;
3. *Knowledge structure cues*—indicated by number of principles, concepts, comparisons, contrasts, etc., stated;
4. *Interest*—indicated by attention-seeking statements, emphasis, problems raised, etc.; and
5. *Vagueness*—indicated by words signaling approximation, unclarity, and lack of assurance on the part of the speaker.

Several of these classes indicate not only lexical information but also other types of linguistic cues. However, and conveniently, the class that turns out to be the strongest predictor of other teaching variables, *vagueness*, is defined solely in lexical terms. In fact, when one studies the actual measurements employed by Hiller *et al.*, *vagueness* turns out to be measured by the number of times any of some 233 words, or in some cases short phrases, appear in a lesson of standard length. Examples of these words, the nine subclasses into which they fall, and average numbers of occurrences of each subclass for lessons lasting 15 minutes are given in Table 9.4. If we take seriously an argument advanced by Gage (see Rosenshine, 1968), teacher *vagueness* should be positively associated with lack of teacher information

Table 9.4   Categories and Example Items Illustrating Vagueness

Category	Number of Different Items in Category	Mean Number of Items Occurring per Lesson*
1. Ambiguous designation (all of this, and things, somewhere, other people)	39	4.7
2. Negated intensifiers (not all, not many, not very)	48	1.2
3. Approximation (about as, almost, pretty much)	25	2.3
4. "Bluffing" and recovery (a long story short, anyway, as you all know, of course)	27	8.3
5. Error admission (excuse me, not sure, maybe I made an error)	14	1.3
6. Indeterminate quantification (a bunch, a couple, few, some)	18	10.3
7. Multiplicity factors (aspects, factors, sorts, kinds)	26	7.8
8. Possibility (may, might, chances are, could be)	17	8.0
9. Probability (probably, sometimes, ordinarily, often, frequently)	19	2.0
	233	45.9

* Average length of 15-minute lessons was 1,892 words.
Adapted from Hiller *et al.* (1969), p. 665.

concerning the subject matter of the lesson and negatively associated with pupil learning. We shall return to these predictions in our empirical review.

Vagueness is obviously only one of many lexical aspects of teaching that might be examined. As a matter of fact, it should be possible to find categories of words that indicate many of the concepts of teaching that have been measured intuitively in research reported in the other chapters of this book. Most investigators have not yet thought about making such simple measurements.

Other surface features   To count those words that fall into a lexical category is to analyze a "surface feature" of discourse. As we shall use the term, "surface features" are those that can be judged by a computer from an accurate transcription of classroom discourse. For example, length of the natural sentence in words is a surface feature, as is length of the uninterrupted utterance or certain sequential features of discourse. Some of these "other" surface features also turn out to have value for the analysis of teaching.

A general program for examining surface features of classroom discourse has been undertaken by Hays (see Hays *et al.*, 1971) as part of a larger research project at the University of Missouri that was directed by M. L. Loflin and B. J. Biddle. In contrast with the program headed by Gage, the Loflin-Biddle program was directed not so much at the validation of an insight stemming from educational theory as at exploration of the many linguistic concepts that might have value for understanding teaching. Thus Hays has explored a wide range of surface features in classroom discourse including frequency of word emission for both teachers and pupils, length of natural sentences, length of uninterrupted speaker utterances, frequencies of words that begin and end sentences and utterances, and simple sequences of both words and sentences.

Simple sentence analysis   The focus of the Loflin-Biddle project, however, has not been surface features but rather the logic and content of classroom discourse. As was suggested earlier, much of the information present in a typical discourse is compressed, elliptical, referential, implicit. Although meaning can be intuited by those who are present, the formal analysis of meaning requires that we make explicit those portions of the discourse that have been left out or compressed. This demands that the discourse record be filled in and converted into a standardized propositional form.

The process of filling in and converting a discourse record is termed by the Loflin-Biddle group discourse *reconstruction*. This process is illustrated in Figure 9.5, which consists of two transcriptions taken from a grade VI social studies lesson. Both transcriptions cover the same materials. The upper transcription is in the form of standard English and was prepared for the analysis of surface features. The lower transcription is the reconstructed record. Note that the latter is in the form of a series of *simplex sentences* each consisting of a clause in which appears a single verb plus associated nominal materials. Information implicit in the original transcription has been filled in parenthetically, and most forms of modification have disappeared to be replaced by additional simplex sentences that represent their meaning In general, then, each natural sentence from the original transcription has been replaced by one or more simplex sentences that make explicit the argument being advanced. (Adjectives are retained as a form of modification however, so that each nominal unit may either be a single word or a noun phrase. Verbs may also be represented by a single word or by a verb phrase of course.)

Discourse records that are in a simplex-sentence format can be analyzed for many variables. In general, the Loflin-Biddle group has chosen to focus on two classes of variables, those applicable to nominal phrases and those pertaining to the verbal phrase or simplex sentence as a whole. *Nominal variables* studied included the following, among others: *realization, modification, form, case, person, number, gender,* and *address form.* Most of these terms will be familiar to readers, and coding categories adopted by the Loflin-Biddle group are but an extension of grammatical distinctions that many of us were taught to make in high school. *Realization* refers to whether the nominal phrase was spoken explicitly or was implicit in the discourse *Case* concerns such issues as whether the nominal phrase indicated an agent who acted, an object upon which action was performed, a location, and so forth. (Since case-modification nouns are rarely present in English, linguists have argued for some time concerning case classification for our language

FIGURE 9.5   Fragment of classroom discourse in original and reconstructed formats. (From Loflin et al., 1973)

Original Format

E   :Teacher::
T   :Pupils::
    Now as you look through a book you are surveying it, just looking it over, seeing what you find in it. This is survey. /Teacher writes on blackboard/ Then after you have surveyed and looked it over /Teacher writes the word question on the blackboard/ questions might come into your mind: what is this?

Reconstructed Format

E   :Teacher::
T   :Pupils::
    001 01 0 Now L1 as 1 you = pupils/ V look through 2 a book
    001 02 1 you = pupils/ V are surveying 2 it = book/ L1 (and|or)
    001 03 1 (you = pupils/) V (are) just looking//over = surveying/ 2 it = book/ L1 (and|or)
    001 04 1 (you = pupils/) V (are) seeing Al *05
    001 05 1 what (?) 2 you = pupils/ V find 3 in it = book/
    002 01 1 This = 1.XX/ V is 2 survey
    003 01 L1 Then L2 after 1 you = pupils/ V have surveyed 2 (it = book/) L3 and(or)
    003 02 L1 (then) L2 (after) I (you = pupils/) V (have) looked// over = surveyed/ 2 it = book/
    003 03 1 questions V might come into 2 mind
    003 04 1 your = pupils/ V (have) 2 (mind)
    003 05 L1 (such as) Al *06V (is) I (a question)
    003 06 1 what (?) V is 2 this (?)?

The Loflin-Biddle group obtained satisfactory reliability through use of a 15-category system.) *Address form* deals with the ways in which people address one another in the classroom. Definitions of the coding categories used for each of these variables may be found in Figure 9.6.

The second class of variables studied applied to *verbal phrases* or to simplex sentences as a whole. Among others, these included: *realization, sign, mode, embedding mechanisms, conjoining, adjoining,* and *meaning feature of link.* Again, some of these categories will be familiar to readers. *Mode* concerns whether the simplex sentence was a demand, an assertion, or a question, and, if the latter, its form. *Embedding mechanisms* are those by which a constituent simplex sentence is attached to the simplex sentence that encloses it. *Conjoining* concerns the use of coordinating conjunctions, whether explicit or implicit, *adjoining* the use of subordinating conjunctions. *Meaning features* concern the various logical categories into which conjoined and adjoined simplex sentences can be sorted. Definitions of the coding categories for the variables would take up too much space here, but a listing of facets and categories is provided in Figure 9.6.

FIGURE 9.6   Codes for nominal units and simplex sentences. (Adapted from Loflin et al., 1973)

Codes for Nominal Units

Lexical Realization
  1) Implicit
  2) Explicit
Modification of Unit
  01) Simple adjective
  02) Multiple adjective
  03) Simple relative clause
  04) Multiple relative clause
  05) Simple prepositional phrase
  06) Multiple prepositional phrase
  07–19) Other combinations
  20) Unmodified
Nominative Form
  1) Noun
  2) Pronoun or proform
Nominal Case
  01) Agentive
  02) Participative
  03) Dative
  04) Commitative
  05) Location
  06) Destination
  07) Temporal
  08) Source
  09) Resultative
  10) Instrumental
  11) Purposive
  12) Justification
  13) Benefactive

  14) Manner
  15) Objective
Person
  1) First person (speaker)
  2) Second person (addressee)
  3) Third person (all other animals or persons)
Number
  1) Singular
  2) Plural
Gender
  1) Feminine
  2) Masculine
  3) Both feminine and masculine
  4) Neuter
  5) Indefinite
Address Form
  0) Nonrelevant
  1) Endearment
  2) First name
  3) Title plus first name
  4) Title plus last name
  5) Last name
  6) General age or sex title
  7) Occupational, positional, or family title
  8) Pronoun
  9) Derogatory

Codes for Verbal Phrases or Simplex Sentences

Verbal Realization
  1) Implicit
  2) Explicit
Verbal Sign
  1) Completely negative
  2) Partially negative
  3) Positive
Sentence Mode
  0) Uncodable
  1) Wh question, basic order
  2) Wh question, reversed order

  3) Wh question, sentence-completion order
  4) Non-wh question, simple yes-no
  5) Non-wh question, tag
  6) Non-wh question, imperative
  7) Non-wh question, coordinated yes-no
  8) Demand
  9) Assertion

Embedding Mechanisms
- 00) Nonrelevant
- 01) For-to complement
- 02) -ing complement
- 03) Possessive -ing complement
- 04) To complement
- 05) Whether, if complement
- 06) Wh- complement
- 07) That complement
- 08) The fact that complement
- 09) Possessive
- 10) Relative
- 11) Appositive
- 12) Comparative
- 13) Matrix sentence
- 14) Verbal nouns

Conjoining Judgment
- 0) Nonrelevant
- 1) Conjoined without deletion
- 2) Conjoined with deletion

Adjoining Judgment
- 0) Nonrelevant
- 1) Adjoined without deletion
- 2) Adjoined with deletion

Meaning Feature of (Conjoining or Adjoining) Link
- 00) Nonrelevant
- 01) Temporal
- 02) Causal
- 03) Concessional
- 04) Conditional
- 05) Purposive
- 06) Inferential
- 07) Adversative
- 08) Additive
- 09) Disjunctive
- 10) Additive/disjunctive

These variables are phrased in terms that are traditional to grammarians, and it is difficult to appreciate what might be their significance for the topic of teaching. Moreover, trying to think about 15 variables at one time is difficult. Let us consider one or two potential implications of these variables and then let the remainder of our discussion be delayed until after presentation of results from the Loflin-Biddle research. Consider *realization*. One of the features of adult civilized discourse is that we learn to make explicit what it is we are saying. Perhaps for this reason teachers tend to pressure pupils toward *explicit* expression. We should expect to find a greater proportion of discourse becoming explicit as pupils become more mature. By the same token, pupils whose language is less explicit should have a harder time in school, and teachers whose language features considerable implicit material may be less effective as teachers.

A similar argument concerns *adjoining*. Much of the logic of classroom discourse concerns the process of tying together a superordinate clause. As his process becomes more formal we should find more explicit use of adjunctive features—and higher education demands that pupils learn to use ormal logic.

To take yet another example, teachers have a number of ways of indicating emotional response to pupils. Teachers who reject their pupils should be more likely to use formal titles or last names in *addressing* their pupils; hose who accept or like their pupils should use more first names or even erms of endearment.

Arguments such as these seem quite plausible once we have a chance o think about them, although each will have to be backed up by evidence of course. Perhaps for this reason the basic notion of examining classroom discourse by means of textual *reconstruction* has already been explored in a second major project. As part of a larger program conducted by E. Scott a the James Cook University (Townsville, Queensland), Cambourne (1971) ha studied discourse features in classrooms, playgrounds, and pupils' homes Cambourne's concepts and procedures differ slightly from those of th Loflin-Biddle group, and it is worthwhile to consider this slightly differen approach.

Cambourne also begins by preparing a transcription of discourse in th form of standard English. This is then broken into a series of nested units representing content, the identity of speakers, and pauses in the languag flow. The smallest of these is the sentence, or "T-unit." Citing Hunt (1965 Loban (1963), and Watts (1947), Cambourne defines the sentence as " grammatically independent clause together with any dependent clause whic may be attached to it" (1971, p. 230). This unit is, therefore, midway i length between a natural sentence, which may contain two or more indepen dent clauses, and Loflin's simplex sentence, which contains not more than on clause. Despite this difference, Cambourne proceeds to treat the *sentenc* in more or less the same way Loflin does the simplex sentence. Abbreviate sentences are reconstructed to "flesh out" their meanings, sentences ar coded for the presence of embedding, conjoining, and adjoining, and th same list of mechanisms is used for coding that was originally developed b Loflin. It is unclear whether Loflin's or Cambourne's methods of reconstruc tion are easier to accomplish, and we suspect that the end-product (fc judgments about sentence complexity) are reasonably comparable betwee the two techniques.

A slightly larger unit used by Cambourne is the "exchange," whic consists of all those sentences uttered sequentially by a given speaker tha are reasonably proximal in time and have but a single topic. Exchanges ar in turn, nested within *encounters,* this last unit consisting of all those ex changes uttered sequentially by speakers that are proximal in time and hav a single topic. In operational terms the boundaries of exchanges and er counters are identified at the same time. Change of speaker denotes th boundary of an exchange. Encounter boundaries occur when either a ser tence appears that "shares no common semantic features with the sentenc which immediately preceded it" (p. 86) or "occurs 10 seconds or later afte the sentence which immediately precedes it" (p. 86).

Little is made by Cambourne of the "exchange" unit. However, *encoun ters* are coded for the identities of those persons who are involved in then As we shall see shortly, Cambourne's concerns are focused on the isolate pupil. Because of this concern, Cambourne sets forth a five-category face for classifying encounters: *individual encounters*—when the pupil is talkin to one other person; *multiple encounters*—when he is talking to two or mor others; *overheard encounters*—when he is listening to others but not speak ing himself; *potential encounters*—when he tries to get others to talk wit him but is unsuccessful; and *talk to self*—when he speaks to himself. As is true for all of Cambourne's operations, high reliability is reported for the encounter code. Clearly, this facet may be used to judge the degree to which a pupil is actively involved in the classroom, and as we shall see, Cambourne established a number of interesting findings for its use.

Research on Classroom Behavior

Let us now turn to the evidence that justifies the use of these complex linguistic concepts. Box 9.2 provides a summary of details and findings from research using linguistic concepts. As already suggested, three groups of persons have been working on the application of linguistic concepts to the study of teaching. The group headed by N. L. Gage at Stanford has as one of its missions the study of teachers' ability to "explain." As originally conceptualized by Gage, this research was to focus on the single central topic of teacher explaining behavior rather than on the many diffuse topics other investigators had looked at in attempting to predict the effectiveness of teaching (see Rosenshine, 1968). In pursuit of this goal a number of different studies were undertaken, most of which are not pertinent to our review because they did not involve direct classroom observation. However, three studies did involve such observation, and these are worthy of our close attention.

BOX 9.2   Application of Linguistic Concepts

STUDIES REVIEWED

Cambourne (1971)	(Cam71)
Hays *et al.* (1971)	(H&a71)
Hiller (1971)	(Hil71)
Hiller *et al.* (1969)	(Hil69)
Loflin *et al.* (1973)	(Lof73)
Rosenshine (1968)	(Ros68)

INSTRUMENT, METHOD OF GATHERING DATA, CODING SYSTEM, UNIT STUDIED, RELIABILITY

Cambourne Semantic Procedure, audiotapes, transcripts, and reconstruction; multi-facet category system; words, phrases, "thought units," and sentences; high reliability (Cam71).

Hays Surface-Feature Procedure, videotapes, transcripts, and computer processing; multifacet category system; words and sentences; absolute reliability (H&a71).

Hiller Lexical Instrument, transcripts and computer processing; multifacet category systems; words and phrases; absolute reliability (Hil69), (Hil71).

Loflin-Biddle Semantic Procedure, videotapes, transcripts, and reconstruction; multifacet category system; words, phrases, simplex sentences, and sentences; high reliability (Lof73).

Rosenshine Explaining Instrument, videotapes and transcripts; multifacet category

Box 9.2 (continued)

---

system; words, phrases, clauses, sentences, movements, gestures; reliability not reported (Ros68).

Field Surveys

(Cam71)   28 pupils (14 each from rural and urban areas), grade I; data collected in four contexts; home-breakfast, home-dinner; playground, classroom; one hour per context

(H&a71)   15 teachers and pupils, male and female teachers, black ghetto and white suburban classrooms, grades I, VI, and XI; social studies; one lesson each

(Hil69)   Same original sample as that of (Ros68) (analysis confined to 32 teachers for the Yugoslav lesson and 23 for the Thai lesson)

(Lof73)   Same as that of (H&a71)

(Ros68)   43 teachers and pupils, grade XII, social studies; two 15-minute lessons, each on Yugoslavia and Thailand (analysis confined to 15 most and 15 least effective teachers)

Presage-Process Experiments

(Hil71)   24 university teachers, social studies; four 2-minute lectures on Yugoslavia or Thailand

FINDINGS

Lexical Concepts

Process Occurrences

None reported.

Context-Process Relationships

None reported.

Presage-Process Relationships

9.2-1   *Teachers' knowledge of subject matter* reduces *teachers' use of vagueness* (Hil71) E.*

9.2-2   *Subject matter* has little effect on *teachers' use of vagueness,* and

9.2-3   *Subject matter* affects *teachers' optimal information amount, knowledge structure cues,* and *interest* (Hil69).

Process-Process Relationships

9.2-4   *Teachers' use of vagueness, verbal fluency, optimal information amount, knowledge structure cues,* and *interest* are relatively unrelated to one another (Hil69).

Process-Product Relationships

9.2-5   *Teachers' use of vagueness* is negatively associated with *pupil achievement* (Hil69).

9.2-6   *Teachers' verbal fluency* is positively associated with *pupil achievement* (Hil69).

9.2-7   *Teachers' optimal information amount* and *interest* are positively associated with *pupil achievement* for "some" topics (Hil69).**

---

* Findings generated experimentally are indicated with an E.
** See text for details.

Other Surface Concepts

Process Occurrence

9.2-8   Each minute of typical classroom discourse involves 125 explicit words and 7 different *utterances* averaging 18 *words* in length (H&a71).

9.2-9   (In comparison with pupils) *teachers* use 3 times as many explicit *words* and *utterances* that involve 5 times as many *words* (H&a71).

Context-Process Relationships

None reported.

Presage-Process Relationships

9.2-10   *Male teachers* (as opposed to female teachers) emit *longer utterances* (H&a71).

9.2-11   *Teachers of black** (as opposed to teachers of white) *pupils emit a larger proportion of total words spoken*—therefore, black pupils speak relatively less than white pupils (except at grade XI) (H&a71).

9.2-12   *Grade XI* (as opposed to grade I or VI) *teachers* emit a *larger proportion of total words spoken* (except for black* classrooms) and longer *utterances* (H&a71).

Process-Process Relationships

None reported.

Process-Product Relationships

None reported.

Semantic Concepts Based on Reconstruction

Process Occurrence

9.2-13   Most *nominal units* in classroom discourse are
either *unmodified* or *modified by a single adjective* (Lof73);
either *objective, agentive, participative, dative,* or *locational* in case (Lof73);
singular (Lof73); and
inanimate, or if animate, *third-person* (Lof73).

9.2-14   About equal numbers of *nominal units* in classroom discourse are
explicitly and *implicitly* expressed (Lof73);
noun or *pronoun* in form (Lof73); and
if animate, *feminine, masculine, both,* or *indefinite* in gender (Lof73).

9.2-15   Most *address forms* in classroom discourse are *pronominal* in form, or make use of *first names* (Lof73).

9.2-16   Most *(simplex) sentences* in classroom discourse
are *positive* in sign (Lof73);
are *assertive* in mode (Lof73);
are *simple in structure* (that is, make no use of *embedding, conjoining,* or *adjoining*) (Lof73), (Cam71);
if adjoined, usually *no deletion* occurs (Lof73), (Cam71);
if conjoined or adjoined, most often involve *additive links* (Lof73), (Cam71).

9.2-17   *Classrooms* (as opposed to *playgrounds* or *homes*) exhibit *longer adult sentences* (Cam71);

* Black lower class versus white middle class—see text.

Box 9.2 (continued)

> more complex adult sentences (that is, use more embedding or adjoining)
> (Cam71);
> more overheard and fewer individual or potential pupil encounters
> (Cam71);
> if individual, shorter pupil encounters (Cam71);
> if overheard, longer pupil encounters (Cam71); and
> if individual, fewer encounters that are pupil initiated (Cam71).
>
> 9.2-18 Classrooms (as opposed to homes) exhibit
> shorter pupil sentences (Cam71); and
> less complex pupil sentences (that is, use less embedding, conjoining,
> and adjoining). Pupil sentences in playgrounds are similar to those
> in classrooms in length and complexity (Cam71).
>
> 9.2-19 Teacher-enunciated nominal units are more likely (than pupil units) to be
> explicitly expressed (Lof73);
> if explicit, plural (Lof73);
> if animate, second person (Lof73); and
> if animate, both feminine and masculine (Lof73).
>
> 9.2-20 Teachers more often address pupils by first names than do pupils (Lof73).
>
> 9.2-21 Teacher-enunciated (simplex) sentences are more likely (than those of
> pupils) to be
> questions or demands (Lof73);
> longer (Cam71); and
> more complex (that is, make more use of embedding, conjoining, or
> adjoining) (Cam71).
>
> *Context-Process Relationships*
>
> 9.2-22 Teachers of black* (as opposed to teachers of white) pupils use
> more first names (except of grade XI and among male teachers) (Lof73);
> and
> fewer additive links (Lof73).
>
> 9.2-23 Black (as opposed to white) pupils use
> more implicit discourse (except at grade XI)† (Lof73);
> fewer masculine and more indefinite nouns (Lof73);
> fewer first names (Lof73); and
> fewer additive links (Lof73).
>
> 9.2-24 Grade I (as opposed to grade VI or XI) teachers use
> more second-person and fewer third-person references (Lof73) and
> more singular nouns (Lof73).
>
> 9.2-25 Grade VI (as opposed to grade I or XI) teachers use
> more conjoining without deletion (Lof73).
>
> 9.2-26 Grade XI (as opposed to grade I or VI) teachers use
> fewer feminine and more indefinite nouns (Lof73).
>
> 9.2-27 Grade I (as opposed to grade VI or XI) pupils use
> more objective nouns (Lof73);
> more inanimate references;
> more first-person and fewer third-person references (Lof73);
> more singular nouns (Lof73);
> more feminine and more masculine nouns (Lof73);
> fewer examples of embedding (Lof73); and
> fewer examples of conjoining (Lof73).
>
> * See text for details.

9.2-28 *Grade VI* (as opposed to *grade I* or *XI*) *pupils* use
    more first-name references (Lof73);
    fewer implicit verbs (Lof73); and
    more additive links (Lof73).

9.2-29 *Grade XI* (as opposed to *grade I* or *VI*) *pupils* use
    fewer feminine nouns (Lof73).

9.2-30 *Urban* (as opposed to *rural*) *classrooms* exhibit
    shorter pupil sentences (Cam71);
    less complex pupil sentences (that is, use less *embedding, conjoining,* or
    adjoining) (Cam71);
    more multiple and *fewer overheard pupil encounters* (Cam71);
    if *individual, shorter pupil encounters* (Cam71); and
    if *multiple, shorter pupil encounters* (Cam71).

Presage-Process Relationships

9.2-31 *Male teachers* (as opposed to *female teachers*) use
    fewer first-person and *more third-person* references (Lof73);
    fewer first names (Lof73);
    more assertions (Lof73); and
    more adjoining without deletion (Lof73).

9.2-32 *Pupils of male teachers* (as opposed to *pupils of female teachers*) use
    fewer nominal units in the *objective case* (Lof73);
    more third-person references (Lof73);
    more masculine and *fewer indefinite* nouns (Lof73); and
    more adjoining without deletion (Lof73).

Process-Process Relationships
None reported.

Process-Product Relationships

9.2-33 *Teachers' use of adjoining without deletion* is positively associated with
    pupil achievement (Ros68).

In the first of these studies, by Rosenshine (1968), only three variables were found to distinguish between effective and ineffective lectures across three different subsamples. One of these concerned gesture and movement rather than linguistic phenomena and was reviewed in Chapter VII. Rosenshine's second finding is also reviewed elsewhere (in Chapter X). Although linguistic in character, it concerns the sequencing of linguistic events rather than event frequencies. Rosenshine's third finding is purely linguistic, however. In general, effective lectures were found to contain more explaining links, that is, "prepositions and conjunctions which indicate the cause, result, means or purpose of an event or idea" (p. 8). Examples given by Rosenshine of such links include, "because," "in order to," "if . . . then," "therefore," and "consequently." In terms suggested by the concepts of Loflin and Biddle, Rosenshine's finding means that effective lectures are more likely to feature *adjoining without deletion* than are ineffective lectures. We argued above that explicit use of adjoining would characterize a discourse that was formal and logical. Apparently the use of formal logic is not only demanded of pupils but is also more likely to lead to pupil comprehension when used by the teacher!

A second study by the Stanford group (reported by Hiller, Fisher, and Kaess, 1969) made use of the same sample of lessons as did Rosenshine. The same criterion of effectiveness was also used. As suggested earlier, the strongest findings reported by Hiller et al. concerned vagueness. In general, vagueness was *negatively* associated with pupil achievement, in fact, it was the strongest predictor of pupil understanding among all variables examined. In addition, the investigators found that incidence of vagueness was relatively independent of incidence of the other four lexical factors and that vagueness was a function of teacher rather than of lesson topic (that is, teachers vague on Yugoslavia tended also to be vague on Thailand).

Why should teacher vagueness be associated with lack of learning by pupils? According to the authors, vagueness occurs when "a performer . . . does not sufficiently command the facts or the understanding required for maximally effective communication" (p. 670). It arises when a speaker tries to present information he has forgotten or never really grasped. As an example of a vague presentation, they quote the following discourse segment:

"And this, of *course*, means, ah, *many factors* in terms of standard of living. Ah, I think in an effort to do this, however, *many* of the underdeveloped areas of Yugoslavia have been *kind* of helped equally, equality. And, ah, *much* of the effort and expense that's been going into underdeveloped areas, and this has served in *almost* a negative fashion." (p. 672)

Thus, if the teacher does not understand the topic, it is small wonder that pupils cannot learn it from her.

Hiller et al. presented several other findings. The next strongest variable in predicting pupil understanding was teachers' *verbal fluency*, and once again this variable appeared related to teacher rather than to lesson topic. In contrast, *optimal information amount, knowledge structure cues*, and *interest* were affected by lesson topic and did not predict pupil understanding for both lessons. (*Optimal information amount* and *interest* did predict pupil understanding for the lessons on Thailand.)

Given the strength of his findings concerning *vagueness*, Hiller (1971) was led to conduct an experimental study designed to test the assumption that vagueness reflects inadequate knowledge and understanding. As predicted, Hiller's major finding was that teachers' knowledge of the topic reduced the amount of vagueness in their lectures. In his discussion of this finding Hiller suggested that his manipulation might have induced anxiety for the low-knowledge group of subjects. However, he suggested that *lack of knowledge* may be an anxiety-provoking experience for teachers in the main, and that it would be interesting to find out whether teachers became vague through confusion, anxiety, or both. Whichever may be the case, the evidence from Hiller's two studies is impressive and suggests that lack of knowledge on the part of the teacher induces vagueness in her presentation, which in turn depresses pupils' understanding. *Vagueness* is surely an interesting variable for future research and for emphasis in teacher education.

The second group of investigators has operated at Missouri under the leadership of Loflin and Biddle. As was previously suggested, this group has attempted to explore a wide variety of linguistic variables in the study of teaching, using both the computer and *reconstruction* of the discourse record so as to examine the logic of classroom exchange. This group has drawn its data from an extensive videotape library that was partially described in Chapter VII in our report on the Adams-Biddle project. As will be recalled, in the Adams-Biddle research a library of videotapes was assembled that represented both mathematics and social studies lessons, male and female teachers, and grades I, VI, and XI. This first set of videotapes was obtained from white classrooms in the suburbs of a major midwestern city. The Loflin-Biddle project made use not only of the Adams-Biddle videotapes but also of a parallel sample of videotapes made in a black lower-class ghetto of another midwestern city. (Most of these latter tapes featured teachers who were black.) Thus, comparisons could be made between classrooms by race-cum-social class, as well as by subject matter, grade level, and male versus female teacher leadership.

To understand the importance of studying racial differences in classroom interaction, consider the well-known fact that black pupils do less well in standard schools than do white pupils. One might consider this to be evidence of racial "inferiority." However, a more sophisticated interpretation can be formed from the idea that blacks might be handicapped for standard educational experiences because of the language they normally speak. Bernstein (1958, 1970) has argued that middle-class persons use language that is "elaborated" (hence more precise, less self-referenced, and more suited for abstract reasoning), while lower-class persons use language that is "restricted." (And, unfortunately for America, most blacks are surely lower class.) American linguists have also begun to develop data to show that the speech of blacks in this country differs from that of whites in systematic ways (see Labov, 1966; Stewart, 1965; and Loflin, 1970). If this argument is correct, we should be able to detect differences in language use between black and white classrooms, and these differences should be expressed in features that make for "success" in the experience of classroom education.

Within this general project, Hays *et al.* (1971) concerned themselves with surface features of discourse. To exemplify the extremely verbal character of classroom interaction, Hays *et al.* report that classroom discourse averaged approximately 125 explicit words per minute, or slightly more than two per second.[2] (This figure *includes* the times given over to pauses and con-

---

[2] At this rate the typical class hour will produce approximately 7,500 words!

fusion wherein explicit words are not spoken.) Of all words spoken, teachers emit approximately three times as many as pupils, thus confirming once again the domination of classroom affairs by the teacher. To look at these findings slightly differently, each minute of classroom discourse produced an average of seven uninterrupted utterances averaging some 18 words in length, while teacher utterances were five times as long as pupil utterances, on the average.

Among presage-process relationships, Hays *et al.* report that male teachers emit longer utterances, on the average, than do female teachers. (This finding, like others from the Loflin-Biddle project, was validated not only for the sample as a whole but also for available analytic breakdowns within the sample.) Such a finding appears to corroborate the earlier findings by Adams and Biddle that male teachers are more likely to control classroom events by standing still and using a loud voice. Hays *et al.* also report an interesting relationship between the proportion of words emitted by teacher and pupils that interact with both grade level and race of the classroom. As it turns out, the grade I and grade VI classrooms featured a pattern of rapid exchange between teachers and pupils, but within this pattern the teachers of *black* pupils dominated the classroom more than did the teachers of *white* pupils. Moreover, the *black* grade XI classrooms looked very much like the black grade VI classrooms, with a continuation of the pattern of rapid exchange between teachers and pupils. However, the *white* grade XI classrooms featured a format that was similar to a university lecture, with long teacher utterances and only occasional, and brief, comments from pupils. These findings suggest that the white pupils are being socialized more adequately for university course work than are the black pupils. Unfortunately, we can as yet only speculate on the effects of these differential treatments, since neither Hays *et al.* nor any other has yet reported process-product research on these discourse features to our knowledge.

The study reported by Loflin *et al.* (1973) concerns the semantic characteristics of nominal phrases, verbal phrases, and simplex sentences, using the concepts that were set forth in Figure 9.6. As will be seen in Box 9.2, a large number of findings were generated in this study. We can interpret only a sample of these findings here.

Among findings for process occurrence, Loflin *et al.* report that teachers are more likely than pupils to use *explicit* discourse units, to enunciate *plural* nouns, to use the *second person*, and to emit nouns that are both *feminine* and *masculine*. Some of these indicate greater maturity of teachers, but some are probably related to the norms of classroom behavior. As an example of the latter, although classroom participants are nearly always addressed by their *first names* or *pronouns*, Loflin *et al.* report that teachers more often use *first* names than do pupils. Finally, it should come as no great surprise to discover that teachers are more likely (than pupils) to enunciate *questions* and *demands*.

A number of black-white differences were also obtained. Not surprisingly (given the fact that race is a *pupil* feature), most of these findings concerned pupils. Black pupils were found to use more *implicit* discourse (except at grade XI), fewer *masculine* and more *indefinite* nouns, fewer *first names*, and more *conditional* and fewer *additive* links. In sharp contrast, teachers of black pupils used *more first names*. However, like their pupils, they also used fewer *additive* links. Of these findings the one most clearly relevant to the Bernstein hypothesis is the use of implicit discourse. If black pupils enter school enunciating a good deal of implicit material, they are clearly handicapped within a school system that stresses the production of explicit discourse. They eventually "catch up" in the production of explicit discourse (at grade XI), but by then they may have been handicapped for competition with white pupils. The use of fewer masculine and more indefinite nouns by black pupils suggests lack of confidence. Interestingly, black pupils are *less* likely to use first names when addressing one another, while their teachers are *more* likely to use first names when addressing them. The first suggests either a subcultural norm (black pupils are more likely to say "Hey, man!" or to use no address form at all) or that blacks are less confident in their peer relationships, while the latter suggests compensation. (Note, however, that most of the teachers of black pupils were also black themselves.)

Analysis by grade level also produced a number of findings in the Loflin *et al.* study. Grade I teachers used more *second-person* and fewer *third-person* references and more *singular* nouns. Grade I pupils used more *objective* nouns, more *inanimate* references, more *first-person* and fewer *third-person* references, more *singular* nouns, more *feminine* and more *masculine* nouns, fewer examples of *embedding*, fewer examples of *conjoining*, and fewer *disjunctive* links. (Most of these appear to be a reflection of the immature verbal style characteristic of the younger grades.) Grade VI teachers used more *conjoining without deletion* and fewer *disjunctive* links. Grade VI pupils used more *first-name references*, fewer *implicit* verbs, and more *additive* links. (It is intriguing to contemplate the similarities between these findings and those generated by black-white comparison. Blacks use less explicitness, fewer masculine nouns, fewer first names, fewer additive links. Grade VI discourse is characterized by greater explicitness, more masculine nouns, more first names, more additive links. Once again, it would appear that black pupils are handicapped for the peculiar patterns of discourse that characterize grade VI interaction.) Grade XI teachers used fewer *feminine* and more *indefinite* nouns. Grade XI pupils used fewer *feminine* nouns.

Presage-process findings concern differences between the discourse characteristics of classrooms led by male and female teachers. Rather surprisingly (to the authors), these differences were substantial. In general, male teachers used fewer *first-person* and more *third-person* references, fewer *first names*, more *assertions*, and more *adjoining without deletion*. To express these findings another way, the language of male teachers appeared less egocentric, less friendly, more fact-oriented, and more characterized by formal logic. Pupils of male teachers differed somewhat from pupils of female teachers in using fewer nominal units in the *objective case*, more *third-person* references, more *masculine* and fewer *indefinite* nouns, and more *adjoining without deletion*. The most interesting finding is the last, for it suggests that pupils are capable of picking up the use of formal logic from their (male) teachers.

To date the Loflin-Biddle group has produced no process-product findings, so we are left in some doubt as to the actual effects of these discourse phenomena on pupil learning or other outcome variables. As we noted previously, however, Rosenshine (1968) found a relationship between teachers' explicit use of adjoining links and pupil achievement. This suggests the following set of relationships: male teachers are more likely to adjoin without deletion, hence to make explicit and formal their logic, and so are their pupils. To adjoin without deletion is to induce greater pupil achievement—therefore male teachers should be more effective! That they are not notoriously more effective suggests either that other factors in classroom discourse are also operative or that these findings (which, it will be recalled, are all based on field surveys and not experiments) are not actually a reflection of cause and effect at all. The adjoining variable appears an interesting one and deserves more investigation.

Of the rest of the Loflin-Biddle variables, the most interesting ones appear to be those associated with the Bernstein hypothesis. Classrooms demand explicit discourse, and to the extent that pupils enter them speaking a language that is implicit they are probably handicapped, be they black or white. In addition, it would appear that blacks are peculiarly handicapped to play the interactive linguistic game characteristic of grade VI classrooms. Indeed, if we take seriously the data advanced by Hays *et al.*, blacks appear less likely to progress beyond this game to the more formal, lecture-oriented pattern of discourse found in grade XI white classrooms.

As was suggested, the research conducted by Cambourne in Townsville was influenced by, and made some use of the concepts of, the Loflin-Biddle group. However, Cambourne was also influenced by other linguists' efforts, as well as by the work of Roger Barker. In addition, his research formed part of a larger project headed by Scott that includes other studies of classroom interaction as yet uncompleted. Within this larger context Cambourne set himself the task of examining the effects of *community size* and *interactive context* on the speech of grade I pupils. A group of 28 pupils was studied. Each volunteered to wear a transmitting microphone on his or her lapel for several hours, and the investigator simply made audiotape recordings of all conversation thus picked up. One full hour of discourse was studied for each pupil within the classroom, one hour while the child was on the playground and one-half hour each when the child was at home during breakfast and during dinner. In addition, the sample was broken—14 subjects being from an urban area, 14 being from rural areas and attending one-room schools. In two respects, then, Cambourne's study provides data that are unusual in studies reviewed for this book. For one, he has examined interaction in rural one-room schools;[3] for the other, he provides data allowing us to compare features of classroom interaction with interaction found in two other environments in which pupils are normally found.

In general, Cambourne examined fewer variables than did Loflin and Biddle. (For example, Cambourne did not study nominal variables at all.) In several cases, however, it is possible to appose findings from Cambourne's and the Loflin-Biddle research, and when this is done each is found to be confirmed. For example, both groups found that the most-often-used link for joining simplex sentences was the *additive* link (Finding 9.2–16).

Cambourne, however, provides a number of findings that are unique to his concepts and sample. First, we learn that classrooms are substantially different from both playgrounds and homes as linguistic environments. In general, teachers use longer and more complex sentences in the classroom than do other adults in either the playground or home; encounters in the classroom are more likely to be overheard and less likely to be individual or potential; individual pupil encounters are shorter; overheard encounters are longer; and individual encounters are less likely to be pupil initiated. Interestingly, *pupil* sentences are *not* substantially different when the classroom is compared with the playground, but both school settings generate shorter and less complex pupil sentences than does the home. As Cambourne points out, these findings suggest that the classroom is a context that demands low verbal involvement on the part of pupils and would appear a relatively poor place to learn language skills, if that learning requires practice on the part of pupils.

Cambourne also advances findings concerning the differences between rural and urban classrooms. Surprisingly, these tend to favor the rural one-room classroom. Urban classrooms are found to exhibit shorter and less complex pupil sentences; more multiple and fewer overheard pupil encounters; and shorter individual and multiple encounters. It is possible that these differences reflect the generally older pupil population of the rural classroom (recall that grade I pupils will surely be among the youngest in such an environment) or other factors in the rural or urban environments. Whatever the explanation, these findings call our attention to the fact that we have as yet but little evidence concerning differences in teaching practices as a function of school size, isolation, amalgamation, or bussing of pupils. Barker and Gump (1964) offer non-classroom research evidence that appears to favor smaller schools. Is it possible that such schools might also produce a more salubrious climate for classroom education?

[3] Compare findings reported by Hogan (1973) that were summarized in Chapter VII. Hogan's research also involved data from one-room schools and also formed part of the Townsville group of studies.

CONCLUSION

This chapter is the second of two in which our major concern is with the exchange of ideas in the classroom. Whereas in Chapter VIII we took up models of intellect that have been generated by psychologists, in this chapter our concern has been with research generated by logicians and linguists.

Although somewhat overlapping in coverage, the two research traditions of this chapter have been pursued by independent groups of investigators. They also differ in their orientation. To analyze teaching from the viewpoint of logic is to use concepts that are familiar to educators, are stated at an abstract level, involve considerable inference, and hence are hard to code reliably. To analyze teaching linguistically is to use concepts that are less familiar, are more concrete, involve little inference, and hence are not only easier to code but in some cases may be handled directly by computers. In comparison, then, findings from research on logic are harder to generate but are more "obvious" in their implications; linguistic findings are easier to generate (apart from the tedium of reconstruction) but need interpretation for the average educator. Finally, the two traditions differ somewhat in their eventual implications. Those pursuing the linguistic tradition have presumed that their concepts will eventually be found to underlie and "generate" other concepts for coding the processes of teaching. (So far this presumption has not been demonstrated with data, although we suspect that it is not wholly wrong.)

The two traditions are similar in the ways they have conducted research. Both have been represented by major programs that involved several or more years of original work. In general, these programs focused on the development of concepts and instrumentation rather than on the induction of effectiveness in teaching. With few exceptions they have concentrated on the observable processes of teaching rather than on presage-process or product variables that might be related to these processes. Moreover, few of their findings have yet been confirmed with experimental research. In a real sense these programs have been free from *Commitments*, except perhaps to the general notion that teaching is a complex, rational, observable process about which we know little as yet. For these reasons the two traditions are more exciting for their concepts than for their findings. Indeed, if we take them seriously, it will be some years before we are able to characterize the teaching strategy of a given teacher, let alone to know what combinations of factors make for effectiveness in the given classroom context. At the same time, some of the variables suggested by these traditions (such as cognitive variety, vagueness, or adjoining deletion) appear worthy of additional, immediate investigation by experimental means.

Together the two traditions have also contributed insight into a problem which has emerged from our review in this and the previous chapter. This is the problem of explaining the finding that higher-level discourse does not relate positively to pupil achievement. We first encountered this finding in Chapter VIII. It was replicated by Tisher (1970), operating in the logical-analysis tradition. Tisher and Nuthall and Lawrence (1965) have both suggested that vagueness might be the root of the problem. Research in the linguistic-analysis tradition has found that vagueness is indeed negatively related to pupil achievement (Hiller *et al.*, 1969) and, moreover, that vagueness is caused by lack of knowledge in teachers (Hiller, 1971). What is now needed is a finding that the incidence of vagueness is, in fact, greater in high-level discourse than in low-level discourse. We would then have a set of presage-process, process-process, and process-product findings that would account for the negative relationship so far found between discourse level and pupil achievement. Subsequently, we might then ask whether high-level discourse that is free of vagueness enhances pupil achievement.

These two traditions are alike also in another of their major implications. Earlier in the chapter we stressed that the proper analysis of logic requires that we consider longer sequences of utterances for their logical properties. This is no less true for linguistic phenomena. We have already seen that the technique of reconstruction requires the use of information found elsewhere in the discourse stream to "understand" (hence to reconstruct) implicit materials. Multisentence units of discourse may also be recognized, as is indicated by Cambourne's concepts of "exchange" and "encounter." We suspect, however, that these latter merely scratch the surface of the problem of sequential linguistic analysis, and that logical and linguistic analysis are alike in requiring the study of longer units of discourse for their proper realization.

Analysis of such longer units is still in its infancy. Nevertheless, several studies have already taken up this complex task, and to these we turn in Chapter X.

RECOMMENDED ADDITIONAL READING

Bellack, A. A., Kliebard, H. M., Hyman, R. T., and Smith, F. L., Jr. *The Language of the Classroom*. New York: Teachers College Press, 1966.
The major report of the research conducted by Bellack *et al.*
Hudgins, B. B. *The Instructional Process*. Chicago: Rand McNally & Company, 1971.
A valuable introductory text on classroom interaction research. It also contains several chapters on cognitive processes in the classroom. Several research studies reviewed in this chapter are also reviewed by Hudgins.
Hyman, R. T. (ed.). *Teaching: Vantage Points for Study*. Philadelphia: J. B. Lippincott Company, 1968.
A book of readings grouped into sections corresponding with the organization of this book. Some of the sections present research studies reviewed in this chapter.

Meux, M., and Smith, B. O. Logical dimension of teaching behavior. In B. J. Biddle and W. J. Ellena (eds.), *Contemporary Research on Teacher Effectiveness*. New York: Holt, Rinehart and Winston, Inc., 1964.

A brief report of the Smith *et al.* research program. (The rest of the book will also be of interest to readers. Various approaches to the study of teacher effectiveness are explored.)

Nelson, Lois H. (ed.). *The Nature of Teaching: A Collection of Readings*. Waltham, Mass.: Blaisdell Publishing Company, 1969.

A book of readings similar in content to Hyman's collection. Several of the research studies reviewed in this chapter are contained in Nelson's book.

Tisher, R. P. The nature of verbal discourse in classrooms, and Association between verbal discourse and pupils' understanding in science. In W. H. Campbell (ed.), *Scholars in Context: The Effects of Environment on Learning*. Sydney, Australia: John Wiley & Sons, Inc., 1970.

A brief report of Tisher's research and some of his findings. (The entire book will also be of interest to readers. Various relevant studies appear in it.)

SEQUENTIAL PATTERNS OF CLASSROOM BEHAVIOR

Teacher: Ah ... Dolores, would you read on, the third paragraph?

Dolores: "Just then the announcer called out, 'The Girl of the Western Plains!' A slim girl, she wore a knee-length, fringed skirt."

Teacher: All right. What's the word FRINGED? ... Billy? ... Fringed, she wore a knee-length, fringed skirt. What is a fringed skirt? ... Shannon?

Shannon: Well, it's like a fringed tablecloth.

Teacher: Yes, but what is the fringe on a tablecloth? That's right.

Shannon: It's kinda of a place. I don't know how to say it.

Teacher: Well, she wore a deerskin jacket, too. Have you ever seen anyone that has a deerskin jacket with fringe on it? Mike, can you explain this fringe?

Mike: Just sort of strips.

Teacher: It's like it's been shredded, isn't it? If I took a piece of paper and took my scissors and made little cuts all the way up through it, that would be like fringe. Uh, your mother may have fringe on the bottom of a tablecloth or maybe fringe on curtains somewhere.

Bill: Or bedspreads.

Teacher: Yes, bedspreads, lots of times.

Mark: Mrs. Vogel, I got a jacket in there that has fringe on it.

Teacher: Oh it does? All right, let's see it. Get that out so we can look at it. And anybody who's not sure what fringe is will sure enough know. (*Mark leaves room to get his coat.*)

Teacher: That's right. That's what we're looking for.

Tom: Where'd you get that?

Teacher: That's the fringe. Okay, Mark; thank you. Jimmy, would you read on please?

As evidenced in previous chapters, most classroom observational research has focused upon the *frequency of occurrence* of various categories of behavior. But lessons are not merely the concretions of more-or-less frequent instructional events. Even informal observation of classrooms reveals that teaching has a *sequential* character such that one type of instructional act is likely to follow and be followed by other acts of specific types. At several stages in earlier chapters we have commented upon the potential value of exploring such sequential relationships. For example, we have wondered whether the importance of teacher praise depends upon what it is that is

321

being praised, or whether pupils could profit from high-level discussion: without first being appraised of the facts on which they were based.

Some of the research already discussed has explored sequential relation ships, although most of these concerned quite short sequences. Users o: Flanders' categories, for example, have tabulated data in a matrix that allow: the study of pairs of categories occurring sequentially in time. The reinforce ment model also involves a short sequence of pupil and teacher acts. Again in Chapter IX we reported findings about the logical demands of teachers questions, the logical properties of subsequent pupil responses, and teache: reactions to the sequence. Study of short sequences has obvious value. Bu classrooms also exhibit longer sequences of events, and to these we now turn

In general, the most difficult problem in sequential analysis is the identi fication of useful sequence units. Lessons exhibit many different features tha vary over time: persons who speak, the content of their speech, the forms o their utterances, their gestures, and so forth. Which of these features is use ful to note in setting the boundaries of sequence units, which indeed allow u: to *find* predictable sequences of classroom events, let alone sequences tha will relate to pupil learning or other events of interest?

Several solutions have already been proposed for this problem. Each leads to a somewhat different set of sequence units. We suspect that none of these solutions is definitive, since the research they have generated is a yet nascent. To that extent this chapter is an exercise in speculation concern ing the sophistication of classroom research yet to come.

BACKGROUND

To a large extent the background for research discussed in this chapte: consists of the concepts and research reported in earlier chapters. It seem: that progression from concern with frequencies of acts to concern with th(patterns formed by those acts over time is a sign of increasing sophisticatior in research on teaching. Of course, other areas of theory in education hav(long since recognized the importance of sequences of instruction. Studen teachers of earlier generations were thoroughly versed in the notion o "lesson steps," which owed much to Herbart's (1895, 1901) work. Mor(recently we have witnessed the programmed learning movement, which i: the example *par excellence* of the utilization of principles of sequencing anc itself owes something to such notions as "schedules of reinforcement," "massed and distributed practice," and so forth, arising from the work o: learning theorists.

No doubt, too, part of the background for the research to be discussec in this chapter is to be found in recent developments in other areas, such a: systems analysis, computer science, and games theory. Indeed, the prominen attempts to conceptualize sequential patterns of classroom interaction hav(

made use of such concepts as strategies, tactics, rules, and moves which create the disturbing (?) impression that classrooms are analogous to battlefields or chessboards.

TACTICAL CONCEPTS

The research to be reviewed here may be sorted into two categories depending on the length and sophistication of the sequence concepts used. For convenience we refer to these categories as *tactics* and *strategy*. By tactics we mean the details of communication among classroom members. Tactical units concern the immediate give and take among classroom members as they concern themselves with but a single topic. Later in the chapter we will take up concepts for strategy, by which we mean the extended and substantive properties of the exchanges among teachers and pupils.

Episodes and Incidents

A number of concepts were introduced in earlier chapters that were defined so as to form parts of longer sequential units of classroom behavior. One of these was the *episode* developed by Smith and his associates at Illinois. This was defined by Smith and Meux as "the one or more exchanges which comprise a completed verbal transaction between two or more speakers" (1962, p. 14). Some of the defining attributes of an episode are that the exchanges occurring within it are pertinent to a single topic and that it passes typically through three phases: an initial or *opening phase*, a *sustaining phase*, and a closing or *terminal phase*. The *opening phase* of an episode is an entry, consisting of a *verbal move* in the form of "a remark or set of remarks (questions, assertions, etc.) signalizing that it will be followed by discussion, and setting the direction of that discussion" (p. 22). The *continuing phase* of an episode "is made up of remarks [verbal moves] which are: (a) either replies or responses to questions; (b) claims, comments, or opinions; (c) questions which sustain the entry or point under discussion; and (d) anomalous questions" (pp. 22-23). The *terminal phase* of an episode may be overt or implicit. If it is overt it may consist of "remarks [verbal moves] which serve expressly to cut off the flow of discussion" (p. 24) or "supplementary or elaborate comments which serve to punctuate the current flow of discussion" (p. 24). If the terminal phase is implicit, "the episode is taken as terminated by the occurrence of remarks which signal the opening of a new episode" (p. 24).

Let us look at examples of three episodes supplied by the authors. (Episode boundaries are indicated by //.)

T: *Now who do you know who was the first person who discovered the Hawaiian Islands? Steve?*

Steve: Was it Captain Cook?

T: That's right. // *Do you know about what time it was,* Steve?

Steve: 1670 something?

T: No, it's not that early. Come down about a hundred years.

Steve: 1770?

T: Yes. It was 1778, actually during the time of our American Revolu tion. // *And do you know what he called the islands?* They weren' Hawaii at the time. Anybody know? Oh, I think this is an easy name to remember—especially around noon. Steve?

Steve: Cook Islands?

T: No. They weren't Cook Islands. That's a good guess, but that doesn' happen to be it. The Sandwich Islands.

Steve: Oh.

T: Do you eat sandwiches at noon, too? // In this particular period, the United States wasn't too interested . . .(p. 15)

Notice that all three episodes begin with a question, which is followed by a response, which is in turn commented upon by the teacher. But notice too that while the first episode consists of a simple question—response— comment sequence, the second continues beyond that simple type of sequence when the teacher directs Steve, and that the second does not conclude with the teacher's agreement but continues until an elaborating comment is made The third episode is interesting in that it continues beyond the point at which the teacher supplies the answer to include Steve's "Oh" reaction and the teacher's rhetorical question. The point of these observations is that while the sequence of question—response—comment is common to all and might be regarded as structurally the core of the episodes, there are variations from that sequence. Thus, the episode depends more on changes of topic for its boundary than on structural characteristics. Consequently, episode one finishes when the topic changes from who discovered the islands to when they were discovered, while the third episode begins with a question on the original name of the Hawaiian Islands.

It is interesting that after having conducted a detailed conceptualization of the types of moves included in opening, continuing, and terminal phases of episodes, Smith and Meux proceeded only to classify episodes into categories of logic on the basis of their entries. Having done so, they did not proceed to analyze different types of episodes to see if the pattern of moves within them was related to their logical import. Nor did they conduct a systematic analysis of the relation between the logical import of the entry and the logical import of other phases of the episode. In effect, the concept of episode was simply dropped from further exploration.

As suggested in Chapter IX, additional exploration of the episode concept was carried out by Nuthall and Lawrence (1965). In addition, the latter authors also modified the episode to produce a unit called the *incident,* defined as "any question or demand . . . and all the subsequent verbal moves which occur up to, and including, the final response . . . to that question or demand. Any introductory comments . . . preceding the initial question, or terminal comments following the last response . . . are also included in the incident" (Nuthall and Lawrence, 1965, p. 21). The latter authors attempted to distinguish the incident from the episode by pointing out that "it is a contextual unit, similar to Smith's episode, but question-centred rather than topic-centred" (p. 20). They also pointed out that the development of the incident was an attempt "to provide a unit of discourse more amenable to psychological, logical, and pedagogical analysis (i.e., in terms of stimulus-response elements, types of cognitive operation involved, and patterns of teaching technique)" (pp. 9–10).

Nuthall has further explained procedures adapted in coding incidents as follows:

> When you tie your unit of discussion to questions (as we did with incidents), a strange phenomenon appears. In class discussion, questions do not get answered one at a time in single linear sequence. Smith and Meux and Bellack (and others) assume that class discussion is orderly and each question is answered as it arises and thereafter superseded by the next question, and so on. This conception of discussion is only tenable if you have a way of hiding away questions that intrude on other questions. Smith and Meux used their "continuant question" category for this. We found that if you take each question seriously, you have to cope with the phenomenon of questions which get answered in the middle of answers to other questions, and so on. In other words, question-answering units are like clauses in sentences. Sometimes they get strung along in sequences, but sometimes they get nested within each other. We coped with this phenomenon by retaining the strict definition of an incident (the question plus its answer(s) etc.) and allowing for incidents to occur within incidents. Incidents that occur within incidents are referred to as *subsidiary incidents*, i.e., they are questions answered within the answering of some more general questions. Incidents that contain subsidiary incidents are called *complex incidents*. Incidents that stand alone are called simple incidents. (Nuthall, personal communication, November, 1972)

Unfortunately, it is difficult to tell from the report by Nuthall and Lawrence what the exact empirical relationship between episodes and incidents was. It seems likely that incidents may occur within episodes, since every time a new question occurs a new incident begins, whereas episodes need not begin with every new question but can include *continuant* questions. However, many episode and incident boundaries should coincide. Thus, whether both units are needed or are equally viable is not clear to us, although we suspect that Nuthall and Lawrence intended the *incident* to replace the *episode*.

Nuthall and Lawrence described verbal moves occurring within incidents in concepts similar to those originally used by Smith and Meux for verbal moves within episodes. The Nuthall and Lawrence classification is presented in Figure 10.1.

FIGURE 10.1   Types of verbal moves in incidents. (Adapted from Nuthall and Lawrence, 1965, pp. 20–21)

Verbal Moves Made by the Teacher

1.1   Introductory comments which provide information or orientation leading up to a demand.

1.2   Questions, directives, or other verbal moves which, by meaning or tone of voice, require a response from the listener.

1.31   Simple comments which indicate briefly the correctness or appropriateness of a preceding verbal move.

1.32   Complex comments which provide information concerning the original question or a response to the original question. Rhetorical questions or verbal moves which repeat the original question with similar wording or emphasis are included in this category.

1.4   Verbal moves which designate who should speak, or give permission for a pupil to speak.

1.5   Responses to pupil questions.

1.6   Verbal moves in which the teacher indicates that the previous response was inaudible, unintelligible, or otherwise in need of repetition.

Verbal Moves Made by the Pupils

2.1   Verbal moves made in response to a request or demand from the teacher or other pupil.

2.2   Verbal moves in which the pupil requests or provides the occasion for a response from the teacher.

2.3   Comments made by pupils which are not requested or demanded by the teacher or other pupils.

An example of an incident from a language lesson with verbal moves coded as above is provided in Figure 10.2. The incident exhibits both an "initial question" and "subsidiary questions" concerned with the same issues.

The incident was also "diagrammed" to provide a representation of the sequential patterns apparent as the teacher guides the discussion toward the required response from pupils. Note especially the recurring question—response—comment pattern of verbal moves.

One of the most important insights in the Nuthall and Lawrence study was the idea that complex incidents could be analyzed for their various sequential components. The type of sequential analysis they suggest is exemplified in Figure 10.3, which contains a complex "explanatory" incident coded for the logical quality of the questions posed and a diagrammatic representation of the sequence of verbal moves. As may be imagined, incidents of this degree of complexity exhibit literally dozens of features that may be studied for their educative significance. Unfortunately, Nuthall and Lawrence merely hint at these features and do not present us any data illustrating their usefulness. Surely the insights represented by this type of analysis should not be ignored.

FIGURE 10.2   An incident from a language lesson. (Adapted from Nuthall and Lawrence, 1965, pp. 21–23)

	Category
Teacher: What does direct speech do to a story . . . Susan?	1.2
Susan: It arouses your interest in it.	2.1
Teacher: It does . . .	1.31
I think we could be a little more specific than that.	1.32
Brian: Puts more life in it.	2.1
Teacher: Yes . . . more life . . .	1.31
I think I could describe a little bit more . . . a little more detail than that.	1.32
Joanne?	1.4
Joanne: It lets you know the characters, sir, in direct speech . . .	2.1
You know what they are . . . what they are like . . . and . . . a . . . things like that.	
Teacher: How can you get the character of the person more clearly stated through direct speech than just . . . describing him . . . ?	1.2[b]
John: By what he says . . . the way he reacts . . . and . . . says something.	2.1[b]
Teacher: The way he reacts and says something . . .	1.31[b]
Can you enlarge on that a little?	1.2[c]
John: Well . . . the way he . . . um . . . says something and gives you his ideas about things.	2.1[c]
Teacher: Yes . . .	1.31[c]
We'll see what Robert has to say.	1.4
Robert: Well . . . if you just talk of a person . . . well they um . . . (*part of statement obscured by coughing*) than putting what he says . . . like if it's . . . um a solemn person . . . they might answer just yes or no.	2.1
Teacher: That's a very good answer Robert . . . I think Robert's put his finger on . . . the essence of using direct speech . . . You can give a fairly clear picture of the type of thinking that person indulges in . . . (etc.)	1.31

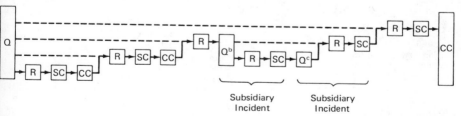

Note: Q=Initial question; Q[b] and Q[c]=subsidiary questions; R=Pupil response (2.1); SC=Simple comment (1.31); CC=Complex comment (1.32). Verbal moves indicating who should speak (1.4) have been omitted from the diagram.

FIGURE 10.3 A complex "explanatory" incident from an arithmetic lesson (Adapted from Nuthall and Lawrence, 1965, pp. 58–59)

Q1. T. What would I pay for six articles if five cost one and three? *Would you explain how to go about doing this sum? How would you go about finding that?*

R1. P. Bring one and three to pence.

C1. T. If I write it down as well ... (T. writes on blackboard: "1. Bring ⅓ to pence.")

Q2. T. *How many is that? How many pence?*

R2. P. Fifteen.

C2. T. Yes?

R3. P. You divide by five ... to find how much one article would cost.
(T. writes: "2. Divide by 5 to find cost of 1, 5 $\overline{)15}$")

R4. P. Three, sir.
(T. writes '3' thus: "5 $\overline{)15}$") with $\frac{3}{}$ above

R5. P. You multiply by six.
(T. writes: "3 multiply by 6")

Q3. T. *Why is that?*

R6. P. To find the cost of six articles.

Q4. T. *What do I multiply by six?*

R7. P. Three, sir.
(T. writes: "3d × 6")

Q5. T. *How will I write the answer?*

R8. P. Put eighteen pence on the end.
(T. writes: "3d × 6 = 18d.")

Q6. T. *How much is that?*

R9. P. One and six, sir.
(T. writes 1/6 beside 18d.)

C3. T. Well ... Is there anyone who can't understand how to do that? ... All right.

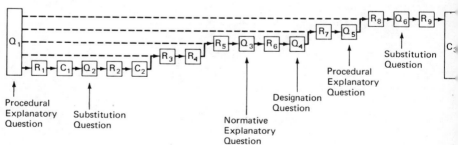

Teaching Cycles

Another approach to the analysis of classroom sequences appeared in the research of the Columbia team (Bellack *et al.*, 1966) that we considered in Chapters VII and IX. The reader will recall that the Columbia group considered the entire public stream of discourse in the classroom to be fractionable into four types of verbal or *pedagogical moves:* structuring, soliciting, responding, and reacting. It will also be recalled that these moves were conceived to form tactical sequences that are termed *teaching cycles.* In actual fact, two different kinds of teaching cycles were defined and used by the Columbia group. These were termed the "formally ordered teaching cycle" and the "temporally ordered teaching cycle," respectively. We find this terminology somewhat wordy and misleading and prefer the terms *structural cycle* and *topical cycle* for the two types.

In general, a *structural cycle* consists of "a series of pedagogical moves that begins either with a structuring move or with a solicitation that is not preceded by a structuring move and ends with the move that precedes a new structuring or a new unstructured solicitation" (p. 194). Thus, in contrast with the Illinois-inspired concepts of episode and incident, the concept of teaching cycle depends primarily on the structured form of communication and is independent of topic. For the Illinois group, then, the internal structure of the sequence, whether an episode or incident, is problematic— an unknown universe to be explored. For the Columbia team the sequence of moves possible within the structural cycle is severely constrained. "Since, by definition, both responding and reacting moves are either actively elicited or occasioned by a previous pedagogical move, neither one can be said to begin a cycle, thus substantially limiting the number of combinations of moves" (p. 194). Given these restraints, it is possible to make a classification of structural cycles in terms of the possible patterns of moves they might exhibit. Such a classification was, in fact, made by the Columbia group and is reproduced as Figure 10.4. Moreover, investigations were then conducted to explore the relative frequencies of these various sequence types.

The *topical cycle* is a slightly longer unit. It was defined by the Columbia team as "beginning either with a structuring move or with a soliciting move that was not preceded by a structuring move and continuing until the last reflexive move" (pp. 204–205). As an example of the difference between these two units, let us consider a sequence of moves between the teacher and a pupil wherein the pupil requests a clarification of the teacher's question. In such cases the pupil's response, and the teacher's subsequent reaction, if any, were generated as much by the original solicitation as by the subsequent clarification or repetition. In terms of *structural cycles* two different sequences have occurred, but only one *topical cycle* has transpired. Thus, judgments concerning the boundaries of topical cycles require the discrimination of topical information. However, little use was made of this information. In fact, the vast majority of topical cycles were found to be constituted of only one structural cycle, and only three types of *augmentation* were actually "allowed" by the research team: repeating, directing performance, and clarifying-expanding. Cycles that involve *repeating* contain information that repeats previous moves. Cycles wherein *directing perform-*

FIGURE 10.4   A classification for structural cycles. (Adapted from Bellack et al., 1966, p. 195)

Teaching Cycles

1. STR					
2. STR	SOL				
3. STR	REA				
4. STR	REA	REA ...			
5. STR	SOL	RES			
6. STR	SOL	RES	RES ...		
7. STR	SOL	REA			
8. STR	SOL	REA	REA ...		
9. STR	SOL	RES	REA		
10. STR	SOL	RES	REA	REA ...	
11. STR	SOL	RES	REA	RES ...	
12. STR	SOL	RES	REA	RES ... REA ...	
13.	SOL				
14.	SOL	RES			
15.	SOL	RES	RES ...		
16.	SOL	REA			
17.	SOL	REA	REA ...		
18.	SOL	RES	REA		
19.	SOL	RES	REA	REA ...	
20.	SOL	RES	REA	RES ...	
21.	SOL	RES	REA	RES ... REA ...	

Code

SOL—Soliciting   RES—Responding
STR—Structuring   REA—Reacting
... —one or more additional moves of the kind designated; e.g., "RES ..." means one or more additional responding moves to the same soliciting move.

ance occurs involve "asides" where someone directs others to a nonverbal performance. *Clarifying-expanding* cycles appear when ideas are refined or expanded within the concepts of an ongoing cycle. We find these three types of augmentation a restricted and somewhat arbitrary universe and suspect that if one were to take seriously the relation between topical boundaries and teaching cycles a much more complex classification of sequential units would appear.

Given the different bases of definition, there is no simple relationship between the Illinois concepts of episode and incident and the Columbia concept of teaching cycle. In general, however, teaching cycles, like incidents, are shorter units of sequence whose structural boundaries will occur *within* the topical boundaries of an episode. In addition, teaching cycles are unlikely to involve exchanges among more than two participants, while an episode might involve several different speakers. For our purposes, however, the most significant difference is that findings have been reported for teaching cycles, while parallel findings concerning the episode and incident have not.

Behavioral Episodes for Individuals

So far we have considered sequential units that involve the interaction among two or more classroom participants. But classroom events are also sequential for the individuals who participate in them, and it is possible to study the sequence of events as they occur to the individual pupil or teacher. Surely the most appropriate unit for this purpose is the (individual) *behavior episode* first proposed by Barker and Wright (1955).

In general, a *behavior episode* consists of a unit of time wherein the individual is going in one direction, engaging in a bounded set of activities, or pursuing an observable goal. Evidence for the existence of the behavioral episode may consist of both the observable behaviors of the person and the observable events to which he may be responding. In general, behavioral episodes exhibit three features. First, they exhibit constancy of behaviors with respect to the end or goal toward which the person is directed. Second, they exhibit a "normal behavior perspective," and so constitute units that may be perceived by either the individual or others. Third, the behavioral episode is presumed to have more potency than its constituent parts, thus unit behaviors appear integrated within the sequence. (Examples of behavioral episodes appear in Figure 4.1, and readers are urged to turn back to it for reference.) In practice, behavioral episodes have usually been employed by persons trained within the Barker tradition and have been judged from specimen records. There is no reason, however, why behavior episodes could not be judged from any kind of classroom transcript that provided sufficient detail of information concerning the behavior of the target person. We suspect, for example, that most classroom transcripts would provide sufficient information for judging the behavior episodes of the teacher, but not enough to judge those of the individual pupils. Figure 4.1 illustrates what is needed by way of detail to judge the latter.

Again, there is no simple relationship between the concept of *behavior episode* and those sequential concepts already reviewed. From the Barker perspective, an individual pupil may be involved in but a single behavior episode that involves his paying close attention to any number of exchanges between the teacher and other pupils on various topics. However, should the pupil himself be called on or choose to enter the stream of classroom discourse voluntarily, a new behavior episode would almost certainly be judged. In addition, pupils may engage in any number of behavior episodes that do not enter the public stream of the classroom, such as when they look for a pencil in their desks or whisper to the pupil at the next desk.

A large number of concepts has been suggested for the coding and classification of behavior episodes (see Barker and Wright, 1955). Unfortunately, few of these have yet been applied to pupil classroom behavior and none at all to teacher classroom behavior that we know of. We review one study (Barker and Barker, 1963), however, in which the *length, spon-*

taneity, and *continuity* of behavior episodes for pupils are studied. Once again, we find these concepts suggestive and wish more research had been published in which they were used.

Classroom Research

Studies reporting findings for tactical sequence units are presented in Box 10.1. Three studies are reported in which data for the Columbia concept of *teaching cycle* were reported (Bellack *et al.*, 1966; Lundgreen, 1972; and Power, 1971). All three studies were reviewed in earlier chapters.

BOX 10.1   Research Involving Shorter Sequence Units

STUDIES REVIEWED

Bellack *et al.* (1966)	(Bel66)
Lundgren (1972)	(Lun72)
Power (1971)	(Pow71)
Resnick (1971)	(Res71)
Barker and Barker (1963; also	(Bar63)
Schoggen *et al.*, 1963)	
Wright and Nuthall (1970)	(W&N70)

INSTRUMENT, METHOD OF GATHERING DATA, CODING SYSTEM, UNIT STUDIED, RELIABILITY

Columbia Instrument, audiotapes and transcripts, multifacet category system, T and P moves, moderate reliability (Bel66), (Lun72), (Pow71).

Resnick Instrument, live observation, single-facet category system, T utterances during three-minute intervals, high reliability (Res71).

Barker Procedures, specimen records, multifacet category systems, individual episodes, reliability not reported (Bar63).

Canterbury Instrument, transcripts, multifacet category system, T and P verbal moves, reliability not reported (W&N70).

DESIGN OF STUDY, SUBJECTS, CONTEXTS

Field Surveys

(Bel66)	15 teachers and pupils, grades X and XII; economics; 4 lessons for each teacher; New York
(Lun72)	9 teachers and pupils, grade XI; mathematics; Göteborg (Sweden)
(Pow71)	4 teachers and pupils, grade VIII; science; 5 lessons for each teacher; Queensland (Australia)
(Res71)	4 teachers and their pupils, self-directed (British) infant classrooms (grade I); both morning and afternoon sessions
(Bar63)	39 pairs of specimen records wherein pupils from Kansas and Yorkshire were matched for sex, age, and social and community characteristics; grades I through VI; academic, music, (indoor) physical education, and outdoor athletic classes; specimen records averaging 29 minutes in length
(W&N70)	17 teachers and pupils, grade III; three nature-study lessons, standardized content; Christchurch (New Zealand)

FINDINGS

Process Occurrence

10.1-1 Most *structural cycles* are short in duration. Structural cycles occur at the rate of 1.8 per minute on the average (Bel66).

10.1-2 Most *topical cycles* are (also) short in duration. Topical cycles occur at the rate of 1.6 per minute on the average (Bel66). About eight tenths of all *topical cycles* are composed of four moves or less (in the self-directed classroom) (Res71).

10.1-3 Most *cycles* are initiated by the teacher. About six sevenths of all structural and topical cycles are teacher initiated (Bel66). *In contradition, it is also found that*

    10.1-3a Most *topical cycles* (about three fifths) are initiated by pupils (in the self-directed classroom) (Res71).

10.1-4 The commonest types of *structural cycles* in *New York, Queensland,* and *Sweden* are

	New York	*Queensland*	*Sweden*
SOL RES REA	26%	37%	22%
SOL RES	22%	18%	16%
SOL	10%	4%	6%
SOL RES REA REA	9%	1%	4%
SOL RES REA RES . . . REA . . .	7%	14%	3%
STR SOL RES REA	6%	9%	6%

(Bel66), (Lun72), (Pow71)

10.1-5 Only a few *topical cycles* (one tenth) are augmented beyond structural-cycle length. Of these, *clarifying-expanding* and *repeating* augmentations are most often encountered, *directing performance* least often (Bel66).

Context-Process Relationships

10.1-6 *Nationality* affects *length of behavioral episodes for pupils.* In particular, *Kansas* episodes (averaging 61 seconds) were shorter than *Yorkshire* episodes (averaging 87 seconds) (Bar63).

10.1-7 *Nationality* affects *spontaneity of behavioral episodes for pupils.* In particular, *Kansas* episodes are more often spontaneously initiated than *Yorkshire* episodes. *Kansas* episodes are also more spontaneously terminated (Bar63).

10.1-8 *Nationality* affects *continuity of behavioral episodes for pupils.* In particular, *Kansas* episodes are more likely to be contained in other episodes than are *Yorkshire* episodes (Bar63).

10.1-9 *Average I.Q. of "steering-group" pupils* co-varies directly with the percentage of cycles that are *solicitation initiated* (Lun72).

Presage-Process Relationships

10.1-10 *Length of teaching experience* varies inversely with teachers' use of *simple reciprocation.* (Teachers with greater experience are more likely to ask pupils to explain or expand their answers.) (W&N70).

Process-Process Relationships

10.1-11 *Lesson format* affects *type of structural cycle.* For example, *assigning*

Box 10.1 (continued)

---

homework exhibits more *structuring-initiated cycles* than do other formats (Lun72).

10.1-12 *Initiator identity* affects *type of structural cycle.* For example, *teachers* are more likely to initiate *SOL RES REA,* while *pupils* initiate *SOL RES* more often (Bel66).

10.1-13 *Initiator identity* affects *length of topical cycles.* Brief topical cycles are more likely to be initiated by *pupils,* longer cycles by the *teacher* (in self-directed classrooms) (Res71).

10.1-14 *Length of topical cycle* is related to *cycle type.* Brief topical cycles feature fewer *questions* and more *directives, permissions,* and *responses* (in self-directed classrooms) (Res71).

10.1-15 *Topical cycles of a given type* tend to be followed by *another cycle of the same type* (Bel66).

10.1-16 *Topical cycles of a given logical process* (for example, defining) tend to be followed by *another cycle of the same process* (Bel66).

10.1-17 *Teacher-initiated topical cycles* are usually (nine tenths of the time) followed by *another teacher-initiated cycle* (Bel66).

10.1-18 *Pupil-initiated topical cycles* are often (six tenths of the time) followed by a *teacher-initiated cycle* (Bel66).

Process-Product Relationships

10.1-19 *A moderate rate of teaching cycles* is (weakly) associated with *high pupil achievement* (Bel66).

10.1-20 *A moderate use of teacher initiation and structuring* is (weakly) associated with *high pupil achievement* (Bel66).

10.1-21 *Use of simple reciprocation—SOL RES* (REA)—co-varies with *pupil achievement.* (*Use of multiple reciprocations* varies inversely with *pupil achievement.*) (W&N70).

10.1-22 *Use of postquestion structuring—SOL STR—*varies inversely with *pupil achievement.* (*Use of prequestion structuring* is not related to *pupil achievement.*) (W&N70).

10.1-23 *Redirection of nonanswered questions to other pupils* co-varies with *pupil achievement.* (Also see findings 8.3-40 and 8.3-41.) (W&N70).

10.1-24 *Use of episode-terminal structuring—. . . STR—*co-varies with *pupil achievement* (W&N70).

Earlier review was also given to Resnick (1971). In this latter study sequential notions appeared, but less formal treatment was given to them than in other research we review. Resnick appears to have discovered the notion of *topical cycle* for himself.

But a single study represents findings for *behavior episodes* in the classroom. (This is both surprising and disappointing. More than a decade ago Barker *et al.,* 1961 published a set of specimen records in which the behaviors of pupils from British and American schools were paired. Then in 1963 the study we review appeared. Since then, nothing, although the Barkers have in preparation a book comparing British and American data.)

Finally, findings are also reported for the ubiquitous Wright and Nuthall (1970) study we have so often encountered in earlier chapters. Among others, this study also reported findings based on the Illinois concept of *episode*.

Quite a number of findings appear in Box 10.1. Among process-occurrence findings, we learn that teaching cycles are of short duration and that most of them are initiated by the teacher. Moreover, only a few topical cycles are augmented beyond the structural-cycle length. Three different studies (in three national contexts) have found that the cycle types most frequently encountered are SOL RES REA and SOL RES. For convenience, we shall refer to these as *simple reciprocation*, thus it is found that simple reciprocation is more likely between teacher and pupils than more complex forms of reciprocation.

Several context-process findings are concerned with nationality. Finding 10.1-4, which we have presented under process occurrence in Box 10.1, can also lead to speculations about national differences. Power (1971), for example, attributed some significance to differences between Queensland and New York when he wrote:

> In Queensland, more cycles were teacher initiated, cycles tended to be shorter and the pattern dominated by teacher soliciting-pupil responding-teacher reacting. . . . The data indicate that the communication pattern in Queensland represents a more formal version of the game played in the United States. . . . [These data] are more characteristic of "subject-centered" classrooms than of "pupil-centered" classrooms. (p. 8)

Since these three studies were conducted independently, however, the findings might have reflected subject-matter or grade-level disparities in the designs rather than nationality. However, sharp differences are also reported for behavior episodes between Kansas and Yorkshire classrooms by the Barkers. We learn that Kansas episodes were shorter on the average, that they were more often spontaneously engendered in the classroom, and that they were more likely to be contained in other episodes (thus less single-minded). Taken together, these several findings suggest not only the power of sequential concepts but also that there may be substantial differences among Western countries in the customs of classroom life.

The last context-process finding reported concerns the concept of "steering group" as used by Lundgren. Recall that in Chapter VII we reviewed findings from Lundgren which suggested that, in part, teaching style varies as a function of the intelligence of the less able pupils in the classroom, whom Lundgren termed the steering group. Now we discover that solicitation-initiated cycles are more likely when the I.Q. of the steering group is high.

But a single presage-process finding appears. Wright and Nuthall report that the tendency for teachers to use *simple reciprocation* (that is, cycles or episodes of the forms SOL RES or SOL RES REA) varies with the length of teachers' experience. Teachers with greater experience are more likely to ask pupils to explain or expand their answers. (We consider an additional finding concerned with *simple reciprocation* below.)

Three types of process-process findings are reported. First, we learn that the occurrence of teaching cycles varies depending on lesson format. Next we learn that teaching cycles will be different depending on whether they are initiated by the teacher or by pupils. Teacher-initiated cycles are more likely to involve reactions by the teacher, are longer on the average, and are more likely to be followed by another teacher-initiated cycle. Finally, we learn a few things concerning the length and sequence of teaching cycles. Brief cycles are said to feature fewer questions, while cycles of a given structural or logical type tend to be followed by other cycles of the same type.

Finally, we turn to process-product findings and receive a pleasant surprise. Often in other chapters we have had to conclude either that process-product evident was missing or that the relationships reported were weak ones. This latter is also true for the two findings generated by Bellack concerning the *rate of teaching cycles* and the use of *initiation* and *structuring* by the teacher. It is *not* true for the four findings reported by Wright and Nuthall, however. In fact, some of the strongest findings they reported concerned features of tactical-sequence use. It was found that teachers who used *simple reciprocation, redirection of nonanswered questions to other pupils,* and *episode-terminal structuring* all generated greater achievement in pupils. In contrast, *use of postquestion structuring* appeared to interfere with pupil achievement. Taken together, these findings would appear to suggest that good teaching is characterized by simple patterns of teacher-pupil interaction and by frequent structuring summaries. However, Wright and Nuthall caution us that their findings were generated against the criterion of a test of low-level knowledge and may not do justice "to the full range of educational objectives in which most teachers are interested" (1970, p. 489). We shall have more to say on this matter in Chapter XII.

In all, these findings suggest that sequential analyses at the tactical level hold the promise of considerable power to represent classroom events, and we suspect that more research effort ought to, and will, be expended on them in the future.

STRATEGIC CONCEPTS

So far we have been dealing with quite short units of sequence, in effect, the details or tactics by which instruction is carried on in the classroom. But surely these tactics are engaged in for larger purposes. In planning the lesson teachers will often begin with one type of activity, move on to a second, and finish with a third. For example, a reading lesson might begin with all pupils reading silently to themselves, then individual pupils may be asked to read aloud while the teacher interrupts and comments, then a general discussion takes place, or perhaps a short test is given, and finally materials are cleaned up and put away. Each of these longer sequences may be considered a *strategy*. Each has common, identifiable elements, and each has cyclical properties as it begins, continues, and ends. Moreover, the sequence of strategic units is also meaningful, for the lesson itself constitutes an even larger sequential unit.

Strategic sequences are longer and more difficult to study than are tactical units. For one thing, fewer of them appear within any given lesson. For another, the boundaries of strategies are difficult to establish, for often the classroom appears to be doing two or three things at once, particularly when in transition. Finally, teachers appear to differ from one another over the strategies they choose, so that only a small range of strategies is likely to appear in the lessons of a given teacher. For these reasons the study of strategic sequences is still in its infancy. Nevertheless, some interesting concepts have been proposed for this purpose, and a few findings are also available.

Thought Units, Complex Chains, and Teaching Modules

As it turns out, the two Taba studies (1964, 1966) made contributions to our thinking concerning sequences in teaching. Most of the emphasis in Taba's first study was given to tactical sequences combining such moves as "raising the level of thought," and Taba (also) seems to have conceptualized instruction to be a series of topical episodes or incidents. Her tactical concepts were not clearly expressed, however, nor were data advanced to support them, and so we have chosen to ignore them in our presentation.

In the second Taba study, however, a somewhat different unit was suggested that appears to us a strategic concept. In Box 8.3 it was reported that the second of Taba's studies found that the pupils of teachers given special training used "complex chains of reasoning" more than pupils of teachers not so trained. Clearly, notions of sequence are involved when one judges "complex chains of reasoning." Let us see what Taba means with this phrase.

Taba (1966) argues for the importance of analyzing sequences of thought as follows:

> Sequential reasoning is a better index of quality of thinking than is frequencies by level. First, sequential reasoning offers proof that generalizations were produced in class, rather than rendered from recall. Also connected thought in itself represents a more sophisticated form of thinking than do single statements, regardless of the level at which they occur. (p. 175)

To give form to this argument Taba conceived discourse to be composed of *thought units* that were, in turn, sometimes assembled into *complex chains of reasoning*. Thought units were conceived as clauses or sentences, while complex chains were the "logically-connected thought paragraphs that con tained factual information, inferences drawn from these data, and inferences upon inferences" (p. 175) or that "pertained to making predictions and ther either to supporting them through facts or logical inference or to evaluating their validity and/or universality" (p. 176). A complex chain was illustrated with the following example (boundaries of thought units being indicated by slashes):

> Well, part of the reasons (for differences in education) that this is so is that Brazil and Argentina, Costa Rica and Guatemala have had more stable governments than Haiti/. So the government has been able to spend its money on education/. But in Haiti the people have always tried to take over a dictatorship/. So they have not been able to spend as much time and money on education. (p. 175)

As we already know, the concept of complex chain was used by Taba as a criterion variable to discriminate between trained and untrained teach ers. Furthermore, Taba argues that the occurrence of these chains can be used to distinguish between generalizations which are produced and those which are recalled. If this argument is valid, then one of the problems in applying category systems such as those based on Bloom's taxonomy may be overcome (see Chapter VIII for a discussion of the problem).

Thought units and *complex chains* are sequential concepts, it is true but they are not concerned with *inter*action in the classroom. A third con cept, the *teaching module*, was developed for this latter purpose. The teach ing module was seen as "a definable sequence of teacher-pupil interaction that results in, or includes, high level pupil thought" (p. 210). The procedure adopted for the identification of teaching modules was to begin by looking for an example of a high-level pupil response defined as any of the follow ing:

1. An inferential explanation . . . e.g., "The colonists had more security because they were more in bunches than the pioneers."
2. A generalization upon a generalization . . . e.g., "The witch doctors are trying to do with wands and cracked eggs what our medical doctors do with words and needles."
3. A logical relationship among inferences . . . e.g., "If you can't educate enough people to teach, then you don't have enough teachers." (Taba 1966, p. 210)

When such an example was found the five pupil thought units immediately preceding and following it were examined, and if there were one or more responses giving factual support following it, the segment was considered to be one of high-level thinking. Once such a segment was located the inter change of thought units between teacher and pupils preceding and following the "signal" response was studied for recurring patterns. This analysis indicated that four types or sequences of teaching modules appeared in the lessons studied. These are represented in Figure 10.5.

The following was given as example of a teaching module:

Thomas: If they brought water into the desert,/ they'd probably make it into a crop land just like the valley. .

T: All right—all these people are here. We said that many people were coming./ What problems might they have?/ Can you think of something that might happen? Donna?

Donna: It would get crowded./ If everyone came in one bunch, it would get crowded.

T: It would get crowded/—was there anything that would happen because of this? Martha?

Martha: Well, if they lived in the valley in that climate,/ in the nights they might freeze/—they might die because the climate is so different.

T: All right, it is a different climate./ Now can you think of any problems that would be presented with all the people coming into this area? Louann?

Louann: Well, it would be so crowded the new people would crowd out the old ones. (Taba, 1966, pp. 212–213)

Comparisons of the classroom discourse of the specially trained and the untrained teachers revealed that teaching modules occurred nearly twelve times as often in the former as in the latter. This suggests that the *teaching module* concept is a valid one, although it appears to us awkward and somewhat arbitrary. However, Taba also reported little difference between the two groups of classrooms in the incidence of high-level pupil responses that seemed unrelated to teaching modules, thus indicating that there are other ways of eliciting high-level responses and that such responses can occur just as often without as with the special training of teachers. In addition, as is too often the case for sequential concepts, little or no results were actually reported by the Taba team for *teaching modules.*

Ventures

The Taba concept of *teaching module* was described by her as "empirical" and "largely subjective" (p. 212). That is, the teaching module arose out of analysis of empirical data rather than being conceptualized in advance so as to guide the research, and the criteria for the identification of modules were arbitrary. A quite different approach to the development of strategic concepts was adopted in the *second* Illinois study (Smith *et al.,* 1967). As we saw in Chapter IX and again in the first part of this chapter, the *first* Illinois study was concerned with the tactical issues involved in logical operations in the classroom. However, even in the first study Smith and

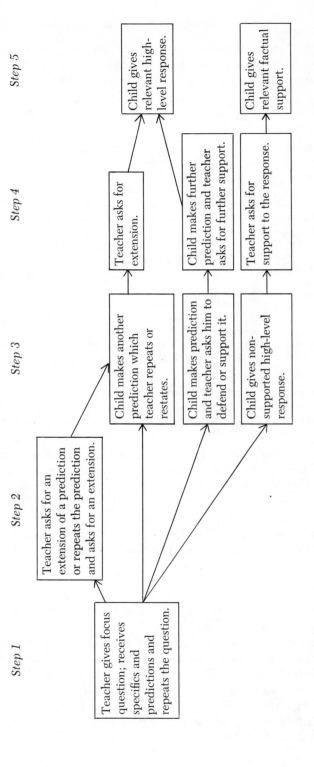

FIGURE 10.5 Diagram of the sequencing of teaching modules found. (Adapted from Taba, 1966, p. 216)

Step 1 *Step 2* *Step 3* *Step 4* *Step 5*

Teacher gives focus question; receives specifics and predictions and repeats the question.

Teacher asks for an extension of a prediction or repeats the prediction and asks for an extension.

Child makes another prediction which teacher repeats or restates.

Teacher asks for extension.

Child gives relevant high-level response.

Child makes prediction and teacher asks him to defend or support it.

Child makes further prediction and teacher asks for further support.

Child gives non-supported high-level response.

Teacher asks for support to the response.

Child gives relevant factual support.

Meux differentiated in their thinking between the tactics and strategies of teaching. As they suggested:

> The means [of teaching] . . . consist in two types of factors: subject matter and instructional paraphernalia. . . . The first of these we call material means and the second procedural means. The procedural means have two aspects: large-scale maneuvers which we call strategies, and smaller movements, constituting tactical elements of strategies, which we call logical operations. (Smith and Meux, 1962, p. 3)

Further,

> "Strategy" refers to a pattern of acts that serve to attain certain outcomes and to guard against certain others. Among the general objectives toward which a strategy may be directed are the following: to insure that certain learnings will be acquired in as brief a time as possible; to induce students to engage in an exchange of ideas; and to minimize the number of wrong responses as the student attempts to learn concepts and principles. (p. 3)

Thus, the Illinois team did not "discover" the notion of strategy, but set out to study it explicitly in their second study.

Following the procedure they had used earlier, the Illinois team began the study of teaching strategies by identifying a *contextual unit*. The unit adopted was termed the *venture*, which was defined as "a segment of discourse consisting of a set of utterances dealing with a single topic and having a single overarching content objective" (Smith *et al.*, 1967, p. 6). Lest the reader be misled by the term "content objective," it should be emphasized that the authors used it not in the sense of the intended outcome of teaching but in the sense of "a central point . . . a sort of conclusion to which the verbal exchanges lead, a sort of theme that seems to pervade the exchanges . . . the import of the venture . . . the central meaning of a segment of discussion" (p. 22). Given the vagueness of these descriptions, it is not surprising that the researchers had difficulty spelling out specific criteria for the identification of ventures and that they relied fairly heavily upon "intuition."

An example of a venture is provided in Figure 10.6. The authors comment upon that venture as follows:

> The topic discussed in this venture is how juvenile delinquency might be decreased. The content element disclosed by the discussion as a whole is that making parents responsible for the damage done by their children, getting children to have respect for their own integrity, and having people refuse to put up with delinquency are the means of reducing the amount of juvenile delinquency. Note that all of the discussion in this venture is concerned with indicating what the means of reducing delinquency are, or else, with supporting or refuting a claim that something is a means of reducing delinquency. (p. 12)

FIGURE 10.6   An example of a venture. (Adapted from Smith et al., 1967, pp 10–11)

S: If all of us had—parents had to pay for all the damage that a child did to somebody's property, what would that prove? Kids would keep on doing it even though the parents pay for it.

B: Would they?

T: What do you think about that?

B: Well, if—if the parents had to pay for it, I think they're—they'd keep the kids home, or—or at least knew where they were going. And, if the kids lied about where they were going, they wouldn't go out again for quite a while. They'd keep a little closer tabs on the kid.

G: Yeah, and the kids would think their parents were getting too strict and they'd start sneaking out and doing things behind their backs. You don' get anywhere.

B: Well, that would bring on more punishment.

G: Well, if they—you know—[inaudible] a little and just [inaudible] or something. They had to pay for it, well, maybe they'd just put their foo down and make them work it out of their allowance and they wouldn't be so free to do anything.

B: I think that's probably what a lot—a lot—a—how—how it would work out in a lot of places. In a lot of homes, parents wouldn't pay it; kid would. I think that would be a better law than—well, you can't hardly I guess—I guess you couldn't do that, though, because you couldn't make a minor pay for something he did.

T: Might make the parents a little more interested in the cases where the parents were at fault.

B: Uh-hum.

T: And, I believe that Mr. Hoover has, on one occasion, said that a great deal of our juvenile delinquency was parental delinquency and possibly making them legally responsible for actions of children, and financially responsible, would cause them to be a little more anxious to see children get what they should.

B: I don't think that—I mean, I don't think—just—the parents having an iron hand over the kids—that's—I don't think that's the answer to it. But if you could get—if you could get a better understanding between the kid and the parents, so the kids would have more respect and have more respect for their own integrity, rather than just be afraid of what would happen if they did do something. I—I think that's the real answer to it but—

T: We all need to learn self-discipline, don't we? That is fairly necessary— in our society. We can't have policemen or other law-enforcement officer stationed at every place, to check up on everybody, all the time. And it' necessary that we have a nation of people who are law-abiding, willing to abide by the law even when they—know there isn't someone there watch ing, to catch them in case they fail to abide by the law.

B: Last night on television, it was just a cowboy serial is what it was, but there was a good point brought out in it. People get the law that they deserve. The kind of law that they deserve.

T: What did—uh—?

B: Well, it was—this town was corrupt, it was run by one man—you know

And the marshal came in and they couldn't get anything done because all the jury was afraid of this one man, you know. And, this one guy brought out that point—that people ought to get the law that they deserve.

T: If they had been willing to insist on better things, law enforcement would have taken effect.

B: Have better law men.

T: One of the reports yesterday said that we would have this problem as long as people are willing to put up with it. And when they had all that they could stand for, then they would clear it up.

As we know, the venture was conceived as a unit of strategy, as opposed to the episode, which is a unit of tactics. The episode is generally a smaller unit than a venture, then, as the authors state in spelling out criteria for ventures: "A venture generally contains more than one episode. A venture is only coextensive with an episode if it is not possible to legitimately consider the episode as part of the discussion of a more inclusive topic having a single overarching content objective" (p. 16). In fact, analyses of a common set of lesson transcripts resulted in the identification of about 3,400 episodes and 637 ventures, indicating that there were on the average about five episodes within each venture.

A second concept developed as fundamental to the exploration of teaching strategies was the concept of "move." Moves in this context are "various kinds of verbal manipulations of the content of instruction . . . and . . . may be thought of as units of content as well as manipulations, depending upon whether one considers them as static or dynamic elements" (p. 53). Moves were regarded as the basic component of strategies and vary in type according to the type of venture in which they occur. Thus, within any one type of venture there is likely to be found a strategy composed of a sequence of moves, each of which is unique to that type of venture. Examples of moves in one type of venture are provided in the following:

The teacher has indicated that there are various biological misnomers, and has been mentioning some of these. The following . . . moves then occur:

Move 1

T: Can you name any other animals that we usually refer to as fish, but they don't belong with the fish at all?

S: The whale is a mammal . . .

Move 2

S: . . . The silverfish is an insect.

T: Oh, we studied one and made a drawing of him.

Move 3

S: Crayfish.

T: The crayfish. We talked about that a while ago . . . (Smith *et al.*, 1967, p. 54)

A distinction needs to be made between the concept of *move* as used in the second Illinois study and the concept of *verbal* or *pedagogical* move used by Bellack *et al.* The difference is that verbal or pedagogical moves are individual utterances that are performed in the control of behavior, while moves in the Illinois study are single or multiperson units of thought which advance the content of the discussion. In the above example *move 1* advances the content of the discussion by providing an example of a biological misnomer. In Bellack's terms it consists of two pedagogical moves, a solicitation and a response. It is possible that moves as used in the Illinois study often have the structure of teaching cycles as used in the Columbia study.

It is a little difficult to understand why the Illinois group introduced the new concept of move. As we know, ventures were conceived as units of strategy for which "logical operations" were described as the components or tactical elements. Unfortunately, the authors provide no discussion of the relationship between logical operations and moves, and we are left to conclude that the former, as identified in the first study, were found to be unsuitable as the basic analytic components of teaching strategies. Nuthall explains the distinction between logical operations and moves as follows:

> Suppose a teacher is engaged in teaching a concept by examining instances of the concept and discussing the attributes of the instances which make them instances. He might begin by asking for the pupil to name an instance. ("Can you give me the name of an instance of X?") and then ask the pupil to give the reasons why he suggested that instance ("Why is that an instance?"). Finally the teacher might ask the pupils to compare this instance with some other instance ("How does this instance differ from the one we discussed before?").
>
> In this discussion, two *moves* occur as part of a *concept venture*. They are (1) instance substantiation (an instance is named and reasons given for its being an instance) and (2) instance comparison (discussing differences and similarities between instances). The particular procedure the teacher used to achieve those two moves was to ask three questions. Those three questions required the pupils to engage in three different logical operations: (i) *stating* (the name of an example), (ii) *explaining* (why it was an example) and (iii) *comparing and contrasting*.
>
> Note two things—(a) the teacher could have achieved the same two *moves* by merely lecturing to the pupils (Smith and Meux's Monologue), or by asking other kinds of questions that got the same general information from the pupils; (b) these same three *logical operations* could occur in any other kind of venture, and be used to get together other information about something quite different.
>
> In other words *logical operations* are almost entirely independent of *moves*. *Logical operations* refer to the kinds of questions teachers ask—they are a tactical element in the discussion. *Moves* refer to the kind of information that is contained in the discussion, i.e., it is the meaning of what is said. *Moves* are the elements you arrive at if you do a detailed *content-analysis* of what you want to teach. *Logical operations* are the elements you arrive at if you want to plan what you (the teacher) will *say* when you teach. (Nuthall, personal communication, November 1972)

The task of classifying ventures according to their "overarching content objectives" led the Illinois team ti identify eight different types of ventures: conceptual, causal, reason, evaluative, interpretative, rule, procedural, and particular. The definitions of these different types of ventures are as follows:

> *Causal venture.* The overarching content objective of this type of venture is a cause-effect relationship between particular events or between classes of events. . . .
>
> *Conceptual ventures.* The overarching objective of this type of venture is a set of conditions either governing, or implied by, the use of a term. . . .
>
> *Evaluative ventures.* The objective of this type of venture is a rating of an action, object, event, policy or practice; or a rating of a class of such things with respect to its worth, correctness, and the like. . . .
>
> *Particular ventures.* The particular venture has as its objective a body of information which clarifies or amplifies a specified topic or group of related topics. The central concern . . . is the answering of questions such as "What happened?" "When did it happen?" "What did it do?" "Who or what did it?" or "What is it like?" . . .
>
> *Interpretative ventures.* The objective of this type of venture is the meaning or significance of a set of words or symbols. . . .
>
> *Procedural ventures.* A venture of this type discloses a sequence of actions by which an end may be achieved. . . .
>
> *Reason ventures.* A venture falling into this category discloses the reason or reasons for an action, decision, policy, or practice. As used here, the term "reason" refers to a consideration which leads a person to perform an action or which justifies his performing the action. . . .
>
> *Rule ventures.* The objective of this type of venture is a rule or several related rules. The term "rule" as it is used here refers to conventional ways of doing things and to analytic relationships which may be used to guide actions. . . . A prescripiton stating what action is to be taken to achieve a given end is not a rule. (Smith *et al.*, 1967, pp. 23–37)

In general, moderately high reliability was reported for the task of sorting ventures into these eight classes. However, no agreement was reached on the identification of causal ventures as distinct from reason ventures. Excluding causal ventures, the reliability coefficients obtained were more satisfactory. Apparently, causal and reason ventures were difficult to distinguish from each other, perhaps, as the authors claim, because the two "are not customarily distinguished in the language and are thus easily confused by naive judges" (p. 42).

Once ventures were classified into these eight types, the task became that of analyzing ventures of each type in search of a categorization of their moves. Surprisingly, the codes developed were quite different for each of the eight venture types. Across all types of ventures some 106 subcategories of moves were identified and grouped into 36 major categories. Little discussion was provided for why different systems should have been evolved for the different venture types, or what might be the relationships among the different classifications. Space will not permit presentation of the details of all these moves. Instead, we will focus merely on the types of moves for which findings are shortly to be reported (Box 10.2).

1. Moves within conceptual ventures:
   (a) *Description move:* a description of a characteristic; the listing of the parts that make up a whole
   (b) *Comparative move:* a discussion of similarities and differences
   (c) *Instantial move:* an identification of an instance or example
2. Moves within causal ventures
   (a) *Cause-identification move:* identifying a condition as a cause of a given effect
   (b) *Cause-description move:* identifying, explicating, evidencing, and explaining causes
   (c) *Relational move:* giving examples of causes, generalizing beyond a specific cause-effect relation
3. Moves within reason ventures
   (a) *Action-identifying move:* mention or discussion of some action, practice, decision, or attitude
   (b) *Reason-giving move:* giving factual or motivational reasons for actions
   (c) *Factual-consideration move:* giving information concerning facts assumed to underlie the actor's deciding upon his action
4. Moves within evaluative ventures
   (a) *Identification or value objects or value term or both*
   (b) *Descriptive move:* description of the attributes of the value object
   (c) *Rating move:* application of rating terms to an object
5. Moves within interpretative ventures
   (a) *Citation move:* quotation or reference to part of a text to be interpreted
   (b) *Extrapolation move:* attempts to elicit judgments about events and actions given in a text
   (c) *Factual-elucidation move:* citing the facts as to what took place in a passage of text
6. Moves within rule ventures
   (a) *Range-of-application move:* indications of situations when it is appropriate to resort to the rule
   (b) *Rule-formulation move:* statements which make rules explicit
7. Moves within procedural ventures
   (a) *Problem-centered move:* information about, or analysis of, the problem or situation
   (b) *Performance-centered move:* descriptions of the performance by which the procedure is exercised in the situation or problem
8. Moves within particular ventures
   (a) *Information about the particular move*
   (b) *Relating the particular move to other events*
   (c) *Appraisal of the particular move*

Moves in the Conceptual Venture

All but one of the studies we review in this chapter were field surveys. The one exception consisted of a process-product experiment conducted by Nuthall (1968b) in which various types of *conceptual* ventures were studied for their impact on pupil learning. Since Nuthall's study involved conceptual ventures, we provide some additional details concerning this one type.

In all, three broad categories of moves were identified by Smith *et al.* (1967) for conceptual ventures: *descriptive moves*; *comparative moves*; and *instantial moves*. *Descriptive moves* included such things as a description of a characteristic of the concept and the listing of the parts that make up the concept, for example:

T: The cerebrum. All right, the cerebrum of course is formed in what—what is its form—the cerebrum? What else goes with the cerebral—what?
S: Spheres.
T: Hemispheres. Cerebral hemispheres. In other words it is divided here—a rather deep impression which seems to divide it into two parts and we call them hemispheres. (Smith *et al.*, 1967, p. 63)

Comparative moves include such things as a discussion of the similarities between the concept and some other thing, for example:

T: Now, what is the *shape*—what is the shape of the cerebellum? If you saw it from, say, the back, what would it appear to be like?
S: Well, sort of like the wings on the side of a moth—or a—
T: Yes, go ahead.
S: That's all.
T: It would appear to be sort of like—uh—the wings of a moth or butterfly. (p. 70)

Instantial moves include such things as identification of an instance or example of a concept, for example:

T: (Continuing) The next book that we're going to read, *Babbitt* by Sinclair Lewis, is one of the finest examples of a novel that is satire. (p. 75)

When conceptual ventures were analyzed in terms of these three broad categories of moves they were found by Smith *et al.* to be of seven types. These were:

Type I. Ventures containing only descriptive moves.
Type II. Ventures containing only comparative moves.
Type III. Ventures containing only instantial moves.
Type IV. Ventures containing descriptive and comparative moves.

Type V.   Ventures containing descriptive and instantial moves.
Type VI.   Ventures containing comparative and instantial moves.
Type VII. Ventures containing at least one of each of the three different kinds of moves.

Venture types I, IV, and V were found to be the most common while types II and VI were least common. Type III was common only in English lessons. Thus, descriptive and instantial moves emerged as the most common tactical elements of strategies for the teaching of concepts. Comparative moves were used much less frequently.

As reported in Box 10.2, the study of sequences of moves within conceptual ventures revealed that the most common strategies consisted of

1. sequences of descriptive moves only;
2. alternating sequences of descriptive and instantial moves; and
3. alternating sequences of descriptive and comparative moves.

Other possible strategies, such as a sequence of comparative moves only or an alternating sequence of instantial and comparative moves, occurred infrequently. One general characteristic of conceptual ventures was the tendency for discussions to keep returning to descriptive moves concerned with some single characteristic of the class of things under discussion.

On the basis of findings of the above types, the authors commented:

> Perhaps the most obvious conclusion which can be derived from the analysis of patterns of moves in concept ventures is that not only is the direct description of a characteristic the most common kind of move, but even when other kinds of moves occur, there is a constant returning of the discussion back to this kind of move. It is interesting to note that this pattern has some similarities with the alternation of exposure to examples and discussions of "generalizations" advocated by a number of writers on the basis of experimental investigations of "discovery learning" procedures. . . .
>
> However, what is observed in discussions in concept ventures is more complex than a simple alternation of "rules" (so far as characteristics can be called "rules") and examples. It is an alternation between "rules" and a variety of other kinds of discussion of which description of instances is only a part. (Smith *et al.*, 1967, p. 92)

Classroom Research

Studies reporting findings for strategic sequences are found in Box 10.2. As previously noted, few data were reported for the Taba sequence concepts, and no findings for them are included in the box. The Illinois concept of venture, however, has already generated at least three studies that we know of. The original study (Smith *et al.*, 1967) made use of the same set of transcripts that had formed the data bank for the first Illinois study; and, as in the earlier study, findings were confined primarily to process occurrence. A second application has been made by Zahorik (1970), who reports process-process relations among ventures and his own classification for teacher reactions that we first discussed in Chapter VII.

BOX 10.2   Research Involving Longer Sequence Units

STUDIES REVIEWED

Smith *et al.* (1967)	(Smi67)
Nuthall (1968b)	(Nut68)
Zahorik (1968, 1970)	(Zah68)
Wright and Nuthall (1970)	(W&N70)

INSTRUMENT, METHOD OF GATHERING DATA, CODING SYSTEM, UNIT STUDIED, RELIABILITY

Illinois Strategies Instrument, transcripts, single-facet category system, ventures and moves, moderate reliability (Nut68), (Smi67).

Zahorik Instrument, audiotapes and transcripts, single-facet category system, teacher feedback (reaction) behavior, high reliability (Zah68).

Canterbury Instrument, transcripts, multifacet category system, T and P verbal moves, reliability not reported (W&N70).

DESIGN OF STUDY, SUBJECTS, CONTEXTS

Field Investigations

(Smi67)   14 teachers and pupils, grades IX-XII, several subjects; five lessons for each teacher

(Zah68)   15 teachers and their pupils, grades III and VI; social studies "discussion" lesson based on the same issues in current events per teacher

(W&N70)   17 teachers and pupils, grade III; three nature-study lessons, standardized content; Christchurch (New Zealand)

Process-Product Experiments

(Nut68)   432 pupils, grades X and XI; sociology; six different treatments manipulated with programmed texts

FINDINGS

Process Occurrence

CONCEPTUAL VENTURES

10.2-1   The most common strategies were
  (a)   sequences of descriptive moves only;
  (b)   alternating sequences of descriptive and instantial moves;
  (c)   alternating sequences of descriptive and comparative moves (Smi67).

CAUSAL VENTURES

10.2-2   The most common strategies were
  (a)   sequences of cause-identification moves only;
  (b)   alternating sequences of cause-identification and cause-description moves;
  (c)   alternating sequences of cause-identification and relational moves (Smi67).

Box 10.2 (continued)

REASON VENTURES

10.2-3   The most common strategy was
    (a)   identification of the action followed by reason giving followed by factual considerations (Smi67).

EVALUATIVE VENTURES

10.2-4   The most common strategy was
    (a)   an identification of the object to be evaluated followed by an alternating sequence of description and rating moves (Smi67).

INTERPRETATIVE VENTURES

10.2-5   The most common strategies were
    (a)   a sequence of citation moves followed by a sequence of extrapolation moves;
    (b)   a sequence of factual elucidation moves followed by a sequence of extrapolation moves (Smi67).

RULE VENTURES

10.2-6   The most common strategy was
    (a)   a sequence of range-of-application moves followed by a sequence of rule-formulation moves (Smi67).

PROCEDURAL VENTURES

10.2-7   The most common strategy was
    (a)   an alternating sequence of problem-centered moves and performance-centered moves (Smi67).

PARTICULAR VENTURES

10.2-8   The most common strategy was
    (a)   a sequence of moves containing information about the nature of the particular, followed by a sequence of moves relating the particular to other events, followed by a sequence of moves appraising the particular with a tendency to return to moves of the first type throughout the venture (Smi67).

Context-Process Relationships

10.2-9   *Subject matter* affects *frequencies of venture types.* (See Table 10.1 for details.) (Smi67).

Presage-Process Relationships

None reported.

Process-Process Relationships

10.1-10   *Phase of venture* affects *type of teacher reaction* (to pupil responses). During the *medial* phase *response-development solicitation* and *different-topic lesson progression* are likely reactions. During the *terminal* phase *simple praise confirmation* and *positive-answer repetition* become more likely (Zah68).

10.2-11   *Type of venture* affects *type of medial teacher reactions* (to pupil responses). The following *medial* reactions are likely:
    for *casual, reason,* and *informatory* ventures—*response-development solicitation;*
    for *conceptual* ventures—*positive-answer repetition.*
    (Terminal reactions are less affected by venture type.) (Zah68).

10.2-12 *Phase of lesson* affects *type of teacher reaction* (to pupil responses). *Introductory phase* generates *positive-answer repetition, lesson progression—different topic,* and *response development. Developmntal phase* exhibits *simple praise—confirmation* and *solicitation repetition—several answers* (Zah68).

Process-Product Relationships

10.2-13 *Ventures containing descriptive and instantial moves* are more effective than *ventures containing comparative moves* in inducing *pupil concept learning* (Nut68)E.*

10.2-14 *Ventures containing instantial moves* are more effective for *pupils with a high level of related prior knowledge* in inducing *pupil concept learning* than they are for pupils with a low level of related prior knowledge (Nut68)E.

10.2-15 *Teacher use of lesson-terminal summaries* co-varies with *pupil achievement.* (Teacher use of lesson-initiatory recapitulation is not related to pupil achievement.) (W&N70).

* Findings generated experimentally are indicated with an E.

The third application of the venture notion appears in the carefully designed experiment that was conducted by Nuthall (1968b). This project was designed to investigate the effectiveness of four alternative strategies for the teaching of two sociological concepts to high school pupils. The four strategies selected for research were (1) a sequence consisting only of descriptive moves, (2) an alternating sequence of descriptive and instantial moves, (3) an alternating sequence of descriptive and comparative moves, and (4) an alternating sequence of comparative and instantial moves. Each strategy was composed of six moves corresponding with six propositions related to each concept, and the strategies were presented in the form of programmed texts to 432 pupils in grades X and XI of five high schools representing a cross section of different types of schools in Illinois. Pupils were tested for prior knowledge in terms and concepts in related areas, and four weeks after the completion of the programmed texts they were given a criterion test to measure the learning of concepts included in the experiment.

One study is also included in Box 10.2 because it reports findings for the sequence of events within the *lesson*—which is, after all, a larger strategic unit. This is (again) the Zahorik study. Finally, Wright and Nuthall (1970) also appear in Box 10.2 because one of their findings concerns strategic sequencing.

Process-occurrence findings from Box 10.2 are confined to a listing of the common strategies found by the Illinois group to appear within each venture type. Details of these may be taken from Findings 10.2-1 through 10.2-8. As an exercise readers may wish to speculate as to which of these findings are generated by theories of instruction, which by Rules of the

Table 10.1   Approximate Percentage Frequencies of Occurrence of
Types of Ventures Within Subject Areas

	Science (%)	Geometry (%)	History/ Social Studies (%)	English (%)
Conceptual	64	26	13	15
Causal	19	0	16	1
Reason	0	0	12	3
Evaluative	2	0	8	11
Interpretative	0	0	2	43
Rule	1	53	1	14
Procedural	7	21	0	0
Particular (extirates)	7	0	48	13
Total	100	100	100	100

Adapted from Smith et al., 1967.

Classroom Game, and which from other causes. Unfortunately, to date we have little additional information as to the significance of these occurrences.

Finding 10.2-9 reports that subject matter affects the frequencies of venture types in the classroom. Details of this finding are found in Table 10.1. In general, science lessons appear to emphasize conceptual ventures; geometry seems to place stress upon rule ventures; history and social science feature particular ventures; while in English the rates of occurrence appear particularly high for interpretative ventures. We suspect that it would be hazardous to generalize the particulars of this table beyond the sample of lessons studied in the Illinois research. However, the suggestion that emphasis on "content objective" is related to subject matter is surely reasonable, given the differences in the structure of knowledge for, let us say, English literature and physics. The frequencies with which conceptual ventures occur across subject boundaries are also worthy of note. At the senior secondary level it would appear that considerable attention needs to be given to concepts in discussion, whatever the subject.

Zahorik reports two different findings for the relationship between ventures and teacher reactions to pupil responses. On the one hand, Zahorik found that type of teacher reaction varied depending on whether ventures were "in process," that is, in the medial phase, or were terminating. Not surprisingly, when ventures were coming to a conclusion teachers were more likely simply to praise or to repeat the answer, while medial reactions were more likely to involve solicitations for response development, or a different topic. Again, type of venture was found to affect the teacher reaction, although this effect was more likely during the medial than terminal phase of the venture. Only four types of ventures were examined by Zahorik, but conceptual ventures were found more likely to exhibit the repetition of positive answers, while causal, reason, and informatory ventures featured solicitations for response development.

Zahorik also reports that phase of the lesson affects teacher reactions. Most of these findings parallel those for the phases of ventures, suggesting that in this respect at least the venture is similar to the lesson as a strategic unit.

When we turn to process-product findings we discover that Wright and Nuthall report that teachers who use summaries at the end of their lessons are more effective than those who do not or who use recapitulation at the beginning of the lesson. This finding parallels one reported for episodes in Box 10.1.

In addition, Nuthall found that strategies involving descriptive and instantial moves were more effective than those involving comparative moves. Moreover, instantial moves were found more effective for pupils with a high level of prior knowledge. These suggested to Nuthall that "elements within a teaching strategy interact with each other to produce a unified effect which, in turn, interacts with the knowledge a student already possesses" (Nuthall, 1968b, p. 582).

CONCLUSION

For many reasons the authors find themselves less satisfied with the presentation of this chapter than with any other. On the one hand it appears to us that any meaningful analysis of teaching *must* involve sequential elements. Indeed, perhaps the greatest single flaw in much of the research we have reviewed is the persistent assumption that appears to underlie much of it—that teaching can somehow be reduced to a scalar value that can be indicated by a frequency of occurrence for some teaching behavior. We suspect, with Taba, that this simply is not true. Rather, effective teaching must consist of sequences of presentations that are planned carefully and conducted sensitively. Moreover, we find the sequential concepts we have reviewed to be insightful, exciting, suggestive—but.

On the other hand most of the research on sequential notions is yet nascent, few findings are reported for even those concepts that have been subjected to research, many of the most interesting ideas have simply not been researched at all, and even the clearest discussions of sequence are couched in murky, intuitive, analogistic phrases suggesting that investigators are still really groping toward solutions to these complex problems. Thus, we can find relatively little evidence to back up our belief that the real breakthroughs in research on teaching should involve sequence.

We also suspect that the Illinois group are on the right track in stressing that smaller units of sequence must be conceived to form parts of larger sequences. We presume that they have not yet found the key to unlocking the exact relationship between these two, and that the key might ultimately be a linguistic one. However, these speculations properly belong in Chapter XII.

RECOMMENDED ADDITIONAL READING

Bellack, A. A., Kliebard, H. M., Hyman, R. T., and Smith, F. L., Jr. *The Language of the Classroom*. New York: Teachers College Press, 1966.

Most relevant to this chapter is the concept of "teaching cycle." Types and incidence of teaching cycles are fully reported and discussed. Many ideas for further research emerge from the discussion.

Lundgren, U. P. *Frame Factors and the Teaching Process*. Stockholm, Sweden: Almqvist & Wiksell, 1972.

An application of Bellack's concept of "teaching cycle" to Swedish classrooms. Relationship between teaching cycles and a variety of other variables are explored. A grand example of insightful research.

Nuthall, G. A., and Lawrence, P. J. *Thinking in the Classroom*. Wellington, New Zealand: New Zealand Council for Educational Research, 1965.

Contains an application of the Illinois logic categories to New Zealand classrooms. A careful diagrammatic approach to the sequential analysis of verbal moves is included. Full of insights pursued in subsequent research at the University of Canterbury.

Smith, B. O., Meux, M., Coombs, J., Nuthall, G., and Precians, R. *A Study of the Strategies of Teaching*. Urbana, Ill.: University of Illinois Press, 1967.

Probably the most sophisticated and complex attempt to analyze sequential patterns in the cognitive domain. Not recommended as light reading but as a challenge to the serious student. Probably many years in advance of its time.

Taba, H. *Teaching Strategies and Cognitive Functioning in Elementary School Children*. Co-operative Research Project No. 2402, U.S. Office of Education. San Francisco State College, 1966.

The concepts of "complex chains of reasoning" and "teaching modules" are presented in this report. Attempts at definition and analysis are primitive and yet suggestive. Could well provide a stimulus for further research.

Taba, H., Levine, S., and Elzey, F. F. *Thinking in Elementary School Children*. Co-operative Research Project No. 1574, U.S. Office of Education, San Francisco State College, 1964.

Of special interest to this chapter are attempts to trace diagrammatically sequences of "pedagogical functions" in relation to thought levels. Few findings are reported for these sequences but many implications for the analysis of teaching follow.

THREE
PUTTING IT ALL TOGETHER

XI
FINDINGS FOR TEACHERS

By now the sensitive reader is bound to have some feeling of being overwhelmed by classroom research. Hundreds of studies have been reviewed, and even more findings have been reported for them. Such numbers would have been difficult enough to handle had these studies fallen into a single research tradition. But they obviously represented a variety of traditions, concepts, approaches, and methods for the study of teaching. Moreover, the research enterprise has reflected limitations of design, instrumentation, samples, and methods of gathering and interpreting data —as a result of which we have felt constrained to question claims that were made in several research traditions for the meaning and applicability of their findings. But surely this research has produced more than massive confusion and unwarranted generalization. What then do we now know about teaching that we did not know two decades ago?

This chapter is the first of two in which we attempt to put together our conclusions concerning the field of research on teaching up to the early 1970s. In it we summarize and interpret findings concerning teaching that are likely to be of interest to teachers and other educators. The chapter has four sections. The first considers the assumptions we must make when we conclude that a "finding" has been made concerning teaching. In the second findings are summarized for major process variables concerned with teaching. The third section provides a brief, interpretative discussion of findings and their limitations. The fourth considers implications of findings for developing empirically based theories of teaching. As we review findings readers will be reminded again of the limitations of the research conducted to date. Nevertheless, the burden of this chapter is to present the authors' best guess as to the state of our knowledge concerning teaching, based on observational studies of teaching conducted to date.

The next and last chapter of the book concerns the state of the art in research on teaching. In it we make recommendations for those who would join us and others in the exciting conduct of empirical research on the processes of instruction.

ASSUMPTIONS AND THE
NATURE OF FINDINGS

The readers, the authors, indeed all educators, would like to learn that definitive knowledge had been developed from research on teaching that could be applied for the improvement of education. Instead, much of the knowledge yet developed must be considered *tentative*. Let us see why this is so, and what we can make out of this as yet tentative knowledge.

What is meant when we presume to have "discovered" useful knowledge in scientific research? What does it take before one is willing to apply in the real world a "finding" that has been unearthed through empirical investigation—whether it be in chemistry, physics, or research on teaching? Let us pretend that we are managers of a chemical firm engaged in the manufacture of plastics. One of our researchers claims to have discovered a more efficient process for making a given type of plastic, and we are considering whether to convert our operations to his process. What would we want to know before making this decision?

One of the first things, of course, would be knowledge of the concepts, used by the researcher and assurance that those concepts were meaningful and had been detected in his research through instruments that were valid and reliable. Moreover, the researcher should have used valid designs in his studies, being careful to keep contaminants out of his laboratory. We would also want to know that the effect he claimed was a strong one, that it was presumably independent of associated events, and that the investigator had ascertained that the variables he thought were causing his effect were actually causative. Moreover, to apply his findings we would want to know over what range of contexts—such as variations in temperature, pressure, or catalysts—the effect was likely to take place. And if these were not problems enough, in the long run we would also want to know *why* the process worked. This means we would like to see some sort of a comprehensible theory that tied the new effect into a body of knowledge.

So it is with teaching—except that the questions are more difficult to answer. Let us assume that we were an educational administrator interested in improving pupil achievement. Some investigator claims to have established a relationship between an observed teaching variable (say *teacher warmth*) and a pupil product variable (*pupil achievement*). To take action in our schools, based on these findings, we would want to know:

> that the concepts used in the finding are meaningful, and that they had been measured with instruments that were valid and reliable;
> that the studies reporting the finding had used valid, uncontaminated designs;
> that the effect claimed was strong, that it was independent of other effects, and that the independent variable claimed for it was truly independent;
> that the effect applied over a wide range of teaching contexts, or if not, to what range it was limited; and finally
> that we understood why the effect took place.

As readers are by now aware, contemporary teaching research meets only some of these five concerns. Let us consider the general status of research on teaching in terms of these concerns to see what we may reasonably expect to conclude from that research.

Literally scores of concepts have now been explored in research on teaching, together with more than a hundred different instruments for their measurement. At the same time, not all instruments used in this field are equally useful. As we know, some instruments suffer from unreliability while others are probably invalid because they are composed of categorical systems that were treated by investigators as mutually exclusive even though they did not form a facet. As a result, some of the concepts developed and used in this research effort are probably not useful. We shall have to sort out the conceptual wheat from the chaff in our review.

At least minor problems have also appeared in most study designs used in teaching research. As we know, some studies have chosen to apply questionable methods (such as the inappropriate use of live observation), have misapplied statistics to field data or have used contaminated manipulations in experimental studies, or have jumped to conclusions that were not warranted in interpreting their data. Nearly all studies, in addition, suffer from small samples that were chosen in a nonrandom manner. Again, this field depends on observation of classroom events for its basic data, and classroom participants may have behaved in ways that were not characteristic because of that awareness. At present we have little ability to estimate the biases introduced into findings because of these latter problems, but those engaged in teaching research presume they are small. Most studies of teaching, then, exhibit at least some design faults. When studies appear that have exceptionally good or poor designs, we should note these facts and use them to strengthen or discount our belief in their findings.

More substantial problems appear for our third concern. Most studies of teaching constitute simple field surveys whose findings report merely that a relationship has, or has not, been obtained between a teaching variable and some other. Only a minority of studies report the strength of that relationship, and such reports are subject to error (see the Appendix). But few studies provide information showing that the relationship is independent of other effects in teaching. To establish definitive information concerning strength and independence of findings requires multivariate field research, and yet multivariate designs have only rarely appeared in teaching research to date. In addition, field surveys cannot tell us whether a given relationship is or is not a causative one. To do this latter requires experiments, and only a minority of findings suggested in field research has yet been subjected to experimental test. In sum, most findings from this field must presently be presumed tentative: because we are not sure how strong they are, because we do not know whether they are independent of other effects, or because they have not yet been validated experimentally. When exceptions to these generalizations appear, we should note them, since they will increase our acceptance of findings.

Even if the above problems were met, contemporary teaching research would still face a contextual challenge. As we know, a finding should be considered valid only to the extent that we know the range of its application. Normally this information may be provided in either of two ways. In some cases it is possible to do definitive field research in which a given relationship is examined across a wide range of contexts. In others this is not feasible, and we judge a finding valid only to the extent that it has been tested by various investigators in different contexts. Both patterns of validation may be observed in teaching research. Unfortunately, however, those findings most likely to have been replicated to date seem to have come from studies with the weakest instruments and designs (see Boxes 5.2, 5.3, 5.4, 5.5, 6.1, and 6.3). Studies involving stronger instruments and designs, particularly those involving videotape instrumentation and contextual variation, have generally not yet been replicated. In general, then, findings from this field have questionable validity due to inadequate information concerning their contextualization and replicability. This does not mean they are invalid, of course, but rather that we should suspend our final judgment about them pending additional research.

The problem of context can also be viewed in a slightly different light. As we know, most of the research in this field has been based on samples of traditional, single-subject lessons that are taught by female teachers to white, middle-class, suburban American pupils of but a single grade level. To what extent do findings from such samples represent classrooms in general, and to what extent do they represent merely the culture of the white, middle-class, suburban American school? At present we simply do not know the answer to this question. Numerous studies have suggested differences in the practices of teaching across context boundaries, and a few studies have begun to take up the effects of context on the relationship between teaching and presage, context, or product variables. Most researchers assume that their findings will generalize to a broad range of classrooms, and surely many will. Moreover, throughout the text the authors have gone along with researchers and have worded findings so as to imply generalization, except when contradicting information was known. But not all findings will generalize (see, for example, Brophy and Evertson, 1973), and once again we urge the suspension of final judgment pending additional research.

Finally, findings from research on teaching become believable to the extent that they are imbedded within explanatory theories. As we know, many studies in this field were generated by simple theories, if not *Commitments*, concerned with the improvement of classroom education. Most of these notions have *not* been well supported by the research that was designed to validate them. But what of the positive findings advanced in various studies—have these yet been integrated into empirically based theories of teaching? In general, no. Most positive findings for the field remain unintegrated, and the stating of empirically based theories for teaching appears to lie mainly in the future, although one may hope that future may not be too distant.

In summary, then, findings from research on teaching must currently be considered tentative on various grounds. This does not mean that findings in this field are invalid. On the contrary, we suspect that the majority will be confirmed in subsequent research. We ask merely that readers join us in suspending their final judgments in the matter. In the meantime, this field has by now generated a truly fascinating array of tentative findings. Let us now review these and some of their more interesting implications for educators.

FINDINGS FOR PROCESS VARIABLES

For convenience our summary is organized in terms of the several research traditions that were reviewed. The assumptions, concepts, and methods of each tradition are first briefly discussed. Then findings are presented for each of the major process variables from that tradition for which results from our earlier research box summaries are collated and rephrased so as to indicate generalizations concerning teaching. Finally, a short commentary on each research tradition is given.

Findings for Climate and Directiveness

The first research tradition reviewed is that associated with the Flanders Interaction Analysis Categories (FIAC) system and its related instruments (see Chapter V and the first section of Chapter VI). As readers will recall, this research tradition appears to reflect some of the major tenets of progressive education, democratic ideology, and group dynamics. Traditional classroom teaching is assumed to be weak because it is cold and authoritarian. On the one hand, teachers are presumed to conduct classrooms in a manner that lacks warmth and responsiveness. On the other, traditional teaching is also presumed to be authoritarian and to make inadequate provision for individualism and the practices of democracy. These assumptions suggest a *Commitment*—that to improve teaching it is necessary to encourage greater warmth on the part of the teacher as well as more classroom democracy and pupil initiative. Much of the research within this tradition appears to reflect this *Commitment*.

This research tradition has been blessed by a great deal of research effort, by the publication of many studies, and by various research instruments. As we have seen, many of the latter have appeared to stem from the pioneering work of H. H. Anderson and Withall. The instrument most often used, however, has been the FIAC system. Not only has this instrument itself been used in many studies but a number of other instruments have also been developed from it. In general, most of these instruments were designed for use in live observation, asked observer to make judgments for time intervals, and provided but a single facet of judgmental categories wherein the categories were presumed to form a mutually exclusive set. These are simple instruments that may be adopted to teacher training as well as to research, hence a second *Commitment:* to demonstrate that teaching can be improved by use of training programs that involve FIAC or related instruments.

Two kinds of findings have been reported for FIAC and its related instruments. On the one hand, it has been assumed by many of the investigators that these instruments were capable of generating a wholistic score that would indicate how warm and democratic (versus cold and authoritarian) the classroom was. We have termed this wholistic dimension "indirectness," although a number of different terms have been applied to it by other investigators. In general, scores indicating "indirectness" were obtained by summing categorical scores from the observational instruments used.

On the other hand, many studies have also reported scores for individual categories of their instruments. We have also reviewed a number of these latter, as they pertain to issues of classroom climate and directiveness. The variables studied have included *teacher praise* (or approval), *teacher acceptance of pupils' ideas,* and *teacher criticism* (or disapproval)—which we have classified as climate variables; and *teacher talk, teacher questions, teacher lecturing, teacher giving directions, pupil talk, pupil initiation, pupil responding,* and *silence and confusion*—which we have associated with directiveness. In general, each of these latter variables concerns a proportionate amount of the phenomenon indicated during the lesson studied. For example, a high score in *pupil talk* indicates that during the lesson studied pupils were found to talk more and other phenomena to occur less.

Let us now consider findings for these several variables.

"Indirectness"   Findings for "indirectness" are indicated in Figure 11.1.[1] Let us consider first those findings concerned with the *occurrence* of "indirectness." In support of the *Commitment* it would appear well established that most classroom teaching is "direct." Moreover, "indirect" teaching would appear likely with pupils of higher social class and greater intelligence, and to be more likely in reading lessons and where computers are used to assist instruction. In addition, "indirectness" is reported to be associated with higher teacher scores on the NTE history and philosophy exam-

---

[1] Figure 11.1 is the first of several figures having a common format. Seven columns are provided in these figures. The column on the left names the process variables for which findings are being summarized and informs the reader from which research box findings are taken. Each of the other columns lists a class of findings taken from the box. Note that process-product findings are differentiated into those that were generated in field surveys and those stemming from experiments. Following each finding a number appears in parentheses. This number indicates the number of independent studies reporting the finding. Findings that are in conflict are bracketed together.

inations, greater teacher ego strength, and lack of teacher authoritarianism. Finally, most, but not all, experimental studies indicate that it *is* possible to train teachers to perform in a more "indirect" manner with educational programs that involve exposure to FIAC or related instruments.

Among findings concerned with the *effects* of "indirectness" it would also appear established that "indirectness" is associated with more pupil talk and more pupil initiations. Finally, we have some evidence suggesting

FIGURE 11.1 **Findings for teacher "indirectness." (Numbers in parentheses indicate number of studies on which finding is based. Braces group together findings that are in conflict.)**

Process variable considered	Process Occurrence	Context-Process	Presage-Process	Process-Process	Process-Product Field Survey	Process-Product Experimental
					Process variable associated with:	Process variable induces:
Teacher "Indirectness"	Most teaching is: "Direct" (11)	Process variable associated with: Higher social class of pupils (1) Higher intelligence of pupils (1) Unrelated to use of computer-assisted instruction (1) Reading lessons (1)	Process variable associated with: Ratings by supervisors as "superior" (1) Unrelated to ratings by supervisor (1) Higher scores on NTE history and philosophy examinations (1) Sex of teacher (males more "indirect") (1) Unrelated to sex of teacher (1) Higher scores on MTAI (2) Unrelated to scores on MTAI (2) Higher scores on ego strength (MMPI) (1) Lower scores on authoritarianism (F scale) (1) Unrelated to scores on EPPS (1) More humanistic (and less custodial) attitudes toward pupils (1) Unrelated to humanistic and custodial attitudes toward pupils (1) Higher teacher expectations for pupil achievement (1) Unrelated to teacher expectations for pupil achievement (4) -------------- Experimental training using FIAC or other such instruments (9) Experimental training produced no difference (1) Experimental training produced short-term increase, long-term decrease (1)	Process variable associated with: More pupil talk (3) More pupil responses (1) Unrelated to pupil responses (1) Less pupil responses (2) More pupil initiations (5) Higher cognitive levels of discourse (2) Unrelated to cognitive levels of discourse (1)	Greater pupil achievement (10) Unrelated to pupil achievement (15) Curvilinear or complex relationships with pupil achievement (3) More positive pupil attitudes (8) Unrelated to pupil attitudes (3) Greater pupil achievement motivation (1) Greater pupil creativity (1) Lower pupil anxiety (1)	Unrelated to pupil achievement (5) Curvilinear or complex relationships with pupil achievement (3) More positive pupil attitudes (1) Unrelated to pupil attitudes (2)

× 5.2)

that greater pupil achievement motivation, greater pupil creativity, and lower pupil anxiety are all associated with "indirectness," although these findings all came from field surveys and may not have indicated a cause-and-effect relationship.

Were these all of the findings reported, "indirectness" would surely have to be concluded a good thing in the classroom. However, from here on the picture becomes muddy. Taking first the rest of the presage-process findings, we learn that "indirectness" is and is not related to high ratings by teachers' supervisors, sex of the teacher, teacher scores on the MTAI, teacher attitudes toward pupils, and teacher expectations for pupil achievement. These findings might have been considered curiosities only except for the equally muddled findings concerned with process and product effects of "indirectness." Among others, we learn that "indirectness" is and is not associated with more pupil responses, the cognitive level of classroom discourse, greater pupil achievement, and more positive pupil attitudes. Of particular interest are the experimental findings concerning the relationship between "indirectness" and pupil achievement. Most of these latter show no relationship, the rest only curvilinear or complex relationships.

Unfortunately for the Commitment, then, we cannot conclude that "indirectness" has the salubrious effects claimed, nor will training teachers to be "indirect" have the positive results hoped for by those who have pursued this line of investigation. What can be made of these findings? At least two interpretations seem possible to us. One is that "indirectness" has a variety of effects, depending on contextual conditions. The other is that "indirectness" is simply not a unitary phenomenon at all and should be abandoned as a variable. Of these two interpretations the latter seems the more likely. Little evidence has been advanced to suggest contextual conditions under which "indirectness" would have differential effects. In addition, as we have suggested, it appears that "indirectness" has the effect of eliding the concepts of classroom climate and classroom directiveness. Our conclusion, then, is that this variable should be abandoned and that teachers should cease to use it in conceptualizing their classroom performances in the future.

Teacher praise (or approval) Let us turn next to those variables more clearly associated with classroom climate (see Figure 11.2). The first of these, *teacher praise*, or approval, is presumed by those holding the Commitment to be in short supply in traditional classrooms. Since teacher praise is presumed to be a good thing, to increase it will have good effects on pupil morale and achievements. Let us look at the evidence.

In support of the Commitment traditional teaching *is* found to be short on praise. Further, teacher praise is found to be associated with positive attitudes held by teachers for pupils (and with white pupils!), with positive attitudes toward the class as a whole, with prior pupil achievement, and with higher teacher expectations for pupils' occupational status.

(Apparently teachers are more likely to praise those pupils whom they like and admire.) Finally, praise is reported to be associated with more positive pupil self-concepts.

So far so good, but from here on the picture again clouds. Incidence of teacher praise is found and is not found to relate to sex of pupils, social class of school, and teacher expectations for pupil achievement. Experi-

FIGURE 11.2   Findings for climate variables.

Process Variable Considered	*Process Occurrence*	*Context-Process*	*Presage-Process*	*Process-Process*	*Process-Product*	
	Most teaching is:	Process variable associated with:	Process variable associated with:	Process variable associated with:	*Field Survey* Process variable associated with:	*Experimental* Process variable induces:
Teacher Praise (or Approval)	Short on praise (10)	Sex of pupil (boys receive more praise) (5) Unrelated to sex of pupils (4)	Positive attitudes toward pupil (3) Positive attitudes toward class (1)		Greater pupil achievement (3) Unrelated to pupil achievement (11)	Curvilinear or complex relationships with pupil achievement (1)
		Lower-class schools (1) Unrelated to social class of school (1) White pupils (1) Prior pupil achievement (1)	Unrelated to dogmatism (2) Higher teacher expectations for pupil achievement (4) Unrelated to teacher expectations for pupil achievement (5) Lower teacher expectations for pupil achievement (2) Curvilinear or complex relationships with expectations for pupil achievement (1)		More positive pupil attitudes (1) Unrelated to pupil attitudes (4) More positive pupil self-concepts(1) Lower pupil non-verbal creativity (1)	
			Unrelated to teacher expectations for pupil behavior (1) Higher teacher expectations for pupil's future occupational status (1)			
(Box 5.3)			Experimental training using FIAC or other such instruments (1) Experimental training produced no difference(1) Experimental training produced short-term increase, long-term decrease (1)			
Teacher Acceptance of Pupils' Ideas	Short on acceptance of pupils' ideas (9)	Higher scores on MTAI (1) Higher concern for pupils (1) Humanistic rather than custodial attitudes toward pupils (1)		More pupil initiations (1)	Greater pupil achievement (1) Unrelated to pupil achievement (6) More positive pupil attitudes (3) Unrelated to pupil attitudes (3)	Curvilinear or complex relationships with pupil achievement (1)
(Box 5.4)			Experimental training in FIAC, etc. (7) Experimental training produced no difference (2)		Lower pupil anxiety (1) Greater pupil creativity (1)	

Figure 11.2 (cont.)

Process Variable Considered	Process Occurrence	Context-Process	Presage-Process	Process-Process	Process-Product	
					Field Survey	Experimental
	Most teaching is:	Process variable associated with:	Process variable associated with:	Process variable associated with:	Process variable associated with:	Process variable induces:
Teacher Criticism (or Disapproval)	Short on criticism (10)	Sex of pupil (boys receive more criticism) (9) Unrelated to sex of pupils (1) Lower grade levels (1) Subjects other than social studies (2) Lower-class schools (1) Unrelated to social class of school (1) Black pupils (1)	Higher scores on NTE English A and Literature examinations (1) Unrelated to scores on MTAI (2) Greater anxiety and hypochondriasis (1) Greater dogmatism (Rokeach scale) (1) Unrelated to dogmatism (Rokeach scale) (1) Greater rejection of pupils (2) Lower indifference to pupils (1) Lower teacher expectations for pupil achievement (4) Unrelated to teacher expectations for pupil achievement (7) Curvilinear or complex relationships with expectations for pupil achievement (1) Lower teacher expectations for pupils' future occupational status (1) Lower expectations for female pupils' obedience and cooperativeness (1) Higher expectations for female pupils' destructiveness (1) ----------------- Experimental training in FIAC, etc. (lowers criticism) (2) Experimental training produced no difference (3) Experimental training produced no short-term change but decreased criticism in the long run (1)	Unrelated to teacher use of praise and acceptance of pupils' ideas (2)	Lower pupil achievement (6) Unrelated to pupil achievement (7) Curvilinear or complex relationships with pupil achievement (1) More negative pupil attitudes (2) Unrelated to pupil attitudes (3) Lower pupil achievement motivation (1) Higher pupil fear of failure (1) Lower pupil self-concept (1) Greater pupil dependency (1) Lower pupil anxiety (1)	

(Box 5.5)

mental studies wherein teachers were exposed to FIAC or related instruments have also produced ambiguous effects with regard to praise. Finally, the majority of studies have found praise unrelated to pupil achievement and pupil attitudes, while one study found it associated with *lower* pupil nonverbal creativity. On the basis of evidence, then, it would appear that unmitigated teacher praise, or approval, is *not* a particularly good thing to encourage in teachers. Even if teachers can be taught to deliver more praise

—and the evidence for this assertion is weak—simply increasing the amount of praise delivered in the classroom is unlikely to have desirable effects.[2]

Teacher acceptance of pupils' ideas The second variable associated with classroom climate is *teacher acceptance of pupils' ideas.* According to the *Commitment*, traditional classrooms will be short on teacher acceptance, and good effects can be obtained by increasing this feature of teaching.

Once again, some support for the *Commitment* appears in the data. Classrooms *are* found to be short on teacher acceptance. Teacher acceptance is also found to be associated with higher scores on the MTAI, with higher concern for pupils, and with humanistic attitudes toward pupils. In addition, teacher acceptance is associated with more pupil initiations in the classroom, lower pupil anxiety, and greater pupil creativity. Finally, and in contrast with findings for teacher praise, most of the experimental studies of teacher-training programs involving FIAC or other such instruments show that greater teacher acceptance *can* be induced.

All of this sounds promising—but once again there are flies in the ointment. Unfortunately, the majority of studies have shown teacher acceptance to be unrelated to pupil achievement, while studies of pupil attitudes have split equally between those that did and did not show positive effects. We must conclude, then, that although teachers can be trained to provide greater acceptance of pupils' ideas, only poor evidence has yet been advanced to indicate pupils would benefit if this were done. Teacher acceptance also seems to be a weak variable.[3]

Teacher criticism (or disapproval) Interestingly, more findings are available for *teacher criticism,* or disapproval, than for either teacher praise or teacher acceptance. According to the *Commitment*, teacher criticism will be a bad thing in the classroom; too much criticism will be present, and positive effects in pupils will be noted when criticism is reduced.

Unfortunately for the *Commitment*, evidence submitted suggests that teacher criticism is *also* in short supply in the classroom. If we take this finding seriously, the rest of the findings in Figure 11.2 are moot, since criticism will not occur with sufficient frequency to matter. But let us assume that a little criticism goes a long way, and though teacher criticism may occur infrequently in the traditional classroom, it should be stamped out completely. What then do we know about the concomitants and effects of criticism? All sorts of things, actually.

We learn that criticism is more likely to be given to boys than to girls, to be associated with lower grade levels, to appear in subjects other than social studies, and to be given to black pupils(!). In addition, criticism is

[2] Contrast this finding with that reported for praise as a positive reinforcer (see Figure 11.5). For those interested in comparing the results of independent reviews, Rosenshine (1971) also concludes that results for praise are "inconsistent" (p. 69).
[3] Rosenshine (1971) concludes that acceptance has "not been shown to be a significant predictor of student achievement" (p. 71) but suggests additional research be conducted on the variable.

associated with higher scores on NTE English A and literature examinations, greater anxiety and hypochondriasis, greater rejection of pupils, greater indifference to pupils, lower teacher expectations for pupils' future occupational status, and higher expectations for female pupils' obedience and cooperativeness (and lower expectations for female pupils' destructiveness). It is *not* found associated with MTAI scores or with the incidence of teacher praise.or teacher acceptance, and findings for relationships with social class of school, teacher dogmatism, and teacher expectations for pupil achievement are ambiguous. Finally, and of greater significance for the *Commitment,* teacher criticism is found associated with lower pupil achievement motivation, higher pupil fear of failure, lower pupil self-concept, greater pupil dependency, and lower pupil anxiety(!). So far teacher criticism sounds like the most promising variable of those associated with classroom climate.

But once again there are problems. For one, the evidence that teacher criticism can be lowered with experimental training involving FIAC or other such instruments is spotty and certainly less strong than the evidence for teacher acceptance. For another, once again we must contend with the annoying problem of contradictory evidence concerning pupil achievement and pupil attitudes. Some studies show these variables to be related to teacher criticism, others do not.

On balance, we suspect that there is rather more evidence concerning *teacher criticism* than for either of the other two climate variables. If we may differentiate between classrooms which are *syrupy* (those high on teacher praise), *responsive* (those high on teacher acceptance), and *warm* (those low on teacher criticism), it would appear that the latter are the more likely to have effects. Our tentative conclusion, then, is that teacher criticism should be avoided. (Unfortunately for this recommendation, it would appear that training programs featuring FIAC or related instruments are not particularly effective in training teachers in this avoidance.)[4]

Teacher talk   We now turn to one of those variables associated with directiveness of the classroom, *teacher talk* (see Figure 11.3). According to the *Commitment,* classrooms should be long on teacher talk, and good effects should be accomplished by reducing the scope of this phenomenon.

Evidence is impressive that classrooms feature a lot of teacher talk. (Numerous studies from other research traditions have also reported the finding that teachers talk a lot.) In addition, we learn that teachers who talk a lot are less likely to be given ratings as "superior teachers" and that talking is more likely in student teachers who lack experience. However. evidence that teacher talk produces negative results is weak. A few studies show positive or negative relationships with pupil achievement and attitudes; the majority show nil effects. In addition, it would appear that training with FIAC or related instruments is not particularly likely to reduce the amount

---

[4] Rosenshine (1971) concludes that "teachers who use a great deal of criticism appear consistently to have classes who achieve less in most subject areas" (p. 61).

of teacher talk. On evidence, then, teacher talk appears a weak variable, and reducing teacher talk *per se* would appear an unlikely prospect for the improvement of teaching.[5]

Teacher questions In contrast with teacher talk the asking of *teacher questions* should presumably be a good thing in classrooms, according to the *Commitment*. After all, the more one asks questions, the more pupils are encouraged to think and to respond.

Unfortunately, the evidence supporting this argument is no stronger for teacher questions than that supporting the argument for teacher talk. We learn that teacher questions are likely to be present in the typical classroom of the order of one fifth of the time and that questions are more likely to be asked at the lower grade levels. (Is this "too few" or "too many" questions? The *Commitment* does not provide us an answer to this question.) Beyond these simple findings the evidence is ambiguous, to say the least. Teacher questions either are or are not more likely to be directed to boys; either can or cannot be induced through appropriate training programs; either are or are not associated with greater pupil achievement; either are or are not associated with more positive pupil attitudes. Teacher questions also appears a weak variable, then, and we can see little evidence in these findings to recommend that teachers either increase or decrease their asking of questions.

Teacher lecturing According to the *Commitment*, classrooms suffer from too much *teacher lecturing*. Classrooms dominated by lecturing will be autocratic places in which the individual pupil has but little opportunity to practice autonomy and independence of thought.

Evidence presented to bolster this argument is even weaker than that for teacher talk and teacher questions. We learn that teachers lecture about one quarter of the time in the typical classroom, and the lecturing increases at the upper grade levels. Greater amounts of lecturing are associated with more experience in student teaching as well as less humanistic attitudes toward pupils, while teachers rated as "superior" are more likely to exhibit shorter lecturing segments. Evidence concerning the effects of training programs on teacher lecturing is ambiguous; evidence concerning the effects of teacher talk is available from but one study, and that study reports *greater* pupil achievement with increased teacher lecturing! On balance, then, we have seen little reason at present to make recommendations for teachers concerning the amount of lecturing they conduct in the classroom.

Teacher giving directions Presumably teachers who spend much of their time *giving directions* are not going to have much time to engage in instruction. Consequently, those interested in improving classroom instruction should want to reduce the amount of time spent in giving directions.

Once again, evidence supporting this argument is either weak or missing. We learn that in the typical classroom teachers spend little time

[5] Rosenshine (1971) reaches a similar conclusion (p. 156).

FIGURE 11.3 Findings for directiveness variables.

Process Variable Considered	Process Occurrence	Context-Process	Presage-Process	Process-Process	Process-Product Field Survey	Process-Product Experiment
	Most teaching is:	Process variable associated with:	Process variable associated with:	Process variable associated with:	Process variable associated with:	Process var induces
Teacher Talk	Long on teacher talk (3)		Lack of experience in student teaching (1) Rating of "less than superior" in teaching (1) ------------------ Experimental training in FIAC, etc., (lowers teacher talk) (1) Experimental training produced no difference (1)		Unrelated to pupil achievement (7) More positive pupil attitudes (1) Unrelated to pupil attitudes (4) Less positive pupil attitudes (1)	
Teacher Questions	Involves teacher questions about 1/5 of the time (3)	Lower grade levels (1) Sex of pupil (boys receive more teacher questions (1) Unrelated to sex of pupils (1)	Unrelated to teacher expectations for pupil achievement (1) ------------------ Experimental training in FIAC, etc. (2) Experimental training produced no difference (2)		Greater pupil achievement (1) Unrelated to pupil achievement (6) More positive pupil attitudes (1) Unrelated to pupil attitudes (5)	
Teacher Lecturing	Involves teacher lecturing about 1/4 of the time (3)	Upper Grade levels (1)	Greater experience in student teaching (1) Ratings of "superior" in teaching (shorter lecturing segments) (1) Lowers teachers' humanistic attitudes toward pupils (1) ------------------ Experimental training in FIAC, etc. (lowers teacher lecturing) (1) Experimental training produced no difference (3)		Greater pupil achievement (1)	
Teacher Giving Directions	Short on teacher giving directions (3)	Lower grade levels (1)	Ratings of "less than superior" in teaching (2) ------------------ Experimental training in FIAC, etc. (lowers teacher giving directions) (4) Experimental training produced no difference (1)			
Pupil Talk	Involves pupil talk about 1/4 of the time (3)	Lower grade levels (1)	Greater experience in student teaching (1) Ratings of "superior" in teaching (1) Unrelated to teachers' humanistic and custodial attitudes toward pupils (1) ------------------ Experimental training in FIAC, etc. (2)		Unrelated to pupil achievement (5)	

370

Figure 11.3 (cont.)

Process Variable Considered	Process Occurrence — Most teaching is:	Context-Process — Process variable associated with:	Presage-Process — Process variable associated with:	Process-Process — Process variable associated with:	Process-Product: Field Survey — Process variable associated with:	Process-Product: Experimental — Process variable induces:
Pupil Responses to Teachers' Initiations	Involves pupil responses about 1/5 of the time (2)		Ratings of "superior" in teaching (1) — Unrelated to teachers' humanistic and custodial attitudes toward pupils (1) — — — — — Experimental training in FIAC, etc. lowers pupil responses (3) / Experimental training produced no difference (2)			Unrelated to pupil achievement (1)
Pupil Initiations	Short on pupil initiation (2)		Ratings of "superior" in teaching (1) / Ratings make no difference (1) — Higher teachers' humanistic attitudes toward pupils (1) — Higher teacher expectations for pupil achievement (1) — — — — — Experimental training in FIAC, etc. (3) / Experimental training produced no difference (1)			
Silence and Confusion (Box 6.1)	Involves silence and confusion about 1/5 of the time (2)	Upper grade levels (1)	Ratings of "less than superior" in teaching (2) — — — — — Experimental training in FIAC, etc. (lowers silence and confusion) (1) / Experimental training produced no difference (2)			

n giving directions, but that more time is spent in the lower grade levels where pupils presumably need more management. Teachers who are rated as "superior" are somewhat less likely to spend time giving directions. Once again, evidence concerning the impact of training programs on this variable is ambiguous; evidence concerning the effects of giving directions on pupils is missing. On balance, we can conclude little, and we make no recommendations concerning whether teachers should or should not spend time giving directions.

Pupil talk Needless to say, to have *pupils talking* is presumed a good thing by those holding the *Commitment*. The picture of the traditional classroom includes the idea that pupils are to sit in solemn silence and speak only when addressed directly by the teacher. Any strategy that results in greater participation by pupils should improve matters.

In support of this general contention we learn that pupils talk only about one quarter of the time in the typical classroom, although pupil talk is somewhat more likely at the lower grade levels. Moreover, pupil talk is reported to increase with greater experience in student teaching and teachers who are rated "superior" are more likely to devote more time to pupil talk. Strikingly, the two studies that have concerned themselves with the matter both report success in increasing the amount of pupil talk with training programs that feature exposure to FIAC and related instruments. All of this seems thoroughly impressive—until we look at the effects of pupil talk on pupil outcomes. Without exception studies report no relationship between pupil talk and pupil achievement. With reluctance then, we must conclude that although it appears quite feasible to train teachers to encourage pupils to talk, no evidence has yet been advanced to demonstrate that this is a good thing to do.[6]

Pupil responses to teacher initiations   Within the tradition being reviewed pupil talk is generally presumed to be classified either as responsive or initiatory. The *Commitment* is somewhat ambivalent concerning pupil responses. On the one hand, pupils should be encouraged to speak more often, while on the other the responsive role is one that involves passivity and submission.

Only a few studies report data specifically for pupil responses. We learn that pupil responses are found to account for approximately a fifth of classroom interaction time. They occur more in classrooms of teachers rated as "superior," but are reduced through training with FIAC. However, responding appears no more beneficial to pupil achievement than nonresponding, and we can find no basis for recommending that teachers should worry merely because pupils in their classrooms respond more or less of the time than do pupils in other classrooms.

Pupil initiation   If evidence is lacking to support the pupil response variable, what about *pupil initiation?* The *Commitment* would surely have this an advisable phenomenon.

In support of the *Commitment* pupil initiation is found to be in short supply in the typical classroom. Girls are found more likely to initiate than are boys, as are pupils who have a history of prior achievement. Greater pupil initiation is also found associated with teachers' humanistic attitudes toward pupils and teacher expectations for pupil achievement. However the rest of the evidence is ambiguous, pupil initiation being associated and not associated with ratings of "superiority" and experimental training programs. This variable appears somewhat more promising than others so far reviewed, although findings associated with product variables are so far in short supply.

Silence and confusion   It is surely too bad that silence and confusion were lumped together in FIAC and related instruments. Confusion is

---

[6] Rosenshine (1971) reaches a similar conclusion (p. 156).

surely something to be avoided at most times in the classroom, while silence may at times be necessary for individual study. Thus, this variable appears to elide two quite different sorts of events.

We learn that the typical classroom involves silence and confusion only about one fifth of the time. Interestingly, they appear associated more often with classrooms at the upper grade levels, and teachers who are rated as "superior" are less likely to exhibit silence and confusion. Evidence concerning the effects of training programs on silence and confusion is ambiguous. Evidence concerning this variable, then, is also weak or lacking.

Commentary As was suggested in Chapters V and VI, it pains us to give such a negative review to a research tradition that has represented not only our own initial *Commitments* in education but also the energetic research efforts of such a broad group of investigators. Nevertheless, it would appear that this group of concepts is remarkably nonuseful for generating recommendations that might be put to use by educators. Of twelve variables examined one ("indirectness") has been rejected as a variable, while for ten variables no recommendations could be made for the improvement of teaching. Only for *teacher criticism*, or disapproval, were we able to make a recommendation that teachers should seek to reduce this classroom process. Evidence concerning the effects of training programs based on exposure to FIAC or related instruments on these variables is also ambiguous, although it would appear on balance that teachers *can* be taught to increase the amount of their "indirectness" (whatever that means), acceptance of pupils' ideas, and effective encouragement of pupil talk.

Why should this tradition have produced so few findings of real value to educators? Two explanations appear to be likely. The first stresses the weakness of the methods used in many of the studies in the tradition. If findings are to depend on the vagaries of live observation and to rest on single-faceted instruments whose categories are not logically exclusive, then is it small wonder that but few findings have been generated? The second explanation suggests that the conceptual posture of the *Commitment* is overly simple. Each of the variables examined is, after all, based on frequency counts that are summarized for the lesson as a whole. It matters not, for example, whether *teacher praise* is given on appropriate or inappropriate occasions; if it is given at all, we are presumably better off, according to the *Commitment*. Would not more findings be generated if more sensitive variables were used?

At present the evidence is insufficient to determine which of these explanations is the more likely—and, in fact, we suspect that both are partially correct. The point is, however, that little evidence has appeared from this tradition to support the general contentions of progressive education concerning the improvement of classroom teaching. On evidential grounds it seems unlikely that teaching can be improved by making classrooms warmer or more democratic places. Indeed, a number of the studies reviewed suggest that such steps are likely to have but few effects on pupil achievement or attitudes. Thus our major finding concerning both climate and directiveness is that, as operationalized in this research tradition, they do not appear promising concepts for the improvements of teaching.

Findings for Discipline and Group Management

If directiveness is not a useful concept for producing findings concerning the managerial success of teachers, what kinds of concepts are more useful? Fortunately, there are two research traditions that have addressed themselves to this question. The first constitutes the studies of Kounin that have focused on the problem of discipline and the management of classroom groups.

As we know from Chapter VI, Kounin's work has been characterized by both flexibility and the development of original concepts. The first of Kounin's three studies concerned deviancy control in the kindergarten classroom. It featured the use of the specimen-record technique, focused on "deviancy control incidents," and used a simple observational instrument. Three concepts were developed for expressing the classroom behavior of teachers: *desist clarity, desist firmness,* and *desist roughness;* and findings were advanced to show that these had effects on subsequent pupil behavior in the kindergarten setting.

Kounin's subsequent studies involved more complex methods and concepts. Data for primary classrooms were collected by means of motion pictures and videotapes, various units of classroom events were studied, and complex codes were developed to explore various aspects of the management problem. Kounin then did something that we suspect is unique in the field of research on teaching. He concluded that the three original variables for which he had already published results were *not* effective for primary classrooms. Instead, he developed a new series of variables that could be shown to relate more strongly to pupil involvement and deviancy: *withitness, overlappingness, smoothness, momentum, group alerting, accountability, valence and challenge arousal,* and *seatwork variety and challenge.* It is findings for these latter that we shall review here.

Before turning to Kounin's findings, however, a word or two of caution concerning the limitations of the research evidence. First, Kounin's research was conducted with primary classrooms only. It remains an open question as to whether his findings would apply at the secondary level, and we suspect that some at least would not. Second, the studies were all field surveys. Thus, it is possible that the cause-and-effect relationship between teacher behaviors and pupil responses assumed by Kounin, and ourselves, will eventually be found in error. Third, Kounin's methods were exploratory and complex, and some of his concepts are difficult to understand. His results also suggest interaction among the various teaching style variables, and it is possible that subsequent research will show these variables to collapse into a smaller number of factors. Fourth, Kounin has yet to validate his teaching variables against product criteria. Instead, teaching is judged to be successful when pupils are found to be involved and free from deviancy, which are process criteria. (To find classrooms where pupils are involved and deviancy free is not bad, but we would also like them to learn something by being there.) Finally, fifth, Kounin has not yet demonstrated that teachers can be trained to change their teaching behavior in respect to his concepts. That they should be able to learn withitness, smoothness, momentum, and the like, seems reasonable, but demonstrations have not yet taken place.

Work involvement Let us now look at Kounin's findings for work involvement. What should the teacher do to keep pupils involved with the tasks of the lesson?

Findings reported by Kounin are summarized in Figure 11.4, which deals exclusively with process-process relationships. As will be seen in the figure, recommendations for work involvement are somewhat different for the recitation and seatwork contexts. In general, for *recitation* the teacher interested in provoking involvement should first of all demonstrate *withitness, smoothness, momentum,* and *group alerting.* It would also help if she exhibited *overlappingness, accountability,* and *valence and challenge arousal.* Let us recapitulate what these words mean.

Withitness means that the teacher "knows what is going on," in effect, has "eyes in the back of her head."

Smoothness means that the teacher maintains the flow of classroom activities, particularly at points of transition.

Group alerting means that the teacher attempts to involve nonreciting pupils in the task, maintains attention, and keeps all "on their toes."

Overlappingness refers to the teacher's ability to deal with two or more things at the same time.

Accountability concerns the degree to which the teacher holds pupils responsible for task performance during the lesson.

Valence and challenge arousal concerns the teacher's ability to stimulate pupil enthusiasm, involvement, or curiosity about academic affairs.

(Details of how these teaching strategies can be accomplished may be found in Chapter VI, or—better—in Kounin, 1970.)

Recommendations for maintaining pupil *involvement* in the *seatwork* context are somewhat different. Above all the teacher should demonstrate *seatwork variety and challenge.* It would also help if she exhibited *withitness, smoothness* and *valence and challenge arousal.* In general,

Seatwork variety and challenge concerns the degree to which pupils are given varied tasks to do.

FIGURE 11.4 Process-process findings for discipline and group management (Box 6.2).

Pupil Behavior Variables

Teacher Behavior Variables	Work Involvement in Recitation	Work Involvement in Seatwork	Deviancy in Recitation	Deviancy in Seatwork	Desist Success	Subsequent Audience Pupil Conformity	Subsequent Audience Pupil Nonconformity	Disruption of Pupil Activities
Desist Clarity	0(1)*		0(1)*		0(1)*	+(1)*		
Desist Firmness	0(1)*		0(1)*		0(1)*	+(1)*	−(1)*	
Desist Roughness								+(1)*
Desist Child Treatment	0(1)		0(1)	0(1)	0(1)			
Desist Intensity	0(1)		0(1)	0(1)	0(1)			
Desist Focus	0(1)		0(1)	0(1)	0(1)			
Desist Withitness	++(1)	+(2)	−−(1)	−−(2)				
Desist Overlappingness	+(1)	0(1)	−(1)	−(1)				
Smoothness	++(2)	+(2)	−(2)	−(1)				
Momentum	++(1)	0(1)	−−(1)	−(1)				
Group Alerting	++(1)	0(1)	−(1)	−(1)				
Accountability	+(1)	0(1)	−(1)	0(1)				
Valence and Challenge Arousal	+(1)	+(1)	−(1)	−(1)				
Seatwork Variety and Challenge	0(2)	++(2)	0(2)	−(2)				
Duration of Seatwork Activities		0(2)		0(2)				

Key: ++ = strong positive relationship reported

+ = positive relationship reported

0 = weak relationship reported

− = negative relationship reported

−− = strong negative relationship reported

* = These findings reported for the first day of kindergarten only

(1) = Finding reported in one study

(2) = Finding reported in two studies

(Somewhat surprisingly, *overlappingness, momentum, group alerting,* and *accountability* appeared to make relatively little difference in the maintenance of pupil involvement in the seatwork context.)

Pupil deviancy What should the teacher do if she wants to avoid pupil deviancy and disruption in the classroom? Once again, the findings are somewhat different depending on whether one considers the recitation or seatwork context. To avoid pupil *deviancy* in *recitation,* above all the teacher should exhibit *withitness* and *momentum.* Also useful would be the exhibition of *overlappingness, smoothness, group alerting, accountability,* and *valence and challenge arousal.* As far as the *seatwork* context is concerned, the most important behavior for avoiding pupil *deviancy* would appear to be *withitness.* Additional behaviors of help would be *overlappingness, smoothness, momentum, group alerting, valence and challenge arousal,* and *seatwork variety and challenge arousal.*

Commentary Despite the limitations of the research that has so far been conducted to support Kounin's findings, we regard these findings as impressive. In sum they appear to support many of the recommendations that used to be made in wholistic "methods of teaching" courses that now seem to be disappearing from the curriculum in favor of methods courses that are focused on a given academic subject or grade level. Perhaps this disappearance is a good thing; it may well be that classroom lectures on methods of teaching are an inefficient way of training teachers to recognize the symptoms of poor classroom management in their own behavior. Surely Kounin found a number of teachers to study who were poor classroom managers, or his findings would have not been generated. And yet we cannot help but believe that the concepts advanced by Kounin were simply unknown to many of his teachers; indeed, several years ago they were unknown to the authors. We have the disturbing feeling that considerable improvement in classroom teaching could be wrought by alerting teachers to Kounin's major concepts and findings.

Findings for Behavior Modification Research

Kounin's findings concern management of the classroom as a whole. In essence, they are responses to the question, "What should the teacher do to increase involvement and decrease deviancy for the groups of pupils in the classroom?" But what if the teacher wants to gain control over the *individual* pupil? Let us presume that the problem is not the control of the group but rather that of bringing into the group a disturbed or hostile pupil. What kinds of recommendations can we make to that teacher on the basis of research on teaching?

The next research tradition we consider has addressed itself to this question. This is the group of studies that has concerned the use of behavior modification by teachers for the control of pupil behavior. As we know from Chapter VI, this tradition grew from a long history of behavioristic research in animal psychology. Intrinsic to this history were several *Commitments:* that control over the behavior of experimental subjects was best achieved with immediate reinforcement, that positive reinforcement was a more effective (and more humane?) means of controlling behavior than negative reinforcement, and that experimental studies were the best means of demonstrating these propositions.

Each of these *Commitments* is reflected in the studies that have been conducted within the classroom behavior modification tradition. The result has been a series of findings that are similar to those of Kounin in that they depend mainly on process criteria to indicate "successful" teaching. Unlike the Kounin studies, however, those in the behavior modification tradition have been exclusively experimental. As a result, we cannot be certain that the range of behaviors exhibited by their (experimental) teachers is likely to be exhibited—or indeed *could* be exhibited—in the typical classroom. We are, of course, more certain of the cause-and-effect relationship between the teaching concepts studied and the pupil behaviors used to establish their success.

As was pointed out in Chapter VI, many of these studies have also suffered from other design defects. Most studies concentrated on only small numbers of classrooms and target pupils who were disturbed. Few studies concerned themselves either with what was happening to the other pupils in the classroom or with the retention of behavioral effects by target pupils after the experimental treatment had ceased. Few studies used control groups, and experimental treatments appeared in many cases to be contaminated with other teacher behaviors. Finally, primitive tools were used for the observation of pupil behaviors, and in some cases teachers were not even observed to find out whether they had exhibited the experimental treatment for which they had been trained!

Target-pupil deviancy   With all these problems it still appears to us that findings are well established for the behavior modification tradition (see Figure 11.5). Let us first take up the problem of *target-pupil deviancy.* How does one bring into line the individual pupil who is constantly misbehaving? We use *praise, material incentives, extrinsic tokens, response manipulation,* or *peer manipulation* as positive reinforcers for *acceptable* behavior. From the evidence it would appear not to make much difference what kind of a "reward" is used provided that it is applied consistently to the target pupil upon the occasion of his doing things which are acceptable. Since *praise* would appear the commodity most easily administered by the teacher, perhaps this should be the reinforcer of choice. (And, in fact, more studies have concerned praise than any other commodity.) But what happens when the teacher uses *criticism* of deviant behavior as a negative reinforcer? Results are mixed: some studies report success, others no success. The message appears clear: praise for acceptable behavior *works,* criticism for deviant behavior is *questionable* when dealing with target-pupil deviancy.[7]

Target-pupil task involvement   Findings for task involvement of target pupils are also straightforward, although fewer studies have considered the problem. Teacher use of *intrinsic tokens* and *response manipulation* as reinforcers of acceptable behavior have both been found to increase pupil involvement. In addition, *material incentives* and *extrinsic tokens* when used for reinforcement have both been found to increase the proportion of correct responses by pupils, while the latter has also been found to increase pupil attendance. Apparently some of the same means that have been found effective for bringing target-pupil deviancy under control are also useful for increasing target-pupil task involvement.

Pupil achievement   Despite the generalization given above, three of the studies reviewed have actually taken a look at the effects of classroom reinforcement on pupil achievement. Two studies have found that teachers can increase target-pupil achievement by use of extrinsic tokens for the reinforcement of correct responses in the classroom. One study also demonstrated (slight) improvement in the achievement of nontarget pupils when they watched target pupils who were subjected to positive reinforcement for correct responses. So, although the evidence is weak, it would appear that positive reinforcement of appropriate responses may also be useful for generating increased pupil achievement.

Commentary   None of these experimental studies has yet taken on the basic question of whether it is practicable to use positive reinforcement for the target pupil in a classroom containing thirty-plus pupils. Elsewhere we review evidence suggesting that the vast majority of teacher reactions to pupils are either neutral or positive in tone—thus suggesting that the typical classroom has a fair amount of praise in it already. Is it possible for the teacher to single out the individual pupil for an "extra dose of praise" whenever that pupil is behaving appropriately? And what happens to the other pupils while this is going on? Such questions require much more careful research in field settings than has yet appeared from the behavior modification tradition. Unfortunately, too, positive reinforcement requires much greater discipline, patience, and energy investment on the part of the teacher than does negative reinforcement. (It is much easier to leave the individual pupil to his own devices and to respond only when he evidences problems than it is to lavish praise on him whenever he does something "right.") For this reason we suspect that teachers will utilize the reinforcement finding only *in extremis*—for those pupils whose behavior has not responded to ordinary classroom treatment. Nevertheless, the evidence

---

[7] Contrast these findings with those reported earlier for the total incidence of *praise* and *criticism* in the lesson.

FIGURE 11.5 Experimental findings from behavior modification research.

Process Variable Considered	Process Occurrence	Context-Process	Presage-Process	Process-Process	Field Survey Process-Product	Experimental Process-Product
		Process variable associated with:	Process variable associated with:	Process variable associated with:	Process variable associated with:	Process variable induces:
Teacher praise (as a positive reinforcer of acceptable behavior)	Most teaching is:			Reduced target-pupil deviancy (6)		
Teacher criticism (as a negative reinforcer of deviant behavior)				Reduced target-pupil deviancy (2) Does not affect pupil deviancy (3)		
Teacher use of material incentives (as a positive reinforcer of acceptable behavior)				Reduced target-pupil deviancy (2) Increased proportion of "correct" responses (1)		
Teacher use of extrinsic tokens (as a positive reinforcer of acceptable behavior)				Reduced target-pupil deviancy (2) Increased pupil attendance (1) Increased proportion of "correct" responses (1)		Increased target-pupil achievement (2)

Teacher use of <u>intrinsic tokens</u> (as a positive reinforcer of acceptable behavior)	Increased target-pupil task involvement (3)	
Teacher use of <u>response manipulation</u> (as a positive reinforcer of acceptable behavior)	Decreased target-pupil deviancy (1) Increased target-pupil task involvement (3)	
Teacher use of <u>peer manipulation</u> (as a positive reinforcer of acceptable behavior)	Decreased target-pupil deviancy (2)	
Teacher use of <u>vicarious reinforcement</u> (as a positive reinforcer of acceptable behavior)	Does not affect nontarget-pupil deviancy (1) Decreases nontarget-pupil deviancy (1)	Slightly increased nontarget-pupil achievement (1)
(Box 6.3)		

seems clear to us. Positive reinforcement *works*, at least for the target pupil.

Findings for the Classroom as a Social System

Chapter VII reports on a series of studies that do not constitute an integrated research tradition. Rather, these studies share a common theme—that classroom events constitute a social system of interrelated parts. This theme owes as much or more to the field of sociology as it does to psychology. Teaching is seen as a phenomenon that grows out of the interaction of curriculum, facilities, customs, actors, and their expectations. Thus teaching, and its consequences, will reflect as much the social group structure of the classroom as it will the actions of the teacher considered in isolation.

This is a clear message. It may even be right, but its implications are more difficult for the individual teacher to handle. Let us assume that the teacher is told that curriculum, pupil roles, group structure, or the physical ecology of the classroom make a significant difference in teaching or its effects. Unless these phenomena are under the control of the teacher—and they may not be—the teacher may feel only frustration over the information given. Some of the results from this study may not constitute findings, then, but only curiosities.

There are other problems. Despite the common theme, the various studies of this group have managed to use a wide variety of concepts. Most have considered themselves exploratory and have developed instruments that were multifaceted. Unfortunately for our purposes, there was but little terminological overlap among the studies reviewed. As a result, the Research Boxes of Chapter VII report a welter of different terms and apparently disparate findings, but little replication.

Again, most of the studies have also constituted field surveys that were concerned with examining the peculiarities of the *genus classroom* rather than with testing propositions about the effectiveness of teaching. In consequence, many results have little apparent relevance for the improvement of teaching. For example, why should we care to learn that pupils are more likely to touch themselves when resting, or that lessons taught by women teachers exhibit more intellectualization about organizational matters than lessons taught by men teachers? Findings such as these become meaningful only when we think about them for some time and then tie the finding to an issue that is under the possible control of educators.

Finally, studies in this group have concerned themselves primarily with process relationships. Scant attention has been paid to product variables. Thus, the major criteria offered against which we can judge classroom phenomena for their effects are those concerned with observable pupil behavior. But are these acceptable as dependent variables? Since the classroom is viewed as a system, some of the pupil behaviors examined at least should be as much a cause of related classroom events as they are a reaction to them. For example, classroom subgroups may be formed either by teacher or pupil initiative. To discover, then, that subgroups are better (or worse) for certain purposes than the total classroom group does not provide secure information that can be used by the teacher. It is possible that the results obtained came from pupil-initiated subgroups and that the results would be different if we considered teacher-initiated subgroups only.

Despite these problems, a careful reading of Research Boxes 7.2 through 7.8 reveals a number of effects that may be interpreted as findings for teachers. For convenience we summarize these on a box-by-box basis (see Figure 11.6).

Lesson format It has often been argued in the hortative literature of education that lessons become ineffective when they are too lengthy. For this reason *duration of the lesson* is a format variable of some potential significance to educators. Unfortunately for the argument, results presented in Box 7.2 suggest that duration of the lesson makes little difference to either pupil involvement or pupil deviancy, at least within the range of lesson lengths examined.[8]

A second variable from the lesson-format group concerns the relationship between structure and function of groups. It is reasonable to presume that teaching will be more effective when structure is matched to function, for teachers who adopt structures that are appropriate to the task will presumably be more effective than those who demand an invariant structure for all tasks. Interestingly, we learn that the match between structure and function varies depending on subject matter and is generally more likely for teachers who are younger and female. But whether this variable is associated with differential pupil products is not yet known.

It has also suggested that lessons using a *probing* format might be better for stimulating pupil interest and the development of logical abilities. This hypothesis was tested in an interesting field experiment, and it was ascertained that probing lessons induced greater ability to make inferences in pupils. In addition, we also learn that probing lessons had differential effects on white suburban and black ghetto classrooms. Apparently, probing is not an unmixed blessing. We suggest that this variable needs further research before a definitive recommendation should be made.

Group structure Educational commentators would have us believe that the typical classroom is dominated by whole-class activities, and that this is a bad thing. After all, pupils are more likely to participate, hence to be more active, in the small group. Let us now look at the evidence for *use of small groups* in the classroom. Results show that traditional classrooms spend most of their time in whole-class activities or in independent seatwork. Use of small groups varies as a function of subject matter, is greater in the lower-grade levels and in multigraded classrooms, and is more likely in classrooms operated by younger teachers. Moreover, pupil

[8] Rosenshine (1971) reaches a similar conclusion from reviewing totally different studies (p. 186).

FIGURE 11.6 Findings for classroom social system variables.

Process Variable Considered	Process Occurrence	Context-Process	Presage-Process	Process-Process	Field Survey Process-Product	Experimental Process-Product
	Most teaching is:	Process variable associated with:	Process variable associated with:	Process variable associated with:	Process variable associated with:	Process variable induces:
Duration of lesson				Unrelated to pupil involvement (1) Unrelated to pupil deviancy (1)		
Close relationship between structure and function of groups		Subject matter (2)	Younger teachers (1) Female teachers (1)			
"Probing" lessons (Box 7.2)						More accurate pupil "increases" (1) Complex or curvili-near relationships with pupil "obser-vations" (1)
Use of small groups in the classroom (Box 7.3)	Involves whole-class activities or inde-dependent seatwork (2)	Subject matter(1) Lower grade levels (1) Multi-graded classrooms (1)	Younger teachers (1)	Greater pupil involvement (1) More intellectual-ization (1) Nonrelevant subject matter (1)		
Discussion concerned with relevant subject matter	Concerned with relevant subject matter (2)	Subject matter(1) Longer exchanges (1)	Younger teachers (1) Male teachers (1)			
Discussion concerned with organization	Concerned with organization about 1/5 of the time (2)	Lower grade levels (1) Use of computer-assisted				

Characteristic	Level	Correlates		Consequences
discussion	zation about 1/5 of the time (2)	Upper grade levels (1) Subject matter(1)		of classrooms(1)
(Box 7.4)				
Centrality of teacher role	Central (3)	Subject matter(1) Lower grade levels (1)	Younger teachers (1) Male teachers (1)	Greater pupil involvement (1) Maintenance of group functions (1)
Teacher contact with individual pupils	Not involved with individual contact (3)	Use of computer-assisted instruction (1) Multigraded classrooms (1)	Younger teachers (1)	
(Box 7.5)				
Passivity of pupil role	Passive (2)	Girl pupils (1) Underachieving pupils (1) Nonuse of computer-assisted instruction (1)		Lower pupil involvement (1) More self-touching by pupils (1)
Pupil self-directed activities (i.e., seatwork)	Not self-directed (2)	Girl pupils (1) Pupils who are not underachievers (1) Use of computer-assisted instruction (1) Multigraded classrooms (1)		Lower pupil involvement (1)
(Box 7.6)				

Figure 11.6 (cont.)

Process Variable Considered	Process Occurrence	Context-Process	Presage-Process	Process-Process	Process-Product Field Survey	Process-Product Experimental
		Process variable associated with:	Process variable associated with:	Process variable associated with:	Process Variable associated with:	Process variable induces:
	Most teaching is:					
Moves emitted by pupils (rather than by teacher)	About 2/5 of moves are pupil emitted (3)	Girl pupils (1)	Teacher familiarity with pupils' names (1)			
Teacher emission of soliciting moves	About 3/10 of all moves to solicit (3)		Teacher familiarity with pupils' names (1)	Standard (rather than "individual-ized") lessons (1)	Pupil perception that teacher solicitations are directed toward them (1)	
	Most solicitations are teacher emitted (3)			Type of pupil response (1)		
Pupil emission of responding moves	About 3/10 of all moves respond (3)	Boy pupils (1)	Teacher familiarity with pupils' names (1)	Standard (rather than "individual-ized") lessons (1)		Unrelated to pupil achievement (1)
	Most responses are pupil emitted (3)	Average I.Q. of "steering-group" pupils (1)		Teacher solicita-tions that are "closed" (1)		
Teacher emission of positive reactions	About 3/10 of all moves react (3)	Lower grade levels (1)		Type of teacher solicitation (1)		Greater pupil achievement (with "thanks and praise") (2)
	Most reactions are teacher emitted (3)	Average I.Q. of "steering-group" pupils (1)				
	Most reactions are positive or neutral (3)					

Teacher emission of structuring moves	About 1/10 of all moves structured (3)			Unrelated to pupil achievement (1)
	Most structuring moves are teacher emitted (3)			Curvilinear or complex relationships with pupil achievement (1)
(Box 7.7)				
Teacher front-and-center location	Front and center (1)	Upper grade levels (1)	Older teachers (1)	Whole-class activities (1)
Teacher use of gesture and movement		Middle grade levels (1)		Greater pupil achievement (1)
Pupil front-and-center location	Involves pupils who are front and center (1)	Subject matter (1)	Older teachers (1)	
		Upper grade levels (1)		
"Stimulation" value of educational media			Complex or curvilinear relationships with pupil involvement (1)	Complex or curvilinear near relationships with pupil achievement (1)
				Unrelated to pupil attitudes (1)
(Box 7.8)				

involvement is greater in small groups, and the discussion there is more likely to involve intellectualization. On the other hand, small groups are more likely to involve themselves with nonrelevant materials than is the classroom as a whole. In the main, then, these findings support the idea that small groups should be encouraged in the classroom, although their activities should be supervised by the teacher so as to keep them on target.

Group function Educational ideology speaks with confusion when concerned with group functions, probably because no consistent vocabulary has yet been adopted for problems in this field. However, most commentators would stress that group discussions should stick to the topic, should avoid overinvolvement with organizational issues, and should involve intellectualization rather than, or in addition to, exchanges concerned merely with facts. Let us look at the evidence concerning *relevant subject matter, organization,* and *intellectualization.*

Evidence is minimal concerning the first two topics. Classroom discussion spends much of its time on relevant subject matter, particularly in longer exchanges, although this emphasis varies as one goes from topic to topic. Younger teachers and male teachers are also more likely to stick to the topic. Emphasis on organizational matters is low, although greater at the lower grade levels and in classrooms involving the use of computer-assisted instruction. There are no problems in either set of findings. Concerning intellectualization, however, we have more interesting results. The typical classroom discussion is *not* found to be intellectual, although intellectualization varies from topic to topic. Intellectualization is more likely at the upper grade levels, in classrooms supervised by younger teachers, and, as we already know, in small groups in the classroom. Unfortunately, we have no product criteria by which to judge the effects of intellectualization. In summary, then, classrooms normally spend much of their time on the topic and little time on organizational matters. They are not particularly intellectual places, however, though we do not yet know the effects of lack of intellectualization.

Teacher roles Many commentators have noted the sharply centralized role of the teacher in traditional classrooms. It has also been argued that teaching would be more effective if it were individualized, if individual contact were encouraged between teacher and pupils. Box 7.5 provides results bearing on these arguments. Concerning *centrality* of the teacher role, most teaching is found to be central, centralization is found to be associated with subject-matter differences and to be more prevalent at the lower grade levels, younger teachers are more likely to exhibit centralization than older teachers, and also men rather than women. Not surprisingly, centralization of role is found associated with the maintenance of group functions. But then comes a surprise; pupils are found to have *greater* involvement when the teacher's role is central than when it is not. We suspect that pupils are used to looking to the teacher for direction and guidance, if not for inspiration, in the traditional classroom. When the teacher wanders off stage, pupils' attention wanders also. This latter finding suggests that traditional classrooms are better managed when the teacher *maintains* a centralized role! (So much for folk wisdom.)

Concerning teacher *contact with individual pupils*, we learn that little of this occurs in the typical classroom and that younger teachers are more likely to be involved with individual contact. We are also told that *if* one wants to increase the amount of individual contact between teacher and pupils, two ways to accomplish this goal are to bring computer-assisted instruction into the classroom and to make classrooms multigraded. Unfortunately, no data have yet been advanced to indicate what happens to pupils when individual contact is increased.

Pupil roles As a general rule, pupils tend to be *passive*, to sit in solemn silence and meek compliance, in the typical classroom. Numerous commentators have suggested that this is a hard role to perform and that classrooms would be better off, particularly at the lower grade levels, if pupils were allowed a more active role. In general, these contentions are supported by the evidence. Pupils *are* found to be passive in the typical classroom. Passivity induces lower pupil involvement and more pupil self-touching behavior. Underachieving pupils are found to be more passive than achieving pupils. We also suspect that overly passive classrooms will be found to depress pupil achievement and morale, but evidence for this theory is not yet available. Should one want to decrease pupil passivity, one strategy open is to use computer-assisted instruction. Finally, in perhaps the most interesting of those findings reported, girls are reported to be more passive than boys in the classroom. This implies that the passive role is likely to work a greater hardship on boys than girls and that inability to behave passively may be one of the reasons why boys have traditionally done less well than girls in American classrooms. From the evidence, then, we would recommend more active roles for pupils.

Moves of the classroom game The idea that classroom interaction might consist of a "game" in which "moves" were made by teacher and pupils is not widespread in educational ideology. Yet our review has located a particularly interesting set of findings based on this analogy. As we know from Chapter VII, these findings are based on the concept that moves can be classified as either *structuring, soliciting, responding,* or *reacting*. Not all types of moves are equally likely. For convenience we shall summarize findings for five variables only: proportion of moves emitted by pupils, teacher emission of soliciting moves, pupil emission of responding moves, teacher emission of positive reactions, and teacher use of structuring moves.

To begin with, about two fifths of all moves in the classroom game are reported to be emitted by pupils. Since the ratio of pupils to teacher is in excess of thirty to one in the typical classroom, this means that individual pupils emit, on the average, about 1/100 as many moves as does the teacher! Girl pupils are likely to emit more moves than are boys, and pupil emission of moves is likely to increase when teachers are familiar with pupils' names. We are not yet told, however, what might be the processual or product effects on pupils of increasing or decreasing the proportion of moves emitted by pupils.

About three tenths of all classroom moves consist of *solicitations*, and of those solicitations nearly all are teacher-emitted. (Teachers also emit the majority of *structuring* and *reacting* moves. Pupils' moves are mainly *responses*.) Pupils, thus, are cast into the passive role of responding to questions and demands but receive few opportunities to structure the classroom environment, make requests of the teacher or other pupils, or state their own reactions to classroom events. Is this bad? It depends, of course, on what is wanted in the classroom. If the teacher is to be the font of wisdom, as well as the source of discipline and control, then these findings are appropriate. If pupils are to be self-directed in learning, they are deplorable. Not surprisingly, we also learn that teacher solicitations are more likely when teachers are familiar with pupils' names and in standard, rather than "individualized," lessons. Type of pupil response is also reported to vary as a function of type of teacher solicitation (about which, more below). Finally, pupils who perceive that teacher solicitations are directed toward them are actually more likely to *have* solicitations so directed (surprise!). But whether solicitations by the teacher are themselves useful or deleterious in the classroom these data do not tell us.

Another three tenths of the moves in the classroom constitute *responses*, most of which come from pupils. Pupil responding is also found associated with teacher familiarity with pupil names and with standard, rather than "individualized," lessons. Pupil responses are also likely to be more numerous when the average I.Q. of "steering group" pupils is high. (Readers will recall that Lundgren, 1972, reported a number of teaching phenomena to vary as a function of the average intelligence of the next-to-lowest I.Q. pupils in the classroom—the "steering group.") Pupil responses are also more likely to appear following teacher solicitations that are "closed." Again (and despite the fact that girls are more likely to emit moves in general), boys are more likely to emit responding moves. Thus, the role played by girls is in several senses more similar to that played by the teacher, perhaps because the teacher is almost always a woman in American classrooms. Ideology would have it that pupil responding is a good thing, but a single study reports this variable to be unrelated to pupil achievement.

So far we have not considered successful findings concerned with pupil products in our review of variables from the classroom game tradition. We now turn to such a variable—teacher use of *positive reactions*. Again, about three tenths of all moves are reactive, most reactions are teacher-emitted, and most reactions are reported to be positive or at least neutral in tone. In addition, positive reactions are more likely at the lower grade levels and are more likely when the average I.Q. of "steering group" pupils is high.

Teacher reactions also vary depending on the type of teacher solicitation. Most of these positive reactions are only mild ones, however. When greater stress is given, that is, when positive reactions are given in the forms of "thanks" and "praise," greater pupil achievement obtains. This finding is important to match with those reported earlier for positive reinforcement. Once again, it would appear that teachers who go out of their way to thank and praise pupils for their responses are likely to generate effectiveness in the classroom.

Finally, teacher use of *structuring moves*. It is often stressed in textbooks or courses on teaching methods that teachers should structure the lesson. Despite such assertions, only about one tenth of all moves structure (although most of these are teacher-emitted). It might be argued, therefore, that more structuring would be better than less structuring. Evidence to test this hypothesis is available, and the support is not overwhelming. (Below we consider findings that suggest structuring may be more or less effective depending on when it is performed.)

Location and other ecological features   The idea that classrooms are physical environments and that their physical features should affect teaching is also not often discussed in educational theory. Should the teacher stand *front and center* or should she be at the side or circulate about the classroom? "It depends." Should the teacher use *gesture and movement*? "It depends." Should pupils be equally involved throughout the classroom? Whoever thought they weren't?

Findings concerning each of these matters are available. Concerning teacher *front and center* location, we learn that teachers normally *are* found there (surprise!), and that this focal location is more likely at upper grade levels, among older teachers, and when whole-class activities are in progress—none of which appears overly significant. Teacher use of *gesture and movement* appears to be greatest at the middle-grade level and, interestingly, is found to be associated with greater pupil achievement. Findings for pupil location come as a surprise. Pupils, too, are more likely to be *front and center* when involved in classroom activities. Moreover, this tendency varies depending on subject matter and is greater at the upper grade levels and for older teachers. We presume that it is desirable for all pupils to participate equally in the classroom. These latter findings suggest that this does not happen in the typical classroom. Teachers may want to take note of this tendency and make special efforts to involve pupils in the rear corners. On the other hand, it may be possible to encourage shy pupils simply by moving them front and center. Finally, findings are also available relating to the "stimulation" value of educational media, although these findings do not suggest that this is a particularly strong variable for improving teaching.

Commentary   Once again, much of this research suffers from a lack of concern with product variables. It is also not clear which of the social processes of the classroom are under the immediate control of the teacher, and, apart from the research reported on computer-assisted instruction, we have as yet little evidence concerning how an educator might go about adjusting the parts of the classroom system. Despite these shortcomings, which we hope will be rectified in future research, the findings so far advanced suggest that it is indeed fruitful to view the classroom as a social system. Educators would do well to bear this in mind when interpreting the findings from more traditional studies that have considered teaching to be under the immediate control of the teacher alone.

Findings for Knowledge and Intellect

In the previous section we reviewed findings suggesting that the majority of classroom discussion is not concerned with intellectualization but rather information dissemination or "fact exchange." Concerned with this phenomenon at least three independent groups of investigators have attempted to devise coding systems that would reveal, and training systems that would encourage, the growth of intellectualism in classroom affairs. Each of these groups has held to the *Commitment* that greater intellectualization in the classroom would be a good thing, and each has sought to validate this *Commitment* with product, as well as process, variables.

The first of these groups developed concepts on the basis of Bloom's *Taxonomy of Educational Objectives.* Central to their orientation is the idea that classroom communications can be sorted into categories ranging from such "low-level" processes as *knowledge* and *comprehension* to "higher-order" categories such as *synthesis* and *evaluation.* The second group made use of a vocabulary developed by Guilford and developed categories that differentiated "convergent" from "divergent" thinking. The third group, led by Hilda Taba, concerned itself not only with the use of "higher thought levels" but also with attempts by the teacher to "lift the thought level" and "extend thought on the same level."

Findings from these three groups were generated through field surveys of existing classrooms and, for two of them, in presage-process experiments in which teachers were trained to exhibit greater intellectualization in classroom affairs. Given the complexity of coding systems developed, as well as the differences among the various training programs, there would be little wonder if many of the results reported had but limited appeal for the general teacher. Rather than attempt to recapitulate these many detailed findings we shall concentrate, instead, on those that bear upon the shared *Commitment* within the tradition—namely, that greater intellectualism in the classroom is advisable (see Figure 11.7).

Teacher use of "higher-order" categories of knowledge Let us first take up findings from the Bloom group that bear on the *Commitment.* Eight different studies from this group have found that most classroom discourse is concerned with *knowledge*, the "lowest-level" category of the system. We also learn that use of "higher-order categories" is greater at upper grade levels, but is unrelated to the subject matter of the lesson or to whether lessons are "process" or "content" oriented. Younger teachers and teachers having less teaching experience are *more* likely to exhibit higher-order categories, while use of these categories is unrelated to MTAI scores or teacher academic background in science. Experimental training, either in the Bloom taxonomy or in SCIS, appears to be effective in getting teachers to use more higher-order categories.

So far so good. But does the use of higher-order categories have desired effects upon pupils? The evidence is hardly encouraging. When teachers use higher-order categories, pupils seem also likely to use them, although one study reports a complex relationship. However, use of higher-order categories has either a complex relationship with pupil achievement or, in an experimental study, is found to be unrelated to this product variable. One possible reason for this discouraging set of findings is found in the apparently inverse relationship between use of higher-order categories and the "abstractness" of the content. Higher-order use appears more likely with concrete content, while abstract content is more likely to be paired with low-level categories. Do pupils benefit more from "higher-order" logic or from abstractness of thought? So far the problem is not resolved. On evidence, then, although use of higher-order concepts can apparently be trained in teachers, its use by teachers seems to encourage similar use in pupils, but the evidence does *not* demonstrate that this induces greater pupil achievement.

Teacher use of "divergent" rather than "convergent" questions We turn next to evidence generated by the Guilford group. In general, the thesis explored is that there is not enough "divergent" thinking in classrooms. In support of this thesis we learn that teaching is mainly concerned with cognitive memory and is convergent. Teacher use of divergent questions is found to vary with pupil group and lesson, (Divergency is more likely during the early part of the lesson.) Use of divergent questions by teachers is also found to be unrelated to divergency in teacher statements and also to teacher reactions to pupil responses(!). However, divergent questions are more likely to provoke divergent responses by pupils. But does divergency have the hoped-for positive effects in pupils? Once again, the evidence is hardly encouraging. One study reports that moderate use of convergent questions is associated with higher pupil achievement than either high or low use. Again, when subjected to the crucial test of product-variable relationships, the *Commitment* generating this research effort is not supported.

Lifting, extending, and higher levels of thought Finally, we turn to findings generated by the Taba group. As we learned in Chapter VIII, the Taba team used complex, and sometimes confusing, concepts for the expression of classroom events, and in a number of cases the findings they have presented are insufficient to judge the success of their research. Nevertheless, findings can be reported for five separate concepts related to the

FIGURE 11.7 Findings for studies concerned with knowledge and intellect.

Process Variable Considered	Process Occurrence	Context-Process	Presage-Process	Process-Process	Field Survey Process-Product	Experimental Process-Product
	Most teaching is:	Process variable associated with:	Process variable associated with:	Process variable associated with:	Process variable associated with:	Process variable induces:
(Bloom Taxonomy) Teacher use of "higher-order" categories of knowledge	Concerned with knowledge (i.e., uses "lower-order" categories) (8)	Unrelated to subject matter of lesson (2) Unrelated to "orientation" of lesson (1)	Unrelated to MTAI scores (1) Teachers having less teaching experience (1) Younger teachers (1) Unrelated to teacher academic background in science (1) ——— Experimental training in use of the taxonomy (3) Experimental training in SCIS science approach (2)	Pupil use of "higher-order" categories (5) Curvilinear or complex relationship with pupil use of categories (1) Teacher use of concrete content (1)	Curvilinear or complex relationship with pupil achievement (1)	Unrelated to pupil achievement (1)
(Box 8.1)						
(Guilford Taxonomy) Teacher use of "divergent" (rather than "convergent" thought in questions)	Concerned with cognitive memory (2) Convergent (1)	Pupil group and lesson (1) Phase of the lesson (divergency encouraged during early phases)(1)		"Divergent" responses by pupils(2) Unrelated to teacher divergency in statements (1) Unrelated to teacher reactions to pupil responses (1)	Curvilinear or complex relationship with pupil vocabulary growth (1)	
(Box 8.2)						

(Taba Taxonomy)

Teacher seeks use of "higher thought levels"
→ Unrelated to experimental curriculum (1)
→ Nature of the cognitive task (1)
→ Experimental training in Taba concepts (1)
→ Pupil use of "higher thought levels" (1)

Pupil use of "higher thought levels"
→ Upper grade levels (1)
→ Unrelated to experimental curriculum (1)
→ Nature of the cognitive task (1)
→ Unrelated to pupil I.Q. (1)
→ Experimental training in Taba concepts (given to teachers) (1)
→ Total number of thought units uttered by pupil (1)
→ Curvilinear or complex relationships with pupil achievement (1)
→ Unrelated to pupil achievement (1)

Pupil use of "more abstract thought units"
→ Unrelated to experimental curriculum (1)
→ Nature of the cognitive task (1)

Teacher seeks to "lift thought level"
→ Experimental training in Taba concepts (given to teachers) (1)
→ Pupil use of "higher thought levels" (1)
→ Unrelated to pupil achievement (1)

Teacher seeks to "extend thought on the same level"
→ Pupil additional use of "thought units on the same level" (1)
→ Unrelated to pupil achievement (1)

(Box 8.3)

395

Commitment. First, *teacher seeks use of "higher thought levels."* We learn that occurrence of teacher seeking higher thought levels is unrelated to experimental curriculum, but varies depending on the nature of the cognitive task. It is reported that teachers can be trained to increase their seeking of higher thought levels, and that when teachers seek, pupils respond with higher thought levels in their responses. These findings look very similar to those of the Bloom group. Unfortunately, no product variables are available to assess the success or failure of teacher seeking higher thought levels.

Pupil use of higher thought levels is also found to relate to the nature of the cognitive task and to be more prevalent at upper grade levels. It is found unrelated to the experimental curriculum. It is also (believe it or not) unrelated to pupil I.Q., although the greater the number of thought units uttered by the pupil, the more likely they are to include higher levels of thought. Experimental training of teachers increases pupil use of higher thought levels. Again, this all sounds very encouraging until we learn that use of higher thought levels bears either complex or no relationships to pupil achievement. This is discouraging.

The Taba group also found evidence indicating an inverse relationship between use of higher-level thought units and concrete concepts. As a result, they also examined, as a variable, *pupil use of "more abstract thought units."* This is also found related to the cognitive task but unrelated to the experimental curriculum. However, teachers who were experimentally trained *were* found able to increase the average level of abstraction of pupil thought units—to what effect in pupil achievement we are not told.

Finally, the Taba group also reported findings for two additional variables: *teacher seeks to "lift thought level"* and *teacher seeks to "extend thought on the same level."* Both of these were found by the Taba group to relate to corresponding pupil activities. Interestingly, they were not checked by the Taba group against pupil achievement or other product criteria. However, another study found them unrelated to pupil achievement.

Commentary Once again, this set of findings is a mixed bag. In general, it has been well established that teacher behavior in the intellectual realm *can* be affected by effective programs of teacher training. Moreover, teachers who ask for a higher level of response from pupils are likely to stimulate pupils to a higher level of response. However, the evidence suggesting that this has positive effects on pupil achievement is spotty, if not negative. It is possible, of course, that the wrong product variables have been chosen for study, that what investigators should have chosen to examine was pupil attitudes toward the subject or pupil ability to handle intellectual materials. But until evidence from such variables is examined we would have to conclude that the case for higher levels of intellectualization has not been made.

Findings for Use of Logic in the Classroom

The next set of studies we review are those concerned with logic in the classroom. As we know, two research groups have contributed to this tradition. The first group began work at Illinois under the leadership of B. O. Smith; the second, at Teachers College, Columbia University, was led by Arno Bellack. The two groups worked independently for the most part, and different observational instruments were developed by the two teams. Nevertheless, the two groups shared an interest in the expression of classroom logic and used concepts, and to some extent vocabularies, that overlapped.

Central to both approaches is the idea that classroom interaction may be broken into a series of "moves" that represent the communications emitted by a single classroom actor. In our earlier review of findings concerning classroom moves we considered the basic classification of move types made in the Columbia system. Now we turn from the enumeration and classification of moves to consider their logical properties.

All studies so far conducted within the tradition have been field surveys. Moreover, greater emphases have been given to descriptions of the classrooms and lessons studied, in logical terms, rather than to the testing of hypotheses concerning teaching. However, several findings have already been generated in this tradition that are of interest to us. These are summarized under four different variables (see Figure 11.8).

Logical complexity The first two of these variables concern the complexity of the logic used in the classroom. It is only reasonable to posit that classrooms which feature simple logic are likely to have somewhat different effects from classrooms that feature complex logic. This hypothesis was tested by independent investigators using somewhat different definitions of logical complexity (see Figure 9.4). One investigator differentiated between "*analytic*," "*empirical*," and "*evaluative*" processes in logic. The classroom was found to be more often concerned with "empirical" processes, while a more equitable use of "analytic" and "evaluative" processes was found to be associated with greater pupil achievement. The other two investigators differentiated between those logical processes placing "lower cognitive demands" and those placing "higher cognitive demands" on participants. Classrooms were found to exhibit lower cognitive demands more frequently than higher cognitive demands, experienced teachers used higher cognitive demands more often, while complex relationships were found between level of cognitive demands and pupil achievement. This latter finding is reminiscent, in both terminology and results, of earlier reported findings concerning levels of knowledge used in the lesson. Again, it seems that logical complexity probably does *not* bear a simple relationship with pupil achievement. On the other hand, the finding that classrooms might be "too empirical" in their orientation is provocative. We suspect that further research is needed on this issue.

FIGURE 11.8 Findings for studies of logic.

Process Variable Considered	Process Occurrence Most teaching is:	Context-Process Process variable associated with:	Presage-Process Process variable associated with:	Process-Process Process variable associated with:	Field Survey Process-Product Process variable associated with:	Experimental Process-Product Process variable induces:
Use of "analytic" and "evaluative" rather than "empirical" processes	More often concerned with "empirical" processes	Subject matter (2) (3) Nationality (4)			Greater pupil achievement (1)	
Use of categories implying "higher cognitive demand"	Low-level (3)		Greater teaching experience (1)		Lower pupil achievement (1) Complex or curvilinear relationship with pupil achievement (1)	
Congruency between teachers' solicitations and pupil responses	Congruent (1)			Unrelated to teachers' reactions to pupils' responses (2)		
Adequacy or appropriateness of pupil responses		"Sequential" and "procedural explaining" questions from teacher (other types of "explaining" questions less likely) (2)		Differential teachers' reactions ("praise" and "solicitation" more likely; "solicitations for additional responses" less likely) (1)		

(Box 9.1)

Congruency and appropriateness The third and fourth variables listed in Figure 11.8 concern relationships of logic between teacher and pupil utterances. All things being equal, one would expect to find close relationships in logic among classroom moves that were in the same episode or teaching cycle. When the teacher asks a question, for example, the pupil should presumably attempt to answer it. This type of logical relationship is termed *logical congruency*, and not surprisingly, most responses of pupils are found to be congruent to the teacher's solicitations. Interestingly, however, the concept of congruency does *not* necessarily extend to the teacher's subsequent reaction to the event. Apparently, teachers are reasonably tolerant of noncongruent responses. Unfortunately, we do not yet know what this tolerance accomplishes in product variables.

Another type of logical judgment concerns whether or not the pupil's answer was a correct one. Even if the pupil's answer is congruent, it need not be the "right" answer. If it is, the answer is termed *appropriate*. As it turns out, some teacher questions are more likely to provoke appropriate answers than are others. Among questions concerned with *explaining,* those requesting "sequential" and "procedural explaining" answers are likely to provoke appropriate answers, other types of explaining questions less likely. Teacher reactions are also likely to vary as a function of the appropriateness of pupils' responses. Appropriate responses are more likely to provoke "praise" and "repetition of the pupil's response" while an inappropriate response is likely to stimulate "solicitations for additional response." We already know from research on positive reinforcement that praise used for rewarding an appropriate response is effective. As we shall see shortly, the redirection of an unanswered question to another pupil is also associated with greater pupil achievement. No investigator has yet studied whether appropriateness *per se* has a relationship with achievement—presumably because it is normally presumed that inappropriate responses are a function of pupil ignorance. If, as we have discovered, inappropriateness is also a function of the vagueness of the question asked by the teacher, this assumption may not be completely valid. (More on vagueness below.)

Commentary The fact that relatively few findings are yet available from the research tradition concerned with logic does not mean that it is following a blind alley. Any number of variables concerned with teaching effectiveness may be derived from the concepts of this tradition, and we suspect that many of these will be explored in the near future. Research on the logic of teaching has great face validity, and the concepts of this tradition will presumably prove necessary in any empirically based theory of teaching. We shall have more to say on this topic in the last section of the chapter.

Findings for Linguistic Concepts

Research within the linguistic tradition is even more of an enigma than is research on logic. Above all, the classroom is a linguistic environment. Most of the symbols exchanged in the classroom are verbal or are based on verbal models, and discussion of the process of symbolizing constitutes a large part of the content of classroom discourse. Many of the judgments we are interested in making about teaching—whether these are concerned with warmth, managerial strategies, intellectual level and content, or logic—are expressed using linguistic symbols. Thus, *if* we had a viable set of linguistic concepts that could be used for disentangling classroom discourse, these concepts ought to generate much of the information of interest to those concerned with improving teaching.

If.

The trouble, of course, is that the field of linguistics is still in its infancy as far as our interests are concerned. Although linguists are now able to make quite sophisticated judgments concerning phoneme usage, lexical choice, syntax, and other surface features of classroom discourse, their ability to make *semantic* analyses is as yet poor. As a result, while excited over the potential linguistic analysis, we must to date put up with a series of somewhat uninteresting, superficial concepts in our search for findings concerning teaching. Let us consider three types of findings (see Figure 11.9).

Lexical concepts   Lexical concepts concern choice of vocabulary. It is reasonable to presume that teachers who are *verbally fluent* will have pupils who achieve more, and data are now available, from a field survey, to support this idea. Moreover, teacher use of *vagueness* also predicts pupil achievement (negatively). In addition, it is found that teachers who lack knowledge of their subject are more likely to use vague words than those who have that knowledge. Three other lexical concepts, *optimal information amount, knowledge structure cues,* and *interest,* fared less well in the data. They were more likely to vary as a function of the subject taught and were related to pupil achievement only in complex ways. In summary, then, vagueness would appear a good thing for the teacher to avoid in the classroom, while verbal fluency appears to be a good thing to possess. Unfortunately, apart from the single finding concerned with subject-matter knowledge, we are not told how to persuade teachers to be more fluent and less vague. One wonders whether these are trainable skills—outside of the traditional course in rhetoric and declamation!

Other surface concepts   A second set of findings concerns the occurrences of utterances in classroom discourse. In general, an utterance is a string of words that is emitted by a single classroom actor. Utterances may, for example, contain many "moves" in the Smith or Bellack sense or may be as short as a single exclamation. It has been noted by many commentators that teachers issue *more utterances* and *longer utterances* in the classroom than do pupils, and the data bear out these assertions. Teachers also are found to speak oftener and for longer periods at the upper grade levels.

Teachers of black pupils are found to speak more often; men teachers are likely to hold forth for a longer period of time once started. It is also claimed by some commentators that these phenomena should be avoided, that teachers should speak less and for shorter periods. Unfortunately, the data do not support the first of these ideas, and no findings have yet been advanced to test the second. We conclude, then, that findings concerning utterance frequency and length are presently of little value in telling us how to improve teaching.

Concepts based on reconstruction   Finally, we turn to findings generated by the process of reconstruction. As we know from Chapter IX, the technique of reconstruction is used to break a discourse record into manageable units of logic and to "fill in" materials that are implicit in the original speech pattern. A number of interesting concepts have been generated through this process. Consider first the use of *implicit reference*. Teachers lay considerable stress upon the use of explicit reference, since it is presumed that implicit reference is "not clear," and explicitness is the hallmark of the professional—be he scientist or lawyer. Thus, we learn that teachers are more likely to use explicitness than are pupils and that black pupils are more likely to use implicit speech, in the early grades, than are whites. Unfortunately, we are as yet provided no data concerning the effects of implicitness, so this finding too is at present a curiosity.

The same is true of the use of *complex sentences*. Teachers are found to use more complex sentences than are pupils. Complexity is more likely to characterize the speech of pupils in the upper grades and in rural, one-room schools. One suspects that the use of complex sentences will also have effects on pupils' achievement, but findings pertaining to this hypothesis have not yet been studied.

A third variable, use of *explicit logic*, has been studied for its effects, however. As we know, logical explicitness is signaled by the retention in explicit speech of words that signal an adjoining relationship, words such as "therefore" and "because." Not surprisingly, much of classroom discourse is found to be characterized by logical explicitness, while male teachers, and the pupils of male teachers, are found to use more explicit logic than female teachers and their pupils. Crucially, however, the use of explicit logic is found to be associated with greater pupil achievement. Apparently this linguistic variable *is* to be encouraged for teachers.

Finally, we examine findings associated with the use of *first names*. First-name use is an indicator of both status and intimacy—at least in the United States. Thus, we learn that teachers are more likely to use first names than are pupils, that first names are more likely to be used by women teachers, and that first names are more likely at the middle grade levels. Surprisingly, and perhaps pejoratively, first names are more likely to be used with black than with white pupils. But again, we do not yet know the educative significance of first-name usage or its lack.

Commentary   With minor exceptions linguistic research has so far

FIGURE 11.9 Findings for studies using linguistic concepts.

Process Variable Considered	Process Occurrence Most teaching is:	Context-Process Process variable associated with:	Presage-Process Process variable associated with:	Process-Process Process variable associated with:	Field Survey Process-Product Process variable associated with:	Experimental Process-Product Process variable induces:
(Lexical Concepts)						
Vagueness		Unrelated to subject matter of lesson (1)	Lack of subject matter knowledge (1)		Lesser pupil achievement (1)	
Optimal information amount		Subject matter (1)			Curvilinear or complex relationship with pupil achievement (1)	
Verbal fluency					Greater pupil achievement (1)	
Interest		Subject matter (1)			Curvilinear or complex relationship with pupil achievement (1)	
(Other Surface Concepts)						
More utterances (by teacher)	Teachers exhibit more utterances than do all pupils together (1)	Teachers of black pupils (1) Upper grade levels (1)				
Longer utterances (by teacher)	Teachers exhibit longer utterances than do pupils (1)	Upper grade levels (1) Male teachers (1)				

(Concepts based on Reconstruction)

Teacher use of <u>implicit reference</u>	Less likely to be implicitly expressed (1)	Black pupils (1)	
Pupil use of <u>implicit reference</u>	More likely to be implicitly expressed (1)	Black pupils (1)	
Teacher use of <u>complex sentences</u>	More likely to be complex (2)	Upper grade levels (1)	
Pupil use of <u>complex sentences</u>	Less likely to be complex (2)	Upper grade levels (1) Rural locations (1)	
Teacher use of <u>explicit logic</u> (adjoining without deletion)	Logically explicit (2)	Male teachers (1)	Greater pupil achievement (1)
Pupil use of <u>explicit logic</u> (adjoining without deletion)	Logically explicit (2)	Male teachers (1)	
Teacher use of <u>first names</u>	Likely to involve first names (1)	Black pupils (1) Female teachers (1)	
Pupil use of <u>first names</u>	Unlikely to involve first names (1)	Middle grade levels (1)	

(Box 9.2)

depended on field surveys in which the sole source of data was discourse records taken from classrooms. This is appropriate during exploratory research. (Actually, it represents an improvement on traditional methods in structural linguistics, which have tended to depend on the use of but one or two informants.) But such studies cannot provide information concerning process-product relationships, let alone experimental validation of such relationships. Moreover, to know that linguistic phenomena in the classroom are associated with desired effects is not to know how to train or select teachers to exhibit these phenomena. Some linguistic phenomena may be a reflection of the teacher's intelligence, sex role, social class background, or other experiences over which the teacher has little control. In the long run we suspect that the linguistic tradition will provide its greatest contribution not by suggesting variables but rather by providing us hard information about how teachers and pupils manage to exhibit the complex phenomena of teaching with which we are concerned.

Findings for Sequence Units

Finally, we turn to findings concerning the sequence of events in the classroom. As suggested in Chapter X, studies that have concerned themselves with sequences of classroom events do not constitute a single research tradition. Rather, concern for the obvious sequential character of the classroom has been expressed by a number of different investigators. Various concepts have been used to express these concerns. For convenience we sorted our review into concepts that were used to express the shorter sequences, or *tactics* of classroom conduct, and those used to express longer, or *strategic,* procedures in the classroom. Both types of units have produced findings of interest to educators (see Figure 11.10,) although research on classroom sequences is still in its infancy.

Tactical units　Most of the research so far conducted on classroom tactics has concerned the teaching episode (or teaching cycle). As we know, this is a unit of events during which the teacher exchanges moves with one or more pupils on a common topic. To use the vocabulary of Arno Bellack, the unit may either begin with a *structuring* statement or a *solicitation,* and usually these come from the teacher. It continues with a *response,* usually from a pupil, then perhaps additional responses or *reactions.* It terminates when the discussion switches to a new topic. As we know from our own classroom experience, teaching episodes are frequent events in the classroom, and it is not surprising that a number of episode characteristics have been examined by investigators.

First, consider *simple reciprocation,* which is a unit of exchange between the teacher and a single pupil. As we know, simple reciprocation usually begins with a teacher question. This is normally followed by a pupil response and may be terminated by a teacher reaction, although the latter is optional. Not too surprisingly, simple reciprocation is found to constitute a large proportion of all teaching episodes in the typical class-room, although this proportion varies with nationality and with length of teaching experience. As it turns out, simple reciprocation is also associated with greater pupil achievement, although the data come from a field survey. If confirmed experimentally, this would mean that simple exchanges be-tween teacher and individual pupil are an effective way of putting across the topic—perhaps better than the uninterrupted monologue or the longer, more complex exchange.

But what does the teacher do when the pupil does not know the answer to her question? Possible tactics include dropping the topic, negative re-inforcement of the mistaken pupil, additional structuring commentary, and so forth. However, the most effective strategy would appear to be *redirec-tion of the question* to another pupil. At least this is found to be associated with greater pupil achievement in field survey data.

If simple reciprocation is an effective teaching strategy, then perhaps *short episodes* will be found to be more effective than long episodes. Not unexpectedly, it turns out that the average episode *is* a short one in the typical classroom, although episode length varies with nationality and the type of episode considered. However, the relationship between episode length and pupil achievement turns out to be a complex one, and no simple recommendation for shorter episodes is in order.

What about *pupil initiation of episodes?* It is often argued that greater pupil initiative should be encouraged in the classroom, and indeed it turns out that the bulk of episodes in the typical classroom are teacher initiated, although again this phenomenon varies with nationality and with type and length of episode. Pupil initiation is also more likely in self-directed class-rooms than in standard classrooms. But we have no data as yet concerning the effects of greater pupil initiation on outcome variables, if any.

Finally, we take up a pair of variables concerned with the positioning of structuring statements in the episode. It is possible for the teacher to give a structuring statement at any of various points in the episode: at its begin-ning, following a solicitation, or at the end of the episode. It turns out that *episode-terminal structuring* is positively associated, and *postquestion structuring* negatively associated, with pupil achievement in field survey data. This makes sense. The teacher who first asks a question and then answers it herself is likely to generate confusion or boredom in pupils. On the other hand, the teacher who ties the episode together with terminal structuring is likely to make its implications clearer for all concerned.

In summary, then, although the data stem from field survey evidence only, it would appear that simple reciprocation, redirection of questions to other pupils, and episode-terminal structuring are teaching tactics to be advocated, while postquestion structuring should be avoided, for good teaching. Although evidence has not been advanced concerning whether

FIGURE 11.10 Findings for sequence units.

Process Variable Considered	Process Occurrence — Most teaching is:	Context-Process — Process variable associated with:	Presage-Process — Process variable associated with:	Process-Process — Process variable associated with:	Field Survey — Process variable associated with:	Experimental — Process variable induces:
(Tactical Units)						
Simple reciprocation— SOL RES (REA)	Concerned with simple reciprocation (3)	Nationality (2)	Lesser teaching experience (1)		Greater pupil achievement (1)	
Redirection of question (to other pupils)					Greater pupil achievement (1)	
Length of episodes (or cycles)	Exhibits short episodes (3)	Nationality (3)		Type of episode (1)	Curvilinear or complex relationship with pupil achievement (1)	
Pupil initiation of episodes (or cycles)	Teacher initiated (1)	Self-directed classrooms (1) Nationality (1)		Type of episode (1) Shorter episodes (1)		
Episode-terminal structuring— ...REA					Greater pupil achievement (1)	
Postquestion structuring— SOL STR	Seldom concerned with postquestion structuring (1)				Lesser pupil achievement (1)	
(Box 10.1)						
(Strategic Units)						
Ventures combining descriptions and instances		Subject matter of lesson (1)			Greater pupil concept learning (1)	
Lesson-terminal summary					Greater pupil achievement (1)	
(Box 10.2)						

406

teachers can be taught these tactics, we suspect that they can indeed be induced through appropriate programs of teacher education.

Strategic units   Two kinds of strategic units were reported in Chapter X. The first consists of the *venture*, which is a discourse segment that has a "single, overarching content objective." Research Box 10.2 reported a large group of results concerning the classification and frequency of occurrence of venture phenomena, but not very many findings that can be put to use by educators. As a matter of fact, the only simple finding that is associated with the venture unit is that *ventures combining descriptions and instances* are found to be more effective in inducing pupil concept learning than three other types of ventures. As interesting as the venture concept may be, we find little to report on it for educators at the moment.

The second strategic unit is the *lesson* itself. Given the obviousness of the lesson as a unit, it is surprising that so few investigators have yet looked at the distribution of teaching phenomena within the lesson. It seems likely, for example, that any number of teaching phenomena—managerial strategies, utilization of logic, intellectualization, and so forth—will be found to vary, depending on whether it is early or late in the lesson. Moreover, distribution of these phenomena during the lesson ought to have an effect on pupil learning or attitudes. And yet we have found only two examples of findings concerned with this type of information. One was the earlier result telling us that "divergent" questions were more likely to be found early in the lesson. In addition, a single field survey found that greater pupil achievement was associated with *lesson-terminal summarization*, which we presume is a good strategy for teachers to follow.

Commentary   The idea that teaching should be effective or ineffective depending on its sequencing has great face validity. Moreover, notions of sequence have been taught for years in courses concerned with "methods of teaching." Consider the old claim that it is more effective to ask the question first and then to nominate the pupil who will answer it, rather than to nominate and then ask. This is a sequence idea. Moreover, we suspect that it is correct and could be validated by data. But to the best of our knowledge it has not yet been tested. We hope and presume that additional findings concerned with sequence phenomena will be appearing in the near future.

DISCUSSION

The authors have occasionally encountered educators who claimed that observational research on teaching had produced little of interest for teachers. Whether these commentators were responding to the findings of research based on FIAC, to the as-yet-limited amount of research relating process variables to product variables, or merely to the well-known fact that researchers have difficulty writing common English is not known. The fact is that this claim is clearly in error. Not only has this field produced information of value to educators, but in some ways that contribution is a massive one.

Perhaps the strongest contribution to date is in the realm of concepts. Literally hundreds of concepts for teaching have now been examined in this research effort, and scores of instruments are now available for their measurement. Some of these concepts represent the application of notions from pre-existing theories of education. Some grew directly out of the observational process itself and had no existence prior to the conduct of research. Moreover, in some cases concepts that had previously been presumed to describe the events of teaching have been found non-operational when applied to the actual observation of classroom events. As a result of this research, then, educators are provided a rich and growing vocabulary of terms known to describe the processes of teaching. These terms constitute a vocabulary that may be used by teachers and other educators for thinking about teaching. As well, they provide a base for additional research in which the processes of teaching are explored and are tied to other events.

A second major contribution has been the debunking of several simple models for the improvement of classroom education. As we know, many studies in this field were generated by simple theories, if not *Commitments*, concerned with the improvement of teaching. Most of these notions have fared rather badly at the hands of studies that were designed to validate them. This does not mean that they are totally worthless. Indeed, we suspect that each of these ideas has a significant place in our understanding of teaching. But those who thought that classroom teaching would be improved "if only" it were warmer or less directive, or that teachers used more divergent questions or a higher level of discourse, are likely to have a sobering experience when they look at the findings of this research field. Even negative findings such as these are a significant contribution.

But what about the positive findings? However tentative these latter may be, it is clear that research on teaching has now generated a wide range of findings covering many aspects of classroom education. Some of these suggest strategies that might be employed by teachers for raising pupil achievement. Some suggest means for improving classroom experiences. Some suggest steps that might be taken to improve the selection or training of teachers. Some suggest ways in which contexts might be manipulated to improve education. Some provide us descriptions of contemporary classroom life. Although tentative, findings such as these represent a clear improvement over hearsay or the unsupported opinions of advocates.

At the same time, it should be remembered that these findings are but tentative. Earlier in the chapter we noted a number of reasons why findings should not yet be considered definitive. Some studies in this field have made use of poor instruments or weak designs. Nearly all samples used have been small and were chosen in a nonrandom manner. Few multivariate studies have yet been conducted, and few results from field surveys have yet been validated experimentally. Most studies have not involved context variation in their samples, and where replication has taken place it appears to have involved studies with weaker design features.

Studies have also concentrated on but a limited range of classrooms to date, primarily traditional American classrooms conducted by female teachers with white, middle-class pupils. Little research has yet appeared concerning self-directed classrooms, open schools, pupils representing ethnic or linguistic minority status, or innovations such as educational television. As a result, some of the findings may reflect the biases and cultural limitations of this specific form of classroom experience. We suspect, for example, that the finding reported in Figure 11.6 wherein centrality of teacher role was reported to be positively related to pupil involvement might well be reversed in open classrooms once pupils became used to self-directed study. Again, differential treatment of pupils by sex may well be reversed in other countries where classrooms are conducted in a more "masculine" manner than is presumably true in the United States.

Another problem concerns the choice of criterion variables against which to validate teaching processes. As readers will have discovered, most attempts to use product variables for this purpose have chosen *pupil achievement*, as measured by standardized achievement tests. This is not only an insensitive variable, but it may be offmark for our purposes. Consider the finding that teacher use of higher cognitive demand leads to lower pupil achievement. It seems possible to us that lower cognitive demand is more efficient for putting across facts, while higher cognitive demand encourages independence of thought. The latter, of course, is not measured by standardized achievement tests. Hypotheses of this sort cannot be tested until more sensitive product criteria are developed and used in research on teaching.

Still another problem concerns the function of *Commitment* and the validity of findings. As readers will know from our earlier chapters, *Commitments* have not only generated several of the research traditions upon which we have reported but have also apparently caused researchers to cling to inappropriate concepts and research tools, and apparently to misinterpret their own findings or those of other investigators. To put it another way, when discussing their research and its implications, educational researchers tend to become advocates rather than reporters. For this reason readers would gain a somewhat different picture of findings and their implications were they to read primary sources instead of the review they have found here. Well, which findings are "correct," the ones claimed by the investigators, or the more conservative ones portrayed here? In some cases investigators may be privy to information they have not yet seen fit to publish, but on the whole we suspect that our interpretations, based on clinical judgments (see the Appendix), are the more accurate.

However, it seems to us that the largest shortcoming concerning these findings is the lack of an integrative theory of teaching with which to make sense out of them. It is quite impossible to keep findings for 75 different variables in one's head. Moreover, some of these variables overlap one another in meaning; many presumably co-occur; some are causative, others resultative, and still others but concomitants of more complex teaching processes than we have yet conceptualized. In the long run we need to know not only what teaching processes occur, when they are likely to appear, with what other processes they co-occur, and what they produce in pupils when present or absent, but also we want to know *why*. In short, a tabulation of findings, however comprehensive it may be, is but a prelude to an empirically based theory of teaching. Although we cannot hope to provide such a theory here—indeed, that is the topic of another book!—it is possible to sketch some of the outlines of this task. To these outlines we now turn.

TOWARD EMPIRICALLY BASED THEORIES OF TEACHING

Let us begin with a truism—any comprehensive theory of teaching must involve three classes of variables: independent variables which determine the events of teaching, process variables that express the events of teaching, and dependent variables that reflect the outcomes of teaching. It is convenient if we organize our discussion in terms of these three variable classes.

Independent Variables

In presenting findings we have differentiated two broad classes of variables, those we have termed *presage* variables and those expressing *context* variation. Presage variables are those associated with the teacher; context variables include conditions associated with pupils, classroom, school, and community. The distinction between these two classes is arbitrary, but as a general rule context variables express conditions to which educators must accommodate, whereas presage variables express strategies for coping and are more likely to be under control by educators. Again, educators hope eventually to build theories of teaching that transcend contextual conditions, whereas presage variables are integral to our concerns within those theories. Let us consider these two classes of variables in turn.

Context variables As we know, only a few context variables have featured in research on teaching to date. Most of these have been associated with classrooms, including *grade level, subject matter, multigradedness,* use of *computer-assisted instruction,* and *experimental curricula.* Many "obvious" classroom variables have not yet received much attention, however, including class size, physical properties of the classroom, other educational media, equipment in the room, or self-directed and "open" classrooms. Only two variables have yet been considered that are associated with school and community: *nationality* and *social class* of the school. So far ignored are such variables as the social structure and size of the school, the use of inspectors, the effects of matriculation examinations, and so forth. Finally, only a handful of studies has yet examined pupil variables, including pupil *sex, race, intelligence,* and *prior achievement.* Slighted have been such obvious variables as pupil impulsiveness, creativity, sociometric status, leadership position in the school, ethnic background, or "reputation."

As yet little is known concerning the functions of these various context variables in theories of teaching, although findings are available for those variables cited in the figures and earlier text of this chapter. Some are presumably irrelevant, some will provide but minor input, some will turn out to generate substantial variation in teaching and its effects. Most of the context variables so far examined *have* proved to affect teaching in at least minor ways. Also, most context variables will have their greatest use in predicting wholistic aspects of teacher or classroom behavior. Pupil variables, in contrast, may also be used for predicting the differential treatment of individual pupils by the teacher. Additional research on context variables is clearly indicated.

Presage variables   To date more studies have considered presage variables than context variation. Of these the variable most often studied has been *experimental training procedures* used in programs of teacher education. Also studied have been *ratings* given to teachers by supervisors, various *inventory scores* designed to measure personality or teaching abilities, teacher *expectations* for pupil achievement and future success, *attitudes toward pupils,* and *academic background.* Surprisingly, only three demographic and background variables have yet appeared in the presage list: teacher *age, sex,* and *years of experience.* (So far ignored, for example, have been teacher intelligence, social class background, birth order, and physical characteristics.)

Presage variables have not had an impressive "track record" in predicting the processes of teaching. It is possible, of course, that those who have investigated presage variables have simply been more scrupulous in reporting negative findings, but if not, we have considerable cause to question the usefulness of such presage variables as ratings by others, inventory scores, experimental training programs, and expectations for pupil achievement. As an example, out of seven findings involving the MTAI, only two report obtaining a relationship with a teaching variable. Again, roughly a third of the findings for experimental training programs report nil success.

Why these results? We can think of three possible explanations. First, it may in fact be true that variations in teaching are more likely to be induced by contexts than by presage conditions, although this is as yet an unresolved question. Second, concentration has heretofore been given to teacher properties and training experiences rather than to demographic variables and formative experiences. The latter would appear to have a better record of success. Third, much of the research to date appears to have concentrated on weak presage variables. Ratings given to teachers by others have questionable validity, most of the inventories so far used were not prepared with knowledge of the processes of teaching in mind, and experimental training procedures have often appeared to reflect *Commitments* rather than clear ideas as to what teaching processes are desirable in the classroom. Information is not yet available to indicate which of these explanations is strongest, and we rather suspect that all three will be found to have some merit.

Where does this leave us with regard to presage variables? Which presage variables are likely to provide us the greatest ability to predict and control classroom events? Two answers may be suggested for this question. On the one hand, some demographic and formative experiences are likely either to have left a significant impact on teachers or to cause continuing, differential response to teachers in pupils. Age, sex, race, and ethnic background exemplify such variables, and we ignore factors such as these at our peril when constructing theories of teaching. On the other hand, much of teaching is presumably *coping* behavior on the part of the teacher and is thus subject to beliefs held by the teacher concerning the curriculum, the nature and objectives of the teaching task, expectations for pupils, and norms concerning appropriate classroom behavior. Thus, a reasonably good prediction of the classroom behavior of the teacher can presumably be obtained by finding out what the teacher thinks she prefers to, ought to, and will do in the classroom. It will presumably take a substantial number of presage variables to predict a substantial proportion of the variance of classroom events, but we suspect that the variables most likely to be effective will stem from the two classes just described.

We must not leave this subject without noting that our review has merely scratched the surface of what is known concerning the influence of context and presage variables. Readers will recall that studies reviewed in this text were limited to those wherein observational research was conducted in the classroom. Many studies have been conducted involving context and presage variables that do not meet this restriction. Thus, a considerable literature is available on such topics as teacher expectations for pupils, teacher authoritarianism, pupil sex and race, grade level, subject matter, or educational television that have not been reviewed here. Those desiring to know of the effects of these variables on classroom events will find our review useful; those wanting to know "all about" teacher expectations or the effects of educational television will have to look elsewhere.

Process Variables

Process variables and their relationships are the heartland of theories of teaching. If our theories accomplish no other purpose, they must at least account for the observable events of the classroom as teachers and pupils come together and engage the complex and multiordinate processes of instruction. As we know, literally scores of process variables have now been studied in observational studies of teaching. These variables represent a number of different research traditions, and yet it would appear that there is considerable overlap among the traditions and their variables. How can we accommodate this variety of variables?

One way to reduce the confusion is to recognize that most of the variables reviewed appear to fall into a limited number of models for "explaining" classroom events. For convenience we shall consider four such models.

The trait model   Perhaps the simplest of all models considers teaching to be a matter of the display of behavioral traits by the teacher. Teachers may be ranked in terms of the degree to which they display a given trait ("warmth," for example, or "directiveness"), and differential effects are obtained in pupils to the extent that this trait is or is not displayed. At least a third of all variables reviewed appear to fall within the scope of this model. These would include teacher *praise, acceptance, criticism, talk, asking of questions, lecturing, giving directions, use of higher-order knowledge, asking divergent questions, use of abstract thought, thought extension, structuring, vagueness, implicit reference, sentence complexity, explicit logic, use of first names, postquestion structuring,* and so forth. As we can see, variables of the trait variety have stemmed from several traditions and represent both high-inference and low-inference variables. Trait models have often appeared in others' thinking about teaching, notably in Ryans' (1960) classic study as well as in the recent review efforts of Rosenshine (1971).

The trait model would appear simple in comparison with the other three models to be reviewed. It tends to ignore the fact that teacher behavior is reactive as well as proactive, to gloss over differential treatment of pupils by the teacher, and to avoid considering teacher management of the classroom group. That it is a simple model does not make it an ineffective one, however. Some of the variables cited above have, indeed, proved to bear relationships with product variables. In addition, it is possible to convert some variables from the more complex models to trait variables by suitable reconceptualization, and investigators have often done this when searching for the determinants of effective teaching. All things considered, however, we find this model to have but limited utility and suspect that its variables are likely to have less long-term usefulness than those to follow.

The interaction model   A second model considers teaching to be primarily a matter of interaction between the teacher and individual pupils. Concepts are set forth for studying the sequences of interaction, and variables are derived from properties of those sequences. Variables appearing within this model include *positive* and *negative reinforcement, congruency, appropriateness, simple reciprocation, redirection, episode length, episode-terminal structuring,* and the like. As can be seen, the interaction model appears to characterize research in the behavior modification tradition, as well as those studies that have concentrated on tactical sequences in instruction. The interaction model is also likely to appear in observational research conducted by social psychologists of other types of face-to-face groups.

The interaction model is surely a more complex one than the trait model. And, as we know, some if its variables are more effective predictors of pupil outcomes than are their trait counterparts. As an example, sheer incidence of praise does not appear to have consistent relationships with pupil achievement, whereas praise used for the positive reinforcement of pupil responses does. However, the analysis of sequences of teacher-pupil interaction is a complex business, and some of those who have used the interaction model have appeared to be satisfied merely to tabulate sequences rather than to explore variables that could be defined for those sequences. In addition, the fact that sequences of teacher-pupil interaction form the data for the model means that it is more difficult to use process criteria to judge success in teaching (see below). Also, this model, too, avoids concern for the classroom group. All things considered, however, we find this model a useful one but would stress the need to combine it with other models so as to obtain an adequate coverage of classroom events.

The social system model   The third model we shall consider views teaching to involve group states, as well as individual states of the teacher and pupils. Actions are taken by the teacher, as well as by pupils, as a result of which systemic conditions are set up in the classroom. These, in turn, produce effects in the behavior and growth of pupils. Two subclasses of variables appear within this model, those concerned with the behaviors of teachers and pupils that affect the state of the system and those that describe the system. Among the former we find many of the concepts used by Kounin, such as *withitness, overlappingness, smoothness, momentum* and the like, as well as variables used to describe the *teacher's role*. Among the latter are included variables for the *structure* and *function* of classroom groups, a number of *format* variables, and those applying to *pupil role*. The social system model owes as much to the discipline of sociology as it does to psychology, and other examples of it may be found in leadership research.

The social system model is more complex than either of the two models already reviewed. Moreover, no study that we have yet discovered appears to exemplify it *in toto*. In defense of the model teachers are well aware that much of their effort is spent in creating an effective classroom climate. Indeed, we are told that in the really well-managed classroom the pupils become self-directed learners, while the teacher's role withdraws from lecturing in favor of consultation and resource management. Moreover, much of the teacher's communications are addressed to the classroom as a whole, and many pupil activities are carried out by groups rather than by individuals alone. Be that as it may, our vocabulary for describing group states in the classroom is still nascent, and findings for this model are more tentative than for the two models already reviewed. The model also appears to ignore the details of teacher interaction with individual pupils. It is also difficult to study classroom climate, and the strategies by which it is maintained, without longitudinal observation of the classroom over a number of lessons—something that most investigators are unwilling to contemplate. All things considered, then, this model also furnishes us with insights concerning the events of teaching, but it must be combined with other models for adequate coverage of the field.

The curriculum model   Finally, we turn to yet another model that appears simple in conception, although its details may be complex indeed. This model views the events of teaching to vary as a function of the curriculum that is imposed on the classroom. Various aspects of the curriculum may be explored, including *lesson formats*, the *physical ecology* of the classroom, *educational media* such as television or the use of computer-assisted instruction, and the like. As used in this model, "curriculum" refers not to a set of prescriptions that are enunciated for the classroom but rather to the complex of events that actually occur in that setting. For example, innovations are often proposed for new ways of conducting the lesson or for the use of educational media. Unless these are reflected in actual changes in the practices of classroom members, a new curriculum has not been effected in the sense we are using it here. The curriculum model is often argued by educational innovators, and it appears similar to models advocated by sociologists when they speak of "the definition of the situation."

Like the social system model, the curriculum model views the classroom as a system of interlocking parts. That system, however, is viewed as a gestalt rather than as a set of components that can be analyzed. In addition, the system is considered a resultant of many causes—lesson plans, pressures from outside the classroom, the physical environment, teacher actions, pupil actions—rather than as something over which the teacher has presumptive control. In defense of the model, *if* it should turn out that lesson formats and the like can be neatly categorized, the model will provide a succinct way of approaching classroom events. The model also alerts us to the fact that the events of teaching may vary as a function of causes other than teacher action alone. So far, however, this model has provoked even less systematic research than the social system model. It also appears to ignore much of the detail of teacher-pupil interaction and to view the teacher more as a victim than as a perpetrator of the lesson. All things considered, the model offers an attractive prospect for the eventual simplification of complex findings concerning teaching, but we suspect that appropriate curriculum variables are more likely to develop from research involving the detailed analysis of classroom events than they are to be developed through insight or theory.

None of these models, then, is adequate by itself to accommodate the events of teaching. Each has some attractive features. The trait and curriculum models offer simplicity of conceptualization and the prospect of providing clear prescriptions for the improvement of teaching. The interaction model focuses our attention on the details of teacher interaction with individual pupils. The social system model reminds us that the teacher must also manage the classroom group. Theories of teaching that utilize but one of these models are not likely to accommodate more than a portion of the events of teaching.

These observations suggest that theories of teaching must accommodate a variety of variables, indeed models, if they are to be effective. And yet most studies reviewed so far have involved the measurement of only a handful of process variables. As a result, little is known today concerning the co-occurrence of process variables, particularly variables that represent two or more research traditions or models. It is possible to speculate at some length concerning the probable relationship between Kounin's managerial variables and the structure of classroom groups, for example, or between logical and linguistic concepts that appear to cover some of the same territory. But until research is conducted in which numerous variables are apposed within a common set of data, these speculations remain untested. One of the major problems hampering construction of theories of teaching is the fact that so few multivariate process studies have yet been conducted. (We shall have more to say on this subject in Chapter XII.)

Dependent Variables

Two types of dependent variables have been used to judge the outcomes of teaching in studies we have reviewed: process variables that describe pupil classroom behavior and product variables. Both types have their advantages. Pupil classroom behavior is observable to teachers, and sensitive teachers undoubtedly utilize this criterion to establish whether a given lesson is or is not "getting across." On the other hand, only in some explanatory models are pupil process variables considered to be the clear results of classroom events. The interactive model, in particular, builds variables that involve both teacher and pupil behavior, and for this model it is difficult to use pupil behavior also to judge outcomes of teaching. In addition, we cannot tell from external appearances what is going on inside the pupil's head, thus pupils may appear to be highly involved in the lesson and yet be learning little. For this reason most educators have insisted that the ultimate validation for improvements in teaching must depend on product measures. Let us consider these two types of measures in turn.

Pupil process variables Given the relative blandness of pupil classroom behavior, it is surprising to discover that more than a dozen pupil variables have now been used as outcome measures for establishing the success of teaching, or its lack. Of these, two variables are used with considerable frequency, *pupil work involvement* and *pupil deviancy*. However, numerous other variables have also been used, including *pupil talk, pupil responses, pupil initiations, "correct" responses, pupil conformity* to model or demand, and *pupil self-touching behavior.* In addition, several variables have also appeared that involved judgments made about the classroom group, including the *maintenance of group functions,* the *intrusion of non-relevant subject matter,* and *cognitive level of the discourse.* While not an exhaustive list, this set of variables would appear to provide a reasonably adequate catalog of observable events against which teachers and researchers can judge teaching for its immediate success.

Little is yet known concerning the co-occurrence of these various pupil process variables. Are pupils who are involved in their work also likely to be free from deviancy? Kounin's research suggests that these two variables are likely to occur under somewhat different conditions, but this does not mean that they may not co-occur. No study has yet been conducted, to our knowledge, concerned with exploring the range of pupil variables that might be used for judging success in teaching. Surprisingly, several studies have appeared in which these outcome measures were themselves used to predict to product variables. In general, this latter strategy has proved a weak one. To the extent that we can depend on those few studies that have so far taken up the matter, pupil classroom behavior and pupil product measures would appear to be only weakly related.

Pupil product variables By far the majority of product findings so far reported have utilized *pupil achievement* on a standardized test as the criterion. More than 100 findings using this variable are tabulated in the figures of this chapter. Substantial results are also reported for *pupil attitudes* to the subject. Beyond these two measures only a scattering of findings are available for such variables as *pupil achievement motivation, pupil creativity, pupil anxiety, pupil self-concept, pupil fear of failure, pupil dependency, pupil vocabulary growth,* and the like. This list, then, is a remarkably limited one. Standardized achievement tests usually measure low-level knowledge rather than understanding or integration of the subject. Quite ignored to date are any number of variables that would be related to claimed goals of classroom education, such as knowledge of school rules, attitudes concerning citizenship, liking for the teacher, or knowledge concerning adult role behavior.

One of the striking things about product-oriented research on teaching to date is how often investigators have *failed* to obtain a predicted relationship. More than half of all findings examined for both pupil achievement and pupil attitudes have reported insignificant relationships. It is possible that these findings have resulted from the wrong choice of process variables, and we have generally given this interpretation in earlier chapters. It is also possible that the product variables chosen are simply weak and unreliable. Once again, no study to our knowledge has yet taken on the task of developing an adequate set of product variables with which to assess the success of teaching in a multivariate fashion. We view this as another major problem standing in the way of theory development (and again will have more to say on the subject in Chapter XII).

In summary, then, adequate, empirically based theories are not now available concerning the determinants, processes, and effects of teaching. Some of the outlines of such theories can be discerned, however, and readers are urged to join us in the exciting task of theory assembly.

POSTSCRIPT

We began this text by encouraging readers to believe that research on the processes of teaching was a vital necessity and that this research has already generated findings useful to educators. This chapter has summarized evidence for these claims. Most of the evidence so far advanced is suggestive rather than definitive. Some of it concerns notions for the improvement of teaching that *don't* appear to work; some of it presents evidence for ideas that *do*. Some of the conclusions reached are tentative because studies of crucial relationships have not yet been conducted, because of limited samples, or because evidence from field surveys has not yet been confirmed with experiments. Little has yet appeared by way of theoretical integration for this field, although the outlines of theories can be discerned. But scores of variables for describing classroom events are now available from this research for which literally hundreds of suggestive findings have been developed! At long last we are beginning to know what is actually going on in the classroom, as well as what produces and results from classroom events. Surely the appearance of this research effort is one of the most significant developments in education during the twentieth century.

XII
RECOMMENDATIONS FOR RESEARCHERS

This chapter discusses problems we have unearthed in reviewing research on classroom behavior and makes recommendations concerning them for researchers and others concerned with teaching. What gaps have been identified in our review of research? What variables are in need of further exploration? Which designs and methods are likely to be profitable in the future? What problems appear to lie in the way of useful research on teaching, and what can be done about these problems? These are questions of interest to researchers, to educators, to those who support research on education, indeed to all who are involved with teaching in any way. Let us consider them now.

The mood of this chapter is somewhat different from that of the previous chapter, which drew a wealth of detail from explicit materials in our substantive reviews. Few citations to earlier comments are given here. Instead, each problem and recommendation is argued in its own terms. Nevertheless, the chapter presupposes that readers are familiar with the content and vocabulary of the rest of the book, and readers will discover that most of the points made here are expansions of earlier observations.

Five sections constitute the chapter. We begin with general problems that are endemic to the wider culture of educational research. Three sections follow concerned with problems of theory, method, and interpretation in studies of research on teaching. Finally, we make a series of recommendations concerning designs for future research in this important field.

THE CULTURE OF EDUCATIONAL RESEARCH

Research on teaching is laid within a larger cultural context. Research on educational matters has been conducted for years within Western societies, and procedures for its accomplishment are well established. These procedures include settings in which educational research is usually performed, mechanisms for its support, and avenues for publication and distribution of its results. In the United States, for example, most educational research is accomplished in university settings, is supported casually or through short-term federal grants, and is published in journals that include not only reports of research but also articles that are philosophic or hortatory in their orientation. Such procedures have produced a history of educational research that runs back to the turn of the century. However, they have some disadvantages for research on teaching, and it is useful to consider the latter.

The culture of educational research is shared by more than researchers, of course. For this reason recommendations within this section are addressed not only to researchers but also to chairmen of school boards, civil servants responsible for research on education, editors of journals, foundation representatives, and others in the educational community.

Lack of Support

Perhaps the greatest problem facing research on teaching processes is lack of support dollars for educational research. Support for research is much greater in other fields than it is in education. For example, research consumes some 10 to 25 percent of the available funds in the automotive and drug industries, while billions of federal dollars are available for research on arms development, space exploration, or cancer research. And yet less than one tenth of one percent of the dollars annually spent on education in the United States is spent for research purposes, nor is the amount appreciably greater in other Western countries.

One can only speculate as to the reasons for this lack of support: disbelief in the effectiveness of educational research; lack of an ideology that stresses the crucial importance of rectifying poor educational conditions; belief that problems in education can be solved through common sense; disputes among local, state, and federal authorities over responsibility for support of educational research. The point is that few dollars are available for support of any form of educational research, and support for research on teaching is no exception to this generalization. "We would not dream of constructing a bridge, distributing a new drug, or placing a man in a rocket to fly to the moon without careful research. However, we daily subject thirty million school children to instructional methods whose effects are largely unresearched" (Biddle, 1974). One can but speculate on the millions of young lives that are warped through this failure.

The difficulty with good research on teaching is that it is simply more expensive to conduct than most types of educational research. As we have noted, to process recordings of classroom lessons requires upwards of one hundred dollars per lesson. These are much more expensive data than pupil achievement scores, for example, or measurements obtained from teacher personality inventories. (They are also far cheaper than data obtained from a neutron accelerator, but then we are used to spending large sums for research in the physical sciences.) If we are serious about research on teaching, as we must be, dollar support for this research must be sharply increased.

Recommendation: *Support for research on the processes, causes, and effects of teaching should be sharply increased from federal, state, and local sources.*

Programmatic Support

Only slightly less important is the problem of programmatic support. Research on teaching tends to make its most significant advances when efforts of an investigative team are supported for several years. Partial examples of this principle may be found in the contributions of groups headed by Kounin, B. O. Smith, Bellack, Gage, Scott, or Nuthall, although none of these programmatic efforts would appear to have been supported securely over time. Programmatic support allows for time to develop concepts, instruments, and innovative designs for research. It allows time for the collection of field data involving variations in context, for conducting a series of related experiments, or for developing curricular materials that are related to empirical information concerning teaching.

And yet the majority of studies we have reviewed have represented one-shot research projects that received minimal or short-term grant support. As we have noted, the information generated by such research is paper thin, and many of these projects have exhibited flaws in conceptualization, design, or interpretation. Short-term grant support may be appropriate in the physical sciences or engineering, where concepts and methods are more firmly established and where knowledge concerning the effects of contextual variables has been backlogged. It is less appropriate in the social sciences. It is particularly inappropriate in the field of teaching research, where data are costly and complex and where we are just beginning to explore the effects of contexts on teaching phenomena. It seems vital that programmatic support be made available to investigative teams who will commit themselves to promising avenues for research on teaching for periods of several years.

Recommendation: *Programmatic support should be made available for research on the processes, causes, and effects of teaching to promising teams of investigators.*

Research Pacing

In Chapter II we reviewed several responses that citizens have expressed concerning our lack of well-established knowledge about teaching. Two of these are likely to affect the researcher directly. The first is the notion that, for one reason or another, it is impossible to develop empirically based knowledge concerning teaching. Researchers are likely to hear plaints to this effect from members of school boards, from some teachers, from physical scientists or humanists, and even from some educational researchers interested in other matters (who should know better). Responses of this sort may be used to justify denying funds to support research on teaching or to support innovative programs in teaching that have not yet been subjected to teaching research.

The second is the idea that teaching research can be expected to provide immediate and definitive answers. It seems strange that after more than seven decades of relatively ineffective research on teacher effectiveness, plus another two on more effective but complex research on the processes of teaching, there should still be persons around who believe that teaching research can produce an immediate and definitive pay-off. One of the authors was once offered more than $100,000 from a federal official if he would produce definitive information on the "improvement" of teaching within a six-month period! Federal support for research is sometimes restricted to projects that promise practical results within a short time, and for this reason researchers too are prone to make exaggerated claims for the definitive significance of their research when they are submitting proposals for research funding.

Let us recognize that truth lies between these extremes of unreasonable pessimism and optimism. Research on teaching can produce useful, empirically based information for the improvement of education—indeed, has already done so. But production of this information will take considerable time and effort.

Recommendation: *Support for research on the processes, causes, and effects of teaching should be asked for and given with the expectation that valuable information can be developed (through programmatic effort) in a period of several years.*

Innovative Programs

Another problem concerns the place of teaching research in programs of educational innovation. As we have seen, most research on teaching is conducted for its own sake, and most of it to date has concerned traditional classroom practices. And yet considerable effort is now being spent to construct innovative programs that should affect, and may even improve, classroom teaching. These include dozens of programs for curricular innovation, new programs for the training of teachers, the adoption of open-plan school buildings and self-directed classrooms, bussing of pupils to achieve racial balance, the adoption of such educational media as television or teaching machines, and so forth, in endless profusion. We find these efforts to be striking evidence of the vitality of Western education.

With minor exceptions, however, most of these programs have been instituted without any attempts to find the effects of the programs on the behaviors of classroom participants. Most innovative programs are instituted without the benefit of research. Where research is conducted it nearly always concerns presage or product variables rather than observational research on the processes of teaching. Thus, the typical program is "validated" through research on the attitudes of teachers using it or through the achievement scores of pupils who are subjected to it. As we know, such research designs are weak, are subject to errors induced through investigator enthusiasms, and provide us little information as to why the innovation *really* works, if indeed it does. Clearly, research on teaching should be built into innovative programs in education on a regular basis.

Recommendation: *Innovative programs that are likely to affect teaching should not be instigated or funded without research on the effects of these programs on the processes of teaching.*

Publication

We next turn to the complex topic of procedures for the publication of research on teaching. As is well known, scientific journals constitute the major avenue for publication in any field. These journals set and enforce standards for research and constitute a repository of information that may be tapped by other researchers or by those who want to apply scientific knowledge to the solution of a practical problem. Each subfield tends to have one or more journals devoted to research within its compass, and these journals are clearly distinct from others in which findings are popularized or their philosophic implications are discussed. When turning to education, however, we find that this neat picture breaks down. Although scientific journals can be found in education, most journals include a melange of research, opinion, philosophy, and exhortation. Many journals are eclectic in their interests, others are devoted to research that is conducted within a state or region rather than in a given subfield. Moreover, a sizable portion of educational research is not now published at all, in any traditional sense, but is rather delivered as papers at conventions or distributed as technical reports of federally funded research projects. As a result, information on any given subfield in education is likely to appear in literally hundreds of different sources, editorial control over the quality of educational research is therefore loose, and consumers have difficulty in keeping up with research on any given topic.

Let us take up these problems in order—first, the diffusion of information. It is unfortunately true that no journal, as distinct from newsletter, is now published that devotes itself to research on teaching. Sufficient research is now available to justify such a journal, and we suspect that it would receive wide adoption among educators.

Recommendation: *A journal should be instigated that is concerned with research on the processes, causes, and effects of teaching.*

A second problem has to do with editorial control over research quality. A number of problems of quality control in research on teaching have been identified in our earlier chapters. These include matters such as failure to provide descriptions of instruments, failure to publish reliability data, misuse of inductive statistics, failure to interpret findings that appear in data tables, failure to publish results, and so forth. We discuss these and related problems of interpretation in greater detail below. The point here is that standards should now be set and enforced for scientific publication for all educational journals that are willing to publish research results.

Recommendation: *Standards for scientific publication in education should be specified for the most prestigious journals in education, perhaps under the sponsorship of national educational research organizations.*

Third is the problem faced by consumers of educational research. The typical consumer meets problems that are immense. For one thing, research of concern to him is likely to be published in any of literally hundreds of sources. For another, its quality varies. For another, the vocabulary with which it is expressed may be unfamiliar to him, for research from a variety of disciplinary traditions may bear on the practical problem with which he is concerned. And again, much of that research is likely to be reported together with advocacy and interpretation, so that it is difficult for him to separate the actual findings from the claims. No wonder that Jeanne Chall (1967) found research on reading to have so little effect on the adoption of reading programs in the schools!

Efforts to alleviate this problem have been underway for several years. Of these, perhaps the most significant is ERIC, the educational retrieval service supported by the U.S. Office of Education. As yet, however, no ERIC center has been set up concerned with observational research on teaching.

Recommendation: *A center should be set up concerned with accumulating and disseminating information from research on the processes, causes, and effects of teaching.*

Information retrieval is but part of the problem, however. Most educators are not equipped to disentangle the intricacies and deficiencies of research on teaching—or any other complex field of educational research. Moreover, educators need "friends in court" who will sort out the facts from the claims and who are willing to give a reasoned judgment concerning what is now known and not known about research on a given problem in education. The two editions of the *Handbook of Research on Teaching*[1] have provided valuable service in this regard, as has the *Review of Educational Research.* In addition, several years ago the Office of Education began to commission reviews of specific subfields in educational research for consumers, although these commissions have fallen on hard times recently. Other reviews (such as those of Simon and Boyer, 1970; and of Rosenshine, 1971) have been supported from independent sources and appear aimed at researchers more than consumers. Perhaps a better current source of informa-

---

[1] Gage (1963a), Travers (1973).

tion for consumers is the commercially published review texts, such as Good and Brophy (1973)—and the book they are now reading! Regular reviews of research on teaching are badly needed.

Recommendation: *Regular reviews of research on the processes, causes, and effects of teaching should be commissioned.*

PROBLEMS OF THEORY

We turn now to core problems for those interested in research on teaching. Perhaps the greatest problem facing this field at the moment is our lack of adequate theories of teaching that would integrate and explain its many findings. Concepts this field has, instruments too, and findings by the score. But what do these findings *mean? Why* is it that a given teaching strategy appears in one type of classroom and not another, and *why* does it work whereas other strategies are found to be less effective? Until adequate, empirically based theories are developed, this field will continue to exhibit a complex and somewhat chaotic visage. Let us consider several aspects of this problem.

Reification of Instruments

One effect of the lack of theory has been to focus the attention of researchers on instruments rather than on concepts, findings, and their interpretation. This focus has a number of ramifications. One is the enormous variety of observational instruments that have now been developed, many without any published rationale. As we have noted, Simon and Boyer's (1970) anthology included 79 different systems, while Rosenshine (1970) claimed to know of 40 others that had been missed by Simon and Boyer. Clearly, the number of observational instruments greatly exceeds the number of orientations into which they may be sorted, and concepts such as "teacher asks a question" appear in literally scores of different instruments.

A number of authors have reacted to the confusion and gross ineconomy of this proliferation of research instruments. For example, Komisar (1968) has said: "We are rapidly approaching chaos in the production, by researchers, of 'new' category systems. No one seems able or willing to tell us *why* certain categories are chosen or how one researcher's categories bear on those of another" (p. 22). Let us, with Nuthall (1968a), call for a reasonable moratorium on the development of new category systems. Nuthall writes: "In future it may be necessary for a creator of a 'new' category system to provide a theoretical justification for his work. Possibly in this way the explanation and understanding of classroom behavior may begin to receive some of the attention it needs" (p. 129).

Recommendation: *New observational instruments for research on teaching should not be developed in the absence of clear theoretical justifications.*

But why have so many different observational instruments appeared? We suspect that two reasons furnish at least part of the answer. For one, investigators have often appeared unwilling to search the literature for observational tools that might meet their needs. There is little excuse for this behavior any longer, given review sources such as Simon and Boyer (1970), Rosenshine (1971), or this text. For another, however, investigators have evidenced some confusion over the nature of workable category systems. As readers know, most observational instruments have presumed to constitute a single facet of concepts that were viewed as mutually exclusive and that could be used for live observation. One can understand the legitimate desire of investigators to make their instruments as simple as possible. And yet many instruments simply have *not* constituted mutually exclusive category systems, and complex rules have had to be adduced by investigators to make such instruments reliable. We cited FIAC as a prime example of this process. But if researchers are used to "making do" with categorical instruments that do not really form a facet of mutually exclusive alternatives, what does it matter if we subdivide categories of an existing instrument or add new categories to it to create a new research tool? Data created by such instruments are difficult to interpret, and, as we know from Chapter V, not particularly valid anyway. We suggest that it is now time to abandon nonfaceted categorical instruments.

Recommendation: *Additional research should not be conducted with categorical instruments where the categories do not constitute mutually exclusive facets.*

What are the alternatives to such instruments? We suggest two answers to this question. Categorical instruments have inherent advantages in that they may be applied to the sequence of classroom events, and we suspect that they are irreplaceable for exploratory research that involves analysis of classroom recordings. Consequently, we recommend the use of multifaceted categorical instruments in exploratory research. Good examples of this use may be found in the work of such investigators as Kounin (1970), Bellack *et al.* (1966), and Wright and Nuthall (1970).

Recommendation: *Multifaceted, categorical instruments are the tools of choice for coding classroom events from recordings.*

But what about the investigator, or teacher-trainer, who wishes to utilize a simple instrument for live observation? What recommendation can we make for his use? For such purposes the multifaceted instrument is clearly an impossibility. Sign systems are quite legitimate for such purposes, however, along with simple, single-faceted category systems that concentrate on only one aspect of the teaching scene. The only difficulty is that we have not yet developed a set of instruments especially for live observation that reflect concepts for teaching which have been well-validated in exploratory research. We view this as a needed step.

Recommendation: *A catalog should be developed of simple instruments for live observation which represent concepts for the improvement of teaching that have been well-validated through exploratory research.*

We envision such a catalog as of considerable value to those who want to use live observation in teacher-training programs, as well as for those who would do simple replication research in new classroom settings. It would also facilitate the development of a standardized vocabulary needed by teachers for describing their craft.

Commitments

A second concomitant of the lack of viable theory concerning teaching has been the appearance of research that was generated by *Commitments* for the improvement of teaching. As we have seen, some researchers have appeared *Committed* to the tenets of progressive education, others to "raising the level" of classroom discourse, others to the use of open-ended questions, others to the use of behavior modification in the classroom, still others to the efficacy of a new program or curriculum. Such *Commitments* are not wholly bad; they serve to motivate researchers and to generate enthusiasm for findings among educators who share the same *Commitments*. But, as we have also seen, *Commitments* have also apparently affected choice of research instruments, interpretation of data, and preservation in research enterprises that were strongly criticized by reviewers. These latter are clearly counterproductive.

Recommendation: *Investigators who hold* Commitments *to a given strategy for the improvement of teaching should take pains to recognize these* Commitments *and not allow them to color their research methods or interpretation of data.*

It is possible to overstress the avoidance of *Commitments*, of course. In Chapter II we suggested that some classroom researchers of the past two decades have appeared to withdraw from concern with the problems of teacher effectiveness and have concentrated, instead, on the study of classroom events for their own sake. This has been a useful thing to do, since we needed a workable vocabulary with which to describe the observable events of teaching. But describing classroom events is one thing and relating them to presage, context, or product variables is quite something else. To validate the "success" of teacher activities by observing the possibly resulting classroom behaviors of pupils is desirable. However, educators are more interested, as indeed they should be, in evidence that a given classroom strategy produces relatively enduring differences in pupil learning, that it works or does not work in various contexts, and that teachers can or cannot be trained to produce it. Thus, researchers should be wary lest their avoidance of *Commitments* leads them to eschew research designs that would provide practical information for the improvement of teaching.

> Recommendation: *Investigators should utilize designs for research on teaching that pair process information with presage, context, or product variables—thus generating information of further practical use to educators.*

We shall have more to say on the subject of design later in the chapter.

Development of Theory

Given our present lack of integrating theories concerning teaching, are there any steps that researchers can take to encourage their development? Indeed, several steps can be recommended.

The first concerns the development of concepts for expressing the processes of teaching. Much of the effort of researchers during the past two decades has been devoted to the development of concepts for expressing classroom events, and literally hundreds of concepts have now been studied for expressing teacher behavior, pupil behavior, classroom group behavior, and other observable events in the classroom. Some of these represent high-inference variables that are hard to judge—such as *enthusiasm* and *clarity*—others—such as *asks a question* or *raises hand*—are low-inference variables that are easier to judge for research purposes. Despite empirical problems with high-inference concepts, we suspect that they are requisite for an adequate theory of teaching. Indeed, Rosenshine and Furst (1971) have suggested that high-inference concepts have a better record as predictors to pupil growth than do low-inference concepts. They also suggested that progress would be made if researchers were to try to discover the low-inference components of high-inference variables that are known to work. This relates to our earlier assertion that linguistic research should be pursued because of its potential for producing the low-inference evidence upon which high-inference judgments are based.

> Recommendation: *Research should be pursued on the low-inference components of high-inference concepts that express classroom events known to work.*

The fact that hundreds of concepts are now available to researchers interested in the study of teaching suggests that we may be nearing the end of a period when researchers are concerned primarily with concept development. We suspect that this suggestion is valid in a limited sense. Much of the development of concepts in the past has drawn ideas from our common vocabulary or from theories of education to which educators had given *Commitments*. The result is a vocabulary of terms and concepts that ranges widely but has little integration. Concepts are meaningful to the extent that they are integrated into conceptual systems, and eventually to the extent that they are involved in explanatory theories that are supported with empirical evidence. We see as particularly significant the development of conceptual *systems* (such as those within the logic and linguistic research traditions) and suspect that future development of concepts for teaching should be systematic in this sense.

Recommendation: *New concepts that are proposed for research on teaching should not be suggested in 'isolation but should be components of a conceptual system or explanatory theory.*

From whence should such systems or theories be taken? Rosenshine and Furst (1971) have suggested that concepts developed in laboratory settings might be mined for the expression of classroom events (also see Travers, 1971). They found little overlap between the variables employed in the typical categorical system used for classroom observation and those involved in laboratory and curricular research. They also cited several examples from the latter that might be incorporated into observational instruments in the future. Nuthall (1968a), however, has expressed less confidence in the value of theories that are used in traditional laboratory research. He writes:

> Traditional psychological theory cannot be of any significant value until the investigators of classroom behavior have themselves produced significant theoretical explanations of classroom events. The need is not for further adaptation and stretching of old theory, but for the creation of new theory which arises directly from the natural grain and details of the behaviour it is intended to explain. (p. 144)

Our review suggests that Nuthall's argument is more likely to prevail than that of Rosenshine and Furst. Two kinds of experiences have appeared to generate the most significant developments of conceptual systems to date. On the one hand, some investigators, such as Kounin or Smith and Geoffrey, have developed concepts by "wallowing" in the complexities of classroom events. On the other, some conceptual systems have been generated by pre-existing theoretical positions that "ought" to apply to classroom events— such as those of logic or linguistics. We suspect that conceptual development is likely to continue to reflect these two kinds of experiences. In the long run, however, theories of teaching must accommodate not only the concepts found useful for expressing classroom events but also the findings that relate contexts, presage variables, processes, and products of teaching. We suspect—and hope—that the time for development of explanatory theories that will accommodate findings as well as concepts is at hand. We also believe that such theories will begin as attempts to explain related groups of findings rather than all events concerned with teaching.

Recommendation: *High priority should be given to the development of explanatory theories concerned with teaching that will integrate concepts already found useful for expressing classroom events, and findings concerning those events.*

MEASUREMENT PROBLEMS

We next turn to problems that are explicitly concerned with techniques that are used for the study of classroom events. As readers will recall from our review of problems in Chapter IV, there are a number of different issues concerning the measurement of phenomena in teaching, and it is now time to make recommendations concerning these issues.

Recording

As readers may have detected, the authors favor the use of recordings for serious research on the events of teaching. Granted that recordings are expensive to prepare and that some of the nonverbal details of the live classroom are lost when recordings are prepared, it still seems to us that preparation of data in the "frozen" form is requisite for the complex judgments coders must make in definitive research on teaching. It would appear particularly important to use recordings when instruments involving two or more facets of information are to be used. In fact, we can think of only three types of classroom research for which the preparation of recordings would not be a method of choice. First, the use of recordings may be superfluous or harmful in exploratory studies that are aimed at concept development rather than concept verification or the generation of findings. Second, recordings are probably not particularly useful for the study of classroom events that unfold over a period of days, weeks, or months. Participant observation is probably a better method to use in these two cases, as illustrated by studies such as those of Smith and Geoffrey (1968) or Rist (1970). Third, recordings may not be necessary for studies wherein coders are called upon to make simple judgments that involve only a few judgments at an acceptable pace. Such studies are best conducted when concepts are well validated, hypotheses to be tested are clear, or a previously established finding is to be checked in a new context. A particularly good example of the use of live observation meeting these criteria may be found in the work of Brophy and Good (1974). Nevertheless, our general recommendation stands.

Recommendation: *Recordings are to be recommended for serious research on the processes of teaching, particularly when two or more facets of classroom behaviors are to be studied.*

This recommendation does not tell us how these recordings should be made. Given our present state of technology, three methods are open for our consideration: specimen records, audio recordings, and visual recordings. It seems to us that the first of these suffers more than the others from observer-induced error. The second may be recommended in those cases where funds are tight, especially when the audio record is supplemented by additional dictation supplied by an observer sitting in the classroom, and where it is desired to concentrate particularly on verbal events in the classroom. The third is to be recommended where funds are sufficient and where it is desired to study nonverbal aspects of teaching.

Recommendation: *Visual or two-track audio recordings should be used for research on teaching, depending on funds available and the nature of the events one wants to study.*

Encoding

Whether or not recordings are used, it is necessary to develop instruments so as to code classroom events, and development and application of such research tools also raises issues about which recommendations should be made. Several recommendations have actually been given concerning instruments in earlier sections. Among others, we have recommended that categorical instruments wherein the categories do not form a facet be abandoned; that new instruments should not be developed in the absence of a clear, theoretical justification; that a catalog of simple instruments should be developed for live-observation purposes that represent well-validated concepts for the improvement of teaching; and that the instruments of choice for use with recordings should constitute multifaceted categorical formats. Let us now consider additional issues concerning instrumentation.

First, what kinds of units should be chosen for analysis? Three choices are available for our consideration: arbitrary units of time, phenomenal units, and analytic units. Arbitrary time units, unless used solely for the purpose of quantification, appear to have little value for future research, since their boundaries do not match those of actual classroom events. Phenomenal units have the advantages of greater immediate reliability and comprehension by untrained coders and consumers of research. However, we suspect that the common vocabulary is simply insufficient for the study of teaching and that analytic units are requisite for most teaching research in the future.

Recommendation: *Investigators should be prepared to cope with analytic units in research on teaching processes.*

Second, what should be the conceptual posture of instruments used for the study of teaching? Should they concern themselves with the intent of actors, with objective characteristics of classroom events, or with the effects of those actions? Our choice would be for the study of objective characteristics. Given the possibility that any given event in teaching may be studied as either a cause or an effect of other events, we should stick to objective characteristics where possible.

Recommendation: *Instruments for research on teaching processes should deal where possible with the objective characteristics of classroom events.*

Third, what about problems of validity and reliability of instruments? As readers know, instruments are valid to the extent that they measure what we expect them to measure and reliable to the extent that they give us the same scores on repeated applications to the same data. Little can be done to assess the validity of observational instruments at present. (Most research to date is exploratory, and instruments are designed for the first-ever measurement of teaching variables rather than as a better way of measuring a variable previously studied.) However, instruments that demonstrate repeated inability to predict to variables with which their concepts should be related will cause us eventually to conclude that the instruments themselves are not valid. In addition, instruments have questionable validity and may, in fact, be unusable when inadequate descriptions are given of the operations that underlie their coding categories.

Reliability is another matter, however. Researchers simply must assume responsibility for evaluating new instruments they have developed in terms of reliability, and instruments should not be used for subsequent research unless acceptable reliability figures are available for them.

Recommendation: *Instruments for research on teaching processes should not be used unless operational descriptions are available for their categories and data are available showing them to be reliable.*

The interesting thing concerning all of our recommendations for measurement problems is that they are not always likely to be policed by researchers themselves. Each recommendation simply lays additional burdens on the researcher that will cost him time and money. Researchers have tended to ignore various of these recommendations in the past and will presumably be tempted to do so in the future. And yet the value of research conducted on teaching will ultimately depend on investigators' willingness to conduct research that reflects high standards. We suggest that standards are most easily set and policed by editors of research journals, hence our earlier recommendation concerning standards for publication of educational research.

INTERPRETATION PROBLEMS

We turn now to a series of problems associated with the conversion of classroom data into findings. Some of these problems are statistical in nature; some concern the interpretation of statistical data in verbal form. Each has appeared in various studies concerned with observational research on the classroom.

Statistics

Surely the statistical error most often found in research on teaching is the substitution of inductive for descriptive statistics. As readers will recall from Chapter IV, descriptive statistics are those concerned with events and relations occurring in the data and are exemplified by measures such as the mean, the variance, or the correlation coefficient. Inductive statistics are measures that tell us whether a descriptive measure is large enough "to count"; that is, whether the result found in the sample is likely to have appeared also in the population. They are exemplified by such statistics as the F, χ^2, and t tests, and results from applying inductive statistics are generally reported in terms of a degree of probability; thus, "this finding was significant at $p < .01$." Finally, we also know that investigators (and editors) use inductive measures to ascertain whether or not a finding was "really" found or not. As a result, inductive statistics are likely to be reported by researchers—and to be insisted upon by editors—rather than the descriptive statistics on which they are based.

Unfortunately, the calculation of inductive statistics for data from classroom research is rarely justified. As we know, most studies so far conducted have involved small samples of classrooms that were chosen in far from random procedures. In addition, many investigators have used an N of events or of persons in computing inductive statistics, which make assumptions about the distribution of those events or persons among classrooms that may or may not be justified. These problems are severe enough, but the real difficulty is that the reader needs to know the *descriptive* information, not the inductive, in order to assess the strength of a given finding. To know that a correlation or mean difference is "statistically significant" does not tell us how large those relationships were found to be. And yet it is exactly the criterion of how large that should be used to ascertain whether a given finding is substantial or picayune.

Recommendation: *Descriptive statistics should be reported for all findings from research on the processes of teaching.*

The misuse of inductive statistics is endemic throughout educational research. The second problem we have noted also is not confined to classroom research alone. This concerns the use of complex statistics where simple statistics might have sufficed. Complex statistical procedures—such as the analysis of co-variance, factor analysis, path analysis, and the like—suffer from two difficulties when applied to observational data. Often the data cannot meet the assumptions on which they are based, and findings are difficult to interpret to the uninitiated reader. Why then are complex statistical procedures used? Presumably for several reasons: they provide answers that are presumed to be "definitive," they display complex result that are difficult to see in data tables, they provide opportunity for the dis play of virtuosity in the investigator, and they "legitimize" research publica tions. As a general rule, the investigator should report the simplest statistic available, or better yet a graph or figure that will display his findings.

Recommendation: *Data from research on the processes of teaching should be presented with the simplest of appropriate statistics.*

Our third problem is a technical one that, while not confined to research on teaching alone, is nevertheless peculiar to research designs that utilize pupil achievement scores for their dependent variables. As we have seen pupil achievement is the variable most often used by researchers as a product measure in research on teaching. Data on pupil achievement are gathered in many school systems on an annual basis, and it takes but little additional effort on the part of the investigator to gather these data in addi tion to the much more complex observational data he is studying concern ing the observable events of teaching. But if we are to validate the effects of a teaching style against the criterion of pupil achievement, how much more valid it must be to use the pupil's gain in achievement "this year" rather than his total achievement score, which presumably reflects his previou, classroom experiences, intelligence, social class background, and othe factors that will introduce error into the evaluation of the effects of the teaching strategy we hope to assess. Thus, unadjusted pupil achievemen scores are not often used. Rather, results are often given in terms of "gair scores" or "adjusted gain scores." But Cronbach and Furby (1970) have pointed out that most studies simply do not meet the assumptions necessary to use complex statistics such as these, or misuse them when they are employed. Instead, they recommend the use of simpler statistics—such as raw pupil achievement scores (and analyses of co-varience)—which are easier to comprehend anyway.

Recommendation: *Research on teaching that utilizes product variables should make use of "raw" pupil scores rather than "gain scores" or "adjusted gain scores."*

Interpreting Data

A wide variety of interpretive errors are represented in the reports of research on teaching. Only a few recur with any frequency, however. Let us confine discussion to these latter.

A series of several problems may be classified under the general rubric of "throwing the results away." Perhaps the most surprising and distressing of these problems is failure by investigators to report findings for data they appear to have collected. We have commented on several studies in the text for which it would appear that extensive data were collected and analyzed, but for which the authors have been unable to find a report of results. Why should investigators have engaged in such apparently self-defeating behavior? Presumably because the investigator became involved with other activities after publication of his initial report, possibly because the findings he obtained did not match his expectations, and in some cases because he was able to achieve "success," such as academic tenure or successful adoption of a curriculum program, without bothering to publish full results. It takes time and energy to analyze and write up the results of complex research projects, and until editors are willing to refuse publication until researchers supply their full results, we suspect that this problem will continue to plague research on teaching. Nevertheless, we feel rather foolish in making the following recommendation:

Recommendation: *Investigators concerned with research on teaching processes should report and publish their complete findings.*

A second problem concerns the variety of types of findings a given study is capable of generating. As readers are aware, findings concerning teaching may be classified into a number of different types of information: process occurrence, context-process, presage-process, and so on. Nearly all studies have collected data that were capable of generating findings for two or more types of information. And yet investigators usually report only one type of finding. Process-occurrence information is most often ignored. Many studies, in addition, were built on samples that would have allowed the checking of the impact of contextual variation on findings, but this too is often ignored. Sometimes, for example, in the Taba studies, even process-product information is slighted. Consequently,

Recommendation: *Investigators concerned with research on teaching should take pains to report findings concerned with all types of information available in the study.*

A third problem concerns failure to see results in data tables. This problem is nearly as strange as the first one discussed above. Surprisingly, numerous studies have appeared in which findings were somehow "missed" by investigators in the data tables they have (fortunately) published. Occasionally a derivative statistic that is reported flatly contradicts tabulated data. More often the investigator seems to have been oblivious to findings that appear obvious to the serious reader of his data tables. Consequently,

Recommendation: *Investigators concerned with research on teaching should take pains to examine their data tables carefully for obvious findings that may appear within them.*

Finally, a substantial group of investigators appear to ignore the theoretical or practical significance of their findings. It is common to find results that are reported without any attempt at interpretation. Sometimes, however, the findings contradict either the argument that was advanced by the investigator or the previously reported findings of others, and these facts were apparently not thought worthy of comment by the investigator. Facts by themselves are difficult for the reader to assimilate, unless he is intimately involved with the research tradition represented by a given study. Consequently, investigators should take pains to interpret the major findings of their studies.

Recommendation: *Investigators concerned with research on teaching should take pains to interpret their major findings for practical and theoretical significance.*

So much for errors of omission. Errors of commission appear less frequently in the interpretation of classroom research. Of these, surely the most heinous is making claims for the efficacy of a new curriculum or program of teacher training on the basis of research when the results of that research are not published, when the sample is inappropriate to the results claimed, or when the data contradict the conclusions advertised. Fortunately, occurrences of this sort are rare.

Two other errors of commission occasionally crop up in classroom research, however, and researchers should be alerted to avoid them, or interpret data correctly when they appear in the reports of others' research. The first concerns the confusion of correlational with cause-and-effect information. As readers know, most research conducted to date on teaching represents field surveys. Data from such studies simply do not constitute definitive evidence concerning causes and effects. To discover that a context is associated with a given type of teaching, or that a type of teaching is associated with certain classroom behaviors of pupils, or even certain products in pupil learning, is not to know that one of these classes of data "causes" the other. Indeed, the relationship may reflect contextual conditions not yet examined, or in the case of classroom events that occur in interaction, the relationship of cause and effect may be reversed. Cause-and-effect explanations may be argued for field survey data (indeed, the authors have done just this throughout the text), but it requires experimental evidence to validate these arguments. And, as we have seen, experiments do not always produce what we expect them to.

Recommendation: *Data from field surveys of teaching processes should be reported in co-variational terms; cause-and-effect interpretations of their findings should be labeled as plausible speculations.*

The second concerns the confusion of process with product criteria for the validation of programs for the improvement of teaching. Throughout this text we have taken the position that improvements in teaching must ultimately be validated against product criteria to be judged "successful." And yet some investigators claim "success" when a given program is validated only in terms of observable differences in pupil behavior or—worse— if changes can be observed in teacher behavior only. Given the problematic relationship between classroom events and product variables, such claims seem specious.

Recommendation: *Programs for the improvement of teaching should be validated with process-product research; validations against process criteria should be labeled as plausible speculations.*

We cannot conclude this section on problems of interpretation without noting, again, that our recommendations are not always likely to be policed by researchers themselves. Errors of interpretation are not likely to cost the investigator as much in time or money as are errors of measurement. Most are likely to recur, however, since they are products of self-deception, thoughtlessness, and occasionally ignorance on the part of investigators. These too require policing by the editors of research journals.

DESIGNS FOR RESEARCH

We now turn to the most interesting and speculative section of the chapter. Until this point our recommendations have concerned themselves primarily with problems to be solved in conducting research on teaching. But all of these problems might be met and yet the research conducted be pedestrian, costly, and uninspired. What kinds of research are likely to produce innovative information concerning teaching? What designs are likely to produce the most information per expenditure of time and funds on the part of investigators?

Process Designs

Since process variables are at the heart of research on teaching, it is appropriate that we begin our design recommendations with their consideration. In general, these involve four different ideas that are not found in many studies concerned with teaching that have been published to date.

The first recommendation has already been given. It will be recalled that we have recommended that investigators should concentrate their efforts on designs for research in which process information is paired with presage, context, or product information so as to maximize potential for producing findings that will be of use to educators. Process information is meaningful in itself as a data source, but it is of greater value to discover what affects the process of the classroom and, in turn, what effects are induced through these processes.

Second, designs are to be recommended in which a variety of different process variables are measured at the same time. Multivariate designs commend themselves to our attention for several reasons. For one, in considering simultaneously a number of different teaching variables it is possible to discover those that are *not* productive as well as those that *are*. For another, relationships *among* various teaching phenomena may be studied, thus providing some indication as to whether teaching phenomena from conceptually independent realms are empirically independent or co-occurring. Finally, it is possible to mine the same (expensive) classroom recordings for a variety of different findings, thus increasing the cost effectiveness of research. Examples of multivariate designs may be found in the studies of Kounin (1970), Adams and Biddle (1970), and Bellack *et al.* (1966), but perhaps the best single example is that of Wright and Nuthall (1970), which illustrates clearly each of the three advantages suggested for multivariate research.

Recommendation: *Research designs should be encouraged that provide measurement of various process variables.*

Third, designs are to be recommended that supply information concerning the differential impact of teaching on individual pupils. We are used to thinking of teaching in terms of wholistic judgments that are made about the teacher's treatment of the classroom group, while even teacher interaction with individual pupils is presumed to be a stylistic matter that varies from teacher to teacher rather than from pupil to pupil. And yet findings have been reviewed which suggest that pupils are treated differentially by teachers in terms of their sex, race, intelligence, and teacher expectations for their ability. Good and Brophy (1971) make a particularly strong argument for research on the differential treatment of pupils and suggest that one of the reasons for relatively weak effects in classroom research to date has been that the teacher simply does not behave in the same way to all pupils. Designs illustrating the collection of data on individual pupils, either as behavers or as targets for teacher behavior, may be found in numerous studies, particularly in those conducted by Brophy, Good, and their colleagues.

Recommendation: *Research designs should be encouraged that provide measurement of the differential treatment and behaviors of individual pupils.*

Fourth, however, there is surely more to teaching than simply the differential behavior and treatment of individual pupils. Kounin's findings remind us that classroom management is a process wherein teachers manifest control over the classroom group, while in many respects the teacher's job is more that of creating an appropriate learning environment than of providing a direct stimulus for the edification of individual pupils. This suggests research in which teacher behavior is considered an independent variable, classroom environment a mediating variable, and pupil response a dependent variable. Designs of this sort would be particularly appropriate for the study of teaching in self-directed classrooms. We are unfamiliar with any studies that exhibit this particular design, although those of Gump (1967) and Perkins (1964, 1965) come close.

Recommendation: *Research designs should be encouraged that provide independent measures of teacher behavior, classroom environmental states, and individual pupil behavior.*

Context Designs

Of all variables that might be studied in research on teaching, context variables are least often considered. We can think of at least two reasons for this neglect. On the one hand, the study of context variation nearly always means that the sample of classrooms for which we collect data must be increased in size, which in turn increases the cost of the study. On the other, teaching phenomena are normally presumed to be invariant as we go from context to context. Assumptions of contextual irrelevance are made in all sciences, hence our willingness to consider a sample representative of a larger universe of events. In the case of research on teaching, most investigators are willing to presume that their findings will generalize to other grade levels, other subjects of instruction, other climes—and we were willing to entertain this presumption, too, in Chapter XI.

The difficulty with the lack of research involving contextual variables is that we have as yet little information with which to check this presumption. Moreover, when contextual information is collected it often turns out that variations in the processes of teaching, if not the relationships between those processes and other variables, are encountered. (As an example, Brophy and Evertson, 1973, have recently reported sharp differences in the success of various teaching strategies, depending on whether pupils were middle class or lower class.) We take it as a high priority, then, that designs involving contextual variation be encouraged. We will suggest three strategies for this purpose.

First, replication of particularly strong studies should be sought with samples of classrooms that represent different contextual conditions from those originally studied. To give two examples: the data collected by Wright and Nuthall (1970) were obtained from grade III classrooms in New Zealand, while those of Kounin (1970) were taken from grades I and II in the metropolitan Detroit area. Both studies should be replicated with other grade levels and in other cultural contexts.

Recommendation: *Research should be encouraged that constitutes replications of strong studies in alternative contexts.*

Second, however, there are problems with the exact replication of research. Often a given study had a design that was constructed for a particular set of conditions that are not likely to be repeated in other contexts. Some studies involve instruments or curricula that are inappropriate to other grade levels, subjects of instruction, or social class contexts. Replication of such studies is impossible in any strict sense, although "functionally equivalent" research may be conducted. A stronger design, however, is to conduct research that provides contextual variation in the sample. We shall refer to such investigations as *comparative studies*. Examples of comparative studies may be found in Abraham *et al.* (1971) or Adams and Biddle (1970), and it is characteristic of such studies that some teaching phenomena will be found to generalize across contexts while others will be found to be context-dependent. We urge that more studies be conducted with comparative designs.

> Recommendation: *Research should be encouraged that involves comparative designs wherein classrooms are contrasted for nationality, social class, ethnicity, curriculum, or educational media.*

Comparative studies are expensive, however, particularly if they involve the collection of classroom recordings. For some time the authors have wondered (with Flanders, 1971; and Rosenshine and Furst, 1973) why it was that those interested in classroom research did not form a consortium or data bank to share their classroom recordings with one another. Literally thousands of hours of classroom recordings have now been made and transcribed at the major centers interested in research on teaching, and it seems a shame that these are not made available to other investigators who would thereby be saved the cost of making and transcribing additional recordings. Presumably one reason why this has not occurred is that designs and standards for the collection of recordings and associated presage, context, or product data have varied, so that investigators have not thought it worthwhile to share their data. But there is no reason why two or more centers might not cooperate in comparative research wherein each sought to collect data that matched those collected at the other centers. Such a design would allow creation of a large data pool for relatively little cost per center. These thoughts suggest two recommendations.

> Recommendation: *A data bank should be set up wherein recordings and transcriptions of classroom lessons are maintained for the use of researchers on a cost-per-copy basis.*

> Recommendation: *Research should be encouraged in comparative designs wherein two or more research centers undertake to collect matched data that may be contrasted for nationality, social class, ethnicity, or other contextual variables.*

Third, collection of at least one type of contextual data does not involve multiplying the number of classrooms studied. We refer, of course, to data concerning the backgrounds of individual pupils in the classroom. The number of variables falling into this class that have so far been studied in research on teaching is pitifully small—sex, intelligence, race, teacher expectations for achievement, and little else. Presumably this is because the teacher "ought" to be able to cope with any pupil, and yet we make a great to-do about teachers' ability to "individualize" instruction to fit the needs of individual pupils. In perhaps the best study yet conducted of individualization Power (1971) discovered that patterns of pupil achievement, and their need for differential treatment, varied as a function of a wide variety of pupil personality characteristics. Power concluded that individualizing instruction is a much more complex problem than is commonly realized and that more attention needs to be given to pupil characteristics. We agree.

Recommendation: *Research should be encouraged that involves the collection of contextual data concerning pupil formative experiences and properties.*

This recommendation clearly fits with our earlier one advocating designs in which the differential treatment and behaviors of individual pupils are studied.

Presage Designs

Perhaps half of all teaching research conducted to date that involves presage variables has been experimental in nature. For convenience we delay discussion of experimental studies for two or three pages and concentrate our attention here on field surveys that have involved presage variables. And when we turn attention to the latter the first thing that strikes us is the concentration that researchers have given to teacher properties—rather than to teacher formative experiences or training features. Interestingly enough, such variables as teacher age, sex, and experience have seldom been explored in relationship to classroom processes, despite the fact that when this is done investigators have nearly always reported findings that were generated by the study. Why have formative and experiential variables been given such short shrift? Presumably because such variables are ignored in educational ideology, or because many investigators were trained in psychology and hope to discover predictive relationships between personality inventories and teacher behavior. Our recommendation is that additional attention be given to variables that express teacher formative and training experiences.

Recommendation: *Research should be encouraged that involves the collection of data concerning formative and training experiences of teachers.*

But what about the research that has already been conducted on teacher properties? What has this research accomplished? Strikingly little, actually. One would have expected that instruments such as the MTAI and NTE examinations would predict differential teacher behavior in classrooms, and yet these expectations have often been frustrated (see Chapter XI). More success can be reported for a few instruments that assess teacher personality variables, such as *anxiety* and *rigidity*, but even here the picture is not a clear one. What is the problem? Why have we so far failed to find teacher properties that would predict classroom events? We suspect that the basic difficulty is that inventories for the measurement of teacher properties were developed independently of knowledge concerning actual classroom behavior. In other words, the tendency has been to devise paper-and-pencil instruments that were derived from theoretical writings rather than from observations of the events of teaching.

One alternative procedure might be to begin with observed classroom behaviors and to work backwards from them to the development of paper-and-pencil instruments. The best example of this process to date may be found in Ryans' Teacher Characteristics Schedule. While Ryans used rating techniques for observing teacher behaviors, his subsequent development of the TCS is a model that might well be emulated by other investigators interested in predicting teacher classroom behavior. Another example of such an instrument may be found in Taylor's (see Taylor *et al.*, 1972) research that was designed to classify teachers on the basis of their descriptions of their classroom roles. Neither instrument has yet been used to predict the details of classroom behavior to our knowledge, but such instruments are surely worth pursuing.

Recommendation: *Research should be encouraged that involves development of paper-and-pencil instruments for measuring teacher properties from variables representing significant teacher classroom behaviors.*

Product Designs

Our recommendations concerning product-oriented research in teaching may be simply summarized: such research should be conducted more often; and it should be conducted with a greater range of product variables than heretofore. Concerning the first point, despite the presumptive importance of process-product information in validating *any* attempt to improve classroom education, surprisingly few studies have yet been conducted that investigate the effects of classroom events on pupil outcomes. Concerning the second point, nearly all studies so far conducted have involved the measurement of pupil achievement with standardized tests. Such tests present difficulties for evaluation of the effectiveness of teaching. For one thing, they represent general information rather than what was specifically taught in the lessons studied. For another, they tend to provide only a single measurement of low-level knowledge of a subject of instruction. These short-comings suggest designs for conducting product-oriented research.

First, let us consider field-survey designs wherein product variables are matched to lesson content. One strategy for accomplishing this is to postpone the construction of the product test until after the lesson has actually been given. Content analysis of lesson transcripts suggests that there may be one hundred or more propositions uttered in the typical lesson. Some of these propositions may be unclear, some may be erroneous, some display prejudice, some come from the teacher, others from pupils. It seems both feasible and practical to use a weekend, for example, to develop a test of pupil knowledge of content that was expressed in Friday's lesson. This test could then be administered to pupils on Monday to study the details of knowledge acquisition.

Recommendation: *Research should be encouraged that involves development of product tests matched to lesson content.*

Another strategy for matching lesson content to product variables is to conduct research in which content is standardized and a product instrument is developed for that specific content. Examples of this design may be found in the research of Bellack and his colleagues (1966), in Wright and Nuthall (1970), but best of all in Hughes (1973). Such designs offer both advantages and disadvantages. Among the former, the product instrument constructed can focus on understanding and integration of the content of the lessons rather than merely on low-level knowledge of facts. Also, one can reduce the impact of "extraneous factors" (such as content variation) on processes or products, thus revealing in clear focus the relationships between teaching strategies and their effects. However, lesson content is difficult to standardize, as Bellack and his colleagues have reported, and it might be that some process-product relationships do not generalize beyond specific content and context, in which case they are of little use.

Recommendation: *Process-product research should be encouraged that involves standardization of lesson content and matched product instruments, but findings from such studies should be validated with different types of contents and contexts.*

Second, let us recognize that standardized achievement tests were constructed for evaluating the achievements of individual pupils and *not* for validating the effects of teaching. Most such tests generate but a single score, that score often represents low-level knowledge, it is generally confined to a single subject of instruction, its focus is on knowledge rather than attitudes, and so forth. Nearly all of these strictures violate our needs for finding out what happens to pupils as a result of teaching. In ideal terms we should like product instruments that provide multiple scores; measures of high-level as well as low-level knowledge; information on pupil knowledge of school rules, adult roles, and other matters in addition to subject matter; and affective as well as cognitive information. This suggests that efforts should now be directed toward developing product instruments that are more appropriate to the validation of teaching.

Recommendation: *Research should be encouraged on the development of multivariate product instruments appropriate for assessing success in teaching.*

Third, even given the limitations of standardized tests, the fact is that they are administered annually to pupils in many school systems, and these records are often kept for some considerable period. Thus, many school systems have a data bank of information that might be mined for research on teaching. Let us see how this might be accomplished. One design (suggested to us by Tom Good and Jere Brophy) is to sort through the data so as to establish sets of teachers who consistently produce better-than-

PUTTING IT ALL TOGETHER

average and poorer-than-average rates of achievement in their pupils, year after year. These teachers might then be observed to assess the differences in their classroom strategies. Variants on this design might involve additional information concerning the backgrounds of pupils for whom differential achievement patterns are discovered and classroom behaviors or treatments are studied.

> Recommendation: *Research should be encouraged in which pupil achievement records are studied so as to select teachers of pupils for processual investigation.*

Experimental Designs

Most of our discussion to this point has concerned recommendations for field-survey research. We now turn to experimental research. As readers know, experiments provide us information concerning cause-and-effect relationships that is difficult or impossible to obtain through field surveys. Thus, experimental information is requisite for definitive information concerning explanatory theory. At the same time, experiments have several disadvantages when compared with field surveys. For one thing, only one or two independent variables can be manipulated in the typical experiment, thus restricting the amount of data generated. Again, some independent variables simply cannot be manipulated at all (such as social class background of the teacher), and for evidence concerning these latter we must be satisfied with field surveys. Finally, experimental manipulations may introduce conditions that are simply never obtained in such purity or emphasis in the real world, thus their results may be actually "unreal."

Despite these difficulties, experiments are irreplaceable. But so are field surveys—for exploratory investigations and the establishment of base-line data that would lead us to validate the occurrence of independent variables for which we might later conduct experiments. This suggests that programmatic research on teaching should involve *both* field surveys and experiments.

> Recommendation: *Effective, programmatic research on the processes, causes, and effects of teaching should involve complementary field surveys and experiments.*

Unfortunately, most programs of research have not followed this recommendation. As we have seen, many field survey findings have not yet been validated by experiments, while in the case of behavioral modification research no field surveys have yet been conducted. It is to be hoped that these shortcomings will be rectified in the near future.

In Chapter IV we suggested that experiments could be conducted on context-process, presage-process, process-process, and process-product relationships. Let us consider recommendations for each of these design types.

Our survey has found few examples of context-process experiments.

This is not surprising, although we bemoan the lack of such research. As we know, contextual variables are often ignored in field surveys too. Variables such as composition of the pupil group, size of school, or equipment available in the classroom are likely to be viewed as conditions to be accommodated rather than as variables to be studied for their effects in the classroom. And yet each of these variables probably has substantial effects on teaching. Particularly surprising is the lack of experimental research on the effects of curricular innovation in the classroom. We advocate more experiments concerning this variable, as well as studies of the process effects of educational media, class size (!), and other manipulable context variables.

Recommendation: *Context-process experiments concerned with the processes, causes, and effects of teaching should be encouraged.*

Numerous presage-process experiments have already appeared within the literature. Most of these have concerned differences among various programs of teacher education, and most have been conducted by investigators *Committed* to a given idea for the improvement of classroom teaching. Most have appeared to be successful in generating differences in the classroom behaviors of teachers or pupils. However, surprisingly, most have not obtained the desired effects in *product* variables. We conclude that presage-process experimentation is highly feasible, but that the variables so far chosen for such research have not been particularly useful.

Recommendation: *Presage-process experiments concerned with teaching should be encouraged, but variables chosen for such experiments should have been validated for their effects through prior field surveys.*

Experiments involving the manipulation of classroom processes are more difficult to conduct than experiments wherein context or process variables are manipulated. The reason for this is that events in the classroom are not played out in isolation from other events. Rather, the classroom is characterized by *inter*action among teacher and pupils, which tends to wash out the clear, independent status of variables we would like to manipulate for their effects on the processes or products of teaching.

To date, this quandary has been solved in two ways. Experiments involving process-process relationships have concentrated on short sequences of teacher acts followed by pupil responses. (Thus, experimental teachers have been instructed to provide a consistent diet of positive reinforcement, or to use reinforcers of a given class, and reactions of pupils to these treatments have been studied.) In contrast, process-product experiments have tended to use standardized curricula that were varied systematically among experimental treatments. The first design has limited use, since many of the teaching processes in which we are interested involve longer sequences of teaching. Studies using it have also apparently been confounded by the intrusion of uncontrolled teacher behavior, in some cases, although process evidence concerning the latter is seldom offered by investigators. The second design suffers from the advantages and disadvantages we considered earlier when discussing designs involving standardization of lesson content. In sum, clean process-process and process-product experiments are difficult to conduct and should presumably be confined to the validation of crucial relationships among variables that have previously been discovered in field surveys or that have strong theoretical status.

Recommendation: *Process-process and process-product experiments concerning teaching should be encouraged, but preferably for the validating of crucial relationships previously discovered in field surveys or with strong theoretical justification.*

Were this the only recommendation to be made concerning the experimental validation of process or product effects of teaching, prospects would appear dim for definitive research on the effects of teaching. However, an alternative strategy is available. Let us assume we are conducting a presage-process or context-process experiment and have succeeded in creating differential teaching phenomena in the classroom. What is to prevent us from also examining the effects of these phenomena in pupil behavior or pupil products? To be strictly kosher, this latter evidence is not experimental, since we have manipulated the antecedents of teaching rather than teaching itself. But surely evidence collected under these conditions is stronger than evidence generated from nonmanipulated field surveys. Thus, if we are careful to spell out the detailed differences obtained among experimental classrooms in teaching behavior, it would appear fruitful to pair this information with process or product variables in quasi-experimental designs.

Recommendation: *Context-process and presage-process experiments should be conducted in which process-process and process-product information are also sought as effects of the experimental treatments.*

However difficult they may be to conduct, experiments involving process-process and process-product relationships are our ultimate means of validating the effectiveness of teaching strategies, and clearly they are irreplaceable in the armory of the researcher concerned with teaching and its effects.

Innovative Designs

Finally, we turn to recommendations concerning innovations in education. Like many other aspects of Western culture, education has been in considerable ferment during the twentieth century. Proposals for new curricula, new educational media, new school buildings, new goals for education appear with astounding frequency. Moreover, many of these proposals are put into practice, and often with the barest imaginable evidence. Equipment for language laboratories, educational television, new curricula for science education, buildings wherein open-classroom education is to be practiced—all have been adopted with little information concerning their impact on teaching and its effects. Some of these innovations are now considered to have failed, others may be retained and become standard features of schools during the next generation. But all have involved the expenditure of untold millions of dollars that were invested on the basis of faith, ideology, and enthusiasm.

We have suggested that *there is a better way* to proceed with educational innovation. This involves building research on the processes and effects of teaching into programs of educational innovation. We have already recommended that innovations not be adopted before they are subjected to research on their effects in the classroom and that a center be set up to store and disseminate results of research concerning such innovations. If these recommendations were to be adopted, untold millions of dollars might be saved.

Research involving innovations is difficult to conduct, however, because of the problem of disentangling the effects of an innovation from those of the enthusiasm of the investigator *for* that innovation. More than one school system has abandoned curriculum A for curriculum B because an enthusiastic researcher has shown the latter to produce more achievement in pupils, only at a later date to abandon B for C, and perhaps still later to return to A—all because teachers were imbued with enthusiasm for new curricula by subsequent investigators. To be effective, then, innovative research must involve control over the enthusiasm of investigators (and experimental teachers).

Recommendation: *Research concerning the impact of innovations on teaching and its effects should be conducted in such a manner as to equalize enthusiasm for the innovation and its alternatives.*

Despite this problem, research on the processes and effects of teaching is vital to the evaluation of innovations and should presumably form one of the core fields of educational research.

POSTSCRIPT

Readers who are not now convinced of the vital importance of research on the processes of teaching will probably never be. What we cannot hope to portray is the exciting challenge, the joy of the hunt, that accompanies research into this fascinating field. One of our motives in writing this book has been to intrigue others into the real need for competent classroom research. If you have interests in this field, welcome to a fascinating career that combines science with an opportunity for needed social service. The need is pressing, the challenge great, the problems remaining to be investigated legion!

APPENDIX
PROCEDURES FOR REVIEW

Some readers may be interested in the procedures used by the authors in reviewing studies and in identifying and assembling findings for this text.

Those who attempt to review empirical research in the social sciences at present face formidable problems. For one thing, little consensus exists among investigators over terms used to express a given concept; thus as many as a score or more different terms may be used by different investigators to mean quite similar ideas. For another, widely varying instruments and procedures may be used to measure the same phenomenon. Many research designs are also possible, each of which has differing implications for the validity of findings. A plethora of statistical techniques are used that overlap in coverage, vary in power, and involve different assumptions. Finally, results may be published in hundreds of journals, and there is little consensus among journal editors concerning grounds for publication or features of the research that must or must not be published.

These problems apply broadly in the social sciences. In addition, those who review studies of teaching must contend with a number of additional problems that are peculiar to this field. As was discussed in Chapter IV, samples of teachers and lessons are generally quite small for studies of teaching, and rarely, if ever, are chosen in a random fashion. Most studies have concerned white, suburban classrooms only, and few studies have exhibited much contextual variation in their samples. Most findings in this field have yet to be replicated in a *single*, additional study (other than the one in which they were first advanced). Findings from field surveys have infrequently been confirmed with experimental research, nor have experiments always been validated with field research. Instruments of questionable validity and reliability are sometimes used. And if these problems were not sufficient, standards of reporting for this field appear even looser than in most other social science fields.

This does not mean that the research enterprise is worthless. But it does impose on the reviewer the need to make a series of clinical judgments as he attempts to sort out concepts and findings for this literature. In general, these judgments are of two kinds. First, the reviewer must decide which studies to retain, and which to omit, in his review. In the case of this text, the authors chose to eliminate from consideration all studies that did not involve formal observation of classroom events. This means that we forewent studies in which classrooms were observed informally (as in Smith and Geoffrey, 1968), in which classrooms were rated (as in Ryans, 1960), or in which teachers or pupils were observed but not in a classroom setting (as in Moore *et al.*, 1973). In addition, we excluded from the review a number of studies whose methods were particularly questionable or for which insufficient data were available to detect findings. Finally, several additional studies were omitted from coverage because they could not easily be apposed to others in constructing integrated reviews.

The second type of clinical judgment required involves the detection, assembly, and expression of findings in some form that readers can easily understand. This, in turn, involves a number of component tasks. Findings must first be detected in studies, a task by no means simple because investigators use several criteria for detecting findings themselves (see below). Findings that express similar ideas, even if they involve different terms, must then be assembled from various studies. If possible, findings should be weighted to express the strengths and weaknesses of the studies that gave rise to them. Finally, findings must then be expressed in some form that enables their appreciation by readers.

Let us consider these component tasks. First, how are findings detected in studies of teaching? By far the majority of teaching studies use derivative statistics for the detection of findings, and of these most studies use *inductive statistics* that provide a test of stated hypotheses for which results are expressed in terms of statistical significance. For example, a given study might report that "experimental teachers produced a significantly greater average achievement score for pupils ($t = 2.456$, p $<$ .02) than did control teachers." In this case, the inductive statistic used is the t-test, applied to a mean difference. Other, common inductive statistics include F, χ^2, the Mann-Whitney U, the Wilcoxon T, and so forth. Such statistics may be applied in various ways, make a variety of assumptions about the data to which they are applied, and have the great advantage of providing the investigator (and his readers) with a clear basis for detecting whether the hypothesis with which he is dealing is supported by his data or not.

Such statistics have many problems when applied to research on teaching. For one, they nearly all presume random samples, and as we know, the samples of this field are not generally chosen in a random manner. For another, the achieving of statistical significances depends on *two* factors: the strength of the obtained relationship and the size of the sample. Unfortunately, most samples used in research on teaching are small, thus effects must be quite sizable before they are judged as significant findings. To put this another way, studies that differ only in their sample sizes may report quite different findings, simply because one had a small sample and the other a larger one. Furthermore, given the small number of teachers in most studies, investigators may be tempted to make inductive judgments using an N of lessons, pupils, or classroom events. Sometimes such judgments are justified; usually they are not but investigators make them anyway. Investigators are also usually able to choose among several inductive statistics that might be used for judging the statistical significance of their data. Some of these statistics make few assumptions about the data but are not very powerful. Others make many assumptions and have greater power. If the weaker statistic is used, a given effect may not quite reach an acceptable level of statistical significance, in which case the investigator is tempted to use the more powerful statistic even though his data do not meet the assumptions needed for use of the latter. Investigators may also use "one-tailed tests" when they should not, which has the effect of apparently generating additional findings that are significant, albeit in a spurious manner.

Despite these problems, inductive statistics are widely used in research on teaching, as well as in other social science fields. Indeed, their use is so reified that investigators may conclude they have no finding at all when a given inductive statistic does not reach a preset level of significance, and editors will often deny publication to studies that do not exhibit examples of inductive statistics that are significant. For these reasons, few instances appear in the published literature in which investigators report the *lack* of a given teaching relationship. To illustrate, let us suppose that we are interested in examining all studies that have considered the effects of *teacher warmth* on *pupil achievement*. Let us also assume that in the real world these two variables are related in a weak though positive fashion. Most studies of this relationship, then, should generate nonsignificant results. But these are less likely to be published than those studies that show significant positive or significant negative relationships. Publication of the latter will tempt us to conclude that teacher warmth and pupil achievement are strongly related to one another and that the direction of their relationship varies as a function of context. Needless to say, such a conclusion gives a false picture of the real world of teaching.

The other method often urged for detecting findings is to make use of *descriptive* statistics that provide measures of the sign and strength of an obtained relationship. To give another example, a study might report that "teacher warmth and pupil achievement were positively and moderately correlated, $r = +.32$." Again, a number of different statistics are used to provide indications of the strength of relationships, including various correlation coefficients, variance scores, mean differences, and so on. Such statistics have several advantages when compared to inductive statistics. For one, they usually make fewer assumptions about the data. For another, they are often easier to compute than are their inductive counterparts. But crucially, they are independent of sample size. A correlation coefficient of a given size is just as likely to be obtained in studies involving small samples as it is in studies where the sample size is large. For this latter reason alone, it is often suggested that descriptive statistics should be used, rather than inductive statistics, for assessing data from several studies that have addressed the same problem.

But descriptive statistics have their problems, too. Perhaps the greatest of these is that descriptive statistics simply are not given in many published studies. Editors often ask authors to delete descriptive statistics from their manuscripts to save space in crowded journals. In addition, most investigators are aware that error may make the measurement of a given descriptive statistic quite variable, particularly when the sample size is small. For this reason, unbiased investigators are loath to interpret or report an isolated descriptive statistic until it reaches statistical significance. They become willing only when the nonsignificant statistic can be compared with others for its meaning. For this reason, nonsignificant descriptive statistics are more likely to be reported for multivariate studies wherein various descriptive statistics can be compared with one another, or for studies that were designed to replicate the prior research of other investigators. They are also more likely to appear when the investigator is *Committed* to the finding cited, for enthusiasm can overcome statistical scruples. As a result of these tendencies, reviewers who use descriptive statistics alone for conducting a review find they must discard the evidence of numerous studies that bear on the topic. In addition, their review may reflect a biased selection of findings.

Another problem concerns the comparability of results when different descriptive statistics are used. How do we compare results from three different studies when one provides mean differences, the second correlation coefficients, and the third analyses of co-variance? In order to make them comparable all such statistics must be translated into a common, derivative statistic. The derivative statistic normally used for this purpose is "the percent of variance in the dependent variable accounted for by the independent variable." But not all descriptive statistics *can* be translated into variances, and for these latter we are out of luck when seeking a common basis for making comparisons for strength of relationships between variables.

Even when translations into a common variance statistic are possible, findings reported for strength of relationship are not always comparable. To illustrate, let us suppose that a given field survey reports that an independent variable, X, appeared to account for 50 percent of the variance of a dependent variable, Y. However, the authors of the study reasoned that part of this relationship may have been induced by contextual factors, M, N, and O, that are known to co-vary with independent variable X. To take care of this possibility they also provided additional statistics, such as analyses of co-variance or partial correlations. When these latter were examined, they concluded that the "residual" effect showed X to account for only 20 percent of the variance of Y. Which is the figure we should believe, 50 percent or 20 percent? Worse, what are we to do with another study that also considered the relationship between X and Y but failed to consider contextual variables or used a different set of contextual factors in its analysis? Most of us would assign greater believability to "residual" variance scores, but these are provided in only a few studies, and the catalog of contextual variables on which they are based varies from study to study.

If this were not enough, even comparable descriptive statistics (such as variance scores given common statistical treatment) may differ in their educative importance, depending on the design of research. As a general rule, any design feature that restricts the range of contextual factors is likely to *inflate* the variance score obtained for a relationship that does involve those factors. Contrast the well-designed field survey in which a wide range of classrooms is surveyed with the experimental study in which grade level, curriculum, teaching aids, and other context features are tightly controlled. In the former we would be lucky to find any single teacher variable that accounted for as much as ten percent of the variance of pupil achievement, while we would be unhappy in the latter if our independent variable controlled as little as ten percent of the variance. But most studies of teaching have poor samples that are contextually limited, thus their results are likely to appear stronger than comparable results from studies with better samples! (In passing, we should also note that design features which restrict the range of the independent or dependent variables are likely to *deflate* the variance scores obtained for their relationship. Designs that call for the selection of a homogeneous sample of teachers or that consider high-achieving pupils only are less likely to obtain findings for those variables.) In sum, the educative importance of a given descriptive statistic varies as a function of design features. Variance scores from broad-based field surveys and tightly controlled experiments cannot usually be compared for strength of their findings in any simple sense.

This problem relates to another often cited for descriptive statistics. How large or how small should such a statistic be before one concludes that a given effect has, or has not, been obtained? This question is answered neatly, if arbitrarily, for inductive statistics—indeed, that is why inductive statistics are used. Descriptive statistics produce no such clear decision concerning the hypothesis with which we are concerned. Let us assume that three studies of equivalent design all produced variance scores concerning the effects of teacher warmth on pupil achievement: $var_1 = +.55$, $var_2 = +.15$, $var_3 = +.01$. Clearly, the first study strongly supported the proposition, while the third produced nearly a nil relationship. But what about the second study; did it support it or did it not? We need more information about study design and the history of related research before we can answer such a question.

Given these last difficulties, it is sometimes argued that descriptive statistics should be reviewed for their sign alone and not their size. Suppose we have data from several studies that pertain to the same relationship. Why not simply count to see on which occasions a positive effect was obtained and on which negative effects were reported? If all or nearly all effects are of one sign, then conclude that a universal finding was obtained. If not, then results are random, or contextual factors are at work. Such a procedure appears useful primarily when sample sizes are small and relationships are weak. (If not, inductive statistics should tell the story.) It is valid only to the extent that all data pertaining to a given relationship are published. But we already know that some nonsignificant findings are *not* published. Moreover, the tendency to avoid publication should be greatest when the real-world relationship is weak. Thus to conduct such a nose count is to tabulate from a biased sample, and possibly from a sample generated by *Committed* investigators. Use of this technique, then, may generate fictitious findings that are not present in the real world.

As can be appreciated, many pitfalls attend the use of either inductive or descriptive statistics in conducting a review of findings. Inductive statistics are more conservative but depend on sample size as well as on the strength of findings obtained and may be misused by investigators. Descriptive statistics are independent of sample size but are subject to error, are not capable of the simple interpretation we would like to give them, and may not be reported at all for many studies. And if these were not problems enough, some studies do not even present their findings using such statistics! Instead, they present findings in the forms of graphs, sociometric diagrams, matrices in which frequencies are displayed, and the like, arguing findings from the results shown by face validity only. Moreover, when tables of basic data are published, it is sometimes possible for the reviewer to discover additional findings in them that were not recognized (or were misunderstood) by the investigator. How does the reviewer handle these latter?

Given these problems, as well as the wide range of designs used in studies of teaching and the nonuniform standards for publication in this field, how should the reviewer proceed? Our position is that these problems require the reviewer to make clinical judgments when assessing the findings of a given study. In brief, the reviewer's task is to decide what conclusions may legitimately be drawn from studies whose reports are before him. In making his decisions he will have to assess the design of the study, its strengths and weaknesses, and the strength and statistical significance of results claimed. The reviewer who is unwilling to make such judgments, who relies on any single criterion to make his decisions for him, will either have to ignore relevant research or will create a review that is biased.

In general, the authors have followed these steps in detecting findings. First, findings were noted as claimed by investigators on the basis of inductive statistics. These claims were then checked against descriptive statistics and data tables (if available) and were corrected (if needed). In those cases where inductive statistics were not used, claims made by investigators were assessed and then allowed, if reasonable, in terms of the data presented. In some cases the authors were able to detect additional findings in the data tables provided by authors, and these too were allowed. Findings claimed without supporting evidence, or findings claimed in violation of evidence, were not allowed. In short, our procedures involved clinical judgments, made use of multiple criteria, and were based primarily on the criterion of statistical significance. (At an early stage of our review the authors also attempted to provide a separate tabulation of variance scores for strength of relationship claimed for all findings cited. This effort was ultimately abandoned because of unavailability and noncomparability of descriptive statistics.)

As will be understood, problems are not over when the reviewer has detected findings. Findings must also be assembled together, should be weighted in some way to reflect the strengths of studies, and should be expressed in some form that is understandable to readers. Given the variety of terms used in classroom research, let alone the numerous concepts and methods for measuring them employed in different studies, assembly of findings that bear jointly upon a given issue is also a matter for judgment. Readers will no doubt detect several instances where the authors have chosen to keep separate the reviews for concepts that are closely related because the concepts were subtly different, because the methods commonly used for their measurement are distinct, or because their findings are disparate. Less obvious are those cases where we have chosen to throw together studies that used different terms or operations for much the same concept. Judgments such as these are subject to error.

No formal method was used in our review for weighting studies in terms of their excellence. Instead, strengths and weaknesses of studies are discussed in the text. As a rule, field surveys of teaching are excellent to the extent that they involve large, randomly chosen, contextually variable samples and a multivariate design. (Additional criteria for excellence are discussed in Chapter XII. Also, *findings* are valid to the extent that they are found to hold across contexts or are replicated by other investigators.) No single study that we are aware of yet meets all of these criteria. Those meeting them partially are praised in the text. Coincidentally, those fields wherein the generally weaker studies have appeared are also those featuring the most replication (see Chapter XI).

Finally, we have chosen in this text to express findings in the form of English-language sentences. This procedure has the advantage of making results intelligible to readers with few skills in statistics. It also helps one to think about the theoretical significance of findings. The procedure has the shortcoming of being unable to express multivariate or curvilinear relationships in any simple way. (On the other hand, few studies to date have considered either multivariate or curvilinear effects. We strongly urge such studies, but for the moment most findings reported in studies of teaching involve but two variables and are stated in simple, monotonic terms.) It also may lull the unwary reader into believing that findings in the field of teaching are other than tentative. Some investigators may also conclude that the authors have crassly misrepresented their results, but this is a price one pays for making clinical judgments.

REFERENCES

Abraham, E. C., Nelson, M. A., & Reynolds, W. W., Jr., 1971. Discussion strategies and student cognitive skills. A paper presented at the annual meeting of the American Educational Research Association, New York.

Adams, R. S. (ed.), 1970. Symposium on Teacher Role in Four English-Speaking Countries. *Comparative Education Review, 14* (1).

Adams, R. S., & Biddle, B. J., 1970. *Realities of Teaching: Explorations with Video Tape.* New York: Holt.

Alexander, W. F., 1970. Abstract of a study of the effects of teacher verbal behavior on manipulative skill development. *Classroom Interaction Newsletter, 5* (2), 46–54.

Allen, D. W., & Cooper, J. M., 1968. *Model Elementary Teacher Education Program.* Washington, D.C.: USOE Bureau of Research. U.S. Government Printing Office FS 5.258:58022.

Allen, G., 1970. The relationship between certain aspects of teachers' verbal behaviour and the number development of their pupils. Paper presented at the Founding Conference of the Australian Association for Research in Education, Sydney.

Altman, H., 1970. Teacher-student interaction in inner-city and advantaged classes using the science curriculum improvement study. *Classroom Interaction Newsletter, 6* (1), 5–16.

American Educational Research Association, Committee on the Criteria of Teacher Effectiveness, 1953. Second report of the *Journal of Educational Research, 46,* 641–658.

Amidon, E. J., & Flanders, N. A., 1961. The effects of direct and indirect teacher influence on dependent-prone students learning geometry. *Journal of Educational Psychology, 52* (6), 286–291. Reprinted in E. J. Amidon & J. B. Hough (eds.), *Interaction Analysis: Theory, Research and Application.* Reading, Mass.: Addison-Wesley, 1967.

Amidon, E. J., & Flanders, N. A., 1963. *The Role of the Teacher in the Classroom.* Minneapolis: Amidon.

Amidon, E. J., & Flanders, N. A., 1967. *The Role of the Teacher in the Classroom: A Manual for Understanding and Improving Teachers' Classroom Behavior* (revised ed.). Minneapolis: Association for Productive Teaching.

Amidon, E. J., & Giammatteo, M., 1967. The verbal behavior of superior elementary teachers. In E. J. Amidon and J. B. Hough (eds.), *Interaction Analysis: Theory, Research and Application.* Reading, Mass.: Addison-Wesley.

Amidon, E. J., & Hough, J. B. (eds.), 1967. *Interaction Analysis: Theory, Research and Application.* Reading, Mass.: Addison-Wesley.

Amidon, E. J., & Hunter, Elizabeth, 1967. Verbal interaction in the classroom: The verbal interaction category system. In E. J. Amidon & J. B. Hough (eds.),

Interaction Analysis: Theory, Research and Application. Reading, Mass.: Addison-Wesley.

Anastasiow, N. J., Sibley, Sally A., Leonhardt, Teresa M., & Borich, G. D., 1970. A comparison of guided discovery, discovery and didactic teaching of math to kindergarten poverty children. *American Educational Research Journal, 7,* 493–510.

Anderson, H. H., 1939. The measurement of domination and of socially integrative behavior in teachers' contacts with children. *Child Development, 10,* 73–89. Reprinted in E. J. Amidon and J. B. Hough (eds.), *Interaction Analysis: Theory, Research and Application.* Reading, Mass.: Addison-Wesley, 1967.

Anderson, H. H., & Brewer, Helen M., 1945. Studies of teachers' classroom personalities, I: dominative and socially integrative behavior of kindergarten teachers. *Applied Psychology Monographs* (6).

Anderson, H. H., & Brewer, J. E., 1946. Studies of teachers' classroom personalities, II: effects of teachers' dominative and integrative contacts on children's classroom behavior. *Applied Psychology Monographs* (8).

Anderson, H .H., Brewer, J. E., & Reed, Mary F., 1946. Studies of teachers' classroom personalities, III: follow-up studies of the effects of dominative and integrative contacts on children's behavior. *Applied Psychology Monographs* (11).

Anderson, R. C., 1959. Learning in discussions: A resumé of the authoritarian-democratic studies. *Harvard Educational Review, 29,* 201–215.

Anthony, B. C. M., 1967. The identification and measurement of classroom environmental process variables related to academic achievement. Unpublished doctoral dissertation, University of Chicago.

Aschner, Mary Jane, Gallagher, J. J., Perry, Joyce, Afsar, Sybil, Jenne, W., & Faar, H., 1965. *A System for Classifying Thought Processes in the Context of Classroom Verbal Interaction.* Urbana, Ill.: University of Illinois.

Ausubel, D. P., 1963. *The Psychology of Meaningful Verbal Learning.* New York: Grune and Stratton.

Bales, R. F., & Gerbrands, H., 1943. The "Interaction Recorder," an apparatus and check list for sequential content analysis of social interaction. *Human Relations, 1* (4).

Balzer, L., 1969. An exploratory investigation of verbal and nonverbal behaviors of BSCS teachers and non-BSCS teachers. Paper presented at the 42nd annual meeting of the National Association for Research in Science Teaching, Pasadena, Calif.

Bandura, A., 1969. *Principles of Behavior Modification.* New York: Holt.

Barber, T. X., & Silver, M. J., 1968. Fact, fiction, and the experimenter bias effect. *Psychological Bulletin Monographs, 70* (6), Part 2.

Barker, R. G., & Barker, L. S., 1963. Social actions in the behavior streams of American and English children. In R. G. Barker (ed.), *The Stream of Behavior: Exploration of Its Structure and Content.* New York: Meredith.

Barker, R. G., & Gump, P. V., 1964. *Big School, Small School: High School Size and Student Behavior.* Stanford, Calif.: Stanford University Press.

Barker, R. G., & Wright, H. F., 1955. *Midwest and Its Children.* Evanston, Ill.: Row, Peterson.

Barker, R. G., Wright, H. F., Barker, L. S., & Schoggen, P., 1961. *Specimen Records of American and English Children.* University of Kansas Publications.

Barr, A. S., 1948. The measurement and prediction of teaching efficiency: A summary of investigations. *Journal of Experimental Education, 16,* 203–283.

Barrish, Harriet H., Saunders, Muriel, & Wolf, M. M., 1969. Good behavior game: Effects of individual contingencies for group consequences on disruptive behavior in a classroom. *Journal of Applied Behavior Analysis, 2,* 119–124.

Becker, W. C., Madsen, C. H., Arnold, Carole, R., & Thomas, D. R., 1967. The contingent use of teacher attention and praise in reducing classroom behavior problems. *Journal of Special Education, 1,* 287–307.

Bellack, A. A., Hyman, R. T., Smith, F. L., Jr., & Kliebard, H. M., 1966. *The Language of the Classroom.* Final report, USOE Cooperative Research Project, No. 2023. New York: Teachers College, Columbia University.

Bendix, E. H., 1966. Componential analysis of general vocabulary: The semantic structure of a set of verbs in English, Hindi, and Japanese. Pub. 41, *International Journal of American Linguistics,* Indiana University Research Center in Anthropology, Folklore, and Linguistics.

Benowitz, L. M., & Busse, T. V., 1970. Material incentives and the learning of spelling words in a typical school situation. *Journal of Educational Psychology, 61,* 24–26.

Bernstein, B., 1958. Some sociological determinants of perception. *British Journal of Sociology, 9,* 159–174.

Bernstein, B., 1970. A socio-linguistic approach to socialisation: With some references to educability. In J. Gumperz & D. Hymes (eds.), *Directions in Sociolinguistics.* New York: Holt.

Biddle, B. J., 1964. The integration of teacher effectiveness research. In B. J. Biddle and W. J. Ellena (eds.), *Contemporary Research on Teacher Effectiveness.* New York: Holt.

Biddle, B. J., 1967. Methods and concepts in classroom research. *Review of Educational Research, 37,* 337–357.

Biddle, B. J., 1970. The institutional context. In W. J. Campbell (ed.), *Scholars in Context: The Effects of Environments on Learning.* Sydney: Wiley.

Biddle, B. J., 1974. *Roles: Expectations, Identities, and Behaviors.* New York: Holt.

Biddle, B. J., & Adams, R. S., 1967. *An Analysis of Classroom Activities.* Final Report, Contract USOE 3-20-002, University of Missouri, Columbia.

Birnbrauer, J. S., Wolf, M. M., Kidder, J. D., & Tague, Cecilia E., 1965. Classroom behavior of retarded pupils with token reinforcement. *Journal of Experimental Child Psychology, 2,* 219–235.

Bloom, B. S., Engelhart, M. D., Furst, E. J., Hill, W. H., & Krathwohl, D. R. (eds.), 1956. *Taxonomy of Educational Objectives: The Classification of Education Goals, Handbook I: Cognitive Domain.* New York: David McKay.

Bondi, J. C., Jr., 1969. The effects of interaction analysis feedback on the verbal behavior of student teachers. *Educational Leadership, 26,* 794–799.

Biddle, B. J., Loflin, M. D., Barron, Nancy, Guyette, T., & Hays, D. G., 1971. Race grade-level, and classroom discourse complexity. Technical Report No. 50, Center for Research in Social Behavior, University of Missouri, Columbia.

Borg, W. R., Kelley, Marjorie L., Langer, P., & Gall, Meredith, 1970. *The Mini Course: A Microteaching Approach to Teacher Education.* Far West Laboratory for Educational Research and Educational Services, Inc., Berkeley, Calif.

Broden, Marcia, Bruce, C., Mitchell, Mary A., Carter, Virginia, & Hall, R. V., 1970. Effects of teacher attention on attending behavior of two boys at adjacent desks. *Journal of Applied Behavior Analysis, 3,* 199–203.

Broden, M., Hall, R. V., Dunlap, A., & Clark, R., 1970. Effects of teach attention and a token reinforcement system in a junior high school special education class. *Exceptional Children, 36,* 341–349.

Brophy, J., & Evertson, C., 1973. Low-inference observational coding measures and teacher effectiveness. Paper presented at the annual meeting of the American Educational Research Association, New Orleans.

Brophy, J., Evertson, C., Harris, T., & Good, T., 1973. Communication of teacher expectations: Fifth grade. Report Series No. 93. Research and Development Center for Teacher Education, University of Texas, Austin.

Brophy, J. E., & Good, T. L., 1970. Teachers' communication of differential expectations for children's classroom performance: Some behavioral data. *Journal of Educational Psychology, 61* (5), 365–374.

Brophy, J. E., & Good, T. L., 1974. *Teacher Student Relationships: Causes and Consequences.* New York: Holt.

Brown, B., Ober, R., Soar, R., & Webb, Jeannine N., 1968. The Florida Taxonomy of Cognitive Behaviors. Institute for Development of Human Resources, the University of Florida, Gainesville.

Bruce, L. R., 1971. A study of the relationship between the SCIS teachers' attitude toward the teacher-student relationship and question types. *Journal of Research in Science Teaching, 8* (2), 157–164.

Bruner, J. S., 1966. *Toward a Theory of Instruction.* Cambridge: Harvard University Press.

Bushell, D. H., Wrobel, Patricia A., & Michaelis, Mary L., 1968. Applying "group" contingencies to the classroom study behavior of pre-school children. *Journal of Applied Behavior Analysis, 1,* 55–61.

Cambourne, B. L., 1971. A naturalistic study of language performance in grade 1 rural and urban school children. Ph.D. dissertation, The James Cook University of North Queensland, Australia.

Campbell, W. J., 1968. Studies of teaching: I classroom practices. *New Zealand Journal of Educational Studies, 3* (2), 97–124.

Campbell, W. J., 1970. Some effects of affective climate on the achievement motivation of pupils. In W. J. Campbell (ed.), *Scholars in Context: The Effects of Environments on Learning.* Sydney: Wiley.

Carline, J. L., 1969. An investigation of the relationship between various verbal strategies of teaching behavior and achievement of elementary school children. Unpublished doctoral dissertation, Syracuse University, Syracuse, New York.

Carline, J. L., 1970. In-service training re-examined. *Journal of Research and Development in Education, 4,* 103–115.

Carlson, Constance S., Arnold, Carole R., Becker, W. C., & Madsen, C. H., 1968. The elimination of tantrum behavior of a child in an elementary classroom. *Behaviour Research and Therapy, 6,* 117–119.

Chadwick, B. A., & Day, R. C., 1970. Systematic reinforcement: Academic performance on Mexican-American and black students. Unpublished paper, Department of Sociology, University of Washington.

Chall, Jeanne S., 1967. *Learning To Read: The Great Debate.* New York: McGraw-Hill.

Chomsky, N., 1965. *Aspects of the Theory of Syntax*. Cambridge: The M.I.T. Press.

Claiborn, W. L., 1968. An investigation of the relationship between teacher expectancy, teacher behavior and pupil performance. Unpublished doctoral dissertation, University of Michigan.

Claiborn, W. L., 1969. Expectancy effects in the classroom: A failure to replicate. *Journal of Educational Psychology, 60*, 377–383.

Clarizio, H. F., 1971. *Toward Positive Classroom Discipline*. New York: Wiley.

Coleman, J. S., 1961. *The Adolescent Society*. Glencoe, Ill.: The Free Press.

Coleman, J. S., 1972. Class integration—a fundamental break with the past. *Saturday Review*, May 27, 1972. New York: Saturday Review.

Coleman, J. S., Campbell, E. Q., Hobson, Carol J., McPartland, J., Mood, A. M., Weinfeld, F. D., & York, R. L., 1966. *Equality of Educational Opportunity*. Washington, D.C.: U.S. Government Printing Office.

Conners, C. K., & Eisenberg, L., 1966. The effect of teacher behavior on verbal intelligence in operation headstart children. Mimeographed report, Johns Hopkins University School of Medicine.

Cook, R. E., 1967. The effect of teacher methodology upon certain achievements of students in secondary school biology. Unpublished doctoral dissertation, University of Iowa.

Cornbleth, Catherine, Davis, O. L., Jr., & Button, C., 1972. Teacher-pupil interaction and teacher expectations for pupil achievement in secondary school social studies classes. Paper presented at the annual meeting of the American Educational Research Association, Chicago.

Cronbach, L. J., & Furby, Lita., 1970. How we should measure "change"—or should we? *Psychological Bulletin, 74*, 68–80.

Dahllöf, U. S., & Lundgren, U. P., 1970. Project Compass 23: Macro and micro approaches combined for curriculum process analysis: A Swedish educational field project. Paper presented at the annual meeting of the American Educational Research Association, Minneapolis.

Dalton, W. B., 1969. The relations between classroom interaction and teacher ratings of pupils: An exploration of one means by which a teacher may communicate her expectancies. Paper presented at the annual meeting of the Southeastern Psychological Association, New Orleans.

Davis, Hazel, 1964. Evolution of current practices in evaluating teacher competence. In B. J. Biddle & W. J. Ellena (eds.), *Contemporary Research on Teacher Effectiveness*. New York: Holt.

Davis, O. L., Jr., & Slobodian, June J., 1967. Teacher behavior toward boys and girls during first grade reading instruction. *American Educational Research Journal, 4*, 261–270.

Davis, O. L., Jr., & Tinsley, D. C., 1968. Cognitive objectives revealed by classroom questions asked by social studies student teachers. In R. T. Hyman (ed.), *Teaching: Vantage Points for Study*. Philadelphia: J. B. Lippincott.

Day, R. C., & Chadwick, B. A., 1970. Modification of disruptive classroom behavior of Mexican-American and black children. Unpublished paper, Department of Sociology, University of Washington.

Dawe, Helen C., 1934. The influence of size of kindergarten group upon performance. *Child Development, 5*, 295–303.

Dell, D., & Hiller, J. H., 1968. Computer analysis of teachers' explanations. In N. L. Gage *et al.* (eds.), *Explorations of the Teacher's Effectiveness in*

Explaining. Stanford Center for Research and Development in Teaching, Technical Report No. 4, School of Education, Stanford University, Stanford, Calif.

Doenau, S. J., 1970. *Catch a Teacher by the Toe.* Sydney, Australia: Galleon Publications.

Domas, S. J., & Tiedeman, D., 1950. Teacher competence: An annotated bibliography. *Journal of Experimental Education, 19,* 101–218.

Elashoff, H., & Snow, R., 1971. *Pygmalion Reconsidered.* Belmont, Calif.: Charles A. Jones.

Emmer, E. T., 1967. The effect of teacher use and acceptance of student ideas on student verbal initiation. Unpublished doctoral dissertation, University of Michigan.

English, H. B., & English, Ava C., 1958. *A Comprehensive Dictionary of Psychological and Psychoanalytic Terms.* New York: Longmans, Green.

Evans, G., & Oswalt, G. L., 1968. Acceleration of academic progress through the manipulation of peer influence. *Behaviour Research and Therapy, 6,* 189–195.

Evertson, C. M., Brophy, J. E., & Good, T. L., 1972. Communication of teacher expectations: Second grade. Report Series 92. Research and Development Center for Teacher Education, University of Texas, Austin.

Evertson, C. M., Brophy, J. E., & Good, T. L., 1973. Communication of teacher expectations: Second garde. Report Series 92. Research and Development Center for Teacher Education, University of Texas, Austin.

Farnsworth, P. R., 1933. Seat preference in the classroom. *Journal of Social Psychology, 4,* 373–376.

Felsenthal, Helen, 1970. Sex differences in teacher-pupil interaction in first grade reading instruction. Paper presented at the annual meeting of the American Educational Research Association, Minneapolis.

Fillmore, C., 1968. The case for case. In E. Bach and R. T. Harms (eds.), *Universals in Linguistic Theory.* New York: Holt.

Finske, Sister M. Joanice., 1967. The effect of feedback through interaction analysis on the development of flexibility in student teachers. Unpublished doctoral dissertation, University of Michigan.

Fishburn, C. E., 1962. Teacher role perception in the secondary school. *Journal of Teacher Education, 13,* 55–59.

Fishburn, C. E., 1966. Learning the role of the teacher. *Journal of Teacher Education, 17,* 329–331.

Flanders, N. A., 1960. *Interaction Analysis in the Classroom: A Manual for Observers.* University of Michigan, Ann Arbor.

Flanders, N. A., 1963. Teacher and classroom influences on individual learning. Paper presented at the Seventh Annual Curriculum Research Institute, Eastern Section, Association for Supervision and Curriculum Development.

Flanders, N. A., 1964. Some relationships among teacher influence, pupil attitudes, and achievement. In B. J. Biddle & W. J. Ellena (eds.), *Contemporary Research on Teacher Effectiveness.* New York: Holt.

Flanders, N. A., 1967. Teacher influence in the classroom. In E. J. Amidon & J. B. Hough (eds.), *Interaction Analysis: Theory, Research and Application.* Reading, Mass.: Addison-Wesley.

Flanders, N. A., 1970. *Analyzing Teacher Behavior.* Reading, Mass.: Addison-Wesley.

Flanders, N. A., 1971. A national coordinated program on teacher effectiveness.

In *How Teachers Make a Difference*. Washington, D.C.: U.S. Government Printing Office.

Flanders, N. A., & Simon, Anita, 1970. Teaching effectiveness: A review of research 1960–66. In R. L. Ebel (ed.), *Encyclopedia of Educational Research*. Chicago: Rand McNally.

Foa, U. G., & Foa, Edna, B., forthcoming. *Societal Structure of the Mind*. Springfield, Ill.: Charles C Thomas.

Fortune, J. C., Gage, N. L., & Shutes, R. E., 1966. The generality of the ability to explain. Paper presented at the American Educational Research Association, Amherst, Mass.

Fowler, Beverly D., & Soar, R. S., no date. Relation of teacher personality characteristics and attitudes to teacher-pupil behaviors and emotional climate in the elementary classroom. Mimeographed report, University of South Carolina.

Freud, S., 1910. *Eine Kindheitserinnerung des Leonardo da Vinci* (A Childhood Memory of Leonardo da Vinci), F. Deuticke, publisher (Germany). Also in J. Strachey (ed.), *Standard Edition of the Complete Works of Sigmund Freud*, Vol. 11. London: Hogarth Press, 1953.

Furst, Norma F., 1967. The multiple languages of the classroom. Paper presented at the annual meeting of the American Educational Research Association, New York. (a)

Furst, Norma F., 1967. The effects of training in interaction analysis on the behavior of student teachers in secondary schools. In E. J. Amidon & J. B. Hough (eds.), *Interaction Analysis: Theory, Research and Application*. Reading, Mass.: Addison-Wesley. (b)

Furst, Norma F., 1967. The multiple laguages of the classroom. Unpublished doctoral dissertation, Temple University, Philadelphia. (c)

Furst, Norma F., & Amidon, E. J., 1967. Teacher-pupil interaction patterns in the elementary school. In E. J. Amidon & J. B. Hough (eds.), *Interaction Analysis: Theory, Research and Application*. Reading, Mass.: Addison-Wesley.

Gage, N. L., 1960. Address appearing in "Proceedings," *Research Resumé, 16*, Burlingame, Calif.: California Teachers Association.

Gage, N. L. (ed.), 1963. *Handbook of Research on Teaching*. American Educational Research Association. Chicago: Rand McNally. (a)

Gage, N. L., 1963. Paradigms for research on teaching. In N. L. Gage (ed.), *Handbook of Research on Teaching*. American Educational Research Association. Chicago: Rand McNally. (b)

Gage, N. L., 1964. Theories of teaching. In E. R. Hilgard (ed.), *Theories of Learning and Instruction*. N.S.S.E. Yearbook No. 63, Part 1. Chicago: University of Chicago Press.

Gage, N. L., 1966. Research on cognitive aspects of teaching. In *The Way Teaching Is: A Report of the Seminar on Teaching*. Washington, D.C.: Association for Supervision and Curriculum Development and the Center for the Study of Instruction of the National Education Association.

Gage, N. L., 1972. *Teacher Effectiveness and Teacher Education: The Search for a Scientific Basis*. Palo Alto, Calif.: Pacific Books.

Gallagher, J. J., 1965. Productive thinking in gifted children. Cooperative Research Project No. 965. Institute for Research on Exceptional Children, University of Illinois, Urbana.

Gallagher, J. J., 1970. Three studies of the classroom. In J. J. Gallagher, G. A.

Nuthall, & B. Rosenshine (eds.), *Classroom Observation*. American Educational Research Association Monograph Series on Curriculum Evaluation, Monograph No. 6. Chicago: Rand McNally.

Goldenberg, R. E., 1971. Pupil control ideology and teacher influence in the classroom. Paper presented at the annual meeting of the American Educational Research Association, New York.

Good, T. L., & Brophy, J. E., 1971. Analyzing classroom interaction: A more powerful alternative. *Educational Technology, 11*, 36–41.

Good, T. L., & Brophy, J. E., 1972. Behavioral expression of teacher attitudes. *Journal of Educational Psychology, 63*, 617–624.

Good, T. L., & Brophy, J. E., 1973. *Looking in Classrooms*. New York: Harper & Row.

Good, T. L., Sikes, J. N., & Brophy, J. E., 1973. Effects of teacher sex, student sex and student achievement on classroom interaction. *Journal of Educational Psychology, 65*, 74–87.

Greenberg, J. H., 1957. *Essays in Linguistics*. Chicago: University of Chicago Press.

Griffith, C. R., 1921. A comment upon the psychology of the audience. *Psychological Monographs, 30* (136), 36–47.

Guilford, J. P., 1956. The structure of intellect. *Psychological Bulletin, 53*, 267–293.

Guilford, J. P., 1959. *Personality*. New York: McGraw-Hill.

Guilford, J. P., 1970. Intelligence has three facets. In H. F. Clarizio, R. C. Craig, & W. A. Mehrens (eds.), *Contemporary Issues in Educational Psychology*. Boston: Allyn and Bacon.

Gump, P. V., 1967. *The Classroom Behavior Setting: Its Nature and Relation to Student Behavior*. Final Report, Contract No. OE-4-10-107, U.S. Bureau of Research, H.E.W.

Gunnison, J. P., 1968. An experiment to determine the effects of changing teacher classroom behavior through training of student-teachers in the use of Flanders Interaction Analysis System. Unpublished doctoral dissertation, Arizona State University, Temple.

Guttman, L. P., 1954. A new approach to factor analysis: The radex. In P. F. Lazarsfeld (ed.), *Mathematical Thinking in the Social Sciences*. Glencoe, Ill.: The Free Press.

Hall, R. V., Axelrod, S., Foundopoulos, Marlyn, Shellman, Jessica, Campbell, R. A., & Cranston, Sharon S., 1971. The effective use of punishment to modify behavior in the classroom. *Educational Technology, 11*, 24–26.

Hanley, E. M., 1970. Review of research involving applied behavior analysis in the classroom. *Review of Educational Research, 40*, 597–625.

Harris, A. J., Morrison, C., Serwer, B. L., & Gold, L., 1968. *A Continuation of the CRAFT Project: Comparing Reading Approaches with Disadvantaged Urban Negro Children in Primary Grades*. New York: Division of Teacher Education, City University of New York.

Harris, A. J., & Serwer, B. L., 1966. *Comparison of Reading Approaches in First Grade Teaching with Disadvantaged Children (the CRAFT Project)*. USOE Cooperative Research Project No. 2677, City University of New York.

Hawkins, W. H., & Taylor, Sandra, 1972. Teacher reactive behavior related to class size and to the teaching of mathematics, social studies and English.

Paper presented at the annual meeting of the Australian Association for Research in Education, Canberra.

Hays, D. G., Kantor, R. N., & Goldstein, L., 1971. Manifest characteristics of interactive sequencing in the classroom. Technical Report No. 41, Center for Research in Social Behavior, University of Missouri, Columbia.

Helmreich, R., 1971. The TEKTITE II human behavior program. NASA-ONR Technical Report No. 14.

Hendrix, Gertrude, 1961. Learning by discovery. *The Mathematics Teacher, 54*, 290–299.

Herbart, J. F., 1895. *The Science of Education.* Boston: Heath.

Herbart, J. F., 1901. *Outlines of Educational Doctrine.* New York: Macmillan.

Herbert, J., 1967. *A System for Analyzing Lessons.* New York: Teachers College Press.

Herman, W. L., Jr., 1967. An analysis of the activities and verbal behavior of selected fifth grade social studies classes. *Classroom Interaction Newsletter, 2* (2), 27–29.

Herman, W. L., Jr., Potterfield, J. E., Dayton, C. M., & Amershek, K. G., 1969. The relationship of teacher-centered activities and pupil-centered activities to pupil achievement and interest in fifth grade social studies classes. *American Education Research Journal, 6,* 227–239.

Hewett, F. M., Taylor, F. D., & Artuso, A. A., 1969. The Santa Monica Project: Evaluation of an engineered classroom design with emotionally disturbed children. *Exceptional Children, 35,* 523–529.

Highet, G., 1954. *The Art of Teaching.* New York: Vintage Books.

Hill, W. M., 1967. The effects on verbal teaching behavior of learning interaction analysis as an in-service education activity. *Classroom Interaction Newsletter, 2* (2), 30–31.

Hill, R. A., & Furst, Norma F., 1969. A comparison of the role of teachers in CAI classrooms and teachers in traditional classrooms. Paper presented at the American Educational Research Association, Los Angeles.

Hiller, J. H., 1971. Verbal response indicators of conceptual vagueness. *American Educational Research Journal, 8,* 151–161.

Hiller, J. H., Fisher, G. A., & Kaess, W., 1969. A computer investigation of verbal characteristics of effective classroom lecturing. *American Educational Research Journal, 6,* 661–675.

Hoehn, A. J., 1954. A study of social status differentiation in the classroom behavior of nineteen third grade teachers. *Journal of Social Psychology, 39,* 269–292.

Hoetker, A. J., & Ahlbrand, W. P., 1969. The persistence of recitation. *American Educational Research Journal, 6,* 145–169.

Hogan, B. A., 1973. A structural comparison of classroom behavior in multi- and single-grade classrooms. Unpublished Ph.D. dissertation, The James Cook University of North Queensland, Australia.

Homme, L., 1966. Contingency management. *Newsletter, 5,* American Psychological Association Division of Clinical Psychology.

Hough, J. B., 1967. An observation system for the analysis of classroom instruction. In E. J. Amidon and J. B. Hough (eds.), *Interaction Analysis: Theory, Research and Application.* Reading, Mass.: Addison-Wesley.

Hough, J. B., 1968. *Specifications for a Comprehensive Undergraduate and*

Inservice Teacher Education Program for Elementary Teachers. Washington, D.C.: USOE Bureau of Research, U.S. Government Printing Office.

Hough, J. B., & Ober, R., 1967. The effect of training in interaction analysis on the verbal teaching behavior of pre-service teachers. In E. J. Amidon & J. B. Hough (eds.), *Interaction Analysis: Theory, Research and Application.* Reading, Mass.: Addison-Wesley.

Houston, W. R., 1968. *Behavioral Science Elementary Teacher Education Program.* Washington, D.C.: USOE Bureau of Research, U.S. Government Printing Office.

Hudgins, B. B., 1971. *The Instructional Process.* Chicago: Rand McNally.

Hudgins, B. B., & Ahlbrand, W. P., Jr., 1967. *A Study of Classroom Interaction and Thinking.* St. Louis: Central Midwestern Regional Educational Laboratory.

Hughes, D. C., 1973. An experimental investigation of the effects of pupil responding and teacher reacting on pupil achievement. *American Educational Research Journal, 10* (1), 21–37.

Hughes, Marie M., 1959. *Assessment of the Quality of Teaching in Elementary Schools.* Salt Lake City: University of Utah Press. (a)

Hughes, Marie M., 1959. *Development of the Means for the Assessment of the Quality of Teaching in Elementary Schools.* Salt Lake City: University of Utah Press. (b)

Hunt, W. K., 1965. *Grammatical Structures Written at Three Grade Levels.* Champaign, Illinois: National Council of Teachers of English.

Hunter, C. P., 1968. Classroom climate and pupil characteristics in special classes for the educationally handicapped. Unpublished doctoral dissertation, University of Southern California.

Hunter, Elizabeth, 1969. The effects of training in the use of new science programs upon the classroom verbal behavior of first grade teachers as they teach science. *Classroom Interaction Newsletter, 4* (2), 5–11.

Hyman, R. T., 1968. *Teaching: Vantage Points for Study.* Philadelphia: J. B. Lippincott.

Hymes, D., 1964. Directions in (ethno-) linguistic theory. In A. K. Romney & R. G. D'Andrade (eds.), Trans-cultural Studies in Cognition. *American Anthropologist.* Special Publication, *66* (3).

Jackson, P. W., 1966. The way teaching is. In *The Way Teaching Is: A Report for the Seminar on Teaching.* Washington, D.C.: Association for Supervision and Curriculum Development and the Center for the Study of Instruction of the National Education Association.

Jackson, P. W., 1968. *Life in Classrooms.* New York: Holt.

Jackson, P. W., & Lahaderne, Henriette M., 1967. Inequalities of teacher-pupil contacts. *Psychology in the Schools, 4* (3), 201–211. Reprinted in M. W. Miles & W. W. Charters, Jr. (eds.), *Learning in Social Settings.* Boston: Allyn and Bacon, 1970.

Johns, J. P., 1966. The relationship between teacher behaviors and the incidence of thought-provoking questions by students in secondary schools. Unpublished doctoral dissertation, University of Michigan.

José, Jean, 1970. Teacher expectancies and classroom interaction. Paper presented at the annual meeting of the American Educational Research Association, Minneapolis.

Joyce, B. R., 1968. *The Teacher Innovator: A Program to Prepare Teachers.* Washington, D.C.: Bureau of Research, U.S. Government Printing Office.

Keeves, J. P., 1972. *Educational Environment and Student Achievement*. Melbourne: Australian Council for Educational Research.

Kerlinger, F. N., 1964. *Foundations of Behavioral Research*. New York: Holt.

Kirk, J., 1967. Elementary school student teachers and interaction analysis. In E. J. Amidon & J. B. Hough (eds.), *Interaction Analysis: Theory, Research and Application*. Reading, Mass.: Addison-Wesley.

Klein, M. F., & Goodlad, J. I., 1970. *Behind the Classroom Door*. Worthington, Ohio: C. A. Jones.

Kliebard, H. M., 1966. The observation of classroom behavior—some recent research. In *The Way Teaching Is: A Report to the Seminar on Teaching*. Washington, D.C.: Association for Supervision and Curriculum Development and the Center for the Study of Instruction of the National Education Association.

Komisar, B. P., 1968. As quoted in G. A. Nuthall, Studies of teaching: Types of research on teaching. *New Zealand Journal of Educational Studies, 3*, 125–147.

Kounin, J. S., 1970. *Discipline and Group Management in Classrooms*. New York: Holt.

Kounin, J. S., Friesen, W. V., & Norton, Evangeline, 1966. Managing emotionally disturbed children in regular classrooms. *Journal of Educational Psychology, 57*, 1–13.

Kounin, J. S., & Gump, P. V., 1958. The ripple effect in discipline. *Elementary School Journal, 35*, 158–162.

Koutsoudas, A., 1966. *Writing Transformational Grammars: An Introduction*. New York: McGraw-Hill.

Kowatrakul, Surang, 1959. Some behaviors of elementary school children related to classroom activities and subject areas. *Journal of Educational Psychology, 50*, 121–128.

Kranz, Patricia L., Weber, W. A., & Fishell, K. N., 1970. The relationships between teacher perception of pupils and teacher behavior toward those pupils. Paper presented at the annual meeting of the American Educational Research Association, Minneapolis.

Labov, W., 1966. *The Social Stratification of English in New York City*. Washington, D.C.: Center for Applied Linguistics.

LaShier, W. S., 1965. An analysis of certain aspects of the verbal behavior of student teachers of eighth grade students participating in a BSCS laboratory block. Unpublished doctoral dissertation, University of Texas.

Lewin, K., Lippitt, R., & White, R., 1939. Patterns of aggressive behavior in experimentally created "social climates." *Journal of Social Psychology, 10*, 271–299. Reprinted in E. J. Amidon & J. B. Hough (eds.), *Interaction Analysis: Theory, Research and Application*. Reading, Mass.: Addison-Wesley, 1967.

Lipe, D., & Jung, S. M., 1971. Manipulating incentives to enhance school learning. *Review of Educational Research, 41*, 249–280.

Loban, W., 1963. *The Language of Elementary School Children*. Champaign, Ill.: National Council of Teachers of English.

Loflin, M. D., 1970. On the structure of the verb in a dialect of American Negro English. *Linguistics, 59*, 14–28.

Loflin, M. D., 1973. Personal communication.

Loflin, M. D., Biddle, B. J., Barron, Nancy, & Marlin, Marjorie, 1973. Sex, race, social class and language in the classroom. Technical Report No. 88, Center for Research in Social Behavior, University of Missouri, Columbia.

Loflin, M. D., Guyette, T. W., Barron, Nancy, & Marlin, Marjorie, 1972. Reconstruction in the analysis of verbal interaction. *American Educational Research Journal, 9* (1), 101–112.

Lohman, E., Ober, R., & Hough, J. B., 1967. A study of the effect of pre-service training in interaction analysis on the verbal behavior of student teachers. In E. J. Amidon & J. B. Hough (eds.), *Interaction Analysis: Theory, Research and Application.* Reading, Mass.: Addison-Wesley.

Lundgren, U. P., 1972. *Frame Factors and the Teaching Process: A Contribution to Curriculum Theory and Theory on Teaching.* Stockholm: Almgrist and Wiksell.

Madsen, C. H., Becker, W. C., & Thomas, D. R., 1968. Rules, praise, and ignoring: Elements of elementary classroom control. *Journal of Applied Behavior Analysis, 1,* 139–150.

McAllister, L. W., Stachowiak, J. G., Baer, D. M., & Conderman, L., 1969. The application of operant conditioning techniques in a secondary school classroom. *Journal of Applied Behavior Analysis, 2,* 277–285.

McCandless, B. R., 1961. *Children and Adolescents: Behavior and Development.* New York: Holt.

McGee, H. M., 1965. Measurement of authoritarianism and its relation to teachers' classroom behavior. *Genetic Psychology Monographs, 52,* 89–146.

McKenzie, H. S., Clark, Marilyn, Wolf, M. M., Kothera, R., & Benson, C., 1968. Behavior modification of children with learning disabilities using grades as tokens and allowances as back-up reinforcers. *Exceptional Children, 34,* 745–752.

Measel, W. W., 1967. The relationship between teacher influence and levels of thinking of second grade teachers and pupils. Unpublished doctoral dissertation, University of Michigan, Ann Arbor.

Medinnus, G., & Unruh, R., 1971. Teacher expectations and verbal communication. Paper presented at the annual meeting of the Western Psychological Association.

Medley, D. M., 1967. The use of orthogonal contrasts in the interpretation of records of verbal behaviors of classroom teachers. Paper presented at the American Psychological Association, Washington, D.C.

Medley, D. M., & Hill, R. A., 1968. A comparison of two techniques for analyzing classroom behaviors. Paper presented at the Annual Meeting of the American Educational Research Association, Chicago.

Medley, D. M., & Hill, R. A., 1970. Cognitive factors in teaching style. Paper presented at the annual meeting of the American Educational Research Association, Minneapolis.

Medley, D. M., Impellitteri, J. T., & Smith, L. H., 1966. *Coding Teachers' Verbal Behavior in the Classroom: A Manual for Users of OScAR 4V.* New York: Division of Teacher Education, City University of New York.

Medley, D. M., & Mitzel, H. E., 1958. A technique for measuring classroom behavior. *Journal of Educational Psychology, 49,* 86–92.

Medley, D. M., & Mitzel, H. E., 1959. Some behavioral correlates of teacher effectiveness. *Journal of Educational Psychology, 50,* 239–246.

Medley, D. M., & Mitzel, H. E., 1963. The scientific study of teacher behavior. In

A. A. Bellack (ed.), *Theory and Research in Teaching*. New York: Bureau of Publications, Teachers College, Columbia University.

Medley, D. M., Schluck, Carolyn G., & Ames, Nancy P., 1968. *Assessing the Learning Environment in the Classroom: A Manual for Users of OScAR 5V*. Research Memorandum. Princeton, N.J.: Educational Testing Service.

Meichenbaum, D., Bowers, K., & Ross, R., 1969. A behavioral analysis of teacher expectancy effect. *Journal of Personality and Social Psychology, 13*, 306–316.

Mendoza, Sonia M., Good, T. L., & Brophy, J. E., 1971. Who talks in junior high classrooms? Paper presented at the annual meeting of the American Educational Research Association, New York.

Meux, M. O., 1967. Studies of learning in the school setting. *Review of Educational Research, 37*, 539–562.

Meux, M. O., & Smith, B. O., 1964. Logical dimensions of teacher behavior. In B. J. Biddle & W. J. Ellena (eds.), *Contemporary Research on Teacher Effectiveness*. New York: Holt.

Meyer, W. J., & Thompson, G. G., 1956. Sex difference in the distribution of teacher approval and disapproval among sixth-grade children. *Journal of Educational Psychology, 47*, 385–396.

Minor, M. W., 1970. Experimenter-expectancy effect as a function of evaluation apprehension. *Journal of Personality and Social Psychology, 15*, 326–332.

Mitzel, H. E., 1957. A behavioral approach to the assessment of teacher effectiveness. Unpublished paper, Division of Teacher Education, College of the City of New York.

Mitzel, H. E., 1960. Teacher effectiveness. In C. W. Harris (ed.), *Encyclopedia of Educational Research* (3rd edition). New York: Macmillan.

Mood, D. W., 1972. Teacher verbal behavior and teacher and pupil thinking in elementary school. *Journal of Educational Research, 66* (3), 99–102.

Moore, J. R., no date. An analysis of teacher and pupil verbal behavior and teacher procedural and evaluative behavior in relation to objectives unique to the PSSC and non-PSSC physics curricula. Unpublished paper, University of Michigan, Ann Arbor.

Moore, J. W., Gagné, E. D., & Hauck, W. E., 1973. Conditions moderating the self-fulfilling prophecy phenomenon. Paper presented at the annual meeting of the American Educational Research Association, New Orleans.

Moreno, J. L., 1934. *Who Shall Survive? A New Approach to the Problems of Human Interrelations (revised edition)*. Washington, D.C.: Nervous and Mental Disease Publishing Co. New York: Beacon House, 1953.

Morsh, J. E., and Wilder, E. W., 1954. *Identifying the Effective Instructor: A Review of the Quantitative Studies, 1900–1952*. Research Bulletin No. AFPTRC-TR-54-44. San Antonio, Texas: USAF Personnel Training Research Center.

Moskowitz, Gertrude, 1967. The attitudes and teaching patterns of cooperating teachers and student teachers trained in interaction analysis. In E. J. Amidon and J. B. Hough (eds.), *Interaction Analysis: Theory, Research and Application*. Reading, Mass.: Addison-Wesley.

Murray, C. K., & Williams, T. L., 1971. The effect of cognitive instruction on secondary and English student teachers and their pupils. Paper presented at the annual meeting of the American Educational Research Association, New York.

Nelson, Lois, 1969. *The Nature of Teaching: A Collection of Readings.* Boston: Blaisdell.

Nelson, M. A., Reynolds, W. W., Jr., & Abraham, E. C., 1971. Discussion paradigms. Paper presented at the annual meeting of the American Educational Research Association, New York.

Neujahr, J. L., 1970. A descriptive study of individualized instruction. Paper presented at the annual meeting of the American Educational Research Association, Minneapolis.

Nuthall, G. A., 1968. Studies of teaching: Types of research on teaching. *New Zealand Journal of Educational Studies,* 3 (2), 125–147. (a)

Nuthall, G. A., 1968. An experimental comparison of alternative strategies for teaching concepts. *American Educational Research Journal,* 5 (4), 561–584. (b)

Nuthall, G. A., 1970. A review of some selected recent studies of classroom interaction and teaching behavior. In *Classroom Observation,* American Educational Research Monograph No. 4. Chicago: Rand McNally.

Nuthall, G., 1972. Personal communication.

Nuthall, G., & Church, J., 1971. Experimental studies of teacher behavior: A preliminary report of the experimental studies of teacher behavior being conducted in the Teaching Research Project, University of Canterbury. Paper presented at the 43rd Congress of the Australian and New Zealand Association for the Advancement of Science, Brisbane, Australia.

Nuthall, G. A., & Lawrence, P. J., 1965. *Thinking in the Classroom: The Development of a Method of Analysis.* Wellington, New Zealand: New Zealand Council for Educational Research.

Nuthall, G., & Snook, I., 1973. Contemporary models of teaching. In Robert M. W. Travers (ed.), *Second Handbook of Research on Teaching.* New York: Rand McNally.

O'Leary, K. D., & Becker, W. C., 1967. Behavior modification of an adjustment class: A token reinforcement program. *Exceptional Children, 33,* 637–642.

O'Leary, K. D., & Becker, W. C., 1968. The effects of a teacher's reprimands on children's behavior. *Journal of School Psychology, 7,* 8–11.

O'Leary, K. D., Becker, W. C., Evans, M. B., & Saudargas, R. A., 1969. A token reinforcement program in a public school: A replication and systematic analysis. *Journal of Applied Behavior Analysis, 2,* 3–13.

O'Leary, K. D., & Drabman, R. S., 1971. Token reinforcement programs in the classroom: A review. *Psychological Bulletin, 75,* 379–398.

O'Leary, K. D., Kaufman, K. F., Kass, Ruth E., and Drabman, R. S., 1970. The effects of loud and soft reprimands on the behavior of disruptive students. *Exceptional Children, 37,* 145–155.

O'Leary, K. D., & O'Leary, Susan G., 1971. *Classroom Management: The Successful Use of Behavior Modification.* New York: Pergamon.

Osborne, J. G., 1969. Free-time as a reinforcer in the management of classroom behavior. *Journal of Applied Behavior Analysis, 2,* 113–118.

Packard, R. G., 1970. The control of "classroom attention": A group contingency for complex behavior. *Journal of Applied Behavior Analysis, 3,* 13–28.

Pankratz, R., 1967. Verbal interaction patterns in the classroom of selected physics teachers. In E. J. Amidon & J. B. Hough (eds.), *Interaction Analysis: Theory, Research and Application.* Reading, Mass.: Addison-Wesley.

Penny, R. E., 1969. Presentational behaviors related to success in teaching. Unpublished doctoral dissertation, Stanford University, Stanford, Calif.

Perkins, H. V., 1964. A procedure for assessing the classroom behavior of students and teachers. *American Educational Research Journal, 1* (4), 249–260. Also reprinted in R. T. Hyman (ed.), *Teaching: Vantage Points for Study.* Philadelphia: J. B. Lippincott, 1968.

Perkins, H. V., 1965. Classroom behavior and underachievement. *American Educational Research Journal, 2,* 1–12.

Powell, E. R., 1968. Teacher behavior and pupil achievement. Paper presented at the annual meeting of the American Educational Research Association, Chicago.

Power, C. N., 1971. The effects of communication patterns on student sociometric status, attitudes, and achievement in science. Unpublished Ph.D. thesis, University of Queensland, Australia.

Premack, D., 1965. Reinforcement theory. In D. Levine (ed.), *Nebraska Symposium on Motivation.* Lincoln: University of Nebraska Press.

Preston, R. C., 1962. Reading achievement of German and American children. *School and Society, 90,* 350–354.

Ragosta, Marjorie, Soar, R. S., Soar, Ruth M., and Stebbins, Linda B., 1971. Sign versus category: Two instruments for observing level of thinking. Paper presented at the annual meeting of the American Educational Research Association, New York.

Resnick, L. B., 1971. Teacher behavior in an informal British infant school. Paper presented at the annual meeting of the American Educational Research Association, New York.

Rexford, G. E., Willower, D. F., & Lynch, P. D., 1972. Teacher's pupil control ideology and classroom verbal behavior. *Journal of Experimental Education, 40* (4), 78–82.

Reynolds, W. W., Jr., Abraham, E. C., & Nelson, M. A., 1971. The classroom observational record. Paper presented at the annual meeting of the American Educational Research Association, New York.

Rian, H., 1969. Teacher leadership and pupil reaction: The authoritarian-democratic dimension revisited. *Scandinavian Journal of Educational Research* (Pedagogisk Forskning), *13,* 1–15.

Risley, T. R., & Hart, B., 1968. Developing correspondence between the non-verbal and verbal behavior of preschool children. *Journal of Applied Behavior Analysis, 1,* 267–281.

Rist, R. C., 1970. The socialization of the ghetto child into the urban school system. Unpublished Ph.D. dissertation, Washington University, St. Louis, Mo.

Roe, Ann, 1953. *The Making of a Scientist.* New York: Dodd, Mead.

Rogers, Virginia M., & Davis, O. L., Jr., 1970. Varying the cognitive levels of classroom questions: An analysis of student teachers' questions and pupil achievement in elementary social studies. Paper presented at the annual meeting of the American Educational Research Association, Minneapolis.

Rosenshine, B., 1968. Objectively measured behavioral predictors of effectiveness in explaining. Paper presented at the annual meeting of the American Educational Research Association, Chicago.

Rosenshine, B., 1970. Evaluation of classroom instruction. *Review of Educational Research, 40,* 279–300.

Rosenshine, B., 1971. *Teaching Behaviours and Student Achievement*. London: National Foundation for Educational Research.

Rosenshine, B., & Furst, Norma F., 1971. Research on teacher performance criteria. In B. O. Smith (ed.), *Research in Teacher Education: A Symposium*. Englewood Cliffs, N.J.: Prentice-Hall.

Rosenshine, B., & Furst, Norma F., 1973. The use of direct observation to study teaching. In M. W. Travers (ed.), *Second Handbook of Research on Teaching*. Chicago: Rand McNally.

Rosenthal, R., & Jacobson, L., 1968. *Pygmalion in the Classroom: Teacher Expectation and Pupils' Intellectual Development*. New York: Holt.

Rossi, P. H., & Biddle, B. J., 1966. *The New Media and Education*. Chicago: Aldine.

Rothbart, M., Dalfen, S., & Barrett, R., 1971. Effects of teacher expectancy on student-teacher interaction. *Journal of Educational Psychology*, 62, 49–54.

Rowe, M. B., 1973. *Teaching Sciences as Continuous Inquiry*. New York: McGraw-Hill.

Rubovits, Pamela C., & Maehr, M. L., 1971. Pygmalion re-analyzed: Toward an explanation of the Rosenthal-Jacobson findings. Paper presented at the annual meeting of the American Educational Research Association, New York.

Rubovits, Pamela C., & Maehr, M. L., 1973. Pygmalion black and white. *Journal of Personality and Social Psychology*, 25 (2), 210–218.

Ryans, D. G., 1960. *Characteristics of Teachers: Their Description, Comparison, and Appraisal*. Washington, D.C.: American Council on Education.

Ryans, D. G., 1963. *An Information-System Approach to Theory of Instruction with Special Reference to the Teacher*. System Development Corporation, Santa Monica, Calif.

Samph, T., 1968. Observer effects on teacher behavior. Unpublished doctoral dissertation, University of Michigan.

Sanders, N. M., 1966. *Classroom Questions: What Kinds?* New York: Harper and Row.

Schalock, H. D., 1968. *A Competency Based, Field Centered, Systems Approach to Elementary Teacher Education*. Washington, D.C.: USOE Bureau of Research, U.S. Government Printing Office.

Schantz, Betty M. B., 1963. An experimental study comparing the effects of verbal recall by children in direct and indirect teaching methods as a tool of measurement. Unpublished doctoral dissertation, Pennsylvania State University.

Schluck, Carolyn, 1971. Using the MMPI to predict teacher behavior. Paper presented at the annual meeting of the American Educational Research Association, New York.

Schoggen, P., 1963. Environmental forces in the everyday lives of children. In R. G. Barker (ed.), *The Stream of Behavior: Exploration of Its Structure and Content*. New York: Meredith.

Schoggen, P. M., Barker, L. S., & Barker, R. G., 1963. Structure of the behavior of American and English children. In R. G. Barker (ed.), *The Stream of Behavior: Exploration of Its Structure and Content*. New York: Meredith.

Schueler, H., Gold, M. J., & Mitzel, H. E., 1962. *The Use of Television for Improving Teacher Training and for Improving Measures of Student-Teacher Performance: Phase I, Improvement of Student Teaching*. U.S. Department of

Health, Education and Welfare, Office of Education, Grant No. 730035. New York: Hunter College of the City University of New York.

Scott, E., 1971. Personal communication.

Sharp, C. S., 1966. A study of certain teacher characteristics and behavior as factors affecting pupil achievement in high school biology. Unpublished doctoral dissertation, University of South Carolina, Columbia.

Silberman, M. L., 1969. Behavior expression of teachers' attitudes toward elementary school students. *Journal of Educational Psychology, 60*, 402–407.

Simon, Anita, 1967. Patterns of verbal behavior in favored and non-favored classes. *Classroom Interaction Newsletter, 2* (2), 47–50.

Simon, Anita, & Boyer, E. G. (eds.), 1970. Mirrors for Behavior II: An Anthology of Observational Instruments. *Classroom Interaction Newsletter,* special edition.

Skinner, B. F., 1971. *Beyond Freedom and Dignity.* New York: Knopf.

Smith, B. O., 1960. A concept of teaching. *Teachers' College Record, 61* (5), 229–241.

Smith, B. O., 1963. Toward a theory of teaching. In A. A. Bellack (ed.), *Theory and Research in Teaching.* New York: Teachers College Press.

Smith, B. O., & Meux, M. O., 1962. *A Study of the Logic of Teaching.* Urbana, Ill.: University of Illinois Press.

Smith, B. O., Meux, M. O., Coombs, J., Nuthall, G. A., & Precians, R., 1967. *A Study of the Strategies of Teaching.* Urbana, Ill.: Bureau of Educational Research, University of Illinois.

Smith, L. M., & Geoffrey, W., 1968. *The Complexities of an Urban Classroom: An Analysis toward a General Theory of Teaching.* New York: Holt.

Smith, L. M., & Hudgins, B. B., 1964. *Educational Psychology: An Application of Social and Behavioral Theory.* New York: Knopf.

Smith, M. B., 1965. Interpersonal relationships in the classroom based on the expected socio-economic status of sixth grade boys. *Teachers' College Record, 36,* 200–206.

Snider, R. M., 1966. *A Project to Study the Nature of Effective Physics Teaching.* Ithaca, N.Y.: Cornell University. U.S. Office of Education Research Project No. S-280. Also available as an unpublished doctoral dissertation, Cornell University.

Snow, R. E., 1969. Unfinished Pygmalion. *Contemporary Psychology, 14,* 197–199.

Soar, R. S., 1966. *An Integrative Approach to Classroom Learning.* Temple University, Philadelphia.

Soar, R. S., 1968. Optimum teacher-pupil interaction for pupil growth. *Educational Leadership, 26,* 275–280.

Soar, R. S., & Soar, Ruth M., 1969. Pupil subject matter growth during summer vacation. *Classroom Interaction Newsletter, 5* (1), 46–59.

Soar, R. S., Soar, Ruth M., & Ragosta, Marjorie, 1971. The validation of an observation system for classroom management. Paper presented at the annual meeting of the American Educational Research Association, New York.

Solomon, G., 1970. The analysis of concrete to abstract classroom instructional patterns utilizing TIP profile. *Journal of Research and Development in Education, 4,* 52–61.

Solomon, G., & Wood, S., 1970. Classroom behavior accompanying TIP profile measures. Unpublished manuscript, West Virginia University.

Sorber, E., 1967. Classroom interaction patterns and personality needs of traditionally prepared first-year elementary teachers and graduate teaching interns with degrees from colleges of liberal arts. *Classroom Interaction Newsletter, 2* (2), 51–55.

Spaulding, R. L., 1963. *Achievement Creativity and Self-Concept Correlates of Teacher-Pupil Transactions in Elementary Schools.* Cooperative Research Project No. 1352, College of Education, University of Illinois.

Sprague, Nancy F., 1971. Inquiry dialogue in the classroom. Paper presented at the annual meeting of the American Educational Research Association, New York.

Stephens, J. M., 1967. *The Process of Schooling: A Psychological Examination.* New York: Holt.

Stewart, W., 1955. Urban Negro speech: Sociolinguistic factors affecting English teaching. In R. Shuy (ed.), *Social Dialects and Language Learning.* Champaign, Ill.: National Council of Teachers of English.

Stolurow, L. M., 1965. Model the master teacher or master the teaching model. In J. D. Krumboltz (ed.), *Learning and the Educational Process.* Chicago: Rand McNally.

Stone, P. J., Dunphy, D. C., Smith, M. S., & Ogilvie, D. M., 1966. *The General Inquirer: A Computer Approach to Content Analysis.* Cambridge: The M.I.T. Press.

Strausser, B., 1967. A conceptual model of instruction. *Journal of Teacher Education, 28* (1), 63–74.

Taba, Hilda, 1963. Learning by discovery: Psychological and educational rationale. *Elementary School Journal, 63,* 308–316.

Taba, Hilda, 1966. *Teaching Strategies and Cognitive Functioning in Elementary School Children.* USOE Cooperative Research Project No. 2404, San Francisco State College.

Taba, Hilda, Levine, S., & Elzey, F. F., 1964. *Thinking in Elementary School Children.* USOE Cooperative Research Project No. 1574, San Francisco State College.

Taylor, P. H., Christie, T., & Platts, C. V., 1972. Towards a typology of science teaching. Unpublished paper, Teaching Research Unit, University of Birmingham, England.

Thomas, W. I., & Znaniecki, F., 1927. *The Polish Peasant in Europe and America.* New York: Knopf.

Thompson, G. R., & Bowers, N. C., 1968. Fourth grade achievement as related to creativity, intelligence, and teaching style. Paper presented at the annual meeting of the American Educational Research Association, Chicago.

Thorndike, R. L., 1968. Review of pygmalion in the classroom. *American Educational Research Journal, 5,* 708–711.

Thorndike, R. L., 1969. But do you have to know how to tell the time? *American Educational Research Journal, 6,* 692.

Tinsley, D. C., Watson, Elizabeth P., & Marshall, J. C., 1970. Cognitive objectives revealed by classroom questions in "process-oriented" and "content-oriented" secondary social studies programs. Paper presented at the annual meeting of the American Educational Research Association, Minneapolis.

Tisher, R. P., 1970. The nature of verbal discourse in classrooms and association between verbal discourse and pupils' understanding in science. In W. J.

Campbell (ed.), *Scholars in Context: The Effects of Environments on Learning*. Sydney: Wiley.

Torrance, E. P., 1966. *Characteristics of Mathematics Teachers That Affect Students' Learning*. Cooperative Research Project No. 1020, U.S. Office of Education.

Traill, R. D., 1971. The effects of using interaction analysis as a means of assisting student teachers to analyze teaching behavior. *Australian Journal of Education, 15* (3), 295–304.

Travers, R. M. W., 1971. Some further reflections on the nature of a theory of instruction. In I. Westbury & A. A. Bellack (eds.), *Research into Classroom Processes*. New York: Teachers College Press.

Travers, R. M. W. (Ed.), 1973. *Second Handbook of Research on Teaching*. American Educational Research Association. Chicago: Rand McNally.

Tuckman, B. W., McCall, K. M., & Hyman, R. T., 1969. The modification of teacher behavior: Effects of dissonance and coded feedback. *American Educational Research Journal, 6*, 607–619.

Van Wagenen, R. K., & Travers, R. M. W., 1963. Learning under conditions of direct and vicarious reinforcement. *Journal of Educational Psychology, 54*, 356–362.

Waimon, M. D., & Hermanowicz, H. J., 1965. A conceptual system for prospective teachers to study teaching behavior. Paper presented at the American Educational Research Association, Chicago.

Wallen, N. E., 1966. *Relationships between Teacher Characteristics and Student Behavior (Part 3)*. Salt Lake City: University of Utah Press.

Wallen, N. E., & Wodtke, K. H., 1963. *Relationships between Teacher Characteristics and Student Behavior (Part 1)*. Salt Lake City: Department of Educational Psychology, University of Utah.

Waller, W., 1932. *The Sociology of Teaching*. New York: Wiley.

Ward, M. H., & Baker, B. L., 1968. Reinforcement therapy in the classroom. *Journal of Applied Behavior Analysis, 1*, 323–328.

Wasik, B. H., Senn, K., Welch, R. H., & Cooper, B. R., 1969. Behavior modification with culturally deprived school children: Two case studies. *Journal of Applied Behavior Analysis, 2*, 181–194.

Watts, A. F., 1947. *The Language and Mental Development of Children*. Boston: Heath.

Weber, W. A., 1968. Relationships between teacher behavior and pupil creativity in the elementary school. Unpublished doctoral dissertation, Temple University, Philadelphia.

Weick, K. E., 1968. Systematic observational methods. In G. Lindzey & E. Aronson (eds.), *The Handbook of Social Psychology* (2nd edition). Reading, Mass.: Addison-Wesley.

Weinreigh, U., 1966. Explorations in semantic theory. In T. A. Sibeok (ed.), *Current Trends in Linguistics III: Theoretical Foundation*. The Hague: Mouton.

Werner, Edwenna, Elder, Rachel, Newman, Jackomina, Lai, Moris, Harano, Joanne, Walton, Deborah, & Baron, Patti, 1971. *Interaction Analysis: Teacher Handbook*. Berkeley, Calif.: Far West Laboratory for Educational Research and Development.

Williams, T. L., 1970. The effect of cognitive instructions on secondary student teachers and their pupils. *Journal of Research and Development in Education,* 4, 73–83.

Wilson, J. H., 1969. The "new" science teachers are asking more and better questions. *Journal of Research in Science Teaching,* 6 (1), 49–53.

Withall, J., 1960. Research tools: Observing and recording behavior. *Review of Educational Research,* 30, 496–512.

Withall, J., 1949. The development of a technique for the measurement of social-emotional climate in classrooms. *Journal of Experimental Education,* 17, 347–361. Reprinted in E. J. Amidon & J. B. Hough (eds.), *Interaction Analysis: Theory, Research and Application.* Reading, Mass.: Addison-Wesley, 1967.

Withall, J., & Lewis, W. W., 1963. Social interaction in the classroom. In N. L. Gage (ed.), *Handbook of Research on Teaching.* American Educational Research Association. Chicago: Rand McNally.

Wittgenstein, L., 1958. *Philosophical Investigation.* Oxford: Basil Blackwell.

Wittrock, M. C., 1966. The learning by discovery hypothesis. In L. S. Shulman & E. R. Keislar (eds.), *Learning by Discovery: A Critical Appraisal.* Chicago: Rand McNally.

Wolf, M. M., Giles, D. K., & Hall, V. R., 1968. Experiments with token reinforcement in a remedial classroom. *Behaviour Research and Therapy,* 6, 51–64.

Wood, S. E., 1970. A multidimensional model for the observation, analysis and assessment of classroom behavior. *Journal of Research and Development in Education,* 4, 84–97.

Worthen, B. R., 1968. A study of discovery and expository presentation: Implication for teaching. *Journal of Teacher Education,* 19, 223–242.

Wright, C. J., & Nuthall, G., 1970. Relationships between teacher behaviors and pupil achievement in three experimental elementary science lessons. *American Educational Research Journal,* 7, 477–491.

Zahorik, J. A., 1968. Classroom feedback behavior of teachers. *Journal of Educational Research,* 62, 147–150.

Zahorik, J. A., 1970. Teacher verbal feedback and content development. *Journal of Educational Research,* 63, 419–423.

INDEXES

NAME INDEX

SUBJECT INDEX

A

Abstractness, 243, 263
Achievement, 379, 409
Action sequencing, 186
Activities, 34, 153, 159
Adams and Biddle Instrument, 202
Address form, 302
Adjoining, 302
Allocation of communicating roles, 190
Analysis, 234
Analytic processes, 397
Application, 234
Application of principles, 257
Appropriateness, 399
Arguments, 297
Aschner-Gallagher Classification System (AGCS), 248, 253
Audiovisual record, 430–431
    defined, 68
Augmentation, 329

B

Bales-Gerbrand Recorder, 205
Barker Procedures, 332
Behavior, autocratic teacher, 99
    democratic, 99
    "dominative" teacher, 97, 99
    individual pupil, 74
    "integrative" teacher, 97, 99
    learner-centered, 99
    pupil-as-emitter, 74
    pupil classroom, defined, 44
    pupil group, 74
    study of teacher, 74
    teacher-as-emitter, 74

teacher-centered, 99
    teacher classroom, defined, 44
Behavior modification, 161, 175, 376, 380
Beliefs concerning teaching, 17
Borg Categories, 240
Brophy-Good System, 108, 112
Businesslike classroom behavior, 60

C

Cambourne Semantic Procedure, 307
Canterbury Instrument, 202, 266, 288, 332, 349
Case, 302
Case classification, 297
Centrality, 388
Clarifying-expanding, 329
Clarity, 60
Classes, 246
Classifying, 280
Classroom culture, 35
Classroom game, the, 34, 178, 294
    findings for, 220
    moves in the, 193, 389
    rules of, 45
Classroom(s), 32, 55
    climate of, 93
    management of, 134
    sequence of events in, 295, 321
    "social-emotional climate" of, 98
    as a social system, 176 ff., 382
Climate, 362
    of classrooms, 93
    findings for, 361
    findings for vairables concerning, 365
    "social-emotional" of classrooms, 98

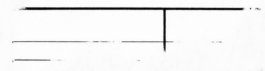